Business

Business

UPDATE

FIRST CANADIAN EDITION

Louis E. Boone

David L. Kurtz

Ronald A. Knowles

DRYDEN

HARCOURT BRACE & COMPANY, CANADA

Toronto Montreal Fort Worth New York Orlando
Philadelphia San Diego London Sydney Tokyo

Canadian Cataloguing in Publication Data

Boone, Louis E.
Business

Updated ed.
Includes index.
ISBN 0-03-922731-6

1. Business. I. Kurtz, David L. II. Knowles, Ronald A. III. Title

HF1008.B66 1999   650   C98-932812-0

Acquisitions Editor: Ken Nauss	Cover Art: Greg Stevenson
Developmental Editor: Su Mei Ku/Martina van de Velde	Typesetting and Assembly: Sharon Foster
Copy Editor: Claudia Kutchukian	Technical Art: Sharon Foster/Rose Zgodzinski
Production Co-ordinator: Sheila Barry/Shalini Babbar	Big Shot Cartoons: Stephen Kennedy
Cover and Interior Design: Sharon Foster	Printing and Binding: Friesen Corporation

This book was printed in Canada.

2 3 4 5   02 01 00 99

ABOUT THE COVER
The cover illustration was created specifically for this book to echo the most important themes and concepts examined in our book, including new technology, globalization, workplace diversity, strategic alliances, teamwork, and creative opportunities in today's business environment.

Preface to the Update Edition

"This is the first time in the history of business that you can be great at what you do and be out of business tomorrow," says Ken Blanchard, author of *The One Minute Manager*. That said, entrepreneurs need to be well-equipped to thrive and survive in today's competitive and rapidly changing business environment.

Our belief that students need the most current information available to help them prepare for the challenges of today's business world was confirmed soon after the First Canadian Edition of *Business* had been released. The overwhelmingly positive response from students and instructors convinced us that students should have access to even more examples of how Canadian business really works to help prepare them for business in the new millennium.

Generally, a textbook and its ancillary support package is updated every three or four years, but the pace of technological innovation and its implications for business world wide dictated that the traditional revision cycle is simply too long to offer current information to today's student. So we decided to break the mould once again in order to stay ahead of today's changing technology.

The result of our efforts is this updated First Canadian Edition of *Business* which features many new focus boxes profiling up-to-the-minute business issues and scenarios, accompanied by a revised ancillary support package and a comprehensive new Web site. At the same time, we have retained all the features that were so well-received in the First Canadian Edition of *Business*, including the focus on career preparation for students, a global business perspective throughout the text, strategies for competing in foreign markets, profiles of Canadian companies that have implemented successful management strategies, and an emphasis on emerging technology, management, and workplace trends.

Updates throughout the text focus on issues that will act as a springboard for class discussion and debate:

→ **Ethical Issues** boxes, such as *Should Profit Be the Bottom Line* (Chapter 1) and *NAFTA and the Plight of the Mexican Worker* (Chapter 4), introduce students to the ethical controversies that exist in the business world and allow them to apply their problem-solving skills to find potential solutions that are socially and environmentally responsible.

→ **Future Trends** boxes on such topics as *Business Opportunities in Europe* (Chapter 3) and *Telehealth Services* (Chapter 10) will help students learn about the future direction of Canadian business.

→ New **Case Exercises** in each chapter, such as *What Goes Around Comes Around* (Chapter 2) and *You're the HR Manager* (Chapter 8), help students apply chapter concepts to real life challenges and situations.

→ Students also need to know what makes our fastest growing companies so successful. How do today's new-age business leaders survive and thrive in the new economy? What are their key business strategies? We worked closely with *Profit Magazine* and their 1997 and 1998 surveys of Canada's 100 fastest growing companies. The result of this collaboration is our new **Lessons From the Best** boxes where students will learn strategies from such business leaders as Tony Franceschini of Stanley Technology Group, a design company in Edmonton, Alberta (Chapter 1), and Eric Bourbeau and Chad Loeven of Les Systèmes Zenon Inc., a sytems integrator in Longueuil, Quebec (Chapter 9).

The new Web site which accompanies this Update Edition helps make *Business* one of the most innovative and technologically advanced learning packages available in Canada. Integrated with the text, this high-tech resource illustrates key chapter concepts with hands-on applications for students, and connects instructors and students alike with countless world wide business resources. From our Web site, users can select the home page for any chapter or appendix in the textbook to access related company profiles, Web exercises, resources associated with chapter topics, links to other sites, interactive simulations, and much more.

Career Preparation

A major thrust of the book resulted from listening to students. Over the past three years, we visited students on dozens of college and university campuses, culminating in our final visit in the spring of 1997. In our surveys, focus group discussions, and one-on-one meetings, students repeatedly expressed their concerns about finding jobs when they graduate. These concerns are so important that we have made a major commitment to addressing them in this book.

Students of the late 1990s are pragmatic. They know how important it is to start preparing early for a career, to match their individual abilities and interests to specific career alternatives, and to create an academic plan to help them secure that first job on their career path. But they need help in accomplishing their objectives.

Your first business course is a perfect setting in which to begin career preparation. As you are exposed to many different aspects of the world of business throughout the course, you can also begin to consider which areas represent potential careers. For this reason, we have interspersed boxes entitled "Where the Jobs Are" throughout the text. These will give you a good sense of what kinds of careers are out there, and what successful people in business have to say about starting a career.

Integration of Global Business

The 1990s business executive must think globally — beyond the "us-versus-them" orientation that is so prevalent in current business education.

Any focus on quality and business competitiveness must include *global* competitiveness. Many books attempt to focus on international issues by placing a chapter on global issues at the end of the text, where it becomes a logical candidate for omission when time runs short. Other texts go a step further and add boxed examples on international topics. Unfortunately, this is not what is meant when instructors plead for an internationally integrated textbook.

In response to this plea, *Business* takes a truly global perspective. Dozens of international examples are interspersed throughout the book's sixteen chapters. Coverage of global issues begins in Chapter 1 but is also integrated into the remaining chapters. We include focus boxes and real examples of Canadian firms — large and small — competing in foreign markets, as well as of foreign firms competing on Canadian turf. As part of our strategy for making the book a truly global text, we have placed the traditional "international" chapter in Part I as a key component of our coverage of the general environment for business.

Teamwork and Communication

Boone, Kurtz, and Knowles' *Business* is the first introductory text to devote an entire chapter to two fundamental concerns of today's business executives: the shift of organizations to working in teams and the importance of effective communication. Coverage includes work teams, special-purpose problem-solving teams, cross-functional teams, team development, conflict resolution, oral and written communication, verbal and nonverbal communication, international business communication, and communication technology.

Quality and Customer Satisfaction

Another first for this book is a separate chapter focussing on the role of quality in business success. Instead of a narrow conception of quality as affecting only production processes, Chapter 6 shows how total quality management can be applied throughout an organization, from human resource management and finance to marketing and information. A unique feature of this chapter is the focus on ISO 9000. The importance of employee involvement, empowerment, training, and teamwork in achieving world-class quality to provide customer satisfaction is examined as well.

Technology

Global economic leadership is related closely to the productivity of a nation's business sector; its people and productivity, in turn, are spurred by technological advances. The importance of technology is stressed from the first chapter of the text and throughout the balance of the book. Special focus boxes in every chapter demonstrate the contributions of technology to our standard of living. Topics include the Internet and the World Wide Web (WWW), the intranet, telecommunications and the information superhighway, databases, the networked and digital economy, fibre optics, and digitization.

Focus on Ethics and Social Responsibility

In our surveys and focus group discussions with faculty and students, ethics and social responsibility were mentioned time and time again as major issues in Canadian business. Not unlike the topic of global business, ethics is usually relegated to a chapter near the end of a business book. Not so in this text.

Discussion of ethical, societal, and environmental concerns begins in Chapter 1 and continues throughout the text. Each of the chapters in Part I devote major coverage to these topics. More specific coverage is included for each business function, including human resource management, production, marketing, and finance.

Focus on Partnerships and Strategic Alliances

Throughout the text, we emphasize how important it is for businesses to form partnerships and strategic alliances. This is one of our major themes. From our own experience, we can tell you that partnerships really do work. So, in this edition, we decided to "walk the talk." Harcourt Brace & Company, Canada, the publisher of this book, formed a partnership with *The Financial Post*. Our examples in the text are current and draw heavily from *The Financial Post*'s "50 Best Managed Private Companies." Thanks to *The Financial Post*, you will see many examples of how our leading Canadian firms have partnered and thrived in the 1990s.

Emphasis on Small Business and Entry-Level Management

Small- and medium-sized firms are two of the main engines driving the Canadian economy into the next millennium. And the fuel is entrepreneurship. In 1997 alone, there were 2.4 million self-employed Canadians. Too often, business books highlight large corporations. In this text, we recognize and have responded to students' growing interest in small business and the many career opportunities found in organizations other than corporate giants. A balanced presentation of applications and examples from over 100 small and large businesses is maintained throughout the text. In addition, Chapter 5 devotes major coverage to entrepreneurship, small business, and franchising.

Numerous business professors have pointed out to us that most business students will find their first jobs at the supervisory management level. However, most textbooks tend to focus on top-management decisions and activities and to neglect discussion of first-line supervisory management. The book provides detailed coverage of first-line management in Chapter 7 and includes many examples of supervisory management activities and concerns.

Fewer Chapters

At sixteen chapters, *Business* is the shortest major book available for the first business course. The book's length and number of chapters are intended to match the time constraints of a one-semester or one-quarter course. Our objective is to permit the instructor to cover all of the text in a single term without facing the dilemma of deciding what important topics to omit when using a text with simply too many chapters and pages to cover.

Big Shot

Those who were born in the mid-1930s and early 1940s are the lucky few who are now running many of our major corporations. They entered the work force during the 1950s and early 1960s when anyone with a briefcase and a smile could get a job. They soared up the corporate ladder, bought big houses in the suburbs for peanuts, and always had an extra car in the driveway. Now they sit on their lofty perches bemoaning the fact that their kids haven't had the spunk to do as well as they have.

Big Shot, our corporate executive, digitized by Stephen Kennedy, is one of these lucky few. He's in his mid-50s and heads his own manufacturing plant, Big Shot Enterprises Ltd. Big Shot can't identify with the younger generations, especially anyone under 30. He is desperately trying to understand the new economy, and has his own special way of dealing with business issues.

Each chapter contains a lesson from Big Shot, a man who does not seem to understand what is going on in the business world these days. Slinky, his executive assistant, tries to clue him in, but Big Shot somehow remains oblivious to the realities of the 1990s. You may not like or agree with him, but we certainly want you to understand how he thinks. Why? Because when you get out into the world of work, the reality is that you are going to meet a lot of people like Big Shot — and you are going to have to learn how to deal with them. If you really cannot identify with Big Shot, don't worry — his is a dying breed.

SUPPLEMENTARY MATERIALS

Harcourt Brace & Company, Canada has spared no expense to make this the premier textbook on the market today. Many instructors teach large classes with limited resources. Supplementary materials provide a means of expanding and improving the students' learning experience. The teaching/learning package provided with the book is designed specifically to meet the needs of instructors facing a variety of teaching conditions and to enhance students' experience in their first business course. The following are descriptions of these materials.

Computerized Test Bank

For most instructors, one of the most important parts of any teaching package is a test bank comprised of questions that accurately and fairly assess student competence in the subject material. Boone, Kurtz, and Knowles' *Business Computerized Test Bank*, prepared by John Moran of InfoBASE, provides over 1600 multiple-choice, true/false, and short essay test items.

The test items have been reviewed and class-tested to ensure the highest quality. Each question is tied to chapter learning outcomes and is rated for level of difficulty so that instructors can provide a balanced set of questions for student exams.

The computerized format allows instructors to select and edit test items from the printed test bank, as well as add their own questions.

Instructor's Manual

The authors devoted a major effort to developing this critical instructional tool. The *Instructor's Manual* provides a clear map of how the integrated teaching/learning package supports every learning outcome discussed in the text. The *IM* contains the following for each chapter:

→ Suggested lesson plan and teaching notes
→ Annotated learning outcomes
→ Answers to review questions
→ Answers to discussion questions
→ Supplemental cases
→ Discussion issues
→ In-class exercises
→ Experiential exercises
→ Guest speaker suggestions
→ Term paper suggestions

Student Workbook

We have prepared a *Student Workbook* to accompany the text. Here you will find experiential exercises and typical text-bank questions and answers.

PowerPoint™ Slides

A comprehensive set of over 300 PowerPoint™ slides is available for adopters of the book. This support material focusses on concepts — and sometimes on actual figures — discussed in the text.

ACKNOWLEDGEMENTS

Special acknowledgement and appreciation must go to our Canadian researcher and our marketing associate, John Moran of InfoBASE and Orville Lahey, for their seemingly endless assistance. We also want to thank Steven Kennedy of ParaDocs Documents Design for digitizing Big Shot and making him come alive.

The authors are extremely grateful for the insightful comments of the following colleagues who reviewed all or part of the manuscript:

Kirk Bailey (Ryerson Polytechnic University)
Dwight Dyson (Centennial College)
Joel Gillis (St. Mary's University)
John Kaszel (The Investment Funds Institute of Canada)
John Lille (Centennial College)
Shelley Lowe (Canadian Bankers Association)
Andrew Peacock (Dalhousie University)
Maureen Peszat (Seneca College)
John Shanks (University of Saskatchewan)
Ron Shay (Kwantlen College)
Mark Webb (The Canadian Securities Institute)

Last, but not least, we thank our good friends at Harcourt Brace: Ken Nauss, acquisitions editor, whose belief in this book made it happen; Su Mei Ku, developmental editor, for her tireless effort and patience in seeing the book through development; Claudia Kutchukian, copy editor, for insightful improvements to the manuscript; Marcel Chiera, editorial manager, for pulling together the design and production team; and Sheila Barry and Shalini Babbar, production co-ordinators, for their good production advice.

A Note from the Publisher

Thank you for selecting *Business*, First Canadian Edition, by Louis E. Boone, David L. Kurtz, and Ronald A. Knowles. The authors and publisher have devoted considerable time and care to the development of this book. We appreciate your recognition of this effort and accomplishment.

We want to hear what you think about *Business*, First Canadian Edition. Please take a few minutes to fill in the stamped reader reply card at the back of the book. Your comments and suggestions will be valuable to us as we prepare new editions and other books.

Brief Contents

Contents

Chapter 8
The Human Resource **187**

Chapter 9
Teamwork and Communication **217**

Chapter 10
Information Technology **243**

PART IV

Production and
Marketing   269

Business in a Global Environment

Nuala Beck, President,
Nuala Beck & Associates Inc., Toronto

"Choose what you love and apply it

in a field with a future.... If it makes your pulse

race, figure out how you can apply it in

the business world....

We're on the edge of an educational revolution."

Chapter 1

Business: Blending People, Technology, and Ethical Behaviour

Learning Outcomes

After studying this chapter, you should be able to

1. Explain what a business is and how it operates within the private enterprise system.
2. Define the roles of competition and of the entrepreneur in a private enterprise system.
3. Outline the basic rights of the private enterprise system.
4. Explain the concepts of gross domestic product and productivity.
5. Identify the degrees of competition that can exist in a private enterprise system.
6. Discuss the major challenges and opportunities facing managers in the late 1990s.
7. Describe the most important qualities that managers should possess.
8. Explain the ethical and social responsibilities of business.

Can the Eaton's Magic Return?[1]

Timothy Eaton opened his first store on Toronto's Yonge St. back in 1869. Some say this signalled the end of bartering and bargaining for goods and the beginning of modern retailing in Canada. Eaton introduced Canadians to the idea of cash sales, fixed-price goods, and the concept of offering satisfaction or your money back — as well as to retailing through catalogues and mail order to serve farmers.

Timothy Eaton was an enlightened capitalist of the Victorian era and a strong supporter of the labour movement who in 1875 led a campaign to reduce the length of workdays. He died in 1906, but by the early 1950s, T. Eaton Co. Ltd. had grown to become the largest employer in Canada after the railways and the federal government. Eaton's was the icon of retail. Judith K. Knelman, who teaches journalism at the University of Western Ontario, remembered the company this way:

[N]o service was too small or burdensome for the Eaton's of my youth, from parking our finny car to trusting little girls who used their mothers' magic charge number.... The two numbers that I remember from my childhood in Winnipeg (some 50 years back) are ... my phone number and my mother's Eaton's account number. Several times a week I'd hear my mother on the phone ordering things from Eaton's on that magic number. Sometimes it would be a fresh salmon, delivered the same day.

Eaton's remained the undisputed doyen of Canadian department store retail — until February of 1997. It was then that shock waves were felt throughout Canada's vulnerable retail sector and some 15 000 Canadian jobs were put in jeopardy as the Eaton's Retail group sought protection from its creditors under the Companies Creditors Arrangement Act (CCAA). This Depression-era law protected the personal interests of the Eaton family and, at the same time, gave the company some breathing space in which to restructure its operations. "It's very tough. It's a great disappointment and I assure you we did not take this step lightly. I truly feel badly about the people who will lose their jobs," said George Eaton, president of T. Eaton Co. Ltd. Asked what his great-grandfather would say of the move, he replied, "I think he'd be disappointed as we all are, but he would have taken the same steps we have."

The company finances had been faltering for years — more than $250 million in losses had been recorded since 1988. By 1996, Eaton's owed about $500 million to lenders, suppliers, and landlords. Revenues had slid from about $2.3 billion in the early 1990s to about $1.7 billion in 1996. Its estimated share of the department store market had fallen from 25 percent in 1992 to around 15 percent at the end of 1995. Nevertheless, the situation seemed to come as a surprise, to George Eaton at least, whose observation at the time was "We obviously thought the retail market was in better shape than it was."

Being a 127-year-old Canadian icon did not protect Eaton's from the savage battles of the 1990s retail market. What happened? Here's what some of the experts had to say:

Passion. "You've got to be passionate in the retail business," says McGill University management professor Henry Mintzberg. Mintzberg, one of Canada's leading management consultants, has often voiced scepticism about companies that hand down their leadership from one generation to the next. It's a gamble whether the next generation will be as smart or as motivated as its predecessors, he says. Some argue that the empire owned by the four Eaton great-grandsons — George, John Craig, Thor, and Frederik — was a chore that took away from their other interests, like thoroughbreds, politics, and charity golf tournaments. They were simply too complacent.

Retail Market. Retail spending in the 1990s slowed to a crawl — about 2 percent per year, compared with 8 to 10 percent in the 1980s. The Eaton family played in a retail environment in which stingy consumers punished stores that fell behind the times. These same market conditions demolished Consumers Distributing Inc., Greenberg Stores Ltd., and Woolco — to name only a few — and wounded many other general Canadian retailers.

The Eaton Corporate Empire

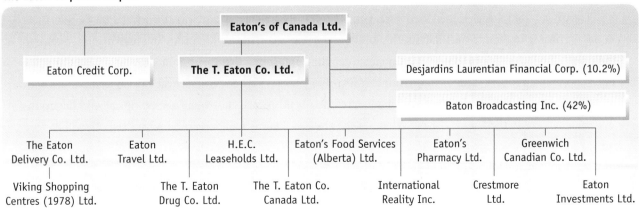

Source: "The Eaton Corporate Empire," *The Globe and Mail*, March 1, 1997, B4. Reprinted with permission from The Globe and Mail.

Competition. Eaton's was a greying relic that simply could not keep up with the new leaner and more colourful stores. This hastened the invasion of giant U.S. retailers such as Wal-Mart. According to a 1997 consumer study by Kubas Consultants, Wal-Mart beat every major Canadian department store in categories such as value for money and customer service.

Customer Focus. Eaton's got caught doing too many things. "Unless you have something distinctive to offer, it's easy to become an also ran," said Ed Strapagiel, a retail consultant based in Toronto. Many of Canada's best retailers were regional players who specialized in niche markets. According to Michael Treacy, a U.S. strategy consultant, "The trick is to grab a greater 'share of the wallet' from a core set of customers rather than trying to be all things to all people."

Quality and Service. "From the consumer's point of view, my belief is they still didn't think the product that they wanted to buy was there and service that they expected was there," said Richard Talbot, a retail analyst with Thomas Consultants International. Other observers were a little more harsh in their criticism: "Eaton's destroyed themselves. They had poor merchandising and they opened dog stores," commented John Winter, a Toronto-based retail analyst. Donald Shaffer, former president and CEO of Sears Canada Inc., says that a store must "deliver on product, price and service. You can't just open up the store and expect customers to come."

Finance. Most observers believed that the heavy losses incurred by Eaton's over the 1990s meant that the company would need a major influx of somewhere between $200 and $300 million. The most pressing need was cash for store renovations, computer technology, and payments to suppliers.

Management. Many argued that Eaton's needed experienced retail management and leadership. Stephen Arnold, professor of marketing at Queen's University said, for example: "I don't think Eaton's can do it internally unless they completely change their management." Professor Donald Thompson at York University's Schulich School of Business also commented that Eaton's management made a fatal mistake in not responding to the changing nature of the retail industry and positioning the company accordingly.

In June of 1997, George Kosich — a 37-year veteran of the Hudson's Bay Co. — was introduced as the new president and chief executive officer of T. Eaton Co. Ltd., replacing George Eaton. "I believe the Eaton's franchise is bruised but certainly not broken. I believe I can make a meaningful contribution to this great company," Kosich said at that time.

The 62-year-old Kosich signed his contract on June 5, 1997 at 10:30 AM and was at work at 2:00 PM that afternoon. According to many retail analysts, this kind of dedication and leadership brought a reassuring presence to the troubled retailer. "It's good news for Canadian retailing and shows that the imminent solution is a Canadian one," commented Albert Plant of the accounting firm Coopers & Lybrand. Will George Kosich lead Eaton's back to its roots as a profitable and respected Canadian retailer? Is this near-catastrophe a wake-up call and the beginning of a new era in the Eaton's legacy? Whatever the answers, Eaton's will have to reinvent itself. All will depend on the commitment of the Eaton family, Kosich's management and business acumen, the patience and support of Canadian consumers, and a solid financial plan.

CHAPTER OVERVIEW

THE EATON'S SAGA is a classic Canadian story of a company that lost its vision and leadership. It lost track of its competitive roots and the needs of the customer. Over time, the company became complacent. For Eaton's, the retail market of the 1990s was a stark reminder of the vagaries of Canadian business. The "Build it and they will come" retail philosophy of the past no longer works in the new competitive economy. Those companies that survive and those that profit in the years to come will have to blend people, technology, and ethical behaviour in a mix that is attractive to the Canadian and the global marketplace.

Many Canadian companies have proven that they have the business acumen to compete and prosper. Many traditional Canadian companies in the retail sector, such as Canadian Tire, and upstarts, such as Mountain Equipment Co-op, McNally Robinson Booksellers Ltd., and Roots Canada Ltd., have been able to make the transition to the new competitive economy. In the high-tech and manufacturing arena, other Canadian companies, like Newbridge Networks and Corel Corporation, are well positioned to compete in the global marketplace, as we will learn later on. Many leading Canadian companies have been able to satisfy the needs of the marketplace and the objectives of the business to make a profit. Throughout this book, we will be highlighting successful Canadian firms like these and sharing their business advice with you.

These are perhaps the most exciting times in Canadian business. As we have noted in the Preface, this book draws on the successful business practices of *The Financial Post*'s "50 Best Managed Private Companies." Each of these companies had a business dream or vision. The ability to realize this dream was made possible by our unique Canadian business system, a complex blend of private and public sector enterprises all trying to achieve their objectives — be they profit or not-for-profit

motives. In this chapter, we begin the study of business by examining these facts: today's business is unavoidably global in nature, and quality products offering customer satisfaction are the result of blending technology, people, and ethical behaviour. Characteristics of successful managers will be identified, and the need to include ethical behaviour and social responsibility as important organizational goals will be explored. The starting place is an understanding of the word "business."

THEY SAID IT

"It's only Canadians who consistently put down Canadians. Our business sector is extraordinarily well recognized outside of our country."

JEFFREY GANDZ, Associate Dean of Business,
University of Western Ontario

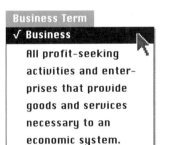

Business Term

✓ **Business**

All profit-seeking activities and enterprises that provide goods and services necessary to an economic system.

WHAT IS BUSINESS?

WHAT DO YOU think of when you hear the word *business*? Some of us think of our jobs, others think of the merchants they deal with as consumers, and still others think of the millions of firms that make up the world's economy. This broad, all-inclusive term can be applied to many kinds of enterprises. Business provides the bulk of our employment as well as the products we enjoy.

Business consists of *all profit-seeking activities and enterprises that provide goods and services necessary to an economic system.* Some businesses produce tangible goods, such as cars, breakfast cereals, and computer chips; others provide services, such as insurance, concerts, car rentals, and lodging.

Business is the economic pulse of a nation, the means through which standards of living improve. Canada enjoys the highest level of human development in the world. In 1997, for the fourth consecutive year, we ranked number 1 on the United Nations Development Program's human-development index — slightly ahead of France, Norway, and the United States (see Table 1.1) Our achievements and world leadership in health, knowledge, and standard of living depend on the continuing strength and vibrancy of our business community.[2]

THEY SAID IT

"There's a total shifting of players going on right now. Frankly, I think we're entering the most exciting period in Canadian retailing history."

JAMES OKAMURA, principal partner, J.C. Williams Group Ltd.,
a Toronto-based retail consulting company

ETHICAL ISSUE

SHOULD PROFIT BE THE BOTTOM LINE?

In the late 1990s, the murders of recording stars Tupak Shakur and Notorious B.I.G. intensified the debate about high voltage rap music known as *gangsta rap*. At the heart of the controversy were the incendiary lyrics of many rap tunes, such as the Geto Boys' "Assassin": "I dug between the chair and whipped out the machete; she screamed, I sliced her up until her guts were like spaghetti."

Gangsta rap has put some recording companies in a tight spot. Stiff criticism

from opponents of gangsta rap led Time Warner to sell its 50 percent share in the Interscope/Death Row rap label to MCA, a company owned by Seagram. The popularity of the label's gangsta rap recording artists has boosted profits (the bottom line) for MCA, now one of the recording industry's fastest-growing companies. "Judging by the recent results, it is clear that Time Warner's loss was our gain," said Ron Meyer, MCA's CEO. However, some disgruntled stockholders have sold their shares in MCA's parent company, Seagram Co., to protest gangsta rap.

1. Do you think the profit motive should dictate, or do you side with

the unhappy Seagram stockholders who believe that recording companies have a social responsibility to monitor the lyrics of music they produce?

2. Can you give other examples of companies that struggle with the balance between profit performance and social responsibility?

Source: Shelley Branch, "Goodbye Gangsta," *Fortune*, July 7, 1997, 40; Thomas S. Mulligan, "Once Again, Anti-Rappers Put the Heat on Time Warner," *Los Angeles Times*, May 16, 1997, D4; William J. Bennett, "Seagram's Share in Gangsta Rap," *Washington Post*, April 18, 1997, A25; and William Chitwood, "Still Peddling Filth for Profit," *Los Angeles Times*, January 19, 1997, B17.

Role of Profits

Profits are a critical ingredient in accomplishing the goals necessary to constantly improve standards of living. **Profits** represent *rewards for the businessperson who takes the risks involved in blending people, technology, and information in creating and marketing want-satisfying goods and services that provide customer satisfaction.* Even though accountants think of profits as the difference between a firm's revenues and expenses involved in generating these revenues, it is

useful to think of profits as serving as an *incentive* for people to start companies, expand them, and provide consistently high-quality, competitive goods and services.

Just as important as profits are the social and ethical responsibilities that successful businesses must meet. This means organizations must act responsibly in their dealings with employees, consumers, suppliers, competitors, government, and the general public if they are to succeed in the long run. We will discuss social responsibility and business ethics more fully in Chapter 2.

Table 1.1 Human Development Index

HDI Rank	Rank 1996	Life Expectancy at Birth (years) 1994	Adult Literacy Rate (%) 1994	Combined First-, Second-, and Third-Level Gross Enrollment Ratio (%) 1994	Real GDP per Capita (PPP$) 1994
1. CANADA	1.	79.0	99.0	100	21 459
2. France	7.	78.7	99.0	89	20 510
3. Norway	5.	77.5	99.0	92	21 346
4. USA	2.	76.2	99.0	96	26 397
5. Iceland	8.	79.1	99.0	83	20 566
6. Netherlands	4.	77.3	99.0	91	19 238
7. Japan	3.	79.8	99.0	78	21 581
8. Finland	6.	76.3	99.0	97	17 417
9. New Zealand	14.	76.4	99.0	94	16 851
10. Sweden	9.	78.3	99.0	82	18 540

LESSONS FROM THE BEST

FIRM DESIGNS CULTURE TO MAKE PROFIT

Stanley Technology Group Inc., an Edmonton design company, has expanded at an eye-popping pace. It has racked up 44 consecutive years of profit and has grown almost seven-fold since 1985. Stanley's roots are in Alberta, where 800 of its 2000 employees are located, with offices in five other provinces, three U.S. states, and the Caribbean. The company's goal is to become one of the top ten design outfits in the world by 2005.

Tony Franceschini, president and CEO, says the company's consistent profit record is built on the understanding that the bottom line (profit) always comes first. "One thing that we've instilled within our staff is a culture of change," he says. "They know that we have to be profitable and they know the shareholder comes first." This philosophy clearly prevails in staffing issues: 30 percent of the 2000 employees are on contract at any given time.

For Stanley, two major benefits of using contract workers are increased productivity and adaptability: "There's no doubt that the person on a contract works harder," says Stephan Pamukoff, a human resources specialist with KPMG. "Their goals are more tangible and definable." Not only does contract work allow the company the flexibility to grow quickly, but it's also a way to recession-proof the firm. According to Mr. Franceschini, Stanley can shrink rapidly if it smells a downturn.

Source: Adapted from Mark MacKinnon, "Firm Designs Culture to Cushion Recession," *The Globe and Mail*, August 31, 1998, B9. Reprinted with permission from The Globe and Mail.

Business Concepts in Not-for-Profit Organizations

Even though our definition of business focuses on the operations of firms whose objectives include earning a profit for their owners, it is clear that the business concepts discussed in this text apply equally to **not-for-profit organizations** — *firms whose primary objective is something other than returning profits to their owners*. This sector includes museums, libraries, religious and human-service organizations, secondary schools, many health-care facilities, colleges and universities, symphony orchestras, fraternal organizations, government agencies, political parties, labour unions, and thousands of other groups.

Although not-for-profit organizations have service objectives not keyed to profitability targets, they still must secure sufficient revenues in the forms of membership fees, ticket sales, donations, and grants to cover their costs. They also deal with the same kinds of issues facing their profit-seeking counterparts: developing objectives aimed at serving their constituencies; planning; building an effective organization; attracting, training, and motivating an effective work force; acquiring financing to improve physical facilities; and offering goods and services aimed at providing satisfaction to their customers, clients, and patients. We will discuss marketing in not-for-profit organizations further in Chapter 11.

> **Business Term**
> **√ Profits**
> Rewards for the businessperson who takes the risks involved in creating and marketing want-satisfying goods and services that provide customer satisfaction.

> **Business Term**
> **√ Not-for-profit organizations**
> Firms whose primary objective is something other than returning profits to their owners.

Business concepts also apply to not-for-profit organizations. The Royal Ontario Museum uses effective and award-winning transit advertisements to attract visitors and sell its service.

THE PRIVATE ENTERPRISE SYSTEM

AN APPROPRIATE PLACE to begin our study of business is to describe the economic system to which the majority of Canadian and foreign businesses belong. The

private enterprise system, or capitalism, is *an economic system founded on the principle that competition among firms determines their success or failure in the marketplace and that this competition, in turn, best serves the needs of society.* Competition is the battle among businesses for consumer acceptance. Sales and profits are the yardsticks by which such acceptance is measured.

In the private enterprise system, firms must continually adjust their strategies, product offerings, service standards, and operating procedures; otherwise, competitors may gain larger shares of the industry's sales and profits. Consider the retailing industry. At one time Consumers Distributing and Eaton's were major forces in Canadian retailing. Over the 1990s, both companies were not able to adjust to market trends. As a result, Consumers Distributing declared bankruptcy in 1996 and Eaton's was closing outlets and struggling to stay alive by 1997. Wal-Mart, in contrast, had become the dominant department store, capturing 25 percent of department store sales in Canada since entering the market in 1994. Why? According to a 1997 study by Kubas Consultants, Wal-Mart had beaten every Canadian department store in categories such as value for money, customer service, and convenience — key competitive areas that keep customers coming back.[3]

Sears Canada Inc. was one company that was able to make adjustments to market conditions and new competition. Over the early to mid-1990s, it responded to a weak retail market by cutting costs and reducing employees. The number of full- and part-time workers, for example, plunged by about 30 percent to 35 000 in 1996, from 51 000 in 1990. By 1997, Sears was positioned to expand in a growing retail market — but not by adding traditional department stores that would compete with Wal-Mart. Sears' growth strategy involved "off-mall" businesses in specialty sectors such as renovations, hardware supplies, and auto parts.[4]

Business Term
√ **Private enterprise system**
An economic system founded on the principle that competition among firms determines their success or failure in the marketplace and that this competition, in turn, best serves the needs of society.

> ## THEY SAID IT
>
> "Some see private enterprise as a predatory target to be shot, others as a cow to be milked, but few are those who see it as a sturdy horse pulling the wagon."
>
> **WINSTON CHURCHILL, British statesman and prime minister**

Competition is the mechanism that guarantees the private enterprise system will continue to offer goods and services that provide high living standards and sophisticated lifestyles. Even not-for-profit organizations, like the Canadian Cancer Society, must compete for contributions with other not-for-profit groups, such as the Heart and Stroke Foundation of Canada, the local symphony, or your own college or university. Similarly, government departments such as Industry Canada compete with private industry in attempting to employ qualified personnel.

Basic Rights of the Private Enterprise System

Certain rights critical to the operation of capitalism are available to citizens living in a private enterprise economy. These, illustrated in Figure 1.1, include the rights to private property, profits, freedom of choice, and fair competition.

Figure 1.1

The right to *private property* is the most basic freedom under the private enterprise system. This system guarantees people the right to own, use, buy, sell, and bequeath most forms of property, including land, buildings, machinery, equipment, inventions, and various intangible properties.

The private enterprise system also guarantees business owners the right to all *profits* (after taxes) earned by the business. Although business is not assured of earning a profit, its owners are legally and ethically entitled to it.

Freedom of choice means that citizens are free to choose their employment, purchases, and investments. They can change jobs, negotiate wages, join labour unions, and choose among many different brands of goods and services. People living in the capitalist nations of North America, Europe, and other parts of the world are so accustomed to this freedom of choice that they sometimes forget its importance. The private enterprise economy maximizes human welfare and happiness by providing alternatives. Other economic systems sometimes limit freedom of choice in order to accomplish government goals, such as increasing industrial production.

The private enterprise system also permits *fair competition* by allowing the public to set rules for competitive activity. This is why the federal and provincial governments have passed laws to prohibit "cutthroat competition" — excessively competitive practices designed to eliminate competitors. Ground rules have also been established to outlaw price discrimination, fraud in financial markets, and deceptive practices in advertising and packaging.

How the Private Enterprise System Works

Capitalism, like other economic systems, requires certain inputs if it is to operate effectively. Economists use the term **factors of production** when they refer to *the four basic inputs of natural resources, capital, human resources, and entrepreneurship*. Not all firms require the same combination of these factors, but each business uses a unique blend of the four inputs.

Natural resources refer to everything useful as a productive input in its natural state, including agricultural land, building sites, forests, and mineral deposits. People who provide these basic resources required in any economic system receive *rent* as a factor payment.

Capital, the key resource of technology, tools, information, and physical facilities, frequently determines whether a fledgling computer firm, like Corel or Nortel, becomes an industry leader or remains small. *Technology* is a broad term that refers to such machinery and equipment as production machinery, telecommunications, and basic inventions. Information, frequently improved by technological innovations, is also a critical factor, since both management and operative employees require accurate, timely information in order to perform their assigned tasks effectively.

Money is necessary to acquire, maintain, and upgrade a firm's capital. These funds may come from investments of company owners, profits, or loans extended by others. Money then can be used to build factories; purchase raw materials and component parts; and hire, train, and compensate workers. People and firms who supply capital receive the factor payment of *interest*. Chapter 16 discusses investing in detail.

Human resources, the third factor of production, include the millions of managers and other employees of the world's businesses. Anyone who works — from Terry Matthews, chief executive officer of Newbridge Networks, to a self-employed gardener — is a human resource. In return for supplying companies with their managerial and other skills, human resources receive the factor payment of *wages* or *salaries*. Chapter 8 discusses human resource management in detail.

The final production factor is **entrepreneurship**, *the taking of risks involved in creating and operating a business*. The entrepreneur is the risk taker in the private enterprise system, the person who identifies a potentially profitable opportunity and then devises a plan and forms an organization to achieve that goal. Some entrepreneurs set up entirely new companies; others revitalize already established firms. If they are successful in their efforts, entrepreneurs receive the factor payment of *profits*.

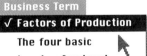

> **Business Term**
> √ **Entrepreneurship**
> The taking of risks involved in creating and operating a business.

> **Business Term**
> √ **Factors of Production**
> The four basic inputs of natural resources, capital, human resources, and entrepreneurship.

Successful entrepreneurs also receive considerable satisfaction of a nonmonetary nature. Clare Davenport is a good example. In 1995, at the age of 30, Davenport left Washington — and a consultant's salary well in excess of $100 000 (U.S.) — and moved back to Ontario to open Blue Dog Bagels. Within two years, she opened four stores in the Kitchener-Waterloo area of Ontario and by 1997 was looking for two additional outlets to open in the Toronto area. More freedom and flexibility and the ability to control her own destiny were big factors in Davenport's decision to go it alone. "I was getting to the point in my career where I was getting entrenched," she said.[5]

The entrepreneurial spirit lies at the heart of the private enterprise system. If no one took risks, there would be no successful businesses and the current economic system could not exist. We will discuss the role of the entrepreneur in more detail in Chapter 5.

Table 1.2 Eight Big Economies in 1997

Country	Canada	United States	Japan	Germany	Britain	France	Italy	Russia
Leader	Jean Chrétien	Bill Clinton	Ryutaro Hashimoto	Helmut Kohl	Anthony Blair	Jacques Chirac	Romano Prodi	Boris Yeltsin
Population (millions)	30	265	125	82	59	59	58	150
Inflation (%)	1.4	2.0	0.9	1.1	2.3	1.0	2.4	14.2
GDP growth rate (%)	3.5	3.6	2.3	2.2	3.0	2.5	1.0	3.0
Unemployment rate (%)	9.4	5.0	3.2	11.1	6.1	12.6	12.1	9.4

TODAY'S BUSINESS IS A GLOBAL BUSINESS

AS ONE OF of the world's most industrialized countries, Canada is a leader on the global front (see Table 1.2). In 1995, Canada rated first in export growth among Group of Seven (G7) nations. Our export trade was a major economic force during the 1990s. For example, the value of our goods and services exported grew by some 60 percent from 1992 to 1995. In contrast, our domestic growth (gross domestic product) grew by only 8.9 percent.[6]

The Canadian small business sector, representing about 52 percent of private sector jobs, has been slow to venture into the international arena. Only about 10 percent of small businesses export. However, there are some encouraging signs that this pattern is beginning to change. One example of this new breed of small business is Oasis Technology Ltd. of North York, Ontario. Oasis is a software company that develops programs for electronic funds transfer. It was on the list of *Profit* magazine's fastest-growing companies in 1996. All of Oasis' revenue — about $13 million — came from exports. "Our strategy has been to attack markets in Latin America, China and the Middle East, which have no real banking infrastructure," says Ashraf Dimitri, who founded the company in 1990.[7]

A particular issue, as we shall see in Chapter 3, is Canada's persistent economic dependence on the United States in both exports (see Figure 1.2) and imports. Over 20 percent of our total exports come from only four large companies — all of which have head offices in the United States. A second major issue is the relatively low value of the Canadian dollar — a lower dollar makes Canadian exports cheaper to buy (see Figure 1.3a). There is some concern, which is shared by Industry Canada, that a higher dollar may result in decreased exports as Canadian goods and services become relatively more expensive in foreign markets.[8]

Productivity: The Key to Global Competitiveness

To compete in a global marketplace, a nation's economy must be productive. **Productivity** is a measure of efficiency. It can be defined as *the relationship between the number of units of goods and services produced and the number of inputs of human and other resources necessary to produce them.* It is a ratio of output to input and can be calculated for a nation, an industry, or a single firm. When a constant amount of inputs generates increased outputs, an increase in productivity has occurred.

Figure 1.2 Canada's Exports

Other, 4%
Other Asia, 5.4%
Japan, 4.5%
EU15, 6.3%

United States, 79.7%

Figure 1.3a Canadian Dollar

Average annual price against U.S. dollar

$1.00
0.90
0.80
0.70
0.60
0

$0.73

'87 '88 '89 '90 '91 '92 '93 '94 '95 '96

Figure 1.3b Merchandise Trade Balance

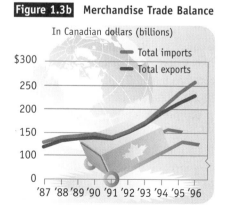

In Canadian dollars (billions)

Total imports
Total exports

$300
250
200
150
100
0

'87 '88 '89 '90 '91 '92 '93 '94 '95 '96

Total productivity considers all inputs necessary to produce a specific amount of outputs. Stated in equation form, it can be written as follows:

$$\text{Total Productivity} = \frac{\text{Outputs (goods or services produced)}}{\text{Inputs (human/natural resources, capital)}}$$

Many productivity ratios focus on only one of the inputs of the equation: labour productivity, or the output per worker-hour. An increase in labour productivity means that the same amount of work produces more goods and services.

C. N. Weber Ltd. is a privately held firm operating out of Kitchener, Ontario. A 140-year-old company with sales of around $100 million in 1996, it supplies goods to hardware retailers and heavy industry. The company invested heavily in technology and built a Web site for its wholesale business. This site improved the firm's productivity by helping it deliver products faster and more efficiently to customers.[9]

Over the 1990s, many Canadian companies like Weber invested heavily in new technology. As a result, people

> **Business Term**
> **√ Productivity**
> The relationship between the number of units of goods and services produced and the number of inputs of human and other resources necessary to produce them.

THE GLOBAL ARENA

MORE GOOD NEWS

We have already referred to the 1997 UN study that ranked Canada first in the world in level of human development. As well, a World Economic Forum study placed Canada fourth in international competitiveness. In a raft of other international studies released in 1997, Canada ranked near the top in international competitiveness and showed consistent improvement over previous years.

Here are the results of a few more studies done in May 1997 (some of these are discussed in more detail elsewhere in this chapter):

→ **Economist Intelligence Unit.** Canada ranked third among countries expected to have the best business environment over the next five years.

→ **Swiss-based International Institute for Management Development.** In world competitiveness, Canada moved to tenth position from twelfth spot the previous year.

→ **Deloitte & Touche Consulting Group.** Deloitte surveyed some 12 000 publicly traded companies in 56 countries. Twenty-three Canadian businesses were identified among the 200 fastest-growing ones in the world. Canada had three companies within the top fifteen. The highest-ranking U.S. firm was twenty-sixth on the list.

→ **Organization for Economic Co-operation and Development (OECD).** The OECD predicted that Canada's real gross domestic product (domestic growth without inflation) would grow by over 3 percent in the late 1990s — the highest of the 29 industrial countries reviewed.

Why has Canada done so well? In addition to internal factors within a company's control, such as strong strategic planning and high productivity, among the key external factors were

→ A relatively low dollar, which made Canadian products less expensive in foreign countries.

→ A strong U.S. economy, which created a healthy demand for our goods and services in the United States, Canada's major trading partner.

→ Federal and provincial deficit reduction, which created more international confidence in the strength of our economy.

→ The Bank of Canada's low inflation policy of the last ten years, which meant lower prices.

→ Free trade agreements with the United States (discussed in Chapter 3), which allowed more U.S. goods into the country and forced Canadian firms to wake up and become more cost-efficient.

Sources: Adapted from Janet McFarland, "Canada Shines in Global Ratings," *The Globe and Mail*, May 26, 1997, B1; and Alan Toulin, "Canada Tipped to Lead OECD in Economic Growth," *The Financial Post*, June 13, 1997, 7. Reprinted with permission from The Globe and Mail and The Financial Post.

CASE EXERCISE

THE PRODUCTIVITY DEBATE

Mouvement des Caisses Desjardins proudly announced, in late 1997, its ambitious plans to improve services, invest in technology and slash over 1320 *caisses populaires*. It planned to replace labour with technology to cut its operation costs and improve productivity. Similar measures had already been taken by the chartered banks. To remain competitive, Desjardins was following suit.

In 1998, another Quebec firm, Cognicase Inc., announced it would increase its R&D work force by some 2000 jobs. With financial assistance from the Quebec government, Cognicase would hire new R&D workers in four areas: software design, including Web applications; development of multiprotocol telecommunications servers; engineering; and the design of multimedia applications.

You would think that massive layoffs, along with concomitant investments in technology and R&D expenditures by companies such as these should increase the country's productivity and standard of living . . . right?

In the spring of 1997, over 200 economists and statisticians from around the world gathered in Ottawa to debate what has come to

were expecting improved productivity gains in the Canadian economy. But, as of 1997, this hadn't happened. The numbers from Statistics Canada in Table 1.3 show that businesses in Canada were just 0.4 percent more productive in 1996 than in 1995. This was the same sluggish growth rate in productivity recorded in 1995 — ironically, much lower than the rate of 2.2 percent in 1994. Even more worrisome to some experts was that Canada's productivity (both business and labour) slipped further behind that of the United States, its major competitor on the world market. Statistics Canada suggested that the widening productivity gap between Canada and the United States may have been the result of U.S. companies being more heavily concentrated in high-growth industries such as computers, office automation, and electronic equipment. John Lester, a senior economist with CIBC Wood Gundy, suggested that many Canadian companies went on a hiring binge in late 1995 and early 1996. The

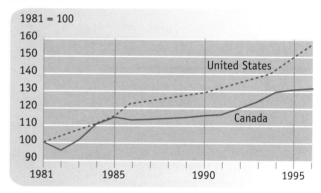

Figure 1.4 Productivity Index

economy did not pick up steam as expected and thus there were too many employees for the level of production, dragging down productivity. Whatever the reasons, as of 1996, there was general agreement that Canadian businesses had to do more to improve productivity. Reports from Statistics Canada, summarized in Figure 1.4, clearly indicate that we are lagging behind the United States in this area. "Canadian manufacturers have to achieve the same levels of productivity performance as their rivals to compete in export markets. You can't depend on a low dollar over the long term," said Jayson Myers, chief economist at the Alliance of Canadian Manufacturers and Exporters.[10]

In some cases, gross domestic product is used as an indicator of a nation's productivity or economic performance. **Gross domestic product (GDP)** is *the sum of all goods and services produced within a nation's boundaries.* According to the OECD, Canada leads the major industrial nations in economic growth — topping even the

Table 1.3 Productivity

Year	Business Productivity Annual % Change	Business Labour Productivity Annual % Change	
	Canada	Canada	U.S.
1991	−1.2	1.1	0.6
1992	0.2	1.6	3.4
1993	0.9	1.0	0.2
1994	2.2	1.8	0.5
1995	0.4	0.5	0.1
1996	0.4	0.3	1.0

be known as the productivity paradox: the empirical absence of any apparent payoffs in productivity growth despite two decades of exploding investments in computers, technology and research, and massive reductions in staffing. From 1961 to 1973, the international productivity of labour (output per unit of labour) and capital (output per unit of capital) increased by an average of 2.4 percent per year (2.2 percent in Canada). From 1974 to 1992 the international average was only 0.9 percent (0.6 percent in Canada). If rising productivity is the foundation of a rising standard of living, the data imply that the world's standard of living really hasn't improved that much.

1. What do you think are the reasons for this paradox?

2. Suppose Canada had a major nuclear accident or oil spill, costing the Canadian taxpayer $1 billion for cleanup. Would this type of environmental catastrophe increase our Gross National Product, which is one indicator of productivity?

3. How would you measure a country's economic and social well-being?

Source: Adapted from Bruce Little, "Productivity Paradox Puzzles Experts," *The Globe and Mail*, April 14, 1997, B1, B7; Konrad Yakabuski, "Cognicase to Create 2000 R&D Jobs," *The Globe and Mail*, September 2, 1998.

United States. The OECD estimates Canada's growth in GDP at about 3.3 percent in 1998 (see Figure 1.5). The major reason for this growth was our exports, which were spurred on by a relatively low Canadian dollar — despite our lower productivity.[11]

How Businesses Compete

Four basic degrees of competition exist in a private enterprise system: pure competition, monopolistic competition, oligopoly, and monopoly (see also Table 1.4). We can classify firms on the basis of the relative competitiveness of their particular industry.

Pure competition is a *market situation in which there are many firms in an industry close enough in size that no single company can influence market prices*. It involves similar products that cannot be differentiated from those of competitors. In a purely competitive market, it is relatively easy for a firm to enter or leave that market. Agriculture is probably the closest example of pure competition (although government price-support programs make it somewhat less competitive), and wheat is an example of a product that is similar from farm to farm.

Monopolistic competition is a *market situation in which firms are able to differentiate their products from those of competitors*. You can see monopolistic competition

> **Business Term**
> ✓ **Gross domestic product**
> The sum of all goods and services produced within a nation's boundaries.

> **Business Term**
> ✓ **Pure competition**
> Market situation in which there are many firms in an industry close enough in size that no single company can influence market prices.

Figure 1.5 OECD Economic Forecasts

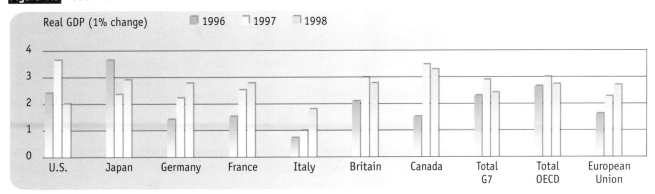

Table 1.4 Types of Competition

Characteristics	Pure Competition	Monopolistic Competition	Oligopoly	Monopoly
Number of competitors	Many	Few to many	Few	No direct competitors
Ease of entry into industry by new firms	Easy	Somewhat difficult	Difficult	Regulated by government
Similarity of goods or services offered by competing firms	Similar	Different	Can be similar or different	No directly competing goods or services
Control over price by individual firms	None	Some	Some	Considerable in a pure monopoly; little in a regulated monopoly
Examples	Small-scale farmer in Alberta	Blockbuster Video	Steel Company of Canada	Hydro-Québec

operating when you watch advertisements that try to persuade you to choose one brand over another. Monopolistic competition gives a firm some power over the price it charges. Think about retail stores, where prices can vary among different brands of aspirin, toothpaste, or shampoo.

Oligopoly is a *market in which there are few sellers.* In some oligopolies, such as steel, the products are similar; in others, such as cars, they are different. The huge investment required to enter the market tends to discourage new competitors. But the primary difference between oligopoly and the previously mentioned types of competition is that the limited number of sellers gives the oligopolist more control over price. In an oligopoly, the prices of competitive products are usually quite similar because substantial price competition would lessen every firm's profits. Price cuts by one firm in the industry typically are met by all competitors.

Monopoly is a *market situation in which there are no direct competitors.* Fewer and fewer markets are regulated in Canada by governments at any level. The trend today is to allow market forces to prevail and to investigate perceived abuses on an individual basis. One market that is regulated by government is that of local telephone service, which continues to be regulated by the Canadian Radio-television and Telecommunications Commission (CRTC). Local telephone service generally has a sole supplier, and in the

> **Business Term**
> ✓ **Monopolistic competition**
> Market situation in which firms are able to differentiate their products from those of competitors.

> **Business Term**
> ✓ **Oligopoly**
> Market in which there are few sellers.

> **Business Term**
> ✓ **Monopoly**
> Market situation in which there are no direct competitors.

public interest firms selling this service are subject to price regulation. The monopoly situation continues to change with the ever-increasing frequency of wireless communication devices being introduced into the marketplace. However, these services are relatively costly and, as such, are not seriously considered a substitute for any but the most affluent customers. In a pure monopoly, a firm would have substantial control over pricing, but in a regulated monopoly, pricing is subject to rules imposed by the regulators. There are few directly competitive products in a regulated monopoly, and entry into the industry is restricted by the government. In fact, in some U.S. states, a public utility periodically must seek voter approval to continue its service.

Most nations contain examples of each type of competition. For example, most businesses in the Czech Republic were state-owned and, until recently, enjoyed monopolies in their respective industries. Today, the Czech economy can be described as an oligopoly that is evolving toward monopolistic competition as more and more Czech entrepreneurs start small, privately owned businesses.

Nowhere is China's rapid move to capitalism more evident than in Guangdong province, Hong Kong's closest neighbour of 66 million people. Guangdong's brand-hungry consumers, with the highest incomes in all of China (average $3900 annually), can buy Adidas and Reebok sneakers ($95 to $130), Quaker oatmeal ($4.50), Skippy peanut butter ($4), Coke and 7-Up (50 cents per can), and Van Heusen shirts ($16). Fast-food fanciers can purchase Happy Meals from the nearest McDonald's outlet.[12]

BUSINESS OPPORTUNITIES AND CHALLENGES IN THE LATE 1990s

EVERY PERIOD IN history has posed particular challenges and obstacles to business, and the current era is no exception. The way that we respond to these challenges today will have a significant impact on Canada — and the world — tomorrow.

Importance of Partnerships and Strategic Alliances

Traditionally, successful firms were headed by visionaries who bested competition in the marketplace to build their organizations. A growing trend of the late 1990s is for firms to improve their competitiveness by teaming up with other companies to create **strategic alliances**, *partnerships formed to create a competitive advantage*. The most common reasons for the growth of strategic alliances in Canada and other industrial countries are

- Improved efficiencies due to size (economies of scale).

- The benefits of resource pooling.

- Reduction of risk and economies of cost sharing.

These partnerships often cross national borders and can involve any size of company, from the tiniest business to two or more industrial giants.

A common perception is that strategic alliances are mostly confined to large firms in the emerging telecommunications and high-tech sectors. Another perception is that the federal government frowns on strategic alliances in that they limit competition. A 1996 Industry Canada study dispelled these myths: "In fact, Canadian small and medium-sized businesses from all sectors are active participants in numerous forms of interfirm cooperation. In addition, the government's position on strategic alliances has now become more clear and positive. Industry Canada believes that 'it is the Bureau of Competition Policy's experience that most strategic alliances do not raise issues under the Competition Act.'"

> **Business Term**
> √ **Strategic alliances**
> **Partnerships formed to create a competitive advantage.**

WHERE

The Jobs Are

Jim Pattison, President and CEO, The Jim Pattison Group, Vancouver, BC

Do What You Like

"Good business opportunities might not mean a lot if you have no interest in that business. It really depends on the individual's own qualities, interests, and education. You can surround yourself with the necessary experts, such as lawyers and tax experts, as I have. I'd go into exactly the same business. I started as a car salesman and it's treated me very well. I learned more in the used car lot than I ever did studying psychology at university. If a young person came to me for advice, the first thing I'd ask them is 'What do you like?'"

Other major findings from this ground-breaking Industry Canada study indicate[13]

- Companies often participate in more than one alliance. The medium number is four.

- About two-thirds of strategic alliances are with foreign companies.

- One in five alliances are with competitors.

- About 13 percent of all alliances are with suppliers.

- Two-thirds of all alliances were rated as "successful."

- The three key reasons for a successful alliance were

  1. Effective support from senior management.

  2. A clear sense of mission and objectives.

  3. A strong leadership team with personal commitment to the alliance's success.

Clearly, as the Industry Canada findings in Table 1.5 show, businesses see strategic alliances as the most important form of strategic approach to expanding and remaining successful, followed by mergers and acquisitions, direct exports, and foreign direct investments.

As a business traveler, wouldn't it be great if the airline you fly most often was linked to other major airlines that could fly you anywhere you wanted to go. Smoothly. Effortlessly. Efficiently. Wouldn't it be great if you had more access to more airport lounges. And when flying on any of these major airlines, you could earn mileage that counts toward higher status in any of their frequent flyer programs. Wouldn't it be great if you could enjoy the same high standards of service whenever and wherever you fly. That's the idea behind Star Alliance™, a network of Air Canada, Lufthansa, SAS, THAI and United Airlines. A partnership that signals a fundamental change in business travel. And these benefits are just the beginning. We will be offering even more in the months ahead. We know you have choices when you fly, and we're making sure Star Alliance is always your best choice. After all, there's no better way in the world to get around the world.

Imagine.

AIR CANADA   UNITED AIRLINES   Thai   Lufthansa   SAS

STAR ALLIANCE
The airline network for Earth.

This "Star Alliance" among giant airlines is the epitome of strategic alliances, marking the way for businesses today and tomorrow.

Importance of Quality

In December of 1996, *The Financial Post* announced its list of Canada's "50 Best Managed Private Companies." These firms, large and small, were major job generators with over 14 000 employees — up 62 percent from 1994. Their total sales exceeded $2 billion, a 66 percent increase from 1994. The leaders of these companies consistently emphasized the importance of quality management — a commitment to *quality* — as a crucial business goal.[14]

International trade was a key factor in the success of these winning companies. Almost 40 percent of their sales came from exports. How did they compete and succeed on the world market? Roger Jarvis, president of Jarvis Travel Ltd. of Calgary, sums it up this way: "Quality has to be thought of as a religion."[15] The results of the "50 Best" are not unique. Canada has proven it can compete on the world market — and it's getting better. In the annual World Economic Forum study released in the spring of 1996, Canada placed fourth in international competitiveness — a considerable improvement from 1995, when it ranked eighth. It should come as no surprise that quality management was a key factor. The World Economic Forum ranked Canada third in overall quality of corporate management, worldwide.[16]

Table 1.5 **Relative Importance of Strategic Approaches by Canadian Companies to Build Global Market Capabilities**
(percentage of all respondents)

Strategic Approaches	Least Important	Important	Most Important
Strategic alliances	8	26	66
Mergers and acquisitions	27	22	51
Exports through own distribution networks	47	18	35
Start-ups (foreign direct investments)	58	16	26

In the last few years, it has become increasingly important for Canadian businesses to meet stringent international standards. This is why many of our leading companies have embraced ISO (International Standards Organization) as the international benchmark for quality. For example, Northern Telecom (Nortel) is one of Canada's leading telecommunications giants, with over 23 000 workers across the country. ISO approval has been key to its global expansion. Smaller companies, such as Pacific Western Brewing Co. of Prince George, BC, have also benefited from quality and ISO standards.

Training and research and development are also key to maintaining the quality edge. Nortel, for example,

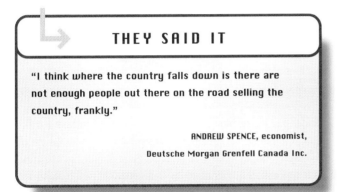

THEY SAID IT

"I think where the country falls down is there are not enough people out there on the road selling the country, frankly."

ANDREW SPENCE, economist,
Deutsche Morgan Grenfell Canada Inc.

announced in 1997 that it would spend $1 million a year to support the Nortel Institute, an advanced institute for telecommunications at the University of Toronto. This one firm alone absorbs one-fifth of the country's bachelor-level graduates in engineering and computer sciences and close to one-third of those with master's degrees or doctorates.[17]

In Chapter 6, we will take a closer look at the importance of quality in achieving business success.

Importance of Technology

Technology involves *the application to business of knowledge based on discoveries in science, inventions, and innovations.* Technological breakthroughs such as videotelephones, orthoscopic surgery, and bullet trains result in new goods and services for consumers, better customer service, lower prices, and improved working conditions. Technology can make products obsolete — cassette tapes and CDs, for example, wiped out the market for vinyl record albums — but just as easily can open up new business opportunities.

Computers and technology are now part of the Canadian personal and business landscape. In 1997, at least $65 billion will be spent in the Canadian information

technology sector alone — an increase of about 66 percent since 1990. Other examples of the pervasiveness of technology include the following:

- In 1997, almost one in three Canadian households owned a computer, and about 8 percent of these were connected to the Internet (see also Figure 1.6). Experts predict that these percentages will grow in leaps and bounds over the next few years.[18]

- Some 22 000 of our schools, libraries, colleges, and universities are connected to the Internet.[19]

- At least 50 percent of employed Canadians use a computer at work.[20]

- About 25 percent of Canada's 2+ million self-employed workers are hooked up to the Internet (see Figure 1.7). In the next few years, up to three-quarters of the self-employed people in Canada will use the Internet as an indispensable business tool according to a 1997 report by the Canadian Federation of Independent Business (CFIB).[21]

- There are about 650 000 teleworkers (those working from home and connected to their employer electronically) in Canada — a number that is expected to double by the next millennium.[22]

This year, companies around the world will spend billions on computer hardware and software. Many of these purchases will involve building new computer networks and expanding existing networks that link employees, suppliers, and customers. Computer networks and electronic mail (e-mail) — a system for sending and receiving written messages through computers — permit more direct exchanges of information within organizations, by-passing formal corporate hierarchies.

Technological developments like networks provide three major benefits for organizations. First, they speed up business operations by allowing people to exchange information and make decisions much more quickly. Second, they by-pass functional boundaries — people in different departments can communicate directly rather than going through formal channels. Finally, computer networks allow people with diverse skills to work together.

Business Term

√ **Technology**
The application to business of knowledge based on discoveries in science, inventions, and innovations.

Changes in technology can create whole new industries and new ways of doing business. Technological innovations, ranging from Web TVs and voice recognition to advanced fibre optics and online services play such an important role in advancing a nation's standard of living that they are featured in every chapter of this text. In Chapter 10, we will take a closer look at how various technologies — especially the Internet — can help business-people make more informed decisions.

Figure 1.6 Computers in Canada

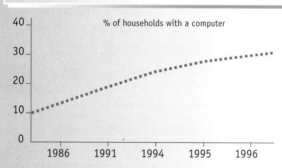

Household Computer Market

- The percentage of Canadian households in 1996 with computers totalled 31.6.
- Of those households, 49.2 percent had a modem and 7.4 percent had access to the Internet.

Growth Triples in a Decade

% of households with a computer

40

30

20

10

0

1986   1991   1994   1995   1996

- Income levels and children determine the likelihood of having a computer in the home.
- 45 percent of single-family households with children under 18 years of age (or about 1.7 million) had a computer compared to 18 percent a decade ago.
- 65 percent of households with an income of over $70 000 reported having a computer.

Internet Penetration

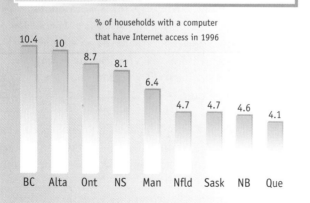

% of households with a computer that have Internet access in 1996

10.4   10   8.7   8.1   6.4   4.7   4.7   4.6   4.1

BC   Alta   Ont   NS   Man   Nfld   Sask   NB   Que

Importance of Focussing on People

Earlier, we noted that people are a crucial input to any economic system. Ironically, perhaps, the growing prevalence of technology makes it even more important for organizations to make effective use of human resources. Computer networks allow employees to work together directly and pool their collective knowledge. This tends to flatten the organizational hierarchy, creating a more informal organization.

More and more organizations are discovering the benefits of *teamwork*, in which employees work together on a project. At the Lotus Notes division of IBM Canada, software writers in Asia and Europe team up via computer networks with their Canadian colleagues to develop new products. It used to take IBM three to four months to create a Japanese version of a new English-language software package; thanks to international teamwork, it now takes three or four weeks.

Teamwork, the focus of Chapter 9, allows organizations to reap the benefits of a wide range of employee skills and compete internationally. Komex International, one of *The Financial Post*'s "50 Best Managed Private Companies" is a successful environmental consulting firm. It has over 100 employees in Calgary and another 50 or so in joint ventures located in the United States and Britain. Sales are in excess of $15 million. Back in 1992, Komex successfully negotiated an environmental study on the impact of an oil pipeline to be laid in Yemen by Canadian Occidental Petroleum. The project was headed by Joseph Wells, Komex vice-president of environmental engineering. The bidding process took two months and involved a team of fifteen professionals, including civil engineers, soil scientists, and social anthropologists as well as vegetation and geomatics specialists. Wells realized that archaeology might play a part, so the team also included the German Archaeological Institute based in Sana'a, Yemen's capital.

THEY SAID IT

"If people run roughshod over archeology, that can cause cultural problems. [In foreign countries], Canadian Occidental Petroleum has made the corporate decision that they would follow the same environmental procedures they would in Canada, even though governments may not require it."

FRED CLARIDGE, president, Komex International Ltd.

Figure 1.7   Small Businesses on the Net

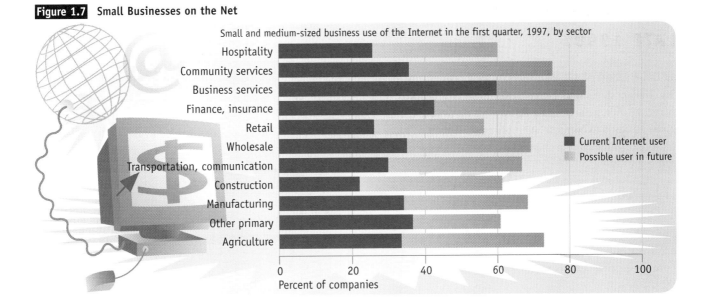

Small and medium-sized business use of the Internet in the first quarter, 1997, by sector

Percent of companies

- Current Internet user
- Possible user in future

Teamwork and partnering not only won the job for Komex in the Middle East, but has led to other work in Europe, South America, Asia, and Africa.[23]

"We empower our people to take the 'bull by the horns,'" says Fred Claridge, president of Komex.[24] More and more businesses are *empowering* their employees by giving them the power, training, and encouragement to analyze situations and make their own decisions. The training process and empowerment begin right at the hiring stage. See Chapter 6 for more on empowerment. People are hired for their attitude, says Isadore Sharp, chairman and chief executive officer of the Toronto-based Four Seasons Hotels, a company he founded in 1960. Four Seasons is a leading Canadian firm that has been identified, among some 238 businesses worldwide, as having a competitive edge in its industry. But Sharp adds that finding employees with the right attitude isn't easy. When the company hired staff for a New York hotel, it looked at 17 000 candidates before winnowing out all but 400. These 400 people were then interviewed 5 times, ending with the hotel manager. However, this elite group is now "out there to demonstrate why they're one of the selected few," said Sharp.[25]

Importance of Outsourcing

Another fast-growing trend in business is **outsourcing**, in which *a company farms out one or more of its in-house operations to outside specialists*. Outsourcing can save money because a company does not have to hire additional staff to perform those functions, thereby producing savings on

salaries and benefits while freeing existing personnel to do other tasks. For example, a firm may outsource its warehousing, payroll, delivery services, or data-processing operations. In 1993, Canada Post signed one of the world's largest outsourcing agreements ever. Heavily invested in older processing systems, Canada Post knew it had to reduce computer operating costs. The purpose of this 10-year,

Business Term

√ **Outsourcing**

Farming out one or more company operations to outside specialists.

$1 billion agreement with SHL Systemhouse was to revamp its technology infrastructure. A major objective was to reduce the company's reliance on mainframe and related costs. Why did Canada Post outsource this project? According to Bruce MacLeod, a corporate manager at Canada Post, "We were looking at ways of concentrating on our core business which is moving mail. In the long term, we felt we would be well served by working with an organization that specializes in the information technology field." Canada Post chose outsourcing because it was more efficient and effective and would allow them to "stick to their knitting" — to deliver the mail on time.[26]

Outsourcing is another recurring theme of this book. In Chapter 3, we will look at outsourcing as a way to enter foreign markets. In Chapters 7 and 8, we will examine different management styles and how outsourcing can enhance the productivity of an organization's human resources. Chapter 9 will explore the importance of teamwork and communication skills, and how these relate to outsourcing, in building an effective organization.

THE MANAGER OF THE LATE 1990s

L EADERSHIP IS A trait that has long been admired. As Italian statesman Niccolò Machiavelli remarked 500 years ago, "There is nothing more difficult to take in hand, more perilous to conduct, or more uncertain in its success than to take the lead in the introduction of a new order of things."[27]

Part III of this book will focus on management. Here, we'll briefly highlight some important issues for the 1990s.

What qualities will the successful manager of the future need? Among the most important will be the ability to manage change, to create and sustain a vision of how an organization can succeed, to apply critical thinking and creativity to business challenges, and to manage an increasingly diverse work force.

Need for a New Type of Manager

Once, managers were encouraged to be "organization people," grey-flannel-suit wearers who worked in a world of strict dress codes and rigid hierarchies. To be successful today, however, an organization must remain flexible and open to change. Businesses must be able to update technologies, identify new marketplace needs, create new goods and services, and stay ahead of global as well as domestic competitors. This creates a need for a new type of manager who can serve as a change agent — one who can perceive the need for change and can manage the change process successfully.

Factors that require organizational change can come from both external and internal sources, and successful managers must be aware of both. External sources might include feedback from customers, developments in the international marketplace, economic trends, and new technologies. Internal factors might arise from new company goals, employee needs, labour–union demands, or problems in production lines.

Managing internationally is a key issue in today's global economy. Some managers may perform well on their home turf but flop when they take on challenging assignments abroad. "Employers with global business should be looking for people with 'international adaptability,'" suggests a survey of successful international CEOs by Hay Group Management Consultants. The best global managers are sensitive enough to change their

behaviours to fit the demands of different cultures. For example, the Hay study showed that Canadian and German CEOs tend to make decisions based on price, quality, or other relatively objective criteria. "The deal's the thing, regardless of personal factors," explains the Hay study, which describes these countries' business culture as "contractual." In contrast, building a personal relationship before doing business is important in such countries as Japan, Singapore, and Brazil. A manager has to understand that making a business decision based on friendship, gender, or ethnic background — rather than on performance — may be very acceptable in Singapore or Brazil. For these countries, Canadian managers may have to adjust their style accordingly.[28]

Need for a Vision

A second important managerial quality is **vision**, *the ability to perceive marketplace needs and what an organization must do to satisfy them*. Thomas Edison, the famed inventor of thousands of products ranging from the electric light bulb to the phonograph and motion picture, was such a person. Not only did he have the ability to make great technological breakthroughs, but he also never forgot to focus on salable solutions to very real problems. As he put it, "Anything that won't sell, I don't want to invent. Its sales is proof of utility and utility is success."[29] This book is filled with examples of business leaders who are driven by a compelling vision. A few are

• Helen Sinclair, who left her high-paying, prestigious, and powerful position as head of the influential Canadian Banking Association (CBA) and launched a new company, BankWorks Trading Inc. (Chapter 15).

• George Cohon, senior chairman of McDonalds Restaurants of Canada Ltd., and vice chairman of Moscow McDonalds (Chapter 3).

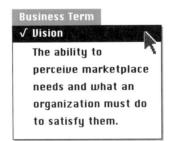

Business Term

√ **Vision**

The ability to perceive marketplace needs and what an organization must do to satisfy them.

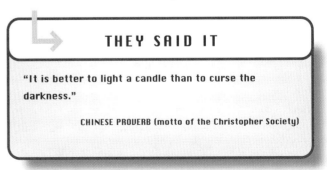

THEY SAID IT

"It is better to light a candle than to curse the darkness."

CHINESE PROVERB (motto of the Christopher Society)

- Kazuko Komatsu, the businessperson who revived the Pacific Western Brewing Company (Chapter 6).

- Terry Matthews, co-founder of Mitel Corporation and Newbridge Networks Corp. (Chapter 10).

Importance of Critical Thinking and Creativity

Critical thinking and creativity are essential qualities in a good manager. **Critical thinking** refers to *the process of determining the authenticity, accuracy, and worth of information, knowledge claims, or arguments.* Perhaps a simpler definition is "informed scepticism." Critical thinkers do not just accept what they hear or see at face value; they evaluate the information and form their own conclusions.[30]

Creativity is *the process of searching for or using novel relationships among objects, people, and ideas.* It has also been defined as *a process of generating new ideas to deal with change.* Creativity is the process of undoing the wall of rationality that gets in the way of everything from inventing to moving office furniture.

CREATIVITY ALERT

The position held by Tom Grueskin at computer supplier Gateway 2000 is Chief Imagination Officer (CIO). "As organizations grow, creativity tends to get blocked. People's roles become more specialized and they tend to distance themselves from the big picture. My job is to supply building blocks of creativity," he says.

Here are some characteristics of creativity:[31]

- Creativity resides in the mind, not in the muscle.

- Jon Henderson, an executive at Hallmark, says creativity is not a question of "'What is it we do?' but 'How do we think?' You can't just order up a good idea or spend money to find one. You have to build a climate and give people the freedom to change."

- You cannot make creativity happen. You have to allow it to happen.

- John Kao, author of *Jamming, the Art and Discipline of Business Creativity*, says that executives must hire creative thinkers and then set the stage for them to

use their talents. Creativity is about changing an organizational environment to allow people to *undo* constraints.

Successful managers design an organization that encourages creativity and critical thinking. These organizations tend to be loosely structured; employees frequently have overlapping responsibilities, work in teams, and enjoy a great deal of flexibility in carrying out assignments. Managers in such companies encourage employees to learn new skills and experiment with new approaches; they reward innovation but do not punish people for making honest mistakes in the process.

> **Business Term**
> ✓ **Critical thinking**
> The process of determining the authenticity, accuracy, and worth of information, knowledge claims, or arguments.

James Collins, a professor at the Stanford Business School who has studied a number of innovative companies, compares creative, critical thinkers to clockmakers as opposed to timekeepers. "A timekeeper churns out product without any thought of where he's headed," explains Collins. "A clockmaker builds a company to last. He or she isn't wedded to any single product or idea.... Entrepreneurs should have a vision for their company first, then experiment, sometimes unsuccessfully, with ideas."[32]

> **Business Term**
> ✓ **Creativity**
> The process of searching for or using novel relationships among objects, people, and ideas; and the process of generating new ideas to deal with change.

DOING WELL BY DOING GOOD

IN RECENT YEARS, headlines have publicized unethical situations and improper conduct on the part of businesspeople and employees. The 1996 Bre-X scandal is a classic case that we will deal with briefly in the next chapter. Here are other examples:

- In the early 1990s, the Alberta Securities Commission (ASC) assessed heavy financial penalties on Larry Ryckman, a flamboyant stock promoter and entrepreneur. The ASC ruled that Ryckman had repeatedly manipulated the province's stock market.

> ### THEY SAID IT
>
> **"This is the first time in the history of business that you can be great at what you do and be out of business tomorrow."**
>
> KEN BLANCHARD, consultant and author of some eighteen books, including his trademark work <u>The One Minute Manager</u>

• In early 1995, two former stockbrokers, Alex Pancer and David (Pud) Foster, pleaded guilty to fraud charges involving $6 million. Pancer and Foster were the owners of the Toronto-based Durham Securities Corp. They used the company to manipulate the market price of shares in Bayridge Developments Ltd. and Astra Resources Ltd.[33]

• In 1996, Justice Joseph O'Brien concluded that former hockey czar Alan Eagleson had deliberately misled his client, Boston Bruin Mike Gillis, in a disability insurance claim. Eagleson told Gillis outside lawyers had been hired when in fact they had not, in order that Eagleson could collect a large fee from Gillis. By doing so, Eagleson "was in serious breach of those duties and of his professional responsibilities." Eagleson was ordered to pay punitive damages.[34]

• In late 1996, police seized thousands of kiddy porn images that had been downloaded from the Internet using a National Defence computer. Police charged a physicist, who was a married father of two with a PhD in physics and a civilian employee of the Defence Department in Ottawa.[35]

Despite the headlines, however, the fact remains that most businesspeople believe in the principles of ethics and social responsibility. **Business ethics** refer to *standards of business conduct and moral values.* They involve the right and wrong actions that arise in any work environment. While sometimes a conflict may appear to exist between decisions that are ethical and those that are practical or profitable, it is nonetheless essential for companies to evaluate their ethical responsibilities in decision making.

Social responsibility is a *management philosophy that highlights the social and economic effects of managerial decisions.* For instance, business decisions can have an impact on the environment. We are becoming increasingly aware that the earth's resources are not limitless. In fact, it is possible for us to run out of natural resources,

> **Business Term**
> √ **Business ethics**
> **Standards of business conduct and moral values.**

The World According to Big Shot

BIG SHOT: Slink, I want you to find out if we have any excess employee pension funds. Check the funds for our managers and directors as well.
SLINKY: Why's that?

BIG SHOT: If there's any excess, find a lawyer with Eaton's experience. We could be in for a large cash injection.
SLINKY: That's not fair. It's not your money.

BIG SHOT: So what! If it's legal it's got to be ethical. Come to think of it, pension funds is how the mob got its start in the States. I must be on the right track this time.

→ Do you agree with Big Shot?

or to pollute our water, land, and air so badly that it will affect the way we live (just ask people in downtown Mexico City, where the air is so filthy that many residents suffer from chronic coughs and bronchitis). Enlightened business managers must find creative ways to make a profit without damaging the environment. A good example of an attempt to protect our fragile ecosystem is the banning of CFC refrigerants that threaten the ozone layer. Since 1994, automobile air-conditioning systems have been redesigned to use CFC-free coolants.

Social responsibility also includes addressing the needs of employees and the general public. With more single-parent families, child care and elder care are becoming crucial needs. At the present time, a relatively small percentage of firms offer child- and elder-care help

> **Business Term**
> √ **Social responsibility**
> Management philosophy that highlights the social and economic effects of managerial decisions.

to employees, whether through subsidies or by sponsoring day-care centres at the work site. Firms providing such programs, however, have found that they reduce employee absenteeism and turnover, and serve as effective recruiting tools.

In Chapter 2, we will explore business ethics and social responsibility in greater detail.

WHAT'S AHEAD

THE STUDY OF business is an exciting, rewarding field involving a global landscape that is always changing. Now that we have introduced some basic terms and issues in the business world of the late 1990s, let's identify several major themes that we will encounter in the remainder of this book. Throughout the text, we discuss five major issues that will be crucial in the coming years:

- Ethics and social responsibility

- The importance of technology

- The need for improved productivity and continuous improvement in quality

- The importance of well-trained human resources who are empowered to make decisions about their work, are flexible enough to succeed in different work areas, and work well with people from different departments inside the organization

- Global competitiveness

Each of the essential business activities and functions — developing objectives and creating plans; establishing an effective work force; fostering teamwork and communication; obtaining and using needed information; and producing, marketing, and financing the firm's output — are the subjects of the following fifteen chapters. We begin our study of business by examining the business environment and its related responsibilities in Chapter 2.

WHERE The Jobs Are

Sam Sniderman, founder, Sam The Record Man, Toronto

Canadian Content

"I'd stay in some form of entertainment business, which will grow more and more, especially home entertainment. If you're hearing that entertainment is now one of the biggest businesses, you're hearing it twenty years too late.

Push Canada and Canadians. We have tremendous amounts of assets in the Canadian talent bank. You'll profit from being involved financially, philosophically, and morally."

SUMMARY OF LEARNING OUTCOMES

1. Explain what a business is and how it operates within the private enterprise system.

Business consists of all profit-seeking activities as well as enterprises — such as not-for-profit organizations — that provide the goods and services necessary to an economic system. A capitalist economy is a private enterprise system in which success is determined by competition among business firms.

2. Define the roles of competition and of the entrepreneur in a private enterprise system.

Competition is the struggle among businesses for consumer acceptance. It is a critical aspect of the private enterprise system that helps to determine which companies succeed. An entrepreneur is a risk taker, someone who finds a profitable opportunity and forms a business to fill that need. Profits are the financial rewards achieved by successful entrepreneurs and businesspeople.

3. Outline the basic rights of the private enterprise system.

Certain basic rights are available to citizens living in a private enterprise economy: the right to private property; the legal and ethical right to any profits that might result from an enterprise; freedom of choice in purchases, employment, and investments; and fair competition.

4. Explain the concepts of gross domestic product and productivity.

Productivity, the relationship between the number of units of goods and services produced and the number of inputs of human and other resources necessary to produce them, is a measure of the efficiency of production. Productivity gains are important to a country's economic health because they lead to higher living standards and greater global competitiveness. A widespread measure of a nation's productivity is its gross domestic product (GDP). As more and more industries compete in a global marketplace, productivity will become an even more crucial factor in a nation's economic health.

5. Identify the degrees of competition that can exist in a private enterprise system.

The four basic degrees of competition in a private enterprise system are pure competition, monopolistic competition, oligopoly, and monopoly. In pure competition, products are similar, there are many firms in a particular industry, and firms are close enough in size that no one company can influence prices. In monopolistic competition, firms are able to differentiate their products from those of competitors, giving companies some control over the prices they can charge. Oligopoly is a market in which there are few sellers, so the firms have more control over prices. Monopoly is a situation in which a firm has no competitors, so it has substantial control over its prices unless they are regulated by the government.

6. Discuss the major challenges and opportunities facing managers in the late 1990s.

Challenges include
- The possibility of forming strategic alliances with other firms to create a competitive advantage.
- An emphasis on quality as a crucial business goal for an entire company.
- Investments in technology that speed up business operations, reduce costs, and allow people with diverse skills to work together.
- The need to make effective use of people through teamwork, empowerment, and training.
- The growth of outsourcing, which can save a company money while offering important business opportunities.

7. Describe the most important qualities that managers should possess.

Among the most important qualities for managers are the ability to manage change, to create and sustain a vision of how an organization can succeed, and to apply critical thinking and creativity to business challenges. Factors that necessitate organizational change can come from both external and internal sources; successful managers must be aware of both. Successful managers design an organization that encourages creativity and critical thinking.

8. **Explain the ethical and social responsibilities of business.**

Most businesspeople believe in the principles of ethics and social responsibility. Business ethics deal with the right and wrong actions that arise in any work environment. Social responsibility is a management phi-

losophy that highlights the social and economic effects of managerial decisions. Ethical and social responsibilities involve being aware of how business decisions can affect the environment, employees, and the general public.

Key Terms Quiz

business ethics
strategic alliance
monopoly
critical thinking
business
creativity
productivity

vision
pure competition
private enterprise system
social responsibility
outsourcing
factors of production
technology

entrepreneurship
not-for-profit organization
profits
oligopoly
gross domestic product (GDP)

1. All profit-seeking activities and enterprises that provide goods and services necessary to an economic system.
2. Rewards for the businessperson who takes the risks involved in blending people, technology, and information in creating and marketing want-satisfying goods and services that provide customer satisfaction.
3. Organization whose primary objective is something other than returning profits to its owners.
4. Economic system in which success or failure is determined by how well firms match and counter the offerings of competitors.
5. Basic inputs into the private enterprise system, including natural resources, labour, capital, and entrepreneurship.
6. Taking risks to set up and operate a business.
7. The relationship between the number of units of goods and services produced and the number of inputs of human and other resources necessary to produce them.
8. Sum of all goods and services produced within a nation's boundaries.
9. Situation in which there are many firms in an industry and none can influence market prices individually.
10. Farming out one or more of a company's in-house operations to an outside specialist.
11. Market having few sellers and substantial entry restrictions.
12. Market situation in which there are no direct competitors.
13. Partnership formed to create a competitive advantage.
14. The application to business of knowledge based on discoveries in science, inventions, and innovations.
15. The ability to perceive marketplace needs and what an organization must do to satisfy them.
16. The process of determining the authenticity, accuracy, and worth of information, knowledge claims, or arguments.
17. A process of generating new ideas to deal with change.
18. Standards of business conduct and moral values.
19. Management philosophy that highlights the social and economic effects of managerial decisions.

Other Important Terms

capital   empowering   monopolistic competition   quality

competition   human resources   natural resources   teamwork

Review Questions

1. Define profit and explain its role in the private enterprise system.

2. What roles do entrepreneurs play in the private enterprise system? What types of people become entrepreneurs?

3. Discuss the basic rights upon which the private enterprise system is based. How does each right contribute to the effective functioning of the private enterprise system?

4. Identify and describe the components of the private enterprise system.

5. What is meant by the term productivity? Why is productivity an important public issue today?

6. Has total Canadian productivity improved over the 1990s? How might Canada's productivity, relative to other countries, affect our international trade?

7. What can a company gain from forming a strategic alliance?

8. Why are critical thinking and creativity important characteristics in a manager?

9. Is it realistic for a profit-seeking company to "do well by doing good"? Defend your answer.

Discussion Questions

1. Apply critical-thinking and creative skills to a problem you have experienced at school or work. What solutions can you devise?

2. Profit sometimes has been described as the regulator of the private enterprise system. Discuss the meaning of this comment.

3. This chapter presents a number of challenges that Canada must face in order to remain competitive in international business. Suppose the prime minister gave you the power to address these challenges. Describe the policies you think Canada should implement to remain competitive in international business.

4. In 1997, Ontario Hydro was drowning in a sea of red ink — it had a debt load of about $35 billion. Ontario Premier Mike Harris was advised to end the 90-year monopoly of Ontario Hydro and allow the province's consumers to buy their electrons on the open market. What are the advantages and disadvantages of allowing free competition in the market for electrical power?

5. Comment on this statement: "All organizations must serve their customers or clients in some way in order to survive."

Answers to Key Terms Quiz

1. business 2. profits 3. not-for-profit organization 4. private enterprise system 5. factors of production 6. entrepreneurship 7. productivity 8. gross domestic product (GDP) 9. pure competition 10. outsourcing 11. oligopoly 12. monopoly 13. strategic alliance 14. technology 15. vision 16. critical thinking 17. creativity 18. business ethics 19. social responsibility

Notes

1. Adapted from Brian Hutchinson, "Merchants of Boom," *Canadian Business*, May 1997, 39–48; Bertrand Marotte (Southam Newspapers), "Eaton's Seeks Bankruptcy Protection," *The Ottawa Citizen*, February 28, 1997, A1; Leonard Stern, "Retail Genius Shaped Heritage," *The Ottawa Citizen*, February 28, 1997, A3; Carolyn Leitch and Paul Waldie, "Family's Business, Political Ties Run Deep," *The Globe and Mail*, March 1, 1997, B4; John Heinzl and Gayle MacDonald, "Ex-Bay Boss to Lead Eaton's," *The Globe and Mail*, June 6, 1997, B1, B15; Judith Knelman (University of Western Ontario), "When Eaton's and I Were Young," *The Globe and Mail*, June 10, 1997, A22; Ann Gibbon and Marina Strauss, "Eaton's Chief Pegs Need at Up to $300-million," *The Globe and Mail*, June 10, 1997, B1, B13; and Elizabeth Church, "If I Ran Eaton's," *The Globe and Mail*, March 6, 1997, B13.

2. Paul Knox, "Canada Still Place to Live, UN Says," *The Globe and Mail*, June 12, 1997, B1, B9.

3. Hutchinson, "Merchants of Boom," 39.

4. Marina Strauss, "Sears Sets Out Growth Strategy," *The Globe and Mail*, June 13, 1997, B4.

5. Ijeoma Ross, "Consultant Sheds Career to Fire Up Bagel Chain," *The Globe and Mail*, June 16, 1997, B5.

6. Business Development Bank of Canada (BDC), *Profit$*, Vol. 17, No. 2, Spring 1997, 1.

7. Gayle MacDonald, "Exports Drive Fast-Growing Firms," *The Globe and Mail*, May 30, 1997, B10.

8. April Lindgren, "Fragile Exports," *The Ottawa Citizen*, October 26, 1996, D1.

9. Patrick Brethour, "Middleman Bucks Trend by Embracing the Web," *The Globe and Mail*, June 18, 1997, B9.

10. Barrie McKenna, "Canadian Productivity Posts Weak Growth in 1996," *The Globe and Mail*, June 6, 1997, B5.

11. Alan Toulin, "Canada Tipped to Lead OECD in Economic Growth," *The Financial Post*, June 13, 1997, 7.

12. Marlene Piturro, "Capitalist China?" *Brandweek*, May 16, 1994, 23–27.

13. Adapted from Sunder Magun (Applied International Economics) for Industry Canada, *The Development of Strategic Alliances in Industries: A Micro Analysis*, Working Paper No. 13, October 1996, Catalogue No. 21-24/14-1996, 15, 22, 23, 27, 29.

14. Rod McQueen, "Canada's 50 Best Managed Private Companies: Peak Performance," *The Financial Post*, December 14–16, 1996, 11.

15. Rod McQueen, "Canada's 50 Best Managed Private Companies: Jarvis Travel Ltd.," *The Financial Post*, December 14–16, 1996, 12.

16. Janet McFarland, "Canada Shines in Global Ratings," *The Globe and Mail*, May 26, 1997, B1.

17. James Bagnall, "Nortel's New Mantra: Built for Speed," *The Ottawa Citizen*, March 6, 1997, C1. Reprinted by permission of The Ottawa Citizen.

18. Ministry of Supply and Services Canada, *The Challenge of the Information Highway*, Final Report of the Information Highway Advisory Council, Catalogue No. C2-229/7-1995E, September 1995.

19. Ibid.

20. Ibid.

21. Gayle MacDonald, "Small Business Gets Connected," *The Globe and Mail*, May 15, 1997, B10.

22. Catherine Mulroney, "Canadians Tiptoe into Telework Era," *The Globe and Mail*, June 10, 1997, C1.

23. Rod McQueen, "Canada's 50 Best Managed Private Companies: Komex International Ltd.," *The Financial Post*, December 14–16, 1996, 38; and personal correspondence with Komex International Ltd.

24. Ibid.

25. Gordon Pitts, "Hotel Chain Hires for Attitude," *The Globe and Mail*, June 3, 1997, B13.

26. SHL Systemhouse, Advertising Supplement, "Outsourcing Centre Helps Canada Post Transformation," *The Globe and Mail*, February 5, 1997, 1.

27. Thomas Stewart, "Rate Your Readiness to Change," *Fortune*, February 7, 1994, 106–10.

28. Margot Gibb-Clark, "What Makes a Successful International Manager?" *The Globe and Mail*, January 18, 1996, B12.

29. Louis E. Boone, *Quotable Business* (New York: Random House, 1992), 146.

30. Nancy Totten, "Teaching Students to Evaluate Information," *RQ*, Spring 1990, 348.

31. Elizabeth Church, "Creativity and All That Jazz," *The Globe and Mail*, September 27, 1996, B10; and Joseph V. Anderson, "Mind Mapping: A Tool for Creative Thinking," *Business Horizons*, January/February 1993, 41–46.

32. Andrew Serwer, "Lessons from America's Fastest-Growing Companies," *Fortune*, August 8, 1994, 42–62; and Richard Daft, *Management*, 3rd ed. (Fort Worth, TX: The Dryden Press, 1993), 362–86.

33. Donn Downey, "Sentencing Put Off for Former Brokers," *The Globe and Mail*, December 10, 1996, B8.

34. Thomas Claridge, "Eagleson $110 000 Loser in Lawsuit," *The Globe and Mail*, December 5, 1996, A14.

35. Andrew Matte, "Child Porn Bust Nabs," *The Ottawa Sun*, December 11, 1996, 4.

Chapter 2

Business: Its Environment and Role in Society

Learning Outcomes

After studying this chapter, you should be able to

1. Discuss the competitive issues that Canada faces in an increasingly global economy.
2. Briefly explain how government regulates business.
3. Summarize the relationship among supply, demand, and price.
4. Describe how the social and cultural environment can affect business.
5. Discuss ways in which the technological environment can affect business.
6. Discuss the role of social responsibility and ethics in the business environment.
7. Outline business's responsibilities to the general public.
8. Identify business's responsibilities to customers.
9. Describe business's responsibilities to employees.
10. Explain business's responsibilities to investors and the financial community.

Destination Canada[1]

The Virgin Group of Companies operates in 17 countries and employs over 9000 staff around the world, including in New York, London, Tokyo, Vienna, Paris, and Amsterdam. Combined sales exceed $1 billion. From its beginnings in England in 1970 as a mail order record company, Virgin has grown 30 times in size during the past 12 years. It's a loosely arrayed confederation of over 100 diverse enterprises embracing retail, travel, hotels, an airline, communications, interactive entertainment, a radio station, book publishing, cola and vodka, and financial services. The Virgin Group is growing fast, is profitable, and is claiming significant shares in new markets worldwide.

Richard Branson is the founder and chair of The Virgin Group of Companies. Branson is an entrepreneur, visionary, and adventure capitalist extraordinaire — a man who prefers the expression "business as recreation" rather than "business as usual." He first coined the name "Virgin" to describe his initial inexperience in business. The name may be shocking to some and sound rebellious to others, although the word itself can also be seen to symbolize honesty, a first experience, and an original and fresh approach.

Virgin Megastore at the corner of Burrard and Robson Streets, Vancouver

The in-store deejay booth — one of the many highlights of this truly spectacular megastore

An impressive decor to match Virgin Megastore's classical section

In December of 1996, Canada got its first glimpse of this new breed of multinational company. The site that had previously housed Vancouver's main library became Canada's first Virgin Megastore. The corner of Burrard and Robson streets, the main intersection of the city's downtown retail and business centre, now houses one of Canada's largest music and entertainment stores — a modern-day landmark. The Virgin Megastore is not your usual music outlet: "Virgin Megastores have met with incredible success throughout the world as exciting and dynamic destinations where shopping meets entertainment," says Ian Duffell, president and CEO of the Virgin Retail Group. A few highlights of the Vancouver store:

- An in-store deejay booth
- A separate classical music room featuring over 8000 titles
- Twenty video/laser viewing stations
- A café for customers who wish to take a break from browsing or shopping
- A satellite up-link and down-link capability

Success for the Virgin Retail Group has come about without the usual trappings of a multinational. Virgin is the ultimate lean enterprise. When the company wants to move into a new business area, a team is assembled that can move fast and seize a business opportunity. There is no cumbersome committee system that delays decision making. Instead, strategic decision making concerning new business ventures is led by Branson himself, but involves a cadre of senior managers summoned on an ad hoc basis.

The Virgin philosophy focuses on building businesses that can create their own growth appeal. A venture must measure up to four core values — quality, competitiveness, innovation, and fun — and a core competence — the ability to manage highly organic growth through alliances and joint ventures. In certain respects, Virgin's organization and management style resembles that of a Japanese *keiretsu*.

Unlike many multinationals, social values and respect for the community are keys to Virgin's global expansion. For example, each Virgin Megastore aims to reflect the values and culture of the local community. It does its own buying, so as to support the local music industry: "The intention is to buy everything from local suppliers and also to promote local artists," said Ian Duffell at the opening of the Vancouver outlet.

CHAPTER OVERVIEW

MOST OF US would agree with the Virgin Group philosophy that business should be ethical and socially responsible. Businesspeople in all industries need to think seriously about the environment in which they operate and the role that they play in society.

This chapter begins by describing five major forces that affect the business environment, forces that are important because they provide the frame of reference within which business decisions are made. We will examine major challenges that have an impact on the competitiveness of Canada in the global market and discuss the role of social responsibility and ethics in business decision making. We will conclude by considering the responsibilities that business owes to the general public, its customers, its employees, its investors, and the financial community.

DID YOU KNOW?

→ **For many Arabs, their signature on a contract is much less meaningful than the fact that they have given their word.**

→ **You should always use your right hand when you accept or pass food in India.**

→ **When most Canadian negotiators** <u>table</u> **a proposal they intend to delay a decision. In Britain,** <u>tabling</u> **means that immediate action is to be taken.**

THE ENVIRONMENT FOR BUSINESS

IT IS CRUCIAL for businesspeople to monitor trends and developments in the business environment continually. Five major environmental forces have an impact on business: competition, regulation, the economy, the social and cultural environment, and technology (see Figure 2.1). Note that some of these factors are beyond a businessperson's control, while others can be changed; a manager who is concerned about a specific piece of legislation, for example, can lobby against it. This section discusses environmental forces in general; later chapters will go into more detail on some of the issues.

Figure 2.1 Environmental Factors That Affect Business

Competitive Environment

As we discussed in Chapter 1, the world is shifting toward an increasingly global economy. Over the 1990s, Canada has been at the forefront of this global movement. It is no coincidence that in 1995 Canada was rated first among the G7 (the world's seven most industrialized countries) in export growth. From 1992 to 1996, the value of our exported products and services grew by more than 60 percent, whereas the value of our domestic demand (gross domestic product) grew by only 8.9 percent.[2] The big challenge today for our Canadian firms — large and small — is to remain competitive in a global marketplace, both at home and abroad. Within our country, for example, Canadian firms like Sam The Record Man or Future Shop face stiff competition from foreign companies like the Virgin Megastore. Similarly, Canadian firms such as Bombardier and Nortel fiercely compete outside our borders in foreign markets.

Traditionally, a firm's competitiveness depended on its ability to keep its costs down. If it could produce something more cheaply, then it could price products lower and outsell the competition. A company's competitiveness also was linked to the resources available in its particular geographic location. Today, however, we are seeing a shift from competition based on costs to competition based on many factors, including product design, product development, and efficient use of technology. Firms succeed or fail based on the quality and service that they provide. Improvements in technology and transportation have made companies independent of their locations. Information can be passed around the world at the speed of e-mail; workers in Ireland or the Bahamas can process data gathered in Asia, for instance, and transmit it to Canada with the touch of a button.

We will examine several competitive issues in an increasingly global economy. These issues include researching and developing better products, improving quality and customer service, improving the competitiveness of the work force, and improving organizational flexibility.

COMPANY WATCH

Fredericton-based Formal Systems is a growing business that has chosen to take an active part in exporting. The company, established in 1990, had sales in excess of $4 million in 1996 — compared with $230 000 in 1993 — and employs more than 90 people. It provides software re-engineering services to Fortune 500 companies and government organizations around the world. Formal has developed technology that helps clients correct the year 2000 software fault as well as technology to switch information systems from mainframe to client-server environments.

In 1996, Formal's exports represented 70 percent of its total revenue. The company attributes much of its success to its decision to export: "We would never have grown so much in such a short time had we not started exporting," said Frank Driscoll, President and CEO. Formal also credits its significant investment in research and development activities. "In 1996, we invested a full 40 percent of our total revenues in R&D," added Ron Hunter-Duvar, Vice President, Research and Development.

Like all companies, JVC must remain competitive by researching and developing better products. In this advertisement the firm markets its CyberCam, a mini digital video camera that is packed with advanced mechatronics.

However, companies like Formal Systems that invest wisely in R&D are able to develop new products efficiently, before competitors beat them to market. Chrysler is another example: it developed its affordable Neon car in 31 months at a cost of $1.3 billion, which is low by industry standards.[3]

Researching and Developing Better Products. A crucial factor in keeping Canada competitive is **research and development**, *the scientific process of developing new commercial products.* R&D, as it is often called, can create totally new industries (such as airplanes and automobiles in an earlier day) and can dramatically change already existing industries (think about how the Internet and computers have transformed so many people's jobs).

Designing and developing a winning new product is not easy. Only 1 out of every 20 to 25 ideas ever actually leads to a new product — and out of every 10 or 15 new products, only 1 becomes a commercial hit.

Business Term
√ **Research and development (R&D)**
The scientific process of developing new commercial products.

Improving Quality and Customer Service. Vital to global competitiveness are improvements in product quality and customer service. Says Jack Welch, chief executive of General Electric, "If you can't meet a world standard of quality at the world's best price, you're not even in the game."

Here's the experience of one successful Canadian company. Back in 1991, Gary Rokas and Dov Rom bought a division of Murata Erie — a money-losing division of Murata Manufacturing Co. of Kyoto, Japan. Apparently, the Canadian operation no longer fit the plans of the $2 billion foreign parent company. Rokas and Rom brought in two more partners, Phillip Siller and Raj Pasricha, and gave the company a competitive entrepreneurial spirit and a new name — Ascent Power Technology. Within five years of the buyout, annual sales of Ascent had increased tenfold from $7 million to $70 million. In 1996, Ascent was one of *The Financial Post*'s award-winning "50 Best Managed Private Companies." It had 700 employees, a strong balance sheet, and plants in Campton, Kentucky, and Mitcheldean, England, in addition to its Canadian facility in Concord, Ontario. According to Rokas, president and chief operating officer, attention to quality and outstanding customer service were the major reasons for Ascent's success, but the initial reorientation was not easy. At the outset, the number of employees had to be cut from 120 to 60.

One of the firm's products is a flyback — a highly specialized encapsulated transformer. Initially, the firm purchased these transformers from the former parent company. As the Japanese yen grew stronger, however, the price of this item grew prohibitive. Ascent began to source from Korea but was unhappy with the quality; returns to the supplier due to poor workmanship ran as high as 25 percent. As a result, Ascent put together a team of engineers and designers and, after considerable investigation, decided to manufacture the flyback. It is now the only North American company with flyback capability. "From day one, we had to work hard. Customers were leery which meant there was no room for error," recalls Rokas. The quality process involved changing from a rigid bureaucratic structure to a more flexible and lean organization — one in which design and manufacturing teams worked with the customer and took ownership of and pride in their work.[4]

Another important aspect of competitiveness is **customer service**, *the aspect of competitive strategy that refers to how a firm treats its customers.* Customers are the lifeblood of any business, and most successful businesses, such as Delta Inns, Nortel, and the Virgin Group of Companies, have made customer service an integral part of their business strategy and corporate culture. However, specific customer service strategies and programs differ from company to company, depending on the particular needs of the client and the type of business. For example, in retail, at Vancouver's Virgin Megastore service means entertainment and fun. Today's consumers want more than value for their dollar as well as service with a smile: "They want to be entertained, through all five

senses — and will endure crowds, parking, public transit and line-ups for the experience. That's where retailers like Virgin Megastore ride the crest of the wave."[5]

Dimatec is an example of a Canadian firm that attributes its success to customer service. A Winnipeg manufacturer of diamond drilling equipment, customer service and quality are part of its corporate culture. Daily meetings focus on quality assurance, maintenance, and sales. Production meetings are held twice a week and engineering meetings weekly. "We now have a constant focus on the customer. We always give the customer the benefit of the doubt. Even if a product has been returned and the problem has been caused by customer misuse, we have on occasion replaced the goods at no charge in order to maintain good relationships," says Ivor Perry, president, general manager, and part owner of Dimatec.[6]

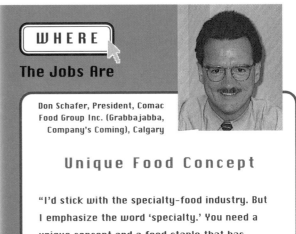

WHERE

The Jobs Are

Don Schafer, President, Comac Food Group Inc. (Grabbajabba, Company's Coming), Calgary

Unique Food Concept

"I'd stick with the specialty-food industry. But I emphasize the word 'specialty.' You need a unique concept and a food staple that has longevity, like coffee or bagels. There is so much growth potential for good specialty-food concepts in this country. With full-service restaurants, you have to do more than feed people — you have to entertain them, give them a reason to go out."

Business Term

√ Customer service

The aspect of competitive strategy that refers to how a firm treats its customers.

Improving the Competitiveness of the Work Force. More and more, human resources are replacing factories and machines as a decisive competitive factor. "The only way we can beat the competition is with people," notes Robert Eaton, CEO of Chrysler. "That's the only thing anybody has. Your culture and how you motivate and empower and educate your people is what makes the difference." It is important for a company to create a culture that encourages employees to innovate and follow up on ideas. Companies then must be able to move new ideas through development and into the marketplace quickly.

DIMATEC INC.

TECHNICAL GUIDE:
IMPREGNATED CORE BITS

Dimatec Inc.'s attention to customer service and quality has made it a very successful company, recognized with ISO 9001 certification (see Chapter 6) and named by *The Financial Post* as one of Canada's "50 Best Managed Private Companies" in 1996.

Just adding new equipment is not enough; workers must be able to use it effectively. Employees must be able to control, combine, and supervise work operations, and they must be motivated to provide the best quality and service possible. The skills that are demanded of the Canadian work force are changing — effective workers in a global economy will be able to ask important questions, define problems, combine information from many different sources, and deal with topics that stretch across disciplines

and cultures. Indeed, the best way for Canadians to prepare for a global economy is to become as educated as possible and to continue that education throughout their lives.

Improving Organizational Flexibility. Organizational flexibility is a key feature of Canada's best-run companies. "Product life cycles are getting shorter and shorter every year in every field. We have to have an adaptability attitude so we can not only respond to the trends, but also offer those new trends to customers," says Pierre Grand'Maison, president and CEO of Thermoplast Inc. Competitive firms like Thermoplast — a successful plastics manufacturer in Laval, Quebec — have a solid vision and strategic plan. But they also have an organizational structure and culture that allows them to change, move quickly, and seize a market opportunity. Successful firms are fluid. They are constantly revising their plans while maintaining their focus and vision. Information is shared freely throughout the organization — there are no secrets. Employees are working in teams. They're constantly asking customers what they need and responding to those needs. If these firms do well, they celebrate. If they don't, they share the pain and try to work out a solution.[7]

Regulatory Environment

Government regulates competition and competitors as well as specific business practices. Provincial and federal government control takes two broad forms: regulating industry and enacting statutes or laws. A **regulated industry** *is one in which competition is either eliminated, and government monitoring substitutes for market controls.* Examples of regulated industries are found in public utilities and other industries closely tied to the public interest, where competition would be wasteful or excessive. For example, only one electrical power company can serve a given market. The large capital investment required to construct a pipeline or electric transmission line or to build and operate a nuclear power plant makes this type of regulation appropriate.

The major weakness of a system that relies solely on government regulation rather than the discipline of free-market forces is that service and performance can deteriorate or not keep pace with technological change. As a result,

Business Term

✓ **Regulated industry**
Industry in which competition is either limited or eliminated, and government monitoring substitutes for market controls.

WHERE WERE THE REGULATORS?

In early May of 1997, an independent geological consulting company, Strathcona Minerals Services Ltd., found Bre-X's supposed Busang gold deposit to be a scam.

This came as a shock to many investors who had been led to believe that Busang, in Indonesia, could contain the world's largest gold deposit. Bre-X Minerals Ltd. was assaulted on several fronts. The Toronto Stock Exchange (TSE) delisted its shares, saying the company "no longer meets the required listing standards"; two of Bre-X's five directors resigned; and the RCMP set out to investigate formal fraud complaints. Bre-X shares had plummeted to about 9 cents — roughly the value of the paper they were written on — from a high of about $300 (on a pre-split basis). "There are tens of thousands of people out there who are really hurting and my heart goes out to them," said Kari Setmeir, a heavy loser.

Some reporters argued that Canada's lax security laws were partly to blame for this fiasco. For example, when the Calgary-based Bre-X graduated to the Toronto Stock Exchange in 1996, it did not have to provide a new prospectus. The TSE accepted the Bre-X prospectus that had been prepared back in 1989 for the Alberta Stock Exchange, when the company's shares began life as penny stocks. The company only had to provide the TSE with a listing statement. Observers speculated that the Bre-X fraud would have been much more difficult to pull off with tighter TSE controls and regulations.

Other industry observers argued that tighter disclosure rules could not have prevented a fraud of such magnitude and sophistication as Bre-X's faked discovery. They said that more government controls would only serve to limit the freedom of the marketplace. Stock market investing, like a horse race, is risky, and investors take their chances and pay the price if they're wrong. Speculative investors — large or small — must be responsible for their own actions. The less government regulation, the better.

What do you think? Was the Bre-X fiasco an anomaly, or was this a case for more government regulation?

Sources: Adapted from Karen Howlett and Janet McFarland, "Where Were the Regulators?" *The Globe and Mail,* May 10, 1997, B1, B8; Andrew Wills, "Bre-X's Winners and Losers," *The Globe and Mail,* May 7, 1997, B1, B6; and John Heinzl, "TSE President Defends Handling of Fiasco," *The Globe and Mail,* May 7, 1997, B1, B8.

some regulated industries are finding that the administrative agencies responsible for them are looking to more competition to improve service. For example, in 1992, the Canadian Radio-television and Telecommunications Commission (CRTC) opened the long distance telephone market to new competition in many parts of the country.

The second form of government regulation, enacting statutes, has led to both provincial and federal laws affecting competition and various commercial practices. For example, businesses in Canada are required to comply with the following acts passed by the federal government and administered by Industry Canada:[8]

- Textile Labelling Act
- Weights and Measures Act
- Competition Act
- Canadian Business Corporations Act
- Small Business Loans Act

Business Term

√ **Deregulation**

The process of eliminating legal restraints on competition in various industries.

Over the 1990s, there was a general trend toward **deregulation,** *the process of eliminating legal restraints on competition in various industries.* The basic economic objective of deregulation is to remove government restrictions, with the assumption of eventually increasing competition and ultimately reducing prices to the consumer. The financial services and telecommunications sectors are two of our major industry groups that have been significantly affected by deregulation over the 1990s.

In the financial industry, for example, revisions in the Bank Act and the revised federal Trust and Loans Companies Act in 1992 gave banks the right to compete with insurance companies, brokerage firms, and investment dealers; as well, trust companies were given full commercial lending powers virtually equal to those of the major banks.

Expect the process of deregulation in financial services to continue. In the spring of 1997, a federal task force set out the federal position on the future of the financial services sector and deregulation: "The cornerstone to our approach is that the government should intervene in the operations of regulated financial institutions only to the minimum extent necessary to carry out a valid public policy objective."[9]

Prior to 1992, the federal government had given the exclusive right to provide long distance telephone services to eleven regional telephone companies. As of 1992, this began to change. The Canadian Radio-television and Telecommunications Commission (CRTC) signalled its deregulation philosophy in the telecommunications industry by allowing other long distance providers and resellers to compete with these eleven regional firms, starting the lucrative market for long distance service. In a landmark decision in 1997, the CRTC continued its deregulation philosophy by allowing other companies to compete in the $7 billion a year local phone market (as of 1998). Canada's phone companies were given the right to compete in the $3 billion a year cable TV market in return for giving up their previously exclusive rights for local telephone services.[10]

> **Business Term**
> ✓ **Supply**
> Sellers' willingness and ability to provide goods and services for sale in a market.

> **Business Term**
> ✓ **Demand**
> Buyers' willingness and ability to purchase goods and services.

Economic Environment

Economics *is the social science of allocating scarce resources and a study of people and their behaviour.* Economists seek to understand the choices people make in using these scarce resources. We all make economic choices every day when we decide what products to buy, what services to use, and what activities we will fit into our schedules.

There are two sides to the study of economics: microeconomics and macroeconomics. *Microeconomics* deals with the study of "small" economic units, such as individuals, families, and companies. Although these economic units may be small, their economic choices may be international in scope. Even individual consumers may become involved in international trade by deciding to buy products made in other countries. International trade is thus part of the study of microeconomics.

Macroeconomics deals with broader issues, like the overall operation of a

> **Business Term**
> ✓ **Economics**
> The social science of allocating scarce resources and a study of people and their behaviour.

country's economy (*macro* means "large"). Macroeconomics addresses questions such as how to maintain adequate supplies of the resources people want. What do we do if the demand for scarce resources exceeds the supply? What government policies will be most effective in improving our standards of living over time?

Two important principles of economics, both micro and macro, are supply and demand. **Supply** *refers to sellers' willingness and ability to provide goods and services for sale in a market.* **Demand** *refers to buyers' willingness and ability to purchase these goods and services.*

The relationship between supply and demand determines another feature: price. As the quantity of a particular product increases, the supply goes up; as the price of that product increases, demand for it goes down. The law of supply and demand states that prices (P) in a market are set by the intersection of the supply (S) and demand (D) curves. The point where the curves meet, known as the *equilibrium price* (E), is the prevailing market price at which one can buy that item (see Figure 2.2).

Figure 2.2 The Law of Supply and Demand

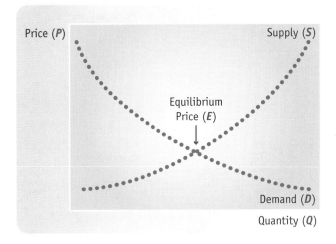

If the actual market price is different from the equilibrium price, people tend to make economic choices that return the prevailing price to the equilibrium amount. For instance, if sellers lower their prices below equilibrium, buyers are likely to snap up all of the available supply quickly. As sellers get more of the product, they are likely to mark up the price so they can increase their profits. On the other hand, if their prices are too high, buyers will purchase less of the product. Sellers

with the result that many Indian firms are exploring new lines of business. "Before, we were in heavy industry because that's where the government let us go," explains Krishan Kumar Modi, head of the manufacturer Modi Group, "but our future is clearly in consumer goods." Through a joint venture with Walt Disney Company, Modi is starting a cable TV service that will broadcast Disney films and TV shows in Hindi and English. He is also hiring and training thousands of salespeople to sell his products door-to-door across India.[11]

will end up competing with one another for customers by lowering their prices to the point where they can sell all of their supply, which is the equilibrium price.

Changes in economic policy can open up new markets. India's economy, for example, has long suffered from strict government regulation of many industries. Government officials used to issue licences that gave certain firms exclusive rights to provide specific goods and services, while high tariffs excluded foreign competitors. By limiting the supply of goods and services, the government curbed competition and kept prices high. Recently, the government has eliminated many of these controls,

Social and Cultural Environment

Political scientist Neil Nevitte of the University of Toronto tells us that Canadian values and beliefs are changing. In his book *The Decline of Deference*, Nevitte says that as a nation we are becoming more permissive and less likely to bend to authority. In our family relationships we are becoming more egalitarian both in our relationships with our spouses or significant others and in our parent–child relationships. As Canadians we are less preoccupied with accumulating material goods and more concerned about what some sociologists call self-actualization. According to Nevitte, increased levels of education have a lot to do with this shift to what he calls postmodern values: "Formal education gives people autonomy in who they are and where they want to go."[12] A snapshot of Nevitte's study is provided in Figure 2.3.

In addition to these changing social values, the age distribution of Canada's population is shifting. For example, David Foot and Daniel Stoffman tell us in their bestseller *Boom, Bust & Echo* that the average age of our population is growing older due to a combination of three major factors:[13]

- Canadians are living longer.

- Fertility rates are expected to remain relatively low at about 1.7 children per woman.

- There is a strong growth in the over-50 population as Canada's boomers (about 10 million Canadians born between 1947 and 1966) begin to enter their twilight years.

Figure 2.3   Are You a Postmodern Person?

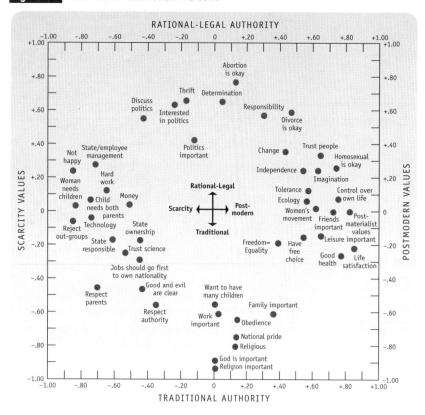

A rapidly expanding population group in Canada, the U.S., and Western Europe share the beliefs listed on this chart as postmodern values. They are people more inclined to be captains of their own fate than traditionalists who defer to authority.

Businesspeople must be sensitive to society's changing values and shifts in demographics, such as population growth and age distribution. These changing variables affect the way consumers react to different products and

THEY SAID IT

"It used to be that hard work and obedience were the values you passed on to children, now it's more imagination and independence."

NEIL NEVITTE, University of Toronto, political science professor

marketing practices. One well-known trend, for example, is the growing popularity of goods and services that offer convenience and save time. Another trend is the growing importance of cultural diversity. Canada's mixed society is composed of various submarkets, each of which displays unique values and cultural characteristics and differs by age, place of residence, buying behaviour, and buying preferences.

One submarket that is growing in importance is the over-50 age group. The relative growth in this segment will have a profound impact on such sectors as real estate, when the boomers begin to sell their homes; finance, as the boomers begin saving for their golden years; and health care, as boomers create a need for new products and services — new pharmaceuticals, for example.

International Business and the Social/Cultural Environment. The social/cultural context for business decision making often is more pronounced in the international sphere than in the domestic arena. Learning about culture and social differences among countries is pivotal to a firm's success abroad. Business strategies and products that work in Canada often cannot be applied or sold directly in other nations.

FUTURE TREND

DEMOGRAPHIC TRENDS CAN SIGNAL BUSINESS OPPORTUNITIES

Which products and services will be in demand in the future? Where will the job opportunities be? If you want to start your own business, demographics (the study of population trends) can be a powerful tool to help you plan for the future. Here are just a few examples of current population trends:

→ The young are losing ground to the old. In the 1920s there were about eight people under the age of 18 for every person over the age of 65. In 1998, the ratio of 18 year olds to 65 year olds dropped from eight to one, to about two to one. This aging trend is expected to continue, and eventually (by the year 2050) we'll have more old than young people. Can you think of business opportunities that will emerge as the Canadian population ages? What about health care for seniors, for example? Where are all these seniors going to live?

→ The 15–24 age group declined by about 17 percent over the 1990s, but will grow about 5 percent by the year 2001. Expect to see music retailers take advantage of this youth trend. Radio stations that still want to convert to the "oldies but goldies" format should perhaps reconsider. What do you think will happen to prices for used cars? They will increase, of course, as more young drivers clamour for road time.

→ Unlike the 1950s and 1960s, Canadian families today average only one or two children (actually it's closer to one). Middle-income parents who could never afford tuition fees of $10 000 for each of four kids can now turn to private education when they have only one child. The Kumon Institute, a Japan-based franchise operation that offers after-school help in math and language for kids, is taking advantage of this trend. Kumon's Canadian enrollment increased from 2000 in 1986 to 27 000 in 1997.

Source: Based on David K. Foot with Daniel Stoffman, *Boom, Bust & Echo: How to Profit from the Coming Demographic Shift* (Toronto: Macfarlane, Walter & Ross, 1996); John Kettle, "Young Losing Ground to the Old," *The Globe and Mail*, September 10, 1998, B12.

TECHNOLOGY

SASKTEL AT LARGE

With the North American market for telephones relatively mature, major suppliers of telecommunications solutions are beginning to shift their attention to regions where growth rates are higher. The lack of existing infrastructure in some countries is proving to be an advantage, allowing them to invest in advanced digital and wireless technology rather than upgrading existing plants. SaskTel is a good example of a Canadian supplier that has taken advantage of this trend.

Since the early 1990s, SaskTel International (SI), a subsidiary of SaskTel that markets the corporation's expertise around the world, has been working closely with the Philippine government and a consortium of Philippine telephone companies. Using locally appropriate technology, including solar power for electricity and water buffalo to haul equipment, SI has been designing and installing digital exchange networks and microwave radio systems. UHF analog radio systems are being used in project areas where topography has impeded microwave technology.

In 1997, SI, the Philippine government, and SR Telecom, a primary supplier and project partner from Quebec, negotiated another contract worth $30 million U.S. that will further expand the rural Philippine telecom network into some of the islands' more outlying communities called "Barangays."

SI has also been active in Africa, working on a major contract in Tanzania to provide a telecommunications cable infrastructure throughout four exchange areas within the capital city of Dar es Salaam. In 1996, SI personnel completed the work three months ahead of schedule, a significant achievement on a two-year project.

Source: Adapted from *SaskTel 1996 Annual Report*, 22–23. Reprinted by permission of SaskTel.

For example, R.C. Purdy Chocolates Ltd. is the largest manufacturer/retailer of chocolates in British Columbia. Total sales are in the $200 million range and the company employs about 600 staff. In 1995, Purdy decided to go international and set its sights on Taipei, the capital of Taiwan. It is a city of 4 million residents with a collective sweet tooth. Despite marketing studies and a very large market potential, the company came nowhere close to its conservative first-year sales forecast: "We recognized we had a lot to learn, but we didn't think there would be as many roadblocks or that they'd be as big," said company owner Charles Flavelle. Problems included packaging preferences (rectangles don't sell, circles and triangles do), hassles in getting products through customs, and hiring and managing staff from a distance. Purdy took some bumps and bruises, but learning from these experiences changed the way it did business. Now this successful Canadian company is aiming at the huge market in China.

Social/cultural factors also influence the types of products a company makes. Returning to Purdy's venture into Asia, despite the research, its management made a major marketing mistake. They assumed that a product popular with Asian Canadians — ice cream bars dipped in chocolate and rolled in nuts — would be a winner in Taipei. It wasn't.[14]

Technological Environment

Over the 1990s, some companies viewed technology as simply an administrative tool for reducing costs and improving worker efficiency. But the more progressive firms realized that technology is a key strategic weapon — without it they simply couldn't compete. Toronto-based Liberty Health Canada is a good example of this kind of company. Liberty sells employee benefit packages that include extended hospital, dental, and drug plans. It took over the operations of Ontario Blue Cross from the Ontario Hospital Association in 1995. Liberty had inherited not only antiquated mainframe equipment but also an increasingly competitive and cost-sensitive market. Corporate customers were intent on trimming insurance costs; at the same time, drug and other costs to the insurer were rising. Since the takeover, Liberty has had no choice but to invest heavily in information technology, much of it to replace big, outmoded mainframe computers with flexible microcomputers linked by client-server networks. Their strategic competitive challenge was to use technology to keep the lid on the company's own costs, while driving down insurance rates and improving customer service. "Given the level of competition in this industry, we've had to do what we've done just to stay competitive. If we hadn't done what we did we wouldn't be in business anymore," said Gerry Byrne, Liberty's senior vice-president of strategic affairs.[15]

New technology results in new goods and services, improvements in existing products, better customer service, and often lower prices through more cost-efficient production and distribution methods. Technology can also quickly make products, like the typewriter, obsolete. But just as quickly, technology can open up new business opportunities and spawn entirely new industries. Lasers, xerography, genetic engineering, and the Internet have all resulted in the development of new commercial opportunities over the past ten years.

Telemedicine is another emerging growth area. Dr. William Feindel at the University of Saskatchewan was among the first to demonstrate the potential of telemedicine in 1956. Some 40 years ago, he used closed-circuit television to transmit live brain-wave tracings. But the high cost and scarcity of long distance circuits prevented physicians from exploiting telemedicine. Today, recent advances in digital communications technology, coupled with declining health-care budgets, have led to a resurgent interest in telemedicine among hospital administrators and physicians. "We think there is a large role for telecommunications providers to help health care institutions provide better service with significant economic savings," said Matthew Lok, of Bell Northern Research Ltd.[16]

SOCIAL RESPONSIBILITY AND ETHICS IN THE BUSINESS ENVIRONMENT

Many business decisions can involve making decisions about what a company "owes" to society. As you will recall from Chapter 1, we define social responsibility as a management philosophy that highlights the social and economic effects of managerial decisions.

Why should a company worry about being socially responsible? Because it does not operate in isolation. In fact, we can think of a business as a set of relationships involving its suppliers, distributors, customers, employees, and other firms — all of the people who somehow are affected by that company's operations. Ultimately, every company interacts with national systems in communications, transportation, education, and health care, as well as global systems of trade agreements, monetary exchanges, factor costs, and environmental restraints.

DID YOU KNOW?

A global survey of managers showed the environment is the number one issue for the 1990s.

→ Singapore has strict laws against littering, spitting, and importing chewing gum.

→ By the year 2000, 15 percent of the population of highly industrialized nations will be over age 65, as compared with less than 5 percent for the typical developing nation.

→ Chinese companies have made several unfortunate brand-name choices for products intended for export to North America. High on the Chinese list of "What Not to Name a Product" are Fang Fang lipstick, White Elephant batteries, and Pansy men's underwear.

This means that social problems, at both national and international levels, affect every company. Many important social issues, such as drug abuse, alcohol abuse, ethnic and gender discrimination, and pollution, can have an impact on any of these relationships. For instance, social problems affect the quality of a firm's most valuable asset: its work force. Drug abuse and alcoholism can make workers less healthy; discrimination against women and various cultural groups may restrict the educational opportunities that these workers receive. This can lead to major financial problems for business. Thus, any steps that a firm can take to resolve social problems can, in turn, help its employees — and in the long run may even improve the company's bottom line. We know, for example, that smoking is the leading cause of preventable disease and death in this country. Alex Tilley, founder, owner,

---

GOOD, BAD, OR UGLY?

Free-market philosophers from Adam Smith to Milton Friedman have denied the legitimacy of the so-called "social contract." Social goals such as job creation and an adequate income for all those who work have little to do with business, whose main concern should be the return to its shareholders. As Albert Dunlap, former CEO of Scott Paper Co., put it: "The point of business is to make a profit. Profit ... is not a dirty word."

and chairman of Tilley Endurables Inc., provides a good example of how one socially responsible Canadian business has responded to the issue of smoking:[17]

> *My stand (ergo, my company's stand) on tobacco is that people who make it, and others who help them sell it are in effect murderers, killing about 40 000 Canadians every year. In my opinion these people should be publicly condemned and shunned by society, so that in time very few will seek to work in that industry. Since no one was doing anything about this, I decided, with some trepidation, to be the first.*
>
> *I added this phrase to our Canadian ads: "We do not welcome to our company-owned stores those who make or promote tobacco products."*
>
> *I wasn't sure at the time how this would affect the company's prosperity. It's been several years now, and I guess it's done us more good than not, although that wasn't at all the purpose of taking this stand. It's just that something had to be done, and I had the forum to do it in.*
>
> *I believe that people are what they do, and what I do reflects upon the honour of my company. The higher the perceived honour of our company, the more likely the kind of people I want as customers, will become our customers.*
>
> *If you don't know the hat, know the hatter.*

In addition to dealing with broad social issues, businesspeople are often confronted with specific ethical issues. We learned in Chapter 1 that business ethics deals with the right and wrong actions that arise in the work environment. Unfortunately, the answers to ethical questions are not always cut-and-dried. Invariably, there are grey zones that can result in an **ethical dilemma:** *a situation in which right or wrong cannot be clearly identified.* Here are a few examples:

- Your boss wants you to bribe some officials in Thailand to get a major contract for the company. She justifies her decision by saying that bribery is common in this country. She also refers to a 1996 study by researchers at a respected Thai university that says Thailand still thrives on corruption. "Corruption isn't all that bad," the Thai researchers argued. "Illegal activities tend to be labour intensive, helping keep Thailand's unemployment rate down to an official 2.6 percent."[18]

  What would you do? Is corruption acceptable to you as long as it is not in your own backyard? Is bribery acceptable because it provides some social benefit in a foreign country?

- What would happen if you accidentally learned that a fellow employee had AIDS? Would you tell your co-workers out of concern for their safety, or would you respect the privacy of this particular employee and not say anything?

These are the kinds of dilemmas and issues that employees and managers must deal with that fall squarely in the domain of ethics. Answers will not be easy to come by. To get you thinking, one model for helping you resolve an ethical dilemma is provided in Figure 2.4.

As an employee, and in your quest to make the right decisions, you are also going to have to deal with the issue of **whistle blowing:** *the disclosure of immoral or illegal acts within an organization.* We caution you, however, that most organizations do

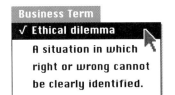

Business Term

✓ **Ethical dilemma**

A situation in which right or wrong cannot be clearly identified.

Figure 2.4 **How to Make Ethical Decisions**

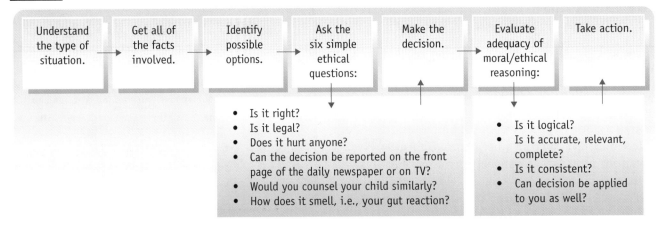

not like to "hang out their dirty laundry" for public scrutiny — or to have it hung out for them! So it is fairly safe to say that whistle blowers are not universally loved and as a result are in short supply. Here is a typical case where it takes a very special kind of person to tell the truth.

Military clerks at the Department of National Defence complained about widespread irregularities in senior officers' hotel and travel claims back in 1994. In one case, an officer even demanded that a clerk rebook a flight to Reykjavik, Iceland, at least seven times in one day. Those orders increased the cost of the flight by about $2000. Four clerks said they complained to their supervisors but nothing was done, according to Access to Information documents released in 1997. In another case a clerk questioned a colonel about discrepancies in his claims, and the colonel replied: "It's my money, give it to me." How were these whistle blowers rewarded for their concern for public spending? Anyone who questioned senior officers about discrepancies in travel claims were later given low scores on their job evaluation sheets, police were told. Some clerks were actually removed from their jobs and were transferred to another directorate because they were "causing too many waves for the higher-ups."[19]

> **Business Term**
> ✓ **Whistle blowing**
> The disclosure of immoral or illegal acts within an organization.

Should you be involved in a situation where whistle blowing is a possible action, the following considerations would be advised:[20]

- Make absolutely certain the situation is one that warrants whistle blowing.

- Examine your motives.

- Verify and document your information.

- Determine the type of wrongdoing you are reporting and to whom it should be reported.

- State your allegations in an appropriate way.

- Stick to the facts.

- Decide whether the whistle blowing should be kept inside the organization or made public.

- Decide whether the whistle blowing should be open or anonymous.

- Decide whether you will stay in or leave your current position before whistle blowing is required.

- Find out how much protection is available for whistle blowers in your industry, province, or federal agency.

- Anticipate and document retaliation.

- Consult a lawyer.

As we saw in the Tilley example, top-level executives are usually the major source of ethical decision making for a business. The ethical standards of a firm are usually governed by a code of ethics, code of practice, or code of conduct. These terms are often used interchangeably, but each can be distinguished according to the dominant source of control, ranging from self-control to imposed control:[21]

- A *code of ethics* states the values and principles that define the purpose of the company. This type of code is usually expressed in credos or guiding principles. Such a code says, "This is who we are and this is what we stand for." See for example Figure 2.5.

  - A *code of practice* interprets and illustrates corporate values and principles, and is addressed to the employee as individual decision maker. In effect it says, "This is how we do things around here." Codes of practice tend to rely on guidelines for decision making, using such concepts as "act and disclose" or "seek advice." This approach takes a view of ethics as "We do what we do because it is our character." Alex Tilley, for example, uses this approach: "I believe that the owner and/or president of a company determines its culture. His or her personal qualities of doing business and treatment of others are disseminated through the rest of the organization: the company ends up with the reputation of its leader."[22]

- A c*ode of conduct* says, "This is what you must or must not do." Codes of conduct typically consist of a set of rules: "Thou shalt not." Usually penalties are identified and systems of compliance and appeal are defined. This approach takes the view of ethics as what is *not* to be done given the consequences.

In practice, corporate codes tend to include elements of all three types, but it is helpful to consider these three basic types as benchmarks (see also Table 2.1).

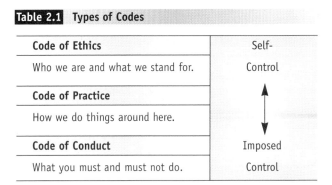

Table 2.1 Types of Codes

Code of Ethics	Self-
Who we are and what we stand for.	Control
Code of Practice	↕
How we do things around here.	
Code of Conduct	Imposed
What you must and must not do.	Control

Figure 2.5   SaskTel's Vision and Values

Our vision

SaskTel will be a highly competitive business, committed to delivering outstanding customer service and value while maintaining our commitment to social responsibility and good citizenship. As a leader in technology, we will anticipate and fulfil our customers' needs for cost-effective communications solutions.

Collectively, our people will be diverse, creative, flexible and highly skilled, accepting challenges and generating personal and corporate successes that will allow all of us to realize increased job satisfaction and security.

We will achieve ongoing market and financial successes by working as one team focused on excellence. SaskTel will grow profitably and diversify both in Saskatchewan and the world, delivering the benefits of advanced communications to our customers and their communities, our employees, owners and partners.

Our values

Honesty, integrity and mutual respect
At the base of all our beliefs is honesty, integrity and mutual respect. These are inherent in everything we do and say.

Open communication
Open communication will create an atmosphere of trust and common purpose. Only through open communication and clearly stating our values will the acceptable behaviors be known and understood in our organization. We believe open communication will foster autonomy and an entrepreneurial spirit among our employees.

Excellence
We believe SaskTel will be successful through excellence:

- Excellence in serving our customers by providing value through price, quality and service.
- Excellence from every person at SaskTel through living our values.
- Excellence in our business through innovative products and processes supporting our customer service.

It is important for employees to know that ethics and social responsibility are priorities for the firm. Here are some suggestions for achieving an ethical corporate culture:[23]

- Develop a written code of ethics, practice, or conduct.
- Make the code as specific to the company as possible.
- Establish an anonymous reporting procedure for internal problem solving.
- Involve all employees in identifying ethical issues.

- Include ethical decision making in employees' performance appraisals.
- Publicize executive priorities and efforts related to social issues.

TO WHOM IS BUSINESS RESPONSIBLE?

"THE NOTION THAT the modern corporation is constituted of shareholders and managers and nobody else is bankrupt," says Professor Michael Deck, executive director of the Centre for Corporate Social Performance and Ethics at the University of Toronto. Professor Deck argues that the corporation must have a responsibility to other stakeholders, such as customers, employees, and community members.[24]

Just what does business owe society? A company must, after all, make money in order to survive in the marketplace. If it goes bankrupt, many people could suffer, including employees, customers, and their families. What happens when, in order to stay in business, a company does things that could be considered harmful to

---

THEY SAID IT

"Corporate ethics programs are emerging as the focal point for internal control. Organizations that fail to manage this part of their business effectively will suffer costs in terms of lost productivity, higher turnover ... and increased exposure to legal action and to fraud."

THE SOCIETY OF MANAGEMENT ACCOUNTANTS OF CANADA,
Codes of Ethics, Practice and Conduct, 1997

Table 2.2 Arguments for and against Social Responsibility

Arguments for	Arguments against
• There are positive results in the long run.	• It takes away from making a profit.
• The needs of society have changed.	• Social costs are business costs.
• The expectations of society have changed.	• Managers are not accountable to society or the public.
• Business has access to resources to help.	• Managers don't have the necessary "social" skills.
• Business has a moral obligation to help.	

society? Table 2.2 lists some of the arguments for and against social responsibility.

The social responsibilities of business can be classified according to relationships a business has with the general public, customers, employees, investors, and the financial community. Many of these relationships stretch beyond national borders. We will look at each of these categories briefly in the rest of the chapter.

Responsibilities to the General Public

Businesses have responsibilities to the general public, including dealing with public health issues, protecting the environment, and developing the quality of the work force.

Public Health Issues. Public health concerns include, but are not limited to, issues such as smoking, drug and alcohol abuse, and AIDS.

In the spring of 1997, the Tobacco Act received royal assent, which meant that it finally became illegal in Canada to advertise tobacco on billboards and in stores. Penalties include fines of up to $300 000 or up to two years in jail. This tough new law came into effect despite the claim by tobacco companies that the Tobacco Act violates Section 2(b) of the Canadian Charter of Rights and Freedoms, which guarantees freedom of expression. "The public health interest is a higher priority than the financial interests of the tobacco industry," said François Damphousse of the Non-Smokers Rights Association.[25]

Smoking is one of the three top risk factors involved in heart disease and stroke in North America. Non-smokers are also in danger since their exposure to so-called "secondhand smoke" increases their risk of contracting cancer, asthma, or respiratory infections. As a result, many employers have banned smoking in the workplace. For example, companies like Tim Horton Donuts have retail outlets that are designated as "smoke-free environments."

Alcohol abuse and substance abuse are also serious public health problems in Canada. Motor vehicle accidents are a major killer, and many serious crashes are caused by drunk drivers. Alcohol abuse has been linked to serious diseases, such as cirrhosis of the liver. For these reasons, public opposition to alcohol advertising is growing steadily. Some brewers have tried to counter these arguments by sponsoring advertising campaigns that promote moderation.

AIDS represents a different type of challenge to business; while no one accuses industry of causing AIDS, firms nonetheless must deal with its consequences. AIDS

GOOD, BAD, OR UGLY?

It was a sunny Saturday in the spring of 1986. The date is hard to remember, but the news is impossible to forget.

David, our fifteen-year-old son, sat on the couch in our family room. He spoke quietly and that made the horror of what he was telling us all the more stark.

David had gone to the hemophilia clinic ... for what was ostensibly a routine six-month check-up. He had scanned down the nurse's chart and had seen "HIV-positive." That was good, right? Positive had to be good!

We took our country's blood supply for granted — safe, available, life-saving. We did so at our peril. We now know that thousands of Canadians who had transfusions in the late 1970s and early 1980s,... were infected with preventable hepatitis. About a thousand people more received blood products contaminated with HIV. Almost half those people have since died of AIDS.

PARTNER IN THE FIGHT AGAINST AIDS

Why would a major beer company make a long-term commitment to helping community groups working on HIV/AIDS public education, prevention, and care? Molson Breweries, Canada's largest brewery, did just that when it was approached by Dancers for Life in Toronto to contribute some beer for an event to raise money for AIDS education and research. Instead, Molson's offered to develop a partnership with them to raise money for AIDS. This was a courageous decision for a company almost completely dependent on young males to buy its products. Associating Molson's with AIDS fundraising risked its product being categorized as a "gay beer," which would not help beer sales.

"Cause-related marketing" has been around for some time. For example, American Express became the lead corporation in the fundraising effort to rebuild the Statue of Liberty in the late 1970s. During the 1988 Olympic year, Petro-Canada sponsored the Canadian Olympic team. Probably the most well-known example is Ronald McDonald House, which has locations near more than 150 hospitals in North America. However, these activities were not controversial nor are they associated with death. It is the rare corporation that will associate its product and name with a cause that is so closely associated with death.

However, the company's commitment was in fact tempered by some realism. Before proceeding with the partnership, Molson's undertook extensive consumer polls to see how their customers felt about AIDS and whether they would be alienated if Molson's sponsored an AIDS cause. The company discovered that AIDS is no longer a gay issue but has become a mainstream issue with men and women of all ages. They also found that it was likely that Molson's involvement would enhance its reputation with Molson's consumers.

(acquired immunodeficiency syndrome) is a fatal disease that breaks down the body's ability to defend itself against illness and infection. What is especially dangerous about AIDS is the long time (typically five years) between first exposure to the AIDS virus and actual development of the disease. While people during this period may not show any symptoms of AIDS and probably don't even know they have it, they are still carriers who can give the disease to someone else. It is this large pool of unknown carriers that accounts for the rapid spread of the disease.

The rapid spread of AIDS means that companies will increasingly find themselves educating their employees about it and dealing with employees who have it. Health care for AIDS patients can be incredibly expensive, and small companies could have trouble paying these health-care costs. Do companies have the right to test potential employees for the AIDS virus? Some people feel this violates the rights of job applicants. Others feel that firms have a responsibility not to place those with AIDS in jobs where they could possibly infect others. These are difficult questions in which a business must balance the rights of individuals against the rights of society in general.

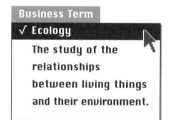

Business Term

√ **Ecology**

The study of the relationships between living things and their environment.

Protecting the Environment. In the winter of 1992, Canadians learned that the ozone layer over Canada was deteriorating faster than scientists had projected. The scare "provided a stark symbol of the way in which the health of the planet is directly affecting our daily lives. It was also a reminder that environmental deterioration can spring nasty surprises and that we are less in control than we like to think."[26] Ecology and environmental issues continue to be important to the public. **Ecology** — *the study of the relationships between living things and their environment* — is now a legal as well as a societal issue for managers to consider. It is for this reason, for example, that in many cases our major banks now require an environmental assessment before accepting a loan proposal.

Pollution. Pollution — tainting or destroying a natural environment — is the major ecological problem today. On a per-capita basis, Canada has one of the poorest records on pollution control in the industrialized world. Pollution can come from many sources. When we burn fossil fuels such as coal and oil for energy, for instance, carbon dioxide and sulphur enter our atmosphere. Both

Over the years, Molson's has helped Dancers for Life raise more than $120 000 for the AIDS Committee of Toronto. It raised $825 000 by holding walk-a-thons for the AIDS Committee of Toronto; sponsored the Laughing Matters Comedy Benefit and the Leontyne Price concert that raised $60 000 for Casey House, a Toronto AIDS hospice; and supported the Eight Ball Gala for the Canadian Foundation for AIDS Research that raised $120 000.

In sponsoring fundraising for AIDS research, Molson's is trying to achieve the following:

→ Raise funds for the AIDS Committee of Toronto.

→ Increase awareness among Toronto beer drinkers of the importance of the fight against AIDS through Molson's sales and marketing efforts.

→ Generate awareness of Dancers for Life and Molson's involvement in the event to attract other like-minded corporate sponsors and generate ticket sales.

→ Communicate Molson's leadership on the AIDS issue to consumers and opinion leaders.

Molson's involvement is partly in the form of cash and partly in the form of efforts by the firm's marketing and publicity departments. They help promote the events and convince advertising agencies and other professionals to offer their services for free.

Molson's has carefully measured the results of its association with this cause. At the end of concerts, Molson's hands out survey cards to gauge the public's reaction to the company's involvement. They also undertake telephone polling. Another benefit noted by Molson's is that the involvement improves employee morale. Molson's has discovered significant benefits in expressing a social conscience.

Sources: This article was put together by Ian Lee, Carleton University, based on Molson Canadian corporate documents; Art Chamberlain, "Firms Do Good, Cautiously," *The Toronto Star*, January 26, 1995; Randall Scotland, "Firms Take Long View of Backing 'Causes,'" *The Financial Post*, October 13, 1994; and *The Lobby Digest & Public Affairs Monthly*, July 1993.

of these chemicals cause environmental problems. The extra carbon dioxide collects in the atmosphere and traps heat, leading to the so-called *greenhouse effect* that allegedly is affecting the earth's climate and its ability to support life. During this century, the amount of carbon dioxide in the atmosphere has soared — we are burning more fossil fuels than ever before. Many scientists fear that this could result in global warming, with disastrous results.

Meanwhile, the sulphur from fossil fuels combines with water vapour in the air to form sulphuric acid. The rain that results is called *acid rain*. Acid rain kills fish and trees and can pollute the groundwater from which we get our drinking water. Acid rain is also dangerous because wind can carry sulphur all over the world. Sulphur from factories in the United States is damaging Canadian forests, and pollution from London smokestacks is destroying the forests and lakes of Scandinavia.

The Recycling Solution. Every time we throw away a plastic box, a newspaper, or a glass bottle, we are adding to the world's trash problem. Garbage just never seems to die; it stays intact in landfills for years, and we're running out of places to put it.

An important solution is *recycling* — reprocessing used materials so they can be reused. Recycling could provide much of the raw material we need for manufacturing, but we need to do a lot more of it.

Conservation. We can divide the complex topic of energy into both short-term and long-term issues. In the short run, the problem is one of **conservation** — *preserving our declining energy resources*. We have seen that burning fossil fuels damages the environment. In any case, our supplies of these fuels are limited and will run out eventually.

In addition to conserving current energy sources, we need to develop long-term solutions to supplying energy by using alternative energy sources. Wind, sun, synthetic fuels, and even garbage and other waste products have all been suggested as substitutes for fossil fuels.

Business Term

✓ **Conservation**

Preserving our declining energy resources.

Developing the Quality of the Work Force. A nation's wealth often has been thought to consist of its money, production equipment, or natural resources. A country's

The municipal government of Metro Toronto uses award-winning advertisements like this one to encourage businesses to recycle and be responsible for everything, beginning with the paper that individual employees use at the workplace.

true wealth, however, lies in its people — an educated, skilled work force is its most valuable asset. It is becoming increasingly clear that, in order to remain competitive, Canadian business must assume more responsibility for developing the quality of its work force.

For the next several years, most new jobs will require at least a college education. Many professions will demand ten years of study beyond high school, and even the least-skilled jobs will require a certain level of reading, computing, and thinking skills. Business must encourage students to stay in school, continue their education, and develop their skills. Companies also must encourage employees to learn new skills, both to help themselves and to help the company remain competitive.

Responsibilities to Customers

Consumer demands are another social-responsibility issue facing business. **Consumerism**, *the public demand for business to consider consumer wants and needs in making its*

decisions, is a major social and economic movement. Ralph Nader is a leading force in this trend.

Since the emergence of consumerism a few decades ago, consumer groups have sprung up throughout the country. Some concentrate on an isolated situation, such as rate hikes by a local public utility, while others attack broader issues. The net effect has been the passage of numerous consumer protection laws. There is little doubt that more such laws will be passed in the years ahead and that these will have a big impact on business.

> **Business Term**
> ✓ **Consumerism**
> The public demand for business to consider consumer wants and needs in making its decisions.

Consumerism is based on the belief that consumers have certain rights, including the right to be safe, the right to be informed, the right to choose, and the right to be heard. Many companies go to considerable effort to ensure that consumer complaints receive a full hearing. Ford

Motor Company of Canada, for example, has set up a consumer appeals board to resolve service complaints.

Responsibilities to Employees

Business's responsibilities to its employees are far-ranging. Issues include family leave, employment equity, multicultural diversity, sexual harassment, and sexism.

> **Business Term**
>
> ✓ **Family leave**
>
> Giving employees a leave of absence from work in order to deal with family matters.

Family Leave. As the number of families with two wage earners increases, employees' responsibilities at home and at work may clash. Some employees care for elderly parents or other relatives, while others find themselves juggling child care or family crises with the demands of their

jobs. **Family leave** — *giving employees a leave of absence from work in order to deal with family matters* — has become an important issue for many workers. Not all family leaves are taken to deal with crises. Some fathers, for instance, are fighting for the right to take a leave when a new child is born in their family.

Employment Equity.[27] By federal law, employment opportunity is a basic right in the Canadian workplace as stated in the Canadian Human Rights Act (CHRA) of 1978:[28]

> *Every individual should have an equal opportunity ... without being hindered in or prevented from doing so by discriminating practices based on race, national or ethnic origin, colour, religion, age, sex, marital status, or conviction for an offense for which a pardon has been granted or by discriminatory employment practices based on physical handicap.*

The CHRA established the Canadian Human Rights Commission, which was given considerable leeway in enforcing its anti-discrimination laws.

Equal opportunity is further promoted through provincial laws and the Employment Equity Act of 1987. **Employment equity** means that *employers must have their work force reflect the wider community in which the business is located, specifically targeting the selection and*

The World According to Big Shot

SLINKY: We can't just lay off employees to avoid employment equity laws. You know very well that company morale is at an all-time low.

BIG SHOT: Tell me, Miss Goody Two Shoes: What did you do with the extra $20 the bank machine doled out to you the other day?

SLINKY: That's different. It's my personal business what I did with the money.

BIG SHOT: Well, this company is my personal business. Tell those who are whining they're lucky to have a job. On second thought, maybe you should get rid of them too.

→ What do you think?

promotion of women, visible minorities, Aboriginal people, and people with disabilities. This Act requires every employer with 100 or more employees, working under federal jurisdiction, to submit an annual report complete with statistics on the four designated groups. The intent of the Act and the spirit of employment equity is to go beyond voluntary efforts at fairness and intentionally hire and promote employees from the designated groups.

Employment equity is also supported through *affirmative action*: the active promotion of programs, policies, and measures designed to ensure an equitable work environment and to rebalance systemic or adverse-effect discrimination. Such programs include analyzing the present work force and setting specific hiring and promotion goals with target dates in areas where women, visible minorities, Aboriginal people, and people with disabilities are involved. Although affirmative action is voluntary in Canada, leading companies like

> **Business Term**
>
> ✓ **Employment equity**
> Ensuring that a business's work force reflects the wider community in terms of the mix of women, visible minorities, Aboriginal people, and people with disabilities.

> **Business Term**
>
> ✓ **Multicultural diversity**
> The racial and cultural blend within a society.

Warner Lambert Canada and responsible municipalities such as Regina, Saskatoon, Toronto, Winnipeg, and Vancouver have adopted affirmative action measures and programs.

Encouraging Multicultural Diversity. *The racial and cultural blend within a society,* referred to as **multicultural diversity**, has always been part of Canadian culture as new immigrants have entered and become part of Canadian society. The challenge for business is to learn how to manage diversity creatively, to benefit from the different viewpoints, experiences, and talents of the various cultures in our society.

Dealing with a culturally diverse work force means understanding what motivates employees and how they function best. Developing a better understanding of people's cultures and behaviours helps businesspeople manage culturally diverse staffs more effectively. Respecting employees' cultural differences is a vital part of management in the 1990s.

Sexual Harassment. Over the last decade, sexual harassment has become a major human rights issue. Research indicates that as many as 40 percent of women are sexually harassed at work. The harassers are men.

The Canada Labour Code describes **sexual harassment** as *conduct, comment, gesture, or contact of a sexual nature that is likely to cause offence or humiliation to any employee.* Human rights legislation, both federal (under the Canadian Human Rights Act) and provincial (Ontario Human Rights Code, for example), prohibits sexual harassment.

Although sexual harassment is not a criminal matter, employers can be held indirectly liable if they are not able to demonstrate that they have done everything possible to protect their employees. This includes education and sexual harassment policies. It is thus in the best interest of employers to be proactive and to resolve sexual harassment in-house.

Many firms have established anti-harassment policies and related employee education programs. An effective harassment prevention program would include[29]

- Issuing a specific policy prohibiting sexual harassment.

- Educating managers, supervisors, and employees about the company's policy against sexual harassment and the appropriate complaint procedures.

GOOD, BAD, OR UGLY?

"It's not fair," said John, a white male in his early fifties. "Employment equity is not supposed to discriminate. Everyone knows I was the most qualified for the job. Why doesn't somebody tell me the truth?"

John was an assistant principal at a local high school. For the third year in a row he had been passed over for a promotion to the principal's level. No one had told him the real reason, but he suspected it was a result of affirmative action.

The local school board had received kudos for its employment equity and affirmative action program. Its new hiring practices reflected the cultural diversity of the surrounding inner-city community and the need to hire more visible minorities. Each year, the board would proudly announce its equity achievements in the local newspaper. Even the federal government had singled it out for a special achievement award.

Affirmative action has been a contentious issue. Some claim that it is reverse discrimination against white males. Others claim that it's the removal of their long-established preferment. What do you think?

- Creating a work atmosphere and culture that encourages sexually harassed staffers to come forward.

- Investigating and resolving complaints immediately and taking disciplinary action against harassers.

Business Term

✓ **Sexual harassment**

Conduct, comment, gesture, or contact of a sexual nature that is likely to cause offence or humiliation to any employee.

Sexism. Sexual harassment is often part of a much bigger problem: sexism. **Sexism** refers to *discrimination against either sex, but it primarily occurs against women.* Some examples of sexism are blatant: a woman being paid less than a male colleague to perform the same job, or a male employee being promoted over a female with more experience. Other instances are more subtle: the only female in a work group may not be introduced to a client or doesn't get a work assignment when a manager passes them out.

Sexism is a global issue. A United Nations study found that women, who account for over half the earth's population, do two-thirds of the world's work, earn one-tenth of the world's income, and own one one-hundredth of the world's property. The 1993 *UN Human Development Report* concluded that no country offers its female citizens opportunities comparable to those enjoyed by their male counterparts.

One important issue concerns equal pay for equal work. In industrialized countries worldwide, women's pay averages just two-thirds that of men. Many women find the route to corporate success blocked by a *glass ceiling* of discrimination. There are several reasons for this; one is that many corporate jobs rely on recruitment by word of mouth and networking, which tends to exclude women and minorities. Women often have less access to training and

CASE EXERCISE

WHAT GOES AROUND COMES AROUND

When Al Dunlap, known as "Chainsaw," headed up Scott Paper Co., he fired one third of the work force, slashed charitable spending, and sold off assets. Some stockholders loved him because this "slash and burn" tactic dramatically increased profits in the short run. In the late 1990s, Al Dunlap moved on to Sunbeam Corp. As CEO, he took the same "take no prisoners" leadership approach and slashed thousands of jobs, just like he had done at Scott Paper.

Dunlap has always insisted that those who run a company must also own a significant amount of stock in the company. The only way to ensure that corporate directors will act in the best interests of the stockholders, he reasoned, is to

have them put their own money on the line. According to Dunlap's business philosophy, if you're in business, you're in business for one thing — to make money. If you can't deliver to shareholders, you shouldn't be there.

It appears that sometimes his system works. In the summer of 1998, Sunbeam was faced with operating losses and falling stock prices. Sunbeam's board unanimously voted to remove Dunlap after he failed to turn the company around as promised. In a one-minute conference call, Dunlap was unceremoniously fired. "There's no question that the system worked here," says Donald Thain, a Canadian corporate governance expert and business school professor at the University of Western Ontario.

Some would say that Al Dunlap got what he deserved. What goes

around comes around. Nevertheless, this classic case highlights the whole issue of corporate governance. Is the average shareholder well served by directors who are loaded up with a company's shares? Should corporate directors be forced to put their own money on the line?

1. Give at least three arguments in favour of directors taking a substantial stake (ownership position) in a company.

2. Give at least three arguments against directors being required to take a substantial stake in a company.

Source: Adapted from Elizabeth Church, "Chainsaw's Own System Cuts Him Down," *The Globe and Mail*, June 19, 1998, B21. Reprinted with permission from The Globe and Mail; Al Dunlap, *Mean Business: How I Save Bad Companies and Make Good Companies Great* (New York: Times Business, 1996).

development programs. Managers' stereotypes can make things worse: managers may assume that a woman with children would not be interested in transfers or promotions that require longer hours. Executive search firms may compound the problem by focussing on white males.[30]

There is some evidence, however, that this glass ceiling may be starting to crack — at least in Canada. More and more women are being appointed to top management jobs. For example, Bobbie Gaunt was appointed president and chief executive officer of Ford Motor Company of Canada in the spring of 1997. Maureen Kempston Darkes was appointed president of General Motors of Canada in the summer of 1994. The difference between the salaries of women and men has also narrowed as a result of a gradual increase in female real earnings and a decline in male real earnings over the 1980s and 1990s. However, single women's pay still averaged about 26 percent less than that of single men in 1994.[31]

Business Term

✓ **Sexism**

Discrimination against either sex, but it primarily occurs against women.

Responsibilities to Investors and the Financial Community

There is probably no place where the public expects a higher level of business ethics than in the arena of financial transactions. Just because a business practice is legal doesn't mean that it is also ethical. When it comes to business's responsibilities to investors and the financial community, the public expects behaviour that is *both* legal and ethical. Ethical business behaviour is not just something that sounds good on paper. When business does not meet its social responsibilities, it can hurt hundreds or even thousands of people. As we learned from the Bre-X scandal, for example, unethical business practices in stock and bond trading can injure people who lose their investments or their jobs. Irresponsible actions can hurt millions of consumers.

SUMMARY OF LEARNING OUTCOMES

1. **Discuss the competitive issues that Canada faces in an increasingly global economy.**

   Shifting toward an increasingly global economy changes the competitive environment, both in Canada and in other countries. The big challenge today is for Canada to develop its ability to compete in a global market both at home and abroad. Currently, there is a shift from competition based on costs to competition based on many factors, such as product design, product development, and efficient use of technology. Firms also will succeed or fail based on the quality and service that they provide. Competitive issues that Canada faces include researching and developing better products, improving quality and customer service, improving the competitiveness of the work force, and improving organizational flexibility.

2. **Briefly explain how government regulates business.**

   Government regulates competition and competitors as well as specific business practices. Government control takes two broad forms: regulating industry and enacting statutes or laws. A regulated industry is one in which competition is either limited or eliminated, and government monitoring substitutes for market controls. The enactment of statutes has led to both provincial and federal laws affecting competition and various commercial practices.

3. **Summarize the relationship among supply, demand, and price.**

   Supply refers to sellers' willingness and ability to provide goods and services for sale in a market. Demand refers to buyers' willingness and ability to purchase these goods and services. The relationship between supply and demand determines another feature: price. The law of supply and demand states that prices (P) in a market are set by the intersection of the supply (S) and demand (D) curves. The point where the curves meet, known as the equilibrium price (E), is the prevailing market price for that item.

4. **Describe how the social and cultural environment can affect business.**

   Businesspeople must be sensitive to society's changing values and to shifts in demographics, such as population growth and age distribution. These variables affect the ways in which consumers react to different products and marketing practices. Canada is a mixed society composed of various submarkets, each of which displays unique values and cultural characteristics and differs by age, place of residence, buying behaviour, and buying preferences. The social/cultural context for business decision making often is more pronounced in the international sphere than in the domestic arena. Learning about cultural and social differences among countries is pivotal to a firm's success abroad. Business strategies that work in Canada often cannot be applied directly in other nations.

5. **Discuss ways in which the technological environment can affect business.**

   New technology results in new goods and services, improvements in existing products, better customer service, and often lower prices through the development of more cost-efficient production and distribution methods. Technology can also quickly make products obsolete, but can just as quickly open up new business opportunities and industries. Applying new technologies in creative ways may give a firm a competitive edge and open up new markets.

6. **Discuss the role of social responsibility and ethics in the business environment.**

   A major concern for a business is profit and maximizing the return on owners' investment. But business does not operate in isolation. We can think of business in terms of a set of relationships involving suppliers, distributors, customers, employees, and other firms. This means that social issues such as drug and alcohol abuse and ethical issues such as bribery and illegal acts are also major concerns for the business community.

7. Outline business's responsibilities to the general public.

The responsibilities of business to the general public include dealing with public health issues, protecting the environment, and developing the quality of the work force. Public health issues include smoking, drug and alcohol abuse, and AIDS. Businesses also should take steps to reduce their impact on the environment (working to minimize pollution, acid rain, and the greenhouse effect; supporting recycling; and conserving and developing our energy resources). Companies must remain alert to changes in environmental regulations since the laws can change quickly. Additionally, it is important to business to develop the quality of its work force, since a well-educated, skilled work force is a nation's, as well as the business's, most valuable asset.

8. Identify business's responsibilities to customers.

Business's most readily identifiable responsibilities are related to its customers. These responsibilities have been heightened by the consumerism movement, which is based on the idea that consumers have certain rights. These include the right to be safe, the right to be informed, to right to choose, and the right to be heard.

9. Describe business's responsibilities to employees.

Relations with employees pose some of the most significant social responsibility and ethical issues facing contemporary business. Issues include family leave, employment equity, multicultural diversity, sexual harassment, and sexism.

10. Explain business's responsibilities to investors and the financial community.

There has been considerable publicity in recent years about business's social and ethical responsibilities to investors and the financial community. Important topics include honest securities trading and responsible investing.

Key Terms Quiz

research and development (R&D)
ethical dilemma
regulated industry
deregulation
economics

supply
demand
ecology
conservation
consumerism

family leave
employment equity
whistle blowing
sexual harassment
sexism

_____ 1. The social science of allocating scarce resources.

_____ 2. Refers to buyers' willingness and ability to purchase products.

_____ 3. The study of the relationships between living things and their environment.

_____ 4. A leave of absence from work in order to deal with family matters.

_____ 5. The scientific process of developing new commercial products.

_____ 6. Refers to the public demand for business to consider consumer needs in making decisions.

_____ 7. A situation in which right or wrong cannot be clearly identified.

_____ 8. The preservation of energy and ecological resources.

_____ 9. An industry in which competition is either limited or eliminated, and government monitoring substitutes for market controls.

_____ 10. Refers to sellers' willingness and ability to provide products.

_____ 11. The elimination of legal restraints on competition.

_____ 12. Discrimination against either sex, primarily occurring against women.

_____ 13. The disclosure of immoral or illegal acts within an organization.

_____ 14. Employers must have their work force reflect the wider community in which the business is located.

_____ 15. Actions of a sexual nature that are likely to cause offence or humiliation.

Other Important Terms

acid rain   code of ethics   greenhouse effect
code of conduct   code of practice   recycling

Review Questions

1. What is meant by the terms _social responsibility_ and _business ethics_? Cite an example of each. Discuss the current status of social responsibility and business ethics in Canadian business.

2. How does government regulate both competitive and specific business practices? Describe the impact of regulation on our financial services and telecommunications industries.

3. Distinguish between microeconomics and macroeconomics. Describe some issues involved in each.

4. What is meant by deregulation? What are its advantages and disadvantages?

5. What contributions can Canadian business make to the job skills of the work force?

6. Explain the importance of R&D in global competitiveness. Find out how Canada rates in regard to R&D expenditures.

7. What are business's responsibilities to the general public? Cite specific examples.

8. Distinguish between sexual harassment and sexism. Cite examples of each. How can these problems be avoided?

9. Is there a need for business to be concerned with ethics? Why or why not?

Discussion Questions

1. Describe specific steps you can take to make yourself a more competitive employee in a global economy. What classes would you like to take? In what areas would you like to get more experience? Share your opinions with the class.

2. Choose a foreign country and a specific occupation (perhaps the job you would like to have after you finish school). Research how that country trains people to hold that particular job. What role does the government play, if any, in this training? Are private companies involved? How does it compare with the career training available in Canada?

3. Some business scholars believe that companies have the obligation to become involved in social responsibility issues such as those discussed in this chapter. Others believe the only social responsibility of business is to make a profit within the rules of free competition. What is your opinion? What arguments do you feel either support or disprove both positions? Explain your answer.

4. Suppose you own a small company with twelve employees. One of them tells you in confidence that he has just found out he has AIDS. You know that health care for AIDS patients can be disastrously expensive, and this could drastically raise the health insurance premiums that your other employees must pay. What are your responsibilities to this employee? To the rest of your staff? Explain.

5. Describe the major social and ethical issues facing the following:
   a. Major shoe manufacturers
   b. Real-estate developers
   c. Detergent manufacturers
   d. Drug companies selling products used to treat AIDS
   e. Managers of stock brokerage firms

Answers to Key Terms Quiz

1. economics 2. demand 3. ecology 4. family leave 5. research and development 6. consumerism 7. ethical dilemma 8. conservation 9. regulated industry 10. supply 11. deregulation 12. sexism 13. whistle blowing 14. employment equity 15. sexual harassment

Notes

1. Based on personal correspondence with Virgin; "Virgin Chooses Vancouver for Their First Canadian Megastore," *The Robson Street Preview*, Vol. 1, No. 1, Summer 1996, 4, 5, 7; The Virgin Group of Companies, Press Release, October 24, 1996; and The Virgin Group of Companies, "The Virgin Philosophy," **http://www.newshook.com/files/virgin-phil.html**, October 24, 1996.

2. Business Development Bank of Canada, "Canadian Exports Surge: Are You Part of the Success?" *Profit$*, Vol. 17, No. 2, Spring 1997, 1.

3. Stratford Sherman, "Are You as Good as the Best in the World?" *Fortune*, December 13, 1993, 95–96.

4. Based on personal correspondence with Ascent Power Technology; Rod McQueen, "Canada's 50 Best Managed Private Companies: Ascent Power Technology," *The Financial Post*, December 14–16, 1996, 16, 17. Reprinted by permission of Ascent Power Technology.

5. "British Columbia's Growth and Economy Entices Investors," *The Robson Street Preview*, Vol. 1, No. 1, Summer 1996, 3.

6. Rod McQueen, "Canada's 50 Best Managed Private Companies: Dimatec Inc.," *The Financial Post*, December 14–16, 1996, 27.

7. Based on personal correspondence with Thermoplast Inc.; Rod McQueen, "Canada's 50 Best Managed Private Companies: Thermoplast Inc.," *The Financial Post*, December 14–16, 1996, 52.

8. Industry Canada, **http://strategis.ic.gc.ca**.

9. John Partridge, "Free Market Urged by Panel," *The Globe and Mail*, May 14, 1997, B1.

10. Lawrence Surtees, "CRTC Rings in New Telco Era," *The Globe and Mail*, May 2, 1997, B1, B11.

11. Peter Fuhrman and Michael Schuman, "Now We Are Our Own Masters," *Forbes*, May 23, 1994, 128–38.

12. Michael Valpy, "The New, Value-Added Canadians," *The Globe and Mail*, October 26, 1996, D5.

13. David K. Foot with Daniel Stoffman, *Boom, Bust & Echo* (Toronto: Macfarlane Walter & Ross, 1996).

14. Gayle MacDonald, "Purdy's Tests Asia's Sweet Tooth," *The Globe and Mail*, June 9, 1997, B7.

15. Tony Martell, "Technology Can Offer a Key Strategic Weapon," *The Globe and Mail*, March 18, 1997, C2.

16. Lawrence Surtees, "Telemedicine Comes of Age," *The Globe and Mail*, April 16, 1996, C1.

17. Alex Tilley, March 27, 1995. Reprinted by permission.

18. Paul M. Sherer, *The Wall Street Journal*, as appearing in "Thai Corruption Thriving, Study Finds," *The Globe and Mail*, December 2, 1996, B6.

19. David Pugliese, "DND Expense Fears Ignored," *The Ottawa Citizen*, June 8, 1997, A1.

20. Adapted from William H. Shaw, "Moral Choices Facing Employees," *Moral Issues in Business*, 4th ed. (Belmont, CA: Wadsworth Publishing Co., 1989), 343–44. Copyright © 1989 by Wadsworth Publishing Co. Reprinted by permission of the publisher.

21. Adapted from The Society of Management Accountants of Canada, *Codes of Ethics, Practice and Conduct* (Hamilton, ON: The Society of Management Accountants of Canada, 1997), 4–5. Reprinted by permission of CMA.

22. Alex Tilley, March 27, 1995. Reprinted by permission.

23. Lynn Sharp Pine, "Managing for Organizational Integrity," *Harvard Business Review*, March/April 1994, 106–17; and Robert McGarvey, "Do the Right Thing," *Entrepreneur*, April 1994, 64–67.

24. Janet McFarland, "Corporate Responsibility Stirs Ethical Debate," *The Globe and Mail*, May 17, 1996, B8.

25. Karen Unland, "Tobacco Makers Lose Bid to Suspend Law," *The Globe and Mail*, April 30, 1997, B5.

26. David Crane, *The Next Canadian Century* (Toronto: Stoddart, 1992), 58.

27. This section is adapted from Richard M. Hodgetts, K. Galen Kroeck, and Michael E. Rock, *Managing Human Resources in Canada* (Toronto: Dryden, 1995), 6, 8, 86, 90, 88, and 126.

Copyright © 1995 by Harcourt Brace & Company, Canada, Limited. All rights reserved. Reprinted by permission of Harcourt Brace & Company, Canada, Limited.

28. Canadian Human Rights Commission, The Canadian Human Rights Act, 1978, section 2(a).

29. Emily MacFarquhar, "The War Against Women," *U.S. News & World Report*, March 28, 1994, 42–48.

30. Richard Klonowski, "Foundational Considerations in the Corporate Responsibility Debate," *Business Horizons*, July/August 1991, 9.

31. Based on Statistics Canada figures of 1994 average income for single male worker $27 309, for single female worker $20 183. John Robert Colombo, ed., *The 1997 Canadian Global Almanac* (Toronto: Macmillan Canada, 1997), 82.

Chapter 3

Global and Economic Forces Affecting Business

Learning Outcomes

| 6 | 12 | 18 | 24 | 30 | 36 | 42 | 48 |

After studying this chapter, you should be able to

1. Explain the importance of international business.
2. Identify the different types of economic systems.
3. Discuss the economic concepts involved in international business.
4. Explain why nations tend to specialize in certain goods.
5. Name the different levels of involvement in international business.
6. Explain countertrade.
7. Identify the main obstacles confronting global business.
8. Explain multinational economic integration.
9. Explain the importance of and outline the key considerations of an international business plan.

"He's Got Ketchup in His Blood"[1]

"People are filled with enthusiasm and running all kinds of private businesses. It's like the gold-rush days, everyone rushing to make their fortune." That's what George Cohon had to say on returning from Moscow, where he had been invited to attend a business awards reception at the Kremlin. He tells us that Russia is "open for business" as almost a quarter of a million small businesses are cutting their teeth on a taste of capitalism and a Big Mac. Cohon is playing a leading role in this new social revolution.

Cohon is senior chairman of McDonald's Restaurants of Canada Ltd. and vice chairman of Moscow McDonald's. He opened his first McDonald's in Moscow in 1991, the culmination of a fourteen-year business vision. He proudly introduced the Big Mac machine to the proletariat. As of 1997, Cohon had opened thirteen outlets in the former Soviet Union. Were they worth it? "Of course," Cohon responded, "290 million people live in the former Soviet Union. The city of Moscow alone has half of Canada's population." Clearly the Russians have responded to the Big Mac invasion — as many as 50 000 people a day line up at the Pushkin Square outlet.

Says Cohon, "You have to look outside of your own backyard. Asia and Africa present major opportunities, as do India and China. I'm sure there will be restaurants in existence as long as people eat, which will be forever." The global reach of McDonald's, which has some 21 000 restaurants, is truly a business

George Cohon, "burgermeister" of McDonald's

"seventh wonder." Why have McDonald's and Canadian entrepreneurs like Cohon been so successful at feeding the world hamburgers? According to some experts, it has more to do with the universal hunger for good service than grilled meat on a bun. Cohon says that the "Russians line up at Pushkin Square every day, not for a hamburger but because they are hungry for things from the West" — things like quality and service. *Fortune* magazine has called McDonald's "the most awesome service machine on the planet." *Pravda*, the major left-wing Russian newspaper, wrote with awe at the ability of the McDonald's training machine and George Cohon to transform Russian service workers into perky fast-food cheerleaders.

But the company's success is not just due to service. Leaders like Cohon who have the entrepreneurial drive and chutzpah and who truly care about the world are also partly responsible for the success of the fast-food chain. *Pravda* described Cohon as a "hero of capitalist labour. Even among the top sharks of the North American business world, George Cohon stands out with his unequalled spirit of entrepreneurship."

Social responsibility and leadership are key components of Cohon's success. For example, to date $4 million has been contributed to the Ronald McDonald Children's Charities of Russia. Cohon is a winner of several philanthropic and humanitarian awards, including the prestigious Order of Canada. He has judiciously combined a capitalist entrepreneurial spirit with a heavy dose of love and humanity.

CHAPTER OVERVIEW

WHETHER YOUR NAME is Acadian Seaplants, a small company in Dartmouth, Nova Scotia, or a corporate giant named McDonald's, successful Canadian companies consider the world their market. Many businesspeople tell us there is hardly any choice: "The continued growth and prosperity of Canada must be linked to a philosophy of looking outward. Canadians must embrace globalization despite its challenges, if for no other reason than there is no alternative for a trade-dependent nation like ours with barely the economic weight of California," says Cedric Ritchie, former chairman of Scotiabank.[2]

Globalization is a reality. Just look at Figure 3.1. Exports of goods and services as a percentage of our gross domestic product (GDP) increased by 13.6 percent between 1993 and 1996. Let's look at other export numbers:[3]

- In 1996, exports of goods and services were in the $300 billion range and accounted for about 43 percent of our GDP. This is the highest percentage in the Group of Seven (G7) leading industrial nations.

The Jobs Are

Jane Somerville,
publisher and president,
Somerville House Books Ltd.

Go Beyond Paper and Canada

"Somerville manages and creates intellectual property, publishing it in a variety of formats, including hardcovers, paperbacks and toys. It's multimedia, which takes us into a whole lot of other industries. We're going beyond paper to fresh, new interactive ideas (the Web, CD-ROM). But it's still publishing. We're just putting words in different formats.

Eighty percent of our revenue comes from the U.S. Our international market now includes Japan, Germany, Portugal, Australia and New Zealand. We couldn't exist if we stayed within Canada."

• Some 3 million working Canadians (one out of every three) owe their jobs to Canada's success in the global marketplace.

• Every $1 billion in exports creates or sustains 11 000 jobs in Canada.

• Export firms expand employment 20 percent faster than nonexporting firms and are 10 percent less likely to fail.

The signing of the Free Trade Agreement with the United States in 1991, and the North American Free Trade Agreement (1994), the formation of the World Trade Organization (1995), and the free trade agreements with Chile and Israel (1996) have all signalled a new era for Canadian business. In Vancouver in November 1997, Canada hosted the Asia-Pacific Economic Cooperation Forum (APEC). As 1997 chair, Canada took the lead in directing APEC's agenda for world trade and investment. Clearly, among the world's trading partners, Canada is now recognized as a leader in international trade.

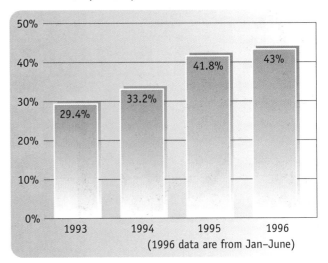

Figure 3.1 Exports of Goods and Services as Percentage of GDP, Canada, 1993–1996

(1996 data are from Jan–June)

In this chapter, we will explore how these activities form the patterns of Canadian trade and world business. We will begin with brief synopses of different economic

FUTURE TREND

BUSINESS OPPORTUNITIES IN EUROPE

The European Union (EU), composed of some 15 countries (1999), is Canada's second most important trading partner after the United States. In 1997 we traded about $15 billion worth of goods and services, a figure that, according to our trade commissioners throughout Europe, could grow substantially if Canadian companies seize opportunities. "The entire European market is ripe for any Canadian company at all that has high quality, high tech products," says Sergio Marchi, Canada's minister of international trade (1998). "The opportunities are endless."

Some of the best opportunities lie in the medical device and information technology sectors. Europe's aging population is a natural market for Canadian high tech medical devices. As in Canada, many European health systems are trying to restrict hospital use and increase home care. In Britain alone there is a $5 billion market for medical equipment and consumables according to Patrick Stratton, a commercial officer with the Canadian High Commission in London.

One firm that has taken advantage of the European market is InfoTech Inc., a small company owned by Winnipeg entrepreneur Zorianna Hyworon. In just two years, InfoTech has created a significant market in the United Kingdom for its specialized health-risk appraisal software.

Like many Canadian companies, InfoTech used the United Kingdom as the base from which to launch its European export drive. As a first step in her market entry strategy, Hyworon wooed the British health education authority with a one-year, exclusive,

private-label version of her product. The following year, she established a non-exclusive agreement and arranged for a master distributor to market the software, "Wellness Checkpoint," to major corporations. "Our systems are being used by more than 40 organizations," says Hyworon. "We're very well positioned and our growth opportunities are tremendous." Peter Doyle, director of KPMG's software and devices practice in Toronto, encourages other Canadian companies to follow this example. "The European market is vast," he says. "We need to get Canadian companies over there and remove or better manage the impediments to doing business in an unfamiliar market."

Source: Adapted from "Breaking into Europe: The Lucrative Frontier," *Profit: The Magazine for Canadian Entrepreneurs*, June 1998, Advertising Supplement.

systems. Next we'll address some of the major terms, issues, and agreements in the international trade arena. We will complete our discussion with a note on Canada's international strategy.

ECONOMIC SYSTEMS[4]

Economic systems can be distinguished along many lines but contain two fundamental principles. The first relates to how an economic activity is co-ordinated, by the market or by a government plan. In today's economy, this question does not demand an either/or answer. Societies must decide which decisions they want made in markets by individual businesses and consumers acting in their own self-interest, and which decisions they want centrally planned so that businesses and consumers act more in the national interest.

The second crucial distinction among economic systems concerns who owns the means of production. Specifically, are businesses privately owned by individuals or publicly owned by the state?

Communism

At one end (sometimes called the left) of the economic or social spectrum is *communism*, a system in which all property is shared by the people of a community under the planned direction of a strong central government. In its extreme form, there is no private property — government owns the property and the means of production and manages the economy through a planned process.

Socialism

Socialism is considered a milder form (a tad to the right) of communism. Under this system, the government owns and operates the key industries that are considered vital to the public welfare, such as transportation, utilities, and

---

Foreign Markets Fuel Canadian Firms

Almost 80 percent of the companies in *Profit Magazine*'s 1998 survey of Canada's 100 fastest-growing firms exported their product. Thirty percent derived at least three-quarters of their revenue from foreign sources. Shown below are the ten hottest companies, ranked by their 5-year growth rate.

Rank	Company, City, Industry	1997 Revenue (in millions)	5-Year Revenue Growth	Exports as a % of Sales
1.	Image Processing Systems Inc., Markham, ON Machine-vision systems	$31.800	27 056	85
2.	RTO Enterprises Inc., Edmonton, AB Rent-to-own furniture and appliances	56.081	12 588	0
3.	Discreet Logic Inc., Montreal, QC Special effects software	101.924	11 326	100
4.	Versent Corp., Mississauga, ON Laser Quest entertainment outlets	52.934	9 804	62
5.	Equisure Financial Network Inc., North Bay, ON Insurance brokerages	56.800	6 820	0
6.	G.A.P. Adventures Inc., Toronto, ON Adventure tour operator	7.838	5 464	82
7.	Tucows Interactive Ltd., Toronto, ON Internet services and shareware	8.634	5 306	20
8.	NTS Computer Systems Ltd., Maple Ridge, BC Specialty computers for school use	20.578	4 344	93
9.	Newcon International Ltd., Toronto, ON Specialty optical equipment	4.426	4 266	90
10.	McGill Multimedia Inc., Windsor, ON Interactive training and marketing software	8.383	3 274	74

Source: "Canada's 100 Fastest Growing Companies," *Profit: The Magazine for Canadian Entrepreneurs*, June 1998, 98-99.

As a result of chronic food shortages and high prices in the days of the Soviet Union, many Russians bought food, such as eggs, from the black market, which sold them approximately 10 percent cheaper than state-owned shops.

West greets East! Civil unrest in East Germany caused the Berlin Wall to come tumbling down in 1989.

health care. Private ownership is allowed in industries that are considered less crucial.

Capitalism

At the other end of the economic spectrum (sometimes called the right) is *capitalism*, a system in which private individuals own the means of production and economic decisions are dictated by the needs of the market. Theoretically, in a purely capitalist state, there would be no government — the collective vote of each consumer in the market would determine what would be produced and what would not be produced.

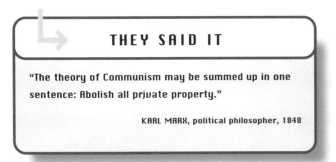

> # THEY SAID IT
>
> "The theory of Communism may be summed up in one sentence: Abolish all private property."
>
> KARL MARX, political philosopher, 1848

Mixed Economies

In practice, most countries do not have a pure communist or capitalist economy. Instead, they have a **mixed economy**, *one that combines government ownership and private ownership*.

The proportions of public and private enterprise vary widely in mixed economies,

Business Term
√ **Mixed economy**
Economic system that combines government owner-ship and private ownership.

and the mix is always changing. Over the 1990s, several countries — including Canada — began *converting government-owned companies into privately held firms*, a development known as **privatization**. Like many other countries — Britain, for example — we moved slightly to the right on the political scale. A major reason for this trend was

Business Term
√ **Privatization**
Converting government-owned companies into pri-vately held firms.

the desire to improve the economy and the belief that private corporations can manage business more cheaply and effectively than governments. In addition, unloading government-run operations had the benefit of raising much-needed cash. For example, Great Britain's government raised more than $23 billion by selling all or part of many state-owned businesses to private owners, including British Airways and aircraft engine maker Rolls-Royce.

Many European countries continued to privatize industries as they moved toward forming a more unified economic community. France now allows private companies to own up to 49 percent of a state-owned industry or bank. Renault, France's state-owned automaker, gave a quarter of its capital to the Swedish company Volvo in return for a similar stake in Volvo. Italy has agreed to sell some of its airline routes currently belonging to state-owned Alitalia to privately owned airlines. The London-based European Bank for Reconstruction and Development, created by Western nations to foster Eastern European business reforms, is scheduled to be privatized.

Similarly, Mexico has started an economic reform program that has privatized more than 1000 state-owned companies, including the Telmex phone company and 18 national banks. The government also introduced a healthy dose of competition by deregulating the trucking industry, which used to make a $500 million profit each year for 15 powerful families. Today, post-deregulation has allowed trucking rates to drop by 25 percent, and 21 percent more trucks are on the road.

In Canada, some Petro-Canada gas stations have been sold to private owners. We may see more privatization — in such areas as liquor sales, airports, and even utilities — in the future.

THE MARKET OR THE PLAN? SOME ISSUES[5]

THE CHOICE BETWEEN *planning* and reliance on *free markets* requires an understanding of just what the market accomplishes and where its strengths and weaknesses lie. Since these issues have been discussed in earlier chapters, we can review them quickly and proceed to a comparison with central planning.

How to Produce Each Good

In a market economy, firms choose the production technique, guided by the price system. Inputs that are in short supply will be assigned high prices by the market. This will encourage producers to use them sparingly. Other inputs whose supply is more abundant will be priced lower, which will encourage firms to use them.

Government taxes and subsidies alter relative prices, and externalities may make the price system malfunction. But on the whole, the market system has no serious competitor as an engine of productive efficiency, as the formerly socialist economies learned.

Planned economies can allow either plant managers or central planners to choose the production techniques. In the former Soviet Union, plant managers had little discretion — which led to monumental inefficiencies, including production curtailments, poor quality, and high costs. Indeed, such problems were among the most serious weaknesses of socialist planning. The truth is that no incentive system has yet been designed that can match the profit motive of competitive firms for keeping costs down.

How Income Is Distributed

In a market economy, the price system determines the distribution of income among individuals by setting the levels of wages, interest rates, and profits. There is no reason to expect the resulting income distribution to be ethically appealing. And, in fact, the evidence shows that capitalist market economies produce sizable inequalities.

Income inequality is certainly one of capitalism's weak points. However, the government has many ways to mitigate inequality without destroying either free markets or private property (for example, through redistributive taxes and transfer payments). In practice, governments in all market economies intervene in the marketplace to alter the distribution of income.

So do governments in planned economies, only more so. For example, they may try to tamper directly with the income distribution by having planners, rather than the market, set relative wage rates. But doing so leads to shortages and surpluses of particular types of labour. So even in the former Soviet Union relative wages were established more or less by supply and demand, and there was considerable inequality in the distribution of wages.

Economic Growth

The rate of economic growth depends fundamentally upon how much society decides to save and invest. In a free-market economy, these decisions are left to private firms and individuals, who determine how much of their current income they will consume today and how much they will invest for the future. Once again, however, government policies can influence these choices by, for example, making investment more or less attractive through tax incentives.

Planned economies have more direct control over their growth rates because the state can determine the volume of investment. They can therefore engineer periods of very high growth if they choose to — an option that both Stalin's Russia and Mao's China exercised successfully, though at great human cost. More recently, Singapore's planned market economy has grown rapidly by forcing individuals to save. One may wonder, however, whether rapid growth is desirable when it is paid for by loss of personal freedom, or even by bloodshed.

Furthermore, the economies of the Soviet Union and Eastern Europe turned in extremely poor growth performances in the 1970s and 1980s, while some of the fastest growth rates were recorded in the market economies of Japan, Taiwan, and Hong Kong. All told, history suggests that no other system can match market incentives for sustaining growth over long periods of time. Indeed, China has become the fastest-growing major economy on earth as it has moved away from planning and toward markets.

Prime Minister Jean Chrétien leads a team of provincial premiers to China in 1994 to promote trade with the fastest-growing economy in the world.

Business Fluctuations

A market economy is subject to periods of boom and bust, to inflation and unemployment. This holds true not only in capitalist market economies like the United States but also in socialist market economies. So even though Marx dubbed the business cycle one of the fundamental flaws of *capitalism*, it is really a problem for *market economies*, be they capitalist or socialist.

Business fluctuations are not much of a problem in highly planned economies because total spending is controlled by the planners and is not permitted to get far out of line with the economy's capacity to produce. So the business cycle was not traditionally a serious problem in, say, China or the former Soviet Union. However, now that these two nations are transforming themselves into market economies, macroeconomic issues have become critical.

ECONOMIC CONCEPTS INVOLVED IN INTERNATIONAL BUSINESS

THE MAIN PATTERNS of international business result from a combination of economic and political factors. To understand trade and world business, let us first look at the concepts of balance of trade, balance of payments, and exchange rates.

Balance of Trade. A country's **balance of trade** is *the relationship between its exports and imports*. If a country exports more than it imports, it has a favourable balance of trade, called a trade surplus. If it imports more than it exports, it has an unfavourable balance of trade, or a trade deficit. Figure 3.2 shows that Canada's balance of trade has steadily become favourable. By the mid-1990s, Canada had a trade surplus of some $19 billion. The major reason for this was the large trade surplus with the United States. For example, in 1995, Canada had a U.S. trade surplus of almost $60 billion. Many analysts have argued that this is the direct result of the Free Trade Agreement and the North American Free Trade Agreement, both of which are discussed in a later section.[6]

> **Business Term**
> ✓ **Balance of trade**
> The relationship between a country's exports and imports.

Balance of Payments. A nation's balance of trade plays a central role in determining its **balance of payments** — *the overall flow of money into or out of a country*. Other factors affecting the balance of payments are overseas loans and borrowing, international investment, profits from such investment, foreign travel, and foreign aid. A favourable

---

DID YOU KNOW?

→ In Canada, people are accustomed to having at least 30 cm of space between them when talking to each other. In India, people are comfortable with half that space.

→ The gesture of sliding a finger across the neck (like slitting one's throat) means "I love you" in Swaziland.

→ To make a sale of construction vehicles in Venezuela, Caterpillar had to take iron ore in payment. The ore was shipped to Romania in exchange for men's suits, which were then sold in London for cash.

→ French fries never are labelled as such in France. Even at a Parisian McDonald's outlet you'll have to ask for <u>pommes frites</u>.

balance of payments, or balance of payments surplus, means that more money is coming into a country from abroad than is leaving it. An unfavourable balance of payments, or balance of payments deficit, means that more money is leaving the country than entering it.

Nations with a deficit normally try to solve this problem by reducing their dependence on foreign goods, reducing investments abroad, devaluing their currency, or increasing their exports. Often these steps involve making politically controversial moves that may reduce the demand for foreign-made goods and also may lead to higher prices and greater unemployment.

Over the first half of the 1990s, Canada had a negative balance of payments. This was not caused by our trade in goods and services, as we now know. The main reason was payments of interest and dividends to foreign corporations and investors. For example, in 1995, payments to foreign companies and individuals (called investment income) was $47.8 billion and receipts to Canadians investing abroad was $17.1 billion. This left a deficit of over $30 billion. Note that our balance of payments deficit declined steadily over the 1990s (see Figure 3.2). The major factors contributing to this decrease were our strength in trade exports and a corresponding devaluation of our dollar.[7]

Exchange Rates. A nation's **exchange rate** is *the rate at which its currency can be exchanged for the currencies of other nations.* A currency's exchange rate usually is quoted in terms of other important currencies. For example, in

THEY SAID IT

"Don't overlook the importance of worldwide thinking. A company that keeps its eye on Tom, Dick, and Harry is going to miss Pierre, Hans, and Yoshio."

AL RIES, chairman, Trout & Ries Inc.

mid-1996 the Canadian dollar was worth about 73 cents U.S. You could buy 68 Japanese yen, 1 German mark, or 3.6 French francs with 1 Canadian dollar.

Exchange rates can have a major impact on a nation's economy. Changes in exchange rates can wipe out or create a competitive advantage quickly, so they are a big consideration in whether or not to invest abroad. If the Canadian dollar rises in price relative to the yen, for instance, this means that a dollar will buy more yen. Japanese products become less expensive, Japanese imports increase, and Canadian firms face greater competition.

Over the first half of the 1990s, the value of the Canadian dollar fell relative to most of the major currencies. In 1993, $1 Canadian could buy 0.52 pound sterling. In mid-1996, this same dollar could buy only 0.46 pound sterling, an 11 percent decrease. This meant that British imports became 11 percent more expensive and Canadian exports were 11 percent cheaper when

Figure 3.2 Balance of Trade and Balance of Payments

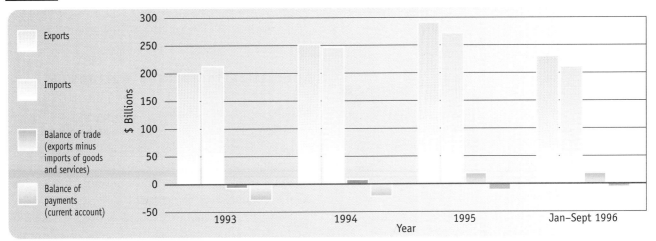

EAST COAST ACADIAN CROSSES WORLDWIDE SEAS

You don't have to be a McDonald's to be successful on the world market. This is what we learned from the winners of the Canada Export Awards Program — a partnership between the Department of Foreign Affairs and International Trade, CIBC, Export Development Corporation, and Bell Advantage (an alliance of Canada's telecommunications companies).

Acadian Seaplants Ltd., a small company in Dartmouth, Nova Scotia, was a 1996 Canada Export Award winner. Acadian Seaplants harvests seaweed and turns it into products that are used by food, botanical, feed, and agro-chemical industries across the world. It represents a new breed of Acadian who has proven that our East Coast Canadians can compete and win in the global marketplace. Acadian exports 91 percent of its products to more than 35 countries. Total sales in 1995 were 89 percent higher than 1993. The company, founded in 1991, currently employs over 100 full-time and 1000 seasonal staff.

What has made Acadian Seaplants so successful? According to its President, Louis Deveau, the company's success is due to its quality product, technology, and aggressive research. It invests heavily in cultivation and harvesting techniques. Its competitive strategy is to invest heavily in technology, product, and market research. As much as 15 percent of its revenues are plowed back into sustainable harvesting technology, resource and technology management science, and cultivation.

Source: Adapted from a special supplement by the Department of Foreign Affairs and International Trade, CIBC, Export Development Corporation, and Bell Advantage. This supplement appeared in "1996 Canada's Export Awards," *The Globe and Mail Report on Business Magazine.*

---

purchased with British currency. Some analysts argue that this was a major factor contributing to our relatively strong balance of payments. It also meant that travelling to a foreign country became relatively more expensive. As a result, our net receipts from tourism, although negative (more money left the country for tourism than came in), did show a gradual improvement over the 1990s.[8]

Devaluation describes *the fall of a currency's value relative to other currencies or to a fixed standard.* Devaluation of the dollar makes Canadian goods sell for less abroad and lowers costs for visiting foreigners. If the dollar buys fewer yen, this increases the prices Canadian consumers pay for Japanese products and decreases the amount of competition for Canadian firms. It also makes it more expensive for Canadian companies to buy assets abroad, but less expensive for foreign firms to purchase Canadian assets.

Most international exchange rates are based on a system called *floating exchange rates*, where currency traders create a market for the world's currencies based on the countries' trade and investment prospects. In theory, this means that exchange rates are free to fluctuate, or "float," according to supply and demand. In practice, exchange rates do not float in total freedom; countries often intervene to adjust their own exchange rates. Also, some currency blocs exist within which exchange rates are linked to one another, and many governments practise protectionist policies that seek to "protect" their economies from trade imbalances. A disadvantage of the floating-rate system is that exchange rates are highly sensitive to every bit of new information that could affect business. For the most part, however, the system works well, and it appears that it will continue as the global basis for determining exchange rates.

> **Business Term**
> √ **Devaluation**
> The fall of a currency's value relative to other currencies or to a fixed standard.

Specialization among Nations

Nations usually benefit from specializing in certain products or commercial activities. By doing what they do best, they are able to exchange surplus domestic output for foreign-made products that are needed. This allows a higher standard of living than would be possible if a country tried to produce everything itself.

However, specialization has its dangers if taken too far. Many less-developed countries depend on one or two primary commodities, such as grain and copper, to earn foreign currency to pay for imported goods. If the price of their main good declines, it becomes much more difficult to import needed goods and services. Other problems can occur when a country depends on foreign nations to supply something that is critical to its economy. A 1996 approach used by the Canadian federal government is a variant of this specialization theory and a planned approach to economic development. In its Canadian International Business Strategy (CIBS) program, the federal government set out international business development strategies for some 27 different sectors. Strategies with the greatest chance of success were those that were developed by federal and provincial governments in close collaboration with industry. For example, the CIBS identified Aboriginal products and services as a targeted industry and subsequent action plans focussed on specific areas of opportunity in this industry.[9]

Absolute Advantage. A country has an *absolute advantage* in marketing a product if it holds a monopoly or produces the product at the lowest cost. Examples of absolute advantage are rare because few countries are sole suppliers, and because rapidly changing economic conditions can wipe out advantages in production costs.

When it comes to gem-quality diamonds, for instance, South Africa traditionally has had an absolute advantage since it possessed a rare domestic source of these gems. However, the discovery of diamond deposits in other areas of the world — such as Canada's far north — has removed South Africa's absolute advantage.

Comparative Advantage. A more practical approach to international specialization is that of *comparative advantage*. A country has a comparative advantage in an item if it can supply that item more efficiently and at a lower cost than it can supply other goods, compared with other nations. For example, if country A can produce a certain good three times as efficiently as country B, and it produces a second good only twice as efficiently as country B, then country A has a comparative advantage in the first good. Country B, even though it produces the second good less efficiently than country A does, has a comparative advantage in this item because that is the one it is relatively more efficient at producing. Worldwide, the greatest supply of both products will result when each country specializes in producing the good in which it has a comparative advantage, that is, country A producing the first good and country B producing the second.

Countries tend to follow this pattern of specialization. A tropical nation, such as Costa Rica, may specialize in agriculture due to its climate and available inexpensive labour. Canadian exports, on the other hand, reflect Canada's comparative advantage — the fact that it is a highly industrialized country with plentiful agricultural and natural resources. Canada therefore exports manufactured items, food products, and natural resources.

Self-Sufficiency. Some countries prefer to be self-sufficient rather than to specialize and trade. Many Central American nations have tried to remain self-sufficient, although this pattern is changing. Other countries seek self-sufficiency only in commodities they regard as strategic to their long-run development, such as energy in Canada, but a few — Israel, for example — try to be self-sufficient in regard to many national-defence items. These countries see the noneconomic advantages of self-sufficiency as being more important to the national welfare than the economic advantages of specialization.

DID YOU KNOW?

"Even though we are an exporting nation, we are not yet a nation of exporters!" François Beaudoin, President and CEO of the Business Development Bank of Canada (BDC) explains that exports contribute to the national balance of payments and eventually help foster a higher standard of living for all Canadians. But, astonishingly, barely 950 firms account for 85 percent of our total exports.

Getting Started in Global Business

Global business involvement is an evolving process for many firms. For example, a small company might start exporting on a limited scale, then expand its overseas efforts as management gains experience and confidence in its ability to operate effectively abroad. The company later may move to even greater degrees of global involvement.

Four levels of involvement in world business are direct and indirect exporting, foreign licensing, overseas marketing, and international production and marketing. As a firm becomes more active internationally, both the risks of and the degree of control over marketing increase.

Direct and Indirect Exporting. **Exporting** firms *produce goods at home and sell them abroad*. (In contrast, **importing** firms *buy foreign goods and raw materials*.) Many

COMPETITIVE STRATEGY

PORTER REVISITED

Michael Porter is a professor at the renowned Harvard Business School. He is a recognized expert on international competitiveness and competitive strategies and has authored fourteen books on the subject. Porter argued, in 1990 and 1991, that Canada was relying too heavily on its past sources of economic strength, such as natural resources. As a result, he said, the country risked missing out on opportunities in a globalized, technology-driven world.

At a Montreal conference in 1996, he revisited the findings of his famous 1990 study *Competitive Advantage of Nations* and his 1991 study *Canada at the Crossroads: The Reality of a New Competitive Environment*. In his update at La Conférence de Montréal, Porter reported that Canada had improved its competitiveness considerably, citing in particular the tremendous growth in exports as evidence of a healthier national situation and global spirit: Companies are more competitive. Governments are responsibly addressing some of their most pressing problems. And rapidly rising exports have given a big boost to the well-being of Canadians. For Canadian companies, increased exports mean increased sales. In turn, increased sales mean increased investment.

According to Porter, investment is the key to prosperity. He did caution, however, that our low-value currency could hardly be considered an effective long-term strategy for prosperity. Canada needs to do more to add value to its economy. Porter added that we need new investment and new products, and we need to tap new markets. To survive in the long run, we must be able to compete, on an equal footing, with the rest of the world.

Source: Adapted from Business Development Bank of Canada (BDC), "Exports Play a Key Role in Canada's Competitive Strategy — Michael Porter," *Profit$*, Vol. 17, No. 2, Spring 1997, 6. Reprinted by permission of BDC.

---

companies engage in *indirect exporting*, often without realizing it, when their products are part of another good that is exported. Electronic components are a common example.

When a firm actually seeks export business, it is engaging in *direct exporting*, the most common form of international business. The company must devote both capital and managerial resources to this effort. Frequently, a firm will co-ordinate its export operation with an in-house "export manager," or it may hire an outside company specializing in export promotion.

While Canadian exporters are mainly large companies, it is not necessary for a company to be big to be successful at exporting. A survey by the Entrepreneur of the Year Institute revealed that almost 70 percent of the respondents were doing business or planned to do business abroad.[10] Calgary-based Vertical Technologies Inc. is typical of the new breed of Canadian small business. Vertical develops software aimed

> **Business Term**
> √ **Exporting**
> **Selling domestic goods abroad.**

> **Business Term**
> √ **Importing**
> **Buying foreign goods and raw materials.**

> **Business Term**
> √ **Foreign licensing**
> **Contract in which a firm allows a foreign company to produce and distribute its products or use its trademark, patent, or processes in a specific geographic area.**

at facilitating the automation of law firm processes. Over the 1990s, the company began to focus on finding export markets for its products and services. In 1996, about 5 percent of Vertical's sales were generated by exports. By 1997, sales were estimated at about $3 million, with exports accounting for 25 percent.[11]

Foreign Licensing. **Foreign licensing** *refers to a contract in which a firm allows a foreign company to produce and distribute its products or use its trademark, patent, or processes in a specific geographic area*. It is a low-cost way for firms to enter new markets. Licensing also provides local marketing information and distribution channels and avoids protectionist barriers.

Overseas Marketing. When a firm gets involved in overseas marketing, it establishes a foreign sales office. The parent company directly controls all foreign marketing, even though the goods and services may come from a variety of sources, such as domestic plants, licensees, or subcontractors.

Sometimes the choice between licensing and overseas marketing can be an important one. When PepsiCo first entered India, it did so via foreign licensing. At first the strategy worked well; within three years Pepsi won 25 percent of India's soft-drink market. However, the company's archrival, Coca-Cola, countered with an overseas marketing coup: it acquired the distribution network and sales offices of Parle Exports, an Indian firm that controlled 60 percent of the country's beverage market. While The Coca-Cola Company will continue to control Indian marketing operations, the pre-established distribution network gives it a big advantage in covering the large country.[12]

International Production and Marketing. Total global business involvement occurs when a company produces as well as markets its products abroad. A firm may enter foreign markets in this way by starting a subsidiary or acquiring an existing firm in the country where it is expanding. Sometimes, too, a company will enter into a **joint venture** with a local firm or government, *sharing the operation's costs, risks, management, and profits with its local partner.* The way in which a company enters a new market may depend on political factors. For example, in late 1996, the Ford Motor Company announced that it would not resume efforts to build cars in Indonesia. According to Wayne Booker, Ford's vice-president of emerging markets, "The situation in the auto industry was very murky. The present regulations in the auto industry are clearly in violation of the [World Trade Organization]." Should the political situation change, Ford will enter Indonesia, as it has in other Asian countries such as Vietnam.[13]

Outsourcing, the practice of contracting production and other business services to outside firms, was introduced in Chapter 1. In many cases, these outside firms are foreign-based. For example, major shoe manufacturers — such as Bata, Nike, and Reebok — contract much of their production to workers in developing countries. Many of Hewlett-Packard's best-selling computer printers are assembled and packaged in Asia.

Countertrade

Sometimes it is difficult to tell who is selling and who is buying in international trade because of the practice of **countertrade**, or *negotiated bartering agreements that facilitate exports and imports between countries.* Some degree of countertrade is involved in an estimated 15 to 30 percent of all international trade.

> **Business Term**
> √ **Countertrade**
> Negotiated bartering agreements that facilitate exports and imports between countries.

> **Business Term**
> √ **Joint venture**
> Sharing the operation's costs, risks, management, and profits with a local partner.

Countertrade typically is used when the buyer has limited foreign currency, so payment must be made in goods. On occasion, however, the buyer pays for the goods and the seller agrees to purchase other merchandise from the buyer or find a customer for the products. Often countertrade may be the only way a firm can enter a particular market. Many developing countries simply cannot obtain enough credit or financial assistance to afford the imports their people want. For instance, a developing country that is dependent on agriculture may lack the means to import such manufactured goods as radios and TV sets, or the machinery to produce these goods itself. Countries heavily in debt also resort to countertrade. Still other nations, such as China, may restrict their imports. Under such circumstances, countertrade can be a good way for companies to distribute their products to new markets in the hope of attracting new customers.

Multinational Corporations. A **multinational corporation** is *a firm with major operations outside its home country.* Canada's top ten exporting companies are multinationals and account for over 30 percent of our total exports. Needless to say, multinationals play a dominant role in Canada's exporting picture. As Table 3.1 shows, most of our top exporters are entrenched in the resource-based and auto industry sectors — despite Michael Porter's optimism (see the box on page 66). Seventeen of our top 50 exporters are in the forest industry sector alone, and the top three exporters are in the auto industry. In addition, many of Canada's largest exporting multinationals are foreign owned — a disturbing picture that deeply concerns our governments, we hope. The top four Canadian exporting companies (in terms of volume) have head offices in the United States and account for over 20 percent of our total exports.[14]

> **Business Term**
> √ **Multinational corporation**
> A firm with major operations outside its home country.

Table 3.1   Top Exporters

Company	Export Sales ($ billions)	Total Sales ($ billions)	Exports as % of Sales	Industry
1. General Motors of Canada Ltd.	17.9	24.9	72	automaker
2. Chrysler Canada Ltd.	13.5	15.7	86	automaker
3. Ford Motor Co. of Canada Ltd.	10.8	20.1	54	automaker
4. IBM Canada Ltd.	5.4	8.5	63	computers
5. Canadian Wheat Board	3.5	3.9	90	grain trading
6. Noranda Inc.	3.0	6.8	44	resources
7. Bombardier Inc.	3.0	5.9	50	engineering
8. Alcan Aluminum Ltd.	2.8	11.0	25	metals
9. TransCanada PipeLines Ltd.	1.9	5.2	36	energy
10. Avenor Inc.	1.6	1.9	84	forest products

Figure 3.3a   Factors Driving Global Expansion

Figure 3.3b   Top Problems in Developing Export Markets

BARRIERS TO INTERNATIONAL BUSINESS

WHILE MANY FACTORS drive global expansion (Figure 3.3a), various barriers to conducting effective world business also exist. Figure 3.3b lists the top ten problems. Some are minor and easily overcome; others are nearly impossible to bridge. In any case, business executives must expect and learn to handle a multitude of problems in attempting to reach world markets.

Cultural Barriers

To succeed in foreign markets, firms must understand cultural factors, such as language, education, social values, religious attitudes, and consumer habits. For example, many Asian cultures place great emphasis on personal relationships as a crucial part of doing business. This helps explain why Japan has been so successful in forming business ties with Pacific Rim nations.

For many Canadian businesspeople, time is a commodity. But in India, time is a process — there's lots of time. This can greatly frustrate some Canadian businesspeople: "What we realized about India and some other countries is that Canadians go with good technical expertise but because of a huge cultural information gap, they become frustrated and get turned off," said Navin Parekh, business adviser at the Conference Board of Canada.[15]

The Disney Corporation provides us with a classic lesson on the importance of cultural understanding. Disney's huge theme park near Paris has been less successful than its counterparts in the United States and Japan. Disney management expected European tourists to behave like Americans, who bring their families to spend a week at a time in Florida's Disney World hotels. However, Europeans' per-capita income is lower than that of American and Japanese tourists, and they prefer to spend it on long vacations. Many EuroDisney visitors are day-trippers who made a brief stop and returned to their Paris hotels in the evening. Another problem is that, unlike snack-happy Americans, Europeans like to eat their meals at set times; long lines formed in front of park restaurants when everyone stopped for lunch at 12:30. Once the tourists got inside, they were less than pleased to discover that the eateries did not serve beer or wine. Complicating the situation were French employees who resented Disney's U.S.-style rules forbidding facial hair, makeup, and fingernails longer than 0.2 inches.[16]

Physical Barriers

A variety of physical barriers also can affect world trade. Location can make a big difference: it is easier for Japan to do business with Pacific Rim nations, for instance, than it is for Canada. According to some experts, location, along with similarities in culture, make it advisable for many Canadian businesses to "cut their teeth" in exporting to the United States. We caution, however, that other analysts believe Canada already relies too much on the States.

Other barriers to trade may be less visible but are important nonetheless. For example, Chile is a "structured and hierarchical society. You really have to watch what you say and to who. It helps if you have someone to introduce you around," warns Susan Nation, a consultant with

> ## THEY SAID IT
>
> "Chile is a developed country, it's not a developing country."
>
> TOM PUGSLEY, vice-president of projects and operations, Falconbridge Ltd.
>
> "Chile is very competitive. You can lose your shirt if you don't do your research."
>
> SUSAN NATION, consultant with Toronto-based Bariston Inc., which helps companies break into foreign markets

Bariston Inc. Spanish lessons are another good investment, although English is spoken by most executives. "It's like speaking French in Quebec. People respect you for making the effort," says Tom Pugsley, a vice-president at mining firm Falconbridge Ltd. who spent eighteen months in Chile. Nation agrees: "If you want to have any friends or business success, you have to speak Spanish."[17]

Tariffs and Trade Restrictions

Global commerce is affected by tariffs and related trade restrictions. These restrictions include import quotas, embargoes, and exchange control.

Tariffs. A **tariff** is *a tax levied on products imported from abroad.* Some require a set amount per kilo, litre, or other unit; others are figured on the value of the good. Tariffs can be classified as either revenue or protective. A *revenue tariff* is designed to raise funds for the government. A *protective tariff*, which is usually higher than a revenue tariff, is designed to raise the retail price of imported items

Business Term
✓ **Tariff**
A tax levied on products imported from abroad.

and improve the competitiveness of domestically made goods. Countries sometimes protect their "infant industries," and their related jobs, by using tariffs to bar foreign-made products.

Trade Restrictions. There are other ways of restricting trade besides using tariffs. An *import quota* sets a limit on the number of certain products that can be imported. The objective of such quotas is to protect domestic industries and their employees or to preserve foreign exchange. The ultimate quota is the *embargo,* a total ban on imported or exported products. Embargoes typically are used for political rather than economic purposes. Until recently, U.S. businesses were unable to do business in Vietnam due to the United States' trade embargo against that country. A week after the embargo ended, more than 34 American firms had already entered the Vietnamese market led by none other than The Coca-Cola Company, which had lined up two joint ventures.

Exchange Controls. Foreign trade also can be regulated by using *exchange controls,* under which firms can buy and sell only through the central bank or other designated government agency. The government can then allocate, expand, or restrict access to foreign exchange in accordance with national policy.

Exchange controls can be used selectively to reduce the importation of specific products or the operation of particular companies (sometimes countries do this to restrict the inflow of goods considered luxuries or unnecessary). Such regulations can be difficult for firms to deal with because they can affect free trade in components or supplies for other products or for overseas production. Often a company will have to negotiate with government officials to agree on what can and cannot be brought into the country.[18]

Exchange controls are not restricted to less-developed countries. Britain, for example, had some form of exchange controls from the time of World War II until the early 1980s.

Political and Legal Barriers

Firms operating abroad often are hindered by local politics and laws. Indonesia's government, for example, prohibits foreign firms from creating their own wholesale or retail distribution channels, which forces outside companies to use Indonesian distributors. Brazilian laws require foreign-owned manufacturers to buy most of their supplies from local vendors. Clearly, managers involved in international business must be well versed in legislation affecting their industry if they want to compete in today's world marketplace.

Dumping. **Dumping**, *selling goods abroad at a price lower than that charged in the domestic market,* is prohibited in many countries. Firms dump products for a variety of reasons, but usually it is to increase market share. This is similar to predatory pricing in the domestic market, since dumping undersells rivals and can force them out of business.

Dumping has become a controversial issue in the global marketplace; since the mid-1980s, over 40 nations

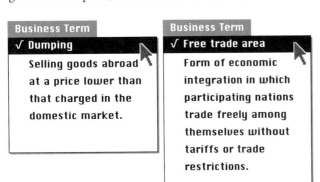

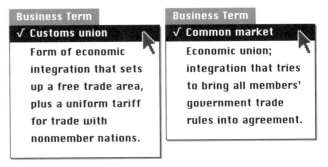

have created their own anti-dumping laws. Since that time, the number of dumping complaints worldwide has risen to roughly 2000.

MULTINATIONAL ECONOMIC COMMUNITIES

SINCE WORLD WAR II, there has been a trend toward multinational economic integration by various means. The simplest approach is to establish a **free trade area** in which *participating nations trade freely among themselves without tariffs or trade restrictions.* Each maintains its own tariffs for trade outside this area. A **customs union** *sets up a free trade area, plus a uniform tariff for trade with nonmember nations.* In a **common market**, or *economic union, members go beyond a customs union to try to bring all government trade rules into agreement.* These partnerships meet with varying degrees of success, but on the whole they have been beneficial to Canada. Widening Canada's network of free trade partners has been and will continue to be a major priority of our foreign trade strategy. Some of the major partnerships/agreements affecting Canada are detailed below.

Free Trade Agreement (FTA)

Amongst considerable political controversy, the Conservative government, led by then Prime Minister Brian Mulroney, signed the historic Free Trade Agreement with the United States in December 1988. This agreement came into effect in January 1989, and the government of the day proudly proclaimed that Canada was "open for business." Canadian companies would no longer be sheltered from American competitors. The **Free Trade Agreement** (**FTA**) was *designed to gradually reduce and eventually eliminate tariff barriers for many products traded between Canada and the United States.* It meant that Canadian companies would have to compete with the Americans based on their own merits. Despite claims by some analysts that Canadian businesses would not be able to compete with their American counterparts on an equal footing, it gradually became clear that Canadians could compete effectively. For example, a 1993 Statistics Canada analysis found that Canada's share of the combined Canadian and U.S. market actually increased in the first three years under the FTA.[19] It was analyses such as this one that encouraged the federal government to sign the North American Free Trade Agreement (NAFTA), which involves Canada, the United States, and Mexico, in 1994.

North American Free Trade Agreement (NAFTA)

The **North American Free Trade Agreement** (**NAFTA**), *a free trade agreement among Canada, the United States, and Mexico*, came into effect in 1994. Although NAFTA has had its critics, the overall impact on the Canadian economy has been beneficial according to most studies. For example, a 1995 study by the Economic Strategy Institute found that exports to the United States were approximately $14 billion higher than they would have been without any free trade agreement. According to some analysts, this translated into about 150 000 new jobs. This rather dramatic north–south shift in our trading has not been without its problems, however. For example, there have been a number of disputes over steel and lumber. As time progresses, most international observers believe that these types of disputes will diminish.[20]

World Trade Organization[21]

The **World Trade Organization** (**WTO**) was established on January 1, 1995, as *the multilateral institution charged*

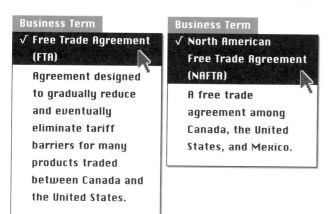

> **Business Term**
> ✓ **Free Trade Agreement (FTA)**
> Agreement designed to gradually reduce and eventually eliminate tariff barriers for many products traded between Canada and the United States.

> **Business Term**
> ✓ **North American Free Trade Agreement (NAFTA)**
> A free trade agreement among Canada, the United States, and Mexico.

> **Business Term**
> ✓ **World Trade Organization (WTO)**
> The multilateral institution charged with the responsibility of developing and administering agreed-upon rules for world trade.

> **Business Term**
> ✓ **General Agreement on Tariffs and Trade (GATT)**
> An international trade accord that sponsored a series of negotiations reducing worldwide tariff levels.

with the responsibility of developing and administering agreed-upon rules for world trade among some 130 member countries. Its role is similar to that of the organization it succeeded — the General Agreement on Tariffs and Trade (GATT), which implemented an agreement of the same name.

The **GATT** was *an international trade accord that sponsored a series of negotiations reducing worldwide tariff levels*. Since GATT was founded in 1948, there have been eight rounds of negotiations, ending with the Uruguay Round. The Uruguay Round commenced in Punta del Este, Uruguay, in September 1986 and concluded at Marrakech, Morocco, in April 1994. At this GATT session, Canada and other countries called for the formation of the WTO to embody the new trade disciplines adopted during those final negotiations. Further progress toward multilateral trade liberalization will take place through future rounds of WTO negotiations.

The goal of the WTO is to stabilize worldwide currencies and prevent protectionist laws that restrict international trade. Other goals include protecting patents and copyrights, lowering trade barriers for services, and improving methods for settling trade disputes.

The WTO agreements are expected to reduce Canadian tariffs by an average of about one-third, with industrial tariffs falling by about one-half. Canada is expected to benefit from tariff reduction abroad on industrial exports, with Japan reducing such tariffs by an average of 56 percent and the European Union by 37 percent.

The following fundamental principles of the WTO are endorsed by the Canadian government, as supplied by the *Forum for International Trade Training (FITT)*:[22]

- **Nondiscrimination among member countries.** Any trade advantage granted to one country is automatically extended to all other countries. This is called the most favoured nation (MFN) clause.

- **Fair competition.** All exporters must enjoy identical customs and fair market access conditions.

CYBERSPACE

The Internet can help businesses. Here are some government Web sites that can help you learn more about our global marketplace.

→ **The Business Development Bank of Canada (BDC)**
   http://www.bdc.ca/site/left

→ **Export Development Corporation**
   http://www.edc.ca

→ **Canadian Commercial Corporation**
   http://www.ccc.ca

→ **Industry Canada – Strategis**
   http://strategis.ic.gc.ca

→ **Department of Foreign Affairs and International Trade**
   http://www.dfait-maeci.gc.ca

→ **Canada Export Newsletter**
   http://www.dfait-maeci.gc.ca/english/
   news/newsletr/canex

→ **U.S. Trade Center**
   http://www.ustradecenter.com

- **Customs tariffs as sole protection.** Customs duties must be used instead of nontariff barriers to ensure that trade barriers are obvious and upfront.

- **Trade liberalization among member countries.** The goal is to facilitate the best market opportunities for every member's businesses.

- **Preferential treatment for developing countries.** The goal is to encourage easier access to the markets of developed countries.

- **Trade dispute settlement by an international jurisdiction.** The purpose of the Dispute Settlement Body is to provide a more efficient dispute settlement mechanism.

- **Stable and predictable trade environment.** This principle speaks for itself.

Other Agreements

In December 1994, leaders of 34 countries agreed that a Free Trade Agreement of the Americas (FTAA) should be negotiated by 2005. In the spirit of this agreement, the governments of Canada and Chile reached a 1997 bilateral free trade agreement. In the opinion of some experts, this agreement will facilitate Chile's eventual accession into NAFTA. A Canada–Israel Free Trade Agreement was also signed in July 1996 and implemented in January

The World According to Big Shot

BIG SHOT: Get FITT on the phone. We're going to export something.
SLINKY: Great, now we'll be a modern business. What's your reason?

BIG SHOT: The wife and kids want to go to Disney World for a holiday.

SLINKY: So?
BIG SHOT: I need a tax deduction.

→ What do you think?

1997. It allows duty-free access to the respective markets for industrial goods.[23]

Asia-Pacific Economic Cooperation Forum (APEC)

Canada's trade and economic orientation has historically been established along trans-Atlantic and continental lines. However, over the 1990s global competition and potential investment began to shift and the Asia-Pacific region emerged as a centre of dynamism and growing importance to Canada.

In 1997, Canada was honoured to chair the **Asia-Pacific Economic Cooperation Forum** (**APEC**). Canada had been a founding member of APEC, which formed in 1989. This is *a group of Pacific Rim economies working to promote open trade:* "Our mission is to improve conditions for doing business in the Asia-Pacific region, which we believe will in turn help spread prosperity for all the region's people," said Paul Gobeil, Chair of the APEC Business Advisory Council.

In 1997, APEC's 18 members represented over 50 percent of global output. APEC's direct investment in Canada was about $11 billion (see Figure 3.4) and Canada's exports to member countries exceeded $25 billion.

European Union

Agreements with other countries that don't involve Canada can also have a significant indirect impact on Canadian trade. Perhaps the best-known example is the *European Union (EU)*. The trade potential of the EU is tremendous — 12 countries, 335 million people, and a market of $5.53 trillion are involved.

To achieve its goal of a "borderless Europe," the union is working to erase barriers to free trade among its members. This is a highly complex process that involves standardizing business regulations and requirements, standardizing trade duties and value-added taxes, eliminating customs checks, and creating a standardized currency known as the European currency unit (ECU). Europe's economic borders were technically dissolved on December 31, 1992, although true economic integration will not take place for several more years.

Consider the difficulty of standardizing a currency when large differences exist in the strength of the members' various

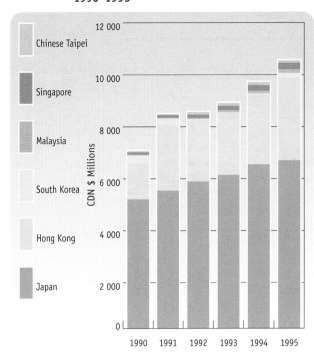

Figure 3.4 Canada's Exports to Selected APEC Economies, 1990–1995

economies; Germany has a strong industrialized economy, for instance, while Portugal's economy is still developing. Another problem is the persistence of cultural traditions that have existed for centuries. For example, Belgium is a small country, but it contains three distinct cultures: Dutch- or Flemish-speaking people in the north, French-speaking people in the south (who view themselves as Walloons rather than Belgians), and a small German community in the southeast.[24]

International Monetary Fund

Originally set up to co-ordinate international financial relations, the *International Monetary Fund (IMF)* lends money to countries that require short-term assistance in conducting international trade. The IMF has played a major role in overseeing agreements between the debtor countries and their lenders to renew their loans while ensuring repayment. Participation in the fund has given debtor countries liquidity (i.e., money or a means of payment) beyond their reserves of gold or foreign exchange. This greatly facilitates trade and investment between nations. The *World Bank* was established to make long-term loans to countries for economic development projects.

Business Term

✓ **Asia-Pacific Economic Cooperation Forum (APEC)**

A group of Pacific Rim economies working to promote open trade.

CASE EXERCISE

PROTECTIONISM REARS ITS UGLY HEAD

During the commercial mercantile age of the 1700s, protectionism was the name of the trading game. Business relied on government to encourage domestic industry, regulate production, control trading, impose tariffs and quotas, and seek raw materials. By the early nineteenth century, this system had given way to the laissez-faire (or free market) philosophy. Economists like Adam Smith, in his classic study *Wealth of Nations*, stressed the value of open competition and trade — without government intervention. The principle of comparative advantage, along with open and competitive markets, was considered the long-term key to a nation's prosperity.

Laissez-faire was the prevailing view during most of the 1990s. Many foreign governments held that money should be allowed to flow freely from country to country, thus allowing capital (financial inflows and outflows) to find the most profitable and productive investments.

In late 1998, protectionism reared its ugly head. Declaring that the free market had failed them disastrously, some Asian and South American countries responded with protectionist policies. The Malaysian government, for example, declared that it would no longer allow its currency to trade outside the country. Apparently technology, and the ability of multinational corporations to transfer capital, was at the root of the problem: large speculative investors had been shifting money from country to country at great

speeds. Some claimed that this was the major cause of the 1998 collapse of many Asian and South American economies, and the dramatic fall of the Canadian dollar.

1. Do you agree with the protectionist view? Or, do you side with the formal American government (1999) view that controls undermine the basic principles of the free market economy and in the long run lead to inefficiencies, lack of productivity, and declining incomes?

Source: Adapted from Heather Scoffield, "Capital Flow Controls Winning Support," *The Globe and Mail*, September 14, 1998, B1, B5; David Wessel and Bob Davis, "'Chinese Solution' Begins to Hold Sway," *The Globe and Mail*, September 4, 1998, B6.

DEVELOPING AN INTERNATIONAL BUSINESS PLAN

EXPERTS ALL AGREE that any firm entering the global marketplace must have an *international business plan*. An excellent plan is provided by the Forum for International Trade Training (FITT), and we suggest that any company or individual seriously thinking about entering the international marketplace get in touch with FITT.[25] Another excellent source is the *Business Development Bank of Canada (BDC)*. Entrepreneurs thinking about exporting should also keep an eye out for the "Going Global" tour in more than 50 cities across Canada organized by the BDC and the Canadian Chamber of Commerce.

Here are five steps suggested in a BDC video entitled *Going Global*:[26]

- **Step 1: Analyze the domestic market.** *Before venturing abroad, you should have a thorough understanding of your company's position in your domestic market. Evaluate all aspects of your operation.*

- **Step 2: Study the export market.** *This involves studying the many countries around the world*

where your product or service might generate interest. Study the country's economic, political, and cultural trends. Evaluate the local competition to see how their products or services compare with your own, in terms of their ability to satisfy customers.*

- **Step 3: Learn the techniques of exporting.** *It is important to become familiar with the various techniques associated with exporting. These include how to finance foreign operations, understanding taxation and legal issues, and managing logistics and customer considerations.*

- **Step 4: Prepare a development plan.** *Building a development plan is a key element which can help you think strategically and focus your export efforts. Essentially, it is a planning tool which outlines the changes your company will need to make in order for your product or service to compete in the global arena.*

- **Step 5: Develop a marketing plan.** *Developing a marketing plan will help you successfully position your company's product or service in terms of price, distribution techniques, promotional efforts, and customer service in the new marketplace.*

SUMMARY OF LEARNING OUTCOMES

1. **Explain the importance of international business.**

   Since most national economies are closely linked today, international business is growing in importance. Exports account for over 40 percent of our economic output and about 30 percent of our jobs. Analysts predict that with the passage of such treaties as NAFTA, our association with such bodies as the World Trade Organization and APEC, and the expansion of Asian, Latin American, and Eastern European markets will make global trade even more important to the Canadian economy in coming years.

2. **Identify the different types of economic systems.**

   Economic systems can be distinguished along many lines. Two are fundamental. The first question is how is an economic activity co-ordinated — by the market or by the plan? The second question is who owns the means of production? Specifically, are they privately owned by individuals or publicly owned by the state? At one end (sometimes called the left) of the economic or social spectrum is communism. Socialism is considered to be a milder form of communism. At the other end of the spectrum (sometimes called the right) is capitalism. A mixed economy is typical of most modern-day societies. It is one in which businesses and industries are publicly and privately owned, in various combinations.

3. **Discuss the economic concepts involved in international business.**

   Economic concepts involved in international business include the balance of trade (the difference between exports and imports), the balance of payments (the difference between inward and outward flow of money), and exchange rates (rates at which currencies can be exchanged for other currencies). Most international exchange rates are based on a system of floating exchange rates, where currency traders create a market for the world's currencies based on the countries' trade and investment prospects.

4. **Explain why nations tend to specialize in certain goods.**

   Countries usually benefit from specializing in certain products or commercial activities. A country has an absolute advantage in making a product if it holds a monopoly or produces the product at the lowest cost. It has a comparative advantage if it can supply the product more efficiently or at a lower cost than it can supply other products, compared with other nations. Some countries refrain from specializing because they want to be self-sufficient, particularly in certain strategic areas.

5. **Name the different levels of involvement in international business.**

   The four levels of involvement in international business are direct and indirect exporting, foreign licensing, overseas marketing, and international production and marketing.

6. **Explain countertrade.**

   Countertrade refers to negotiated bartering agreements that facilitate exports and imports between countries. It often is used when a buyer has limited foreign exchange. In other instances, a seller agrees to buy certain products from the purchaser in order to expedite the original sale. The practice of countertrade is expected to grow in the future.

7. **Identify the main obstacles confronting global business.**

   A wide variety of obstacles face world business. Examples include cultural and physical barriers, tariffs and trade restrictions, and political and legal barriers. Cultural barriers (language and different business customs) can be a problem. Physical barriers, such as geographic distance or poor transportation systems, can also affect world trade. Trade restrictions, such as tariffs, import quotas, embargoes, and exchange controls, may discriminate against particular products, companies, or nations. Other barriers to trade include different national laws and marketing requirements, as well as political factors.

8. **Explain multinational economic integration.**

Multinational economic integration is the removal of barriers between countries to the movement of goods, capital, and people. Three formats, with increasing levels of integration, exist: the free trade area, the customs union, and the common market or economic union.

9. **Explain the importance of and outline the key considerations of an international business plan.**

Experts all agree that any firm entering the global marketplace must have an international business plan. The five-step process suggested by the Business Development Bank of Canada (BDC) is as follows: **Step 1**: *Analyze* the domestic market. **Step 2**: *Study* the export market. **Step 3**: *Learn* the techniques of exporting. **Step 4**: *Prepare* a development plan. **Step 5**: *Develop* a marketing plan.

Key Terms Quiz

balance of trade
tariff
balance of payments
free trade area
devaluation
multinational corporation
World Trade Organization (WTO)

countertrade
exchange rate
customs union
North American Free Trade
   Agreement (NAFTA)
dumping
mixed economy

common market
Free Trade Agreement (FTA)
importing
privatization
exporting

_____ 1. An international bartering agreement in which an exporter must buy something in order to sell something.

_____ 2. A multilateral institution, established in 1995, that is responsible for developing and administering agreed-upon rules for world trade.

_____ 3. Selling domestic goods abroad.

_____ 4. The relationship between a country's exports and imports.

_____ 5. A free trade agreement that came into effect for Canada in 1994.

_____ 6. Buying foreign goods and raw materials.

_____ 7. A corporation that operates in different foreign countries.

_____ 8. A historic Canada–U.S. free trade agreement that came into effect in 1989.

_____ 9. The rate at which a country's currency can be exchanged for other currencies.

_____ 10. An economic system having a mix of government ownership and private enterprise.

_____ 11. A tax levied against imported products.

_____ 12. The trend of substituting private ownership for public ownership.

_____ 13. The flow of money into and out of a country.

_____ 14. A form of economic integration that maintains a customs union and seeks to bring other trade rules into agreement.

_____ 15. A form of economic integration in which a free trade area is established for member nations and a uniform tariff is imposed on trade with nonmember nations.

_____ 16. Selling goods abroad at a price lower than that charged in the domestic market.

_____ 17. The reduction in value of a country's currency.

_____ 18. A form of economic integration in which participants agree to trade among themselves without tariffs or trade restrictions.

Other Important Terms

absolute advantage
Business Development
    Bank of Canada (BDC)
capitalism
comparative advantage

embargo
European Union
exchange controls
FITT
floating exchange rates

GATT
import quota
international business plan
International Monetary
    Fund (IMF)

joint venture
socialism
World Bank

Review Questions

1. Is it possible for a nation to have a favourable balance of trade and an unfavourable balance of payments? Defend your answer.

2. Differentiate among private enterprise, communism, and mixed economies. Discuss the current status of each of these economic systems.

3. What is the role of the WTO in promoting international trade? What is its relationship to GATT?

4. Distinguish between the concepts of absolute advantage and comparative advantage.

5. Identify the levels of involvement in international business and give an example of each.

6. What is meant by countertrade? Why do you think this has become such an important part of international business?

7. How have the FTA and NAFTA been beneficial to Canada?

8. Describe three types of barriers that firms may face in international business. Give an example of each.

9. Explain the difference between a revenue tariff and a protective tariff. What type of tariff is Canada most concerned with today? Why?

10. What initial steps would a firm take if it wanted to export?

Discussion Questions

1. Keep a list of your purchases for a week. How many of the items you bought were foreign-made? Discuss what you have learned from this exercise.

2. Unlike Canada, the United States enforces a ban on trade with Cuba for political reasons. Given the change in the former Soviet Union, should the United States now resume trade with Cuba? What would be the advantages and disadvantages of doing so? Explain your answer.

3. The People's Republic of China resumed control of Hong Kong in 1997. Discuss the impact of this situation on international business.

4. Analyze a government-owned business or Crown corporation in Canada — perhaps even in your own community. How does its government-owned status make it different from businesses that are privately owned? Do you think that it would be more or less efficient if it were privatized (or would it make any difference)? Explain your answer.

5. Acadian Seaplants Ltd. and McDonald's have been successful international exporters. Why? Is there any major difference in the philosophies of the two firms?

Answers to Key Terms Quiz

Notes

1. Adapted from Donna Jean Mackinnon (SouthamStar Network), "Delivering Capitalism — on a Bun," *The Ottawa Citizen*, April 29, 1997, E3. Reprinted with permission — The Toronto Star Syndicate; and Kara Kuryllowicz, "The Best Businesses to Get into Now," *Profit*, December/January 1997, 62. Reprinted by permission of George Cohon and Kara Kuryllowicz.

2. Quoted in Colin Campbell with Carol Hood, *Where the Jobs Are: Career Survival for Canadians in the New Global Economy*, 2nd ed. (Toronto: Macfarlane Walter & Ross, 1997), 18.

3. Minister of Supply and Services Canada, *Canada's International Business Strategy*, 1997–1998, Catalogue No. C2-226/1-1998E, 5; and Campbell with Hood, *Where the Jobs Are*, 21.

4. Parts of this section are excerpted from ECONOMICS: PRINCIPLES AND POLICY, Seventh Edition by William J. Baumol and Alan S. Blinder, 897–98, copyright © 1997 by Harcourt Brace & Company, reprinted by permission of the publisher.

5. Excerpted from ibid., 899–900, copyright © 1997 by Harcourt Brace & Company, reprinted by permission of the publisher.

6. Department of Foreign Affairs and International Trade, "Pocket Facts: Canada — Economic Indicators," *Trade and Economic Analysis*, 1996.

7. Statistics Canada, "Balance of International Payments," *Canadian Dimensions*, **http://www.statcan.ca/english/ Pgdb/economy/economic/econ01.htm**.

8. Department of Foreign Affairs and International Trade, "Pocket Facts: Canada — Economic Indicators."

9. Minister of Supply and Services Canada, *Canada's International Business Strategy*, 1997–1998, 1.

10. Entrepreneur of the Year Institute, *First Annual Survey of Canadian Entrepreneurs*, 1994, 11.

11. Business Development Bank of Canada (BDC), "Increasingly Focused on Exports," *Profit$*, Vol. 17, No. 2, Spring 1997, 6.

12. Subrata Chakravarty, "For Want of a Lever," *Forbes*, February 14, 1994, 18.

13. Associated Press, "Ford on Hold in Indonesia," *The Globe and Mail*, April 30, 1997, B7.

14. "Top Exporters," *The Globe and Mail Report on Business Magazine*, July 1996, 96.

15. Juliet O'Neill, "Corporate Culture Shock," *The Ottawa Citizen*, March 10, 1997, C1. Reprinted by permission of The Ottawa Citizen.

16. Jolie Solomon, "Mickey's Trip to Trouble," *Newsweek*, February 14, 1994, 34.

17. Elizabeth Church, "How to Conduct Business in Chile," *The Globe and Mail*, November 15, 1996, B11.

18. Michael Czinkota and Ilkka Ronkainen, *International Marketing* (Fort Worth, TX: The Dryden Press, 1993), 139.

19. Statistics Canada, *Trade Patterns: Canada–United States 1981–1991*, 1993, Catalogue No. 65-504E, 5, as cited in Forum for International Trade Training Inc., *FITT Skills: Global Entrepreneurship*, Module 1, 1997, 38.

20. Campbell with Hood, *Where the Jobs Are*, 16.

21. This section is based on Minister of Supply and Services Canada, *Canada's International Business Strategy*, 3; Forum for International Trade Training Inc., *FITT Skills: Global Entrepreneurship*, 142; and World Trade Organization, "Fact Sheet," **http://ffas.usda.gov/ffas/fas-publications/ fas-factsheets/wto.html**.

22. Forum for International Trade Training (FITT), *Skills, Global Entrepreneurship* (Ottawa: FITT, 1997), 142.

23. Minister of Supply and Services Canada, *Canada's International Business Strategy*, 3.

24. Art Weinstein, "A Primer for Global Marketers," *Marketing News*, June 20, 1994, 4–5; and Allyson Stewart, "Europeans Embrace Tastes of Ethnic Food," *Marketing News*, January 17, 1994, 10.

25. You may contact FITT by telephone: (613) 230-3553 (local Ottawa), toll-free: 1-800-561-3488, fax: (613) 230-6808, or e-mail: **corp@fitt.ca**.

26. Excerpt from Business Development Bank of Canada (BDC), "Step-by-Step Guide to Going Global," *Profit$*, Vol. 17, No. 2, Spring 1997, 6. Reprinted by permission of BDC.

Getting Started

Michael Cowpland, President and CEO,
Corel Corporation, Ottawa

"We're writing Java [multi-format interactive]

software for client-server applications,

because it's a huge new field filled with

opportunity. It could transform computers over the

next 10 years. Why would I do anything other

than computers? I'm not going into something

I know nothing about. I know computers."

Chapter 4

Developing a Business Strategy and Plan

Learning Outcomes

```
6        12        18        24        30        36        42        48
```

After studying this chapter, you should be able to

1. Identify the components of a mission statement.
2. Define objectives and how they differ from the mission statement.
3. Explain competitive differentiation and identify methods businesses use to create it.
4. Define planning and distinguish among the various types of plans.
5. Explain SWOT analysis and how it is used in corporate planning.
6. Describe SBUs and give examples.
7. Define forecasting and differentiate between qualitative and quantitative forecasting.
8. Outline the components of the business plan.

Corel Plans, Develops, and Goes for the Juggernaut[1]

Corel Corporation was founded by Dr. Michael Cowpland in 1985. In slightly more than a decade this Canadian company has become an internationally recognized developer and marketer of PC graphics, office suites, and multimedia software. By 1997, for example, Corel held a 75 percent share of the Windows™ illustration software market with its award-winning CorelDRAW™. Total company sales were in the $350 million range, and the Corel team was servicing over 250 million users in more than 70 countries and in 20 different languages. "It could not have happened without a strong company vision, careful planning and a committed team," says Cowpland. Successful companies have strong leadership, and Corel is no exception. Cowpland, Corel's CEO, is an industry guru and winner of the 1996 Ursaki award as Canada's Sales and Marketing Executive of the Year.

A pivotal moment for Corel came in March of 1996 when the company moved into the big leagues and acquired the renowned WordPerfect™ business productivity applications. Corel had a plan to carefully, but quickly, re-engineer this world — to place WordPerfect™ software into a market-leading line of powerful productivity suites. The company's determined vision to offer the best office software available, combined with a world-class research team, allowed it to capture first place in U.S. office suite retail sales for four consecutive months in 1996, bringing to a halt Microsoft's monopolization of the business applications market. "The company's pulled off a major coup in being able to make a dent in the

Corel's products are up against strong world competition.

Microsoft juggernaut. Normally when you're in the [software] market, it's a one-way street and here we are pushing them back," said Cowpland.

Cowpland also realizes that to succeed against the industry leviathans, Corel can't go it alone. The company has to maintain its commitment to aligning itself with strong partners who have established distribution channels. Thus, Corel's plan for future domination in software technology also includes its continued commitment to partnerships, alliances, and licensing agreements with such companies as Packard Bell, NEC Inc., Novell Inc., and Netscape.

Corel has weaknesses as well as strengths. With so much opportunity in the software market, sometimes the company has found it difficult to maintain its strategic focus on software development. Analysts point out that it is important for Corel not to get sidetracked and to continue to concentrate on specific market niches, like the medical profession, where it can expect to command a higher market share and profit margin. They also point out that the company should continue to simplify its CorelDRAW™

product offering, emphasizing the most needed and desired features. Lastly, analysts stress that Corel must continue to focus on customer support and quality improvement — ensuring above all that its new product lines get to the market on time.

The key to Corel's future is a planned focus on software niche opportunities and a major opportunity, according to industry analysts, is Java™ technology. Java™ is a universal programming language that increases the speed and performance of Internet applications. It also holds the promise of making irrelevant the differences among computer operating systems; software written in Java™ code can be used on any system. Corel was the first major software firm to seize the Java™ opportunity. It introduced Corel Office for Java™ in mid-1997, representing another industry breakthrough. This was the first full-feature suite of office productivity applications written entirely in the Java™ language. Corel plans to be a world leader in Java™ software applications.

No company exists in a vacuum, however, and Corel faces some serious threats. Competition is vicious in the high-tech arena. Giant cash-rich companies such as Microsoft would like nothing better than to run this Canadian upstart right out of business. For example, Microsoft has already introduced a new lower-priced office suite called Home Essentials™ to compete with Corel Office Professional™. It could also introduce, or encourage a third party to introduce, a competitive graphics software aimed at undercutting CorelDRAW™. Cowpland deflects warnings about the size of the task in going head to head with companies such as Microsoft. His objectives are clear and targeted. For example, in 1997, Corel launched a series of products aimed at niche markets for office suites, including the medical and legal fields as well as a construction industry package. The company also has a strategic plan to attack markets that have been overlooked or that its competitors have given up on. Corel developed, for example, a WordPerfect™ suite that is backgrounded for aging operating systems such as DOS and Windows 3.1.

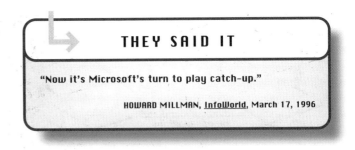

THEY SAID IT

"Now it's Microsoft's turn to play catch-up."

HOWARD MILLMAN, *InfoWorld*, March 17, 1996

Cowpland is pragmatic about the realities of the computer industry. He knows that the average new product has less than a 50 percent chance of success. One generation's computer colossus can be the next generation's struggling also-ran. No one can really predict whether Corel will continue to be successful. But, according to Cowpland, "identifying and maximizing exciting market opportunities in software, such as Java, is paramount. The key to the long-term survival of Corel will be its highly motivated and talented team of employees."

CHAPTER OVERVIEW

I N THIS CHAPTER, we discuss how companies like Corel develop a business strategy and plan. First, a company writes a mission statement, which includes what products or services it plans to provide, its potential customers, and its philosophy of business. Next, a company sets its objectives — that is, the major goals that it hopes to meet over the short or long term. Establishing these objectives leads to the company's next step: creating a competitive differentiation, whether by hiring and keeping the best workers, producing high-quality output, inventing a unique product, streamlining logistics, reducing costs, or using the finest computer technology.

Next, the organization makes specific plans to meet its objectives. For example, strategic planning involves establishing actions and allocating resources, whereas tactical planning includes implementing the activities specified by the strategic plans. Tactical planning also tends to be for a shorter term than strategic planning. Both types of planning are necessary to achieve organizational objectives.

One specific form of planning relies on SWOT (strengths and weaknesses, opportunities and threats) analysis, a process that was carried out at Corel. The strategic business unit is another important planning tool as a company splits itself into logical divisions, each with its own objectives and planning.

Planning must be underpinned by forecasting, which is figuring out the likely financial status of a company, based on its objectives, over the short and long term. Forecasting can be qualitative (based on

people's opinions and judgement) or quantitative (using mathematical formulas based on historical data and different business theories). Various methods of forecasting are described in this chapter.

The chapter concludes with a summary of how to create a business plan.

DEVELOPING THE ORGANIZATION'S MISSION STATEMENT

B EFORE PLANS AND strategies are formulated, it is necessary to determine a company's vision or larger purpose. By developing a **mission statement**, *a written explanation of a company's purpose and aims*, a company can define its general goals and rationale. Mission statements are normally connected to the values and vision of the firm. A company's values are things that its employees, management, and owners find important — health, ecology, and safety, for example. The organizational vision is an inspiring picture or ideal state of how the firm wants to be perceived at some point in the future. As a result, mission statements may include what goods or services are to be provided and what the market will be, as well as information on treatment of employees and the company's belief system or values.

Mission statements may be written by a company's founder as the company is set

Business Term

√ **Mission statement**

A written explanation of a company's purpose and aims.

up, or they may be developed based on input from management and workers. As companies grow and change, mission statements may be rewritten to reflect new goals and attitudes. Mission statements generally are aimed at guiding the people within a firm, but they also can be used to inform customers of a company's point of view. Here are two examples:

- Crestar Energy Inc., Calgary: "Building a successful resource company respected by our employees, their families, business associates and the community."[2]

- Canadian Mountain Holidays, Banff: "To challenge and enrich ourselves and our guests by sharing safe, world-class, wilderness, mountain adventures."[3]

In some cases the basic or guiding principles of the company are embedded in the mission statement. For example, Starbucks Coffee Company, the leading retailer, roaster, and brand of specialty coffee, sums up its mission in 101 words:[4]

Starbucks Mission Statement
Establish Starbucks as the premier purveyor of the finest coffee in the world while maintaining our uncompromising principles as we grow. The following six guiding principles will help us measure the appropriateness of our decisions:
1. *Provide a great work environment and treat each other with respect and dignity.*
2. *Embrace diversity as an essential component in the way we do business.*
3. *Apply the highest standards of excellence to the purchasing, roasting, and fresh delivery of our coffee.*
4. *Develop enthusiastically satisfied customers all of the time.*

COMPANY WATCH

"If you can recite the company's mission statement, the $100 bill is yours." Michael Cannata, president of Cybermation Inc., a Markham, Ontario, based firm, tells his employees. At every quarter, they are updated about the firm at a breakfast meeting that always concludes the same way. Cannata picks a name from a hat, waves a $100 bill, and challenges the selected employee to recite the corporate mission. The answer is "to develop and maintain enthusiastic customers."

---

5. *Contribute positively to our communities and our environment.*
6. *Recognize that profitability is essential to our future success.*

Once the mission statement is written, the next step is to establish organizational objectives.

SETTING ORGANIZATIONAL OBJECTIVES

OBJECTIVES *are guideposts that managers use to define standards of what the organization should accomplish in such areas as profitability, customer service, and employee satisfaction.* Figure 4.1, for example, shows a few of Scotiabank's objectives. In general, more and more businesses are setting objectives other than profitability. As consumer concern about environmental issues mounts, many firms find that becoming environmentally responsible pays off with customers. Other businesses channel some of their profits into socially responsible causes, such as funding educational programs and local charities. Managers continually evaluate performance in terms of how well the organization is moving toward its objectives.

Functions of Objectives

In contrast to the mission statement, which delineates the company's goal in general terms (as in Starbucks' stated aim to "apply the highest standards of excellence to the purchasing, roasting, and fresh delivery of our coffee"), objectives are more concrete. The activities and decisions at all levels of a company are influenced greatly by the objectives of the organization, which serve three important functions: providing direction, setting standards, and providing motivation.

Business Term
√ **Objectives**
Guideposts that managers use to define standards of what the organization should accomplish in such areas as profitability, customer service, and employee satisfaction.

Providing Direction. By specifying end goals for the organization, objectives direct the efforts of managers. For example, senior managers in all locations of Norwest Soil Research Ltd. work closely to set their monthly financial

Figure 4.1

Scotiabank

Banking on strength
Building shareholder value

Risk Management

Effective risk management is the critical factor for success in banking. Scotiabank has consistently emphasized the management of credit and market risk. On these measures of strength, the Bank has been a leader in Canada and among the best in the world for many years.

Diversification

Scotiabank is diversified by geography, products, and customers across four business lines: domestic, corporate, investment, and international banking. Our commitment to diversification minimizes overall risk and broadens the Bank's income streams.

Productivity

Cost control is a strength that is deeply rooted in Scotiabank's culture. We operate efficiently, paying close attention to detail. Our productivity ratio is consistently one of the best among major North American banks.

Customer Service

Scotiabank's goal is to meet the needs of every customer. Our bank-wide commitment to provide the very best products and services is another strength upon which we build market share and revenue growth, year after year.

goals. They discuss the upcoming month's expected results at weekly "huddles." At the end of each month, major

Norwest Soil Research Ltd. is a model organization when it comes to providing direction to its employees.

department heads meet to compare their projected results with the actual results. Each manager then conducts a "post-huddle meeting" with his or her staff to develop strategy and find ways to improve, meet, or exceed forecasts. Employees are encouraged to pinpoint problems, bring up ideas, and suggest solutions. This process of objective-setting has resulted in improved self-confidence and morale for all workers, in addition to a significant improvement in both revenue and earnings.[5]

Setting Standards. Objectives function as standards for the manager since they offer tangible benchmarks for evaluating organizational performance. Objectives include, for example, specific sales targets or profit expectations. Without such standards, the manager has no means of deciding whether work is good or bad. If performance appears unsatisfactory, management can refocus the organization in the direction of its objectives.

Providing Motivation. Finally, objectives encourage managers and workers to do their best. A certain percentage of defect-free products, for example, might be set as a goal, and bonuses, profit sharing, or other incentives can be linked to accomplishing it. At Norwest Soil Research Ltd., employees are motivated in part through an employee-ownership and profit-sharing program. In 1997, for example, employees owned 40 percent of the company, and each received a $2000 profit-sharing bonus.[6] An employee ownership program is also in place at Corel.

Management by Objectives

As well as defining the goals of the entire company ("increase sales by 13 percent"), objectives can be used at the level of the individual employee ("reduce output errors by 5 percent"). A widely used management technique aimed at improving worker motivation and performance is **management by objectives** (**MBO**), which *involves employees in setting their own goals, lets them know in advance how they will be evaluated, and bases their performance appraisals on periodic analyses of their progress toward agreed-upon goals.*

The MBO approach was popularized in the early 1950s by management writer and consultant Peter Drucker, who described it this way:[7]

> *The objectives of the district manager's job should be clearly defined by the contribution he and his district sales force have to make to the sales department, the objectives of the project engineer's job by the contribution he, his engineers, and draftsmen make to the engineering department. ... This requires each manager to develop and set the objectives of his unit himself. Higher management must, of course, reserve the power to approve or disapprove his objectives. But their development is part of a manager's responsibility; indeed, it is his first responsibility.*

The five-step sequence used by most MBO programs is illustrated in Figure 4.2.

Through the MBO process, the manager and the employee reach an understanding about the employee's major areas of responsibility and required performance level. This understanding forms the basis of the worker's goals for the next planning period (usually six months).

Employee goals should be in numerical terms whenever possible — reducing scrap losses by 5 percent, for example, or increasing sales of pocket calculators by 15 percent. Once these goals are established and agreed upon, the worker is responsible for achieving them.

At the end of the period, there is a formal review in which the worker and the manager discuss performance and determine whether the goals were achieved. They analyze any unmet goals, devise corrective measures, and set new goals.

> **Business Term**
> ✓ **Management by objectives (MBO)**
> Program that involves employees in setting their own goals, lets them know in advance how they will be evaluated, and bases their performance appraisals on periodic analyses of their progress toward agreed-upon goals.

Benefits of MBO

The chief purpose of management by objectives is to improve employee motivation. Since workers participate in setting their goals, they know both the job to be done and precisely how they will be evaluated. An MBO program also can improve morale by improving communication between employees and managers. In addition, it enables workers to relate their performance to overall organizational goals. Finally, it serves as a basis for decisions about salary increases and promotions.

Problems Inherent in MBO

The success of MBO programs is affected greatly by the degree of management support and involvement. Also,

Figure 4.2 Steps in Management by Objectives

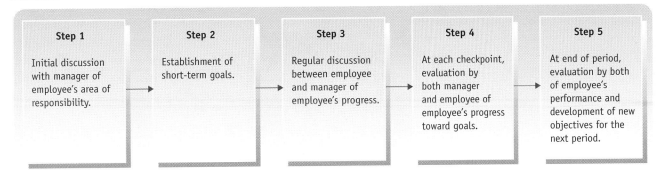

Step 1	Step 2	Step 3	Step 4	Step 5
Initial discussion with manager of employee's area of responsibility.	Establishment of short-term goals.	Regular discussion between employee and manager of employee's progress.	At each checkpoint, evaluation by both manager and employee of employee's progress toward goals.	At end of period, evaluation by both of employee's performance and development of new objectives for the next period.

management must make a conscious effort to avoid over-burdening the MBO system with too much paperwork and record keeping. A potential problem is that, in many organizations, workers' goals constantly change. In such situations, it is difficult to measure results accurately.

The corporate environment can thwart an employee's success at attaining goals. For example, if there is little co-operation or trust between departments, or a lack of planning as a whole, an employee whose work depends on others delivering their work on time will not be able to achieve her or his goals.

Some managers have difficulty in communicating with individual employees and in formulating short-term performance goals. However, when goals are assigned rather than agreed to, the result is typically resentment and lack of commitment on the part of the employee. MBO will succeed only when both managers and subordinates feel comfortable with it and are willing to participate in it.

External factors can also affect the success of MBO programs. For instance, a recession or other economic, political, or social condition can reduce sales of a company's product, thereby preventing salespeople from attaining their sales targets.

CREATING A COMPETITIVE DIFFERENTIATION

O NCE A COMPANY has developed a mission statement and has set objectives, it still faces the challenge of competing with other companies with similar missions and objectives. A company may do this by selling more of its product, cutting overhead, increasing efficiency, and instituting internal improvements that allow greater profit per sale.

A **competitive differentiation** is *any aspect of a company or its performance that makes it more successful than its competitors*. As depicted in Figure 4.3, methods of creating a competitive differentiation include improving management of human resources, using total quality management, developing new products, improving logistics within the company through just-in-time techniques, using up-to-date computer technology, reducing overhead and prices, and creating strategic alliances or partnerships. An individual company may use more than one of these techniques.

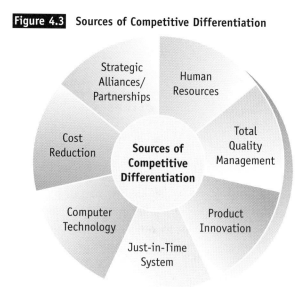

Figure 4.3 Sources of Competitive Differentiation

Human Resources

Starbucks CEO Howard Schultz has never forgotten being financially insecure: "My dad was a blue-collar worker. He didn't have health insurance or benefits, and I saw first-hand the debilitating effect that had on him and on our family." Schultz determined never to treat workers the way his father was treated. This determination motivated Schultz to provide Starbucks employees with a benefits plan unprecedented in the retail service industry, where many workers are part time and turnover is traditionally high. Starbucks employees who work more than twenty hours a week receive health insurance — including preventive medical, vision, and dental coverage — plus stock options and, of course, coffee.

Says Schultz, "More than half of our retail sales force is part-time workers. That tells me that the majority of our customers are coming into contact with part-timers. How we treat our people is directly related to how we treat our customers and to the quality of our product. It's inarguable that our part-timers are key to the company's success."

Employee turnover at Starbucks is less than 50 percent, which is a relatively low rate for food retailers. Since Starbucks provides extensive training for each worker, says Schultz, "the longer an employee stays with us, the more we save." In addition, employee pilfering is low.

Schultz feels that employee loyalty is one of Starbucks' main strengths, and says that, when the workers became stockholders, "All kinds of [employees] started com-

Business Term

✓ **Competitive differentiation**

Any aspect of a company or its performance that makes it more successful than its competitors.

ing up with ways to save money and improve productivity." He adds, "Our only sustainable competitive advantage is the quality of our work force. We're building an international retail company by creating pride in — and a stake in — the outcome of our labour."[8]

A low turnover rate at Starbucks, in comparison with other retail service companies, is a result of its good employee benefits.

Another company that has built a competitive advantage through human resources is Kanke Seafood Restaurants Ltd. Bud Kanke, owner of this chain of three Vancouver restaurants, is a strong advocate of staff training and goal setting: everyone — even the bussers — at all three restaurants has to pass through a company-wide training program that costs the firm about $200 000 per year. Additionally, each of his 30 managers, including chefs, must fill out a two-page goal-setting plan: "Setting and achieving goals is the highest and most effective form of self-motivation that exists. Reaching your goals generates self-satisfaction and confidence," says Kanke. Kanke is also a strong advocate of empowerment. Christine Renner, manager of one of the restaurants, constantly reminds servers that they should see themselves as running a microbusiness: "For the next five hours, these six tables are your shop — show me what you've got."

At Kanke Restaurants, employee performance is recognized daily, and top performers are rewarded with financial incentives, free meals, and even weekend getaways. A disciple of the pat-on-the-back approach to rewards, Kanke argues that "Psychological studies have shown that recognition is of more value to staff members than dollars." The company also believes that motivated

staff need to know the financial score. This means that the company's numbers are posted for all to see.[9]

Total Quality Management

Total quality management (TQM) is a competitive method based on setting quality as a strategic objective and viewing the organization as an entire system with all members contributing to the final results. With TQM, workers are trained to be more assertive and knowledgeable. Through quality circles, groups of up to ten employees meet voluntarily as often as once a week, workers get the opportunity to define, analyze, and solve quality-related problems.

TQM requires that quality be part of the process from start to finish, which includes investing money up front so that products are made correctly the first time. Although TQM costs more at first, the expenses associated with poor product quality — such as downtime, repairs, rework, and employee attrition — are lessened considerably. In TQM, one definition of "quality" is "pleasing the customer"; customers are considered to be partners.

> ### THEY SAID IT
>
> "Quality has to be thought of almost as a religion."
>
> ROGER JARVIS, president, Jarvis Travel Ltd.

Product Innovation

Constant innovation is the competitive advantage and key to survival for many Canadian firms. "We have to have an adaptability attitude so we can not only respond to the trends, but also offer those new trends to customers," says Pierre Grand'Maison, CEO of Thermoplast Inc. in Laval, Quebec. "In 1990 we still had products that were made in 1980. In 1996, 40 percent of the products we had in 1993 [were] gone. Three years from now [1999], at least 50 percent of our products will have been replaced." Since 1993, Thermoplast — one of *The Financial Post*'s "50 Best Managed Private Companies" — has invested heavily in innovation, spending $6 million on new equipment. As a result, quality and productivity have improved by over 30 percent, and the company is now positioned to compete successfully in the plastics industry.[10]

TECHNOLOGY

PEN NOTEBOOKS AND FLASH TECHNOLOGY

All businesses, new and old, must choose the appropriate computer system based on their computing requirements and financial resources. Once initial decisions are made, businesses must monitor their computer use to determine the right time to update equipment. Yet this all may be easier said than done. New developments in technology occur so frequently that some computers are old-fashioned by the time they leave the manufacturer, and a business may feel pressured to always purchase the newest, and therefore most expensive, equipment. But buying cutting-edge technology can be problematic, as some inventions never live up to their hype.

One innovation that initially offered less than advertised was pen computing. Pen computers accept handwritten input, theoretically offering keyboard-shy users a chance to join the computer revolution. However, people's writing varies widely, and early pen computing software couldn't detect the sometimes minute differences between "c" and "e" or "i" and "l." Pen computers may someday be as ubiquitous and useful as cellular phones or fax machines, but businesses that invested in the first models did not get their money's worth.

In contrast, flash technology may genuinely be a computing miracle. Flash memory chips, which replace hard disks, combine the flexibility of random access memory

Just-in-Time System

A *just-in-time (JIT) system* is a method of streamlining manufacturing or service provision by eliminating wasted time and space. By reducing "non-value-added time" (for instance, the time a partially assembled product sits on a table awaiting a missing part or a finished product is stored in a warehouse) and boosting "value-added time," JIT decreases overhead and increases profits.

Although JIT may sound appropriate only to large manufacturing companies, it can be helpful for the smallest service business as well. For instance, a self-employed electrician can benefit from the JIT approach. By limiting the parts kept on hand, arranging appointments with no wasted or non-value-added time in-between, and striving to do a perfect job the first time out, the electrician will improve his or her income through JIT methods.[11]

JIT has its critics as well as its supporters. Economist George Newman writes, "Transportation costs rise sharply as you switch from carload to less-than-carload shipments, from rail to truck, from public to private carrier. ... If a batch is faulty, you may discover it too late, and in any case you have no backup stock to substitute. You have no safety cushion against any unpreventable disruption due to bad weather, traffic tie-ups, or strikes, leading to a snowballing of your losses." As for JIT's strengths, Newman points out that working in partnership with suppliers, streamlining procedures, and raising quality expectations are all just basic good-business procedures.[12]

Computer Technology

Many firms benefit from advances in computer technology. Mail-order companies keeping databases on people's buying habits tailor their mailings to the most responsive audience. Bookstores track inventory and find out instantly which distributor has the book a customer is seeking. A retailer checks in seconds whether a buyer's credit card is good. Computers allow employees in different cities to work together on a sales proposal while looking at the same "paperwork" on their computer screens. With computers, movie makers create images so real that the animation cannot be differentiated from film. This book was formatted using a computer.

A taxi equipped with Digital Dispatch technology arrives at the designated address — an apartment in a scary part of town. The driver is leery of leaving the vehicle to ring the buzzer. Instead, he simply uses his onboard data system to activate a prerecorded telephone message to the customer saying, "Your taxicab has arrived. Please go out now. We thank you for using Yellow/Checker Cab." Digital Dispatch Systems in Richmond, BC, is just one Canadian business that has created a competitive differentiation through computer technology. In 1996, Yellow/Checker Cab Co. of Dallas, Texas, installed in its 500-car fleet the Digital Dispatch system with a backup Pentium host computer in case of failure. "These systems are very sophisticated. It's a highly competitive market so taxi companies are constantly looking for an edge," says

with the longevity of read-only memory. These chips are lighter than hard disks, use less electricity, and never crash. They've been described as "close to the ideal memory." However, the design of flash memory chips will continue to evolve for years, and it may be difficult for businesses to determine the best time to upgrade their computers when next year's flash technology will be even better.

In the midst of this whirlwind of constantly changing technological wonders, the Gillette Company discovered that, for its employees, less can be more. Gillette salespeople use handheld, pen-based computers on sales calls. These devices have 20 MB hard drives, 2400 cps modems, and DOS 3.3; in the high-tech world of today, they are the equivalent of writing with a quill dipped in ink. Yet these easy-to-use computers, which allow Gillette reps to check off boxes rather than input data with a keyboard or by hand, are exactly right for the many first-time computer users in the Gillette sales force. And their ability to transmit data to a central database via phone jacks allows Gillette to form daily summaries of sales in different stores and locations.

While some businesses, particularly those that use computers in manufacturing and design, may need to purchase new technology almost continually, others may find that last year's model works just fine. The challenge is to match the computer technology to the user and the work being done.

Sources: Adapted from Tony Seideman, "On the Cutting Edge," *Sales & Marketing Management*, June 1994, 18–23; Roberta Salvador, "What's New in Pen Computing?" *Electronic Learning*, March 1994, 14; Richard Brandt, "The Coming Firefight over Flash Chips," *Business Week*, February 1, 1993, 68; and Gregory T. Pope, "Memories Are Made of This," *Discover*, January 1993, 94.

Digital President, Vari Ghai. Although taxi fleets predominate, the firm has also found other uses for its products. It now sells its computer equipment for shuttle buses, couriers, public transit vehicles, and airport ground vehicles like snowplows to keep them off active runways. "These systems are so accurate that operators in a tower know where the plows are to within five feet," says Ghai.[13]

Cost Reduction

One method of creating a competitive differentiation is simply to charge less for the product. The challenge becomes discovering how to offer low prices yet still make a profit. Wal-Mart solved this problem by insisting on the lowest possible prices from suppliers. Its guaranteed *everyday low pricing (EDLP)* entices people into the store without the need for expensive advertising campaigns. Many other retailers, such as The Brick, also have adopted EDLP as a basic business strategy.

Strategic Alliances/Partnerships

For many Canadian companies, the creation of *strategic alliances* and partnerships has become a key differentiation strategy. Digital Dispatch Systems, for example, has formed strategic alliances with corporate giants such as Raytheon and Honeywell. These partnerships mean that

American Express partnered with Loyalty Management to offer even more benefits to its customers. This 1997 collateral proved to be so successful that Amex bested program objectives by more than 60 percent.

Digital Dispatch can take on private-label deals and can also work with end users who would otherwise pay no attention to a small firm. "The Toronto Transportation Commission demands an $8-million performance bond. You have to be a $100-million company to arrange that. But if we're with Honeywell, as a small company, we're suddenly taken seriously," says Vari Ghai.[14]

Some Canadian companies are even forming alliances with their competitors to penetrate foreign markets. Xantrex Technology Inc. of Burnaby, BC, whose clients include MIT and the U.S. Marine Corps, has a strategy to create partnerships with its competitors in certain markets to get its products sold in the United States.[15]

THE PLANNING PROCESS

ONCE THE MISSION statement has been developed, the objectives defined, and the competitive differentiation determined, it is time to plan the actions that will allow the company to anticipate the future and achieve company objectives. **Planning** *is the process of anticipating the future and determining the best courses of action to achieve company objectives.* In other words, planning answers the questions of what should be done, by whom, where, when, and how.

> **Business Term**
> √ **Planning**
> The process of anticipating the future and determining the best courses of action to achieve company objectives.

Planning is a perpetual process. When a business is being started, managers may focus the majority of their time on planning. Later, as business conditions and laws change, the business will need to change as well. Therefore, companies must monitor their operations frequently and make necessary adjustments to their plans.

At Weston Forest Corp. in Mississauga, Ontario, for example, planning is a continuous process involving a five-point checklist:[16]

- Analyze the marketplace and isolate niche opportunities.

- Find innovative ways to differentiate your approach.

BUSINESS TIP

Henry Mintzberg, a respected Canadian business professor and author, describes planning as a formalized procedure to produce an articulated result in the form of an integrated system.

Why Bother, According to Planners?

→ Organizations must plan to co-ordinate their activities.

→ Organizations must plan to ensure that the future is taken into account.

→ Organizations must plan to be "rational."

→ Organizations must plan to control.

- Establish a structure and implement a process to support and service a marketing plan.

- Train employees about how and why those niches matter.

- Communicate measurable success along the way.

Ongoing analysis and comparison of actual performance with company objectives enables the company to adjust plans before problems become crises. Accomplishing other managerial functions also depends on sound, continual planning.

Types of Planning

Planning can be classified on the basis of the scope involved. Strategic planning, tactical planning, operational planning, adaptive planning, and contingency planning are the primary categories (see also Table 4.1).

Table 4.1 Types of Plans

Type	Description	Example
Strategic	Establish overall objectives; position the organization in terms of its environment; can be short- or long-term	RNG Equipment Inc. plans to continue growing based 50% on internal growth and 50% through acquisition.
Tactical	Implement activities and resource allocations; typically short-term	Teknion Furniture Systems will launch two new product lines during the next nine months.
Operational	Use quotas, standards, or schedules for implementing tactical plans	At the 6-month point, a new employee of KL Group Inc. is given $1000 worth of shares in the company and can buy more shares annually.
Adaptive	Adapt to change in business situation and environment; emphasize focus and flexibility	Bank of Montreal targets its advertising at new homeowners and computer users.
Contingency	Plan for emergencies, unforseen events	Union Carbide plans a comprehensive strategy for dealing with a major chemical leak.

Strategic Planning. The most far-reaching type is **strategic planning**, *the process of determining the primary, longer-term objectives of an organization, adopting courses of action, and allocating the resources necessary to achieve those objectives.* The strategic planning process is reflected in the firm's mission statement. For example, Northern Telecom Ltd. (Nortel) has this mission statement: "To deliver market leadership through customer satisfaction, superior value, and product excellence." Nortel spends more than 14 percent of its sales on research — a co-ordinated effort that flows down 30 global product lines. Its research is tied closely to its mission and to what customers say they want, and not to what researchers and engineers think is important.[17] Strategic plans tend to be both broad and long-range, focussing on those organizational objectives that will have a major impact on the organization over several years.

When strategic planning becomes too vague, the resulting plans are often ineffective or irrelevant. Intel CEO Andrew Grove says, "You look at corporate strategy statements, and a lot of them are such pap. You know how they go: 'We're going to be the world class this and a leader in that, and we're going to keep all our customers smiling.'" Grove has found that a strategy statement is valuable only if it is used as a constant guide for the actions of managers and workers.[18]

Business Term

✓ Strategic planning

The process of determining the primary, longer-term objectives of an organization, adopting courses of action, and allocating the resources necessary to achieve those objectives.

Business Term

✓ Tactical planning

Implementing the activities specified by strategic plans.

Business Term

✓ Operational planning

Creating the work standards and tasks needed to implement tactical plans.

Tactical Planning. **Tactical planning** *involves implementing the activities specified by strategic plans.* Tactical planning tends to focus on the current and near-term activities (usually one year or less) required to implement overall strategies. For example, in the spring of 1996, Corel had a cost-reduction tactical plan to introduce its Corel WordPerfect Suite™ software at "bargain basement prices." Some governments, schools, and universities were charged as little as $50 — which covered Corel's manufacturing costs. Public institutions were even allowed to make as many copies of the software as they needed. This was Corel's short-term strategy to win back WordPerfect™ customers from the Microsoft package. Although strategic and tactical planning have different time frames, both must be integrated into an overall system that is designed to achieve organizational objectives.

Operational Planning. **Operational planning** *creates the work standards and tasks needed to implement tactical plans.* This involves choosing specific work targets and the right employees to carry out the plans. Operational plans often are stated in terms of quotas, standards, or schedules. For example, the management of a major publishing house expects its sales representatives to make 20 customer contacts per day, with the first one at 8:00 AM or earlier.

Adaptive Planning. Planning, whether strategic, tactical, or operational, needs to be fluid and forward-looking enough to adapt to changes in a business's situation and environment. To succeed, companies must emphasize focus and flexibility in making plans; that is, they must include **adaptive planning:** *planning that allows changes in response to new developments in the business's situation and environment.* *Focus* means figuring out and then building on what the company does best. *Flexibility* means developing scenarios of future activities to be ready to take advantage of opportunities when they occur.

For example, if a company's main customers are baby boomers who are new parents, plans should be made for the eventual aging of the customer base. Alcohol, cigarette, and candy manufacturers must consider the changing mores and growing health consciousness of their customers when making plans. A company with international markets must plan for changes in the strength of the dollar versus other currencies.

Contingency Planning. One of the more contemporary aspects of planning is **contingency planning**, or *planning for emergencies.* Many firms have developed management strategies to speed recovery from accidents, such as airline crashes, factory fires, chemical leaks, oil spills, product tampering, and product failure. Contingency planning is more important now than ever; over half of the worst industrial accidents in this century have taken place since 1977.

Many firms designate a crisis manager to be in charge of handling emergencies that may arise and to create an effective crisis-prevention program. When such an event occurs, it is essential that the firm involved tell the truth.

> **Business Term**
> ✓ **Adaptive planning**
> **Planning that allows changes in response to new developments in the business's situation and environment.**

> **Business Term**
> ✓ **Contingency planning**
> **Planning for emergencies.**

Accepting responsibility, even though it may hurt short-term profitability, is critical, since early honesty means so much in the court of public opinion.

The crisis manager also must ensure that the firm faces the public and makes amends. These may range from product replacements to payments of medical or monetary claims. Finally, the underlying cause of the problem must be determined and systems established to make certain that it does not recur. Hiring a highly regarded independent research group to deduce the cause of the problem frequently is recommended as a method of ensuring objectivity.

Perhaps an even greater responsibility for the crisis manager is to minimize the possibility that emergencies will occur in the first place. Effective crisis-prevention programs include providing special training to keep workers alert to dangers, delegating decision making and authority in a crisis to those who run the operation, improving internal communication systems, avoiding overworking employees, and ensuring that technology does not take away workers' ability to evaluate a situation. The most effective policy for crisis prevention is to give employees information at the right time, plus to give them adequate training in handling emergencies and decision making.[19]

Planning at Different Organizational Levels

Although managers spend some time in the act of planning virtually every day, the total time spent and the type of planning done differ at different levels of management. Table 4.2 illustrates this point. In general, members of top management, including the board of directors and the chief executive officer, spend a great deal of time on long-range planning, whereas middle-level managers and supervisors focus on short-term tactical planning.

Table 4.2   Planning at Different Management Levels

Primary Type of Planning	Managerial Level	Examples
Strategic planning	Top management	Organizational objectives; fundamental strategies; long-term plans
Tactical planning	Middle management	Quarterly and semi-annual plans; departmental policies and procedures
Operational planning	Supervisory management	Daily and weekly plans; rules and procedures for each department

Employees at all levels can benefit themselves and the company by making plans for meeting goals.

Planning and the Managerial Functions

Each step in planning gets more specific than the last. From the global mission statement to the general objectives to the specific plans, each phase must fit into a comprehensive planning framework. The framework also must include small functional plans, aimed at individual employees and work areas and relevant to individual tasks, that fit within the overall framework, allowing the objectives to be reached and the mission to be achieved. Planning is a key managerial function, and planning activities extend into each of the other functions — organizing, leading, and controlling (see Figure 4.4).

Organizing. Once plans have been developed, the next step typically is **organizing**, *the means by which management blends human, technical, and material resources through a formal structure of tasks and authority.* It involves classifying and dividing work into manageable units by determining specific work activities necessary to

> **Business Term**
>
> √ **Organizing**
>
> **Process of blending human, technical, and material resources through a formal structure of tasks and authority.**

Figure 4.4 **Managerial Functions**

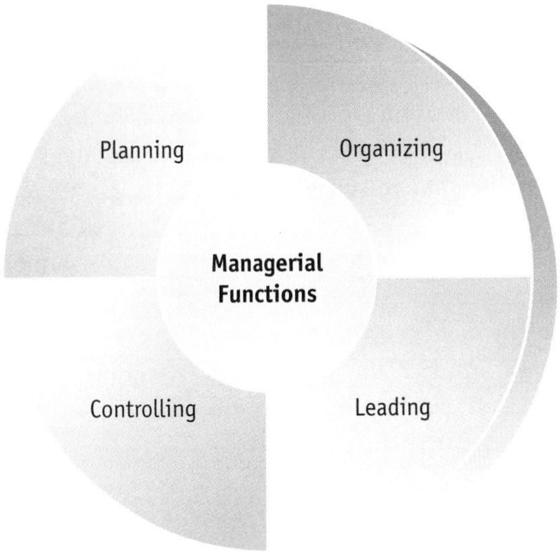

accomplish organizational objectives, grouping work activities into a logical pattern or structure, and assigning activities to specific positions and people.

Included in the organizing function are the important steps of staffing the organization with competent employees capable of performing the necessary activities and assigning authority and responsibility to these individuals. Organizing is discussed in more detail in Chapter 5 and staffing in Chapter 8.

Leading. Once plans have been formulated and an organization has been created and staffed, the task becomes

ETHICAL ISSUE

NAFTA AND THE PLIGHT OF THE MEXICAN WORKER

Maria Trinidad Delgado Navarro is a 28-year-old mother of three. Maria was fired from her job because she was seen hanging around coworkers who wanted to bring an independent union to their factory, located outside Mexico City. She tells a tough tale of threats, violence, low wages, asbestos, and dangerous machinery at her old job.

Maria worked for Itapsa, an auto parts plant. Itapsa is a subsidiary of the multinational company Echlin Inc., which

has plants in all three NAFTA countries and over 2000 employees in Canada.

Under NAFTA, Canadian and U.S. companies, like Echlin, that operate plants in Mexico are required to abide by Mexican labour law. In this way, NAFTA and its side-agreement on labour is supposed to protect the rights of Mexican workers. But some companies, like Itapsa, have been accused of openly contravening the intent of the NAFTA agreement, as well as their social responsibilities. "We saw so many violations of our rights as workers. The conditions were so bad, as were the machines," Maria says.

In late 1998, Maria and some of her colleagues from the Itapsa plant found themselves at the centre of Canada's first case under the notorious NAFTA labour side-agreement. The process is lengthy, and some critics claim that NAFTA lacks the teeth to deal with labour disputes such as this. Nevertheless, with the help of Canadian labour unions, Maria hopes that her case will, at the very least, expose to Canadians the plight of the Mexican worker.

Source: Adapted from Heather Scoffield, "Mexican Case Puts Spotlight on NAFTA," *The Globe and Mail,* August 29, 1998, A11.

that of **leading**, or *guiding and motivating employees to accomplish organizational objectives*. Directing includes explaining procedures, issuing orders, and seeing that mistakes are corrected.

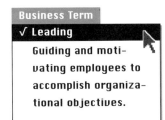

> **Business Term**
> √ **Leading**
> Guiding and motivating employees to accomplish organizational objectives.

The leading or directing function is most important at the supervisory level. If supervisors are to "get things done through people," they must be effective leaders. However, middle and top managers also must be good leaders and motivators, and they must create an environment that fosters such leadership.

Controlling. Controlling is the function of *evaluating the organization's performance to determine whether it is accomplishing its objectives*. The basic purpose of controlling is to determine how successful the planning function

> **Business Term**
> √ **Controlling**
> Evaluating the organization's performance to determine whether it is accomplishing its objectives.

has been. The four basic steps in controlling are establishing performance standards, monitoring actual performance, comparing actual performance with established standards, and, if performance does not meet standards, determining why and taking corrective action.

ASSESSMENT AND EVALUATION

THROUGHOUT THE PLANNING process, it is continually necessary to assess organizational resources and evaluate risks and opportunities, since developmental and marketing plans can be influenced by both internal and external pressures. Production, marketing, finance, technology, and employee talents are some of the internal resources that need to be monitored frequently and evaluated for both strengths and weaknesses. Objectives and functional plans then can be oriented toward a company's strengths, with other objectives aimed at overcoming the company's weaknesses.

Organizations also must monitor outside factors, including environmental legislation, technological developments, successes and failures of competing companies, and changing social trends. In addition, uncontrollable factors, such as the weather and the value of the dollar relative to other currencies — and their effects on the availability of supplies and the viability of foreign markets — must be assessed frequently.

SWOT Analysis

SWOT analysis is *an organized method of assessing a company's internal strengths and weaknesses and external opportunities and threats*. SWOT allows the formulation of a practical approach to planning based on a realistic view

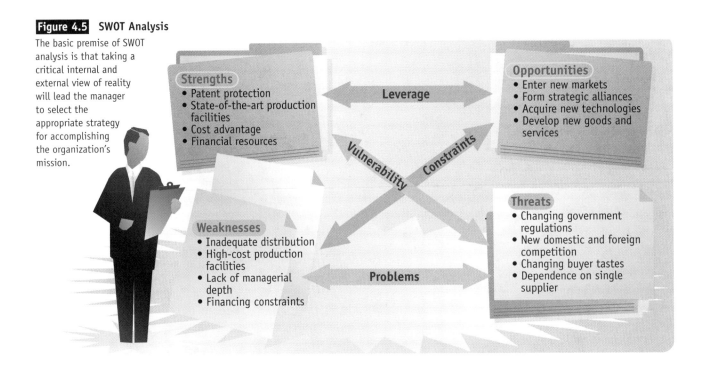

Figure 4.5 SWOT Analysis

The basic premise of SWOT analysis is that taking a critical internal and external view of reality will lead the manager to select the appropriate strategy for accomplishing the organization's mission.

Strengths
• Patent protection
• State-of-the-art production facilities
• Cost advantage
• Financial resources

Opportunities
• Enter new markets
• Form strategic alliances
• Acquire new technologies
• Develop new goods and services

Weaknesses
• Inadequate distribution
• High-cost production facilities
• Lack of managerial depth
• Financing constraints

Threats
• Changing government regulations
• New domestic and foreign competition
• Changing buyer tastes
• Dependence on single supplier

Leverage   Vulnerability   Constraints   Problems

of a company's situation. Figure 4.5 provides the basic premise of SWOT analysis.

When strengths and opportunities mesh, a company has leverage in the marketplace. A hypothetical example would be a sun-protection products manufacturer that is well stocked with high-strength sunscreen when TV weather reports start announcing UV ratings as a regular feature.

On the other hand, when external threats assail a company's weaknesses, the company has a problem to deal with. This would occur if, when UV ratings start being publicized, the sun-protection products manufacturer already has focussed its line by producing and heavily advertising suntan lotion, rather than sunscreen, having judged that consumers are no longer taking the skin cancer threat very seriously. (Note that one company's opportunity can be another company's threat.)

In cases where opportunity knocks but a company's weaknesses render it unable to answer, a constraint exists. In such a case, the sun-protection products manufacturer finds itself limited by lack of inventory and cash just as newly publicized UV ratings motivate more consumers to purchase sunscreen.

The combination of an outside threat with an inside strength is called a *vulnerability*. This might occur if the manufacturer's top-selling sunscreen becomes the focus of false rumours that it contains carcinogens.

Any company can be assessed through SWOT analysis at any point in its history. Corel was discussed in terms of its strengths, weaknesses, opportunities, and threats at the opening of the chapter.

Business Term

✓ **SWOT analysis**

An organized method of assessing a company's internal strengths and weaknesses and external opportunities and threats.

Ottawa, Orem, and Dublin offices. Each group has differing objectives. The Ottawa team develops graphics, desktop publishing, and computer-aided design (CAD) applications, including CorelDRAW™, Corel VENTURA™, Corel Webmaster Suite™, and Java™ applications. The Orem team develops business applications, which include Corel WordPerfect™, Corel Presentations™, and Corel Quattro Pro™. The Dublin office is responsible for developing of European localized products.[20]

A *spinoff* occurs when an SBU breaks away from its parent firm and forms a completely new company. Analysts generally like spinoffs because they bring clarity — and often higher market value — and a spirit of entrepreneurship to the original company. For example, in June of 1997, Corel created a new company — Corel Computer Corp. This was its first spinoff — a hardware company formed from Corel's network computer and video conferencing equipment units. Corel Computer Corp., a wholly owned subsidiary of Corel Corp., will concentrate on the sales and distribution of hardware products.

Business Term

✓ **Strategic business units (SBUs)**

Divisions within a company, each with its own personnel, objectives, products, and planning.

Technology experts applauded this move because it allowed Corel to focus its efforts on its core strength — software — as determined by its SWOT analysis.[21]

Strategic Business Units

One technique for evaluating and assessing the present success and future plans of a firm is to break the company down into **strategic business units** (**SBUs**). *Each SBU is its own organization, with its own personnel, objectives, and products — and its own planning.* SBUs are a mechanism for large corporations to instil an entrepreneurial spirit within the organization without breaking off divisions into separate corporations.

SBUs are also a useful tool in evaluating business performance since they relate specific outcomes to the specific goals of a unit. As discussed at the start of this chapter, Corel has expansive and varied goals. As a case in point, Corel's research and development team is composed of three strategic business groups based in the company's

FORECASTING

FORECASTING *is the estimation or prediction of a company's future sales or income.* Forecasts can be short term (under one year), intermediate (one to five years), or long term (over five years). They can be **qualitative** (*subjective*) or **quantitative** (*based on historical data and mathematical methods*). Look at Table 4.3 for a quick explanation and examples of forecasting methods.

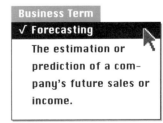

Business Term

✓ **Forecasting**

The estimation or prediction of a company's future sales or income.

Forecasts are important because they guide the planning process and help decision making. On the other

Table 4.3 Forecasting Methods

Type	Explanation	Examples
Qualitative	Subjective estimate or prediction of future events or outcomes	Customer surveys, sales-force estimates, opinions of key executives and industry experts
Quantitative	Estimates or predictions of future events or outcomes based on statistical techniques	Test markets, trend analysis, exponential smoothing

hand, they are also problematic, as they can become outdated and incorrect as a result of changes in consumer spending habits, unexpected moves by competitors, and the like.

Qualitative Techniques

Let's look at qualitative forecasting techniques first. They include sales-force composite, managerial opinion, jury of executive opinion, Delphi technique, and buyer surveys.

Sales-Force Composite. With the *sales-force composite*, salespeople are asked to forecast short-term sales based on their extensive knowledge of their territories. Results are compiled by district, by region, and nationally. This technique is useful, but limited. Although salespeople may not be able to anticipate changes in the competitive marketplace, they might be naturally reluctant to make forecasts that add to their sales quota. Because of these limitations, the sales-force composite is best used in tandem with other forecasting methods.

Managerial Opinion. During budgeting and planning stages, a manager may be asked to predict the sales results in her or his particular units. Although managers are likely to know their operations well, they may feel pressured, much as salespeople do, to bias their predictions one way or another. Some managers will underestimate their predictions so that they can surpass the forecast easily and look good; other managers may overestimate their predictions to get more staff and a larger budget. In any case, even the most straightforward of managers can be just plain wrong.

Jury of Executive Opinion. The *jury of executive opinion* averages the forecasts of top executives from all divisions.

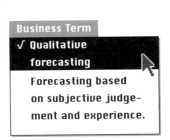

Business Term

√ **Qualitative forecasting**

Forecasting based on subjective judgement and experience.

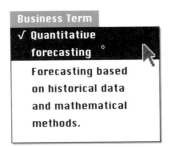

Business Term

√ **Quantitative forecasting**

Forecasting based on historical data and mathematical methods.

This technique works better with experienced managers who are well informed about sales and changing trends. The jury of executive opinion, which is particularly suited to short-term forecasting, is useful in the development of new products.

Delphi Technique. The *Delphi technique* uses an anonymous panel of individuals from both outside and inside the company. Each person is sent a questionnaire, then the answers are compiled and averaged. Instead of just using that data, another questionnaire, adjusted to account for the answers received thus far, is sent out. The technique is not considered complete until a consensus is reached. Although an expensive and lengthy process, the Delphi technique can forecast technological advances and long-term company success.

Buyer Surveys. Another form of forecasting relies on information culled from *buyer surveys*, based on mailed questionnaires and telephone or personal interviews. This expensive technique has some serious limitations; people may not reveal their true buying habits, and, even if they plan to make a certain purchase, ultimately they may not do so. Buyer surveys are best used for short-term or intermediate forecasting for companies with a limited customer base.

Quantitative Forecasting

The second category of forecasting techniques is quantitative in nature. Test markets, trend analysis, and exponential smoothing are included in this group.

Test Marketing. Companies sometimes do *test marketing* by distributing new products in limited test areas. Management can then assess the best prices, promotional strategies, and packaging for their products. The success of a product in a few areas often can be extrapolated to a larger region or the whole country. Test marketing is expensive and risks tipping off competitors as to a company's plans, but is essential in many instances.

Trend Analysis. *Trend analysis* is a mathematical approach to forecasting that assumes that the trends of the past will continue in the future. If, for instance, sales of a particular item have been increasing at 10 percent each year, trend analysis assumes that the 10 percent growth will continue. This approach has two major limitations: it requires extensive historical data, and it is unable to predict shifts in market direction.

Exponential Smoothing. *Exponential smoothing* is a form of trend analysis that considers recent historical data as more important than older data. Therefore, it is a more realistic indication of future sales.

Other Forecasting Components

Other helpful components of forecasting include environmental and industrial forecasting. Environmental forecasting focuses on outside considerations, such as consumer confidence, governmental attitudes, and currency exchange rates, while industry forecasting judges how well the industry is doing as a whole. Industry-wide forecasts may be available from trade associations and their related publications.

CREATING A BUSINESS PLAN

RITTEN **business plans** provide an *orderly statement of goals* for ready reference at all times. They give a sense of purpose to the organization, and they provide guidance, influence, and leadership. They readily communicate ideas about goals *and the means of achieving them* to associates, employees, and others. Plans set standards against which achievements can be measured.

Planning usually works best if the whole organization participates. Planning can combine ideas and communicate information while making everyone a part of the team.

The business plan may be informal and kept completely within the mind of the manager or business owner, or it may be formal, with written copies and schedules and

The World According to Big Shot

LITTLE GUY: Dad, how does a busy guy like you keep track of so much?
BIG SHOT: Simple, I keep the important plans in my head.

LITTLE GUY: Cool. Why's that?
BIG SHOT: So the competition won't know my next move.

LITTLE GUY: Talking about important plans, what's the plan for our holidays?
BIG SHOT: Haven't thought of that. I think your mom wrote something down.

→ What do you learn from Big Shot's example?

deadlines. It may be used only by people inside the organization, or it may be used to communicate the business's goals to banks or financial backers. Although there is no single format for a business plan, almost all plans include the time frame, money involved (both income and outflow), and units of achievement (subjective and numerical). The business plan also should include methods to be used to achieve goals, procedures to be followed, and values the organization wants to uphold. Planning should include forecasting as well as forethought. Perhaps most importantly, plans should always be open to revision.

> **Business Term**
> ✓ **Business plan**
> An orderly statement of a business's goals and the means of achieving them.

If you are starting a business, the process of writing the business plan forces you to examine the business thoroughly and objectively. It is almost impossible to create a market for goods or services without considering the various marketing ramifications. The marketing section of the plan should include an analysis of the target market, the competition, and the plans for distribution, advertising, pricing, and location. It should cover the background of the industry and industry trends, as well as the potential of the new venture. It also should point out any unique or distinctive features of the business and explain the reasons for a particular start-up date.

The plan should include an operating plan forecast, a plan for obtaining capital, and a description of how funds will be spent. In addition to the standard financial statements, a business plan ought to contain an analysis of when the break-even point will occur. Plans written to obtain funding should provide résumés of the principals in the business.

Executive Summary

The *executive summary* should be the first item in the plan, although ideally it will be the last part written. This summary contains the who, what, where, when, why, and how of the business plan in brief.

Evaluations of Owners/Managers and Industry

The introduction to the plan should be a general statement of the concept, purpose, and objectives of the proposed business, along with an overview of the industry. It should give a brief description of your education, experience, and training and should refer to the résumé(s) included later in the plan.

Before writing a plan, answer some questions: How would you explain your idea to a friend? What is the purpose of your business? In what way is your idea different from existing businesses? What is the state of the industry you are entering? Who is your customer or what is your client base? How will your goods or services be marketed? How much will you charge? How will you finance your business? What qualifies you to run this business?

Give special attention to what you intend to call your business. Does the name reflect the business's goals? Is it already registered by someone else? Does it have any hidden meanings to other people? What does it mean phonetically in other languages? Is it offensive to any religious or ethnic group?

Trade journals are an excellent source of industry-related information. Industry Canada and the local library also can assist you with your research. In addition, it helps to talk to suppliers in the industry and to local licensing authorities. How many similar firms have succeeded? How many have failed? Why? What risks are specific to your industry? What are the typical mark-ups? Expenses? Profit percentages?

> ## THEY SAID IT
>
> "Business isn't magic and you don't need to be lucky to win. Results can flow by starting with a plan and by doing the basics of management, sales and production. Business is like the movie, _Field of Dreams_, you know, build it and they will come. Well, do it and success will come."
>
> MICHAEL RUSCIGNO, president and CEO, Intelatech Inc.

Marketing Plan

The *marketing* part of your plan is the core of your business rationale and must answer many questions. Who is your market? What is the profile of your average customer, including age, sex, family size, annual family income, location, buying patterns, and reasons for buying from your business? What is your competitive advantage? How will you determine the price of your goods? Where will your business be located? Who are your direct competitors?

FUTURE TREND

HIGH TECH OPPORTUNITIES FOR HIGH TUITION

We are entering the dawn of a new age for Canadians. The future of Canadian business, education, and jobs will depend largely on information technology.

Until recently, many universities and colleges have been slow to respond to this new reality as they face declining enrollments and reduced funding. Now, many are using a "competitive differentiation" strategy to compete with the private sector, establishing strategic business units (SBU) with trendy three-letter acronyms such as AIT (Algonquin Information Technology). Next, they form a partnership with industry leaders such as IBM or Microsoft to add credibility to the program.

Tuition for an intense 9–12 month IT program can be as high as $20 000. Primary target customers are "adult learners" who already have a degree or diploma and want to enhance their marketability. Sometimes they are able to negotiate Employment Insurance (EI) funding, following a rigorous application process, but in most cases fees come out of their own pockets.

Such relatively high tuition fees have raised eyebrows. Some reason that the students who have $20 000 probably don't need the course to begin with, and argue that high tuition fees constitute a barrier to entry that undermines the principle of universal access to education. Others take a more Darwinian (survival of the fittest) approach: if the market will bear these fees, in the long run, they may help our schools survive their financial woes. Further, they argue, these programs satisfy a social and economic need. Classrooms are being filled with quality students, many of whom are getting jobs in the $35 000 to $40 000 range.

1. If your school has a competitive differentiation strategy, describe it. If not, explain how your school can differentiate itself.

2. Has your school established a technology institute? Did it go the SBU route? Why? If your school does not operate a technology institute, would you recommend one, using a SWOT analysis?

3. Should your school be allowed to establish a separate unit and charge high fees as long as the market will pay them?

4. Should this type of training be carried out by publicly-funded institutions, or be left to the private sector?

Marketing plans must consider rental, leasing, or purchase costs and explain the influence of traffic volume, neighbouring businesses, demographics, parking, accessibility, and visibility. Labour costs, utility access and rates, police and fire protection, zoning restrictions, and other government rules and regulations also must be discussed.

Other topics to be included are whether the firm will be a sole proprietorship, partnership, or corporation; when it will be necessary to hire employees and what their job descriptions will be; the lines of authority in the business; a risk-management plan, including detailed information on insurance; what suppliers you will use and how you have assessed their reliability and competence; and whether you will extend credit to your customers.

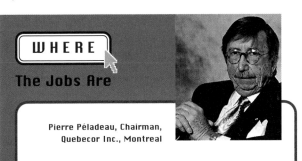

WHERE

The Jobs Are

Pierre Péladeau, Chairman, Quebecor Inc., Montreal

Do What You Know Best

"If I were starting in business, I would go back to the newspaper business. It's a good money-maker and is a lot of fun. It's new every day and full of expectations. Besides that, it's the business I know best."

Financial Plan

The *financial* part of the business plan requires particular attention to detail. If you are using your plan as part of a request for financing, your banker will look at your management skills and experience, the risk, your collateral, and your ability to repay a loan. If you are writing a plan to obtain venture capital, however, the venture capitalist will look at profits and upside potential and not so much at downside risks.

If you have made certain assumptions in the body of your plan, tie them into the financial section. If you plan two retail outlets, for example, your cash-flow projections should show how you are going to pay for them. The bankers or investors analyzing your plan may not know whether it costs $250 or $25 000 to install an exotic high-tech part, but they do know that a telephone system for 50 people costs more than $250 per month. Carelessness with seemingly insignificant variables can undercut credibility.

Itemize expenses on a month-by-month basis; do not simply project an annual amount. If you have $100 000 in costs, don't assume that this means more than $8000 each month. Some expenses will be paid monthly and some annually. If you have a lot of annual payments up front, you will be running back to your financiers in the first month to explain why your cash-flow projection was off. This is not a good way to start.

Your plan must include all assumptions you are making about the conditions under which you intend to operate. It also should include detailed profit-and-loss and cash-flow projections.

After you have assembled your business plan, add a table of contents so that the reader can turn directly to those parts of the plan that are of most interest. Make sure the plan is presented in an attractive and professional format.

SUMMARY OF LEARNING OUTCOMES

1. Identify the components of a mission statement.

A mission statement is a written explanation of a company's purpose and aims. It may include what products are to be produced and what the market will be, as well as information on treatment of employees and the company's belief system or morals.

2. Define objectives and how they differ from the mission statement.

Objectives are guideposts that define standards for what the organization should accomplish in such areas as profitability, customer service, and employee satisfaction. In contrast to the mission statement, which delineates the company's goal in general terms, objectives are more concrete.

3. Define competitive differentiation and identify methods businesses use to create it.

A competitive differentiation is any aspect of a company or its performance that makes it more successful than its competitors. Methods of creating a competitive differentiation include improving management of human resources, using total quality management, developing new products, improving just-in-time logistics, using efficient and up-to-date technology, reducing overhead and prices, and creating strategic alliances or partnerships.

4. Define planning and distinguish among the various types of plans.

Planning is the process of anticipating the future and determining the best courses of action to achieve company objectives. It answers the questions of what should be done, by whom, where, when, and how. It is a key management function that extends into each of the other management functions — organizing, leading, and controlling. Planning is generally classified on the basis of scope and purpose. Major categories of planning include strategic planning, tactical planning, operational planning, adaptive planning, and contingency planning.

5. Explain SWOT analysis and how it is used in corporate planning.

SWOT analysis is an organized method of assessing a firm's internal strengths and weaknesses and external opportunities and threats. SWOT provides a realistic view of the company's position and is used in the overall planning process.

6. Describe SBUs and give examples.

Strategic business units are divisions within the organization, each with its own personnel, objectives, products, and planning. In some cases an SBU will spin off and form a new company, as was the case with Corel Computer Corp.

7. Define forecasting and differentiate between qualitative and quantitative forecasting.

Forecasting is the estimation or prediction of a company's future sales or income. Qualitative forecasting is subjective and relies on the judgement and opinions of managers, the sales force, customers, and others. Qualitative techniques include the sales-force composite, the managerial opinion, the jury of executive opinion, the Delphi technique, and buyer surveys. Quantitative forecasting is based on historical data and mathematical methods. Quantitative techniques include test marketing, trend analysis, and exponential smoothing.

8. Outline the components of the business plan.

The business plan includes the executive summary; evaluations of the business owner(s) and/or manager(s) and of the industry, and a discussion of the business's organization and structure; the marketing plan; and the financial plan.

Key Terms Quiz

tactical planning	SWOT analysis	forecasting
strategic planning	leading	controlling
mission statement	operational planning	adaptive planning
qualitative forecasting	quantitative forecasting	planning
business plan	organizing	strategic business units (SBUs)
management by objectives (MBO)	competitive differentiation	
objectives	contingency planning	

_____ 1. Planning that involves implementing the activities specified by strategic plans.

_____ 2. A program designed to improve motivation through employee participation in goal setting and defining factors used in performance evaluations.

_____ 3. Refers to planning that allows changes in response to new developments in the business's situation and environment.

_____ 4. Anticipating the future and determining the best courses of action to achieve company objectives.

_____ 5. Refers to planning for emergencies.

_____ 6. Evaluating the company's performance to determine whether it is accomplishing its objectives.

_____ 7. A written explanation of a company's purpose and aims.

_____ 8. Refers to any aspect of a company and its performance that makes it more successful than its competitors.

_____ 9. Determining the long-term objectives of the organization, adopting courses of action, and allocating the resources necessary to reach the objectives.

_____ 10. Refers to guiding and motivating workers to accomplish organizational objectives.

_____ 11. Refers to work standards and tasks that implement tactical plans.

_____ 12. The process of blending human, technological, and material resources through the design of a formal structure of tasks and authority.

_____ 13. Guideposts in defining what the business aims to achieve in areas such as profitability, customer service, and social responsibility.

_____ 14. Refers to forecasting based on subjective judgement and experience.

_____ 15. Divisions within a company, each with its own personnel, objectives, products, and planning.

_____ 16. The analysis of a business based on its internal strengths and weaknesses and external opportunities and threats.

_____ 17. The description of the business's goals and the means for achieving them.

_____ 18. Refers to forecasting based on mathematical models.

_____ 19. The estimation or prediction of a company's future sales or income.

Other Important Terms

buyer surveys	jury of executive opinion	strategic alliances
Delphi technique	just-in-time (JIT) system	test marketing
everyday low pricing (EDLP)	sales-force composite	total quality management (TQM)
exponential smoothing	spinoff	trend analysis

Review Questions

1. Distinguish between strategic and tactical planning. Identify instances of each at Corel.

2. What is a mission statement? Identify its primary components.

3. How do objectives differ from mission statements? Cite specific examples.

4. What is meant by competitive differentiation? How do firms implement it?

5. What is SWOT analysis? Apply SWOT analysis to a local firm.

6. Explain the concepts of leverage, problems, constraints, and vulnerability as they relate to SWOT analysis and Corel.

7. Explain the SBU concept. Cite specific examples for a firm with which you are familiar.

8. Differentiate between quantitative and qualitative forecasting. Also, identify the time period used in each type of forecasting.

9. Outline the major forecasting methods, then define each.

10. What is a business plan? What elements are included in a business plan?

Discussion Questions

1. You have decided to start one of the following businesses: an importing/exporting firm, a music store, a delivery service, a supermarket, or a clothing store. Choose one and write a mission statement for your business.

2. How might the business you selected create a competitive differentiation?

3. How might SWOT analysis and SBUs help your business?

4. As the owner of the business selected in Question 1, what forms of forecasting would you use?

5. Outline a brief business plan for your business. Include strategic plans, tactical plans, operational plans, adaptive plans, and/or contingency plans, as appropriate.

Answers to Key Terms Quiz

1. tactical planning 2. management by objectives (MBO) 3. adaptive planning 4. planning 5. contingency planning 6. controlling 7. mission statement 8. competitive differentiation 9. strategic planning 10. leading 11. operational planning 12. organizing 13. objectives 14. qualitative forecasting 15. strategic business units (SBUs) 16. SWOT analysis 17. business plan 18. quantitative forecasting 19. forecasting

Notes

1. Adapted from Corel Corporation, *Annual Report*, 1996; Marleau, Lemire Securities Inc., "Marleau, Lemire Report on Corel," *Ottawa Business Journal*, March 17, 1997, 23; Bruce Blackie, "Cowpland Takes Pitch to the World," *The Ottawa Sun*, February 25, 1997, 20; and personal correspondence with Corel Corporation.

2. Michael Fuller with Alan Hobson, *Above the Bottom Line* (Toronto: Macmillan Canada, 1993), 39; and personal discussions with Crestar Energy Inc.

3. Ibid., 40; and personal discussions with Canadian Mountain Holidays.

4. *Starbucks Mission Statement*, copyright 1996. Reprinted by kind permission of Starbucks Coffee Company.

5. Gayle MacDonald, "An Open-Book Approach to Motivation," *The Globe and Mail*, March 31, 1997, B9. Reprinted by permission of Norwest Soil Research Ltd.

6. Ibid. Reprinted by permission of Norwest Soil Research Ltd.

7. See also Kathy Heine, "How We Measure Performance," *Monsanto Magazine*, April 1992, 7–11; and Peter Drucker, *The Practice of Management* (New York: Harper & Bros., 1954), 128–29.

8. Matt Rothman, "Into the Black," *Inc.*, January 1993, 59–65.

9. Based on personal discussions; and Robert Williamson, "Motivation on the Menu," *The Globe and Mail*, November 24, 1995, B7.

10. Rod McQueen, "Canada's 50 Best Managed Private Companies: Thermoplast Inc.," *The Financial Post*, December 14–16, 1996, 52.

11. Marvin W. Tucker and David A. Davis, "Key Ingredients for Successful Implementation of Just-in-Time: A System for All Business Sizes," *Business Horizons*, May–June 1993, 59–65.

12. George Newman, "As Just-in-Time Goes By," *Across the Board*, October 1993, 7–8.

13. Adapted from Rod McQueen, "Canada's 50 Best Managed Private Companies: Digital Dispatch Systems," *The Financial Post*, December 14–16, 1996, 24, 27.

14. Ibid., 27.

15. Rod McQueen, "Canada's 50 Best Managed Private Companies: Xantrex Technology Inc.," *The Financial Post*, December 14–16, 1996, 52.

16. Excerpt from Rod McQueen, "Canada's 50 Best Managed Private Companies: Weston Forest Corp.," *The Financial Post*, December 14–16, 1996, 31.

17. Northern Telecom, *The Anatomy of a Transformation*, March 1997, 2; and James Bagnall, "Nortel's New Mantra: Built for Speed," *The Ottawa Citizen*, March 6, 1997, C1. Reprinted by permission of The Ottawa Citizen.

18. Ronald Henkoff, "How to Plan for 1995," *Fortune*, December 31, 1990, 70–79.

19. John Carey, "Getting Business to Think about the Unthinkable," *Business Week*, June 24, 1991, 104–7.

20. Corel Corporation, *Annual Report*, 1996, 14, 15.

21. Patrick Brethour, "The Art of the High-Tech Spinoff," *The Globe and Mail*, April 2, 1997, B9.

Chapter 5

Starting and Organizing the Business

Learning Outcomes

```
  6      12      18      24      30  ↖  36      42      48          ⇧
```

After studying this chapter, you should be able to

1. Identify and explain the three basic forms of business ownership.
2. Compare the advantages and disadvantages of the forms of business ownership.
3. Discuss the levels of corporate management.
4. Explain how private ownership, public ownership, and collective ownership (co-operatives) differ.
5. Explain the vital role played by entrepreneurs and small businesses in the Canadian economy.
6. Compare the advantages and disadvantages of small business.
7. List the advantages and disadvantages of franchising.
8. Outline the popular methods of small business operation in the global market.

Business Is a Strategic Game[1]

After racing for Canada in the 1984 Summer Olympics in Los Angeles and winning 150 times worldwide, cyclist Louis Garneau realized it was time to do something else: "I said, 'I need a job.' I didn't want to travel any more after all that global travelling. So with my experience in sports and art, I started [my own] company."

Like most small business start-ups, the launch was modest. Garneau began the business as a sole proprietorship, working out of his father's garage and using funds from a prize he had received upon graduation, with a bachelor's in plastic arts, from Laval University. Rather than use the prize money to continue his education for a master's degree, he bought a sewing machine and started making bicycle shorts for his friends on the Canadian cycling team. Garneau had a vision: he saw big opportunities in the sports apparel business, which he believed was dominated by boring, old-fashioned products. Garneau started his company with energy, determination, and a dream. His career as a racer provided both the experience to lead a team and the will to succeed. "I was determined to drive my business like a bike race," he recalls.

When the time was right, Garneau moved out of the garage and incorporated. Today, Louis Garneau Sports Inc. is a $35 million company with over 500 employees. The company manufactures clothing, helmets, and accessories for cycling; cross-country ski clothing; swimsuits; and children's wear at plants in Quebec, Vermont, and France. It controls about 50 percent of the market

Louis Garneau heads one of "Canada's 50 Best Managed Private Companies."

for cycling and cross-country skiing accessories in Canada and is the only Canadian manufacturer of bicycle helmets and sunglasses.

While Garneau is pleased with the success of his company, he is also aware that such tremendous growth brings its own organizational challenges. A major task of Garneau and his management team is to maintain the company's roots as an entrepreneurial, risk-taking business. That is why he has organized the structure of the company to take advantage of the strengths of a small business — even as it becomes a world leader in its industry. His organization is lean, with only a few management layers. His operations are decentralized into eleven factories. Each plant is considered a profit centre with its own set of responsibilities and goals. Garneau and his financial team carefully follow the profitability of each of these strategic business units on a weekly basis. The company also relies on about twenty carefully selected sales distributors — these motivated entrepreneurs only make money if they sell. Distributorships also reduce the administrative selling costs and allow Garneau to focus on manufacturing, the core strength of his company. Additionally, Garneau works to maintain direct face-to-face communication and a small-company attitude among the employees. For example, he often rolls up his sleeves and gets involved with new-product development.

Innovation, quality, and adaptability are central to Garneau's organizational culture. For example, the 1990–91 recession forced Garneau to quickly expand his product lines: "Our motto became 'innovate or die.' The company rallied around this recessionary adversity and created a new line of helmets. The factories quickly retooled, and within a few years Garneau helmets became one of the top three product lines in the world. Helmets now represent almost 40 percent of the company's sales.

Garneau also had a global vision and was able to make the leap into international sales because of the quality of his helmets and his passion for business excellence. "Designing a helmet is like creating a sculpture," he says. The Garneau lines now sell in the United States, Europe, South America, Japan, and Australia in addition to Canada. Olympic and world champions such as Myriam Bedard and Curt Harnett wear Garneau products. In May of 1996, Garneau moved a step closer to his vision to dominate the world cycling marketplace. He bought a company in France — Group Axone — and has now become the leading supplier of bicycle clothing in France.

Over the next few years Garneau intends to consolidate his business and go for market penetration in the United States and Europe. "Business is a game. I'm the captain of my team and I tell them where we're going in the next five to ten years. The planet is not very big and it is possible for Canadians to win the race. We just have to be confident," concludes Garneau.

CHAPTER OVERVIEW

THROUGHOUT THE 1990S, Canadians began to lose confidence in large corporations and governments that, forced by changing economic demands, laid off workers, downsized middle management, and created an aura of complete economic chaos and uncertainty. As a result, Canada is now deeply entrenched in a business environment that demands innovation, proactivity, and risk taking. A new breed of entrepreneur has emerged. Canadians like Louis Garneau, Beverley MacIntyre (see the Company Watch box) and Michael Cowpland (highlighted in the last chapter) have thrived in this changing economic climate by starting and owning their own businesses. In this chapter, we will look at organizing the business and the issues facing small business owners and entrepreneurs and their start-up companies.

THEY SAID IT

"We can't wait for government to create jobs. Canadians have to think about manufacturing, not just services. But if you don't have the product, forget about it."

LOUIS GARNEAU, CEO, Louis Garneau Sports Inc.

We begin with one of the most common questions asked by people wanting to own their own business: "Should I incorporate?" Any business, large or small, must choose a type of legal ownership that best fits its needs. We will look at the advantages and disadvantages of three major forms of business ownership. This entails considering many variables, including financial resources, financial liability, the needs of the business, and the skills of the people involved.

Next we'll discuss the importance and characteristics of entrepreneurship, as well as small business trends and issues both in Canada and in the world economy.

FORMS OF PRIVATE OWNERSHIP

THERE ARE THREE major forms of private business ownership: sole proprietorships, partnerships, and corporations. Each has its own advantages and disadvantages, which we will now discuss (see Table 5.1).

COMPANY WATCH

The voice at the other end of the telephone was gritty and determined. Its owner, Beverley MacIntyre, is talking from Dieppe, which is just outside Moncton, New Brunswick. "I have always wanted to make a difference, whatever I do," she says. "That's very important to me." Six years ago, she and an associate, Terry Miller, started BKM Research & Development Inc. The company talks to employers, figures out what skills they're looking for, then creates a training program to teach clients. Often, this involves bringing in industry experts to help out, and in December 1996, BKM launched another teaching option in the virtual-solutions division that offers educational support to business via the Internet. Currently, BKM offers its services in Atlantic Canada and in the Caribbean. Around 83 percent of BKM's full-time graduates find work, says MacIntyre, so "we must be doing something right."

Sole Proprietorships

The most common form of business ownership, the **sole proprietorship**, is also the oldest and the simplest because there is no legal distinction between the sole proprietor as an individual and as a business owner. As the name implies, this is *a business that is owned by one person*. The business's assets, earnings, and debts are those of the owner. Although sole proprietorships are common in a variety of industries, they are concentrated primarily among small businesses, such as repair shops, small retail outlets, and service organizations.

> **Business Term**
> ✓ **Sole proprietorship**
> A business that is owned by one person.

Sole proprietorships offer advantages not found in other forms of business ownership. They are easy to form or dissolve and give the owner flexibility and the right to retain all profits after taxes. A minimum of legal requirements makes it easy to go into and out of this form of business. For example, if you operate your business under your own name, there is no legal need to register your business. However, if you want to use a name other than your own, you must register with the provincial government. (Responsibility for proprietorships comes under provincial jurisdiction. Sole

Table 5.1 Advantages and Disadvantages of Each Form of Private Ownership

Form of Ownership	Advantages	Disadvantages
Sole Proprietorship	• Easy to form and dissolve • Owner has control over all aspects • Owner retains all profits after taxes	• Unlimited financial liability • Financing limitations • Management deficiencies • Lack of continuity
Partnership	• Easy to form • Complementary management skills • Expanded financial capacity	• Unlimited financial liability • Interpersonal conflicts • Lack of continuity
Corporation	• Limited financial liability • Specialized management skills • Expanded financial capacity • Economies of larger-scale operation	• Difficult and costly to form and dissolve • Tax disadvantage • Legal restrictions

Each form of ownership has its strong points — and at least a couple of drawbacks.

proprietors should also check with their respective provincial and local governments regarding licensing requirements.) Ownership flexibility is another advantage; the owner can make management decisions without consulting others, take prompt action when needed, and keep trade secrets where appropriate.

A disadvantage of the sole proprietorship is that the owner is financially liable for all debts of the business, and the business's financial resources are limited to the owner's personal funds and money that can be borrowed. Financing limitations can keep the business from expanding. Another disadvantage is that the owner must be able to handle a wide range of management and operational tasks; as the firm grows, the owner may not perform all duties with equal effectiveness. Finally, a sole proprietorship lacks long-term continuity, since death, bankruptcy, retirement, or change in personal interests can terminate it.

Partnerships

Another option for organizing a business is forming a **partnership**, *an association of two or more persons who operate a business as co-owners by voluntary legal agreement.* Partnerships have been a traditional form of ownership for professionals offering a ser-

THEY SAID IT

"Me and the [two kids] keep reminding her that this better not be a business that just bumps along making a modest amount of money. We have repeatedly pointed out that dog food is not something we want to eat in our dotage."

JAMIE COATSWORTH, partner at Coopers & Lybrand, referring to his wife, Helen Sinclair, and her business venture with partner Danica Lavoie – BankWorks Trading Inc.

Business Term

✓ **Partnership**

An association of two or more persons who operate a business as co-owners by voluntary legal agreement.

vice, such as physicians, lawyers, and dentists. It is customary, and strongly recommended, that partners sign a "partnership agreement" covering such matters as

- Purpose of business
- Name of firm
- Duration of agreement
- Place of business
- Capital to be contributed by each partner
- Division of business income
- Rights of management
- Procedure for termination or reorganization of partnership

Partnerships come under provincial jurisdiction and as such are required to register with appropriate provincial authorities, each of which has its own specific requirements. For example, in Nova Scotia, the partnership declaration must be filed with the Registrar of Joint Stock Companies before the business is started. In British Columbia, the declaration must be filed with the Registrar of Companies and should be filed within three months after formation of the business. Consideration must also be given to licences or permits that may be required by any of the three levels of government.

There are two traditional types of partnerships: limited and general. In a **general partnership**, *each partner has a hand in managing the business and assumes unlimited personal liability for any debts* (i.e., each member is "jointly and severally" liable for the full amount of the debts).

A **limited partnership** *is composed of at least one or more limited partners and at least one general partner. The general partner assumes both management duties and the downside risk.* A limited partner's liability is limited to the amount of his or her original investment as long as he or she has had no hand in the management of the business.

A more recent form of partnership is the strategic alliance. As we discussed in Chapter 1, a strategic alliance occurs when one or more firms combine specific business activities for a specified period in the pursuit of a common goal. A **joint venture**, *a partnership formed for a specific undertaking that results in the formation of a new legal entity*, is one type of strategic alliance. Strategic alliances also come in many other forms, such as precompetitive R&D consortia, co-production and co-marketing partnerships, and cross-licensing and cross-equity agreements. Today, alliances exist between producers and their suppliers/distributors and even between rival firms.[2]

A major advantage of partnerships is that they are relatively easy to form. The legal requirements involve merely registering the business and taking out the necessary licences. Another advantage is the opportunity for professionals or consultants to combine complementary skills. Partnerships offer expanded financial capability through the combined resources of the partners. They also usually give greater access to borrowed funds than do sole proprietorships.

Like the sole proprietorship, most partnerships have the disadvantage of unlimited financial liability. Each partner is responsible for the debts of the firm, and each is legally liable for the actions of the other partners. Partners must pay the partnership's debts from their own funds if those debts exceed the partnership's assets. It is also much harder to break up a partnership than it is to dissolve a sole proprietorship. Rather than simply withdrawing the business's funds, the partner who wants out must follow the terms and conditions of the partnership agreement — which most likely will include finding someone to buy his or her interest in the firm. If no partnership agreement exists, dissolution of a partnership can become a sticky and often costly legal issue.

Corporations

A **corporation** or limited company *is a legal entity with the authority to act and have liability separate and apart from its owners.* In Canada, corporations or limited companies can be incorporated and operate under the authority granted by provincial or federal law. **Stockholders** *are people who acquire shares of stock in a corporation,* thereby becoming part-owners of the business. *When all or a majority of a corporation's stock is owned by another corporation, it is a* **subsidiary** *of that corporation,* which is usually called the *parent company.*

Corporate ownership has its advantages. First, because corporations are considered separate legal entities, the stockholders have limited financial risk; if the firm fails, they lose only the amount they have invested. It should be noted, however, that most major creditors are aware of this legal advantage and often require shareholders — especially start-up companies — to provide personal guarantees. Corporations can draw on the specialized

Business Term

√ **General partnership**

Partnership in which each partner has a hand in managing the business and assumes unlimited personal liability for any debts.

Business Term

√ **Limited partnership**

Partnership composed of at least one or more limited partners and at least one general partner; the general partner assumes both management duties and the downside risk.

Business Term

√ **Joint venture**

Partnership formed for a specific undertaking that results in the formation of a new legal entity.

Business Term

√ **Corporation**

A legal entity with the authority to act and have liability separate and apart from its owners.

skills of several employees, unlike sole proprietorships and partnerships where managerial skills usually are confined to the abilities of the owners. Expanded financial capability, another advantage, allows a corporation to grow and become more efficient than if it had been set up as a sole proprietorship or partnership. People outside the business may invest in it by buying shares of stock, and the corporation's size and stability may make it easier for the business to borrow additional funds. A large corporation can finance projects internally by transferring money from one part of the business to another. Longer manufacturing runs usually mean more efficient production and lower prices, thus attracting more customers.

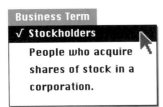

Business Term

√ **Stockholders**

People who acquire shares of stock in a corporation.

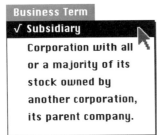

Business Term

√ **Subsidiary**

Corporation with all or a majority of its stock owned by another corporation, its parent company.

A disadvantage of incorporation is that, as a separate legal entity, a corporation is subject to federal and provincial taxes on its profits. In addition, any dividends — payments to stockholders from profits — also are taxed on an individual basis. Furthermore, corporate ownership involves many legal problems not encountered by sole proprietorships and partnerships.

Corporate Management. There are generally several levels of management in a corporation. The stockholders elect a **board of directors**, which becomes *the governing authority for the corporation*. Members of the board — many of whom are nonemployees — set overall policy, authorize major transactions involving the corporation, and hire the chief executive officer (CEO). The CEO and other members of top management set corporate policy, make most of the major corporate decisions, and manage the overall operations of the company. The next level is middle management, which co-ordinates the operational functions of the company and serves as liaison between top management and lower levels. The bottom tier of management includes supervisory managers, who co-ordinate the day-to-day operations of the firm, supervise employees, assign specific tasks to the staff,

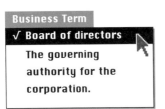

Business Term

√ **Board of directors**

The governing authority for the corporation.

Figure 5.1 Levels of Management in a Corporation

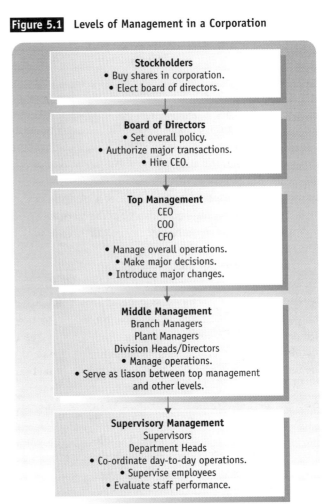

Levels of management in a corporation are often defined by job function.

and are often responsible for evaluating employees' job performance. Figure 5.1 provides a brief summary of the levels of management.

GOOD, BAD, OR UGLY?

David Leighton and Donald Thain are professors emeritus at the Richard Ivey School of Business at the University of Western Ontario. In their book Making Boards Work, they say that directors of corporate boards are increasingly under pressure. The old code of behaviour boils down to "Be a good guy. Cool it. Don't push. Avoid a hassle. Don't cause confrontation." The authors' advice to directors is to speak up, despite the social awkwardness. The more difficult new professional code is "Take responsibility. Rational analysis. Integrity. Ethics. No cover-ups. Don't back down."

Corporate Growth. Corporate growth became a major economic, political, and social issue over the 1990s. Successful corporations traditionally were able to expand internally through effective business management practices. However, the 1990s saw many Canadian firms grow as a result of acquisitions or mergers and strategic alliances.

> ### THEY SAID IT
>
> **"Successful companies are not just followers. We want to be irreverent, to be renegades, to be different."**
>
> RICK CAMILLERI, President, Sony Music Canada

Mergers and Acquisitions.[3] A **merger** *refers to two or more firms that combine to form one company.* In an **acquisition**, *one firm purchases the property and assumes the obligations of another firm.* Over the 1990s, mergers and acquisitions were especially predominant in the financial services and high-technology sectors.

In the financial services industry, federal government deregulation in the late 1980s and early 1990s opened the door for banks to own brokerages, trust companies, and other financial services. This was a major reason leading to mega-mergers in this sector. For example, RBC Dominion — owned by the Royal Bank of Canada — purchased the family-owned Richardson Greenshields of Canada Ltd., the Royal Bank bought Royal Trust, the Bank of Nova Scotia purchased Montreal Trust, and the Toronto Dominion Bank absorbed most of Central Guaranty Trust.

Regarding the high-tech sector, in 1995 alone, U.S. firms offered more than $2.5 billion for the purchase of Canadian software and computer companies. One of the largest transactions took place in the fall of 1995 when U.S. giant MCI Communications Corporation bought SHL Systemhouse Inc. for $1 billion U.S. A major reason for all these high-tech buyouts by foreign companies was that the ownership shares of similar Canadian businesses traded at lower prices than their American counterparts. A lower Canadian dollar made foreign acquisitions even more attractive.

Some business and government leaders became concerned about this situation.

Kevin O'Leary, president of Softkey International Inc., for instance, said that "Canada is losing some of its proprietary technology and momentum in the technology growth industry."[4] Buyouts also mean domestic firms lose many of the non–research and development jobs as administrative functions are moved to the parent company. However, from a stockholder or owner point of view, selling was hard to resist: "It's pretty tough for a board of directors to not greet these offers with open arms. At the end of the day they are there to maximize shareholder value," said David Gurney, president and CEO of Softquad International Inc.[5]

Strategic Alliances.[6] In recent years, growth through strategic alliances has become a popular mechanism for corporate expansion. The main reason: the environment in which companies operate has changed dramatically over the 1990s. Many companies have been forced to rethink their priorities from a traditional emphasis on planning, control, and managed growth — through internal expansion or mergers or acquisitions — and to focus on speed, innovation, flexibility, and cost — through strategic alliances.

Normally, an alliance consists of three essential elements:

- **Independence.** Members of the alliance remain independent after negotiating the collaborative arrangement.

- **Shared control.** Members of the alliance share control over the performance of its functions and tasks, and also share in its benefits.

- **Strategic contribution.** Partners make a strategic contribution to the alliance, such as knowledge, technology, critical skills, equity capital, or products.

In the past, governments believed that interfirm co-operation was harmful to the economy because of its anti-competitive effect. As a result, these agreements were discouraged directly or indirectly. The government stance today, however, is radically different. Most business alliances are now seen as beneficial to the economy and are being promoted by various policy initiatives. For example, it is generally agreed that technology consortia are the most effective mechanism to advance frontier technology. Figure 5.2 illustrates the range of interfirm strategic alliances.

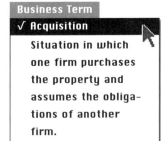

Business Term
✓ **Merger**
Situation in which two or more firms combine to form one company.

Business Term
✓ **Acquisition**
Situation in which one firm purchases the property and assumes the obligations of another firm.

Figure 5.2 Range of Interfirm Strategic Alliances

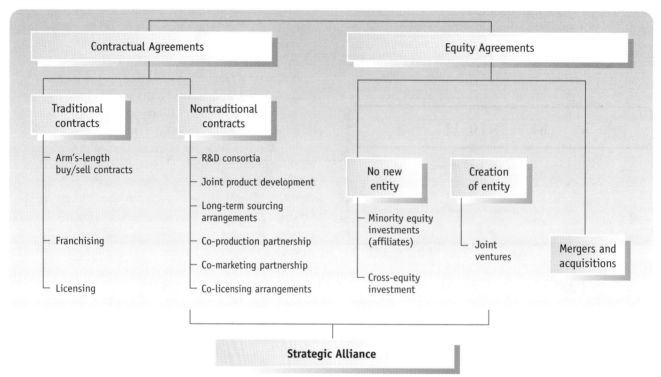

PUBLIC AND COLLECTIVE OWNERSHIP

ONE ALTERNATIVE TO private ownership is some form of **public ownership**, *in which a government unit or its agency owns and operates an organization.* A well-known form of public ownership is the **Crown corporation**, *a corporation owned by the federal or a provincial government.* Examples of major federal Crown corporations include Canada Mortgage and Housing, Export Development Corp., Canada Post Corp., and Atomic Energy of Canada. Examples of provincial corporations include Ontario Hydro, Caisse de dépôt et de placement du Québec, New Brunswick Power Corp., and Saskatchewan Power Corp.

Why do we have Crown corporations? The traditional reasoning has been that certain services, such as roads and utilities, are so important to public welfare that they should not be entrusted to private ownership and control. Crown corporations also provide special nonprofit, economic, or social functions for the

> **Business Term**
> ✓ **Public ownership**
> Enterprise owned and operated by a government unit or its agency.

The Saskatchewan Wheat Pool is one of Canada's largest co-operatives.

public. For example, the Bank of Canada, as a Crown corporation, is responsible for regulating credit and currency. Crown corporations have also been established to assist economic development or research in particular regions of the country. For example, a major objective of the Caisse de dépôt et de placement du Québec is to support the province's economic agenda.

As we discussed in Chapter 3, a trend of the 1990s was the *privatization* of government enterprises. Government downsizing led to contracting out and selling government services to private enterprise. For instance, a private firm would receive a contract to perform a regular service, such as selling motor vehicle, alcohol, or fishing licences. Canada Post closed many of its post offices and franchised out postal services to local entrepreneurs. Even some roads — like highway 407 just north of Toronto — became privately owned, allowing builders to recover their investments by charging tolls. Most experts predict that this trend to privatization will continue as governments seek ways to downsize and pare down expenses.

Another alternative to private ownership is a **co-operative**, *an organization that is operated collectively by its owners.* Co-operatives often are created by large numbers of small producers who want to be more competitive in the marketplace. Well-known co-operatives include the Saskatchewan Wheat Pool, the Desjardins Group, Vancouver City Savings, and The Co-operators. Although many co-operatives begin as small local organizations whose members exercise control and accumulate profits as a return on their investment, others are big businesses and must deal with the same challenges and constraints as their competitors: they face problems in raising capital, hiring quality managers, and exercising control over operations. Table 5.2 lists some of Canada's largest private and Crown corporations and co-operatives.

Business Term

√ **Crown corporation**

A corporation owned by the federal or a provincial government.

Business Term

√ **Co-operative**

An organization that is operated collectively by its owners.

the system efficient and effective; create jobs and improve economic growth; create new ventures and opportunities for others through their initiatives and innovations; and provide a spirit of energy, initiative, and potential for progress.

Literally hundreds of research studies have attempted to determine the common skills and behavioural traits of the successful entrepreneur. The simple result of all this research is that most entrepreneurs cannot be cloned. They tend to defy stereotyping and generalization: "I have seen people of the most diverse personalities and temperaments perform well in entrepreneurial challenges," concludes business guru Peter Drucker.

THE IMPORTANCE OF ENTREPRENEURSHIP

AN ENTREPRENEUR *is the agent of change in the private enterprise system: a person who seeks a profitable opportunity and takes the necessary risks to create a new business.* Entrepreneurs are the fuel of the private enterprise system who provide the competitive zeal that keeps

WHERE

The Jobs Are

Lois Stevenson, Director, Entrepreneurship Development, Atlantic Canada Opportunities Agency, Moncton, NB

Entrepreneurship in Technology and Tourism

"There are lots of opportunities, even in areas that we think have reached the declining stages of the life cycle. But I suggest entrepreneurs look at new industries with lots of growth potential, for example, software development, information technology and businesses relating to Internet access. Young people have an edge if they think about entrepreneurship as a career and mix it with the Internet, telecommunications, CD-ROM and computer animation — growth areas that didn't exist five years ago.

There's also a lot of potential in tourism. It's the world's No. 1 growth industry. It's a growing industry in Atlantic Canada and that will continue with the trend to eco- and adventure tourism. People want to visit more isolated places. The scenery, water and game in Newfoundland and northern New Brunswick can draw tourists. You have to look at your landscape through new eyes."

Table 5.2 Canada's Largest Private Corporations, Crown Corporations, and Co-operatives, 1995

Company	Revenue ($ million)	Profit ($ million)	Assets ($ million)
Private Companies (Top 5)			
General Motors of Canada	30 893	1 391	10 954
Ford Motor Co. of Canada	19 100	10	na
Chrysler Canada	13 691	83	4 875
Sun Life Assurance of Canada	10 615	407	65 996
IBM Canada	10 310	na	na
Crown Corporations (Top 4)			
Federal			
Canada Post Corp.	4 748	−69	2 565
Canada Mortgage and Housing	1 581	84	16 163
Export Development Corporation	965	44	9 428
Canadian Commercial Corp.	893	1	384
Provincial (Top 4)			
Ontario Hydro	8 730	855	49 495
Hydro-Québec	7 667	390	52 182
Caisse de dépôt et de placement	2 939	2 867	52 547
Insurance Corp. of BC	2 428	141	4 353
Co-operatives (Top 4)			
Financial			
Desjardins Group	8 348	314	73 878
Caisse Centrale Desjardins	387	17	5 428
Vancouver City Savings CU	387	21	4 368
Desjardins Life Assurance Co.	1 434	66	4 218
Nonfinancial (Top 4)			
Saskatchewan Wheat Pool	2 821	33	1 112
Federated Co-operatives	2 124	130	836
Alberta Wheat Pool	1 531	11	496
Manitoba Pool Elevators	184	6	282

The following personality traits, to some degree, are common among our most successful entrepreneurs:[7]

- **Goal-oriented relationships.** Their relationships tend to be task- or goal-driven as opposed to activity-oriented or socially motivated.

- **Driven opportunists.** Entrepreneurs are driven by opportunity. They are motivated by the belief that they can satisfy a need through an innovative activity.

- **Agents of change.** Entrepreneurs invariably identify their primary motivations as "seeing a need and acting on it."

- **Moderate risk takers.** Entrepreneurs are innately curious and take calculated risks.

> **Business Term**
>
> √ **Entrepreneur**
>
> The agent of change in the private enterprise system; a person who seeks a profitable opportunity and takes the necessary risks to create a new business.

- **High energy people.** They wake up excited in the morning because they believe they can control and change their lives and the lives of others. They crave the excitement of the unknown and tire quickly when situations become repetitive.

- **Independent souls.** Entrepreneurs have a need for freedom — a need to control their own destiny, and be their own boss.

- **Entrepreneurial family background.** Many entrepreneurs grew up in an entrepreneurial environment. They learn the skills at an early age, and are expected to continue the family tradition.

If you would like to test your entrepreneurial bent, we have provided you with a questionnaire in the *Student Workbook*.

THE ROLE OF SMALL BUSINESS[8]

ACCORDING TO THE Canadian Federation of Independent Business, a **small business** *is a firm that is independently owned and operated and is not dominant in its field.* Small businesses are often described by the federal government as having less than 100 employees in the manufacturing sector and fewer than 50 employees in the service sector. When measured by revenue, one government program — the **Small Business Loans Act (SBLA)** — identifies small businesses as those that have an annual revenue of less than $5 million. Using credit as a yardstick, the banking community generally agrees that smaller businesses have loan authorizations of less than $500 000.

Small business is the engine that drives any private enterprise system — and Canada is no exception. This sector is the major contributor to job creation, productivity, economic growth and wealth, and the social fabric of our country (see also Table 5.3).

- Canada has over 2.3 million small businesses with fewer than 100 employees.

- Including the self-employed, more than 99 percent of all businesses in this country are small businesses.

Business Term

✓ **Small business**

A firm that is independently owned and operated and is not dominant in its field.

Business Term

✓ **Small Business Loans Act (SBLA)**

Federal program designed to help new and existing businesses obtain term loans directly from their financial institutions for purchasing and improving fixed assets.

- Small businesses account for over 50 percent of private sector employment and 43 percent of economic output.

- Small business accounts for more than a quarter of all business sales, a third of all profits, and a fifth of all assets.

- Over 660 000 new jobs were created between 1993 and 1996 — the majority of which were created by small businesses.

Financing Small Business Growth

Small businesses obtain financing mainly from traditional sources, including bank loans and personal savings, government sources, and venture capital.

Small businesses tend to rely on traditional sources of financing: banks or other financial institutions (51 percent of small businesses), credit cards (44 percent), retained earnings (40 percent), personal savings (39 percent), and personal loans (28 percent).[9] As of June 30, 1996, the seven major chartered banks had authorized over $60 billion in loans to small businesses (i.e., credit authorizations under $1 million). This represents a 4.4 percent increase over the previous year.[10]

Table 5.3 Number of Businesses in Canada

	1981		1991		1994	
	Number	%	Number	%	Number	%
Self-employed	678 000	49.3	1 146 000	55.4	1 393 000	59.9
Employer business						
< 5 (employees)	522 358	38.0	678 447	32.8	707 886	30.5
5–19	125 928	9.2	174 966	8.5	163 155	7.0
20–49	30 024	2.2	43 588	2.1	38 330	1.6
50–99	10 049	0.7	13 897	0.7	11 638	0.5
100–499	7 753	0.6	9 334	0.4	8 486	0.4
500+	2 030	0.1	2 020	0.1	2 023	0.1
Subtotal	698 142	50.7	922 252	44.6	931 518	40.1
All businesses	1 376 142	100.0	2 068 253	100.0	2 324 518	100.0

Table 5.4 Current Sources of Financing for Small Businesses	
	Percentage
Bank	51
Credit cards	44
Retained earnings	40
Personal savings	39
Supplier credit	38
Personal loans	28
Government	15
Loans from friends/relatives	12
Do not have business financing	9
Export financing	1
Public equity	1
Venture capital	1

Note: Figures add to more than 100 percent because firms may use more than one source of financing at any given time.

Fifteen percent of small businesses use government sources of financing. This includes having a loan guaranteed under the Small Business Loans Act or the Farm Improvement and Marketing Cooperatives Loans Act (FIMCLA), as well as acquiring loans from the Business Development Bank of Canada (BDC) and other government programs.[11]

Only 1 percent of Canadian small businesses take advantage of venture capital financing. According to a Canadian Bankers Association study, only $670 million of venture capital was invested in small businesses in 1995, leaving over $2.3 billion of available funds unused.[12]

Microbusinesses and Self-Employment

Industry Canada defines *microbusinesses* as self-employed individuals and businesses with less than five employees. Microbusinesses are growing faster than any other type of business in Canada. As Figure 5.3a shows, this sector is growing faster than the total labour force — an 18.7 percent growth in self-employment compared with 7.4 percent for the labour force as a whole. In 1990, 13.9 percent of the labour force was self-employed; in mid-1996 this figure was 15.5 percent.[13]

As you can see in Figure 5.3b, the biggest increase in self-employment has been in the finance, insurance, and real-estate sector. The only industry that saw a decline in self-employment was farming.

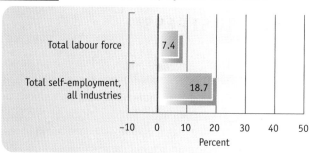

Figure 5.3a Growth in Self-Employment, 1990–1995

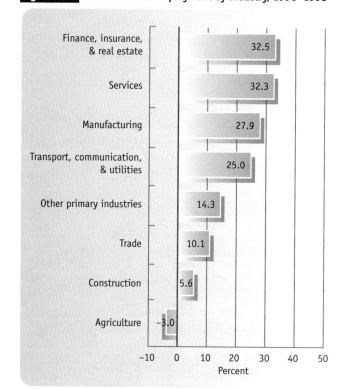

Figure 5.3b Growth in Self-Employment by Industry, 1990–1995

DID YOU KNOW?

Young people aged 15–24 own about 15 percent of all microbusinesses. These enterprising individuals have found a way out of the trap of needing experience to get a job, but not being able to get a job to get the experience. The popularity of self-employment probably also stems from the higher-than-average unemployment rate for the 15–24 age group: 16.6 percent in September 1996. In comparison, the overall Canadian unemployment rate in 1995 was about 9 percent.

Young entrepreneurs like John Warrillow, owner of Brass Tacks Communications, and Justin Poy of Justin Poy Media enjoy the challenges of running their own businesses and like to be in control of their own futures in this economy of constant change and uncertainty. Says Poy, "To survive in today's business world, entrepreneurs must have the ability to rapidly adapt to change."

Technology, Innovation, and the Information Highway

Advances in information technology have transformed the workplace and created many opportunities for small business. Nowadays, small businesses can access distant markets and up-to-date information through the same technology big business uses. Many experts believe small businesses have the advantage in using this technology to compete with large corporations and to launch new entrepreneurial ventures because they are more flexible and responsive to change.[14]

Small business is leading the way in innovation and research and development. As Figure 5.4 shows, small R&D firms of 1 to 49 workers are much more prevalent in the economy — growing by 35 percent between 1990 and 1993 — and are growing faster than R&D firms with over 50 employees.

COMPETITIVE STRATEGY

THE RISE OF THE GOLD COLLAR WORKER

According to "Home Business — the New Reality," a report prepared for the government by Barbara Orser and Ted James, working at home has become a major trend in the way Canadians do business. About one out of every four Canadian households operates some form of *home-based business*. These 2 million Canadian households create jobs, stimulate local economies, and provide a growing commercial market. Most of these home businesses are not "fly-by-night" and have been in operation for more than one year (44 percent — one to three years, and 35 percent — more than three years). Almost half of the home workers are self-employed; 14 percent are substituters (employees who spend part of their day at

home); and 39 percent are supplementers (employees who bring work home). According to these statistics, chances are that you will be working out of your home in the future — even if you have another real job.

Here are some major reasons for the home-based trend:

→ **Cocooning**. Many Canadians are attempting to reduce outside stresses by spending more leisure and work time at home.

→ **Computerization**. New high-tech equipment and software such as fax machines, personal computers, modems, and photocopiers have made it a lot easier and more convenient to operate out of the home.

→ **Two-Income Families**. It makes it a lot easier to work out of the home when both parents are trying to raise a family and make a living.

→ **Growth of the Service Industry**. A service business generally has lower start-up costs, operational expenses, and equipment costs, making it much more sensible to run your operation out of the home.

→ **Higher Productivity**. Studies show that productivity increases by 20 percent to 60 percent when employees can work during peak times at their own pace.

→ **Increased Efficiency**. The home worker saves on transportation, rental, furniture, and equipment costs.

Source: Excerpted from Lee A. Eckert, J.D. Ryan, and Ronald A. Knowles, *Canadian Small Business: An Entrepreneur's Plan*, 2nd ed. (Toronto: Dryden 1995), 157. Copyright © 1995 Harcourt Brace & Company, Canada, Limited. All rights reserved. Reprinted by permission of Harcourt Brace & Company, Canada, Limited.

Figure 5.4 Number of R&D Firms by Employment Size

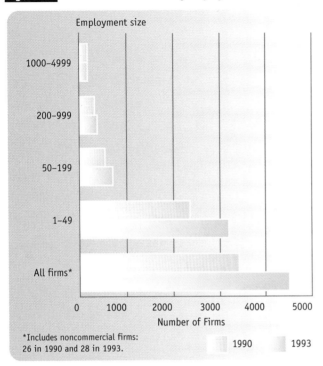

Employment size

*Includes noncommercial firms:
26 in 1990 and 28 in 1993.

1990   1993

Figure 5.5 Current Industrial R&D Expenditures, as Percentage of Sales, by Firm Sales Size, 1993

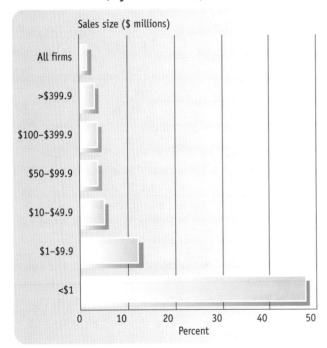

Sales size ($ millions)

As well, small R&D firms (those with sales of less than $1 million) spend a higher percentage of their revenues on R&D. In 1993, they spent 48 percent of their revenues on R&D compared with only 1.7 percent for all firms (see Figure 5.5).

WAKE-UP CALL

What happened? A mini-revolution has hit the Canadian economy in the last six years and the main force driving the change has been small and medium-sized enterprises.

Why? Many of the giant companies — built on the traditional economy, from the railroads to the forest product firms — drastically downsized, starting in the late 1980s. This sent thousands of well-qualified people into the marketplace. As downsizing was taking place, these large companies began outsourcing. A reservoir of creative energy was unleashed of experienced, brighter individuals from corporate Canada to build new companies.

So... If anyone tells you they can't see these new monuments to our entrepreneurial spirit, tell them to simply look around.

Small Business: Strengths and Weaknesses

Small businesses are not simply smaller versions of large corporations. Their legal organization, market position, staff capability, managerial style and organization, and financial resources generally differ from bigger companies, which gives them some unique advantages.

Small firms are usually the first to offer new concepts and new products in the marketplace; Corel Corp., highlighted in Chapter 4, and Louis Garneau Sports Inc., in this chapter, are classic success stories. Small companies often can be more flexible than large corporations, allowing them to tailor their services to the needs of their customers. They can provide a product more cheaply than large firms because they have small staffs and lower overhead costs.

Certain types of industries and markets lend themselves better to smaller firms. Large companies may choose not to pursue limited markets because high overhead costs force them to set minimum sales targets, but this situation provides substantial opportunities for small, lower-cost competitors. Economic and organizational factors may dictate that an industry consist essentially of small firms; upscale restaurants are an example.

Small firms sometimes have a variety of disadvantages, however, including poor management, inadequate financing, and government regulation. Small firms can be more vulnerable during a recession since they have fewer resources to fall back on. On average, nearly 62 percent of all businesses dissolve within the first six years of operation (see Figure 5.6).

While these problems can be overcome, it is important to think carefully about all of these issues before starting a company.

Often, small companies fail because the people who start them are ill-prepared as managers, with little training or education in running a business. They may be so excited about their projects that they neglect paperwork

and fail to write a business plan. Government regulation can also create problems — small businesses often lack employees to do the paperwork required by the government, so it either doesn't get done or the owners have to do it on their own time.

Inadequate financing is yet another leading cause of small business failures. Of the financial obstacles that face small companies, uneven cash flow, shown in Figure 5.7, is the biggest problem. This may be because many companies start with inadequate capital and lack the resources to carry them through difficult periods, and because cash inflows don't always match cash outflows.

TECHNOLOGY

A HELPING HAND FOR SMALL BUSINESSES

There's a destination on the information highway that small and medium-sized Canadian businesses can call their own — **www.bdc.ca**. This is a Web site managed by the Business Development Bank of Canada (BDC) that includes more than 300 hyperlinks to small business resources available from coast to coast.

Here's a sample of the resources that users can find all in one place under **www.bdc.ca**. Alternatively, they can head directly to the sites using the addresses provided.

Small Business Loans Act (SBLA). This is a federal act as well as a program designed to help new and existing businesses obtain term loans directly from their financial institutions for purchasing and improving fixed assets.
- **strategis.ic.gc.ca/sc_mangb/ smallbus/engdoc/sbla.html**

Canadian Technology Network. Here is a site helping Canadian businesses looking for technological assistance. Advisers work with individual entrepreneurs to identify needs and to find the right source of assistance for almost every technology imaginable.
- **ctn.nrc.ca**

Canadian Business Service Centres. This site provides a comprehensive list of programs available to small and medium-sized business for the Canadian government and its partners. The database can be accessed regionally, by industry sector, by business requirement, or by department.
- **reliant.ic.gc.ca**

Strategis. Industry Canada, in partnership with the business community and universities has created the largest, most comprehensive business information Web site in Canada. It contains over 75 000 reports, 600 000 pages of text, and 2 GB of statistical data. You can get updated information ranging from business diagnostic and benchmark-

ing data to all the government forms you need to incorporate.
- **strategis.ic.gc.ca**

On-line Small Business Workshop. This online site covers all the business basics in "how-to" fashion from the initial product idea to marketing, researching, sales forecasting, financing, planning, and everything in-between.
- **www.sb.gov.bc.ca/smallbus/ workshop/workshop.html**

CONTACT! — The Canadian Management Network. This is the primary Canadian source on the Internet for business management information and advice. It describes and gives access to a full range of small business support organizations in Canada and provides a wide range of educational material and tools to help entrepreneurs start a business.
- **strategis.ic.gc.ca/sc_mangb/ contact/engdoc/search.html**

Source: Adapted from Business Development Bank of Canada (BDC), "A Canadian Small Business Web Site: www.bdc.ca," *Profit$*, Vol. 17, No. 1, 1997, 8. Reprinted by permission of BDC.

Figure 5.6 Survival Rate of Businesses

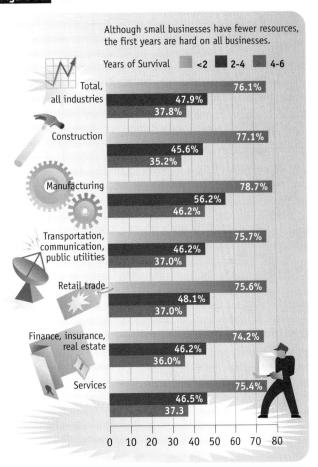

Although small businesses have fewer resources, the first years are hard on all businesses.

Years of Survival | <2 | 2-4 | 4-6

Total, all industries: 76.1% / 47.9% / 37.8%

Construction: 77.1% / 45.6% / 35.2%

Manufacturing: 78.7% / 56.2% / 46.2%

Transportation, communication, public utilities: 75.7% / 46.2% / 37.0%

Retail trade: 75.6% / 48.1% / 37.0%

Finance, insurance, real estate: 74.2% / 46.2% / 36.0%

Services: 75.4% / 46.5% / 37.3

Figure 5.7 Greatest Financial Obstacles Faced by Small Businesses

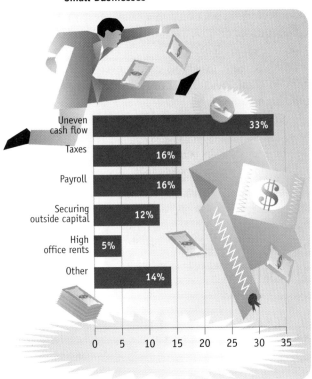

Uneven cash flow: 33%
Taxes: 16%
Payroll: 16%
Securing outside capital: 12%
High office rents: 5%
Other: 14%

Franchising

The franchising concept has played a major role in the growth of small business. A **franchise** *is a business agreement that sets the methods a dealer can use to produce and market a supplier's good or service.*

The dealer, or **franchisee**, *is usually the owner of a small business who is allowed to sell the goods or services of a supplier, or* **franchisor**, *in exchange for some payment* (usually a flat fee called a franchise fee, future royalties or commissions, and in many cases future advertising fees). Total costs can vary widely. The franchisor typically provides building plans, site selection help, managerial and accounting systems, and other services to assist the franchisee. The franchisor also provides name recognition for the small business owner who becomes a franchisee. This image is created by advertising campaigns to which the franchisee typically contributes.

Although the number of franchises in Canada represents only about 5 percent of all businesses, according to the Franchise Association of Canada, as much as 48 cents of every dollar spent on services and retail purchases in Canada is done at a franchise. More than 60 000 Canadians are employed in the franchise industry, which is growing at about 7 percent annually. For instance, Buns Master Bakery Systems Inc. has 102 franchised outlets in Canada and the United States (1997).[15] First Choice Haircutters has 136 franchised outlets (1995).[16] Franchising is also popular worldwide. In the United States, for example, total sales from franchising are expected to top the $1 trillion mark by the year 2000. Franchise sales in Australia are expected to hit the $50 to $60 billion range by the end of the decade.[17]

COMPETITIVE STRATEGY

GROWING WITH MR. LUBE

Don Hamilton moved from Vancouver to Kamloops, bought a Mr. Lube franchise, changed his lifestyle, and became, in his own words, "an entirely different and happier person."

A 25-year veteran and former Vice-President of Stores at Woodward's chain of department stores in British Columbia, Hamilton seized the opportunity to use his acquired business skills in a different business setting when The Bay bought Woodward's.

Hamilton's decision sparked a massive change: opting for franchising, which would allow him to be his own boss while having a franchisor to depend on for ongoing

Mr. Lube has proven to be a good franchise for people like Don Hamilton of Kamloops.

support, Hamilton traded in suits and starched shirts for the striped shirt and black pants of a Mr. Lube franchisee.

He sold his house in Vancouver, which was a one-and-a-half-hour daily commute to his office and, with his wife Jan, bought a successful six-year-old Mr. Lube in Kamloops. His business is now a ten-minute commute "on a bad traffic day" from his new home.

Hamilton is a prime example of why franchising is growing. The restructuring of the Canadian economy, the increase in mergers and acquisitions, and the subsequent downsizing of many companies have meant that more people are deciding to open their own business. This trend is expected to continue.

Sources: Based on personal discussion with Don Hamilton; and Mr. Lube, Advertising Supplement, "Franchising Good Potential for Business Success," *Canadian Business Magazine*, 1994. Reprinted by permission of Mr. Lube.

The World According to Big Shot

BIG SHOT: If we sell five franchises, the company will net $100 000 just from the initial franchise fees. Think how much more we can make from the royalties.

SLINKY: That will fix our cash problem. What will we franchise?
BIG SHOT: Does it matter? There're lots of hot products out there with a slew of people wanting to start a business.

SLINKY: I'll find a franchise expert and get him started.
BIG SHOT: Remember, only pay him on commission when he sells a franchise.

→ What do you think?

Franchising: Strengths and Weaknesses

The franchising concept does not eliminate the risks for someone considering investing in a small business; it merely adds alternatives. In fact, the failure rate of franchises is close to that of independent businesses.[18]

> ### THEY SAID IT
>
> "Franchising is the best marketing concept since the door-to-door salesman."
>
> BIG SHOT

Existing franchises have a performance record on which the prospective buyer can make comparisons and judgements. In addition, a widely recognized name gives the franchisee a tremendous advantage. Car dealers, for instance, know their brand-name products will attract a given clientele. A franchise also gives the small business owner a tested management program and often offers valuable business training. The prospective franchisee usually does not have to worry about setting up an accounting system, establishing quality-control standards, or designing employment application forms.

On the negative side, franchise fees can be expensive. Good franchises with tested management systems, proven performance records, and widely recognized names usually sell for more than those without such benefits. Prospective franchisees must decide whether the expenses involved are a fair exchange for what they will receive. Another potential drawback is that the franchisee is judged by what her or his fellow franchisees do. A strong, effective program of managerial control is essential to offset bad impressions created by unsuccessful franchises.

> ### THEY SAID IT
>
> "True entrepreneurs will die of frustration in a franchise system because they want to do everything their own way."
>
> MAC VOISIN, President of M&M Meat Shops Ltd., a franchise chain of 135 outlets

WHERE
The Jobs Are

Michael Bregman, Chairman & CEO, The Second Cup Ltd., Toronto

Advice from the mmmuffin Man

"You can make money in a wide range of different businesses, but you're more likely to succeed if you stick to what you love and know best. Consulting, financial services, and foodservice don't require a lot of start-up capital, but I know and love foodservice so I'd stick with it. In our case, we started with a muffin store and quickly franchised.

Foodservice offers opportunity, but it's trendy. Something can be hot one minute and stagnate the next. We have our eye on a number of categories, for example, bagels, which will grow explosively. It's limited only by your imagination and common sense."

According to some franchise experts, encroachment is the number one issue in the franchise industry. Allegations of **encroachment** *normally occur when a franchise chain directly or indirectly competes with an existing franchised outlet.* Frank Zaid, a Toronto franchise lawyer, says that encroachment disputes are numerous, but this situation has not become public yet. Ted Levitt, another franchise lawyer agrees: "A lot of this [encroachment] gets hassled out on the doorstep of the courts," he says. Franchise chains prefer to avoid going to the courts, so they make a compensating deal with

> **Business Term**
> ✓ **Encroachment**
> Direct or indirect competition between a franchise chain and an existing franchised outlet.

the franchisee. Traditionally, encroachment has meant that a franchisor would open a store near an already existing franchise outlet. However, encroachment became an even more complicated issue in the 1990s as franchise chains scrambled for growth through new distribution channels. H & R Block, for example, now offers tax services

BUSINESS TIP

Before signing on the dotted line, a would-be franchisee should ask:

→ Does the franchisor offer exclusive territories?

→ Does the franchisor have plans for future distribution channels?

→ Is there a dispute mechanism to determine the impact of new outlets on existing franchises in the same area?

→ Does the franchisor have a compensation policy for such cases?

→ Would you be compensated for the impact of lost sales or would you only be given right of first refusal on nearby franchises?

→ Does the franchisor reserve all rights to itself and none to you? If so ... consider walking away!

→ AND ... Get your answers written in the franchise agreement!

on the Internet; you can buy a Tim Hortons coffee and doughnut at your local ESSO station; and the Body Shop distributes catalogues by mail. Established franchisees are finding it more and more difficult to protect their territory. Franchisors argue that for mature franchise systems with plenty of locations in every market, it becomes difficult to penetrate new locations without stepping on some existing franchisee's toes. Disgruntled franchisees, on the other hand, claim that flooding an area does not give them a chance to make a profit. It's a win–win situation for the franchisor. When a besieged owner eventually fails, the franchisor simply sells the store and banks another franchise fee.[19]

Small Business Goes Global

Historically, the Canadian small business sector has not been a significant participant in the global marketplace. For example, in the early 1990s only about 3 percent (in dollar value) of our manufacturing exports came from the small and medium-sized (SME) business sector. However, over the 1990s there was some encouraging evidence that this pattern was beginning to change. Firms such as Louis Garneau Sports Inc., highlighted in the opening story to this chapter, were on the leading edge of the exporting trend. With the development of a worldwide economy and the trend to "go global," more smaller Canadian firms are now exporting. For example, in 1990 there were about 66 000 SME exporters. By the mid-1990s, this number had increased more than 35 percent to just over 89 000. In addition, the value of exports from SMEs increased from $13.5 billion to about $24 billion over this same period. However, small business is still not a dominant factor in the export market: the percentage of SMEs that export remains well below 10 percent. The federal government wants this to change and has targeted exporting by small business as a key economic growth sector. It is estimated, for example, that if just 2 percent more SMEs were to start exporting, Canada would benefit from the creation of up to 85 000 new jobs.[20] Licensing, franchising, and exporting through intermediaries are three possible ways for small and medium-sized companies to enter the international market.

Under a licensing agreement, one firm allows another to use its intellectual property (trademarks, patents, or technical knowledge) in exchange for royalties. For instance, a firm that has developed a new type of software might license the process to other companies abroad.

Franchising can be another way for small firms to enter foreign markets. Worldwide, franchising is expanding rapidly: it is growing by 2.5 percent a year, compared with an overall global growth in business of 2.3 percent.[21]

Sometimes export success comes from exporting through intermediaries that can provide services small companies cannot afford on their own. An **export management company** *is a domestic firm that specializes in performing international marketing services as a commissioned representative or distributor for other companies.* Another option for small firms wishing to export is to work with an **export trading company**, *a general trading firm that plays a varied role in world commerce by importing, exporting, countertrading, investing, and manufacturing.*

Business Term

✓ **Export management company**

A domestic firm that specializes in performing international marketing services as a commissioned representative or distributor for other companies.

Business Term

✓ **Export trading company**

A general trading firm that plays a varied role in world commerce by importing, exporting, countertrading, investing, and manufacturing.

CASE EXERCISE

MENTORING: A KEY STRATEGIC WEAPON

Much of what is learned in business comes from experience. Entrepreneurs need day-to-day practical help and advice — the kind which may not come from a business book. That is why savvy entrepreneurs rely on the age-old practice of mentoring, a mutually beneficial relationship between a seasoned business person and a less-experienced entrepreneur or protégé.

A mentor (some use the term coach or advisor) is someone who has a "passion to help, and not just a hankering to make money," says David Horowitz, CEO of Priva Inc., a Montreal distributor of reusable adult-incontinence products. Priva is a *Profit* 100 success company.

Horowitz believes that the ability to confide in someone with decades of experience has been a key strategic weapon. For example, his mentor, Jim Godber, told him that "Companies going into the next millennium can no longer differentiate their company by their products, but by what they stand for." In 1997, after a few mentoring sessions, Horowitz turned this advice into a creative market-blasting brand awareness program — the National Caregiver of the Year Award. By 1998, this one mentoring idea alone had nearly doubled Priva's sales to $4.1 million.

Horowitz says, "I hope other entrepreneurs seek mentors — it's so rewarding." But he also warns that mentors mean business. "They can be hard on the ego. They'll point out your weaknesses; they'll push you hard; they'll expect results — and they're a long-term commitment."

We suggest you take Horowitz's suggestion and find a mentor — if you want to be successful, that is.

1. What do you think are the essential qualities of an effective business mentor?

2. Although we strongly suggest you get a mentor, mentoring relationships do not always succeed the first time. What are some problems you might encounter?

Source: Adapted from Diane Luckow, "Psst! Want to Get In on the Latest Trend to Achieve Personal and Business Success? Hire a Mentor," *Profit: The Magazine for Canadian Entrepreneurs*, June 1998, 156-58.

SUMMARY OF LEARNING OUTCOMES

1. Identify and explain the three basic forms of business ownership.

The three legal forms of business ownership are sole proprietorship, partnership, and corporation. The sole proprietorship, a business owned and operated by a single person, is most common. A partnership is operated by two or more people as co-owners. A corporation is a legal entity separate from its owners.

2. Compare the advantages and disadvantages of the forms of business ownership.

The advantages of sole proprietorships are (1) retention of all profits, (2) ease of formation and dissolution, and (3) ownership flexibility. The disadvantages are (1) unlimited financial liability, (2) financing limitations, (3) management deficiencies, and (4) lack of continuity.

The advantages of partnerships are (1) ease of formation, (2) complementary management skills, and (3) expanded financial capability. The disadvantages are (1) unlimited financial liability, (2) possible interpersonal conflicts, (3) lack of continuity, and (4) complex dissolution.

The advantages of corporations are (1) limited financial liability, (2) specialized management skills, (3) expanded financial capability, and (4) economies of larger-scale operation. The disadvantages are (1) high taxes and (2) legal restrictions.

3. Discuss the levels of corporate management.

Stockholders own the corporation, the board of directors governs it, and top management is responsible for its actual operation. Middle management co-ordinates the operational functions of the company and serves as liaison between top and lower levels of management. Supervisory managers co-ordinate the day-to-day operations of the firm, supervise employees, assign specific tasks to staff, and often are responsible for evaluating employees' job performance.

4. Explain how private ownership, public ownership, and collective ownership (co-operatives) differ.

Private ownership refers to ownership by an individual or individuals, regardless of whether the organization is set up as a sole proprietorship, partnership, or corporation. One alternative to private ownership is public ownership, in which a government unit or its agency — such as a Crown corporation — owns and operates an organization on behalf of the population served by the unit. Another alternative to private ownership is the co-operative, which provides for collective ownership of production, storage, transportation, and/or marketing activities.

5. Explain the vital role played by entrepreneurs and small businesses in the Canadian economy.

Entrepreneurs and small businesses play an important part in the private enterprise system. They provide independence and bring competitive fervour to the economy. According to the Canadian Federation of Independent Business, a small business is a firm that is independently owned and operated and is not dominant in its field of endeavour. Small businesses are found in nearly every industry, including farming, retailing, services, and high technology. Small businesses, especially home-based and microbusinesses, account for the bulk of all Canadian commercial enterprises and provide a major portion of national output and employment.

6. Compare the advantages and disadvantages of small business.

Small businesses have some distinct advantages over larger competitors, including ease of introduction of innovations, the ability to provide better service and lower costs, and the ability to fill isolated niches. They also have disadvantages, including poor management, inadequate financing, and government regulation.

7. **List the advantages and disadvantages of franchising.**

The advantages of the franchising approach to small business are access to performance records on which to make comparisons and judgements, a widely recognized name, and tested management systems. Disadvantages include the high cost of buying and starting some franchises, as well as the restrictions that come from fitting into a corporate culture that has already been established. Another disadvantage is that when some franchise outlets fail, this can affect consumers' attitude toward all the outlets.

8. **Outline the popular methods of small business operation in the global market.**

With the development of a worldwide economy, more Canadian small firms are going global. Licensing, franchising, and exporting through intermediaries are three possible ways for small and medium-sized companies to enter the international market. Export management companies and export trading companies can provide specialized services that small firms cannot handle themselves.

Key Terms Quiz

corporation
board of directors
partnership
subsidiary
sole proprietorship
export management company

stockholders
small business
merger
acquisition
co-operative
entrepreneur

franchise
public ownership
franchisee
franchisor
Small Business Loans Act (SBLA)

_____ 1. The governing body of a corporation elected by the stockholders.
_____ 2. Ownership and operation of an enterprise by a government department or agency.
_____ 3. An agreement that sets the methods a dealer can use to produce and market a supplier's good or service.
_____ 4. Refers to ownership (and usually operation) of an organization by one person.
_____ 5. A legal entity with authority to act and have liability separate and apart from its owners.
_____ 6. A supplier of a franchise that provides various services in exchange for payments by the franchisee.
_____ 7. A procedure in which one firm acquires the property and assumes the obligations of another firm.
_____ 8. A business owner who is licensed to operate under the rules and regulations of a franchisor.
_____ 9. A firm that performs international marketing services as a commissioned representative or distributor for other companies.
_____ 10. A corporation with all or a majority of its stock owned by another corporation.
_____ 11. A risk taker in the private enterprise system, specifically a person who creates a new business.
_____ 12. Ownership of a business by two or more persons.
_____ 13. People who acquire the shares of, and therefore own part of, a corporation.
_____ 14. Refers to two or more firms that combine to form one company.
_____ 15. An organization that is operated collectively by its owners.
_____ 16. A firm that is independently owned and operated and is not dominant in its field of endeavour.
_____ 17. A federal program designed to help new and existing businesses obtain term loans directly from their financial institutions for purchasing and improving fixed assets.

Other Important Terms

Crown corporation
encroachment
export trading company
general partnership

home-based business
limited partnership
microbusiness
parent company

privatization
Strategis

Review Questions

1. What are the main reasons Louis Garneau Sports Inc. has become a successful Canadian business?

2. What is meant by a sole proprietorship? Why is it the most popular form of business ownership? Are there any disadvantages to this form of business ownership?

3. What are the advantages and disadvantages of partnerships?

4. How would you define a corporation? What are the advantages of the corporate form of business ownership?

5. What is a co-operative? How does it differ from other business enterprises?

6. Define entrepreneurship and small business. Why are entrepreneurs so important to private enterprise?

7. Outline the advantages small firms have over larger ones. Cite an example of each advantage.

8. Why is financing such a problem for small business? Explain how this disadvantage can be overcome.

9. What is franchising? What are the advantages and disadvantages of franchising?

Discussion Questions

1. Assume that you and your brother or sister are about to open a family restaurant. What factors would determine your choice of a form of business ownership for a new enterprise? Why?

2. Choose an entrepreneur or small business owner in your area. Interview her or him about the experience of owning a business. What advice does this person have about starting a business? What mistakes do new business owners commonly make? Share your findings with the class.

3. Assume you are involved in establishing the following businesses. What forms of business ownership would you use?

a. Toronto Blue Jays (professional baseball team)
b. Dry-cleaning franchise in Halifax
c. Management consulting firm in Vancouver
d. Small foundry in Hamilton

4. Choose a franchise company that operates outlets both in Canada and in other countries. Compare the operations of the Canadian outlets with those in at least two foreign countries. Are they different? If so, in what ways? (For instance, you could compare the menu of a North American fast-food franchise with its menus in other nations.) If there are differences, explain why you think they exist.

Answers to Key Terms Quiz

1. board of directors 2. public ownership 3. franchise 4. sole proprietorship 5. corporation 6. franchisor 7. acquisition 8. franchisee 9. export management company 10. subsidiary 11. entrepreneur 12. partnership 13. stockholders 14. merger 15. co-operative 16. small business 17. Small Business Loans Act (SBLA)

Notes

1. Based on personal discussion with Louis Garneau Sports Inc.; and Rod McQueen, "Canada's 50 Best Managed Private Companies: The Cycling World's Tour de Force," *The Financial Post*, December 14–16, 1996, 29. Reprinted by permission of The Financial Post.

2. Sunder Magun (Applied International Economics) for Industry Canada, *The Development of Strategic Alliances in Canadian Industries: A Micro Analysis*, Working Paper No. 13, October 1996, Catalogue No. C21-24/14-1996, 3. The views expressed in this working paper do not necessarily reflect those of Industry Canada or the federal government.

3. This section is based on Minister of Supply and Services Canada, *Taking Care of Small Businesses: Report of the Standing Committee on Industry*, October 1994, 34; Janet McFarland, "Merger Mixes Similar Styles," *The Globe and Mail*, August 30, 1996, B9; and Jeffrey Hodgson (Bloomberg News Service), "Americans See Benefits in Buying Canadian High-Tech," *The Ottawa Citizen*, October 18, 1995, B1.

4. Jeffrey Hodgson (Bloomberg News Service), "Americans See Benefits in Buying Canadian High-Tech," B1.

5. Ibid.

6. This section is based on Magun, *The Development of Strategic Alliances in Canadian Industries*, i, ii, 3, 6. The views expressed in this working paper do not necessarily reflect those of Industry Canada or the federal government. Reproduced with the permission of the Minister of Public Works and Government Services Canada, 1997.

7. See also Ron Knowles and Debbie White, *Issues in Canadian Small Business* (Toronto: Dryden, 1995), 26–39.

8. This section is based on Industry Canada, *Your Guide to Government of Canada Services and Support for Small Businesses: Trends and Statistics*, 1996–1997, Catalogue No. C1-10/1997E; and John Manley and Paul Martin for Industry Canada, *Growing Small Businesses*, February 1994, 1–7. Reproduced with the permission of the Minister of Public Works and Government Services Canada, 1997.

9. Industry Canada, *Your Guide to Government of Canada Services and Support for Small Businesses*.

10. Canadian Bankers Association, *Business Credit Statistics*, June 1996.

11. Ibid.

12. Ibid.

13. Industry Canada, *Your Guide to Government of Canada Services and Support for Small Businesses*.

14. Ibid.

15. Based on personal inquiry to Buns Master Bakery Systems Inc.

16. Canadian Franchise Association, *The Official Guide to Franchising Opportunities in Canada*, 1995, 10, 18.

17. Lee A. Eckert, J.D. Ryan, and Ronald A. Knowles, *Canadian Small Business: An Entrepreneur's Plan*, 2nd ed. (Toronto: Dryden, 1995), 366; "Franchise Flurry," drawn from the newsletter of accountants Richter Usher & Vineberg, *The Globe and Mail*, April 7, 1997, B7; and Peter Henrys, "Look Before You Leap," *Business Victoria*, August 1993, 5.

18. "Debunking Some Myths about Franchising," *Money*, September 1991, 34.

19. John Southerst, "When Partners Become Rivals," *The Globe and Mail*, May 8, 1995, B5.

20. Industry Canada, *Your Guide to Government of Canada Services and Support for Small Businesses*.

21. Peter Henrys, "Look Before You Leap," 34.

Chapter 6

The Role of Quality in Business Success

After studying this chapter, you should be able to

1. Explain the importance of quality and customer satisfaction in achieving a competitive advantage.
2. Discuss the role of the organization and top management in applying total quality management (TQM).
3. Relate TQM to various functions within an organization, including production, human resource management, marketing, technology, and financial management.
4. Identify the major methods of securing feedback from customers, employees, and suppliers.
5. Describe how organizations can work toward continuous process improvement.
6. Define ISO 9000 and explain its importance as a TQM strategy.
7. Define benchmarking and explain its contributions to quality and customer satisfaction.
8. Identify the components of employee involvement and their impact on quality and customer satisfaction.

"Quality Is Job One"[1]

When a woman in the United States complained that she got locked out of her Windstar minivan after a box of laundry detergent fell on the power lock switch, George Turczyn and his TQM team sprang into action.

Turczyn heads a group of engineers, financial analysts, and computer-assisted design assistants who work at the Windstar assembly plant of Ford Motor Co. of Canada Ltd. in Oakville, Ontario. The plant vehicle team (PVT) found a similar detergent box, repeated the incident, and discovered that the switch was unprotected. Within 90 days, they had designed a protective guard, made the necessary tooling modifications with a supplier, and told the woman that the part could be installed at her dealer when she was ready.

This kind of customer response is just one example of the PVT team mandate of continuous improvement: finding ways to boost the quality of the Windstar or to make the minivan less expensive by cutting the cost of parts or making it easier to put together. One of the most dramatic examples of quality improvement by the PVT team was the savings generated by switching the backing on the Windstar's trim panels from a foam to a cotton product generated from recycled clothing. "Improve the quality, lower the cost and get it done rapidly. A customer doesn't have to see it. [With this cotton product], we reduced the cost, slightly improved the sound quality and created a market for recycled clothing," says Turczyn. It was improvements like these that shaved a total of $264 million (U.S.) on every 1996, 1997, and 1998 model of the Windstar and added about $64 million to the company's bottom line.

The ideas for cost savings and quality improvements come not only from external customers but also from team members, plant workers, or officials who bring problems to the team's attention or from interchange with colleagues in other assembly plants. Quality is an organizational priority at Ford.

The PVT teams at Ford plants across the world learn from one another by putting their ideas in a computer database. They visit other Ford assembly plants, and twice a year PVT managers hold a one-week benchmarking conference where they study best

At Ford, quality is truly Job One.

practices and share the lessons they have learned. Turczyn says that "Success is measured not just by how much is saved, but by applying ISO standards and examining all the standard industry quality studies such as the J.D. Power & Associates surveys." The results of Ford's "Quality Is Job One" program are clear. For example, the company's new vehicle quality study, an internal examination of Ford vehicles, shows that Windstar's quality indicators have improved by 35 percent in the two years the PVT team has been operating. "You can walk right out to the floor and watch it happen," says Michael Everett, a designer on the Windstar PVT.

CHAPTER OVERVIEW

MANAGING FOR QUALITY to provide complete customer satisfaction is essential for surviving and thriving in today's competitive global marketplace. Over the 1990s, many Canadian companies, ranging from the massive Ford Motor Co. of Canada to small entrepreneurial companies like Pacific Western Brewing Co., have learned the hard-won lesson that long-term success requires delivering superior-quality goods and services at good value. Quality-conscious companies have a strong corporate leadership vision and culture, and involve employees in finance, production, marketing, and every other business function so they can understand and satisfy customer needs and wants. In fact, many companies com-

mitted to quality are so customer-focussed that they manage their businesses according to their customers' definition of quality.

This chapter discusses the vital role of customer-focussed quality in building competitive advantage. We start by examining the importance of quality and customer satisfaction to help you understand why this issue is a critical challenge facing Canadian firms, as well as foreign companies operating in Canada. Quality really is "job one," beginning with corporate values and vision, the subject of the next section. We then discuss ways to apply total quality management to each function of the organization and how to obtain feedback. Finally, we examine the critical quality issues of continuous process improvement, ISO 9000, benchmarking, and employee involvement.

IMPORTANCE OF QUALITY AND CUSTOMER SATISFACTION

Quality describes *the degree of excellence or superiority of an organization's goods and services.* Quality is a broad term that encompasses both the tangible and the intangible characteristics of a good or service. Tangible characteristics include such physical traits as durability and reliability. Also included in the overall definition of quality is the intangible component of **customer satisfaction**, *the concept that a good or service pleases buyers because it meets their emotional needs and quality expectations.* Many experts argue that the true measure of quality is whether a firm has satisfied its customers. For example, BMW's quality manufacturing

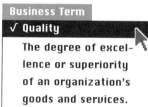

Business Term

√ **Quality**

The degree of excellence or superiority of an organization's goods and services.

offers customer satisfaction to motorcycle purchasers of varying lifestyles; the only commonality is an appreciation of travelling the open road and a desire to spend less than $10 000 for two-wheeled transportation.

Organizations throughout the world are offering high-quality goods and services to create customer satisfaction through **total quality management** (**TQM**), *an approach that involves a commitment to quality in achieving world-class performance and customer satisfaction as a crucial strategic objective* for the entire company. In a total quality organization, marketers develop products people want to buy, engineers design products the way customers want to use them, production workers build quality into every product they make, salespeople deliver what they promise to customers, information-systems specialists use technology to ensure customer orders are filled correctly and on time, and financial managers help determine prices that give customers value.

A TQM strategy does not produce quick results. Studies indicate that it takes an average of two to three years to realize initial benefits.[2] But does quality pay in the longer term? Do quality improvements benefit an organization? Absolutely — studies show that a long-term committment to quality programs can boost company revenues by as much as 40 percent, while decreasing production costs 20 to 50 percent, saving 40 percent on space and inventory, cutting production time by as much as 70 percent, and building strong customer loyalty.

Business Term

√ **Customer satisfaction**

The concept that a good or service pleases buyers because it meets their emotional needs and quality expectations.

Business Term

√ **Total quality management (TQM)**

An approach that involves a commitment to quality in achieving world-class performance and customer satisfaction as a crucial strategic objective.

At the same time, a growing number of quality-conscious organizations are stressing *return on quality*. Leading companies such as Ford of Canada, IBM, and Xerox Canada focus their efforts to improve quality on measures that produce tangible customer benefits while lowering costs or increasing sales.

In addition to providing financial returns from reduced costs, increased satisfaction, and added sales, quality-improvement programs are essential if firms are

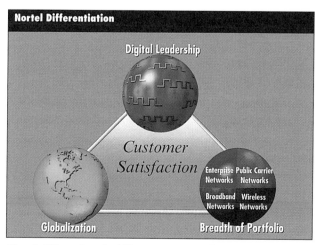

Nortel Differentiation

Digital Leadership

Customer Satisfaction

Enterprise Networks Public Carrier Networks

Broadband Networks Wireless Networks

Globalization

Breadth of Portfolio

Nortel differentiates itself from competitors by ensuring customer satisfaction.

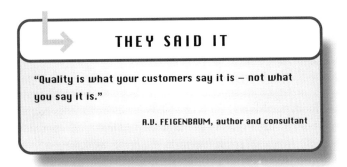

to stay abreast of their competitors. As more companies worldwide apply the principles of total quality management, standards rise. Chey Jong-Hyon, chairman of Korean petroleum products maker Sunkyong Group, notes, "If we merely try to be excellent, our gap with the world's top companies will remain because they keep improving. Only by seeking super-excellence can we reach their level or overtake them."[3] Figure 6.1 illustrates the positive impact that quality has on an organization.

Figure 6.1 How Quality Improvements Benefit an Organization

Quality improvements affect an organization both internally and externally.

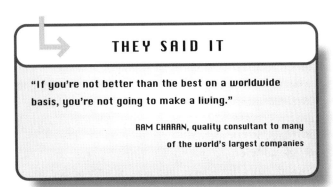

APPLYING TQM THROUGHOUT THE ORGANIZATION

ORGANIZATIONS TODAY RECOGNIZE that improving quality is a critical strategy for building competitive advantage. Within the organization, higher quality leads to increased productivity and lower costs. Externally, quality improvements increase customer satisfaction and lower prices, which in turn boosts market share. Ultimately, a successful commitment to total quality should result in increased earnings and profitability.

TQM often is viewed as primarily affecting production by increasing efficiency on the shop floor. In this section, we will correct this too-narrow view by examining the organizational values and their application to all business functions, including production, human resource management, marketing, information processes, and financial management. Often, TQM programs fail because the philosophy is misunderstood or its applications are mismanaged. Table 6.1 outlines common reasons why TQM either fails or succeeds.

Value-Adding Chain

Effective TQM begins with a commitment and vision by the entire organization to add value for its customers and employees. Building corporate value can be depicted as the function of a five-link chain, shown in Figure 6.2, that connects the corporate vision to the customers' requirements:[4]

- **Culture.** The norms, values, rituals, and relationships within the organization spur people to design systems that fit the culture.

- **Systems.** The operating, administrative control, and reward systems direct employee and management behaviour in the desired direction.

- **Performance.** Employee behaviour is influenced by the integration of culture and systems.

- **Results.** Performance produces operating results such as quality, productivity, and service outcomes.

- **Value.** The final link — value — achieves competitive advantage and customer satisfaction.

Top Management Involvement

John Roth was appointed CEO of Northern Telecom (Nortel) Ltd. in the fall of 1997. Even before taking on

Table 6.1 Why Some TQM Programs Fail and Others Succeed

Reasons for Success	Reasons for Failure
Active and aggressive driving by top management	Little top management support
Fundamental changes in culture, structure, and processes	Training, tools, and techniques emphasized, not fundamental change
Well-articulated strategies	Lack of an overall strategy
Concepts integrated into the fabric of the company	Philosophy not integrated with end-to-end processes
Persistent, long-term results	Some initial results, but fading within three years or so

Figure 6.2 The Value-Adding Chain

this position, Roth had already articulated a succinct vision to guide the company. Six months before officially becoming CEO, he announced the new company vision and direction: "My strategy is to be in *every* high growth area of telecommunications." Faced with the global trends of deregulation and increased competition, Roth said Nortel could no longer succeed with its old approach, in which the company's engineers were left to choose what products to make and what markets to tackle. "Our customers now make those choices. And for us to be their preferred supplier of choice, we must make products for all their networks and we must serve the entire global market."[5]

As exemplified by Nortel — Canada's pre-eminent high-technology manufacturer — effective TQM programs require the involvement of top managers who believe that the success of their firm is based on quality and customer satisfaction.

Quality advocate W. Edwards Deming created a classic set of guidelines for top managers, called his "14 Points for Quality Improvement," that encourage managers to view their organizations as systems that use the knowledge and skills of all employees to improve quality (see Table 6.2). Managers are responsible for communicating the goals of total quality management to all staff members, and for encouraging them to improve themselves

Table 6.2 Deming's Fourteen Points for Quality Improvement

1. Drive out fear.
2. Eliminate quotas and numerical goals.
3. Break down all barriers between departments.
4. Eliminate inspection by building products right the first time.
5. Institute a vigorous education program.
6. Remove barriers that rob workers of their right to pride of workmanship.
7. Institute leadership with the aim of helping people do a better job.
8. Eliminate slogans, exhortations, and production targets.
9. Adopt a new philosophy to awaken managers to the challenge, to learn responsibilities, and to take on leadership.
10. End practice of awarding business based on the price tag. Move toward single supplier and base long-term relationship on loyalty and trust.
11. Improve constantly and forever the system of production, marketing, and service.
12. Put everyone to work to accomplish this transformation.
13. Institute job training.
14. Create constancy of purpose toward the improvement of goods and services to become competitive, stay in business, and provide jobs.

Deming's Fourteen Points for Quality Improvement are designed as guidelines for managers in accomplishing quality objectives.

and take pride in their work. Research determines customers' needs and wants. This information is then used to design and redesign functional, dependable goods and services; to remove defects by reducing variations; and to build relationships of loyalty and trust with suppliers to improve incoming materials and to decrease costs.

TQM and Production

Early efforts to improve quality in the production process consisted mostly of end-of-the-line inspections: workers were positioned at the end of the assembly line to weed out finished products that failed to meet quality specifications. While the end-of-the-line inspection is still used today, it is increasingly viewed as a backward approach. It does nothing to correct the manufacturing errors that created the problems in the first place. In addition, it can be time-consuming and ineffective, since inspectors do not always catch defective products. Finally, it is expensive. Samsung's Chairman Lee Kun Hee estimates that every year 6000 of his firm's 36 000 employees spend their time identifying and then repairing an average of 20 000 defective products.

The quality movement began as an attempt to improve product quality by improving the production process itself. An early approach still used today is **statistical quality control**, *a system using statistical procedures to gather and analyze data to pinpoint and correct problem areas.* It involves developing control charts for detecting variations in the manufacturing process that could produce defective products. By controlling these variations, statistical quality control builds quality into the production process rather than relying on inspection to find defects.

Today, production control has evolved from a statistical quality concept of testing *after* the manufacturing process into a company-wide quality assurance process that contains a series of controls *during* each stage of the production process. According to the Quality Management Institute, a division of the Canadian Standards Association, **quality assurance** is *repeating good performance on every contract through a system of documented procedures that are known, understood, and operated by all personnel, including management, employees, and suppliers.*[6] As evidence of quality assurance, The International Organization for Standardization (ISO) certification, discussed in a later

> **Business Term**
> √ **Statistical quality control**
>
> A system using statistical procedures to gather and analyze data to pinpoint and correct problem areas.

> **Business Term**
> √ **Quality assurance**
>
> Repeating good performance on every contract through a system of documented procedures that are known, understood, and operated by all personnel, including management, employees, and suppliers.

section of this chapter, is rapidly becoming a prerequisite for Canadian firms. An ISO-certified product or service means that the product or service has undergone thorough testing through all stages of production and development.

Quality has a domino effect on the supply chain. Organizations seeking to improve their own production systems also will demand better quality and quicker response time from their suppliers. For example, the big three automakers — Ford, Chrysler, and General Motors — have made quality assurance a top priority. By the end of 1997, their ISO standards (QF 9000, which is an extended version of ISO) had been extended to all of their suppliers. Nortel, Canada's telecommunications giant, has made ISO a prerequisite for all its suppliers. "Requiring suppliers to be ISO certified sets a good foundation for any quality system. We support quality measures in both service and manufacturing organizations," says Milan J. Kosturik, Nortel's assistant vice-president of customer satisfaction. In other words, any supplier who is not ISO-approved will find it increasingly difficult to compete or do business with large, successful Canadian firms.[7] Moreover, to be globally competitive, quality must be assured. As Figure 6.3 shows, consumers demand it, and their opinions can earn a country the reputation of a quality leader.

Figure 6.3 Quality Leaders in Manufacturing

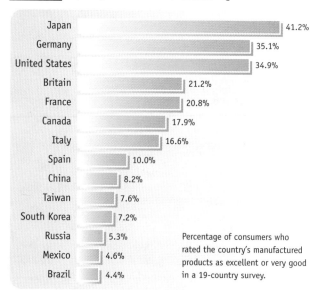

Japan	41.2%
Germany	35.1%
United States	34.9%
Britain	21.2%
France	20.8%
Canada	17.9%
Italy	16.6%
Spain	10.0%
China	8.2%
Taiwan	7.6%
South Korea	7.2%
Russia	5.3%
Mexico	4.6%
Brazil	4.4%

Percentage of consumers who rated the country's manufactured products as excellent or very good in a 19-country survey.

TQM and Human Resource Management

So far in this chapter we have discussed customer satisfaction in terms of **external customers** — *people or organizations that buy or use another firm's good or service.* However, TQM also emphasizes the importance of **internal customers** — *individual employees or entire departments within an organization that depend on the work of other people or departments to perform their jobs.* For example, a Compaq Computer employee processing an order for a new PC is the internal customer of the Compaq salesperson who completes the sale, just as the person who buys the product is the salesperson's external customer. Employee involvement in the decisions that affect the company's success is a key human resource motivational component of TQM and quality service. This was one of the major findings of a 1996 National Opinion Survey conducted by the Angus Reid Group for the Royal Bank.[8] When employees view their colleagues as internal customers, they are motivated to deliver higher-quality goods and services to their co-workers. They accept the responsibility of helping fellow employees do their jobs better and add further value to the production and marketing processes.[9]

Any department that in some way adds value to the end user's product is, in fact, an internal customer in need of information. Consider how clearly the product design engineer at a firm, such as Ford of Canada, must understand who the end users are and what needs they have. In this case, the design engineer becomes one of the marketing department's internal customers. If the marketing department does not clearly identify the target customer to the design engineer, it has delivered unsatisfactory customer service.

> **Business Term**
>
> √ **External customers**
>
> People or organizations that buy or use another firm's good or service.

> **Business Term**
>
> √ **Internal customers**
>
> Individual employees or entire departments within an organization that depend on the work of other people or departments to perform their jobs.

TQM and Marketing

With TQM, customer satisfaction becomes a primary goal of marketing. Jon Nicholls is chairman of Integrated Communications & Entertainment Inc. (ICE) — one of *The Financial Post*'s 1996 "50 Best Managed Private Companies." Nicholls and all 110 of his employees believe that the prime objective of ICE is quality service, and that means total satisfaction of customer needs: "If we produce a sales meeting for a client, we're obliged to make it an exciting, memorable event. If you're dealing with specialness, then you better make everything special. We have a saying around here that if a client says 'that was good,' we know it wasn't good enough."[10]

Successful Canadian companies have learned that TQM must focus first and foremost on the customer. Quality marketing means customer-driven marketing, which has an impact on the entire marketing process from the idea stage to product design, distribution strategy, promotion, pricing, and selling functions.

TQM and Technology

Effective information systems support TQM programs by improving customer service, reducing service costs, and boosting employees' productivity. Over the 1990s, technology investment has been a major focus of successful Canadian firms like appliance parts distributor Reliable Parts in Coquitlam, BC, and auto repairer/dealer Birchwood Automotive Group in Winnipeg, Manitoba.

Over the first half of the 1990s, the market for replacement appliances dropped 35 percent. According to Doug Loughran, president of Reliable Parts, this was due to improved quality: manufacturers gradually improved appliances to contain fewer items that could wear out. "An appliance may now be five to eight years old before it needs a part," says Loughran. Despite a declining market for parts, Reliable — one of *The Financial Post*'s "50 Best Managed Private Companies" — maintained its market share and increased its return on investment. Its focus on technology and customer service has been a major factor contributing to this success. For example, an electronic data interchange arrangement allows dealers to dial in to Reliable's mainframe, look up prices, do model number searches, and chat with other dealers. The entire

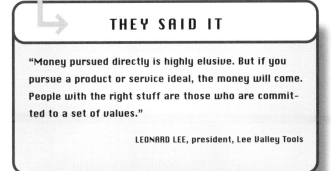

THEY SAID IT

"Money pursued directly is highly elusive. But if you pursue a product or service ideal, the money will come. People with the right stuff are those who are committed to a set of values."

LEONARD LEE, president, Lee Valley Tools

QUALITY BEER WITH THE RIGHT MIX

In 1991, the Pacific Western Brewing Co. closed its doors. This little Prince George brewery in BC, had been forced out of business by domestic competition. It just couldn't compete with the likes of Molson and Labatt.

That's when Kazuko Komatsu, a seasoned businessperson with twenty years of successful marketing and exporting experience, decided to buy the company. Komatsu is allergic to alcohol, so why would she purchase a failed brewing company and hurl herself into the vigorously com-

petitive world of Canadian brewing? With her marketing and exporting experience, she knew there was an export market for quality Canadian beer — especially in Japan.

When Komatsu bought the company, she could have just purchased the assets. Instead she also retained the unionized staff. She didn't have to take the union certification that went with it, but she chose to take the employees because they had failed in their bid to buy the brewery. She knew they really cared and were committed to the business. "It showed that the employees wanted to continue to work there. It meant they were concerned about the product, the company, and the area.

The union was also very important. People need a job, and you cannot do business with hatred. You also need experienced employees who are concerned about the company," she said. So she hired a consultant and, over three years, trained the nearly 100 employees at the Prince George brewery to produce the consistent quality of beer required to qualify for ISO certification.

Since 1991, Pacific Western has expanded almost every year, and by 1997 it was producing about 340 000 hectolitres of beer a year. That's not huge by brewery standards, but Komatsu claims that quality beer takes longer to brew and is difficult to mass-produce. In

price list can be downloaded so the work can be done offline and orders can be sent automatically.[11]

TQM and technology also played a major role in award-winning Birchwood Automotive Group's success. The company's sales and service are monitored daily by a call centre. It also has an information system that allows service representatives to contact over 20 000 customers per year. Errors in repair time or charges are dealt with quickly. Even more modest customer service matters, like the temperature of the coffee in the waiting room, are dealt with promptly: "We don't have to wait for the manufacturer's monthly customer survey report," says Mark Chipman, president of Birchwood.[12]

While information technologies can improve customer service, they also can detract from it if not used properly. Voice mail and e-mail are good examples. They began as communication media for people within an organization and have evolved into a virtual receptionist for many firms. As companies took the hatchet to costs, they often cut the number of secretaries and support staff, leaving workers to pick up the slack with help from voice mail and e-mail. These systems can save money and time, but if poorly designed or implemented they can frustrate and eventually alienate customers, who may then decide to get in touch with the competition instead. As for voice

mail, telecommunications consultant Tom Hunse says, "These days, the [primary] user of voice mail is the [out-of-office] caller. It's not the way you want to treat a customer or client when they call." Hunse suggests the following guidelines for a high-quality voice-mail system:[13]

- Offer callers the option of talking to a human operator at any time during the message.

- Change the message daily to reflect the specifics of your schedule.

- Ask callers to leave a detailed message. This way, the necessary information will be ready when the call is returned.

- Check for messages regularly, at least three times a day. Return all calls within 24 hours.

A 1996 report by the Conference Board of Canada, a business research group, found that the use of e-mail became so incessant that it was gumming up the works of some major companies. "I know people who routinely get 50 to 100 E-mails per day and some receive as many as 500," said David De Long, a research fellow at Ernst and Young. Some companies began to take action by shutting down the e-mail system during selected periods of the day

Quality at Pacific Western Brewing Company is further assured by its ISO 9000 certification.

1997, Pacific Western–produced beer was the third most popular imported beer in Japan behind the giant Budweiser and Heineken brands. Pacific Western was also the first Canadian brewery to export to Russia. The main reason for the company's success in foreign markets has been its attention to quality and customer satisfaction. For example, the company doesn't force Canadian preferences on the Japanese, who prefer a stronger taste of hops: "You cannot force Canadian products. In Japan, they have been eating and drinking for a long time, and they cannot immediately change [to Canadian tastes]," says Komatsu. Quality, according to Pacific Western, is knowing exactly what its international customers want and producing a world-class product that satisfies the needs of those target customers.

Pacific Western's concept of quality also extends to the behaviour and values of its employees. This means understanding and respecting other cultures. On a 1997 trade mission to Japan, for example, Komatsu noticed that a number of Canadian companies did not make respectful comments about Japan and "in those cases, I thought they should not have been there."

Sources: Based on personal correspondence with Pacific Western Brewing Company; and adapted from Daphne Bramham (Vancouver *Sun*), "Managing the Right Brew," *The Ottawa Citizen*, March 22, 1997, E7. Reprinted by permission of Pacific Western Brewing Company and the Vancouver *Sun*.

or charging user fees to their divisions. However, as of 1998, someone has yet to offer any real solutions to the e-mail disease, which still remains a frustrating problem for many employees and customers.[14]

TQM and Financial Management

Applying TQM to financial management means establishing clear quality goals and linking them to employee compensation and financial returns for the company. According to an Angus Reid survey, about 23 percent of Canadians participate as owners in a profit-sharing arrangement.[15] For companies like Corel Corp., where employees share in the ownership, high-quality customer service is linked directly to the firm's profits — and to long-term returns for its owner-employees. However, North American studies indicate that performance measures play a role in determining senior managers' compensation in less than 25 percent of all companies. Lack of clear, quality-oriented financial objectives can derail projects and waste precious funds.

> **Business Term**
> √ **Feedback**
> **Messages returned by the audience to the sender that may cause the sender to alter or cancel an original message.**

IMPORTANCE OF FEEDBACK TO QUALITY

A S A FIRST STEP in improving quality, a company must compile feedback to use in measuring its present performance. **Feedback** consists of *messages returned by the audience to the sender that may cause the sender to alter or cancel an original message.* Feedback can be obtained from customers, employees, and suppliers.

Customer Feedback

Choosing the best way to obtain and measure customer feedback is often a challenging task for management, since *gaps* — differences between actual and perceived quality of goods and services — may exist. Xerox CEO Paul A. Allaire describes such a gap that existed a few years ago at the headquarters of the firm that invented the photocopying market: "We were fairly arrogant, until we realized the Japanese were selling quality products for what it cost us to make them."[16]

In a few instances, management receives a positive surprise in learning that a favourable gap exists; that is, their products are better than expected. If firms are to avoid unfavourable gaps, they must go beyond traditional performance measures and focus on exploring what drives customer behaviour, then formulate their mission statements, goals, and performance standards based on customer perceptions.

Many companies measure customer satisfaction by monitoring purchasing behaviour over a period of time and surveying customers periodically regarding their experiences with company products and service personnel. As we mentioned earlier, Birchwood Automotive contacts over 20 000 customers per year to monitor its service and quality performance. Measuring customer satisfaction is standard operational procedure for customer-service-oriented companies like Shoppers Drug Mart, Canada Trust, and Future Shop. Some companies use customer comment cards regularly to obtain feedback.

Toll-free telephone lines can be an effective customer feedback system. About more than two-thirds of North American manufacturers offer toll-free numbers, compared to just 40 percent a decade ago. One reason for installing these lines and printing the number on packages is that consumers often associate the promotion of toll-free numbers with high-quality goods and services. Also important is the fact that talking to customers yields valuable information. Customer feedback and customer satisfaction measurement are discussed in more detail in Chapter 11.

Employee Feedback

Employee feedback is one area where Canadian companies can improve. According to a 1996 Angus Reid/Royal Bank survey, only 45 percent of Canadian workers rated their companies as good or excellent in feedback (see Figure 6.4).[17] Effective managers are not "one-minute" managers — they take the time to solicit and respond to employee feedback.

Figure 6.4 How Canadians Rate Their Workplace

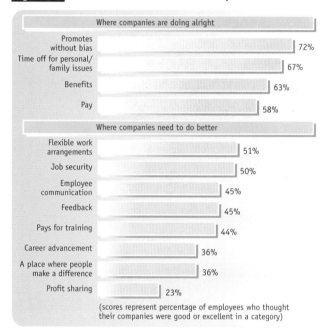

Where companies are doing alright

Promotes without bias	72%
Time off for personal/family issues	67%
Benefits	63%
Pay	58%

Where companies need to do better

Flexible work arrangements	51%
Job security	50%
Employee communication	45%
Feedback	45%
Pays for training	44%
Career advancement	36%
A place where people make a difference	36%
Profit sharing	23%

(scores represent percentage of employees who thought their companies were good or excellent in a category)

The World According to Big Shot

BIG SHOT: I think we're going to be OK.

SLINKY: How's that?
BIG SHOT: The managers tell me we've got world-class quality.

SLINKY: Do you believe them?
BIG SHOT: Of course I do. Now we can forget about all that ISO stuff.

→ Do you agree with Big Shot?

TECHNOLOGY

LEVI'S SIZES UP ITS CUSTOMERS

Marketing consultants, Don Peppers and Martha Rogers, authors of *Enterprise, One to One*, are strong advocates of *mass customization*: the ability of companies to customize products and services efficiently and cost-effectively in large quantities. Clients participate in the product's design, so they are more likely to be satisfied with the result, they say. Examples of mass customization include Dell Computer Corp.'s direct sales to customers which cover more than 14 000 configurations; LensCrafters mass customization of eyeglass lenses in an hour, and the Levi's customer-fit products for women. Here's how the Levi's program works:

Step one. Customer visits one of the 32 Levi's stores in Canada that offer the "personalized pair" program. Her waist, hips, inseam, and rise are measured, and she tries on some store samples. She requests different features and other samples are selected. She then decides on a size and leg style.

Step two. Salesperson taps into a computer the customer's measurements and code for the sample she likes best. Client provides name and address and is asked to complete a short survey.

Step three. Overnight, the order is downloaded to the plant in Stoney Creek, Ont. Orders are grouped based on colour. An operator produces a bar-code label with a customer number that is permanently fixed to the pocket lining of the jeans. A computerized cutting machine generates the pattern pieces based on customer's sample selection. Label is made.

Step four. Within three days, the jeans are ready and measurements checked. Information goes into computer system to track progress. Jeans go to a plant for washing.

Step five. Within three weeks of fitting, jeans arrive at the store. The customer is called to pick them up or have them delivered.

Source: Adapted from Elizabeth Church, "Levi's Sizes Up Its Customers," *The Globe and Mail*, April 11, 1997, B9. Reprinted with permission from The Globe and Mail.

Methods of obtaining employee feedback vary. Many leading firms ask employees to complete standardized surveys. Others actively solicit ideas from employees through brainstorming, questionnaires, or retreats and then to reward individuals and teams for their suggestions. Ford Motor Company and Pacific Western Brewing Company are typical examples of companies that actively listen to and reward their employees.

Carlyle Computer Products is another good example. Each year, President Derek Johannson takes a two-week tour of Carlyle Computer's seven offices. In an annual program that's called "If I were president ...," Johannson meets each employee for a twenty-minute one-on-one session to hear their ideas about running the company. The success of this approach is evidenced in the company's being a repeat winner (1993 and 1996) of *The Financial Post*'s "50 Best Managed Private Companies." Johannson believes that one of the main reasons is that he and his managers take the time to truly listen to employees and to make a point of thinking about and responding to every employee idea.[18]

Employee recognition is one of the areas most in need of improvement in corporate Canada. Being rewarded and recognized for good work — either through profit sharing, time off, or "employee of the month" awards — means a great deal. Quality researcher Kathryn Troy suggests that organizations develop a recognition program that honours skilled employees and gives them a chance to tell other employees what they do. "It sounds hokey, but it's successful," Troy explains. "Almost all of the total quality graybeards who have been at it for years have well-established recognition programs. Corning, Xerox, Motorola, and Milliken — they all have them."[19]

Supplier Feedback

Another element of total quality management involves giving feedback to and receiving it from suppliers. This means thinking in terms of customer–supplier partnerships that require members to consider each other as their customers. For example, a manufacturer orders its parts from another company (the supplier) and the two form a partnership. The manufacturer becomes the supplier's customer. In recent years, companies have started to demand higher levels of quality from their suppliers, and suppliers must comply if they want to maintain the business relationship.

CONTINUOUS PROCESS IMPROVEMENT

IN RECENT YEARS, Japanese quality programs have migrated across the Pacific and are being implemented throughout North America. **Continuous process improvement**, or *kaizen* as it is called in Japanese, is *the process of constantly studying and making changes in work activities to improve their quality, timeliness, efficiency, and effectiveness.* Continuous improvement results in value-added goods and services that meet customer needs and innovations that exceed customer expectations. This process must be ongoing, since customers' needs, wants, and expectations are always changing.

> **Business Term**
> ✓ Continuous process improvement
> The process of constantly studying and making changes in work activities to improve their quality, timeliness, efficiency, and effectiveness.

The quality of work processes to a large extent determines the quality of the resulting goods and services and can give the organization a competitive advantage. Continuous process-improvement efforts focus on three major objectives: reducing cycle time, reducing variation, and eliminating waste.

Reducing Cycle Time

Cycle time is *the time it takes to complete a work process or activity* from beginning to end. The concept of cycle time is closely associated with a term that became a business buzzword of the early to mid-1990s: **re-engineering** — *the process of mapping out delivery chain processes in detail to identify areas in which to reduce cycle time or errors by applying tech-*

> **Business Term**
> ✓ Cycle time
> The time it takes to complete a work process or activity.

nology in those key steps. This concept was first popularized by Michael Hammer and James Champy in their book *Reengineering the Corporation*, highlighted as a good read in the next chapter. When a company re-engineers a process, management systems, job designs, and work flows are evaluated carefully and then are modified in an effort to improve efficiency and reduce cycle time. Ford Motor Company's vendor payment system kept 400 accounting department employees awash in a sea of paperwork. When Ford's top management learned that rival Mazda performed the same work with only five workers in its accounts

> **Business Term**
> ✓ Re-engineering
> The process of mapping out delivery chain processes in detail to identify areas in which to reduce cycle time or errors by applying technology in those key steps.

payable division, they realized that re-engineering was needed. Computers now match receipt records, purchase orders, and invoices and then prepare cheques automatically. Today, the same work is performed by only 100 Ford employees, and vendors are paid immediately upon receipt of a shipment.[20]

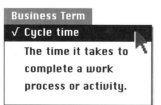

TIERS OF JOY

In 1998, Hunjan Tools & Mould Ltd., of Markham, Ontario, was a first-time PROFIT 100 company, with profits over $1 million and a five-year growth of 802 percent. Founded in 1986, the company manufactures plastic injection-moulded auto parts including cupholders and glove boxes. CEO Bal Hunjan attributes the company's success to continual investments in training and new technology. For example, in 1997, Hunjan Tools spent eight percent of its $8.7 million revenues on R&D and training.

When Hunjan Tools became an ISO-approved supplier, its market potential increased significantly. It was awarded "Tier 1" standing with General Motors, which meant that it could sell directly to GM. Bal Hunjan says it took his company two years and considerable investment to get the QS9000 certification necessary for this primary-supplier status.

One approach used to map out cycle time and find areas for improvement is the **PDCA cycle**, *a step-by-step process of planning, doing, checking, and acting,* depicted in Figure 6.5. In the *planning* step, employees analyze their work and determine what changes might improve it. In the *doing* step, they implement these changes. During the *checking* step, they observe the effects of the change. *Acting,* the final step, changes work activities to bring about improvement. Throughout the cycle, employees are asked to examine their own jobs in relation to how they affect customer satisfaction.

> **Business Term**
> √ **PDCA cycle**
> A step-by-step process of planning, doing, checking, and acting.

people-based service providers such as lawn-care firms, plumbing and appliance repair firms, recruiting agencies, lawyers, and accountants. In fact, it is sometimes difficult even to assure consistency in the services provided by different employees of the same firm.

Quality programs are used to train employees to use statistical controls and problem-solving methods to reduce variations. The goal is to reach the highest possible performance standard so that customers can depend on consistently high quality each time they purchase a good or service.

Figure 6.5 The PDCA Cycle

The PDCA cycle allows employees and management to analyze cycle time and find areas for improvement.

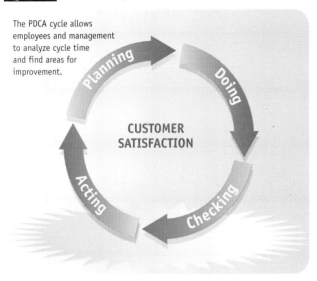

Total quality organizations apply the PDCA cycle to all business processes, from planning long-term strategies to adjusting short-term details of customer service.

Reducing Variation

All work processes, goods, and services have some degree of variation. This can result from such factors as poor market research, faulty machinery or outdated technology, inadequately trained employees, inefficient work procedures, and defective parts and materials from suppliers.

Product variation in the creation and marketing of services is strongly influenced by whether the service is equipment-based or people-based. Standardization of intangible products is simpler for equipment-based industries like computer time-sharing, motion picture theatres, automated car washes, and dry cleaners. Eliminating product variation is much more difficult for

Eliminating Waste

To economically produce and market goods and services that satisfy customers, quality companies concentrate on eliminating waste. Waste includes any work activity that does not add value to the product.

Wasted time and resources cost companies enormous amounts of money. The *costs associated with poor-quality products and production processes, such as scrap, rework, and loss of customers,* are called the **costs of quality**. These costs have internal and external dimensions. Most internal quality costs are measurable; examples include discarding unusable parts, reworking defective parts,

> **Business Term**
> √ **Costs of quality**
> Costs associated with poor-quality products and production processes, such as scrap, rework, and loss of customers.

inspecting and discarding faulty goods, redesigning inferior products, and retraining employees. External costs are more difficult to measure. They include lost sales, missed marketing opportunities, frequent repairs, negative word-of-mouth advertising, bad publicity, and loss of customers to competitors.

ISO 9000[21]

QUALITY ASSURANCE HAS evolved from the more traditional quality-control activity of inspecting and testing a percentage of products after the manufacturing process to the International Organization for Standardization's **ISO 9000** series of standards — described by the ISO as *the minimum requirements for a quality assurance* *system to create and promote worldwide quality standards.* Quality controls are inserted at each stage of the production process so that it becomes difficult to create a product that will be rejected upon final inspection. A continuous process of improvement ensures that if faults exist, they are identified and corrected prior to any further value being added.

The ISO 9000 series, first introduced in 1987 by the Switzerland-based International Standards Organization, were established to help companies improve operating efficiency and productivity and reduce the costs associated with inconsistent quality. ISO standards represent an international

> **Business Term**
>
> √ **ISO 9000**
>
> The International Standards Organization's minimum requirements for a quality assurance system to create and promote worldwide quality standards.

consensus on the essential features of a quality system to ensure the effective operation of any business, whether in the public or the private sector. ISO has now become a major element in supplier management strategy, especially for many leading Canadian companies like Ford of Canada and Nortel who rely heavily on the export market.

ISO standards apply to products as well as to anything related to them — software manuals that accompany software, for example.

Table 6.3 **ISO 9000 Standards**

Six standards are associated with the ISO 9000 series.

ISO 9000

is essentially a set of guidelines for the selection and use of the appropriate systems standards: ISO 9001, 9002, and 9003.

ISO 9001

is a model for quality assurance in design, development, production, installation, and servicing.

ISO 9002

is a model for quality assurance in production, installation, and servicing.

ISO 9003

is a model for quality assurance in final inspection and testing.

ISO 9004

is a multi-part guide for the application of the various elements of a quality management system.

ISO 9004-2

is a guideline for service industries used in conjunction with ISO 9001 and ISO 9002 for registration purposes.

The total ISO process is rigorous and can become quite complicated, but the registration process boils down to four areas:

- **Primary requirement.** The company must develop and maintain a consistent quality management system — a set of documented procedures containing the "best practice" of the company and available to all personnel as a single source record.

- **Secondary requirements.** ISO 9000 requirements include systems for customer-related activities such as contract review, document control, ensuring staff are issued with correct documentation and software required to perform tasks, and so on. These secondary requirements must be documented and met.

- **ISO examinations.** An independent assessor reviews the company procedures for ISO compliance. A written report either confirms compliance or highlights areas of deficiency.

- **Follow-up.** Once registration is achieved, auditors return twice a year to ensure the management system is operating effectively.

Figure 6.6 illustrates a typical registration process.

It can take a company as little as three months or as long as several years to comply with ISO standards. Costs include the time spent on the ISO registration by company personnel, consultants used to help with the development and implementation, and registration fees.

Will the quality of quality service stop at ISO 9000? Not if companies like General Motors, Ford, and Nortel have their way. "Ultimately, we'll be looking for zero defects in manufacturing," said a GM spokesperson. "It's a whole new concept, a paradigm shift for us. Rather than rewarding fewer [supplier] defects, we'll be looking for zero defects."[22]

> **WAKE-UP CALL**
>
> ISO 14000 environmental standards have been developed to help organizations achieve environmental and economic gains through the implementation of effective environmental management systems. The initial version of the 14000 series consists of six standards covering environmental management systems, environmental auditing, environmental performance evaluation, life cycle assessment, environmental labelling, and environmental aspects in products.

Figure 6.6 A Typical ISO 9000 Registration Process

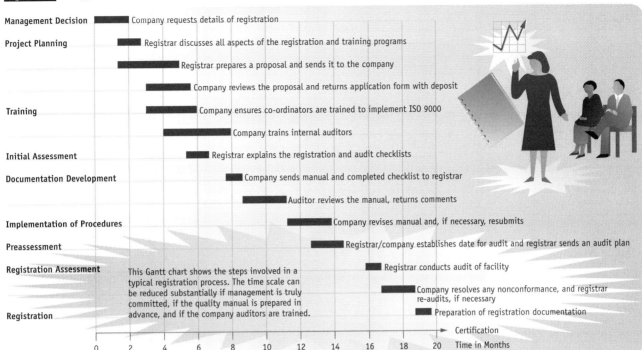

This Gantt chart shows the steps involved in a typical registration process. The time scale can be reduced substantially if management is truly committed, if the quality manual is prepared in advance, and if the company auditors are trained.

BENCHMARKING

I N TODAY'S GLOBAL marketplace, it's vital for Canadian companies to know how they compare not just to other Canadian companies but to ones from other parts of the world too. It is essential for both small and large companies to know their relative strengths and to have a quantitative basis on which to make improvements.

Most quality-conscious organizations rely on an important tool called **benchmarking**. This approach to creating a world-class organization consists of *identifying how business leaders achieve superior performance levels in their industry and continuously comparing and measuring a firm's own performance against these outstanding performers.*[23] It involves learning how the world's best goods and services are designed, produced, and marketed, and then using the information to help improve the company's own operations. The purpose of benchmarking is to achieve superior performance that results in a competitive advantage in the marketplace.

The five-phase sequence of applying benchmarking begins with planning (see Table 6.4). In this phase, participants select the companies they want to benchmark and determine how they will col-

lect the needed data. Next comes the analysis phase: team members study their own company practices and compare them with those of firms considered best in their industries. The third step, integration, begins with communicating the results of this comparison to the members of the organization. Goals and action plans then are developed to incorporate these superior practices. The fourth phase, action, involves putting these plans in place and monitoring their progress. The new processes are measured against the benchmarks, which are replaced as needed. In the final stage, maturity, the organization achieves leadership in its industry by integrating the best industry practices into all organizational functions.[24]

Planning and Analysis

The benchmarking process should focus on **critical success factors**, *activities and functions considered most important in gaining a competitive advantage and achieving long-term success.* These factors vary among organizations. For one firm, a critical factor might be satisfying customers with excellent service; for another, it might be bringing products to the marketplace faster.

> **Business Term**
>
> √ **Benchmarking**
>
> **Identifying how business leaders achieve superior performance levels in their industry and continuously comparing and measuring a firm's own performance against these outstanding performers.**

Table 6.4 Steps in the Benchmarking Process

Planning Phase

1. Select benchmarking candidates.
2. Identify organizations to use in making comparisons.
3. Select data-collection methods and collect needed data.

Analysis Phase

4. Identify gaps between company practices and industry-best practices.
5. Forecast future performance levels if identified benchmarks are implemented.

Integration Phase

6. Communicate benchmarking findings and gain acceptance.
7. Establish functional goals.
8. Develop action plans.

Action Phase

9. Implement plans and monitor progress.
10. Review benchmarks and replace as needed.

Maturity Phase

- Achievement of leadership position.
- Benchmarking fully integrated throughout the organization.

The ten steps to benchmarking can be applied to all business procedures and practices.

After deciding what to benchmark, a firm must identify other organizations recognized as performance leaders. In identifying leaders, companies may look internally, to competitors, or to firms in other industries. In *internal benchmarking*, comparisons are made between similar functions performed in different departments or divisions within the firm. *Competitive benchmarking* involves comparisons with direct product competitors. Reports in magazines, such as *Consumer Reports*, are well-known competitive benchmarks that compare competing brands of products, such as stereos or coffeemakers. The J.D. Power consumer satisfaction rankings compare initial quality assessments of auto purchasers. In *functional benchmarking*, firms make comparisons between the functions of firms in different industries.

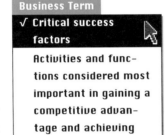

Business Term

√ **Critical success factors**

Activities and functions considered most important in gaining a competitive advantage and achieving long-term success.

Integration, Action, and Maturity

Firms use benchmark findings to implement improvements, such as setting new performance goals, changing current processes by adapting the best practices of the

benchmark partners, and measuring the progress of the new work practices. Benchmarking results should be communicated to employees so they understand the reasons for change, the opportunities for improvement, how they can help implement these changes, and how these changes affect the organization's overall business strategy.

For instance, a recent benchmarking project at Xerox concerned the company's cost centres. Management wanted to remake them into money-making profit centres. Employees at the Business Systems Group's logistics and distribution cost centre established benchmarks by gathering data on how to operate a successful profit centre. Information sources included vendors, other companies with similar cost centres, and noncompeting firms in various industries. This information was used to establish market values for the functions that centre employees performed. Based on these values, the staff negotiated service levels with managers of Xerox departments, who used the services of the centre and then developed level-of-service targets. Finally, the centre began marketing its services to outsiders. Within two years, this external business began generating a profit.

Many firms strive for a *zero defects* standard as a performance goal. H.J. Heinz production facilities use an error-free standard of 99.9997 percent, which translates into 3.4 defects per million units. Xerox uses a standard of 1 mistake per 1000 transactions recorded by its accounting department, and it is working toward a goal of 1 mistake per 1 million.

Today, benchmarking is a major component of most firms' quality programs. AT&T, Metropolitan Life, IBM, and thousands of other large and small firms use benchmarking as a standard tool for measuring quality. Increased interest in benchmarking has spawned a number of associations, councils, and specialized consulting firms.

ENCOURAGING EMPLOYEE INVOLVEMENT

BOOSTING CUSTOMER SATISFACTION and promoting companywide quality is usually dependent on **employee involvement**, *practices that motivate employees to perform their jobs better through empowerment, training, and teamwork* (see Figure 6.7). The idea behind employee involvement is to unleash the energy, creativity, and talents

PROBE BENCHMARKING

A good example of a benchmarking program is PROBE (**Pro**moting **B**usiness **E**xcellence), which was first introduced in Canada in December of 1996. It has been in existence and used widely throughout Europe since the early 1990s, and now includes more than 16 countries and 1000 companies from around the world. The PROBE benchmarking program was developed by IBM and is sponsored by the Quebec Alliance of Manufacturers and endorsed by Industry Canada: "We have to encourage Canadian business —

especially small and medium-sized businesses — to reach world-class status. In this regard, PROBE is very useful as an entry level benchmarking tool," says Margaret McCuaig-Johnston, Director-General of Manufacturing and Process Technologies at Industry Canada. At a cost of about $4000, the PROBE benchmarking process includes:

- The assignment of a PROBE facilitator

- The establishment of a multi-level, multi-function project team

- A comprehensive self-assessment covering all areas of the operation

- An analysis of the firm relative to other companies on the PROBE database

- An action plan to address key areas of improvement

- A 15-page report on the key organizational strengths and weaknesses

More information on PROBE can be found on their Web site: http://www.can.ibm.com/consult/probe.

Source: Adapted from PROBE, Advertising Supplement, "Benchmarking Key for Manufacturers," *The Globe and Mail*, April 9, 1997, C7. Reprinted by permission of Alliance of Manufacturers & Exporters Canada.

---

of all employees. Bringing out workers' best qualities makes them feel better about themselves and their work. It also helps them to feel a sense of ownership and thus take greater pride in their work.

Empowerment

As we discussed in Chapter 1, **empowerment** is *the practice of giving employees the authority to make decisions about their work without supervisory approval.* Empowered employees have increased responsibility for implementing the organization's vision and strategy. For example, in the production process, empowered assembly-line workers can

Figure 6.7

Empowerment, training, and teamwork all add to a firm's commitment to quality through employee involvement.

stop the line when they detect a problem and then find a way to fix it.

Empowerment taps the brainpower of all employees to find better ways of doing their jobs and executing their ideas. Organizations that empower employees nurture their capacity to improve and create. John Wilesmith of Rank Xerox summarizes the major benefit of empowerment as "getting more from your work force, tapping the wisdom and knowledge of every employee, believing that with every pair of hands you hire, you get a free brain."

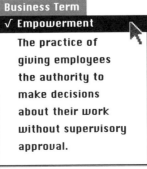

Business Term	Business Term
√ **Employee involvement**	√ **Empowerment**
Practices that motivate employees to perform their jobs better through empowerment, training, and teamwork.	The practice of giving employees the authority to make decisions about their work without supervisory approval.

The ISO international quality standard first gained a following with big manufacturing firms such as Ford Motor Company. But a growing list of smaller firms are now beginning to adopt the ISO benchmark. Many of these smaller firms receive their certification under the ISO 9002 quality system standard.

Mark O'Sullivan, who heads KPMG's ISO registration practice for Canada, estimates that about 20 to 25 percent of his clients now come from smaller service companies. "It's a way for a small business to 'level the playing field' by implementing the same types of quality as its biggest rivals," he says. These are companies like Merlin Motors Inc. in Saskatoon — the first Ford dealership in North America to become ISO 9002 approved. According to Al Elsasser, the head of quality for the family-owned business, it

Training

In order for an employee to become involved on even the most basic level, a thorough understanding of the job or process is required. Employee training provides workers with a wide range of learning experiences. It begins with management sharing knowledge about the organization's visions, values, and strategies. To help identify with the purpose of their work, employees should be able to answer these questions:

- Who are our major competitors?

- What are our company's strengths and weaknesses compared with those of competitors?

- How are we performing in measures such as sales, profits, and market share?

- Who are our target customers?

- What are our customers' needs and expectations?

- How satisfied are our customers with our goods and services?

Teaching employees the technical skills needed to measure and monitor the quality of their work is another aspect of training. Technical training, which varies depending on employees' jobs, can involve learning how to use quality tools, such as statistical quality control and problem-solving methods, as well as learning more about customers' needs.

The importance of quality training is underscored by the huge investments organizations make in educating and developing employees. TQM training alone can cost anywhere from $300 000 for a company with fewer than 3000 employees to $12 million for a corporation with 13 000 workers.[25]

Business Term

√ **Team**

A small number of people with complementary skills who are committed to a common purpose, approach, and set of performance goals.

Business Term

√ **Quality circle**

A small group of employees from one work area or department who meet regularly to identify and solve problems.

Teamwork

The final component of employee involvement is teamwork. A **team** is *a small number of people with complementary skills who are committed to a common purpose, approach, and set of performance goals.* They all hold themselves mutually responsible and accountable for accomplishing their objectives. Quality organizations group employees into teams and teach them team-building skills. The value of these groups is that, by working collectively, employees achieve higher performance levels, respond more quickly, and become more flexible in meeting customer needs.

Three types of employee involvement teams are quality circles, cross-functional teams, and self-managed teams. A **quality circle**, an idea that originated in Japan, is *a*

was a way to build morale as well as improve quality. Elsasser also says that the designation helped establish a management system and focus the attention of its 80 employees on the primary goal of serving customers.

Another early adopter was Histovet Surgical Pathology, in Guelph, Ontario. Histovet is a research lab that analyzes tissue samples from veterinary clinics across North America. Co-owner,

Anne Wilcock (who is also a specialist in quality management at the University of Guelph), says that having a fail-safe system in place is essential because of the nature of their work: "When you are dealing with people's pets, there is no room for error." ISO 9002 also helped the company manage its growth. "We're experiencing high growth. We just wanted to make sure it was controlled growth," says Wilcock.

1. Using the discussion and examples in your textbook, list the advantages of a small business for instituting quality standards such as ISO.

Source: Adapted from Elizabeth Church, "Service Firms Follow the Flow to ISO," *The Globe and Mail*, August 24, 1998, B11. Reprinted with permission from The Globe and Mail.

small group of employees from one work area or department who meet regularly to identify and solve problems. A quality circle in one city's police department redesigned the headquarters' layout to provide a private area for detectives to use for conducting interviews. An employee group for camping equipment maker Coleman Co. suggested design improvements to a propane lamp valve that now saves the company $50 000 a year.

The second type of employee involvement team, the **cross-functional team**, involves employees from different departments who work on specific projects, such as developing a new product or solving a complex problem. A cross-functional team might include members from manufacturing and production, accounting, customer service,

Business Term

√ **Cross-functional team**

A group of employees from different departments who work on specific projects, such as developing a new product or solving a complex problem.

Business Term

√ **Self-managed team**

A group of employees who work with little or no supervision.

and other areas. Each member brings valuable and differing experience to the project.

The **self-managed team**, the final type of employee involvement team, is a group of employees who work with little or no supervision. Team members schedule their own work, are trained to do other employees' jobs, are responsible for the quality of their work, and are accountable for performance results. Self-managed teams have the advantage of requiring the company to have fewer layers of management to direct employee activities.

Depending on the objective of the task, teams can range in size from several employees in one work area to hundreds of employees from different company locations around the world. Chapter 9 discusses teamwork in greater detail.

SUMMARY OF LEARNING OUTCOMES

1. **Explain the importance of quality and customer satisfaction in achieving a competitive advantage.**

   Quality describes the degree of excellence or superiority of an organization's goods and services. Customer satisfaction is the concept of a good or service pleasing buyers because it has met their emotional needs and quality expectations. The true measure of quality is whether a business has satisfied its customers. Quality and customer satisfaction directly affect the bottom line and are crucial to an organization's continued existence, both domestically and internationally.

2. **Discuss the role of the organization and top management in applying total quality management (TQM).**

   Effective TQM requires a commitment and vision by the entire organization to add value for its customers and employees. Quality programs begin with the involvement of top managers who believe in the importance of quality and customer satisfaction. Managers should view their organizations as systems that use the knowledge and skills of all employees to improve quality. Managers are responsible for communicating the goals of total quality management to all staff members, and for encouraging them to improve themselves and take pride in their work.

3. **Relate TQM to various functions within an organization, including production, human resource management, marketing, technology, and financial management.**

   The quality movement started as an attempt to improve product quality by improving the production process through statistical quality control. Today, production control has evolved into a companywide quality assurance process that contains a series of controls at each stage of the production process. Improving production often means demanding better quality from suppliers. Applying TQM to human resource management involves motivating workers and offering helpful services. An effective motiva-

   tional technique centres on the concepts of internal and external customers. With TQM, customer satisfaction becomes a primary goal of marketing. TQM affects the marketing function in several ways, including product design, distribution strategy, promotion, and price. Effective information processes can support TQM programs by improving customer service and boosting employees' productivity. Applying TQM to financial management means setting clear quality goals and linking them to financial returns and employee compensation.

4. **Identify the major methods of securing feedback from customers, employees, and suppliers.**

   As a first step in boosting customer satisfaction, a company must compile feedback and measure its present performance. When measuring customer satisfaction, there may be gaps between actual quality and perceived quality. Some companies measure customer satisfaction by monitoring customers over a period of time. Many use toll-free telephone lines to obtain feedback. Effective managers take time to solicit and respond to employee feedback, either informally or formally, and to recognize skilled employees. Exchanging feedback with suppliers means thinking in terms of customer–supplier partnerships. Companies have started to demand higher levels of quality in their suppliers' products, and suppliers must comply if they want to maintain the business relationship.

5. **Describe how organizations can work toward continuous process improvement.**

   Continuous process improvement involves constantly studying work activities and, when necessary, making changes to improve their quality, timeliness, efficiency, and effectiveness. Continuous improvement efforts focus on improving quality by reducing cycle time, reducing variation, and eliminating waste. Re-engineering and the PDCA cycle are tools for identifying ways to reduce cycle time and errors.

6. Define ISO 9000 and explain its importance as a TQM strategy.

The ISO 9000 series of standards are the minimum requirements for a quality assurance system to create and promote worldwide quality standards. ISO standards are designed to ensure the effective operation of any business, whether in the public or the private sector, and represent an international consensus on the essential features of a quality system. Quality controls are inserted at each stage of the production process so that it becomes difficult to create a product that will be rejected upon final inspection. ISO has now become a major element in supplier management strategy for Canadian companies.

7. Define benchmarking and explain its contributions to quality and customer satisfaction.

Benchmarking is a process in which an organization continuously compares and measures itself against business leaders anywhere in the world to gain information that will help it improve its performance.

Benchmarking can be applied to all business procedures and practices. The process of benchmarking includes five key steps: planning, analysis, integration, action, and maturity. Today, benchmarking is a major component of many firms' quality programs.

8. Identify the components of employee involvement and their impact on quality and customer satisfaction.

Employee involvement refers to practices that motivate employees to perform their jobs better through empowerment, training, and teamwork. The idea behind employee involvement is to unleash the energy, creativity, and talents of all employees. Empowerment is the practice of giving employees the authority to make decisions about their work without supervisory approval. Employee training consists of a wide range of learning experiences. The value of teamwork is that, by working collectively, employees produce higher performance levels, respond more quickly, and become more flexible to customer needs.

Key Terms Quiz

quality assurance
customer satisfaction
total quality management (TQM)
PDCA cycle
re-engineering
cycle time
benchmarking

critical success factors
internal customers
quality circle
statistical quality control
cross-functional team
quality
continuous process improvement

self-managed team
costs of quality
external customers
ISO 9000
empowerment
employee involvement

1. The degree of excellence or superiority of an organization's goods and services.
2. The concept of a good or service pleasing buyers because it has met their emotional needs and quality expectations.
3. An approach that involves a commitment to quality in achieving world-class performance and customer satisfaction as a crucial strategic objective.
4. International standards for quality management and quality assurance.
5. A system of locating and measuring quality problems on production lines.
6. Organizations that buy or use another firm's good or service.
7. Employees or departments within an organization that depend on the work of other people or departments to perform their jobs.
8. The process of constantly studying and making changes in work activities to improve their quality, timeliness, efficiency, and effectiveness.
9. The time it takes to complete a work process or activity.

_____ 10. A process in which existing processes in the delivery chain are mapped out in detail, and technology is applied to key steps to reduce cycle time or errors.

_____ 11. A step-by-step process of planning, doing, checking, and acting.

_____ 12. The costs associated with poor quality, such as scrap, rework, and loss of customers.

_____ 13. The process in which an organization continuously compares and measures itself against business leaders.

_____ 14. Those factors most important in gaining a competitive advantage and achieving long-term success.

_____ 15. Practices that motivate employees to perform their jobs better through empowerment, training, and teamwork.

_____ 16. The practice of giving employees the authority to make decisions about their work without supervisory approval.

_____ 17. A small group of employees from one work area or department who meet regularly to identify and solve problems.

_____ 18. A group of employees from different departments who work on specific projects, such as developing a new product or solving a particular problem.

_____ 19. A group of employees who work together on projects with little or no supervision.

_____ 20. Repeating good performance on every contract through a system of documented procedures.

Other Important Terms

competitive benchmarking
feedback
functional benchmarking
gaps

internal benchmarking
mass customization
return on quality
team

value-adding chain
zero defects

Review Questions

1. Define the concepts of quality and customer satisfaction.
2. How does total quality management help an organization compete more effectively?
3. Why is it important for senior management to support quality programs?
4. Distinguish between external customers and internal customers.
5. How can a firm determine whether it is satisfying its customers?
6. What is meant by customer–supplier partnerships?
7. What are the goals of continuous process improvement?
8. Explain the differences between the ISO 9000 system of quality assurance and benchmarking as TQM tools.
9. What criteria might a firm use to choose a suitable benchmark partner?
10. How can managers encourage employee involvement?

Discussion Questions

1. Explain some of the TQM policies and strategies that have made companies like Ford, Pacific Western Brewing Company, and Nortel successful international exporters.

2. Apply continuous process improvement to a service or procedure at your college or university. At the present time, does this service satisfy customers as much as it could? If not, why not? How might you analyze and resolve any problems?

3. Identify an organization in your city or area that you consider to be a world-class competitor in terms of quality and customer satisfaction. Defend your choice.

4. In designing its Aurora car, Oldsmobile attempted a new approach to product development. It created assembly-line "stop stations" where groups of five employees work at their own pace to bolt the Aurora body together. Helping the three-year development process was a rotating group of 50 hourly workers and engineers. In the final stages, Oldsmobile formed another group comprised of employees from marketing, public relations, engineering, and manufacturing, as well as several Oldsmobile dealers. This group developed a dealer training program and an advertising campaign for the Aurora. Relate the Aurora product-development process to the chapter's discussion of benchmarking, empowerment, training, and teamwork.

5. Choose two companies that have active total quality management programs (possibilities include such firms as IBM, Ford, and Nortel). Compare the various initiatives involved in each company's programs. How are they alike? How do they differ?

6. Choose a company in your area that is ISO 9000–approved. Find out if and how ISO has been helpful to them in selling their product or service within Canada and abroad.

Answers to Key Terms Quiz

1. quality 2. customer satisfaction 3. total quality management (TQM) 4. ISO 9000 5. statistical quality control 6. external customers 7. internal customers 8. continuous process improvement 9. cycle time 10. re-engineering 11. PDCA cycle 12. costs of quality 13. benchmarking 14. critical success factors 15. employee involvement 16. empowerment 17. quality circle 18. cross-functional team 19. self-managed team 20. quality assurance

Notes

1. Based on personal discussion with Ford Motor Co. of Canada Ltd.; and Greg Keenan, "Ford Team Puts Savings in Driver's Seat," *The Globe and Mail*, January 3, 1997, B7. Reprinted with permission from The Globe and Mail.

2. See, for example, James Martin, *The Great Transition* (New York: American Management Association, 1995), 242–43.

3. Louis Kraar, "Korea Goes for Quality," *Fortune*, April 18, 1994, 153.

4. Adapted from M. Dale Beckman, David L. Kurtz, and Louis E. Boone, *Foundations of Marketing*, 6th Cdn. ed. (Toronto: Dryden, 1997), 440.

5. Lawrence Surtees, "Next Nortel Chief to Roam Wider Circuits," *The Globe and Mail*, April 21, 1997, B1–B2.

6. Quality Management Institute Inc. (QMI), Advertising Supplement, "Quality Becomes Job One for Many Canadian Companies," *The Globe and Mail*, December 16, 1996, 1.

7. QMI, Advertising Supplement, "ISO for Me, ISO for You," *The Globe and Mail*, December 16, 1996, 4.

8. Angus Reid survey, conducted for Royal Bank Human Resources, "Workplace 2000 Under Construction: A Snapshot of the New Reality," 1996.

9. Colleen Barrett, "Coworkers Are Customers, Too," *Sales & Marketing Management*, July 1994, 31–32.

10. Rod McQueen, "Canada's 50 Best Managed Private Companies: Integrated Communications and Entertainment Inc.," *The Financial Post*, December 14–16, 1996, 34.

11. Rod McQueen, "Canada's 50 Best Managed Private Companies: Reliable Parts," *The Financial Post*, December 14–16, 1996, 47.

12. Rod McQueen, "Canada's 50 Best Managed Private Companies: Birchwood Automotive Group," *The Financial Post*, December 14–16, 1996, 20.

13. Stephanie Barlow, "Voice of Reason," *Entrepreneur*, March 1993, 52.

14. Judith H. Dobrzynsk, "How to Cope with Message Overload," *The Globe and Mail*, May 2, 1996, B11.

15. Angus Reid survey, conducted for Royal Bank Human Resources, "Workplace 2000 Under Construction: A Snapshot of the New Reality," 1996.

16. Louis E. Boone, *Quotable Business* (New York: Random House, 1992), 113.

17. Angus Reid survey, conducted for Royal Bank Human Resources, "Workplace 2000 Under Construction: A Snapshot of the New Reality," 1996.

18. Rod McQueen, "The 50 Best Managed Private Companies: Carlyle Computer Products," *The Financial Post*, December 14–16, 1996, 21.

19. Cyndee Miller, "TQM Out; Continuous Process Improvement In," *Marketing News*, May 9, 1994, 5, 20.

20. Michael Hammer, "Reengineering Work: Don't Automate, Obliterate," *Harvard Business Review*, July–August 1990, 104–12.

21. This section is based on various companies and organizations, Advertising Supplement, "Canada & ISO 9000," *The Globe and Mail*, December 16, 1996, 1–5.

22. Quality Management Institute Inc. (QMI), Advertising Supplement, "Quality Becomes Job One for Many Canadian Companies," *The Globe and Mail*, December 16, 1996, 2.

23. Susanne Hatherley, "Benchmarking for the Best Reasons," *Business Victoria*, April 1994, 12.

24. Louis E. Boone and Dianne Wilkins, "Benchmarking at Xerox: A Case Study," *Proceedings of the Academy of Business Administration London International Conference*, June 1994.

25. Rahul Jacob, "TQM: More than a Dying Fad?" *Fortune*, October 18, 1993, 66–72.

Management: Empowering People to Achieve Business Objectives

d~Code, "think-tank" consulting firm, Toronto

What does d~Code tell its private sector clients about human resources?

- Provide stability through constant change.
- Provide employability not employment.
- Provide calculated, risk-taking environments.
- Provide fulfilment.
- Provide opportunities for cross-generational co-operation.

The Organization and Its Management

After studying this chapter, you should be able to

1. Discuss the need for organizational structure, and list the steps involved in the organizing process.
2. Evaluate each of the five basic forms of organization, and explain the differences between new-style and old-style organizational structures.
3. Explain the impact of downsizing, delayering, and outsourcing on today's organizations.
4. Identify the skills required for managerial success.
5. Explain the concept of leadership, and identify the three basic leadership styles.
6. Describe the role of intrapreneurship in modern organizations.
7. List the steps in the decision-making process, and contrast programmed and nonprogrammed decisions.
8. Discuss the importance of time management.

It's a Matter of Trust[1]

In the early 1990s, Domtar Inc., a paper products company based in Montreal, was drowning in a sea of red tape and red ink. According to Soosan Daghighi, assistant dean of executive programs at the University of Toronto, Domtar was a traditional hierarchical Canadian organization with the usual signs of *rigor mortis*.

If the company was to have any chance to survive, it would have to restructure its organization and totally rethink its business strategy. In their plan for survival, senior management at Domtar decided that this was every employee's problem and thus everyone should be involved in the solution. They wanted employees at all levels to be involved in developing ideas to improve customer satisfaction, responsiveness to market changes, and profitability.

Since the early 1990s, Domtar has been gradually moving away from a bureaucratic "telling" structure to a more team-oriented "learning" company. For example, over 1000 employees have attended a week-long training seminar developed by the University of Toronto and the University of Sherbrooke. Here, there is no time for doodling or daydreaming. By the end of one week, each

employee is expected to come up with an idea to save the company $10 000 by either cutting expenses or increasing revenues. This one program alone has boosted Domtar's net income by $20 million in less than two years.

Stan Jacobson, a general manager in Toronto, says that the success of the Domtar transformation will take time to "develop a critical mass" and will depend on trust between managers and employees: "If they don't trust that I'm really giving them the responsibility and the authority and I don't trust they can make the decisions, this is never going to work."

Managers and workers alike at Domtar are pleased with its management strategy. Employees and managers are working together to reduce absenteeism and downtime, and as of 1996 the company was back in the black.

Figure 7.1 If you don't know the meaning, please see the answer on page 185.

CHAPTER OVERVIEW

MIKE HARRIS, Pat Quinn, and Michael Cowpland are all managers. In 1998, Harris was the Premier of Ontario, Quinn the President of the Vancouver Canucks hockey club, and Cowpland the Chief Executive Officer of Corel Corporation. Managers preside over organizations as diverse as Domtar, the University of British Columbia, Toronto's Hospital for Sick Children, and your local Tim Hortons donut shop.

The importance of effective management to organizational success cannot be overestimated. Analyses of small business failures usually list poor management as one of the leading causes. When asked about their career objectives, many students in an introductory business course will reply, "I want to be a manager."

In this chapter, we will examine the meaning of management and its universal applications. First, we will identify the three levels of management in a typical or traditional organization and will discuss a few international management issues. We will look at the different types of organizational structures and how the architecture of these structures has changed and is changing to meet the needs of the new Canadian economy. We will also outline the current trends of downsizing, delayering, and outsourcing; the skills required for managerial success; and the process of managerial decision making. Finally, we will examine the

importance of effective time management, and we will discuss new career opportunities for displaced managers.

MANAGEMENT PRINCIPLES ARE UNIVERSAL

MANAGEMENT *is the process of achieving organizational objectives in an effective and efficient manner through planning, organizing, leading, and controlling.* This definition has two important concepts:[2]

1. The four functions of planning, organizing, leading, and controlling, which were first introduced in Chapter 4.

2. The attainment of organizational goals in an effective and efficient manner. Effectiveness is the extent to which an organization achieves its stated objectives: that is, do managers "walk the talk" or do what they say they are going to do? Efficiency is the use of minimum resources — people, technology, money, and raw materials — to produce a planned objective.

Getting things done with people and other resources and providing direction and leadership are what managers do. These activities are universal and apply to

Business Term

✓ **Management**

The process of achieving organizational objectives in an effective and efficient manner through planning, organizing, leading, and controlling.

not-for-profit organizations as well as profit-seeking firms. The local library administrator, the head of the Salvation Army, and a Boy Scout troop leader all perform managerial functions similar to those performed by their counterparts in industry. Service-oriented agencies benefit from effective management as much as profit-oriented ones do.

ORGANIZATIONAL STRUCTURE

The Management Pyramid

The local Pizza Pizza franchise has a very simple formal organization — an owner/manager, an assistant manager, and a few part-time employees. By contrast, large organizations have a complex managerial structure. Toyota, for example, has a chairman of the board, a president, four executive vice presidents, six senior managing directors, and twelve managing directors, as well as a board of auditors. Are all of these people managers? The answer is yes, since they are all engaged in combining human and other resources to achieve company objectives.

Chapter 5 pointed out that a firm's management can be divided into three categories: top management, middle management, and supervisory management. Although all three categories contain managers, each level stresses different activities. **Top management** *is the highest level of the management hierarchy and is staffed by executives who develop long-range plans and interact with the public and outside entities, like the government.* **Middle management** is more involved than top management in specific operations within the organization. Middle managers are *responsible for developing detailed plans and procedures to implement the general plans of top management.*

Supervisory management, or *first-line management*, includes people who are directly *responsible for the details*

> **Business Term**
> √ **Top management**
> The highest level of the management hierarchy, staffed by executives who develop long-range plans and interact with the public and outside entities, like the government.

> **Business Term**
> √ **Middle management**
> Those people responsible for developing detailed plans and procedures to implement the general plans of top management.

of assigning workers to specific jobs and evaluating performance daily or even hourly. Supervisory management is the level at which most people obtain their first managerial experience. They may have such job titles as supervisor, chairperson, department head, group leader, or section chief. In each case, the position involves co-ordinating the work of operative employees in accomplishing tasks assigned by middle management. The first-line manager is often as much a teacher, an expediter, and an assistant as a supervisor. Because she or he interacts continuously with the members of the work team, effective human relations skills are extremely important at this level of management.

Effective communication links must exist among all levels of management. It is also important that each level be responsible for the decisions that legitimately should be made at that point in the organization.

At any level, managers need the ability to lead and motivate other people, the ability to work in a team, the skill to formulate and carry out long-range plans, the courage to take risks, and the ability to relate to others. The lack of some of these abilities often prevents people from moving up the managerial ladder.

> **Business Term**
> √ **Supervisory management**
> First-line management; those people directly responsible for the details of assigning workers to specific jobs and evaluating performance.

You have probably worked with managers who have years of experience and know their job or company inside out, but are ineffective managers. Lack of managerial skill or experience is a major cause of failure among small businesses.

ORGANIZATION

THE FUNCTIONS PERFORMED by managers in accomplishing the goals of the organization — planning, organizing, leading, and controlling — were discussed in Chapter 4. *Organizing* was defined as the means by which management blends human, technical, and material resources through a formal structure of tasks and authority. It is the process of arranging work, dividing it among employees, and co-ordinating it so plans can be carried out and objectives can be accomplished. Organizing can be seen in sports teams, social clubs, religious groups, and work activities. Even groups of animals — bees, ants, baboons, and beavers — have organization. An **organization** can be defined as *a structured grouping of people working together to achieve organizational objectives*. Three key elements are present in an organization: human interaction, goal-directed activities, and structure.

Business Term

✓ **Organization**

A structured grouping of people working together to achieve organizational objectives.

In the organizing process, managers first determine the specific activities that are necessary to meet the organization's plans and objectives (see Figure 7.2). Next, they group these activities into a logical structure, assign them to specific employees, allocate resources for their completion, and co-ordinate the activities of the assigned personnel. Finally, they evaluate the results and make changes as needed.

For a small business, the formal steps of organizing are relatively simple. The owner/manager of the local dry-cleaning outlet employs a few people to sell the outlet's services, launder and dry-clean clothing, and make deliveries. The owner usually handles purchasing tasks (detergents, plastic wrappers, etc.). The owner also assigns jobs to employees and directs business operations in pursuit of profits and growth. The tasks of co-ordinating work schedules and training new employees are relatively uncomplicated. Should one employee prove less effective in operating the check-out terminal, he or she can be reassigned to one of the cleaning tasks.

But as a company grows, the need for organization increases. With increased size comes specialization and more employees. Rather than a single salesperson, the manager works with a sales force; rather than one bookkeeper, an entire accounting department is utilized. The large number of personnel and the accompanying specialization make it impossible for one person to supervise

all operations. Some formal organization is therefore necessary.

Although a small firm experiences fewer organizational problems than a large one, both must have a formal structure to ensure that people perform tasks designed to accomplish company objectives. In a dry-cleaning company, for example, specific duties are assigned to wrappers, pressers, and other personnel.

As we have seen, the starting point in designing the appropriate organizational structure is to focus on the activities necessary to reach goals. Management analyzes the jobs to be performed and employs people who are both willing and qualified to perform the jobs. Co-ordinating workers' activities is another important responsibility, because employees must "pull together" if the firm is to operate smoothly.

A well-defined organizational structure also should contribute to employee morale. Employees who know what is expected on the job, who the team leader or supervisor is, and how their work contributes to organizational objectives are more likely to form a harmonious, loyal work force.

Figure 7.2 **Steps in the Organizing Process**

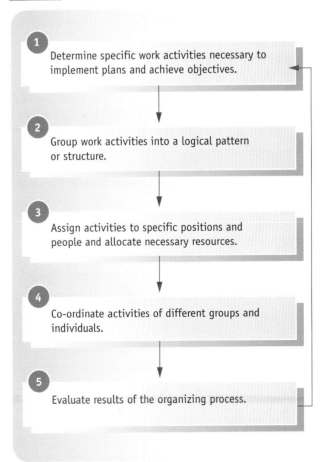

1 Determine specific work activities necessary to implement plans and achieve objectives.

2 Group work activities into a logical pattern or structure.

3 Assign activities to specific positions and people and allocate necessary resources.

4 Co-ordinate activities of different groups and individuals.

5 Evaluate results of the organizing process.

A company objective of "providing customers with quality products at competitive prices" does not tell a mechanic that production machinery should be inspected regularly and defects repaired. Company objectives are often broad and do not specify individual work activities. Consequently, they must be divided into specific goals for each employee in the organization.

Hierarchy of Objectives

A *hierarchy* or *classification of organizational objectives* extends from the overall objectives of the entire firm to specific objectives of the firm to specific objectives established for each employee. The broader goals of increasing profitability, sales, market dominance, and service are broken into objectives for each division, factory, department, work group or team, and employee. Once this has been accomplished, each person can see his or her contribution to the overall organizational goals. The number of levels in the hierarchy depends on the size and complexity of the firm. Smaller firms usually have fewer levels than larger ones. But as we will see later on, large firms are quickly shedding their corporate levels in their struggle for efficiency, productivity, and profits.

Departmentalization

A key functional characteristic of the organizational structure is **departmentalization**, *the subdivision of work activities into units within the organization.* Employees are grouped into units or departments. This lets individuals specialize in certain jobs and thus become efficient in them. For example, a marketing department may be headed by a marketing vice president and may include sales, advertising, and marketing research. A human resource department may include recruitment, training, employee benefits, and industrial relations.

> **Business Term**
> √ **Departmentalization**
> The subdivision of work activities into units within the organization.

Five major forms of departmentalization exist. They are

- Functional (e.g., marketing, sales, administration, finance)

- Product (e.g., coffee, soap, clothing, computers, software)

- Geographic (e.g., Western Canada, Eastern Canada, United States, Europe)

- Customer (e.g., retail, wholesale, business)

- Process (e.g., research, testing, cutting, painting)

Figure 7.3 shows departments organized according to functions performed, geographic regions covered, and types of customers served. Deciding what forms to use involves balancing the advantages and disadvantages of each. The experience and judgement of top management come into play in such decisions.

It is not unusual for several of these forms to be used in a single organization. But the most common form is

Figure 7.3 Various Forms of Departmentalization Used in One Company

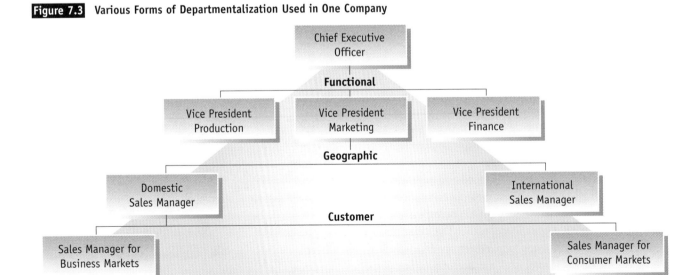

Figure 7.4 Organization Chart for a National Hockey League Team

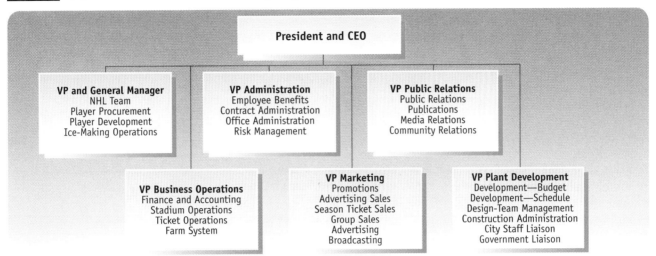

functional departmentalization — especially at the upper level of larger organizations. For example, large transportation companies such as Air Canada and CP Rail are likely to be functionally departmentalized (finance, personnel, administration, etc.) at the upper level of their organizational charts and then to branch out to geographic or regional departments (domestic, U.S., and overseas services, for example) at the middle management levels. A large manufacturing company, such as Bombardier Inc., would most likely branch out along product lines — for example, snowmobiles, aircraft, and urban transit equipment. Other manufacturers may instead rely on process departmentalization with separate departments for, say, cutting material, heat-treating it, forming it into final shape, and painting it.

Delegation

As the organization grows, the manager must assign part of her or his activities to subordinates or team members in order to have time to devote to managerial functions. *The act of assigning activities to others in the organization* is called **delegation**. Staff or team members to whom the tasks are assigned thus receive *responsibility*, or an obligation to perform those tasks. Along with responsibility goes *authority*, the power to make decisions and to act on them in carrying out responsibilities. Problems can arise if managers delegate responsibility without giving the necessary authority, too. Delegation of authority and responsibility make the subordinate accountable to

the supervisor. *Accountability* means that employees are responsible for the results of how they perform their assignments and that they must accept the consequences of their actions.

In larger organizations, authority and responsibility tend to move downward as supervisors delegate them to subordinates. However, accountability moves up the ranks. The final accountability for employees' performance rests with their managers, who in turn are accountable to their bosses. So it is crucial for managers to select the best-qualified employees when delegating.

Organization Charts

The authority and responsibility relationships of most organizations are shown in the *organization chart*. In order to know what and where things are being done, large organizations require a blueprint showing the division of work, chain of command, and departmentalization of activities. This provides all employees with a visual statement of these relationships, enabling them to see how their work relates to the overall operation of the company and to whom they report. Figure 7.4 shows, for example, the organizational chart for a National Hockey League team.

Because the organization chart specifies each area of responsibility and authority, it also can help managers co-ordinate activities. However, since the chart reflects the organization at only one point in time, it should be updated periodically to reflect changes.

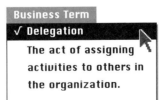

Business Term
√ **Delegation**
The act of assigning activities to others in the organization.

A NEW BREED OF MIDDLE MANAGER

As we learned in the opening Domtar segment, the early to mid-1990s was a period of turmoil and change for many Canadian companies. Bureaucratic corporate structures began to crumble as companies welcomed a new era with leaner, more customer-responsive organizational structures.

The traditional focus of the middle manager was on planning, controlling, and monitoring, and these functions worked well in a static economy. But the changing economy of the 1990s has broadened the role of the middle manager and has begun to create a demand for a new kind of skill set: "The middle managers who are in demand now are a different breed from a decade ago," says Carolyn Farquhar, a research associate at the Conference Board of Canada.

Based on a 1998 study of five large Canadian corporations, the Conference Board identified five distinct roles for this new kind of middle manager:

→ **Action-oriented.** The new middle manager must be able to translate business strategy into action. Middle managers bridge the gap between strategic plans and operations by testing different assumptions and providing feedback on options that work.

→ **Agents of change.** A primary responsibility of the new middle manager is to help ease people through changes they face. This change-agent role emphasizes coaching employees in a number of areas, from concerns

TYPES OF ORGANIZATIONAL STRUCTURE

ORGANIZATIONS CAN BE classified into five main types according to the nature of their internal authority relationships: line, line-and-staff, committee, matrix, and network or virtual organization. These categories are not mutually exclusive. In fact, most of today's business organizations combine elements of one or more types of organizational structure.

Line Organization

Line organization, the oldest and simplest organizational structure, is *based on a direct flow of authority from the chief executive to subordinates.* The line organization is simple. The *chain of command* — the set of relationships that indicates who gives direction to whom and who reports to whom — is clear, so "buck-passing" is extremely difficult. Decisions can be made quickly because the manager can act without consulting anyone other than an immediate supervisor.

> **Business Term**
> ✓ **Line organization**
> Organizational structure based on a direct flow of authority from the chief executive to subordinates.

> **Business Term**
> ✓ **Line-and-staff organization**
> Organizational structure that combines the direct flow of authority present in the line organization with staff departments that serve, advise, and support the line departments.

But an obvious defect exists within line organizations: each manager has complete responsibility for a number of activities and cannot possibly be an expert in all of them. This defect is very apparent in medium- and large-sized firms, where the pure line form fails to provide specialized skills so vital to modern industry. Executives in this type of organization become overburdened with administrative details and paperwork and have little time for planning.

Line-and-Staff Organization

The **line-and-staff organization** *combines the direct flow of authority present in the line organization with staff departments that serve, advise, and support the line departments.* Line departments are involved directly in decisions affecting the operation of the organization. Staff departments lend specialized technical support.

The major difference between a line manager and a staff manager is in authority relationships. A *line manager* forms a part of the main line of authority that flows throughout the organization. Often line managers are involved directly with

such as how to obtain resources for a new project, to how they can develop their career plans.

→ **Opportunists.** The new middle manager must know how to broker opportunities for innovation or for collaboration across departments. This role emphasizes the ability to bring teams together — a vital skill for the future, according to the Conference Board.

→ **Communicators.** The new middle manager is often the source of essential information about customers, suppliers, or industry departments. But the mere corporate sharing of this information is not good enough. The new manager must be able to add value and to leverage that information to facilitate teamwork, production, and efficiency.

→ **Project managers.** Most team projects are no longer simple add-ons to the normal work. Many team projects are now interconnected — from production to finance to sales. A middle manager's role is to make sure that team projects are coordinated to meet departmental/functional objectives and time frames.

According to the Conference Board, this new type of middle manager is making a comeback. It could very well be the start of a new trend.

Do you have the conceptual, human, and technical skills to work as a new breed of middle manager? We suggest you get started by completing our "Management Aptitude Questionnaire" (Figure 7.8 on page 173).

Source: Adapted from Margot Gibb-Clark, "Middle Managers Make Comeback," *The Globe and Mail*, September 24, 1998, B15. Reprinted with permission from The Globe and Mail.

the critical functions of production, finance, or marketing. A *staff manager* provides information, advice, or technical assistance to aid line managers. They do not possess the authority to give orders or to compel line managers to take action, although they do have the necessary line authority to supervise their own departments (see Figure 7.5). Examples of staff managers in medium- and large-sized organizations include the director of research, the advertising manager, the legal counsel, and the director of engineering.

Figure 7.5 **Line-and-Staff Structure for a Manufacturing Company**

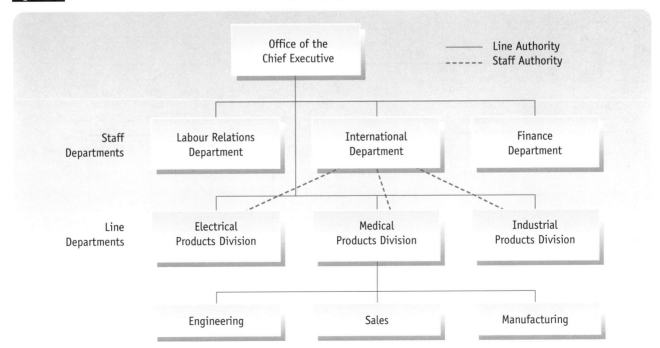

Committee Organization

Committee organization is the organizational structure in which authority and responsibility are held jointly by a group of individuals rather than by a single manager. It typically is used as part of the regular line-and-staff structure.

The committee structure often exists throughout the organization. For example, various firms have used the Office of the CEO concept, in which the duties of the chief executive officer are shared among two or more executives. Typically, the responsibilities are split along functional lines, with one person handling manufacturing, another marketing, and so on. Committees also are used in other areas, such as new-product development. The new-product committee may include managers from such areas as accounting, engineering, finance, manufacturing, marketing, and research. Including representatives from all areas involved in developing new products generally improves planning and company morale because diverse perspectives — production, marketing, and finance — are considered.

But committees tend to be slow and conservative, and decisions often are made through compromise based on

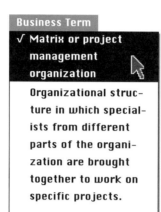

Business Term

√ **Matrix or project management organization**

Organizational structure in which specialists from different parts of the organization are brought together to work on specific projects.

conflicting interests rather than by choosing the best alternative. The definition of a camel as "a horse designed by a committee" provides an apt description of some committee decisions.

Matrix Organization

A growing number of organizations are using the **matrix** or **project management organization** — *a structure in which specialists from different parts of the organization are brought together to work on specific projects* (see Figure 7.6). Like the committee form, the matrix organization typically is used as a subform within the line-and-staff structure.

The matrix organization is built around specific projects or problems. Employees with different areas of expertise gather to focus on these specific problems or unique technical issues. An identifying feature of such organizations is that some members of the organization report to two superiors instead of one. Project members receive instructions from the project manager (horizontal authority), but maintain membership in their permanent functional departments (vertical authority). The term

Figure 7.6 Matrix Organization

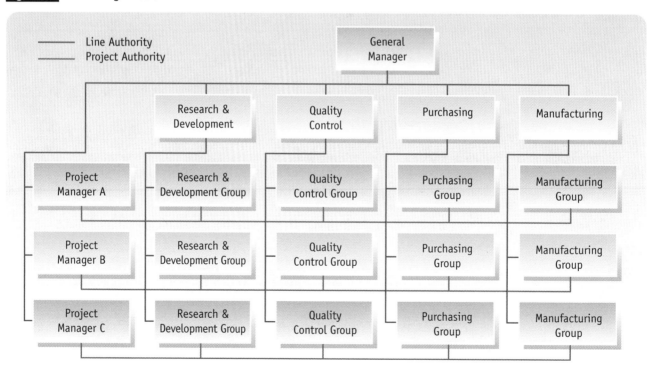

matrix comes from the cross-hatching of the horizontal authority–responsibility flow over the vertical flows of the traditional line-and-staff organization.

The major benefits of the matrix structure lie in its flexibility and the ability it offers to focus resources on major problems or projects. However, the project manager must be able to mould individuals from diverse parts of the organization into an integrated team, and team members must be comfortable working for more than one boss.

The project-team approach offers built-in flexibility for adapting to a changing business environment. It also provides an outlet for employees' creativity and initiative by gathering hand-picked groups of employees — and perhaps even outside contractors — who possess the right skills for a particular project. When the problem is solved or the project ends, the group dissolves and the employees return to their regular jobs. In the future, as the need arises, they may become part of a different group assembled to solve a different problem. General Electric CEO John Welch is a strong advocate of this approach. Says Welch, "What we value most is boundary-lessness. It's the ability to work up and down the hierarchy, across functions and geographies, and with suppliers and customers."[3]

Network or Virtual Organization

A **network** or **virtual organization** *is one in which the major functions are broken up into strategic business units (SBUs) or companies that are brokered by a small headquarters or core organization.* Two basic types of virtual corporation are the federal organization and the shamrock organization, illustrated in Figure 7.7. The corporate core purchases or outsources functions such as manufacturing, production, and R&D. This central hub is expected to promote competition among its business units or outside suppliers, which act like profit centres.

Compaq Computer Corporation and the Bank of Montreal's Mbanx are examples of businesses that are increasingly becoming virtual because of their growing reliance on alliances with outside companies and part-

> **Business Term**
>
> √ **Network or virtual organization**
>
> Organizational structure in which the major functions are broken up into strategic business units (SBUs) or companies that are brokered by a small headquarters or core organization.

WHERE
The Jobs Are

James W. Moir, President and CEO, Maritime Medical Care Inc., Halifax

Virtual Hospitals

"Telemedicine is a new venture for us. PC-based, desktop hardware will deliver medical services through two-way, interactive video communications. Rather than be in the office of a specialist at some centre of excellence in a major city, you can sit in your GP's office in the Northwest Territories and watch your GP conduct the consultation via two-way desktop interactive. Nurses in remote areas would be able to handle diagnosis and treatment if they were electronically linked to GPs. The specialist can see you and the GP and even conduct a physical exam.

We're creating virtual hospitals and we'll be conducting remote operations. Surgeons will wear gloves that are wired to robots in other locations. The surgeon sees the robot and the patient on a wall-sized screen. The robot emulates the surgeon, but if the surgeon's hands are shaky, the robot will make the correction.

Those in technology have tended to seek opportunity where the barriers are easier to break down, but this [health care] is the last frontier."

ners. Some experts are predicting that the virtual corporation, typified by the faceless Mbanx, will become the predominant organizational structure of the next millennium since network organizations

- Promote flexibility and customer focus.

- Reduce bureaucratic inefficiencies since staff overhead and administrative costs are much lower relative to a traditional organizational structure.

- Improve an organization's global competitiveness.

- Promote efficiencies through outsourcing. Most of the workers are contractors whose services are purchased on an as-needed basis.

COMPETITIVE STRATEGY

CHARACTERISTICS OF A VIRTUAL COMPANY

In their book *Agile Competitors and Virtual Organizations*, Steven L. Goldman, Roger N. Nagel, and Kenneth Preiss point to the following characteristics of a virtual company:

→ It is created to take advantage of a specific, customer-driven, time-based opportunity.

→ It is disbanded when the opportunity ceases to exist.

→ Its main raison d'être is customer needs. The purpose of a virtual company is to translate a well-defined market problem or need into an opportunity.

→ It relies on a connected web of alliances (e.g., partnerships, joint ventures, strategic alliances, new corporations, co-operative agreements).

→ It relies on mutual trust and teamwork. A virtual company is designed to disband at the hint of mistrust.

→ A guiding principle of the virtual corporation is to outsource its requirements rather than insource. Competition among suppliers is promoted and expected.

→ Selling duties are delegated to selling agents or resellers.

→ Its corporate structure is linked by a web of prequalified partners or associates. This web of associates replaces core functions such as manufacturing, warehousing, and supplies.

→ More aggressive virtual corporations have floating members rather than fixed membership.

→ It shifts the emphasis from in-house knowledge to outside expertise.

→ It uses loads of technology to connect internationally.

Source: Adapted from Steven L. Goldman, Roger N. Nagel, and Kenneth Preiss, *Agile Competitors and Virtual Organizations* (New York: Van Nostrand Reinhold, 1995). Reprinted by permission of the publisher.

Figure 7.7 Two Types of Virtual Corporations

a) Federal Model*

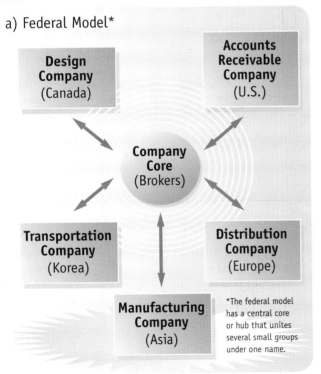

*The federal model has a central core or hub that unites several small groups under one name.

b) Shamrock Model

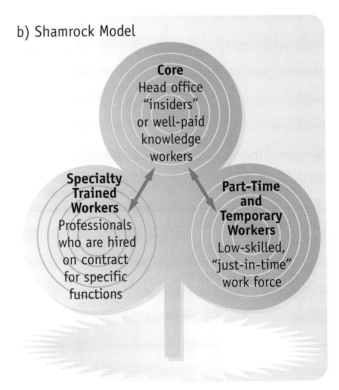

COMPETITIVE STRATEGY

HENRY MINTZBERG'S ORGANIZATIONS

Henry Mintzberg, one of Canada's foremost management gurus, has proposed an alternative framework of five basic forms of organization. There is no "one best" structure. A selected form would depend on the needs of the company and market-place.

The Machine Organization. Classic bureaucracy, highly formalized, specialized, and dependent on the standardization of work processes for co-ordination; common in stable and mature industries with mostly ration-alized, repetitive operating work.

The Entrepreneurial Organization. Nonelaborated, flexible structure, closely and personally controlled by the chief executive, who co-ordinates by direct supervision; common in start-up and turnaround situations as well as in small business.

The Professional Organization. Organized to carry out expert work in relatively stable settings, hence emphasizing the standardization of skills and the services to be carried out by autonomous and influential specialists with administrators serv-ing for support more than exercis-ing control.

The Adhocracy Organization. Organized to carry out expert work in highly dynamic settings, where the experts must work co-operatively in project teams, co-ordinating the activities by mutual adjustment in flexible, usually matrix, forms of structure; found in high-technology industries and product development situations.

The Diversified Organization. Any organization split into semi-autonomous divisions to serve a diversity of markets, with the "headquarters" relying on financial control systems to standardize the outputs of the divisions.

Source: Reprinted with the permission of The Free Press, a Division of Simon & Schuster from THE RISE AND FALL OF STRATEGIC MANAGEMENT: Reconceiving Roles for Planning, Plans, Planners by Henry Mintzberg, 397–98. Copyright © 1994 by Henry Mintzberg.

Comparing the Five Forms of Organization

In summary, Table 7.1 compares the five forms of organi-zation. Line organization is a form that has typically been used by smaller businesses. Line-and-staff and the newer matrix structures are the main forms of organizational structures for medium- and large-sized firms. In theory, they combine the line organization's rapid decision-mak-ing capability and effective, direct communication with the staff specialists' expert knowledge needed to direct diverse and widespread activities. Committee organiza-tion is used by large companies with several functional areas that need to be co-ordinated. It is also used to deal with special projects, like developing a new product. The matrix or product management organization has distinct advantages when used in combination with committed teams. The network or virtual corporation is the newest form of organizational structure used especially by many high-growth technology companies. This virtual concept lends itself to reduced labour and administrative costs in addition to increased flexibility.

CHANGES IN ORGANIZATIONAL STRUCTURES

> **THEY SAID IT**
>
> "The Times They Are a'Changin'"
>
> Singer/songwriter BOB DYLAN's classic 1960s tune

Major Trends

During the 1990s, the organizational structures of Cana-dian business were being affected by three major trends:

Technology. A few short years ago, managers at Mohawk Oil in Burnaby, BC, couldn't use e-mail or pick up their voice-mail messages when they were out of town. Today, that's all changed. Technology and innovation are central

Table 7.1 Five Forms of Organization

Advantages	Disadvantages
Line	
Simple and easy for both managers and subordinates to understand Clear delegation of authority and responsibility for each area Quick decisions Direct communication	No specialization Overburdening of top executives with administrative details
Line-and-staff	
Specialists to advise line managers Employees report to one superior	Conflict between line and staff unless relationships are clear Staff managers make only recommendations to line managers
Committee	
Combined judgement of several executives in diverse areas Improved morale through participation in decision making	Committees slow in making decisions Decisions are the result of compromises rather than a choice of the best alternative
Matrix	
Flexibility Provides method for focussing strongly on specific major problems or unique technical issues Provides means of innovation without disrupting regular organizational structure	Problems may result from employees being accountable to more than one boss Project manager may encounter difficulty in developing a cohesive team from diverse individuals recruited from various parts of the organization Conflict may arise between project managers and other department managers
Network or Virtual	
Company can focus on its core competency Global competitiveness Reduced labour costs Work-force flexibility and challenge Reduced administrative costs	Lack of hands-on control Weakened employee loyalty Lack of organizational control

to the company's business strategy.[4] Mohawk is typical of the Canadian business community. In the 1980s it was cheaper to use workers than machines — thus technology was a frill. But by the 1990s, labour was twice as expensive as technology, according to a 1995 Conference Board of Canada study. Almost overnight, technology had become a necessity. Canadian firms are now using technology to reduce labour and material costs and improve customer information.

Global Competition. During the 1970s and 1980s, Canada's productivity growth, especially in manufacturing, lagged behind that of almost every other major country. The signing of the Free Trade Agreement (1991) and the North American Free Trade Agreement (1994) (see Chapter 3) signalled the dawn of a new era in Canadian business. To compete in this new world economy, Canadian companies have had to restructure in an attempt to reduce labour costs and improve their productivity.

Demographics. David Foot and Daniel Stoffman, in their book *Boom, Bust & Echo*, clearly explain the Canadian

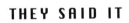

THEY SAID IT

"[S]tructure is best defined in terms of <u>departmentalization</u>, and <u>matrixes</u> and <u>committees</u> are best explained as methods of <u>co-ordinating activities</u> and <u>facilitating communication</u> across the departments in organizations. Matrixes and committees are not structures per se, but methods of horizontal co-ordination.... In reality, none of the organizations which claim to have matrix structures actually have organizational charts that look like Figure 7.6."

RON SHAY, Kwantlen University College

LESSONS FROM THE BEST

SLM'S CULTURAL EDGE

SLM Software Inc. is a Toronto company that sells software systems for electronic banking. Its 1998 revenues were in the $40 million range with at least 80 percent coming from outside Canada. Today, it has 500 or so employees who speak 15 languages (including several dialects) and operates in 35 countries on four continents.

In 1993, SLM's revenue was only $2.5 million, of which 30 percent came from outside Canada. Why has this small Canadian company been so successful in penetrating the world market? According to Govin Misir, SLM's Guyana-born president and CEO, "the company has incorporated cultural awareness into the way it does business." His golden rule: "If they stretch out their hand, I'll stretch out mine."

Here are some of the ways SLM makes cultural awareness part of doing business:

→ **Hiring.** Cultural awareness begins with hiring. Prospective employees are asked if they have had experience with cultures outside North America and whether they speak foreign languages. While such experience wouldn't be enough to get someone a job at SLM, it would give them an edge.

→ **Cultural Preparation.** Corporate multiculturalism goes beyond speaking in a customer's tongue. The company sends its more seasoned travellers abroad to find new markets and discover what is considered proper behaviour.

→ **Common Ground.** When they touch down on a new project, employees' first priority is to find common ground with the new customer. "It's like running a United Nations," says Yogi Bharratt, SLM's production controller and co-ordinator of a $4 million Iranian project.

→ **Cultural Awareness.** SLM trains its staff to understand and respect the cultural mores of clients. For example, employees are not to shake hands with women or drink alcohol in Tehran.

→ **Employee Respect.** The company keeps employees abroad only for short time-periods to minimize the chance of burnout.

→ **Coaching.** There are no briefing books or travel guides at SLM. It relies on informal conversations between employees — bolstered by mentoring and coaching from managers — to spread the unwritten words on conduct.

Source: Adapted from Tyler Hamilton, "SLM Builds U.S. Presence with Bankline Acquisition," *The Globe and Mail*, September 24, 1998, B6; Patrick Brethour, "Software Company Lands in Tehran," *The Globe and Mail*, October 16, 1996, B15. Reprinted with permission from The Globe and Mail.

---

demographic conundrum: "The baby boom resembles a rectangle while the corporate structure looks like a triangle or pyramid. ... We have been trying to promote a rectangle up a triangle, and it can't be done. The rectangle exists because a huge number of baby boomers entered the work force in the 1960s and 1970s. By the mid-1980s they were clogging up the corporate pyramid. There weren't enough openings for them at the top nor were there enough people for them to manage at the bottom."[5] The phenomenon of "plateauing," or career blocking, had begun.

The Restructuring Revolution

In recent years, Canada and every other industrialized country has seen the effects of the trends described above. Almost overnight, many of Canada's largest corporations, such as Domtar in our opening story, reshaped their organ-

izations into leaner, faster, and more efficient structures. Some companies, like IBM Canada, *delayered* their organization, going from some ten levels of corporate hierarchy to four or five. Other companies chose the **downsizing** route — simply *laying off employees across the board without changing the basic corporate structure.* Still others "re-engineered" their organization — they changed the whole process and structure of their business.

The effects of this 1990s management revolution were massive layoffs and plant closings and increased productivity.

> **Business Term**
> ✓ **Downsizing**
> Laying off employees across the board without changing the basic corporate structure.

Massive Layoffs and Plant Closings. Reports of layoffs and plant closings — in both the public and the private sectors — filled the media during the 1990s. Many hard-working Canadians feared for their jobs as thousands of employees at IBM Canada, The Royal Bank, Sears Canada, and the federal government — to name only a few major employers — were forced to look for new jobs. Restructuring was the main culprit. According to a Royal Bank study by economist Frank Sweet, 165 000 jobs, or 40 percent of all jobs lost between 1990 and 1992, were casualties of restructuring. In contrast, during the period 1981–82, only 9 percent of the total jobs lost were due to restructuring.[6] Table 7.2 cites a few examples of companies that cut massive numbers of jobs between 1995 and 1996.

Table 7.2 Job Deaths: Selected Examples, 1995–1996

Bank of Montreal	1400
Canadian National Railways	8700
Cara Operations	2850
CIBC	5700
The Thomson Group	5600

Productivity Increases. A new leaner and meaner corporate structure began to evolve. By the mid-1990s, new types of management structures had clearly emerged in the Canadian business community. For the first time in

Canadian history, the profits and productivity of our larger corporations were increasing while employment and wages were decreasing. Increased profits did not necessarily lead to increased employment.

GOOD, BAD, OR UGLY?

According to Richard Lipsey, a celebrated Canadian economist, the future looks rosy for Canada. "Insofar as the past is any guide, such an upheaval [restructuring] should be followed by a period of sustained secular boom within a more stable economic structure beginning around the start of the next millennium and lasting for a period measured in decades."

Writer and social activist Ted Schmidt, however, has a different vision of Canada's economic future: "Make no mistake, a social disaster of monumental proportions is on the horizon. ... [i]n the jobless recovery of part-time and temporary workers, in the growing numbers of poor people, in the forfeiting of bright futures and the disappearance of hope. ..."

The World According to Big Shot

BIG SHOT: Slinky, there's too much fat in this company. I'm going to re-engineer and become a virtual organization. Get our VP of Human Resources. I want him to fire everyone — except you, of course. When he's done, make up a pink slip for him.

Vic Patterson: OK Big Shot, everybody's fired. By the way, who's going to do the work tomorrow?
BIG SHOT: Don't know. That's stage 2.
Vic Patterson: Who's going to answer the phone when the customer calls tomorrow?
BIG SHOT: I'll know a lot more when stage 2 is done.

BIG SHOT: Next time we can save money by e-mailing their pink slips. Slinky, you'd better call an outsourcing firm to do our work and answer the phones.

→ What do you think of Big Shot's approach?

As for the future, some experts predict booming times ahead. Richard Lipsey is an economics professor at Simon Fraser University and a fellow of the Canadian Institute for Advanced Research. This respected Canadian economist says that *if history repeats itself*, our future generations will be the benefactors of the price Canadians had to pay for restructuring.[7] On the other side of the coin, some social activists predict doom and gloom for the Canadian work force. Their basic assumption is that greedy corporations will continue to reduce wages and downsize their work force in the blind pursuit of higher profits and improved corporate return on investment.[8]

The Cost of Downsizing

What does the corporate report card say now that the lean and mean company is commonplace? Has downsizing/ delayering been an effective strategy for making Canadian companies more competitive? The answer to these questions is "in some cases yes and in some cases no."

According to a 1996 survey by the Canadian Institute of Management (CIM), 54 percent of managers said that downsizing was necessary for Canadian companies to compete internationally.[9] Companies that cut the number of levels in their corporate hierarchy in half were strong indicators that serious structural change was required. General Electric, as an example, downsized its worldwide operations, invested heavily in training, and reaped the economic benefits — revenues increased from $27 billion to $60 billion and profits tripled to $4.4 billion.[10]

But some economic experts question whether job cuts and improved productivity go hand in hand. A financial analysis of 140 000 factories, for example, revealed that while 55 percent of productivity gains came from downsized companies, 45 percent came from companies that were hiring more workers. In addition, management must consider how downsizing affects the workload and behaviour of remaining employees.[11] According to the 1996 CIM survey, 42 percent of Canadian managers said that downsizing is destroying Canadian consumer confidence and individual purchasing power. Caryne Vigon, national administrator for the CIM, said that the survey showed many middle managers were concerned that the cuts made by companies had been too deep. Almost 13 percent said they had been laid off in the last two years. This was a similar result to the CIM's 1994 survey.[12]

Mark Mentzer, a University of Saskatchewan commerce professor, says, "Downsizing is an extremely ill-conceived managing tool." Armed with his study of 250 of Canada's biggest companies over eight years, Mentzer concludes that profits don't usually grow when companies cut jobs. He cites the example of a retail outlet that fires its sales staff "and then wonders why sales have dropped."[13] Henry Mintzberg, a distinguished Canadian management expert, agrees with Mentzer. He says that many of the layoffs are unconscionable since the organizational fat was created by senior managers in the first place.

But what about those who survive downsizing? Many corporate managers think that these employees should feel grateful that they still have a job. Not so, say the experts — the survivors of the downsizing revolution often feel bitter and betrayed: "While they work harder doing the work of their fired colleagues, they wonder when the next wave of layoff rounds will come," says Mark Mentzer.[14] Many experts are predicting that the long-term human cost of downsizing could add up to a new generation of angry employees who lack loyalty and trust — just the skills needed by the new-generation corporation.

We end this discussion by pointing out that downsizing doesn't always mean layoffs. Many companies have been able to cut their work force by offering early retirement plans, voluntary severance programs, and reassignment. What is important to remember is that the decision to downsize must be accompanied by a commitment to quality and growth, not just a reduction in costs. Two important components of successful downsizing/delayering are employee empowerment and outsourcing. Empowerment ensures that the remaining employees are able to carry on the operations of the firm; outsourcing allows outside experts to perform functions previously done in-house. (See Chapters 1 and 6 for more about empowerment and outsourcing.)

Empowering Employees

As organizations downsize, remaining workers must somehow renew their enthusiasm and take on new tasks and responsibilities. As whole management levels vanish, the remaining managers must assume control of more employees than ever before.

As we discussed in Chapter 6, *empowering* employees — giving them additional decision-making authority and responsibility — helps organizations deal with these changes. It frees managers from hands-on control of subordinates and motivates workers by making their jobs more interesting. All too often, traditionally tall organizations have discouraged employees by eliminating much of their power in making decisions affecting their jobs. The challenge for management is to find ways to encourage employee creativity, innovation, and empowerment. A

DOWNSIZING IS PERSONAL

On a cloudy day in the fall of 1996, Peter was summoned to the President's cherrywood office. As Head of Internal Audit at an Edmonton hospital, Peter wanted to use this occasion to brief his boss on a major fraud case and get his recommendations approved.

"Good morning Peter, please sit down," said his boss. "I'm sorry to inform you that your services are no longer required here at the hospital."

The President waited for a split second to make sure that Peter had understood the message. Then he continued, "As you know, for some time now we have been facing a financial and organizational crisis. The decision has been made to downsize. Staff functions such as Internal Audit that offer little contribution to the bottom line or patient care have been eliminated. Please, I don't want you to take this situation personally. Nor does this administrative decision reflect on your professional competence or contribution to the hospital. I would be very pleased to write you a letter of recommendation."

Next, the Vice-President of Human Resources was asked to escort Peter to his office. The VP silently watched at the office door as Peter boxed a few personal possessions, and then he whisked Peter off to the parking garage. By 9:45 AM that same day, Peter found himself at home, lying on the sofa with the phone in his hand. He was trying to remember his wife's number at work. Somehow he had to tell her what had happened. At this point, he was neither angry nor depressed; he was simply numb and speechless. It had all happened so quickly and ruthlessly.

Such a scene is typical of today's downsizing.

John Stoten, an associate with Western Management Consultants, a firm that deals with human resource issues, says that the downsizing phenomenon has led to a loss of dignity as well as fear and stress for many Canadian workers. Mark Mentzer, a University of Saskatchewan commerce professor, agrees. He studied the employment numbers and bottom lines for 250 of Canada's biggest companies over eight years. Mentzer's conclusion? Downsizing is "a sick fad." Even the survivors of the slashes must realize that they too will go through a gamut of emotions similar to those experienced when faced with divorce and death.

Sources: John Stoten's view is from Dennis Hryciuk (SouthamStar Network), "Surviving the Stress and Chaos of Downsizing," *The Ottawa Citizen*, September 9, 1995, E4; and Mark Mentzer's quote is from "Study Finds 'Dim-Witted' Downsizing Sign of Mismanagement by Fad," *The Ottawa Citizen*, October 26, 1996, D7, based on a study by Mark Mentzer, published in *Canadian Journal of Administrative Sciences*, September 1996.

good example is provided by Hershey Canada. At its Smiths Falls plant in eastern Ontario, employees are empowered to stop the production line without management permission if the wrapping operation is not running smoothly. Employees are not only empowered, they are obligated to act, so there is a responsibility dimension to the job enrichment. The Domtar case at the beginning of this chapter sets out another good example of how Canadian firms can use teamwork, training, and empowerment to lead a company from red to black.

Chrysler has also set a good example on how restructuring can be accomplished in a positive way. Where senior management traditionally had been responsible for all decision making, today six platform teams run the business. Each team includes all individuals involved in the production of a specific car, Jeep, minivan, or truck. The team makes all decisions associated with its vehicle. Senior management's role consists of ensuring that the team's decisions are in line with company goals. Employee empowerment has enabled Chrysler to cut its product development from four-and-a-half years to an average of three years.[15]

The bottom line? Maybe this is wishful thinking on our part, but look for the slash-and-burn, cowboy style of downsizing to gradually peter out in the late 1990s and be replaced by a more empowered, value-based, and civil style of management restructuring. As Canadian pollster Angus Reid says, "Civility is more than just a Canadian social virtue; it's an essential precondition to effective economic performance. It's critical to whatever competitive advantage Canada holds in the world market place."[16] We hope he's right.

Outsourcing

Remember from Chapter 1 that another important development accompanying the corporate downsizing trend is **outsourcing**, *relying on outside specialists to perform functions previously performed by company employees*. Outsourcing began on a small scale, typically with peripheral contracting functions such as maintenance, cleaning, and delivery. Today, outsourcing has expanded to outside contracting of such fundamental tasks as production of one or more items in the product line, accounting and legal services, warehousing, and transporting finished goods. It has become a major part of competitive strategies used by such corporate giants as IBM Canada Ltd., Magna International Inc., and General Motors, as well as microbusinesses such as the Markham-based Baranti Group Inc. and Wellness Innovations Corp.

Baranti is a seven-employee firm based in Markham, Ontario. Since the beginning of the 1990s, the company has become a virtual R&D, design, and manufacturing

> **Business Term**
> ✓ **Outsourcing**
> **Relying on outside specialists to perform functions previously performed by company employees.**

department for its clients. Baranti is an outsourcer to firms who want specialized or capital-intensive electronic product design and manufacturing. Its 50 or so customers range from small operations to behemoths like Sony and IBM. In the fall of 1996, IBM sold Celestica, a manufacturing division of IBM Canada, to Onex Corp., a mega holding company with about $3 billion in assets. IBM wanted to focus on services and networking computing. This meant that Celestica — North America's third-largest electronics manufacturer — did not fit IBM's strategic vision. IBM would now outsource its manufacturing to Celestica. Onex, in turn, could provide Celestica with the necessary capital to expand its manufacturing presence.[17]

Outsourcing typically is used in service industries ranging from housekeeping (81 percent) to office movers (29 percent). But as the downsizing revolution has grown, so has outsourcing's importance as a quality component in every major industry. The key to success in outsourcing is a 100 percent commitment by both parties. Outsourcing is a partnership in the purest sense of the word.[18]

Outsourcing complements downsizing in a variety of ways. It reduces the need for employees to perform certain tasks. It also allows a firm to continue performing the functions it does best, while hiring other firms to do tasks that they are more qualified to handle — so it allows for specialization.

Another benefit of outsourcing is that it gives the firm the ability to negotiate the best price from among competing bidders and to avoid the long-term human resource costs associated with in-house operations. Firms that outsource also have the flexibility of changing suppliers at the end of the contract. A firm like IBM Canada that decides to contract its manufacturing needs to a firm such as Celestica can later decide to perform this function with company personnel should the service provided by the outside supplier prove unsatisfactory.

Industries that rank high among candidates for outsourcing are our technology, transportation, and communications sectors. In the technology sector, high-tech firms, for example, often contract out their manufacturing. This allows them to concentrate on their core business. For example, Canada's Corel Corporation — the world's second-largest software developer in 1997 — contracts out much of its manufacturing, allowing it to focus on software development.

For the heavily unionized transportation and communications industries, outsourcing has been a tool not

Baranti Group Inc., a Markham, Ontario-based "outsourcer," has become the "virtual" research and development (R&D), design, and manufacturing departments to its clients.

only for refocussing their core competencies, but also for reducing labour costs and improving productivity. However, this corporate strategy to reduce unionized workers and salaries has caused employee stress and labour unrest. General Motors, for example, took a crippling strike in both Canada and the United States over the outsourcing issue in 1996. In the mid-1990s, Bell Canada outsourced its inside telephone line operation to Entourage Technology Solutions, a small spinoff company based in Longueuil, Quebec. In this case, disgruntled former Bell employees had to take about a 29 percent pay cut to work at Entourage.[19] Despite the growing labour unrest, the trend toward outsourcing seems unstoppable.

SKILLS REQUIRED FOR MANAGERIAL SUCCESS

F ACE IT: you have agonized several times in the past about whether you have what it takes to be a good manager. Certainly you have many strengths, but are they the right combination to make you successful, happy, and productive as a manager? Or should you focus your education more toward acquiring narrower skills that would make you a valued specialist rather than a leader of people? The evaluation form in Figure 7.8 has been used by such business giants as Ford and Xerox to find out how people behave in such areas as teamwork, communication, and change. Even though it is designed to be completed by managers, their bosses, and co-workers, simply completing

it without input from others should offer some insight on how you might rate as a manager.[20]

Every manager, regardless of level in the organization, must possess skills in three basic areas: technical, human relations, and conceptual. Although the importance of each skill varies at different levels, managers use all three types at some time during their careers.

Technical Skills

Technical skills refer to *the manager's ability to understand and use the techniques, knowledge, and tools of a specific discipline or department*. A manager in the human resource department, for instance, must understand the technical details of workplace laws. Technical skills are particularly important for first-line managers, who frequently are involved with production employees who operate machinery, salespeople who

> **Business Term**
> √ **Technical skills**
>
> The manager's ability to understand and use the techniques, knowledge, and tools of a specific discipline or department.

Sun Microsystems, Inc. offers Java™-based courses to help today's workers meet the demand for computer skills.

Figure 7.8 Management Aptitude Questionnaire

Directions: Rate each of the following questions according to this scale:

❏ 5 I always am like this.
❏ 4 I often am like this.
❏ 3 I sometimes am like this.

❏ 2 I rarely am like this.
❏ 1 I never am like this.

___ 1. When I have a number of tasks or homework to do, I set priorities and organize work around the deadlines. C

___ 2. Most people would describe me as a good listener. H

___ 3. When I am deciding on a particular course of action for myself (such as hobbies to pursue, languages to study, which job to take, special projects to be involved in), I typically consider the long-term (three years or more) implications of what I would choose to do. C

___ 4. I prefer technical or quantitative courses rather than those involving literature, psychology, or sociology. T

___ 5. When I have a serious disagreement with someone, I hang in there and talk it out until it is completely resolved. H

___ 6. When I have a project or assignment, I really get into the details rather than the "big picture" issues.* C

___ 7. I would rather sit in front of my computer than spend a lot of time with people. T

___ 8. I try to include others in activities or when there are discussions. H

___ 9. When I take a course, I relate what I am learning to other courses I have taken or to concepts I have learned elsewhere. C

___ 10. When somebody makes a mistake, I want to correct the person and let her or him know the proper answer or approach. * H

___ 11. I think it is better to be efficient with my time when talking to someone, rather than worry about the other person's needs, so that I can get on with my real work. T

___ 12. I know my long-term vision for career, family, and other activities and have thought it over carefully. C

___ 13. When solving problems, I would much rather analyze some data or statistics than meet with a group of people. T

___ 14. When I am working on a group project and someone doesn't pull a full share of the load, I am more likely to complain to my friends rather than confront the slacker. * H

___ 15. Talking about ideas or concepts can get me really enthused and excited. C

___ 16. The type of management course for which this book is used is really a waste of time. T

___ 17. I think it is better to be polite and not to hurt other people's feelings.* H

___ 18. Data or things interest me more than people. T

Scoring Key: Add the total points for the following sections. Note that starred (*) items are reverse scored:
1, 3, 6, 9, 12, 15 Conceptual skills total score _____
2, 5, 8, 10, 14, 17 Human skills total score _____
4, 7, 11, 13, 16, 18 Technical skills score _____

Source: "Management Aptitude Questionnaire," Copyright Dorothy Marcic 1997; Vanderbilt University, www.marcic.com.

must explain the technical details of their firm's products, or computer programmers working on a complicated assignment.

We are deeply entrenched in a technology revolution. This means that computer literacy and Internet literacy are critical technical skills required by the Canadian work force. Naturally, our managers must be at the forefront of this technological tidal wave. Notwithstanding these technological competencies, in general for managers technical skills become relatively less important. However, top executives in many large organizations often start out as technical experts. For example, a vice president of information systems probably has experi-ence as a computer analyst, while a vice president of marketing might have a background in sales.

Human Relations Skills

Human relations skills are *"people" skills involving the manager's ability to work effectively with and through people.* Human relations skills concern communicating with, leading, and motivating workers to accomplish assigned activities. In addition, the ability to interact with superiors and people outside the immediate department or work area is important. The ability to create

Business Term

✓ **Human relations skills**

"People" skills involving the manager's ability to work effectively with and through people.

a work environment in which organizational members will contribute their best efforts is a crucial managerial skill at every level.

Good *communication skills* are an important component of effective human relations. All of us tend to assume that people understand exactly what we mean, but good managers make it a point to check whether their communications come across the way they mean them to. This also involves paying attention to nonverbal communication, such as tone of voice, facial expression, and posture. Studies show that as much as 93 percent of a message's emotional impact comes from such nonverbal signals.

Conceptual Skills

Conceptual skills refer to the *ability to see the organization as a unified whole and understand how each part of the overall organization interacts with other parts*. These skills involve a manager's ability to "see the big picture" by acquiring, analyzing, and interpreting information. Such skills are especially important for top-level managers, who must develop long-range plans for the future direction of the organization.

Frank Stronach, CEO and major shareholder of Magna International Inc., is known for his ability to visualize where the auto industry is heading and then to get there first. For example, when the major auto manufacturers decided to outsource, Magna was first in line with the manufacturing systems and reputation for just-in-time delivery.

Business Term

✓ **Conceptual skills**

The ability to see the organization as a unified whole and understand how each part of the overall organization interacts with other parts.

Managerial Skills: Who Needs What?

All managers within an organization need to possess technical, human relations, and conceptual skills. However, the relative importance of each skill differs for each level of management (see Figure 7.9). Supervisory managers, who spend much of their time dealing with operative workers, must be strong in technical and human relations skills. They spend relatively little time, however, in long-range planning and other conceptual tasks. Top managers, on the other hand, need strong conceptual skills and human relations abilities, but spend little time dealing with technical matters. Middle managers require a blend of all three skills.

In general, conceptual and human relations skills transfer well from one department, company, or industry to another. Technical skills, however, are harder to transfer, due to the unique characteristics and requirements of many such skills. Furthermore, even though people may be great managers within a single functional area (such as engineering), moving into top management may require additional skills. Their success as top managers depends on their ability to understand the contributions made by all departments, not just the one with which they are most familiar.

Figure 7.9 **Managerial Skills at Each Managerial Level**

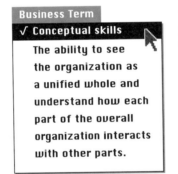

	Technical Skills	Human Relations Skills	Conceptual Skills
Top Management			
Middle Management			
Supervisory Management			

The relative importance of different managerial skills varies at different managerial levels.

LEADERSHIP

LEADERSHIP, the most visible component of a manager's responsibilities, is *the act of motivating or causing others to perform activities designed to achieve specific objectives*. Because of the importance of effective leadership in organizational success, it is not surprising that a great deal of research has been done into the characteristics of a good leader. Great leaders do not all share the same qualities, but three traits are often mentioned: they are driven by a *vision*, they are *motivational* and inspirational (they have the ability to ignite others to action), and they have the faith, *trust*, and loyalty of their followers (i.e., leaders are defined by their followers).

Leadership research focuses on different styles of leadership and on the circumstances under which each style might prove successful. This approach to leadership is known as the *contingency theory*. It argues that management should adjust its leader-

Business Term

√ Leadership

The act of motivating or causing others to perform activities designed to achieve specific objectives.

ship style in accordance with the situation at hand. We will now examine specific approaches to leadership styles.

Leadership Styles

Leadership involves the exercise of *power* — the ability of one person to influence the behaviour of another. This power may result from one or more sources. Leaders secure some power from their position in the organization. As managers, they are responsible for directing the activities of their subordinates. In other cases, their power comes from their expertise and experience: first-line supervisors who were once expert carpenters are likely to be respected by their crew of carpenters. Other leaders secure power from the force of their personalities. Followers of such charismatic leaders may grant them power because they want to please them or become more like them.

The way in which a leader uses available power to lead others is referred to as *leadership style*. A continuum of leadership styles exists, within which we can identify three basic styles. At one end of the continuum are *autocratic leaders*, who make decisions on their own without consulting others. The autocratic leader reaches a decision, communicates it to subordinates, and requires them to implement it. *Democratic leaders*, the second type, involve their subordinates in making decisions. A democratic sales manager, for example, allows sales personnel to participate in setting sales quotas, while an autocratic sales manager simply assigns quotas for each salesperson. The most democratic style of leadership belongs to *free-rein leaders*, who believe in minimal supervision and leave most decisions to their subordinates and team members.

The current trend is toward democratic and free-rein leadership. As companies downsize and eliminate layers of management ranks, lines of authority become shorter and the employees who remain must assume greater responsibility. "Whips and chains are no longer an alternative," explains leadership author Warren Bennis. "Leaders must learn to change the nature of power and how it's employed."

Terry Matthews, CEO of Newbridge Networks Corporation, is a well-respected leader in the business community. Newbridge is a world leader in designing, manufacturing, and servicing a family of products and systems for multimedia applications. In 1995 Matthews knew he had to "relax the reins" a little and transfer some of his power to his senior managers. As a

Terry Matthews, CEO of Newbridge Networks, is a well-respected leader in the business community.

result, he and his senior managers implemented Action '95 — a plan that called for a more flexible, decentralized management structure. The company formed five product groups that supplied regional business teams, which in turn would sell to specific customers.[21]

Which Leadership Style Is Best?

Appropriate leadership style is a function of the leader, the team, and the situation. In short, the best leadership style is one that adapts to the circumstances at hand. Some leaders are uncomfortable in situations characterized by high participation of subordinates in decision making. Some followers do not have the ability or the desire to assume such responsibility. Furthermore, the specific situation helps determine which style will be most effective. Problems requiring immediate solutions may have to be handled without consulting subordinates. When there is less time pressure, participative decision making may work best.

In many cases, democratic leaders will ask for advice from others but will make the final decisions themselves. A leader who usually prefers a free-rein style may be forced by circumstances to be autocratic in making a particular decision. For example, if there is to be a 10 percent reduction in staff, those subject to being fired are not likely to be consulted on who should go.

After devoting many years to research to determine the best types of leaders, experts agree that no single best style of leadership exists. Rather, they contend that the most effective leadership style depends on the power held by the leader, the difficulty of the tasks involved, and the characteristics of the workers. Both extremely easy and extremely difficult situations are handled best by leaders who emphasize the accomplishment of assigned tasks. Moderately difficult situations are handled best by leaders who emphasize participation and good working relations with subordinates.

CORPORATE CULTURE

THE MOST APPROPRIATE leadership style depends greatly on **corporate culture**, *the value system of an organization*. Managerial philosophies, workplace practices, and communication networks are included in the concept of corporate culture.

The corporate culture typically is shaped by the leaders who founded and developed the company and by those who succeed them. One generation of employees passes on a corporate culture to newer employees. Sometimes this is part of formal training. New managers who attend McDonald's Hamburger University may learn skills in management, but they also acquire the basics of the organization's corporate culture. Employees can absorb corporate culture through informal contacts as well, by talking with other workers and through their experiences on the job.

In the early 1990s, Moore Corporation Ltd., a Canadian business forms multinational, had lost market share to international competitors. Throughout the 1980s and early 1990s, while its competitors developed new products, strategies, and technologies, Moore sat still. In response to dwindling market share, Reto Braun was hired as CEO in 1993 to inject new competitive life into the company. One of Braun's primary tasks was to change the corporate culture from one of complacency to one of aggressive customer service. In this case, time was of the essence, so he adopted an authoritative style and quickly replaced those managers who did not buy into the principle of total customer service. Managers who could not hustle for customers were quickly replaced with new "hungry for business" managers.[22]

Corporate culture has a major impact on the success of an organization. In organizations with strong cultures,

> **Business Term**
> √ **Corporate culture**
> The value system of an organization.

everyone knows and supports the organization's objectives. In those with weak cultures, no clear sense of purpose exists. In fact, the authors of the classic book *In Search of Excellence* concluded that the presence of a strong corporate culture was the single common thread among many diverse but highly successful companies, such as General Electric and McDonald's.[23]

INTRAPRENEURSHIP

CHANGE AND ITS impact on Canadian business is a major theme of this book. As we discussed in Chapter 5, entrepreneurs are the spirit of innovation — they are agents of change. Canada has a rich history of entrepreneurship and invention ranging from the invention of the telephone by Alexander Graham Bell to the creation of corporate giants like Mitel, Newbridge, and Corel by corporate entrepreneurial legends Terry Matthews and Michael Cowpland.

Historically, major innovations have often been the domain of a single inventor or small business. In order to survive and compete, the successful larger corporations have had to change and innovate. Many corporations are encouraging **intrapreneurship**, *entrepreneurial-type activity within the corporate structure.* IBM Canada, Shell Canada, and EBA Engineering Consultants in Calgary are well known for their intrapreneurial flair.

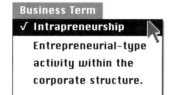

Business Term

✓ **Intrapreneurship**

Entrepreneurial-type activity within the corporate structure.

Hewlett-Packard (HP) is an example of a company that fosters intrapreneurship. A few years ago, HP manager Jim Olson became an intrapreneur when he realized that the company was not involved in the rapidly growing areas of television and telecommunications. Following approval by other members of HP top management, his first step was to recruit a team of engineers and managers, who spent the next several months visiting TV networks, production houses, and trade shows. Team members returned to HP, plunged into research and design, and created fourteen new products in nine months. One is the VidJet Pro, a studio tool that files video images along with the videotape so customers can see what's on a tape without having to watch it. Other new products include a machine that monitors the quality of video signals, and a video server that feeds movies into interactive TV. The division is building components of high-tech TV systems for Pacific Telesis and Time Warner, and is negotiating deals with major telephone companies as well. Olson notes that his intrapreneurship arrangement with HP gave him the best of both worlds: he had the huge company's financial support and expertise, but also had the freedom to innovate. "We're street fighters here," he says. "We're like a start-up."[24]

Although the intrapreneur may begin by assembling a special team task force or working within the confines of a matrix structure, a successful project may result in an entirely new subsidiary of the corporation. In some cases, a separate company is formed at the outset. For example,

Figure 7.10 **Sample "Affiliate" Companies**

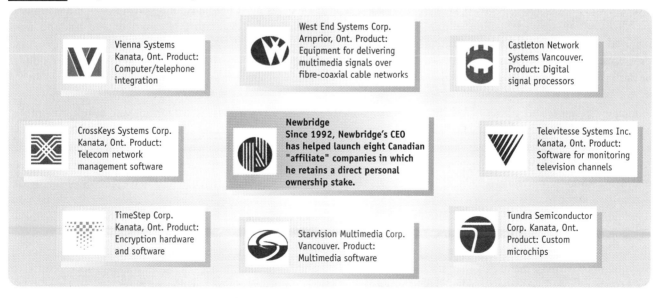

the creative genius of Terry Matthews, CEO of Newbridge, has been responsible for more than eight "affiliate" companies (see Figure 7.10), a form of "start-up" in which Matthews, other private investors, and Newbridge hold equity positions. Newbridge affiliates are a mechanism for the corporation to diversify using a virtual organizational structure. This structure allows large firms to support and profit from the creatively driven talents of entrepreneurs, some of whom are employees. As well, these infant affiliate companies (sometimes referred to as spinoffs) have a much improved chance of success because they have access to the management expertise of a large corporation. They are born with a well-defined customer base (the parent organization and its customers), access to financing, and the necessary manufacturing and marketing expertise that are already in place in the parent corporation.[25] While the disadvantages of this approach are identical to those described earlier regarding the matrix organization, the advantages lie in the available financing and necessary manufacturing and marketing expertise already in place in a large company. In addition, the intrapreneuring option permits many firms to retain valuable entrepreneurially oriented employees who might otherwise leave the company and start their own businesses.

MANAGERIAL DECISION MAKING

ONE OF THE most important tasks of a leader is decision making. Managers earn their salaries by making decisions that enable their firms to solve problems as they arise. In addition, managers continually are involved with anticipating and preventing problems. The decision-making process can be described in five steps. In a narrow sense, it can be thought of as simply choosing among two or more alternatives — the chosen alternative being the decision. But in a broader sense, **decision making** *involves recognizing that a problem or opportunity exists, developing alternative courses of action, evaluating alternatives, selecting and implementing an alternative, and following up* on the effectiveness of the decision by getting feedback (see Figure 7.11). Whether the decision to be made is routine or unique (such as a decision to construct a major new manufacturing facility), the systematic step-by-step approach will be effective.

> **Business Term**
> ✓ **Decision making**
> Recognizing that a problem or opportunity exists, developing alternative courses of action, evaluating alternatives, selecting and implementing an alternative, and following up.

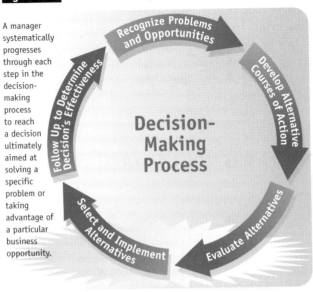

Figure 7.11 Decision-Making Process

A manager systematically progresses through each step in the decision-making process to reach a decision ultimately aimed at solving a specific problem or taking advantage of a particular business opportunity.

Recognize Problems and Opportunities

Develop Alternative Courses of Action

Evaluate Alternatives

Select and Implement Alternatives

Follow Up to Determine Decision's Effectiveness

Decision-Making Process

Types of Decisions

We can classify decisions by their relative uniqueness. A *programmed decision* involves simple, common, frequently occurring problems for which solutions have already been determined. Examples of programmed decisions include choosing the starting salary for a computer programmer, determining reorder points for raw materials used in production, and selecting price discounts offered to customers who make large-quantity purchases.

Organizations develop rules, policies, and detailed procedures for making such decisions consistently, quickly, and inexpensively. Since such solutions eliminate the time-consuming process of identifying and evaluating alternatives and making new decisions each time the situation occurs, they free managers to devote time to more complex problems.

A *nonprogrammed decision* involves complex, important, and nonroutine problems or opportunities. Because nonprogrammed decisions typically are made in situations that have not occurred before, identifying alternatives, evaluating them, and implementing the best ones become critical tasks. In fact, managers often are evaluated on their ability to make nonprogrammed decisions.

For a good example of the importance of leadership and nonprogrammed decision making, let's return to Moore Corporation. In the spring of 1995, Moore's U.S.

division was in trouble. The U.S. compensation scheme was notoriously unpopular with the sales force and there were fundamental problems with their order system. U.S. revenue was on a deep slide. Reto Braun, the newly hired Canadian CEO, acted quickly. First he accepted the resignation of the man in charge of the U.S. division. Next he made an unusual nonprogrammed decision to take over the helm of the U.S. operation himself. He initiated and supervised a complete overhaul of the order entry system to improve throughput. Braun made a second nonprogrammed decision when he devised an effective new sales incentive program. By the fall of 1995, the U.S. division was back on track. Braun hired a new U.S. division head and returned to Canada as CEO of the worldwide company.[26]

TIME MANAGEMENT

MANAGERS ARE BUSY people who are expected to accomplish a lot of goals in a limited amount of time. **Time management**, or *the effective allocation of one's time among different tasks*, is a key element of managerial success today.[27] The starting point for time allocation is to place a value on working time. In other words, what does your time cost the organization? Once you know the value of your time, you can quickly identify the activities that are most cost-effective for you.

> **Business Term**
> ✓ **Time management**
> The effective allocation of one's time among different tasks.

Time Management Guidelines

Numerous time management guidelines have been suggested over the years. Some of the best known include (1) always leaving at least a quarter of your time unscheduled, (2) assigning priorities to tasks, (3) breaking big jobs into smaller ones, and (4) when taking on something new, giving up something old. Following are some other generally accepted time management ideas.

Establish Goals and Set Priorities. Make a list of your long- and short-term projects. Look at the list regularly and revise it as needed. Arrange the items on the list in order of their importance, and then divide the items into specific tasks. Then start at the top of the list and get to work. Do not get upset if your priorities change by the hour — just revise your list and get on with the work. Schedule your daily activities on an hour-by-hour appointment calendar.

Learn to Delegate Work. Part of setting priorities is deciding whether you really need to do a project. One management professor notes that there are really only six things a top manager always should do: plan, select the team, monitor their efforts, motivate, evaluate, and reward them. Consider delegating the other tasks to a subordinate. Here are some questions to ask yourself in deciding what to delegate: Is this project truly necessary? (Will anyone really read this report you're slaving over?) Would this project benefit one of my subordinates? (One of your employees may be eager for the experience and opportunity to try something new.) Is this what my bosses think I should be spending my time on? (If not, can someone else do it instead?)[28]

Concentrate on Most Important Activities. Learn the Pareto Principle of time management: you can achieve 80 percent of your goals in only 20 percent of your time if you work on those tasks critical to the completion of the overall project and avoid those that contribute little to the outcome.

Do Most Important Work When Most Alert. Work on high-priority items when you are mentally alert and on low-priority items when your energy has ebbed.

Group Activities Together. Set aside a period of time to read all your mail and answer all your phone calls. This will help you make the most efficient use of your time.

Learn How to Handle Interruptions. Incoming phone calls, unscheduled visitors, and even the mail can play havoc with your schedule. You can control these interruptions by having your assistant handle all but essential calls when you are working on an important task, by working in another office where no one will be able to find and interrupt you, by setting times when subordinates can talk to you and times when they cannot except for emergencies, and by learning how to deal with long-winded callers. Interrupting yourself also wastes time. Instead of getting yet another cup of coffee or walking down the hall to chat with a friend, try to finish what you are doing, even if the job is difficult or unpleasant. Just think how good you will feel when it's done!

A notebook computer, pager, and cellular phone help Harriet Donnelly, AT&T managing director of consumer products. She manages her time well no matter what time zone she's in. Donnelly typically leaves her home on Monday morning to travel to her other offices in California, Japan, or Europe. Once arrived, she may spend all day in meetings and not return to her hotel room before 9 or 10 PM. She uses her flight time to prepare presentations on her computer, and stays in touch with headquarters via voice mail and e-mail. "You can get hooked on working this way," says Donnelly. "It takes away the nine-to-five restrictions that many people are still limited by. The bad part is that I work more hours, but I feel very productive."[29]

New technologies, like Nokia Data's cellular phone that can be connected to a laptop, give workers the ability to better manage their time and communicate with their clients and colleagues even outside the workplace.

NEW OPPORTUNITIES FOR MANAGERS

AS WE HAVE seen, business organizations have undergone a revolution in structure. The tasks and responsibilities expected of managers within these organizations have also changed, as they manage diverse groups of employees, create flexible work teams, assume broader spans of control, and encourage intrapreneurship. In numerous cases, downsizing and delayering have eliminated many managers' jobs.

While traditional supervisory and middle management positions might be getting more scarce, other opportunities will be available for those with good management skills. Some middle managers leave large corporations for smaller firms. Another option is to become a *contract manager*, someone on a temporary appointment. Temporary management is a fast-growing area in Canada, the United States, and Europe, where a manager may contract with an employer to work for a specified period of time.

An increasing number of managers decide to start their own companies. This is a market push phenomenon that began in the early to mid-1990s. Corporate downsizing motivated Steve and Anne Og to open their own computer shop. Sheila Mather was another corporate refugee who branched out on her own when a retail chain restructured in the early 1990s. She now runs a successful holistic fitness company — targeted at the stress-prone high-tech sector.[30] Many former managers are finding that their skills are in demand as consultants in such industries as engineering, manufacturing, and marketing.

MANAGING ACROSS BORDERS

MOST BUSINESS EXPERTS agree that to thrive in the twenty-first century, Canada must be able to compete successfully in the world marketplace. Thus, many of our companies face an important decision: choosing and training managers to oversee international operations and foreign-based offices. Placing a manager overseas can be expensive and difficult, for both the company and the manager. Culture shock and the stress of an unfamiliar environment can make it harder for the manager to perform well. The prevalence of two-income families complicates matters, since the manager's spouse may not be able to find comparable work in the new country. Many companies are responding by choosing foreign managers more carefully. Some firms hire psychologists to help pick managers most suited to the challenges of working in a different country. Employees who are being considered for such transfers must take a written test, go through management interviews, and complete a self-assessment checklist to judge their own "cultural adaptability." Other companies assist overseas managers and families by boosting the language and cultural training available, finding new jobs for spouses, and paying tuition costs for family members who want to study abroad.

"But the key to a business's success in the global market place is the ability to cultivate a global mindset among all its employees," says Harry Lane, a professor specializing in international business at the University of Western Ontario's Richard Ivy School of Business.[31]

CASE EXERCISE

WHAT WAS YOUR FIRST CLUE, J.P.?

When it comes to the first foreign contact by Canadian mining companies, geologists do most of the negotiating. Yet they typically have no formal training in dealing with other cultures. Nevertheless, Frank Turner, a geologist with a major Canadian mining company, still wonders how he could have been so naïve.

As a young geologist, Frank had been invited by a community of Afghan villagers to attend a feast. He and two companions were presented with a brace of roasted chickens, which they promptly devoured. He later learned of his cultural gaff while leafing through a book on Afghan customs: although the Afghans first brought the chicken to him, he was only supposed to eat a small amount. According to the custom, it would then be passed to the elderly men, the younger men, and the children.

North American concepts of time, decision-making, family, or status are not universal. Morna Flood Consedine, a principal consultant with Maracon & Associates Inc. in Montreal, says that failure to recognize this can send a foreign venture into the dumpster just as surely as showing up in Saudi Arabia with a bottle of scotch.

But you don't have to be an ocean away to feel the impact of cultural differences, as Texan J. P. Bryan, former CEO of Gulf Canada Resources Ltd. learned. In 1996, he gave a speech urging Canada to take a hard line on Quebec secession. One remedy, he suggested, was to send separatists back to France on a boat. "Canadians didn't want to hear this from an American," he later recalled. "In retrospect, I probably should have kept my mouth shut." What was your first clue, J. P.?

David Eaton, of the Boston-based David Eaton Group, says that he has also experienced cultural differences between Canadians and Americans, though often they may seem more subtle. He cites a tense situation in which he had to build social bridges between a U.S. company and its newly-acquired Canadian subsidiary.

The Canadians needed to understand that the brash "can-do" U.S. approach was not a chauvinistic display of plumage. The Americans had to learn that the "less in-your-face" Canadians — who typically required the facts before making a decision — were not necessarily wimps.

1. Meet with your friends, co-workers, or classmates and choose a foreign country. What are some of the cultural/social differences between Canada and your selected country?

2. If you were in charge and your company planned to do business in another country, how would you prepare the staff to become more culturally aware?

3. Suppose you chose to contract the services of a cross-cultural trainer to help your staff. What kind of training would you expect?

Source: Adapted from Carey French, "Globetrotters Taught to Mind Their Manners," *The Globe and Mail*, September 29, 1998, C10; Jacquie McNish, "Running Canada Inc. by Remote Control," *The Globe and Mail*, September 14, 1998, A6. Reprinted with permission from The Globe and Mail.

SUMMARY OF LEARNING OUTCOMES

1. **Discuss the need for organizational structure, and list the steps involved in the organizing process.**

The organizing process and its resulting structure form the basis for organizational planning to reach organizational objectives. The need for structure increases as organizations grow in size. Once organizational objectives and plans have been developed, organizing involves the following five steps:

a. Determine specific work activities necessary to implement those plans and accomplish objectives.

b. Group work activities into a logical pattern or structure.

c. Assign activities to specific positions and people and allocate the necessary resources and authority to carry them out.

d. Co-ordinate activities of different groups and individuals.

e. Evaluate the results of the organizing process.

2. **Evaluate each of the five basic forms of organization, and explain the differences between new-style and old-style organizational structures.**

Five forms of organizational structure are used: line, line-and-staff, committee, matrix, and network. The line organization is the simplest form, but it suffers from a lack of specialization by management. This poses a problem for larger organizations. The line-and-staff form assigns authority to line managers and adds staff specialists to provide information and advice. However, conflict can arise between line and staff members if their relationship is unclear.

The committee form of organization rarely is used as the sole organization structure, but is often incorporated to some extent within the line-and-staff structure. Because committees can be composed of representatives of a number of areas in the organization, they ensure that each area is represented in the decision-making process. However, they are relatively slow in making decisions, which often end up being compromises among conflicting interests. The matrix form of organization, another subform of the line-and-staff structure, permits large multiproduct firms to focus organizational resources on specific problems or projects. Because of its "team" approach and the fact that team members are accountable to more than one manager, conflict can occur.

The network or virtual corporation is a relatively new form of organizational structure. The major functions of this organization are broken up into strategic business units (SBUs) or categories that focus on specific customer needs. Each functional need by the core organization can then be outsourced to the SBU, which is expected to operate like a separate business. This virtual concept lends itself to small business and the "new economy" corporate needs — especially for technology companies — of risk taking, proactivity, and innovation.

3. **Explain the impact of downsizing, delayering, and outsourcing on today's organizations.**

Delayering means reducing the number of corporate layers in the organizational structure. Downsizing means reducing the number of employees. Large Canadian firms have been downsizing and/or delayering in an effort to reduce costs and make the firm more efficient. Downsizing and delayering result in a flatter organization structure that requires empowerment of workers to make decisions previously made by their supervisors. Outsourcing or contracting out is the practice of relying on outside specialists to perform functions previously performed by company employees. Relying on outside contractors to perform needed functions also simplifies the organization by eliminating the need for company employees in these areas.

4. **Identify the skills required for managerial success.**

The three basic managerial skills are technical, human relations, and conceptual. Technical skills, which involve the manager's ability to understand and use the techniques, tools, and knowledge of a specific discipline or department, are most important for first-level managers. Human relations skills, which involve working effectively with and through people to accomplish goals, are important for managers at every level. Conceptual or visualization skills, which involve the manager's ability to see the "big picture" of the organization as a whole and how each part contributes to its overall functioning, are relatively more important for top management.

5. **Explain the concept of leadership and identify the three basic leadership styles.**

Leadership is the act of motivating or causing others to perform activities designed to achieve specific objectives. The three basic leadership styles are autocratic, democratic, and free-rein. The best leadership style depends on three elements: the leader, the followers, and the situation. Today, the general trend is toward greater participation of subordinates in decisions that affect them.

6. **Describe the role of intrapreneurship in modern organizations.**

The term *intrapreneurship* refers to various attempts to make large organizations more entrepreneurial. Intrapreneurship units achieve the innovative dynamics of a smaller firm. These units are given free rein (and sometimes financial incentives) to accomplish their assigned objectives.

7. **List the steps in the decision-making process, and contrast programmed and nonprogrammed decisions.**

The decision-making process consists of five steps:
a. Recognizing problems and opportunities
b. Developing alternative courses of action
c. Evaluating alternatives
d. Selecting and implementing the chosen alternative
e. Following up to determine the effectiveness of the decision

Programmed decisions involve simple, frequently occurring problems or opportunities for which solutions have been determined previously. Such decisions are made quickly by reference to a rule or procedure, and managers need spend little time in identifying and evaluating alternatives. By contrast, nonprogrammed decisions involve more complex, relatively unique situations. Their solution requires considerable management involvement in identifying and evaluating alternatives.

8. **Discuss the importance of time management.**

Time management refers to the process of allocating one's time among different activities. Given the variety of goals management is expected to accomplish in a limited amount of time, it has become evident in recent years that time management is a major ingredient in managerial success. The starting point in effective time management is to know what one's time is worth so that it can be allocated in a cost-effective fashion.

Key Terms Quiz

line-and-staff organization
management
human relations skills
conceptual skills
leadership
outsourcing
top management

delegation
time management
corporate culture
line organization
middle management
intrapreneurship

matrix or project management organization
supervisory management
technical skills
decision making
organization

_____ 1. The achievement of organizational objectives through people and other resources.
_____ 2. The highest level of the management hierarchy, staffed by executives who develop long-range plans and interact with the public and outside entities, like government.
_____ 3. Those people responsible for developing detailed plans and procedures to implement the general plans of top management.
_____ 4. Those people directly responsible for the details of assigning workers to specific jobs and evaluating their performance.

_____ 5. A structured grouping of people working together to achieve organizational objectives.

_____ 6. The act of assigning activities to subordinates or team members.

_____ 7. Relying on outside specialists to perform functions that were previously performed by company employees.

_____ 8. Organizational structure characterized by the direct flow of authority from the chief executive to subordinates.

_____ 9. Organizational structure that combines the direct flow of authority present in the line organization with staff departments that serve, advise, and support the line departments.

_____ 10. Organizational structure in which specialists from different parts of the organization are brought together to work on specific projects.

_____ 11. The manager's ability to understand and use the techniques, knowledge, and tools of a specific discipline or department.

_____ 12. "People" skills involving the manager's ability to work effectively with and through people.

_____ 13. The ability to see the organization as a unified whole and understand how each part of the overall organization interacts with other parts.

_____ 14. The act of motivating or causing others to perform activities designed to achieve specific objectives.

_____ 15. The value system of an organization.

_____ 16. Entrepreneurial-type activity within the corporate structure.

_____ 17. Recognizing that a problem or opportunity exists, developing alternative solutions, evaluating alternatives, selecting and implementing an alternative, and following up on the decision.

_____ 18. The effective allocation of one's time among different tasks.

Other Important Terms

accountability	democratic leaders	organization chart
authority	departmentalization	organizing
autocratic leaders	downsizing	power
chain of command	free-rein leaders	programmed decision
committee organization	leadership style	responsibility
contingency theory	network or virtual organization	
contract manager	nonprogrammed decision	

Review Questions

1. Explain the statement "Management principles are universal." Do you agree or disagree with it?

2. Describe some traits that would make a manager a good candidate for a foreign transfer. Would you be a good candidate for such a transfer? Why or why not?

3. On what level of management would each of the following persons be listed?
   a. Department head
   b. Chief operating officer
   c. Supervisor
   d. Branch manager
   e. Mayor
   f. Dean

4. Identify and briefly explain the three skills required for managerial success. Which skills are relatively more important for top management? Which are more important for first-line managers?

5. MacDugal's Paper Distributors has long observed St. Patrick's Day as a paid holiday for its employees. Donald MacDugal, company president, noticed that the next St. Patrick's Day will fall on a Wednesday. He wonders whether the Monday of that week should be declared a company holiday instead. Using each of the steps in the decision-making process, describe how you would make this decision.

6. Classify each of the following as either a programmed or a nonprogrammed decision. Defend your answers.
   a. Determining the registrar's office system for processing student requests for dropping and adding courses
   b. Making a retail store manager's decision about the number of women's blouses to order
   c. Creating a hospital's procedure for admitting new patients
   d. Pondering management's decision to relocate corporate headquarters from Edmonton to Vancouver

7. What is departmentalization? What are its major forms?

8. Explain why so many organizations have been downsizing, delayering, and outsourcing during the 1990s.

9. Summarize the major strengths and weaknesses of each type of formal organizational structure.

10. What is meant by corporate culture? Describe the corporate culture of a firm in your area.

Discussion Questions

1. Describe the skills that you think would be helpful to someone working in a matrix organization and a network organization. What can you do to prepare yourself for a successful career in both of these types of structures? Try to be specific.

2. Give an example of a firm in your area that should use the following forms of departmentalization. Defend your answers.
   a. Product   d. Functional
   b. Geographic   e. Process
   c. Customer

3. The typical professional sports team is owned by wealthy individuals who enjoy being involved with a particular sport. The owners usually make the major policy decisions, but a hired general manager oversees facilities, equipment, vendors, and personnel matters. He or she also may have responsibility for player personnel decisions such as trades, new-player drafts, and assignment of players to minor leagues. The field manager, or head coach, is in charge of the team's actual performance. This person assists the general manager in matters concerning players. Other personnel include team doctors, assistant coaches, trainers, equipment managers, secretaries, scouts, and ticket sales personnel. Draw an organization chart for a professional sports team and discuss the strengths of this structure.

4. In recent years, Canadian firms have eliminated many management and professional jobs. Discuss how you feel this will affect the Canadian workplace in the next decade. Explain how managers displaced by the downsizing trend may be able to take advantage of the growing practice of outsourcing.

5. Napoleon always refused to reply to letters for six months because he believed that most of the problems raised in the correspondence would be either solved or forgotten in that time. Comment on Napoleon's unique approach to time management.

Meaning of the Chinese Characters

When an organization is faced with adjusting to change, a crisis situation often develops. The Chinese have a revealing way of expressing the word "crisis": the upper character represents danger, while the lower one conveys hidden opportunity. When faced with change, we all encounter the same options suggested by the Chinese symbols — dangerous negative results or new positive opportunities.

Answers to Key Terms Quiz

1. management 2. top management 3. middle management 4. supervisory management 5. organization 6. delegation 7. outsourcing 8. line organization 9. line-and-staff organization 10. matrix or project management organization 11. technical skills 12. human relations skills 13. conceptual skills 14. leadership 15. corporate culture 16. intrapreneurship 17. decision making 18. time management

Notes

1. Adapted from Janet McFarland, "How Domtar Workers Added $20 Million to Profit," *The Globe and Mail*, October 20, 1995, B9. Reprinted with permission from The Globe and Mail.

2. Richard L. Daft, *Management*, 3rd ed. (Fort Worth, TX: The Dryden Press, 1993), 8.

3. John Byrne, "The Horizontal Corporation," *Business Week*, December 20, 1993, 76–81; and "A Master Class in Radical Change," *Fortune*, December 13, 1993, 82–90.

4. Elizabeth Church, "Strategy," *The Globe and Mail*, October 22, 1996, B17.

5. David Foot and Daniel Stoffman, "The Great Canadian Job Funk," The Globe and Mail, May 25, 1996, D1. See also Foot with Stoffman, *Boom, Bust & Echo* (Toronto: Macfarlane Walter & Ross, 1996), p. 58

6. The Royal Bank study is cited in Colin Campbell, *Where the Jobs Are* (Toronto: Macfarlane Walter & Ross, 1994), 18.

7. See, for example, Bruce Little, "Economist Predicts Booming Future," *The Globe and Mail*, November 6, 1996, B4.

8. See, for example, Ted Schmidt, "Have You Lived through a 'Worker Imbalance Correction'?" *Catholic New Times*, November 3, 1996, 16.

9. The CIM survey is cited in "What Managers Think of Downsizing," *The Globe and Mail*, August 19, 1996, B3.

10. Stefan Fatsis, "Amid Trouble, Companies Restructure Hierarchies," *Mobile Register*, December 27, 1992, 5E.

11. "Downsizing Often Costly Cut," *Mobile Register*, July 10, 1994, 1F, 2F.

12. Cited in "What Managers Think of Downsizing," B3.

13. Quoted in "Study Finds 'Dim-Witted' Downsizing Sign of Mismanagement by Fad," *The Ottawa Citizen*, October 26, 1996, D7.

14. Ibid.

15. Stefan Fatsis, "Corporate America Retooling," *Seattle Post-Intelligencer*, December 26, 1992, B6.

16. "Pollster Casts an Observant Eye on Canadians," *The Financial Post*, November 9, 1996, 30.

17. Information drawn from Greg Ip, "Outsourcing Becoming a Way of Life for Firms," *The Globe and Mail*, October 2, 1996, B8.

18. "Out Is In," *Entrepreneur*, May 1994, 12.

19. Ip, "Outsourcing Becoming a Way of Life for Firms," B8.

20. Michelene Maynard, "Evaluations Evolve from Bottom Up," *USA Today*, August 3, 1994, 6B.

21. Michael Salter, "Dream BIG...then BIGGER," *The Globe and Mail Report on Business Magazine*, June 1996, 56–60. Reprinted by permission of the author.

22. Information drawn from Shona McKay, "A Paper Tiger in the Paperless World," *Canadian Business*, April 1996, 25–29.

23. Thomas J. Peters and Robert H. Waterman, Jr., *In Search of Excellence* (New York: Harper & Row, 1982).

24. Kevin Maney, "Giant Goes from Stodgy to Nimble," *USA Today*, May 18, 1994, 1B, 2B.

25. Michael Salter, "Dream BIG ... then BIGGER," 56–60.

26. McKay, "A Paper Tiger in the Paperless World," 25–29.

27. Alan Deutschman, "The CEO's Secret of Managing Time," *Fortune*, June 1, 1992, 135–46.

28. Walter Kiechel III, "Overscheduled, and Not Loving It," *Fortune*, April 8, 1991, 105–7.

29. Adapted from Alison Sprout, "Saving Time around the Clock," *Fortune*, December 13, 1993, 157.

30. Lee A. Eckert, J.D. Ryan, and Ronald A. Knowles, *Canadian Small Business, An Entrepreneur's Plan*, 2nd ed. (Toronto: Dryden, 1995), 8, 159.

31. Patrick Brethour, "Software Company Lands in Tehran," *The Globe and Mail*, October 16, 1996, G15.

Chapter 8

The Human Resource

After studying this chapter, you should be able to

1. Explain the importance of human resource management and the responsibilities of a human resource department.
2. List the different needs in Maslow's hierarchy, and the two main categories of Herzberg's two-factor theory.
3. Distinguish among Theory X, Theory Y, and Theory Z managers.
4. Explain how recruitment, selection, orientation, training, and evaluation contribute to placing the right person in a job.
5. Outline the different forms of employee compensation.
6. Explain the concept of job enrichment and how it can motivate employees.
7. Summarize the role of labour unions and list their primary goals.
8. Outline the sources of power, or "weapons," of labour and management.
9. Identify the major human resource concerns for the twenty-first century.

Fashion This

"Investing the time in putting together a human resource plan really paid off," says George Paulus, the former manager of Bundschuh Fashions Ltd. of Calgary. "It forced me to think. The more I started thinking about planning, the more I started considering different options for things like recruiting, training, and organizing our staff for production."

Bundschuh is a clothing manufacturer that was established in the late 1980s to provide Western Canadian retailers and distributors with local contract sewing and design services. The company fills a market niche for local consumers and retailers who demand more variety and faster response times. Bundschuh's goal is to help its customers reduce inventory costs and enhance cash flow. Despite its relative isolation from traditional fashion clothing markets, the company has performed very well: sales were expected to increase more than 30 percent over the late 1990s.[1]

The way the company treats people and trains them has had a significant bearing on Bundschuh's success. Here is its human resource (HR) advice:[2]

- **Establish a training culture.** "If we're looking for growth in our area, Alberta, where there certainly isn't an excess of experienced seamstresses, we have to be prepared to recruit people and then spend the time training. It usually takes about six months to bring new employees up to speed," says George Paulus. Training is expensive, but Paulus is convinced that it is still the best option for the company and for the community: "We could bring in workers from Hong Kong, but we'd rather create jobs for people already in the community."

- **Plan and budget for training.** "Training does not only apply to production workers," adds Paulus. "We require middle managers that are not only good managers, but who have experience in the industry. We have to train them internally, which means sometimes even bringing in a consultant to advise on better production and employee management."

- **Make training everyone's responsibility.** Bundschuh bases its planning process on *staff* surveys as well as management requirements, which enables the company to match employees with the jobs they're best suited to.

- **Quantify and evaluate training.** Bundschuh has an HR plan that keeps track of the skills and duties needed for every job. This plan lists each employee's skills as well as the skills she or he is most interested in acquiring. By matching these inventories with production forecasts, senior managers are able to organize and anticipate staffing requirements. "We're constantly evaluating all of the employees in the company, to facilitate retraining and promotion," Paulus says. "It is essential that all companies, large or small, go through a similar process. The cost benefits are hard to quantify now; but by eliminating delays in product sales, in the future, our returns will be substantial."

- **Reduce costs by training staff.** HR planning is done at Bundschuh with the ultimate goal of being the most efficient plant. "In the future, we may be competing against Mexican clothing manufacturers and we think we can do it, as long as we keep a firm eye on our labour costs," says Paulus.

- **Work in teams.** According to George Paulus, "We organize ourselves like the Japanese, which means that we work in teams, set goals, cross-train all employees, and provide achievement bonuses to motivate employees. The cross training is especially important because it enables our employees to be much more flexible. This makes the entire production process more flexible."

- **Reward employees.** Bundschuh doesn't forget that money is a strong motivator. The company provides financial bonuses for successful training.

CHAPTER OVERVIEW

AS WE DISCUSSED in Chapter 7, the importance of people to the success of any organization is the essence of management. Getting things done with people and other resources and providing direction and leadership are what managers do. This chapter addresses the critical issue of human resource management. We will examine the way organizations recruit, train, and motivate people. We will also discuss employee training, development, and counselling, and will consider issues in labour–management relations. Finally, we will take a look at human resource concerns of the next century, including the opportunities and challenges of managing older workers, two-career couples, part-time employees, and a global work force.

THEY SAID IT

"Only 7 percent [of the Canadian work force] agree with the statement 'My company cares about me.'"

JOHN WRIGHT, Senior Vice President, Angus Reid Group

HUMAN RESOURCE MANAGEMENT: A VITAL MANAGERIAL FUNCTION

IN THIS CHAPTER we emphasize people — the human element of business — and their importance in accomplishing an organization's goals. Most organizations devote considerable attention to **human resource management**, which can be defined as (1) *the process of acquiring, training, developing, motivating, and appraising a sufficient quantity of qualified employees to perform the activities necessary to accomplish organizational objectives*; and (2) *developing specific activities and an overall organizational climate to generate maximum worker satisfaction and employee efficiency.*

While the owner/manager of a small organization is likely to assume complete responsibility for human resource management, larger organizations use company specialists called *human resource managers* to perform these activities in a systematic manner. The position is becoming increasingly important because of increased competition, growth in the use of outsourcing and part-time workers, a new emphasis on cost control, complex wage and benefit programs, and a changing work force. Human resource managers assume primary responsibility for forecasting personnel needs, recruiting, and aiding in the selection of new employees. They also assist in training and evaluation, and administer compensation, employee benefits, and safety programs.

We can view human resource management in two ways. In a narrow sense, it refers to the functions and operations of a single department in a firm: the human resource, or personnel, department. Most firms with 200 or more employees establish such a department. In a broader sense, though, human resource management involves the entire organization, even when a special staff department exists. After all, general management also is involved in training and developing workers, evaluating their performance, and motivating them to perform as efficiently as possible.

The core responsibilities of human resource management include human

Business Term
✓ **Human resource management**
Process of acquiring, training, developing, motivating, and appraising a sufficient quantity of qualified employees to perform the activities necessary to accomplish organizational objectives; and developing specific activities and an overall organizational climate to generate maximum worker satisfaction and employee efficiency.

resource planning, recruitment and selection, training/management development, performance appraisal, and compensation and employee benefits. Trained specialists from the human resource department typically share such responsibilities with line managers, ranging from the company president (who is involved in overall planning) to first-line supervisors (who may be involved in preliminary interviews with applicants and employee training), and — in companies practising worker empowerment — even employees. By accomplishing these critical tasks, the human resource department achieves its overall objectives of (1) providing qualified, well-trained employees, (2) maximizing employee effectiveness in the organization, and (3) satisfying individual employee needs through monetary compensation, employee benefits, advancement opportunities, and job satisfaction.

HOW NEEDS MOTIVATE PEOPLE

ROBERT LEVERING, AUTHOR of *A Great Place to Work* (Random House, 1988), concludes that any manager can turn a bad workplace into a good one through "the three Rs": granting workers more *responsibility* for their jobs, sharing the *rewards* of the enterprise as equitably as possible, and ensuring that employees have *rights*. These include establishing some kind of grievance procedure, allowing access to corporate records, and giving employees the right to confront those in authority without fearing reprisals.

The presence of the three Rs in an organization should contribute to employee morale. **Morale**, *the mental attitude of employees toward their employer and job*, involves a sense of common purpose with respect to other members of the work group and to the organization as a whole. High morale is a sign of a well-managed organization, because workers' attitudes toward their jobs affect the quality of the work done. One of the most obvious signs of poor manager–worker relations is poor morale. It lurks behind absenteeism, employee turnover, slowdowns, and wildcat strikes. It shows up in lower productivity, employee grievances, and transfers.

Business Term
✓ **Morale**
The mental attitude of employees toward their employer and job.

WORKPLACE TREND

BUY AND BURN

Rick, a high-technology employee, had been working 70-hour weeks for the last nine months. As far as he could remember, the only day he had had off in the last year was Christmas. Near the end of the project, he got an urgent voice-mail message from his boss demanding he call immediately to solve a technical problem. Twenty minutes into the conversation with his superior he was terminated.

What Rick thinks he experienced is an ugly high-tech industry phenomenon known as "buy and burn," a pattern in which some young employees are lured, often by substantial starting salaries, only to be abruptly dumped by their employers after a few years of 70-hour work weeks.

Neil Hill, vice-president of marketing at Cognos Inc., a Canadian company and a world leader in business information software, has this view on the issue: "Poor management is probably endemic in the software industry. ... Many software companies don't have very mature management structures. As a new industry, we have lots of people who have been lifted up through the hierarchy by the success of the company." According to another industry expert: "The typical programmer turned manager comes out of a very hard-skill education system, and has never been exposed to the softer side of people management. So they think that the way they work is the way everyone should be treated." Management weaknesses frequently spawn a greater and more pervasive problem: a lack of clear corporate direction. This often means poor employee selection.

"Yes we have a buy and burn vision in the software industry," says

---

Burnout, a byword in business today, is evidenced by low morale and fatigue. The most likely burnout candidates are those who care most about their jobs and the company. They experience burnout when they feel a sense of futility and a lack of accomplishment. According to Dr. Marilyn Hayman, a psychologist and corporate consultant, employee stress and burnout can be reduced if employees and managers believe that they have the power and authority to resolve problems.[3] Kenneth Pelletier, a stress-management consultant and psychiatrist, believes a manager can inspire workers and prevent burnout by showing appreciation for effort. Appreciation is, according to Pelletier, "the most underestimated benefit."[4]

What factors lead to high employee morale? Interestingly, managers and employees give different answers. In one classic study (see Table 8.1), managers thought that the most important factors involved satisfying employees' basic needs for money and job security. Employees, however, want to be appreciated, to be treated sympathetically, and to feel like part of a team. Jim Gannon of the Royal Bank of Canada agrees. Armed with a 1996 Angus Reid survey sponsored by his bank, Gannon notes that the happiest people are those who feel they are working in jobs they were trained for, with the skills they need to get ahead, and that their efforts count.[5]

Table 8.1 **What Contributes to High Morale?**

	Most Important	Less Important	Least Important
Manager Opinions	Good wages Job security Promotion and growth with company	Good working conditions Interesting work Management loyalty to workers	Tactful disciplining Full appreciation for work done Sympathetic understanding of personal problems Feeling "in" on things
Employee Opinions	Full appreciation for work done Feeling "in" on things Sympathetic understanding of personal problems	Job security Good wages Interesting work	Promotion and growth with company Management loyalty to workers Good working conditions Tactful disciplining

Managers and employees have quite different opinions regarding what factors contribute to high morale.

Paul Swinwood, president of the Software Human Resource Council of Canada. "There's no other word for it. There are some companies — a minority — that are known for hiring young people, burning them out, and passing them on."

Swinwood defines the employee skill set as a "four-legged stool."

→ **Attitude.** Employees must have the attitude that they are responsible for making the project successful. One way is to get the software developers involved right from the start. Graham Mackintosh of Cognos agrees: "When Impromptu 3 (Cognos's business query and reporting tool) was just getting under way, I took every developer and got them involved in the initial design process."

→ **Aptitude.** They must have the ability to work in a fast-changing, stressful environment.

→ **Communication skills.** They have to understand how to communicate not only with their own work groups but also with clients around the world. They must be "customer friendly" and have a clear understanding of the needs of the client base.

→ **Proper training.** Proper human resource management pays off. Cognos, for example, has two developers who have been with the firm for over 20 years and who have been responsible for more than 80 percent of its core innovations.

Managers and employees must recognize that constant upgrading of technical skills is part of the job and managers must budget accordingly. Training must be viewed as an investment, not a cost.

Sources: Adapted from Karyn Standen, "Buy and Burn," *The Globe and Mail Report on Business Magazine*, November 1996, 168–73. Reprinted by permission of the author.

Other studies agree with these results. The Angus Reid survey noted above, for example, found that people running their own business or people working for smaller businesses reported a great deal of satisfaction in their work. U.S. studies have come to this same conclusion. An Opinion Research Center survey found that many Americans would rather work for a small company than a large corporation. Says one researcher, "This desire is interesting, when you consider that benefits and pay are generally better in big corporations, and most people know that."[6]

Maintaining high employee morale also means more than just keeping employees happy. A two-day work week, longer vacations, or numerous work breaks easily could produce happy employees. But truly high morale results from an understanding of human needs and the ability of the organization to make satisfying individual needs consistent with organizational goals.

Business Term

√ **Need**

Lack of something useful; discrepancy between a desired state and the actual state.

Business Term

√ **Motive**

Inner state that directs us toward the goal of satisfying a felt need.

Each of us is motivated to take actions designed to satisfy needs. A **need** is simply *the lack of something useful*. It reflects a gap between an individual's actual state and his or her desired state. A **motive** is *the inner state that directs us toward the goal of satisfying a felt need*. Once the need — the gap between where a person is now and where he or she wants to be — becomes important enough, it produces tension and the individual is *moved* (the root word for *motive*) to reduce this tension and return to a condition of equilibrium. See also Figure 8.1.

Figure 8.1 The Motivation Process

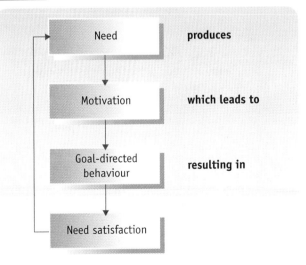

Let's look at an example. If you have been in class or worked at your job until 1 PM, your immediate need may be for food. Your lack of lunch is reflected in the motive of hunger. So you move — literally — to address your need by walking to a nearby restaurant, where you buy the $2.69 special (hamburger, fries, and soft drink). By 1:20 you have satisfied your need for lunch. Now you are ready to satisfy your next need: getting to your 2:00 class on time! The principle behind this process is that a need produces motivation, which leads to goal-directed behaviour, resulting in need satisfaction.

Maslow's Needs Hierarchy

Psychologist Abraham H. Maslow developed a widely accepted list of human needs (Figure 8.2) based on these important assumptions:

• People are wanting animals whose needs depend on what they already possess.

• A satisfied need is not a motivator; only those needs that have not been satisfied can influence behaviour.

• People's needs are arranged in a hierarchy of importance; once one need has been at least partially satisfied, another emerges and demands satisfaction.

Figure 8.2 Maslow's Hierarchy of Human Needs

Maslow's hierarchy of needs illustrates the order in which needs are satisfied.

Everyone has needs that must be satisfied before higher-order needs can be considered. On the bottom level of *Maslow's needs hierarchy* are *physiological needs* — the most basic needs, such as the desire for food, shelter, and clothing. Since most people in industrialized nations today can afford to satisfy their basic needs, however, higher-order needs are likely to play a greater role in worker motivation. These include *safety needs* (protection from physical harm, a sense of job security, and avoidance of the unexpected); *social needs* (the desire to be accepted by members of the family and other individuals and groups); and *esteem needs* (the needs to feel a sense of accomplishment, achievement, and respect from others). The competitive urge to excel — to better the performance of others — is an esteem need and an almost universal human trait.

At the top of the hierarchy are *self-actualization needs* — the needs for fulfilment, for realizing one's potential, for using one's talents and capabilities totally. Different

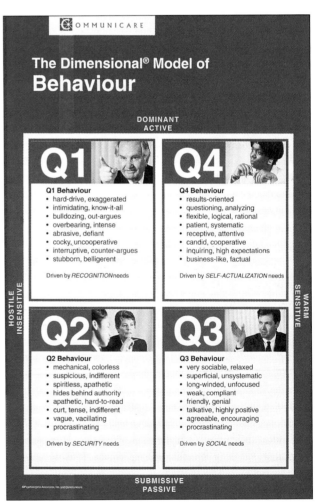

Adopting Maslow's needs hierarchy, Communicare helps North American organizations develop effective behavioural and communication skills to maximize the productivity of their employees.

people have different self-actualization needs: one person may feel fulfilled by writing a poem, another by running a marathon, and someone else may not attain self-actualization until listed in the *Guinness Book of World Records*. For Steve O'Donnell, a writer with "Late Show with David Letterman," self-actualization means "a pat on the back, making Dave happy, the thrill of hearing the audience laugh — that's what matters most." Organizations seek to satisfy employees' self-actualization needs, whatever they may be, by offering challenging and creative work assignments and opportunities for advancement based on individual merit.[7]

A major contribution of the needs hierarchy is the concept that, for most people, a satisfied need is no longer a motivator. Once physiological needs are satisfied, the individual becomes concerned with higher-order needs. There obviously will be periods when an individual is motivated by the need to relieve thirst or hunger, but interest most often is directed toward satisfying safety, belongingness, and other needs on the ladder.

Herzberg's Two-Factor Theory

Research conducted by psychologist Frederick Herzberg in the late 1960s led to another popular theory of motivation called the *two-factor theory*. His study, focussing on various job factors that might prove to be sources of dissatisfaction or satisfaction, identified two main categories: maintenance (or hygiene) factors and motivational factors.

Herzberg found that *maintenance, or hygiene, factors* — the lower level of needs in the Maslow hierarchy — such as working conditions, pay, and job security — worked only in the area of job dissatisfaction. He reasoned that abundant hygiene factors would remove dissatisfaction but were not strong employee motivators. For example, unsafe working conditions or job insecurity caused by downsizing would cause people to be dissatisfied, but their removal would not lead to a higher level of employee motivation or satisfaction.

The major sources of employee motivation, according to Herzberg, were the higher-level needs, the upper levels of Maslow's hierarchy. *Motivational factors* include job-centred factors such as the need for recognition, responsibility,

advancement, and growth potential. These motivators influence job satisfaction and must be in place before employees can be motivated to excel at their work. The manager's role is to provide hygiene factors to meet basic needs (remove the dissatisfiers) and then to use motivational factors to propel workers to greater achievement and satisfaction.

Theories X and Y

Maslow's theory became popular with managers because it is relatively simple and seems to fit the facts. After all, few of us are interested in self-actualization when we're starving. Business organizations have been extremely successful in satisfying the lower-order physiological and safety needs. The traditional view of workers as ingredients in the production process — as machines, like lathes, drill presses, and other equipment — led management to motivate them with money. Today's managers have been forced to reconsider their assumptions about employees and how best to motivate them.

Psychologist Douglas McGregor, a student of Maslow, proposed the concepts of Theory X and Theory Y as labels for the assumptions that different managers make about worker behaviour and how these assumptions affect their management style. **Theory X** *assumes that employees dislike work and must be coerced, controlled, or threatened to motivate them to work.* Managers who accept this view feel that the average person prefers to be directed, wishes to avoid responsibility, has relatively little ambition, and wants security above all. Such managers are likely to direct their subordinates through close and constant observation, continually holding over them the threat of disciplinary action, and demanding that they closely follow company policies and procedures.

If people behave in the manner described by Theory X, this may be because the organization satisfies only their lower-order needs. If, instead, the organization enables them to satisfy their social, esteem, and self-actualization needs too, employees may start to behave differently. McGregor labelled this thinking **Theory Y**, *an assumption that employees like work and, under proper conditions, accept and seek out responsibilities to fulfil their social, esteem, and self-actualization needs.* The Theory Y

Business Term

✓ **Theory X**

Managerial assumption that employees dislike work and must be coerced, controlled, or threatened to motivate them to work.

Business Term

✓ **Theory Y**

Managerial assumption that employees like work and, under proper conditions, accept and seek out responsibilities to fulfil their social, esteem, and self-actualization needs.

manager considers the expenditure of physical and mental effort in work as natural as play or rest. Unlike the traditional management philosophy that relies on external control and constant supervision, Theory Y emphasizes self-control and direction. Its implementation requires a different managerial strategy that includes worker participation in major and minor decisions previously reserved for management.

CYBERSPACE

The Internet is a gold mine of information on human resources, practical tips for managing people, and management strategies. To get started, you might want to visit

http://www.fastcompany.com/resources.

Theory Z

The trend toward downsizing, empowering, and increased employee participation in decision making has led to a third management style, labelled **Theory Z**. This approach *views involved workers as the key to increased productivity for the company and an improved quality of work life for the employee.* Long-term employment for employees and shared responsibility for making and implementing decisions are characteristics of Theory Z organizations. Evaluations and promotions are relatively slow, and promotions are tied to individual progress rather than to the calendar. Employees receive varied and nonspecialized experience to broaden their career paths.

The move toward the participative management style that characterizes the Theory Z approach is dramatically reshaping Canadian companies. As we saw in the last chapter, many companies are adopting flexible, "communication-friendly" organizational structures to reap the benefits of the team approach to solving problems. Increasingly, managers are asking workers how to improve their jobs — and then giving them the authority to do it.

Bundschuh Fashions, featured at the beginning of this chapter, is one company that goes to unusual lengths to learn about and work with its employees. Kanata, Ontario-based CrossKeys Systems Corporation, an affil-

Business Term

√ **Theory Z**

Management approach that views involved employees as the key to increased productivity for the company and an improved quality of work life for the employees.

iate of Newbridge Networks that has $10 million in sales, is another example of a company that attempts to seek long-term relationships with its employees. In four years, CrossKeys grew from 2 employees to more than 200. "There's a great deal of learning, understanding and basic knowledge which has to keep being accumulated in order to create our software. Our objective is not to squeeze out from an employee everything they know in a short period of time. We build and add to the capacity of an employee," says Bruce Litton, director of business relations at CrossKeys.[8]

BUILDING THE TEAM

Recruitment and Selection

Given the importance of a high-quality employee team in achieving organizational success, it is not surprising that human resource management is such an important function. The entertainment industry visionary Walt Disney expressed it this way: "You can dream, create, design, and build the most wonderful place in the world, but it requires people to make the dream a reality."

Not just people, but well-trained, well-motivated people are required. The recruitment and selection process plays a major role in convincing such people to become a part of the organization. Writer Leo Rosten made this observation: "First-rate people hire first-rate people. Second-rate people hire third-rate people."

Recruitment is expensive; it can include interviews, tests, medical examinations, and training. The human resource manager must ensure that potential employees have the necessary qualifications for the job, since an employee who leaves the firm after a few months can cost a company up to $75 000 in lost productivity, training costs, and employee morale. A poor employee who stays with the company can cost even more.

To ensure that potential employees have the necessary qualifications for the job and that they either possess needed skills or are capable of learning them, most firms use a six-step approach to recruitment and selection (see Figure 8.3). Rejection of an applicant may occur at any of these steps.

Businesses use both internal and external sources to find candidates for specific jobs. Table 8.2, for example,

Figure 8.3 Steps in the Recruitment and Selection Process

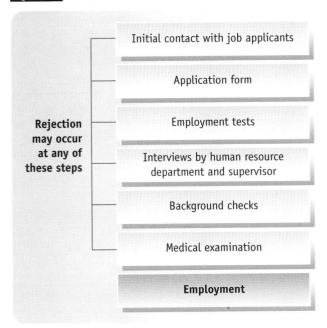

Rejection may occur at any of these steps

- Initial contact with job applicants
- Application form
- Employment tests
- Interviews by human resource department and supervisor
- Background checks
- Medical examination

Employment

Atlantic Canada Careers

"We help navigate careers in Atlantic Canada"

Atlantic Canada Careers is an innovative Internet career networking service for individuals who seek challenging new employment opportunities, and for progressive organizations who want to attract top calibre people.

INDIVIDUALS

Atlantic Canada Careers is a discrete networking service for anyone planning a career move or keeping an eye on the market. It is of interest to people working in Atlantic Canada, qualified Maritimers "living away" looking for the right opportunity to "come home" to, or would-be Maritimers attracted to our region.

ORGANIZATIONS

Atlantic Canada Careers is an innovative and inexpensive job recruitment channel for progressive organizations who want to broaden their recruitment advertising reach, to attract top calibre candidates. Firms can place careers ads, conduct a resume bank search, or market themselves through a corporate profile.

To find out how you can join these leaders, call Jeff Chisholm and check out Atlantic Canada Careers

www.atl-can-careers.com | (902) 425-9555

Besides helping individuals to find the right job, Atlantic Canada Careers, an innovative Internet career networking service, also helps businesses recruit suitable candidates for specific jobs.

lists various sources that companies might use for recruiting potential employees. Many firms have a policy of *hiring from within* — that is, considering their own employees first for job openings.

Internal staffing is usually most suited for the middle- to higher-level jobs and professional staff. For example, EDO Canada, a Calgary-based company that manufactures a marine integrated navigation system (MINS), has had difficulties in hiring a sufficient number of aeronautical engineers. A crucial part of the com-

pany's hiring process is thus maintaining an inventory of all the skills within the company. This inventory describes the skills, lack of relevant skills, and career goals of every employee. It means that the company is

Table 8.2 Recruiting Sources

Internal Sources	External Sources
Posting and bidding	Recommendations and referrals
Employee requests	Newspaper advertisements
Seniority lists	Advertising in trade, professional, or business journals
Skills inventories	Private employment agencies
Assessment centres	Public employment services
Search committees	High schools; trade and technical schools
	Professional, sales, and business organizations
	Recruiting at professional, technical, or business conventions
	College recruiting
	Executive search firms
	Unsolicited ("walk-in") applicants
	Career centres and job fairs
	Minority candidate offices and women's career centres
	Community organizations (Jaycees, the Y, women's clubs)
	Direct mail solicitation
	Telephone recruiting

Table 8.3 Some Laws Relevant to Human Resource Management Practices

Jurisdiction	Human Rights	Employment Standards
Federal	Canadian Human Rights Act Equal Wages Guidelines Employment Equity Act	Canada Labour Code Fair Wages and Hours of Labour Act Holidays Act Wages Liability Act
Alberta	Individual's Rights Protection Act	Employment Standards Code Family Day Act
British Columbia	Human Rights Act	Employment Standards Act Skills Development and Fair Wage Act
Manitoba	Human Rights Act Pay Equity Act	Employment Standards Act Construction Industry Wages Act Vacations with Pay Act Payment of Wages Act Remembrance Day Act
New Brunswick	Human Rights Act Pay Equity Act	Employment Standards Act Days of Rest Act
Newfoundland	Human Rights Code	Labour Standards Act Remembrance Day Act
Nova Scotia	Human Rights Act Pay Equity Act	Labour Standards Code Remembrance Day Act
Ontario	Human Rights Code Pay Equity Act	Employment Standards Act One Day's Rest in Seven Act Wages Act
Prince Edward island	Human Rights Act Pay Equity Act	Minimum Age of Employment Act Employment Standards Act
Quebec	Charter of Human Rights and Freedoms	Labour Standards Act National Holiday Act
Saskatchewan	Human Rights Code	Labour Standards Act National Holiday Act
Northwest Territories	Fair Practices Act	Labour Standards Act Wages Recovery Act
Yukon	Human Rights Act	Employment Standards Act

better able to draw on the capabilities of its own staff before going outside to hire. A senior personnel administrator explains: "Both the company and the individual benefit from the training and development of existing employees to fill vacancies: employees have higher motivation and morale which results in greater job satisfaction and higher productivity."[9]

If qualified internal candidates are not available, management must look for people outside the organization. External recruitment is common for entry-level jobs and the highest-level positions in the organization, such as chief executive officer. Most organizations use external recruitment strategies to some extent. Accounting firm Coopers & Lybrand, for example, has developed a unique recruitment tool — an interactive and menu-driven computer disk that it gives out to university students as a way to expose them to the accounting profession.[10] Outside sources for potential job applicants include colleges, advertisements in newspa-

pers and professional journals, public employment agencies, unsolicited applications, and recommendations by current employees.

Canadian laws relevant to human rights and employment standards involve both the federal and the provincial governments (see, for example, Table 8.3). This is a particularly complicated issue for human resource managers, especially since only about 10 percent of employee rights legislation comes under federal jurisdiction and about 90 percent comes under provincial jurisdiction — and provincial jurisdiction can vary extensively. Failure to follow these requirements may prevent the firm from profiting from the strengths of its own diverse work force; it also can result in stiff penalties and bad publicity. In addition to these laws, employers must be aware of various other legal restrictions governing hiring practices.

Employees, for their part, must be aware of legal restrictions governing their own behaviour. For example, if a company is going to terminate an employee without severance pay, it must prove that it has just cause to fire the individual. To do that, a company must document and prove serious misconduct on the part of the employee. As well, a growing number of communities ban smoking in workplaces and public areas. Many employers have policies against hiring smokers; some penalize current employees who smoke by charging higher premiums for health insurance and other benefits.

Orientation, Training, and Evaluation

Newly hired employees usually complete an orientation program, which is the joint responsibility of the human resource department and the department in which the person will work. Another major function of the human resource department is developing and maintaining a

well-trained, productive labour force. Employee training should be viewed as an ongoing process throughout an employee's tenure with the company.

On-the-job training, in which *employees are trained for job tasks by allowing them to perform them under the guidance of an experienced employee,* is a frequently used method. A variation of this approach is *apprenticeship training,* a program wherein an employee learns a job by serving as an assistant to a trained worker for a relatively long time period. On-the-job training is the most widely used training method in Canada. In 1993, for example, the federal government alone spent almost $4 billion to help Canadians improve

> **Business Term**
> ✓ **On-the-job-training**
> Training employees for job tasks by allowing them to perform them under the guidance of an experienced employee.

ETHICAL ISSUE

IT'S A MATTER OF ETHICS

Get ready for some heated discussions. Read the following human resource scenarios. Explain how you would respond to each one, using the ethics decision-making model below.

Situation 1: You are the HR manager for a department store. Your brother-in-law has been out of work for eight months, and has appealed to you to put him on the short list for a plum job in the store — a job that he is qualified to do. However, there are internal candidates who are better qualified for the position. The company does not have a policy against hiring relatives. You don't know if you should put your brother-in-law on the short list. What would you do, and why?

Situation 2: You are the HR manager in a medium-sized company

that is downsizing. A good friend is the marketing manager for this company. Unfortunately, you have just learned that she will be fired three days from today, as part of the restructuring process. You also know that she is planning to close a deal on a house tomorrow. You are sure that she will not be able to afford the house if she is fired. She has no idea that she could lose her job. Should you tell her? Why or why not?

Situation 3: About six months ago, you started a consulting business as a training specialist. There is a lot of competition for training consultants and you have been struggling from the start. But finally, your first client has offered you a sizable training contract. The only problem is that you have just finished a tour of the company premises and you realize that this company uses chemicals that pollute the environment. You

happen to have strong beliefs about the evils of pollution, but you really need this contract. What would you do, and why?

An Ethics Decision-Making Model
To help you answer these ethical dilemmas, ask yourself the following questions:

→ Is it legal?

→ Is it right?

→ Would the outcome of the decision harm you or others?

→ Would you be comfortable if the decision were public knowledge?

→ What is your gut feeling?

Source: From Diane White and Indira Somwaru, *Cases in Human Resources Management* (Toronto: Harcourt Brace & Comany, 1994), pp. 155-56. The ethics decision-making model is adapted from Michael E. Rock, *Ethics to Live By; To Work By* (Toronto: Concept Press, 1992).

their on-the-job training.[11] This spending was important when we consider that the "average" Canadian worker received only 7 hours of training a year, compared with 17 hours in Australia, 170 hours in Sweden, and 200 hours in Japan.[12]

Off-the-job training involves some form of *classroom training*, in which classroom techniques — lectures, conferences, audiovisual aids, programmed instruction, or special machines — are used to teach employees difficult, high-skill jobs. A **management-development program** is *training designed to improve the skills and broaden the knowledge of current and potential managers.* Such programs often are conducted off the company premises. Organizations such as Levi-Strauss Canada Ltd., Labatt Breweries of Canada Ltd., and the Royal Bank of Canada are among the dozens of giant companies that have established college-like institutes offering specific programs for current potential managers.[13]

Another important human resource management activity, **performance appraisal**, is *the evaluation of an individual's job performance by comparing actual performance with desired performance.* This information is used to make objective decisions about compensation, promotion, additional training needs, transfers, or terminations. Such appraisals are not confined to business. Professors appraise student performance through assignments and examinations, while students appraise instructors by completing written evaluations.

Effective training programs often include both training and performance appraisal. Consider the Hewlett-Packard Interactive Network, which combines a classroom training format with interactive video. HP instructors present the telecourses in special studios; then the information is beamed to HP offices and factories around the world. Students provide feedback to instructors by speaking into microphones or by typing responses into networked computers. Instructors, who have electronic seating charts for each online site, provide immediate performance appraisals by polling students; test results can be displayed instantly on computer-generated charts. Since the company began using the interactive network, the cost of new-product seminars has fallen by more than 98 percent. The network is so cost-effective that Hewlett-Packard has turned it into a profit-maker by selling the service to other companies.[14]

Business Term

√ **Management-development program**

Training designed to improve the skills and broaden the knowledge of current and potential managers.

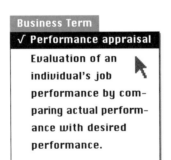

Business Term

√ **Performance appraisal**

Evaluation of an individual's job performance by comparing actual performance with desired performance.

Employee Compensation

One of the most difficult functions of human resource management is to develop an equitable compensation and benefits system. Because labour costs represent a sizable percentage of total product costs, wages that are too high may result in products that are too expensive to compete effectively in the marketplace. But inadequate wages lead to high employee turnover, poor morale, and inefficient production.

The terms *wages* and *salary* are often used interchangeably, but they do have slightly different meanings. *Wages* represent compensation based on the number of hours worked or the amount of output produced. They generally are paid to production employees, retail salespeople, and maintenance workers. *Salary* is employee compensation calculated on a weekly, monthly, or annual basis. White-collar workers, such as office personnel, executives, and professional employees, usually receive salaries.

A satisfactory compensation program should attract well-qualified workers, keep them satisfied in their jobs, and inspire them to produce. The compensation policy of most companies is based on five factors: (1) salaries and wages paid by other companies in the area that compete for the same personnel, (2) government legislation, (3) the cost of living, (4) the ability of the company to pay, and (5) the workers' productivity.

Many employers seek to reward superior performance and motivate employees to excel by offering some type of *incentive compensation*, an addition to a salary or wage that is given for exceptional performance (see Figure 8.4). Hay Management Consultants Ltd. has confirmed a growing trend toward extending incentive programs to all workers.[15] Model companies like 3M Canada and Pillsbury Canada have found that effective employee benefit programs should consist of three key elements: corporate profitability, a team component, and an individual component.[16] Effective incentive compensation plans reward employees for goals related to quality as well as productivity. For example, the SkyDome — Toronto's high-profile sports and entertainment centre — credits its incentive program, which is based on both quantitative and qualitative standards, with helping it exceed its revenue targets.

Figure 8.4 Four Forms of Incentive Compensation

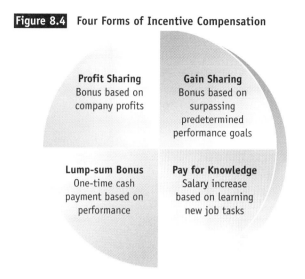

Profit Sharing
Bonus based on company profits

Gain Sharing
Bonus based on surpassing predetermined performance goals

Lump-sum Bonus
One-time cash payment based on performance

Pay for Knowledge
Salary increase based on learning new job tasks

These four types of incentive compensation are designed to reward exceptional performance by the individual work team.

Employee Benefits

The typical organization provides many benefits to employees and their families besides wages and salaries. **Employee benefits** are *rewards such as pension plans, insurance, sick leave, child care, and tuition reimbursement given entirely or partly at the expense of the company.* Most benefits are governed by federal and provincial laws. Federal and/or provincial laws require some mandatory

benefits such as income protection programs for times when income has been disrupted through loss of a job, inability to work due to illness, work accidents, and retirement. What are known in Canada as universal coverage programs — such as Old Age Security (OAS) and Guaranteed Income Supplement (GIS) — are mainly funded by the federal government.[17] However, there are four major mandatory programs that require contributions by employers and employees and in some cases by the provincial government:[18]

> **Business Term**
> √ **Employee benefits**
> Employee rewards such as pension plans, insurance, sick leave, child care, and tuition reimbursement given entirely or partly at the expense of the company.

- Canada and Quebec pension plans: for retirement, disability, and survivors' and death benefits

- Workers' compensation: for disability benefits and spouses' and dependents' pensions

- Health insurance

- Employment insurance

Other benefits may be provided voluntarily. Examples include health insurance, pensions and retirement programs, paid vacations and leave time, and employee services, such as tuition-reimbursement programs.

Great-West Life, one of the strongest financial institutions in North America, is a leading provider of group insurance benefits at the workplace.

Employee benefits are a large and rapidly growing component of human resource costs. For example, payroll taxes such as employment insurance and workers' compensation have risen over 300 percent since 1980.[19] According to a 1996 payroll survey by KPMG Management Consultants, the wages and salaries of workers represent only about 58 percent of the total payroll of a firm; the remaining 42 percent comprises benefits such as social insurance payments, employment insurance premiums, vacation pay, workers' compensation premiums, health insurance, and so on. In 1993 alone, companies in Canada spent about $94 billion on benefits — a 50 percent increase from 1989.[20] Hence, cost containment has become a critical consideration for any company and human resource manager.

An increasingly common method of controlling benefits costs is to offer *flexible benefit plans*, or *cafeteria-style benefits*. The most common flexible program offers everyone a core package of benefits and then lets people choose extra benefits according to their needs. For example, an older person can opt for dental or eye care, whereas a young worker just starting a family can choose more health-care insurance.[21] Companies like Noranda Inc. and Canadian General Tower have used this flexible benefits system with considerable success.[22] Businesses are also finding that a flexible benefits program gives their recruiters an edge in the increased competition for college graduates.[23]

Job Enrichment

In their search for ways to improve employee productivity and morale, a growing number of firms are focussing on the motivational aspects of the job itself. Rather than simplifying the tasks involved in a job, they seek to enrich the job by making it more satisfying and meaningful. **Job enrichment** involves *redesigning work to give employees more authority in planning their tasks and deciding how the work is to be done, and allowing them to learn related skills or to trade jobs with others.*

A recent survey of 77 major companies found that job enrichment plays a crucial role in determining which new

> **Business Term**
>
> ✓ **Job enrichment**
> Redesigning work to give employees more authority in planning their tasks and deciding how the work is to be done, and allowing them to learn related skills or to trade jobs with others.

The World According to Big Shot

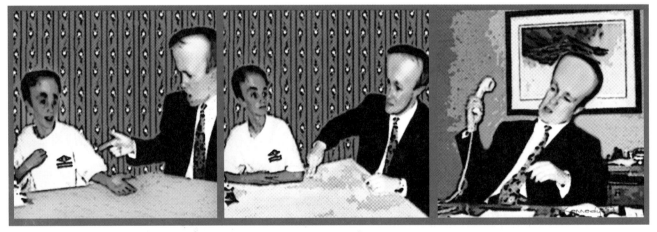

BIG SHOT: Your teacher says that you're not getting along with your classmates. Why's that?
LITTLE GUY: Dad, you told me that leadership was getting extraordinary performance from ordinary people. I told my group that I expected much better work from them if they were going to work for me.

BIG SHOT: Son, when you're working with your classmates you have to think of their feelings or they'll exclude you. But when you're in business, you can be ruthless. For now, you'd better try to be more co-operative — understand?
LITTLE GUY: Thanks, Dad. I think I understand now.

BIG SHOT: You know, Slinky, last night I realized how important it is for fathers to spend quality time with their sons. I think the Little Guy is going in the right direction now. Call him and arrange another session for sometime next month.

→ What can you learn about leadership from Big Shot's example?

products succeed and which do not. Successful product-development teams enjoy full support from top management and are given the authority to manage the project themselves.[24]

Job Enlargement. *Job enlargement* sometimes is used interchangeably with job enrichment, but it differs in that it is merely an expansion of a worker's assignments to include additional, but smaller, tasks. Rather than performing two tasks, a worker might be given four similar tasks. Enlarging a job might lead to job enrichment, but not necessarily. Job enrichment occurs only when the new tasks give an employee greater authority and responsibility for the end result. Enrichment means that employees have more opportunity to be creative and to set their own pace within the limits of the overall schedule.

Job Rotation. *Job rotation* has also been identified as a form of job enrichment. Technically, however, it differs in that it increases the *number* of jobs or tasks an individual performs without increasing the complexity of any *one* job. Job rotation has a greater motivational potential when the jobs are challenging rather than simplified. For example, Bell Canada periodically rotates line managers and personnel officers into each other's positions. The program is designed to ensure that managers remain productive and stimulated. Exposure to unfamiliar areas gives managers an opportunity to expand their knowledge of corporate operations and to learn another area of the company through hands-on experience.[25]

Management by Objectives. *Management by objectives* (*MBO*), discussed in Chapter 4, is a recognized method of enriching the workplace. As such, MBO has been widely adopted in many successful North American companies such as Black and Decker and DuPont as a method of improving employee morale and productivity. Major benefits include improved[26]

- **Performance.** Productivity can be improved at all company levels because employees and managers are committed to achieving mutually agreed-upon objectives.

- **Motivation.** Employees are motivated because they are involved in the decision-making process and are given the responsibility and accountability to accomplish their objectives.

- **Communication.** Relationships between managers and subordinates are improved by having explicit discussions about objectives and defining the required activities that will help achieve their goals.

Flexible or Alternative Work Schedules. Recent studies of employees, ranging from clerks to senior managers, tell us that the number one stress factor for employees is time pressure.[27] Flexible work schedules are a good way for companies to attract and motivate talented employees and enrich their jobs. Flexible schedules include flextime, compressed work weeks, job sharing, and home-based work, explained below.

A work-scheduling system that allows employees to set work hours within constraints specified by the firm is called **flextime**. Most employers offering flextime designate certain "core hours" when employees are required to be on the job, such as between 9 AM and 3 PM.[28] Meetings typically are scheduled during these core hours. In general, flextime is more common in insurance, finance, retailing, and government positions than in manufacturing jobs. Its use is more widespread in Europe than it is in North America. Other alternative work-scheduling practices include a *compressed work week* — where employees work the same number of hours in fewer than the typical five days — and *job sharing*, the division of one job assignment between two or more employees.

Home-Based Work. More and more companies offer employees a fifth option of **home-based work** — *working at the same job, but at home instead of in the office*. Home-based workers are sometimes called *telecommuters* because they may "commute" to work electronically via home computer to the company's computer system. Technologies such as personal computers, electronic mail, and fax machines make working at home easier than ever before.

The number of telecommuting employees — those working from home while hooked up to their company's computer via phone lines — is expected to more than double in North America before the next millennium. Many industry observers believe telecommuting to be an employment wave of the future. In

Business Term

✓ **Flextime**

Work-scheduling system that allows employees to set work hours within constraints specified by the firm.

Business Term

✓ **Home-based work**

Program allowing employees to work at the same job, but at home instead of in the office.

With telecommuting becoming more and more common, computer makers such as Apple are advertising their products to telecommuters, or home-based workers.

Canada, telecommuting is forecasted to grow by 15 percent to 20 percent per year to yield about 700 000 telecommuter homes by the year 2000. Worker productivity as a result of telecommuting typically increases 10 to 40 percent, job satisfaction improves, and company costs on things such as real estate are reduced. For example, BCE Inc., Bell Canada's parent, has more than 5000 employees telecommuting either full or part time. Each teleworker represents an annual savings of about $3000 to Bell. Of IBM's 12 000 employees in Canada, at least 700 work full time from the home and another 4000 "can work from the home on any given day," says IBM spokesperson Mike Quinn.[29]

Telecommuting dramatically changes the employee–employer relationship. Successful telecommuters need to be self-disciplined, reliable, computer literate, and able to do without much supervision; they also need bosses who are comfortable with setting goals and managing from afar.[30] It remains to be seen whether telecommuters continue to enjoy working in isolation.

LABOUR–MANAGEMENT RELATIONS

IN NATIONS THROUGHOUT the world, employees have joined together to increase their power to achieve the goals of improved wages, hours, and working conditions. These efforts have, to a considerable extent, succeeded; today's workplace is far different from the one existing at the turn of the century, where child labour, frequently unsafe working conditions, and a 72-hour work week (six 12-hour days a week) were commonplace.

Today, the people who head organizations that provide necessary goods and services, the people who do the work, and the government organizations that maintain the society comprise the various industrial relationships. With the growing interdependence among nations around the world and the increasing number of multinational corporations, understanding labour–management relations becomes imperative for business students.

Table 8.4 Congress Affiliation of Union Membership

Membership	%
CLC (Canadian Labour Congress)	57.8
AFL-CIO as well as CLC	21.2
CLC only	36.6
CNTU (Confederation of National Trade Unions)	6.2
CFL (Canadian Federation of Labour)	5.2
AFL-CIO as well as CFL	5.0
CFL only	0.2
AFL-CIO only (American Federation of Labor/Congress of Industrial Organizations)	4.1
Other federations	4.5
Unaffiliated international unions	0.2
Unaffiliated national unions	18.7
Independent local organizations	3.2
TOTAL	100.0

Labour Unions

A union or **labour union** generally refers to *an organization of employees that has been granted the exclusive legal authority to bargain on behalf of the employees with their employer with respect to the terms and conditions of employment.* Often the term labour union is used synonymously with trade union, craft union, federation, and staff association, among others.[31] Labour unions can be found at the local, national, and international levels. A *local union* represents union members in a specific area, such as a single community, while a *national union* is a labour organization consisting of numerous local chapters. An *international union* is a national union with membership outside Canada, usually in the United States. A *federation* is a union of unions that represents the broad interests of the labour movement. There are both national and provincial federations, and many unions are affiliated with both levels. The *Canadian Labour Congress (CLC)* is Canada's largest federation.[32]

According to the Canadian Labour Congress, as of 1996, approximately 35 percent of Canada's full-time workers were unionized. This is in sharp contrast to the United States, where only about 15 percent of the full-time labour force belong to a

union. The highest frequency of union membership is in our public sector (approximately 55 percent unionized), and the lowest union membership is in the retail sector (only 7 percent unionized).[33]

Today, labour relations are primarily a concern of the provincial governments. All provinces have labour relations statutes that reflect the principles of four acts and in particular the federal Industrial Relations and Disputes Investigation Act:[34]

- **Constitution Act.** Sections 91 and 92 divide the power for regulating between the provincial and federal governments.

- **Trade Unions Act.** Requires unions to be registered.

- **Criminal Law Amendment Act.** Removes criminal sanctions for organizing in restraint of trade provided the union is registered under the Trade Unions Act.

- **Industrial Relations and Disputes Investigation Act.** The basic principles of this act are
  - Employee freedom of association and union recognition.
  - Compulsory bargaining rights for certified trade unions.
  - Postponement of the right to strike until after government intervention through conciliation.
  - Prohibition of unfair labour practices by both employers and trade unions to protect individual rights and the collective bargaining process.
  - Establishment of legal status and enforceability of the collective agreement.
  - Provision for resolving disputes arising out of the collective bargaining agreement without resorting to strike.
  - Establishment of regulatory bodies with investigation and control powers.

Business Term

√ **Labour union**

Organization of employees that has been granted the exclusive legal authority to bargain on behalf of the employees with their employer with respect to the terms and conditions of employment.

The Collective Bargaining Process

The primary objective of a labour union is to improve the wages, hours, and working conditions of its members. This goal is achieved primarily through **collective bargaining**, *a process of negotiation between management and union representatives for the purpose of arriving at mutually acceptable wages and working conditions for employees.*

Issues covered in collective bargaining include wages, work hours, benefits, union activities and responsibilities, grievance handling and arbitration, and employee rights and seniority. As is the case in all types of negotiations, the collective bargaining process is one of demands, proposals, and counterproposals that ultimately result in compromise and agreement. The initial demands merely represent a starting point in negotiations. They are rarely, if ever, accepted by the other party without some compromise. The final agreement depends on the negotiating skills and relative power of management and union representatives.

Union contracts, which typically cover a two- or three-year period, are often the result of days and even weeks of discussion, disagreement, compromise, and eventual agreement. Once agreement is reached, union

> **Business Term**
> √ **Collective bargaining**
> **Process of negotiation between management and union representatives for the purpose of arriving at mutually acceptable wages and working conditions for employees.**

members must vote to accept or reject the contract. If the contract is rejected, union representatives may resume the bargaining process with management representatives, or union members may strike to obtain their demands.

Once ratified by the union membership, the contract becomes a legally binding agreement for all labour–management relations during the period specified. Some contracts are only a few pages in length, while others can run hundreds of pages.

Settling Union–Management Disputes

According to the Workplace Information Directorate, Labour Canada, in 1995, there were some 370 work stoppages — mainly due to striking workers. Although these

CASE EXERCISE

YOU'RE THE HR MANAGER

You're the chairperson of a major Canadian company. It's the kind of business in which the company's leader must be seen as highly ethical and moral.

You've heard rumours from a number of sources that your president and CEO, a married man, has had an affair with a volunteer summer student in her early 20s. The president has worked for the company for six years and has done well in moving the business forward.

At the next board meeting, you confront the president and he emphatically denies the rumour. To quell the gossip, he issues a memo to employees denying the affair. Relieved, you put the matter out of your mind.

Yet rumours persist. The president continues to deny any personal

relationship with the volunteer. At the next shareholders' meeting, the issue is raised again and the president denies it. The media picks up the story and it hits the papers.

Soon after, another employee advises you that she saw the president in his office late one evening, kissing the volunteer. This time, you speak to the volunteer directly. Initially, she denies the affair, but after assurances that she won't get into trouble, she admits to the affair — in lurid detail. It is clear to you that, while the two have not consummated the relationship, there has been inappropriate office conduct.

Again you confront the president. This time he breaks down and admits to a fling with the volunteer. He is contrite and apologizes, but reminds you that there is no company policy which discourages this kind of action.

You convene the board of directors and call the company's employ-

ment lawyer to decide what to do. You are upset about the president's lack of judgement and persistent lying. You know that you can always dismiss an employee without cause, upon payment of a significant severance package, but your question is: Can you dismiss this employee *with* cause?

1. Can the president be dismissed for any of the following: Sexual harassment? Dishonesty? Violating workplace policy?

2. Is his conduct so inconsistent with the values of the organization so as to warrant dismissal?

3. Do the president's behaviour and his lying reveal a character flaw so severe that continued employment is untenable?

Source: Mary Porjes, "How Employment Law Would View Bill Clinton," *The Globe and Mail*, September 22, 1998, B17.

strikes make newspaper headlines, at least 90 percent of all union–management negotiations result in a signed agreement without a work stoppage.[35] The courts are the most visible and familiar vehicle for dispute settlement, but most disputes are settled by negotiation. There is real motivation to make negotiations work, since so much time, money, and personnel costs are involved in court trials. Dispute resolution mechanisms, such as grievance procedures, mediation, and arbitration, are quicker, cheaper, and less complicated procedurally, and receive less publicity.

The union contract serves as a guide to relations between the firm's management and its employees. The rights of each party are stated in the agreement, but no contract, regardless of how detailed, will eliminate the possibility of disagreement. Such differences can be the beginning of a *grievance*, a complaint — by a single worker or by the entire union — that management is violating some provision of the union

> **Business Term**
> ✓ **Mediation**
> Process of settling union–management disputes through recommendations of an impartial third party.

> **Business Term**
> ✓ **Arbitration**
> Process of bringing an impartial third party into a union–management dispute to render a legally binding decision.

Mediation is *the process of settling union–management disputes through recommendations of an impartial third party*. Although the mediator does not serve as a decision-maker, union and management representatives can be assisted in reaching an agreement by the mediator's suggestions, advice, and compromise solutions.

When disputes cannot be solved voluntarily through mediation, the parties can turn to **arbitration** — *bringing in an impartial third party, called an arbitrator, who renders a legally binding decision*. The arbitrator must be acceptable to the union and to management, and his or her decision is legally enforceable. In essence, the arbitrator acts as a judge, making a decision after listening to both sides of the argument. Ninety percent of all union contracts in North America call for the use of arbitration if union and management representatives fail to reach an agreement.

Weapons of Unions and Management

Most differences between labour and management are settled through the collective bargaining process or through a formal grievance procedure.

Serious differences between the union and management can result in strikes, lockouts, walkouts, slowdowns, picketing, and even violence. Strikes and lockouts are the most common reactions to serious differences. Typically they do not last more than 90 days, but if there appears to be a major impasse, resolution methods such as arbitration are introduced. Strikes and lockouts have proven costly for both sides.

A *strike* is a refusal on the part of unionized employees to work until a dispute has been settled or a contract

DID YOU KNOW?

John Kervin, a University of Toronto professor who has studied negotiations and worked as a bargaining consultant, says that negotiations are particularly hard on people without experience. One of the biggest sources of stress is the sporadic nature of talks, with long periods of waiting while the other side meets and puts together a proposal. "Then there's a great deal of flurry of activity and great deal of pressure because a mistake in understanding something can cause great consequences down the road. ... Hotels [the site of many negotiations] may be the only ones who really enjoy bargaining."

contract. Almost all union contracts require these complaints to be submitted to a formal grievance procedure, typically beginning with the employee's supervisor and moving up the company's chain of command. If the highest company officer cannot settle the grievance, it is submitted to an outside party for mediation or arbitration.

The OPSEU strike against the Ontario government in spring 1997 shut down cities for a day.

signed. Examples include the 1996 Canadian Auto Workers strike, which cost General Motors of Canada at least $1 billion,[36] and the 1994 NHL players strike. In Canada, workers do not have the legal right to withhold their labour when a dispute arises. The only time they have the right to go on strike is after a collective agreement has expired. The general rule is "Work now, grieve later." A *lockout* is a deliberate withholding of labour by the employer.

THEY SAID IT

"Back in the early 1980s when I was the Minister of Employment, I think that the numbers of people who were what you call 'long-term unemployed' was around 4 percent; it is now 13 percent. Also, the nature of the jobs themselves has changed fundamentally. Suddenly, the fastest-growing job market in Canada is overtime, part-time work, individual work, and self-employed work, not the work that was based, as we traditionally knew it, on large companies providing secure systems of benefits and pay rates over a large number of years."

LLOYD AXWORTHY, MP, former Minister

of Human Resources Development

The Future of Organized Labour

Over the 1990s, unions have struggled to maintain their numbers and traditional role. In the future, various economic and social developments will further challenge and perhaps change the face of Canada's union movement. Four major trends include

- Continued globalization of Canadian companies.

- Gradual fragmentation of the workplace.

- Increased telecommuting.

- Growth in the traditionally nonunion sectors, such as the contract and part-time work force and the small business sector.

Many experts feel that the future of organized labour worldwide lies in continuing to build a co-operative relationship with management. The rate of strikes in Great Britain has reached its lowest in over a century. Union workers at Dutch steelmaker Hoogovens reached

a compromise with managers by agreeing to a wage freeze and early retirement for 600 workers in exchange for job guarantees for the rest. Union members at an AT&T facility in the United States helped managers design a work-team system that improved phone-repair and quality-control procedures. The new system proved so cost-effective that AT&T moved 100 jobs back to the United States from Mexico.[37]

HUMAN RESOURCE CONCERNS FOR THE NEW CENTURY

A NUMBER OF ISSUES will continue to grow in importance during the next few years: adjusting corporate policies to reflect the aging work force, responding to the needs of two-career couples, assisting in breaking the so-called glass ceiling, adjusting to the growing ranks of part-time workers, and managing in an increasingly global environment.

Older Workers

Back in 1961, 45 percent of the Canadian population was over age 30. By 1990, this percentage had increased to about 56 percent. Projections by Statistics Canada tell us that, by the year 2011, it will rise even further to about 61 percent.[38] Canada's population and work force are aging. The 1960s counterculture slogan "Never trust anyone over 30" has increasingly become dated.

As the Canadian population ages, more and more companies will offer their older workers **worker buyout plans** in an attempt to reduce payrolls. These involve *financial incentives to encourage voluntary retirement or separation* and typically include financial packages containing a cash bonus, continuation of such employee benefits as insurance coverage, and higher than normal retirement benefits (to cover the gap between retirement and the onset of Canada Pension Plan and RRSP payments).

In addition to reducing company payrolls, worker buyouts may contribute to the morale of remaining workers, who see tangible evidence of management's attempts to maintain job security

Business Term

√ **Worker buyout plans** Financial incentives to encourage voluntary retirement or separation of older workers.

by resorting to buyouts rather than layoffs. Also, unclogging job and promotion opportunities improves the upward mobility of younger employees.

However, business pays a price when it loses older workers. These employees are often the most experienced and knowledgeable, and many employers find that they are simply more effective than less experienced workers. Some companies reward and retain experienced employees by offering nonfinancial incentives. Semiconductor manufacturer Intel, for example, copies the faculty practices of many universities by giving its employees an eleven-week paid sabbatical every seven years.[39]

> **Business Term**
>
> √ **Glass ceiling**
>
> **Invisible barrier that keeps women and minorities from advancing to top management.**

Two-Career Households

Since 1970 there has been a resurgence of female workers entering the labour force leading to a dramatic increase in the number of two-career households — from about 40 percent of all households in 1971 to 60 percent in 1993.[40]

THEY SAID IT

"On an hourly basis, we pay more to park a car in a downtown parking lot than we do for child care."

JUDITH MAXWELL, President,
Canadian Policy Research Networks

An important human resource challenge will involve meeting the specific job-related needs of two-career households. Issues frequently arise when a manager, professional staff member, or highly skilled employee is hired from another geographic area. Relocation services for the spouse often are required to attract the new employee. For example, IBM has been known to reimburse spouses for up to $500 in job-search expenses. Other firms aid spouses by providing employment leads and financial assistance until the spouse locates a job in the new city.

These services pay off for both employees and employers. Flexible work arrangements, part-time work options, high-quality child care, and parental-leave programs are effective ways for firms to attract, retain, and motivate workers.

The Glass Ceiling

Although the number of women in professional and ownership positions has risen, women are still in charge of only about 33 percent of Canadian companies (1996).[41]

Over the past three decades it has been difficult for women to advance beyond a certain level within many business organizations. Where this level falls in the corporate hierarchy varies from company to company. It has been coined the **glass ceiling** because it is *an invisible barrier that keeps women and minorities from advancing to top management*. "The [corporate] culture is more important than policy," says human resource consultant Rose Jonas. "If the culture doesn't change, nothing will change for women."[42]

A few of the results of outdated corporate culture are as follows:

- Women are assumed to be less career-oriented than men, so they are not offered the same advancement opportunities as men.

- Women are not given demanding and challenging jobs because it's assumed they don't handle stress well.

- Women are often left out of the "boys' club" in a company and therefore do not have the same information-sharing and networking opportunities as male colleagues.

More and more women in the 1990s have been proving that the glass ceiling can be broken: Diane McGarry, CEO and chairwoman of Xerox Canada (1997); Sheelagh Whittaker, president and CEO of Electronic Data Systems (EDS) Canada (1997); and Catherine Swift, president of the Canadian Federation of Independent Business (1996) are only a few examples. Wolf Gugler, a senior associate with executive search consultants Westcott Thomas & Associates Ltd., Toronto, says he's recommending more

THEY SAID IT

"I've always said that we'll have true equality when we have as many incompetent women in positions as we have incompetent men."

SHEELAGH WHITTAKER, President and CEO, EDS Canada

WORKPLACE TREND

STUDY SHOWS POWER OF FEMALE-LED FIRMS

An increasing number of Canadian women are running businesses and their companies are creating jobs at four times the national average, a new study says.

The study, conducted by Dun & Bradstreet Information Services, found that nearly a third of Canadian companies have a woman in charge. Between 1991 and 1994, the number of such companies increased by close to 20 percent — to 702 800 from 586 800.

That compares with a rise of under 9 percent in the number of all businesses in Canada during the period.

The ground-breaking research also found that companies run by women employed 1.7 million people in 1994, an increase of 13 percent from three years earlier. The average increase in all companies for the same period was 3.1 percent.

"Women-led firms are a powerful and growing force throughout our Canadian economy," said Michele Fraser, an academic adviser to the study, who unveiled the results yesterday.

Ms. Fraser said the study, called Myths and Realities, The Economic Power of Women-Led Firms in Canada, is important because it provides the first hard numbers on businesses led by women in Canada.

Until now, Canadians have been forced to rely on anecdotal evidence or generalize on U.S. research.

But Ms. Fraser, a senior instructor at the University of Calgary's faculty of management, said the results, which confirm trends that many have suspected, provide women with the ammunition to prove that they are an important force in the economy.

"There is still the notion that women are small potatoes ... that people are saying they are important because it's politically correct. With these numbers we can say, 'No, it's real.'"

The $200 000 study, funded by Bank of Montreal's Institute for Small Business, also found that businesses run by women have about the same survival rate as the average commercially active firm in Canada and are just as likely to pay their bills on time.

It also showed that companies with women in charge tend to be smaller than average. More than 87 percent had fewer than 10 employees, compared with the national average of just over 81 percent.

While the research — based on Statistics Canada and Dun & Bradstreet data — shows that close to half of businesses run by women are still concentrated in the retail sector, it also points to a movement away from this trend.

Between 1991 and 1994, the number of female-led firms both in retail and in personal services fell by 4.9 percent, while companies run by women grew in other nontraditional industries such as agriculture, mining, and the financial–real estate area.

and more women to his clients. He notes that back in the late 1980s, when he presented a short list of five candidates to a client, chances were that one of the names would be a woman. Now, the list might contain two or more female candidates, depending on the business. Baby boomers generally accept the idea of having a woman at the helm, which has opened the doors that were closed by sexist attitudes of the past. Today, there are many more women who are carrying degrees from the same professional schools as men.[43]

Growing Use of Part-Time Employees

One result of increased automation and downsizing during the 1990s is growth in the number of part-time employees.

Sometimes referred to as just-in-time employees, this sector of the Canadian work force has doubled since the late 1970s, growing to over 2.2 million by 1996. Today, more than one in five working people are part-timers (working less than 30 hours per week according to the Statistics Canada definition).[44] Internationally, part-time workers in industrialized nations number more than 60 million.[45]

Part-time work today has been created as a result of such management trends as compressed work weeks, job sharing, flextime, and home-based work. The need for two-career households and flexibility in the labour force also has contributed to the number of part-time workers.

There are a number of advantages for firms in hiring part-time employees. Since part-time wage rates typically are 60 percent of regular full-time wages, companies can reduce their labour costs significantly. Part-time

The researchers define female-led businesses as any company where a woman is president, owner, co-owner, CEO, chairwoman, or partner.

Barbara Caldwell, a Markham, Ont., consultant and entrepreneur who works with female business owners, says the report will be a "tremendous boost" to female entrepreneurs and will force financial institutions and other companies to acknowledge their importance.

"Now that we have the results, there are no more excuses. We are lighting the way, I think, not only for women who are established but for women who are looking for career opportunities."

If response is the same as to a similar U.S. study in 1995, it may do just that.

Julie Weeks, director of research of the U.S. National Foundation for Women Business Owners, says the U.S. study prompted many companies to sit up and notice a market that they had overlooked.

Source: Elizabeth Church, "Study Shows Power of Female-Led Firms," *The Globe and Mail*, August 21, 1996, B8. Reprinted with permission from The Globe and Mail.

Where Women Are in Charge

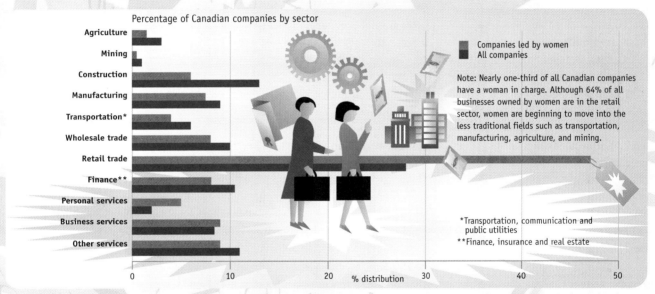

Source: Based on "Myths and Realities, The Economic Power of Women-Led Firms in Canada," a 1996 study conducted by Dun & Bradstreet Information Services and Bank of Montreal's Economics Department, with funding from Bank of Montreal's Institute for Small Business. Reprinted by permission of Dun & Bradstreet Information Services and Bank of Montreal.

workers usually receive fewer benefits, which reduces yet another major company expense. Part-time employment can also be an effective strategy for companies to benefit from the experience of the "retired" work force.

However, the benefits of part-time employment must be weighed against the negative long-term implications. For example, overreliance on part-timers may leave the company without an experienced, well-trained work force, especially in a downsized organization.

Managing in a Global Economy

Traditionally, Canada has relied on the United States for the vast majority of its foreign trade. For example, as of 1997 the United States accounted for about four-fifths of

Canada's merchandising exports and two-thirds of our imports. If human resource managers are to believe the futuristic predictions of our economic and international pundits, expect to see this close Canada–U.S. trade dependence to gradually change in the next millennium. New trade links will be forged with other trading blocs and countries such as those in Europe, the Pacific Rim, and South America. This means that many of our corporations will have to "globalize" their executives to prepare them for the new international marketplace. The new manager will have to "think globally and act locally." For example, a Canadian CEO who uses a participatory style in Vancouver will have to learn to exercise a more centralized style in Brazil. As well, Canadian managers will have to become more sensitive to the cultural needs of foreign managers working in Canada.[46]

WORKPLACE TREND

REINVENTING WORK AND THE WORKPLACE

1. High Performance Human Resource Management (HRM)

Most workplaces in Canada (probably as much as 70 percent) are still based on the traditional industrial model where jobs and work rules are rigidly defined, wages are tied to the job, and management has many prerogatives.

Gordon Betcherman completed a major study called *The Canadian Workplace in Transition* which describes the new HRM strategies that are happening in about 30 percent of workplaces. According to Betcherman, these new high performance strategies have resulted in positive outcomes for employment, efficiency, and financial performance of the firm. Characteristics of this new high performance strategy are:

→ **A flexible work organization.** Work rules and job descriptions are fluid.

→ **A commitment to training** — for both managers and non-managers.

→ **Incentives to increase employee involvement.**

→ **Policies to promote employee–employer collaboration.** The sharing of financial rewards, performance, information, and privilege are encouraged and actively promoted.

The key characteristics of these new workplaces are trust and commitment. For example, unions have to give a little on the traditional notion of job control. Management has to release some of its hierarchical prerogatives.

2. Nurture Knowledge-Based Industries

Fostering the growth of knowledge-based industries is the second element in reinventing work and the workplace. A 1994 study by John Baldwin of Statistics Canada says that the key factor that distinguishes the most successful of these companies (measured by market share and by profits) is innovative activity. He also notes that success of these knowledge-based industries lies in this order:

1. management skills
2. human resources
3. marketing and
4. financing.

3. Learning and Career Ladders

One of the great tragedies of the 1990s is the number of young people who are floundering without access to entry-level jobs that give them promise of personal growth and career development. Without meaningful job experience, they are unable to get their lives started.

Employers and unions can make a huge contribution here by designing positions for programs such as co-operatives, internships, and apprenticeships. In this way, they can give young people a chance to learn and to show what they can do.

They must also reach out to the community and take on the role of catalyst. For example, they can adopt a school, help start up a day-care centre, or launch a mentoring program. Such programs help to shape the expectations and the aspirations of our future labour force. They offer an image of a life with possibilities, as opposed to a life as a dead-end.

4. Redefine Work

In the longer term, we have to redefine work. At the moment, some of the most important and productive work in our society is not paid employment — most child care, mentoring youth, and supporting the elderly so they can live independently. As a result, these services are underproduced.

The basic message here is that many fruitful strategies for jobs and adjustment will have to come from the leadership of business and labour in this country.

Employers can get involved by inviting unions and employees to participate in the decision making. By definition, this will make the workplace into a learning-centred institution, where both employers and employees are focussed on building work skills. Employers must also get directly involved in the community with such programs as co-operative education, internships, creating mentoring programs, and partnerships.

Within the workplace, unions can also promote high-performance strategies. A proactive participation by unions will force a major change in management and employee attitudes and in how decisions are made. Most of the important decisions will be made away from the bargaining table — they will involve the choice of technology, the design and delivery of training, sharing of information, focussing on quality, changing work rules, and so on. Like management, unions will also have to get involved in community employment initiatives such as mentoring, partnerships, and co-operative education.

Source: Excerpt from Judith Maxwell, President, Canadian Policy Research Networks Inc., "Summary of Proceedings," *Jobs Conferences* (Ottawa: Canadian Labour Market and Productivity Centre, April 1994), 6–15. Reprinted by permission of Judith Maxwell.

SUMMARY OF LEARNING OUTCOMES

1. **Explain the importance of human resource management and the responsibilities of a human resource department.**

   Most organizations devote considerable attention to human resource management, which can be defined as (1) the process of acquiring, training, developing, motivating, and appraising a sufficient quantity of qualified employees to perform the activities necessary to accomplish organizational objectives; and (2) developing specific activities and an overall organizational climate to generate maximum worker satisfaction and employee efficiency. A human resource management department is responsible for handling human resource planning, developing job descriptions and job specifications, screening job applicants, developing and administering testing programs, interviewing prospective employees, orienting and training new employees, and administering employee compensation, benefits, and safety programs.

2. **List the different needs in Maslow's hierarchy, and the two main categories of Herzberg's two-factor theory.**

   Psychologist Abraham Maslow proposed a hierarchy of human needs consisting of physiological needs (food, shelter, clothing), safety needs, social (belongingness) needs, esteem needs, and self-actualization needs. Maslow pointed out that satisfied needs are not motivators. The two categories of Herzberg's two-factor theory are maintenance or hygiene factors and motivational factors. Hygiene factors such as working conditions remove dissatisfaction but are not employee motivators. Motivational factors that satisfy higher-level needs such as recognition are the principal motivators.

3. **Distinguish among Theory X, Theory Y, and Theory Z managers.**

   Traditional Theory X managers view workers as being lazy, disliking work, and requiring close and constant supervision. Theory Y managers assume that employees want to satisfy social, esteem, and self-actualization needs through work as well as through other

activities. They emphasize employee self-control and self-direction. A Theory Z organization is more likely to include long-term employment, shared decision making, relatively slow promotions and evaluations, and varied and nonspecialized job assignments. The Theory Z approach emphasizes involved workers as the key to increased productivity and improved quality of work life.

4. **Explain how recruitment, selection, orientation, training, and evaluation contribute to placing the right person in a job.**

   The recruitment and selection process involves locating potential employees, evaluating each application, administering employment tests, arranging for medical examinations, and interviewing. Once hired, the employee completes an orientation program, which is the joint responsibility of the human resource department and the department in which the employee will work. Another major function of the human resource department is developing and maintaining a well-trained, productive labour force. Employee training should be viewed as an ongoing process throughout an employee's tenure with the company. Evaluation is the process of comparing actual performance against desired performance to make objective decisions about compensation, promotion, additional training needs, transfers, or terminations.

5. **Outline the different forms of employee compensation.**

   A satisfactory compensation program should attract well-qualified workers, keep them satisfied in their jobs, and inspire them to produce. The compensation policy of most companies is based on five factors: (1) salaries and wages paid by other companies in the area that compete for the same personnel, (2) government legislation, (3) the cost of living, (4) the ability of the company to pay, and (5) the workers' productivity. Incentive compensation programs, such as profit sharing, gain sharing, bonuses, or pay-for-knowledge plans, often are added to a salary or wage to reward superior performance and boost employee morale.

6. Explain the concept of job enrichment and how it can motivate employees.

Job enrichment (which can include job enlargement, job rotation, management by objectives, flexible or alternative work schedules, and home-based work) involves redesigning work to give workers more authority in planning their tasks and deciding how the work is to be done, and allowing them to learn related skills or to trade jobs with others. This approach can improve employee productivity and morale by focussing on the motivational aspects of the job itself, and making it more satisfying and meaningful.

7. Summarize the role of labour unions and list their primary goals.

A labour union generally refers to an organization of employees that has been granted the exclusive legal authority to bargain on behalf of the employees with their employer with respect to the terms and conditions of employment. The primary goals of labour unions are improving the wages, hours, and working conditions of their members.

8. Outline the sources of power, or "weapons," of labour and management.

Most differences between labour and management are settled through the collective bargaining process or formal grievance procedures. Serious differences between union and management can result in strikes, lockouts, walkouts, slowdowns, picketing, and even violence. Strikes and lockouts are the most common reactions to serious differences. In Canada, workers do not have the legal right to withhold their labour when a dispute arises. The only time a worker has the right to go on strike, for example, is after a collective agreement has expired.

9. Identify the major human resource concerns for the twenty-first century.

Current issues in human resource management include (1) finding cost-effective ways to retain valuable older workers, (2) meeting the needs of two-career households, (3) breaking through the glass ceiling, (4) managing a growing number of part-time employees as a result of increased automation and downsizing, and (5) managing in a global economy.

Key Terms Quiz

employee benefits
morale
collective bargaining
Theory Y
worker buyout plan
labour union
on-the-job training

motive
human resource management
glass ceiling
need
Theory Z
job enrichment
performance appraisal

Theory X
management-development program
flextime
mediation
arbitration
home-based work

_____ 1. Process of acquiring, training, developing, motivating, and appraising a sufficient quantity of qualified employees to perform necessary activities; and developing activities and an organizational climate conducive to maximum efficiency and worker satisfaction.

_____ 2. The mental attitude of employees toward their employer and job.

_____ 3. Lack of something useful; discrepancy between a desired state and the actual state.

_____ 4. Inner state that directs individuals toward the goal of satisfying a felt need.

_____ 5. Managerial assumption that employees dislike work and must be coerced, controlled, or threatened to motivate them to work.

_____ 6. Managerial assumption that employees like work and, under proper conditions, accept and seek out responsibilities to fulfil their social, esteem, and self-actualization needs.

_____   7. Management approach emphasizing employee participation as the key to increased productivity for the company and improved quality of work life for the employee.

_____   8. Training employees for job tasks by allowing them to perform them under the guidance of an experienced employee.

_____   9. Training designed to improve the skills and broaden the knowledge of managers and potential managers.

_____ 10. Defining acceptable employee performance levels, evaluating them, and then comparing actual and desired performance to aid in determining training, compensation, promotion, transfers, or terminations.

_____ 11. Employee rewards, such as pension plans, insurance, sick-leave pay, and tuition reimbursement, given entirely or partly at the expense of the company.

_____ 12. Redesigning work to give employees more authority in planning their tasks and deciding how the work is to be done, and allowing them to learn related skills or to trade jobs.

_____ 13. Organization of employees with exclusive legal authority to bargain with their employer on behalf of the employees.

_____ 14. Negotiation between management and union representatives concerning wages and working conditions.

_____ 15. Process of settling union–management disputes through recommendations of an impartial third party.

_____ 16. Process of bringing an impartial third party into a union–management dispute to render a legally binding decision.

_____ 17. Work-scheduling system that allows employees to set work hours within constraints specified by the firm.

_____ 18. Program allowing employees to work at home, sometimes linked to their employers by terminals hooked to a central computer.

_____ 19. Financial incentive designed to encourage older employees to retire voluntarily.

_____ 20. Arbitrary barrier that keeps women and minorities from advancing to top management.

Other Important Terms

apprenticeship training	Herzberg's two-factor theory	physiological needs
burnout	incentive compensation	safety needs
cafeteria-style benefits	international union	salary
Canadian Labour Congress (CLC)	local union	self-actualization needs
esteem needs	lockout	social (belongingness) needs
federation	management by objectives (MBO)	strike
flexible benefit plans	Maslow's needs hierarchy	telecommuter
grievance	national union	

Review Questions

1. Explain the primary functions of a human resource department. Which of these responsibilities are most likely to be shared with line departments?

2. Based on Maslow's hierarchy of human needs, which needs are being referred to in the following statements?
   a. "The new General Motors Canada labour agreement will guarantee the jobs of at least 80 percent of all GM workers through to the year 2008."
   b. "This is an entry-level job here at Marx Clothiers, and we pay minimum wage for the first six months."
   c. "We have just organized a company basketball team. Why don't you try out Thursday afternoon right after work?"
   d. "Semareh won our Employee of the Month award this month due to her exceptional performance."
   e. "We pay a 20 percent bonus for employees who work the midnight shift."

3. Write brief job scenarios of three people employed in an organization implementing Theory X, Theory Y, and Theory Z management. Relate each of these employees to Maslow's needs hierarchy and Herzberg's two-factor theory, and list factors that might be used by managers in motivating each employee.

4. Identify several methods of work structuring that should result in job enrichment. Can you think of situations where job enrichment would not be effective? List them and explain your reasoning.

5. Why do many firms follow the policy of hiring from within? What problems are involved in following such a policy?

6. Explain what Judith Maxwell means by "reinventing work and the workplace" (see Workplace Trend on page 210).

7. What is a labour union? List the primary goals of labour unions.

8. Explain the major mechanisms for settling union–management disputes.

9. Why are more firms using part-time workers? Is this trend beneficial or detrimental to Canadian business? Explain your answer.

Discussion Questions

1. Discuss the issues involved in managing in a global economy.

2. Consider your most recent (or current) job supervisor. Would you describe this person as a Theory X, Theory Y, or Theory Z manager? Why do you think your boss has adopted this management approach?

3. Discuss the type of compensation plan you would recommend for each of the following:
   a. Jewellery repairperson
   b. Retail salesperson
   c. Assembly-line worker in an electronics factory
   d. Professional athlete

4. Explain why major firms, such as IBM Canada, operate without unions. Does the provision of job security eliminate the need for unions? Explain your answer.

5. A survey of 2010 workers performing 23 different jobs gave the following "Most Boring" awards: assembly-line worker, forklift-truck driver, machine tender, and monitor of continuous-flow production. By contrast, these jobs were ranked at the "Least Boring" end of the scale: physician, professor, air traffic controller, and police officer. Identify some common characteristics of each group of jobs.

6. Women-led firms are a powerful and growing force throughout the Canadian economy. Do you believe the "glass ceiling" for women is beginning to crack? Why or why not?

Answers to Key Terms Quiz

1. human resource management 2. morale 3. need 4. motive 5. Theory X 6. Theory Y 7. Theory Z 8. on-the-job training 9. management-development program 10. performance appraisal 11. employee benefits 12. job enrichment 13. labour union 14. collective bargaining 15. mediation 16. arbitration 17. flextime 18. home-based work 19. worker buyout plan 20. glass ceiling

Notes

1. Excerpt from Industry Canada and Bank of Montreal, "Bundschuh Fashions Ltd.," *Strategies for Success: Participant's Workbook*, 1992, Catalogue No. C2-198/1992E, 150. Reproduced with the permission of the Minister of Public Works and Government Services Canada, 1997, and the Bank of Montreal.

2. Based on personal interviews with Bundschuh Fashions Ltd.

3. See, for example, Dr. Marilyn Hayman and Terry Hayman, *Hurdles: Human Leaps in the Corporate Race* (Carp, ON: Creative Bound, 1992).

4. Brian Dumaine, "Cool Cures for Burnout," *Fortune*, June 20, 1988, 78–84.

5. Margot Gibb-Clark, "Canadian Workers Satisfied but Anxious," *The Globe and Mail*, October 8, 1996, B13.

6. Anne Fisher, "Morale Crisis," *Business Week*, November 18, 1992, 78–80.

7. Alan Farnham, "How to Nurture Creative Sparks," *Fortune*, January 10, 1994, 94–100.

8. Karyn Standen, "Buy and Burn," *The Globe and Mail Report on Business Magazine*, November 1996, 173; and personal telephone interviews with CrossKeys.

9. Industry Canada, "EDO Canada," *Participant's Workbook: Strategies for Success*, 1992, 133; and personal telephone interviews with EDO.

10. Rosanne Bonanno, "Coopers & Lybrand Uses High Technology to Recruit University Graduates," *Canadian HR Reporter*, Vol. 7, No. 19, November 3, 1993, 24, as cited in Richard M. Hodgetts, K. Galen Kroeck, and Michael E. Rock, *Managing Human Resources in Canada* (Toronto: Dryden, 1995), 275.

11. Margot Gibb-Clark, "Job Training Trail a Maze-ing Venture," *The Globe and Mail*, August 7, 1993, A4, as cited in Hodgetts, Kroeck, and Rock, *Managing Human Resources in Canada*, 410.

12. "Private Sector Not Pulling Its Weight in Training Workers for New Economy," *The Toronto Star*, July 17, 1993, D4, as cited in Hodgetts, Kroeck, and Rock, *Managing Human Resources in Canada*, 410.

13. Sandy Fife, "Family Ties," *The Globe and Mail Report on Business Magazine*, March 1993, 38–41, 43, 45–47, as cited in Hodgetts, Kroeck, and Rock, *Managing Human Resources in Canada*, 410–11.

14. Lewis Perelman, "Kanban to Kanbrain," *Forbes ASAP*, June 6, 1994, 85–95.

15. Norma R. Fritz, "A Close-Up of What's New in the HR Picture," *Personnel*, March 1989, 6–7.

16. Leslie Goodson, "Pay as You Pay," *Human Resources Professional*, September 1992, 21–25.

17. Rabindra N. Kanungo and Manuel Mendonca, *Compensation: Effective Reward Management* (Toronto: Butterworths, 1992), 324.

18. Thomas H. Stone and Noah M. Meltz, *Human Resource Management in Canada*, 3rd ed. (Toronto: Holt, Rinehart and Winston, 1993), 627–28.

19. Lynda Hurst, "Has Time Come for a 4-Day Week?" *The Toronto Star*, March 5, 1994, A8.

20. Bruce Little, "Statistics Belie Perception of Less Help for the Needy, Part II," *The Globe and Mail*, January 20, 1994, A1, A6, as cited in Hodgetts, Kroeck, and Rock, *Managing Human Resources in Canada*, 665.

21. Joseph R. Meisenheimer II and William J. Waitrowski, "Flexible Benefits Plans: Employees Who Have a Choice," *Monthly Labor Review*, December 1989, 17–23, as cited in Hodgetts, Kroeck, and Rock, *Managing Human Resources in Canada*, 689.

22. Kanungo and Mendonca, *Compensation*, 334; and Margot Gibb-Clark, "Flexible Benefits Let Employees Tailor Coverage," *The Globe and Mail*, June 24, 1991, B4.

23. Elisabeth K. Ryland and Benson Rosen, "Attracting Job Applicants with Flexible Benefits," *Personnel*, March 1988, 71–72, as cited in Hodgetts, Kroeck, and Rock, *Managing Human Resources in Canada*, 527–28.

24. Brian Dumaine, "Payoff from the New Management," *Fortune*, December 13, 1993, 103–10.

25. J.R. Hackman and G.R. Oldham, *Work Redesign*, (Reading, MA: Addison-Wesley, 1980); and Stone and Meltz, *Human Resource Management in Canada*, 457.

26. "Delegation," *Small Business Report*, July 1986, 71–75; Robert C. Ford and Frank S. McLaughlin, "Avoiding Disappointment in MBO Programs," *Human Resource Management* 21, Summer 1982, 44–49.

27. See for example Karen Peterson, "Job Stress, Satisfaction Can Co-Exist," *USA Today*, July 6, 1994, D1.

28. Sue Shellenbarger, "Firms Make the Most of Flexible Scheduling," *The Wall Street Journal*, April 12, 1994, B1.

29. Robert Brehl (*The Toronto Star*), "Study Predicts Telecommuting to Double in the Next 3½ Years," *The Ottawa Citizen*, November 9, 1996, E4. This article was based on a 1996 study by the Yankee Group described in their report "Meeting the Telecommuter Challenge," and on several North American studies.

30. Sue Shellenbarger, "Some Thrive, But Many Wilt Working at Home," *The Wall Street Journal*, December 14, 1993, B1, B10.

31. Hodgetts, Kroeck, and Rock, *Managing Human Resources in Canada*, 527–28.

32. Ibid., 539.

33. John Godard, *Industrial Relations, The Economy and Society* (Toronto: McGraw-Hill Ryerson, 1994), 95–97.

34. Adapted from Hodgetts, Kroeck, and Rock, *Managing Human Resources in Canada*, 540–43.

35. Based on data provided by Labour Canada.

36. John Heinzl and Oliver Bertin, "Deal Spells Relief for GM Contractors," *The Globe and Mail*, October 23, 1996, B1.

37. David Hage, "Unions Feel the Heat," *U.S. News & World Report*, January 24, 1994, 57–61.

38. Cited in David Crane, *The Next Canadian Century* (Toronto: Stoddart, 1992), 49.

39. Brian O'Reilly, "The New Deal," *Fortune*, June 13, 1994, 44–52.

40. See for example *Characteristics of Dual Income Families*, Statistics Canada, Catalogue No. 13–215, 1993.

41. Based on Dun & Bradstreet study reported in Elizabeth Church, "Study Shows Power of Female-Led Firms," *The Globe and Mail*, August 21, 1996, B8.

42. Rochell Sharpe, "The Waiting Game," *The Wall Street Journal*, March 29, 1994, A1, A10.

43. John Heinzl, "Women Take Charge at Canadian Units," *The Globe and Mail*, November 29, 1996, B10.

44. John Kettle, "Kettle's Future," *The Globe and Mail*, November 1, 1996, B12.

45. "Number of Part-Time Workers in U.S. Triples Since 1970," *Mobile Press Register*, June 1, 1994, 4E.

46. Madelaine Drohan, "Dependence on U.S. Leaves Canada 'Vulnerable': WTO," *The Globe and Mail*, November 20, 1996, B6. This article was based on a 1996 World Trade Organization (WTO) report.

Chapter 9

Teamwork and Communication

After studying this chapter, you should be able to

1. Distinguish between the various types of teams found in organizations.
2. Identify the characteristics of an effective team and the different roles played by team members.
3. Summarize the stages of team development.
4. Relate team cohesiveness and norms to effective team performance.
5. Describe the factors that can cause conflict in teams, and discuss conflict resolution styles.
6. Explain the importance of effective communication skills in business.
7. Compare the different types of communication.
8. Identify and explain several important considerations in international business communication.
9. Summarize important developments in communications technology and how they affect business communication.

The Chip Prime at Nortel

Back in 1881, Charles Fleetford Sise, a former New England sea captain, was unable to find an adequate domestic supply of telephone equipment. If he couldn't source an alternative Canadian supplier, he would lose his Canadian patent rights to the telephone — invented, of course, by Alexander Graham Bell in 1874. The fear of losing the patent rights for Canada led Sise to begin his own manufacturing branch of The Bell Telephone Company of Canada. Thirteen years later, a separate company called Northern Electric was born. It would eventually become Northern Telecom (Nortel) Limited in 1976. Today, Nortel is a leading global provider of digital network solutions with worldwide revenues in the $10 billion range (1996). Its corporate mission is to be the leading architect of global communications networks.[1]

Many at Nortel attribute their success to teamwork culture, the sponsor, and the chip prime. Marty and Dave are two Nortel employees. Marty is the sponsor — in the old days they would have called him the project manager. Dave is a chip prime. He's the team leader — they used to call him a supervisor. Here is what they have to say about how and why they make things happen at Nortel:[2]

- **Self-managed teams.** Teams work on an ongoing basis to bring the product to the customer. The team, not the individual, takes ownership for the success and failure of its project. It is accountable and responsible for its actions.

- **Sponsor.** Marty, the sponsor, is responsible for setting the goals, choosing the teams, and reviewing performance. The sponsor — who usually represents more than one team — is required to meet the needs of senior management and the customer. One of the sponsor's main jobs is resource allocation — shifting people from team to team to speed up the slower teams. "When I meet with team leaders, I want to know if their projects are on time and meet the customer needs. If not, then the teams have to be changed," says Marty.

- **Team leader.** The team leader — in some cases called the chip prime — is chosen by the sponsor based on experience, skills, and past performance. Chip primes must know what the company wants, how the project satisfies the company, and customer needs. Coaching and facilitating take up a large part of his/her day. "The key to our success is the chip prime," says Marty. "Give us a great chip prime and we'll deliver a product on time, below projected cost, and a happy customer."

- **Team members.** The team members are expected to be tightly knit, to support one another, and to work in harmony to achieve aggressive team goals. "Great teams are emotionally attached to their work and to other members of the team," says Dave.

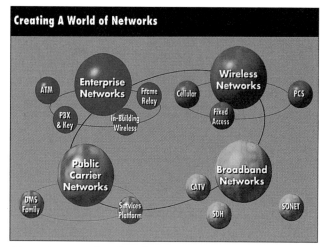

Through teamwork and product innovation, Nortel has become a leading provider of digital network solutions.

CHAPTER OVERVIEW

TEAMWORK WAS INTRODUCED in Chapter 1 as one of the major business opportunities and challenges of the late 1990s.

In this chapter, we examine the types and characteristics of successful teams, discuss sources of team conflict, and explore ways to resolve disagreements that might arise among team members or between teams. We also look at the importance of communication in promoting teamwork, and discuss the factors that facilitate effective communication both inside and outside an organization. Finally, we consider some guidelines for effective international communication and look at the latest developments in communications technology.

TEAMWORK

AS WE DISCUSSED in Chapter 6, a **team** is *a small number of people with complementary skills who are committed to a common purpose, approach, and set of performance goals.* All team members hold themselves mutually responsible and accountable for accomplishing their objectives.

As the Nortel experience illustrates, employee teams are a successful trend in business, and the ability to work effectively in teams is a more important skill than ever before. A recent survey of North America's 500 largest corporations, for example, found that teamwork is the topic taught most frequently in today's employee training programs.

Some teams, such as the management and work teams at Nortel, work together over an extended period of time. Others collaborate for much shorter periods. For example, CEO Joseph Day of the German– Japanese joint venture Freudenberg-NOK asks each of his employees to serve on special problem-solving task forces called GROWTTH (Get Rid of Waste Through Team Harmony). Each GROWTTH team spends no more than three days at one of the company's fourteen U.S. plants. The task force's assignment is to analyze work processes and make recommendations for improvement. In a typical year, about 40 different teams visit each factory. Every visit results in several practical suggestions being made and then implemented. Although many deal with relatively small changes, the overall impact of the combined recommendations is significant cost savings and improvements in quality. Says Day, "What we are doing is what any company will have to do to survive a decade from now."[3]

Business Term

√ **Team**

A small number of people with complementary skills who are committed to a common purpose, approach, and set of performance goals.

Quality organizations group employees into teams and, if necessary, teach them team-building skills. The value of working collectively is that employees produce at higher performance levels, respond better, and become more flexible in meeting customer needs. A few well-known examples include the following:

- **GE Canada.** At the beginning of the 1990s, GE was faced with two challenges. Externally, it faced a world economy characterized by slower growth and stronger international competition. Internally, the company had to "find a way to combine the power, resources, and reach of a big company with the hunger, the agility, the spirit, and the fire of a small one," said John F. Welch, Jr., Chairman and CEO, General Electric Company. The solution — from the top down — was self-managing teams. For example, GE's Pooled Financial Services unit eliminated 40 percent of its staff and cut out two organizational levels. A new structure composed of self-

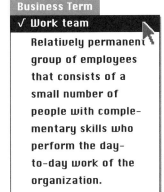

Business Term

√ **Work team**

Relatively permanent group of employees that consists of a small number of people with complementary skills who perform the day-to-day work of the organization.

Business Term

√ **Cross-functional team**

Group of employees from different departments who work on specific projects.

managing teams emerged with a resulting increase in efficiency and improved quality.[4]

- **Shell Canada.** Shell's lubricant plant in Brockville, Ontario, combines teamwork with large-scale computerization. Team members are divided into "job families" that are empowered to solve problems ranging from dealing with suppliers and customers to scheduling work activities and training. A commitment to teamwork has improved production, reduced absenteeism, and increased the customer base.[5]

- **EBA Engineering Consultants Ltd.** EBA reorganized the old-style hierarchical organization at its Calgary office into a client-based team structure. The result was happier customers and employees and a resulting rise in productivity.[6]

- **Infocorp Computer Solutions Ltd.** This small Winnipeg software company thrives on teamwork and building long-term relationships with its customers. As part of the Infocorp culture, teamwork has paid off particularly in the international market with the company's Asian strategic alliances.[7]

Types of Teams

The benefits of the team approach, coupled with the downsizing of the traditional organizational structure, have produced a virtual rainbow of forms or categories of teams. Some of the more common types or classifications include the following:

- **Work teams** *are relatively permanent in nature and consist of small numbers of people with complementary skills who perform the day-to-day work of the organization.* A team of Nortel design engineers assigned with the task of producing a series of new products is an example of a work team.

- **Cross-functional teams** *involve employees from different departments, such as finance and marketing, who work on specific projects.* Tasks vary from developing a new product to interviewing prospective employees.

Business Term

✓ **Self-managed team**

Group of employees who work with little or no supervision.

Business Term

✓ **Problem-solving team**

Temporary combinations of workers who gather to solve a specific problem and then disband.

- **Self-managed teams** *involve groups of employees who work with little or no supervision.* They are most effective when they combine employees with a range of skills. Team members schedule their own work, are trained to do other employee jobs, are responsible for the quality of their work, and are accountable for performance results.

- **Problem-solving teams** *are temporary combinations of workers who gather to solve a specific problem and then disband.* They have specific missions that can be broad (find out why customers are not satisfied) or narrow (solve the overheating problem in generator number 4). Once the task is completed, the problem-solving team usually breaks up.

- **Quality circles** *are small groups of employees from one work area or department who meet regularly to identify and solve problems.* This was a popular concept in the 1980s. By the mid-1990s, the percentage of major firms using quality circles to solve minor quality problems had declined, primarily due to the fact that the limited scope of activities they focus on typically produces only modest increases in productivity.

- **Virtual teams** *consist of employees who communicate with one another using the computer and in many cases the Internet.* These teams are well-suited to employees who are geographically separated.

- **Management teams** *are groups consisting of managers from various functional departments* like sales and production. Management teams normally co-ordinate the work among the teams within larger organizations.

In some cases it can become quite confusing if you are trying to precisely categorize a particular type of team. This is because all of these categories are not necessarily mutually exclusive. For example, a cross-functional team may be formed to solve a specific problem and may even be self-managed. In this case it could also be classified as either a problem-solving team or a self-managed team.

Business Term

✓ **Quality circle**

Small group of employees from one work area or department who meet regularly to identify and solve problems.

Business Term

✓ **Virtual team**

Group of employees who communicate with one another using the computer and in many cases the Internet.

Business Term

✓ **Management team**

Group of managers from various functional departments.

TEAM CHARACTERISTICS

TEAMS ARE CAPABLE of increasing productivity, raising morale, and nurturing innovation. However, these benefits result only if the right type of team is chosen for the task and the right people are on the team.

Teams consume time, energy, and money. They must, therefore, be formed carefully. To be effective, team members should receive training support, strong communication links, and specifics about the jobs they must perform. One major pitfall for many companies using teams is the tendency to create teams when they are not really needed. Some people are better left to work alone, and some tasks can be better accomplished by individuals. Before a team is formed, management should analyze the work to be done, decide whether a team approach is preferable, and then select the best type of team.

Effective teams share a number of characteristics. Two of the most important are the size of the team and the roles played by its members.

Team Size

Rubbermaid organizes its home-products division into teams of five to seven people, one each from manufacturing, research and development, finance, marketing, and other departments. Each team focuses on a particular product line, such as bathroom accessories. The team approach works so well that Rubbermaid's introduction of new products averages one a day, 90 percent of which achieve their target sales.[8]

Effective teams can have anywhere from five to twelve members, but many proponents of teams believe the ideal size is about seven people. Groups of this size are big enough to benefit from a variety of diverse skills, yet small enough that members can communicate easily and feel part of a close-knit entity.

While teams smaller and larger than this size also can be effective, they create certain challenges for a team leader. Participants in small teams (two to four members) want to get along with one another, tend to be informal, discuss more personal topics, and make fewer demands on team leaders. Large groups with more than twelve members are a greater challenge for team leaders since decision making becomes more centralized and participants may feel less committed to team goals. Large teams also tend to have more disagreements, absenteeism, and membership turnover. Subgroups may form, leading to possible conflicts among various factions. As a general rule, teams of more than twenty people should be divided into subteams, with each of these smaller groups having its own members and goals.

Team Roles

Over time, team members tend to play certain roles, which can be classified as task specialist or socio-emotional (see Figure 9.1). People who assume the **task specialist role** *devote time and energy to helping the team accomplish its goals.* These are the group members who are active in proposing new solutions, evaluating the suggestions of others, and asking for more information. They may bring up new ideas, summarize the discussion so far, and attempt to energize the group when interest drops. Team members who play a **socio-emotional role** *devote time and energy to providing support for group members' emotional needs and social unity.*

Business Term

✓ **Task specialist role**

Role played by team members who devote time and energy to helping the team accomplish its goals.

Business Term

✓ **Socio-emotional role**

Role played by team members who devote time and energy to providing support for group members' emotional needs and social unity.

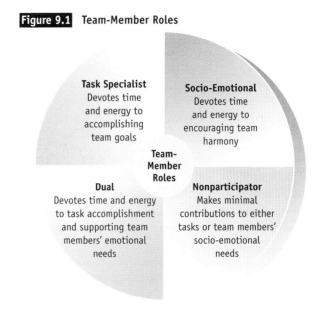

Figure 9.1 Team-Member Roles

Task Specialist
Devotes time and energy to accomplishing team goals

Socio-Emotional
Devotes time and energy to encouraging team harmony

Team-Member Roles

Dual
Devotes time and energy to task accomplishment and supporting team members' emotional needs

Nonparticipator
Makes minimal contributions to either tasks or team members' socio-emotional needs

They encourage others to contribute ideas, and they may change their own opinions in order to maintain team harmony. They attempt to reduce group tensions and reconcile conflicts.

Some team members may play a *dual role*, in which they contribute to the team's task and support members' emotional needs at the same time. Those able to assume a dual role may become team leaders because they satisfy both types of needs. And, finally, some people may fall into a *nonparticipator role*, in which they contribute little either to the task or to members' socio-emotional needs.

The challenge for managers is to ensure that teams are balanced with members capable of performing each type of role. Both the task specialist and the socio-emotional roles are important, and too much of either type can impair a group's ability to function. Teams filled with task specialists may be productive in the short term but unsatisfying over a longer time period, since team members may become unsupportive and will not convey enough personal concern for one

DID YOU KNOW?

When geese fly in formation, they travel about 70 percent faster than when they fly alone.

another. Teams filled with socio-emotional types can be satisfying but unproductive, since participants may hesitate to disagree with or to criticize one another.[9]

TEAM PROCESSES

SHOULD ALL COMPANIES organize their employees into teams? No — not all firms are suited to the team format. Furthermore, some departments within a firm thrive on using the team concept, while others do not. "Teams are great, but some work needs to be accomplished solo," says Kathleen Emery, vice president of the consulting firm Designed Learning Inc. "Be selective. When work makes sense to be done in teams, then do it; when it doesn't, don't. Teams aren't the answer to every situation."[10]

Furthermore, a study of 45 team projects found that certain types of teams are more effective than others, depending on the goal of a particular project. A cross-functional team made up of employees in several departments can be an effective way to develop an entirely new good or service. However, a vertical team from a single department, such as product engineering, may be a better choice if the goal simply is to modify an existing product. Since it takes time for members of cross-functional teams to establish their roles and begin working together productively, such delays could allow a competitor's modifications to reach the market faster.

If management decides to use a team approach, the first step should be to agree on precisely what needs to be accomplished. The focus then should move to identifying customer needs and the best ways to achieve customer satisfaction. Management should meet with all employees who are associated with a particular facet of the project to discuss team goals and the best ways to do the work. This may involve restructuring some jobs and cross-training employees to perform more than one task.[11]

Managers can increase the likelihood of forming effective work teams by using a systematic approach. Such an approach (see Figure 9.2) begins with analyzing successful teams in other organizations and includes team-member involvement in planning and implementation accompanied by built-in flexibility and a willingness to modify plans when necessary. Note that the final step relates to determining an appropriate compensation plan for team members. This can be difficult, since compensation must motivate individual team members while still encouraging them to act as a team. Managers should devote time to selecting the best ways to reward individual achievements and added responsibilities.

Figure 9.2 Nine Steps to Better Work Teams

1. Study other companies' teams that have successfully met challenges similar to yours.

2. In the planning and implementation process, include appropriate union members, employee representatives, and all team members.

3. Seek and encourage feedback from all participants throughout the process.

4. Set realistic deadlines and distribute training and implementation schedules to team members, management, and others affected by the new system.

5. Be prepared to slow down if the process becomes overly complicated.

6. Regularly evaluate the original plan and make adjustments if necessary.

7. Keep everyone informed of all developments throughout the process.

8. Be prepared to handle team fears, anger, confusion, and resistance.

9. Develop a plan to a address compensation issues such as how individual achievement will be acknowledged, how added responsibilities will be reflected in a team member's pay, and how company profits from the project will be shared with team members.

A frequently used approach is to give team members a chance to provide input on compensation issues and perhaps make the final decision themselves. Management should avoid using individual incentive programs, such as contests and personal bonuses, since they foster competition rather than co-operation within groups. "Don't set up a reward system that acknowledges individual achievement at the expense of the team," suggests consultant Ron Johnson.[12]

Stages of Team Development

Once a manager has formed a team, the group goes through five stages of development: forming, storming, norming, performing, and adjourning (Figure 9.3).

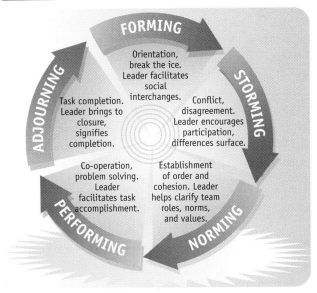

Figure 9.3 Five Stages of Team Development

FORMING
Orientation, break the ice. Leader facilitates social interchanges.

STORMING
Conflict, disagreement. Leader encourages participation, differences surface.

NORMING
Establishment of order and cohesion. Leader helps clarify team roles, norms, and values.

PERFORMING
Co-operation, problem solving. Leader facilitates task accomplishment.

ADJOURNING
Task completion. Leader brings to closure, signifies completion.

The first stage, *forming*, is an orientation period during which team members get to know one another and find out which behaviours are acceptable to the group. During this early phase, team members are curious about what is expected of them and whether they will fit in. An effective team leader provides time for participants to become acquainted and converse informally.

During the next phase, *storming*, participants' individual personalities begin to emerge as they clarify their roles and expectations. Conflicts may arise as people disagree over the team's mission and jockey for position and control of the group. Subgroups may form based on common interests or concerns. At this stage, it is important that the team leader encourage everyone to participate, allowing them to work through their uncertainties and conflicts. Teams must move beyond this stage in order to become truly productive.

As teams move on, they enter the *norming* stage. Differences are resolved, members accept one another, and consensus is reached about the roles of the team leader and other participants. The norming stage is usually brief, and the team leader should use it to emphasize the team's unity and the importance of its objectives.

Next comes the *performing* stage. This phase is characterized by problem solving and a focus on task accomplishment. At this point, team members interact frequently and handle any conflicts constructively. The team leader focuses on task performance and encourages all team members to contribute.

The *adjourning* stage occurs as groups disband following completion of a task. During this phase, the focus is on wrapping up and summarizing the team's experience and accomplishments. The team leader may recognize participants' contributions with some type of ritual, perhaps by handing out plaques or awards.[13]

Team Cohesiveness

Teams tend to be most productive when they are highly cohesive. **Team cohesiveness** is *the extent to which team members are attracted to the team and motivated to remain a part of it.* This cohesiveness typically increases when members interact frequently, share common attitudes and goals, and enjoy being together. When cohesiveness is low, morale suffers.

Managers at GM's Saturn Corp., for example, learned first hand the importance of team cohesiveness. Saturn workers, organized into teams that handle a variety of tasks, enjoy an unusual level of control over operations. When the Saturn program first began, these teams were highly cohesive. One reason was that many new hires shared a common interest in becoming part of the Saturn experiment. Another was the company's extensive training program. All new workers received up to 700 hours of training in such team-building skills as conflict management and communication. But even at firms such as Saturn, teamwork has its drawbacks.

Recently, in an effort to cut costs, managers reduced new-employee training to 175 hours and refocussed the training emphasis on job-specific tasks rather than interpersonal skills. Furthermore, a new union agreement commits management to limit new hires to GM workers who have been laid off from other plants. Many of these applicants are less committed to the team concept. "These folks are tougher to integrate into Saturn," admits human resource management chief Timothy Epps. The resulting tensions have produced occasional conflicts among employees and their union representatives, which in turn have led to lower team cohesiveness.[14]

Team Norms

A **team norm** is *a standard of conduct that is shared by team members and guides their behaviour.* Norms are not formal, written guidelines; they are informal standards

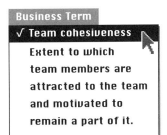

Business Term

✓ **Team cohesiveness**

Extent to which team members are attracted to the team and motivated to remain a part of it.

that identify key values and clarify team members' expectations.

In the Saturn project, conflicts among employees reflect differing norms. The original Saturn workers were attracted to the company by the promise of greater co-operation with management and a larger role in running the factory. Many of them share a view of Saturn as a great experiment in labour–management relations. As one assembly worker put it, "We are the future of the North American car industry, if it has a future." Opposing this norm is the belief, held by some new hires who had been laid off at other GM plants, that Saturn's labour leaders are allied too closely with its management. While most Saturn employees continue to support the company's innovative labour system, a growing minority — 29 percent in a recent election — support a shift to a more traditional approach.[15]

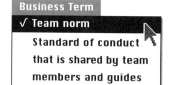

Business Term

√ **Team norm**

Standard of conduct that is shared by team members and guides their behaviour.

TEAM CONFLICT

OF ALL THE skills that a team leader must possess, none is more important than the ability to manage conflict. **Conflict** is an *antagonistic interaction in which one party attempts to thwart the intentions or goals of another.* A certain amount of conflict is inevitable in teams, but too much can impair the ability of team members to exchange ideas, co-operate with one another, and produce results.

Causes of Conflict

Conflict can stem from many sources. It frequently results from competition for scarce resources, such as information, money, or supplies. In addition, team members may have personality clashes or conflicting ideas about what the team should accomplish. Poor communication also can cause misunderstandings and resentment. Finally, conflict can result when job responsibilities or team roles are unclear.

If not managed properly, conflict can destroy a business. Interweb Printing, Canada's sixth-largest printing company, had to manage conflict as it delayered its organizational structure. To survive the technological revolution of the 1990s, Interweb went through an eight-year decentralization process. At the beginning

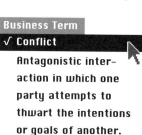

Business Term

√ **Conflict**

Antagonistic interaction in which one party attempts to thwart the intentions or goals of another.

of this process, the company had a conventional bureaucratic organization with six hierarchic levels. Today, says René Hetu, president and founder of Interweb, "We have only three levels in the organization — myself, the resource people, and the front row workers. There are no vice presidents. The whole purpose is to give better service and better quality to customers because now we can get everybody involved." This was a difficult transition for Interweb, but the company managed it properly and humanistically. Interweb reached its goal

> ## DID YOU KNOW?
>
> In their book, <u>Corporate Culture/Team Culture: Removing the Hidden Barriers to Team Success,</u> Jacalyn Sherriton and James Stern explain that most companies encourage teamwork but reward and promote the "superstar." Team players eventually get frustrated and give up. The corporation has to change its culture to support teamwork, "But before you change it you have to know what it is" — and that may take some time and a lot of work. Culture includes everything from the personality of the CEO to the dress code.

by investing heavily in training, profit sharing, and a lot of teamwork. "We could not have succeeded without our participative management philosophy and the involvement of our personnel," concludes Hetu.[16]

Styles of Conflict Resolution

Conflict resolution styles cover a continuum ranging from assertive to co-operative. There is no one best way to manage conflict. The most effective style varies according to the particular situation. Resolution styles include

- **The competing style.** A decisive, assertive approach that might be expressed as "We'll do this my way." While it does not build team rapport, the competing style can be useful for unpopular decisions or emergencies.

- **The avoiding style.** Neither assertive nor co-operative, the most effective style when the cause of conflict is trivial or a no-win situation, when more information is needed, or when open conflict would be harmful.

- **The compromising style.** A moderate degree of both assertiveness and co-operativeness that works well when two opposing goals are equally important, when combatants are equally powerful, or when there is pressure to achieve some sort of immediate solution.

- **The accommodating style.** Involves a high degree of co-operativeness, which can help maintain team harmony. A team member may choose to back down if an issue is more important to others in the group.

- **The collaborating style.** Characterized by a high degree of both assertiveness and co-operativeness. While this approach can be time-consuming and require lengthy negotiation, it can achieve a win–win situation. It is useful when consensus from all parties is important, or when the viewpoints of all participants must be merged into a mutually acceptable solution.

The disruptive impact of conflict can be reduced by focussing team or group members on broad goals that go beyond the immediate sources of disagreement, as exemplified in the Saskatoon Chemicals case. An adversarial relationship existed between union and management at Saskatoon Chemicals. After a bitter strike in the late 1980s that resulted in changes in shift scheduling, both union and management decided that they were going to do things differently. They realized the real issue was the breakdown in the relationship between union and management — there was a lack of communication and trust between the two sides. A third-party facilitator was called in to help mediate their differences. In a two-day discussion, there was a lot of open dialogue about what union and management could do and what the core objectives of the two parties were. When both sides looked at their objectives honestly, they found out that the workers' wants and needs were not that unrealistic, and neither were the company's goals and objectives. The workers wanted some job security, a predictable schedule, and some input into retirement considerations. The company was concerned about quality, costs, liability, and the environment. A focus on broad-based goals by the company and the union was the beginning of a true partnership — both sides are now committed to the change process, and there is as much of a sense of ownership and commitment on the union side as there is on the management side.[17]

When conflict results from ambiguous or overlapping responsibilities, teams can handle it by clarifying participants' respective tasks and areas of authority. The leader, for example, may encourage the opponents to negotiate an agreement. This works well if they are able to deal with the situation in a businesslike, unemotional way. Stubborn disagreements may be turned over to a mediator, an outside party who will discuss the situation with both sides and make a decision.

Perhaps the team leader's or manager's most important contribution to conflict resolution is to facilitate good communication, as shown by the Saskatoon Chemicals example. Ongoing communication ensures that team members perceive one another accurately, understand what is expected of them, and obtain the information they need. The better they communicate, the more likely they are to work co-operatively as a team. Communication is the key to effective conflict resolution. In the remainder of this chapter, we will discuss the importance of effective communication and will look at how good communication skills promote success both inside and outside the organization.

THE IMPORTANCE OF EFFECTIVE COMMUNICATION

COMMUNICATION can be defined as *the meaningful exchange of information through messages*, and it is essential to business. Managers, for example, spend 80 percent of their time in direct communication with others, whether on the phone, in meetings, or in conversation. The other 20 percent is spent on desk work, much of which is also communication in the form of writing and reading.

Communication skills are just as important for other businesspeople as well. Consider a few examples: communication with the marketplace, in the form of market research, helps a company learn what products people want and what changes to make in existing goods and services; communication among engineers, marketers, and production workers enables a company to create products providing customer satisfaction; and communication through advertising and personal sales presentations creates a favourable image for the company and persuades customers to buy.

Business Term
√ **Communication**
The meaningful exchange of information through messages.

COMPETITIVE STRATEGY

THE POWER OF BRAINSTORMING

"We're open-minded and always listen to new ideas. Sales and engineering regularly meet with us to brainstorm, work on new ideas, and develop action plans. We encourage calculated risk taking," says Ivor Perry, president and general manager of Dimatec Inc. Dimatec is a diamond drilling supplies company based in Winnipeg, Manitoba, with about 60 employees and more than $8 million in revenue (1997).

Many successful Canadian companies, like Dimatec, have found brainstorming to be an effective tool for generating new ideas, increasing sales, and reducing costs.

Brainstorming is the establishment of an environment in which innovative thinking can occur.

Here are some suggestions for brainstorming:

→ Plan a brainstorm. Brainstorms don't just happen over a cup of coffee.

→ Identify the objectives or goals of the brainstorm.

→ Set a realistic time limit. There is no need for an "all nighter" — unless, of course, you plan for it.

→ Get someone to record the ideas.

→ Arrange to meet where everyone feels comfortable. The CEO's office, for example, is not normally a good brainstorming location.

→ Follow the five basic rules of a brainstorm:
  1. Always try to improve an idea.
  2. Encourage seemingly crazy ideas — the more the better.
  3. Quantity of ideas is more important than quality.
  4. Try to "add value" to other people's ideas by mixing and matching.
  5. Most of all, try to have fun and reward yourselves!

Source: Information on Dimatec Inc. — the first paragraph is from Rod McQueen, "Canada's 50 Best Managed Private Companies: Dimatec Inc.," *The Financial Post*, December 14–16, 1996, 27. Reprinted by permission of The Financial Post.

Every communication follows a step-by-step process that can be thought of as an interaction among six elements: sender, message, channel, receiver, feedback, and context (see Figure 9.4). First, the *sender* composes the *message* and sends it through a communication carrier, or *channel*. *Encoding* is the translation of a message into understandable terms and in a form capable of being transmitted through the communication medium selected by the sender. There are many channels to choose from, including written messages, face-to-face conversations, and electronic mail. The *receiver* consists of the audience that receives the message and interpret its meaning. *Decoding* is the receiver's interpretation of the message. *Feedback* from the audience — a response to the sender's communication — helps the sender determine whether the message was interpreted correctly. Every communication takes place in some sort of situational and cultural *context*. The context can exert a powerful influence on how well the process works. A conversation between two people in a quiet room, for example, may be a very different experience from the same conversation held outdoors, on a freezing cold day, next to a noisy construction site.

Figure 9.4 **The Communication Process**

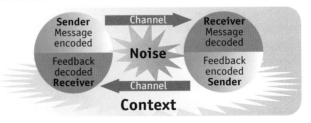

Senders need to pay attention to audience feedback, even solicit it if it is not forthcoming, since this response clarifies whether their message was perceived in the way they intended. Even with the best of intentions, sender and audience can misunderstand each other. A major technology company announced a 10 percent pay reduction to its employees by means of e-mail that was signed by the president. The immediate effect was the opposite of what was expected. Employees greeted the message with amusement rather than disappointment — it had arrived at each employee's desk on April Fools' Day!

Basic Forms of Communication

People communicate in many different ways. Some methods — calling a meeting of team members or writing a formal mission statement — are obvious. Others, ranging from gestures and facial expressions during a conversation to leaning forward when speaking to someone, are much less obvious, even though they can have a significant impact on the message being communicated. It is convenient to discuss communication based on the following forms, outlined in Table 9.1: oral and written, formal and informal, verbal and nonverbal.

Oral Communication. Managers spend a great deal of their time communicating orally, whether in person or on the phone. Some businesspeople prefer to communicate this way, feeling that oral channels allow them to convey their true message more accurately. A vital component of oral communication is **listening**, *the skill of receiving a message and interpreting its genuine meaning by accurately grasping the facts and feelings conveyed*. While listening is the first communication skill we learn in life and the one we use most often, it is also the one in which we receive the least formal training.

> **Business Term**
> √ **Listening**
> Skill of receiving a message and interpreting its genuine meaning by accurately grasping the facts and feelings conveyed.

It is tempting to think that listening is easy — after all, it seems to require no effort. This is deceptive, however. While the average person talks at a rate of roughly 150 words per minute, the brain can handle up to 400 words per minute. This discrepancy can lead to boredom, inattention, and misinterpretation. In fact, immediately after listening to a message, the average person can recall only half of it. Several days later, the percentage of the message that can be recalled falls to 25 percent or less.

Noise, interference with messages being transmitted, can occur as a result of physical factors — poor radio reception or misunderstanding a conversation with a co-worker, for example. In other instances, misinterpretations produce faulty communication.

Table 9.1 **Forms of Communication**

Form	Description	Example
Oral communication	Communication transmitted through speech	Personal conversations, speeches, meetings, voice mail, telephone conversations, video conferences
Written communication	Communication transmitted through writing	Letters, memos, formal reports, news releases, e-mail, faxes
Formal communication	Communication transmitted through the chain of command within an organization to other members or to persons outside the organization	Internal — memos, reports, meetings, written proposals, oral presentations, meeting minutes; and external — letters, written proposals, oral presentations, speeches, news releases, press conferences
Informal communication	Communication transmitted outside formally authorized channels without regard for the organization's hierarchy of authority	Rumours spread through "the grapevine"
Verbal communication	Transmission of messages in the form of words	Meetings, telephone calls, voice mail, video conferences
Nonverbal communication	Communication transmitted through actions and behaviours rather than through words	Gestures, facial expressions, posture, body language, dress, make-up

Certain types of listening behaviours are common in both business and personal interaction. They include

- **Cynical listening.** Defensive listening that occurs when recipients of a message feel its goal is to take advantage of them.

- **Offensive listening.** Listening to catch the speaker in a mistake or contradiction.

- **Polite listening.** Mechanical listening done to be polite rather than to communicate. Polite listeners are usually inattentive and spend their time rehearsing what they want to say when the speaker finishes. Former major-league baseball player Tom Paciorek was referring to this type of listening when he defined boredom as "having to listen to someone talk about himself when I want to talk about me."[18]

THEY SAID IT

"The role of the manager is to shut up and listen to how things are going. We always ask 'What would you do differently if you had my job?' and then listen."

GREG KIESSLING, President, KL Group Inc.

- **Active listening.** A form of listening that requires involvement with the information and empathy with the speaker's situation. In both business and personal life, active listening is the basis for effective communication.

Written Communication. Effective written communication reflects its audience, the channel being used, and the degree of formality that is appropriate. When writing a formal business document, such as a complex report or an important letter, it is important to plan in advance and construct the document carefully. Table 9.2 shows the process of writing a formal document, which can be divided into five stages: planning, research, organization, composition and design, and revision.

Written communication via e-mail and computer networks may call for a less formal writing style. "The medium favours the terse," says Crawford Kilian, a writing instructor at Capilano College. "Short paragraphs, bulleted lists, and one-liners are the units of thought here." Electronic writers often communicate through a combination of words, acronyms, and *emoticons*, little faces called "smileys" that are constructed with punctuation marks and convey some of the message's emotional content (see Figure 9.5). While electronic mail may be more informal, it is still important to write well. "It's so competitive that you have to work on your style if you want to make any impact," says software designer Jorn Barger.[19]

Table 9.2 Written Communication: A Five-Stage Approach

Stage	Description
Planning	Writer determines the objective of the document, assesses the audience's needs and current knowledge about the topic, and decides the best way to write the document. Although thorough planning takes time, it saves time in the long run by helping the writer focus on what really has to be communicated.
Research	Writer investigates the subject systematically to discover relevant facts, opinions, and beliefs. The amount of research needed depends on the nature of the document and the amount of information available. A simple memo often requires little or no research; a long report may call for extensive preparation.
Organization	Writer determines the sequence in which ideas will be presented and the logical connections between those ideas. These choices will determine the format and overall approach of the document. Two often-used alternative approaches include showing a series of causes and effects or identifying a problem and then proposing a solution. The organization of the document should reflect the chosen alternative.
Composition and design	Writer composes a rough draft of the document. Draft will reflect decisions made about tone, writing style, and level of formality. Design issues involve decisions regarding how best to arrange information on the page and what design is more readable for the document's intended audience.
Revision	Through a series of revisions, the writer transforms the rough draft into a finished document. This stage includes assessing the document's wording, clarity, and readability; eliminating any errors; and rewriting as necessary. The writer also may decide to incorporate suggestions from other people, perhaps supervisors or co-workers, into the final draft.

The systematic five-step approach is a logical progression of the steps involved in converting an idea into a polished document.

Figure 9.5 Emoticons

:-)	Sarcastic; "Don't hit me for what I just said."
:-(	Depressed or upset by a remark
:-|	Indifferent
>:->	Devilishly sarcastic
;-)	Winking at a suggestive remark
:-7	Wry
:-/	Sceptical
:-&	Tongue-tied
:-P	Sticking out tongue
:-[	Sour
:-D	Laughing at someone
:-@	Screaming
:[)	Drunk
X-)	Dead
+-:-)	A priest or minister
0:-)	Like an angel
c=:-)	A chef
[:o)	A clown
:-Q	A smoker
:-?	A pipe smoker
:-E	A vampire
8-)	Wearing sunglasses
::-)	Wearing normal glasses
:-#	Wearing braces
:-{}	Wearing lipstick
(-:	Left-handed

Writers on the Internet use a variety of emoticons, or "smileys," in their messages. Note how much they resemble faces when you look at them sideways.

Formal Communication. Communication that follows a company's official organization chart reflects **formal communication channels**, *information channels within the chain of command or task responsibility defined by an organization.* The most familiar is probably *downward communication*, which occurs when someone who holds a senior position in the organization communicates with subordinates. Managers, for example, may communicate downward via e-mail, formal presentations, policy manuals, notices posted on bulletin boards, and reports printed in company newsletters.

> **Business Term**
> √ **Formal communication channels**
> Information channels within the chain of command or task responsibility defined by an organization.

Informal Communication. **Informal communication channels** *exist outside formally authorized channels without regard for the organization's hierarchy of authority.* A familiar example of an informal channel is the **grapevine**, *an internal information channel that transmits information through unofficial, independent sources.* Research shows that many employees cite the grapevine as their most frequent source of information. Grapevines are rapid disseminators of information. While a message sent through formal channels may take days to reach its audience, messages that travel via grapevines can arrive within hours. Grapevines also are surprisingly reliable. They pass on accurate information 75 to 96 percent of the time. However, even a tiny inaccuracy can distort an entire message.

> **Business Term**
> √ **Informal communication channels**
> Information channels outside formally authorized channels without regard for the organization's hierarchy of authority.

> **Business Term**
> √ **Grapevine**
> Internal information channel that transmits information through unofficial, independent sources.

Nonverbal Communication. So far, we have been considering different forms of verbal communication: communication that conveys meaning through words. Perhaps of equal importance is **nonverbal communication**, *communication that is transmitted through actions and behaviours.* Gestures, posture, eye contact, tone of voice, even the clothing we wear — all of these are nonverbal communication cues. Nonverbal cues become important during oral communication since they can distort the intended meaning of a message.

Nonverbal cues can have a far greater impact on our ability to communicate than we realize. One study, for instance, divided face-to-face conversations into three sources of communication cues: verbal (the actual words spoken), vocal (the pitch, tone, and timbre of a person's voice), and facial expressions. The researchers found that the relative weights of these factors in message interpretation were as follows: verbal, 7 percent; vocal, 38 percent; and facial expressions, 55 percent.

Even personal space — the physical distance between people who are engaging in communication — can convey powerful messages (see Figure 9.6). A continuum of personal space and social interaction has four zones: intimate, personal, social, and public. In North America, most business conversations occur within the social zone, between roughly 4 and 12 feet (about 1 m to 3.6 m) apart. If one person tries to approach closer than that, the other is likely to feel uncomfortable or threatened.

Interpreting nonverbal cues from members of other cultures can be especially challenging. Concepts of appropriate personal space, to name just one example, can be quite different. Latin Americans insist on conducting business while standing closer than most Canadians and Northern Europeans find comfortable. The result is that culturally inexperienced Canadians back away to preserve their personal space, causing Latin Americans to perceive them as cold and unfriendly. To protect themselves from such a personal "threat," experienced Canadians use desks or tables to separate themselves from their Latin American counterparts. "The result," explains cultural anthropologist Edward T. Hall, "is that the Latin American may even climb over the obstacles until he [or she] has achieved a distance at which he [or she] can comfortably talk."[20]

People usually are sending nonverbal messages, even when they make a conscious effort not to do so. Some-

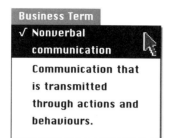

Business Term
√ **Nonverbal communication**
Communication that is transmitted through actions and behaviours.

times nonverbal cues may serve to "leak" a person's true attitudes and thoughts. A discrepancy between verbal and nonverbal messages may indicate that someone is not being truthful. Generally, when verbal and nonverbal cues conflict, receivers of the communication tend to believe the non-verbal elements.

Consider what happened at Lauzon Ltd. of Papineauville, Quebec, where employees used to meet with the owner and president, David Lauzon, in the hallway and get a decision. The company grew rapidly and Lauzon had to impose a new management structure, company policies, and procedures. This meant that employees would now have to go through official channels. Employees thought the owner didn't care about them anymore. Francine Houle, the human resources manager, said that the company took eighteen months "consolidating the changes" and trying to convince employees that the president's door was still open but that the company was growing and everyone would have to learn to operate within this new structure.[21] Mr. Lauzon's verbal message said, "My door is still open," but his nonverbal message said, "I don't have as much time for you anymore." The lesson here is that senior managers and owners must be acutely aware of the nonverbal signals they send to employees when major decisions are made.

Figure 9.6 Personal Space

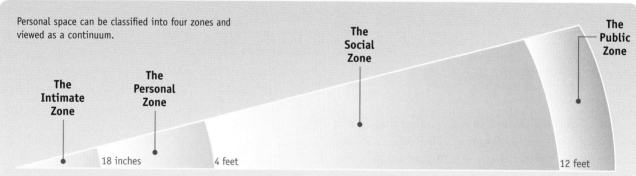

Personal space can be classified into four zones and viewed as a continuum.

The **Intimate Zone**

The **Personal Zone**

The **Social Zone**

The **Public Zone**

18 inches   4 feet   12 feet

- In the **Intimate Zone**, within 18 inches of each other, good friends and family members engage in activities like comforting, lovers make love, and competitors in sports events wrestle and tackle. Not only can partners touch and hug each other, but they are aware of each other's body heat and body odour. If people whisper, they can be heard.

- In the **Personal Zone**, from 1.5 to 4 feet, less intense exchanges are allowed. Touch is more limited, and body heat and odour are unnoticeable (unless odour is strong). Speech becomes louder, and looking becomes more important than in the intimate zone: not only is it easier to focus, but you can also see more of the other person.

- In the **Social Zone**, from 4 to 12 feet, exchanges are more formal. Typical are those between business associates. They can touch at the closer end of the range, and then only if one or both lean toward the other. Visual cues become more important, and voices become louder.

- The **Public Zone**, 12 feet and more, is characteristic of brief standing exchanges, such as calling to a friend across a street, or formal exchanges between a speaker (perhaps a teacher or minister) and an audience. Voices have to be loud, and it is impossible to see much facial expression detail.

COMMUNICATIONS INSIDE THE ORGANIZATION

INTERNAL COMMUNICATION involves *communication through channels within an organization*. Examples include memos, meetings, speeches, phone conversations, even a simple conversation over lunch. Internal communication may be relatively simple in small organizations since it is often face to face. Unclear instructions can be remedied by further conversation. But communication problems increase as the organization grows. Messages, many of which are transmitted in writing, often pass through several hierarchical layers in a formal organization. The distortion of the original message as it flows through several intermediaries is illustrated in the Big Shot cartoon. The sender of the message must continually be aware of the recipient and make certain the message is both clearly written and likely to be interpreted correctly.

> **Business Term**
> √ **Internal communication**
> **Communication through channels within an organization.**

As we'll learn in the next chapter, computers, the Internet, intranets, entranets, and e-mail can facilitate internal communication within large organizations, and may even make companies less formal. "Businesses that have pervasive use of electronic mail operate differently," says Intel CEO Andrew Grove. "It squeezes all the slack out of the system."[22] It also removes time and geography constraints, improves the accuracy of information being exchanged, and can be an effective means of building customer relationships by maintaining customer–supplier contacts and supplying such information as product modifications and price changes. E-mail combined with a graphics environment is poised to become

The World According to Big Shot

Big Shot came upon a memo he had written to his Company Commander during his time in the armed forces. "Those were the days," he thought nostalgically.

Memo from Executive Officer to Company Commander
Tomorrow evening, at approximately 2000 hours, Halley's Comet will be visible in this area, an event that occurs only once every 76 years. Have the troops fall out in the battalion area in fatigues, and I will explain this rare phenomenon to them. In case of rain, we will not be able to see anything, so assemble them in the theatre and I will show them films of the comet.

Company Commander to Lieutenant

By order of the Executive Officer, tomorrow at 2000 hours, Halley's Comet will appear above the battalion area. If it rains, fall the troops out in fatigues, then march to the theatre where this rare phenomenon will take place, something that occurs only once every 76 years.

Lieutenant to Sergeant

Tomorrow at 2000 hours, be in fatigues. The phenomenal Halley's Comet will appear in the theatre with the Executive Officer, something that happens every 76 years. If it rains, the Executive Officer will order the comet into the battalion area.

Sergeant to Squad

When it rains tomorrow at 2000 hours, the phenomenal 76-year-old General Halley, accompanied by the Executive Officer, will drive his comet through the battalion area in fatigues.

→ What does this tell you about communication?

one of the hottest waves of communicating within the business world and beyond. Consider Ron Murch's experience. Back in 1995, Murch, a senior instructor at the University of Calgary, needed a special type of yo-yo — one with a map of the world on it — to hand out as a trinket at a "Going Global" business conference in Banff. Using e-mail over the Internet, Murch quickly located his yo-yo from a Florida vendor who found a supply in China. The Florida vendor scanned a picture of the yo-yo onto his firm's home page and gave Murch the address. Said Murch, "I was talking to [the vendor] on the phone and looking at the picture on the screen two minutes later." The bottom line: Murch delighted the people who received the yo-yos because of "the manner in which [they] were obtained."[23] Benefits such as these explain why North American businesses sent over 6 billion e-mail messages last year. If each message had 50 words, it would be like sending 1000 manuscripts the length of *War and Peace* every day.[24]

E-mail speeds up internal communications at Boston Chicken, a fast-growing restaurant chain. Managers use networking software to collaborate on team projects and develop menus, solve distribution problems, and plan the chain's expansion. Online records of sales and cost breakdowns help them monitor the business. President Bruce Harreld and other managers pay particular attention to the database of customer gripes, which can be sorted by region or type of complaint. "We look for patterns," says Harreld. "The messages go back to the regional level and, as of this fall, back to the store itself electronically, so that everyone sees."[25]

E-mail has a downside, however. Information overload is a major e-mail issue confronting Canadian business. First, business executives have increasingly reported being deluged with e-mail messages. Knowing how to filter information is growing in importance as executives are bombarded with messages. Elizabeth Hunt, director of the Voice Centre, a Toronto communications consulting firm, says that the greatest complaint she hears from executives about e-mail is "too much information is being sent to me just because you can do it." Ted Cadsby, a vice-president of marketing with the Canadian Imperial Bank of Commerce, says that "to be an executive in this day you really have to be disciplined about your priorities. You can easily get drowned in a bombardment of information and messages."[26]

SAS Institute Inc. offers its award-winning Web-enabled software and custom-built data-warehousing solutions to help businesses manage and use information more effectively.

Business Term
✓ **Centralized network**
Communication of team members through a single person to solve problems or make decisions.

Business Term
✓ **Decentralized network**
System in which team members communicate freely with other team members and arrive at decisions together.

Communicating in Teams

Communication in teams can be divided into two broad categories: centralized and decentralized. In a **centralized network**, *team members communicate through a single person to solve problems or make decisions.* In a **decentralized network**, *members communicate freely with other team members and arrive at decisions together.*

Which type of network is more effective? It depends on the nature of the problem or decision at issue. Research has shown that centralized networks usually solve simple problems more quickly and accurately. Members simply pass information along to the central decision-maker. However, when problems are complex, a decentralized network actually works faster and comes up with more accurate

CASE EXERCISE

ONE PLUS ONE DOES NOT EQUAL TWO

MSM Transportation Inc., a Bolton, Ontario, trucking firm, carries freight from Southern Ontario into the United States. In the early days of MSM, tough times forced the partners to reach into their savings to reinvest in the company, a sacrifice each partner could not have made by himself. Today, MSM is a successful *Profit* 100 company.

When Robert Murray and Mike McCarron started out in the late 1980s, they knew their partnership would bring more to the table than start-up capital. They were combining different types of management expertise, plus two very different personalities. McCarron, the company's managing partner and primary marketer, is a relationship builder, outgoing, passionate, and, he admits, impulsive. Murray, MSM's president, comes across as quiet, thoughtful, and more of a long-term thinker. Oil and water, you say? Of course.

But Murray says the duo's strength lies in the fact that they can disagree, argue feverishly, work it out, and move on. With two partners who share a similar vision for the company, if not the same temperament, debate becomes a positive force that generates new ideas and better decisions. In an industry notorious for its lack of marketing and financial skills, MSM benefits from both personalities. "One plus one does not equal two," notes Murray. "My partner makes me ... better at what I do, because we question each others' assumptions and strategies."

1. Using Figure 9.1, describe the team roles of the two partners.

2. Suppose Murray and McCarron had a conflict. What style of conflict resolution do you think they would use? Why?

3. What do you think would be the main form of communication between these two partners?

4. It appears that Murray and McCarron have a highly cohesive team relationship. Based on this case, list and describe at least four characteristics of a cohesive team.

Source: Adapted from Rick Spence, *Secrets of Success from Canada's Fastest Growing Companies* (Toronto: John Wiley & Sons, 1997) 98-99.

answers. Team members pool their data, provide greater input into the decision, and emerge with a higher-quality solution. This research indicates that organizations should use centralized team networks to deal with simple problems, but should set up decentralized teams to handle more complex issues. Members of decentralized teams should be encouraged to share information with one another and generate as much input into the solution as possible.[27]

Decentralized teams work well for the complex process of new-product development, as exemplified at Downsview, Ontario-based Teknion Furniture Systems. "There will continue to be strong pressure for new products, reduced lead times, and cost reduction," says David Feldberg, president and CEO. To compete internationally and meet meteoric changes and demands from across the corporate world — including cheaper space and higher employee turnover — Teknion expanded its product lines. In 1997 alone, the firm launched two new products into the international market. To compete and thrive, the firm works in cross-functional teams that rely heavily on input by everyone. Says Feldberg, "We've become more international in scope. ... Our philosophy is to build strong teams in every market." Design ideas come from outside firms as well as an internal design group that receives ideas from worldwide distributors. For example, the firm has a team it calls a "special cell" that re-engineers a product to suit specific customer requirements that are not standard. This cell responds to about 1200 such requests monthly while maintaining its usual four-week lead time. Another team known as the "run-thru cell" handles order management. This cell acknowledges an order within two hours of receipt and guides the order from manufacture to shipment.[28]

ProShare, an Intel Corp. division producing computer-based video-conferencing products, facilitates decentralized information sharing by allowing team members to view one another on their desktop computer screens as they work together on documents, spreadsheets, and other applications. One satisfied customer is Unisys's airline systems division, which sells computers and software to airlines. "Each time we go to the video, we'll probably save from $75 to $100," says Gary Hart, director of sales and marketing. "It's the kind

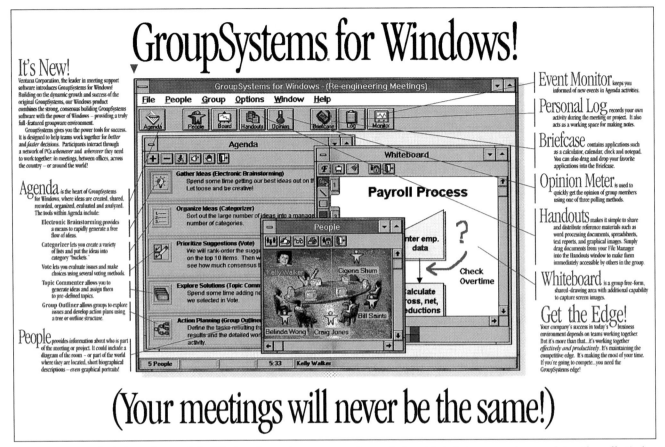

Ventana Corporation's GroupSystems® for Windows is meeting-support software designed to help team members work together effectively. Participants interact through a network of PCs whenever and wherever they need to work together: in meetings, between offices, across the country, or around the world.

of sale where a lot of people are involved — program managers, project managers, legal, marketing, as well as myself and the sales rep. The savings will come from eliminating overnight couriers when preparing proposals for an airline."[29]

COMMUNICATIONS OUTSIDE THE ORGANIZATION

EXTERNAL COMMUNICATION is *the meaningful exchange of information through messages between an organization and its major audiences*, such as customers, suppliers, other firms, the general public, and government officials. Businesses use external communication to keep their operations functioning and to maintain their position in the marketplace.

The central focus of a company's external communication, of course, is the customer, since creating goods and services that provide customer satisfaction is the ultimate purpose of business. Every interaction with customers — whether it is a sales presentation, order fulfilment, routine dealing, or one-time transaction — should create good will and contribute to customer satisfaction.

Consider customer complaints. According to management authors Tom Peters and Nancy Austin, organizations tend to treat complaints in one of two ways: "The first, the most typical, views the complaint as a disease to be got over, with memory of the pain rapidly suppressed. The second views the complaint as a luscious, golden opportunity." Wise businesspeople see a complaining customer as one who can be retained once the complaint has been resolved.[30]

Effective communication can help a firm win back lost customers. When KFC Japan experienced a 10 percent decline in business in a single year, Toshiki Nakata, deputy general manager, commissioned a market survey to find out why. A surprising number of respondents stated that, while they liked KFC's food, they thought it was very expensive. Nakata promptly announced a "value strategy" that targeted the chain's largest customer group in Japan: 18- to 26-year-olds who buy from urban outlets near railway and subway stations. KFC lowered the price on its biggest-selling meal by 16.8 percent (to 500 yen) at city stores. "We call it our one-coin price," says Nakata. KFC regained 10 percent of its lost customers within a few months of the one-coin price taking effect.[31]

We already have seen how personal computer–based video conferencing facilitates internal communication. It offers similar benefits for communication outside the firm. For example, the video-conferencing network is a key communication line at the University of Manitoba. In the winter of 1996, the northern community of Thompson, Manitoba, didn't have a radiologist available to read X-rays. Working with a video-conferencing network set up by a partnership between the University of Manitoba and Lucent Technologies Canada, the X-rays were transmitted through the telephone system to another radiologist in Winkler, Manitoba. He was able to read the X-ray, talk to the attending physician in Thompson, and offer consultation. Using PictureTel equipment, medical students and practising physicians on the university campus went on rounds with physicians in teaching hospitals across the Winnipeg River at St. Boniface General Hospital and up north at Thompson General Hospital. The University of Manitoba also co-operates with the University of Saskatchewan to share courses where faculty isn't available in both places.[32]

> **Business Term**
> ✓ **External communication**
> Meaningful exchange of information through messages between an organization and its major audiences.

LESSONS FROM THE BEST

THE FRIENDS OF ZENON

Does teamwork always require a formal arrangement or a partnership, as was the case with MSM Transportation? Not according to the experiences of many *Profit* 100 companies.

Most entrepreneurs have family, colleagues, associates, and friends that could be called on to help problem-solve or work on cross-functional teams, and to take semi-official responsibility for the company's welfare. Some creative companies establish a more permanent board of advisors, composed of key players such as accountants, lawyers, and mentors. This was the case at Les Systemes Zenon Inc., a systems integrator in Longueuil, Quebec.

Co-founders Eric Bourbeau and Chad Loeven set up "the Friends of Zenon," a group of advisors who consult on strategy and head off any problems they see looming. "It's like a board of directors," says Bourbeau. The voluntary, unpaid board is made up of experts from related technology fields, the company's lawyer, an accountant, and a venture capitalist who has seen it all before. "We're very cautious and don't want to lose our focus," Bourbeau explains. "Before we make any potentially risky decisions we go to those guys and we check everything out. That way we have enough qualified people around us to make sure we rarely do anything stupid."

Source: Adapted from Rick Spence, *Secrets of Success from Canada's Fastest Growing Companies* (Toronto: John Wiley & Sons, 1997), 102.

INTERNATIONAL BUSINESS COMMUNICATION

PEPSICO MARKETERS DECIDED to build sales in China, so they created a promotional campaign based on the theme "Come Alive with Pepsi." Sales were poor, which surprised them until they discovered that the direct Chinese translation of their slogan was "Bring your ancestors back from the dead." Managers ordered a hasty rewrite.[33]

As this example shows, businesspeople who want to succeed in the international marketplace must ensure that their communications are linguistically and culturally appropriate. Communication snafus occur even among English-speaking countries. For example, the British term for "trucks" is "lorries." Britons call the hood of a car a *bonnet* and the trunk the *boot*. Windshields are *windscreens*, tire is spelled *tyre*, and the elevator is simply a *lift*. Even two English-speaking countries can be "separated by a common language," as the playwright George Bernard Shaw once said.

It is helpful to understand the cultural context that surrounds and influences every attempt at international business communication. Anthropologists divide cultures into two basic types, low context and high context (see Figure 9.7). *Communication* in **low-context cultures** *tends to rely on explicit written and verbal messages.* Examples include Switzerland, Germany, Scandinavia, and Canada. *Communication* in **high-context cultures**, however, *is more likely to depend not only on the message itself, but also on everything that surrounds it,* such as nonverbal cues and the personal relationship between the communicators.

Western businesspeople must be careful to temper their low-context style to the expectations of colleagues and clients in high-context settings. While Canadians

> **Business Term**
> ✓ **Low-context cultures**
>
> Cultures in which communication tends to rely on explicit written and verbal messages.

> **Business Term**
> ✓ **High-context cultures**
>
> Cultures in which communication is likely to depend not only on the message itself, but also on everything that surrounds it.

tend to be more direct, wanting to "get down to business" soon after shaking hands or sitting down to a meal, businesspeople in Mexico or the Near East prefer to become acquainted first. When conducting business there, it is wise to allow time for relaxed meals during which business-related topics are avoided and businesspeople can engage in small talk and discuss their families and countries. They may get together for several meetings before any business actually is transacted.

With regard to technology and international culture, e-mail users (many of whom think grammar and editing should be sacrificed for brevity and informality) may find their foreign responses a little frosty. Canadian businesses must realize that e-mail, although growing exponentially, is still in its infancy stage in many parts of the world. For example, in 1997, Greece started using e-mail as a "cross-border" tool rather than an internal communications mechanism — e-mail is "mainly used by international companies for communications outside the country," says Nicholas Moraitis, assistant general manager at the Bank of Nova

> **THEY SAID IT**
>
> "The first EDSer [Electronic Data Systems employee] to see a snake kills it. At GM, the first thing you do is organize a committee on snakes. Then you bring in a consultant who knows a lot about snakes. Third thing you do is talk about it for a year."
>
> **H. ROSS PEROT, American computer industry executive and former presidential candidate**

Figure 9.7 Low- and High-Context Cultures

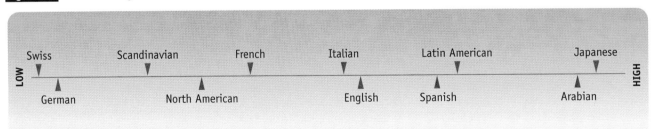

Eleven global regions denote a continuum of low- to high-context cultures.

TECHNOLOGY

CANADIAN HELICOPTER AND STENTOR ALLIANCE LINK TO BETTER COMMUNICATE

Running air ambulance missions in the jungles of Ecuador teaches the importance of sound, reliable telecommunications links.

Trevor Lewis of Canadian Helicopters (CHC) says: "Communications is a vital link in terms of safety and just keeping track of where the aircraft are." CHC is the world's largest commercial helicopter operation. From headquarters in St. John's, Nfld., it manages a fleet of over 230 aircraft located in 20 countries around the world. It also operates a large repair and overhaul business. CHC's quest for reliable, efficient telecommunications for its global operations led [it] to "Concert" — a communications system distributed in Canada by the telecommunications companies of Stentor Alliance — to provide seamless, reliable, state-of-the-art telecommunications to over 50 countries. Concert simplifies telecommunications by ensuring that customers have a uniform network design as well as a centralized billing system. "A major benefit for us is that Concert gives us one point of contact that can address all of our issues. If we have a problem in Aberdeen we can get network support right here in Canada," Mr. Lewis says. "Being in over 20 countries we're dealing with time zone differences, language, even cultural issues. The one point of contact helps us overcome all this."

Thanks to Stentor Alliance and Concert Services, CHC has saved money and time; has improved its performance; and is now planning expansion in Asia and other European countries.

Source: Adapted from Canadian Helicopters, Advertising Supplement, *The Globe and Mail*, December 10, 1996, D2. Reprinted by permission.

Scotia in Athens. What this means is that Canadian businesses ought to be very careful not to commit a cultural *faux pas* by using some of the emerging e-mail shortcuts. "I'd watch it very carefully," says Calgary management consultant Talaat Abdel-Malek. To avoid cultural gaffes, Canadians communicating through e-mail should shun symbols and phrasing that may leave foreign recipients confused or annoyed.[34]

COMMUNICATIONS TECHNOLOGY

WE HAVE ALREADY seen how various communications technologies — computers, video conferencing, e-mail, and networks — can influence the communication process. And the numbers point to their contribution to the world of business (see Figure 9.8, for example).

These technological advances can improve the speed and efficiency of communication by making it easier to create, organize, and distribute messages. They also facilitate international transactions by minimizing time differences and making all areas of the world more accessible.

For example, communication throughout Europe is made easier by the continent's fast-growing wireless

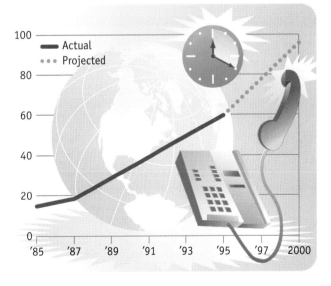

Figure 9.8 Global Minutes of Telephone Traffic, 1985–2000 (billions)

— Actual
••• Projected

telecommunications networks. Europe now has over 2 million digital cellular subscribers, and the market continues to expand by 133 percent a year. Businesspeople already can talk via digital cellular telephones in most of Europe's cities.[35]

In the next chapter, we will examine further the role of these and other communications technologies in business.

SUMMARY OF LEARNING OUTCOMES

1. **Distinguish between the various types of teams found in organizations.**

   A team is a small number of people with complementary skills who are committed to a common purpose, approach, and set of performance goals for which they hold themselves mutually accountable. There are various types of teams. The most common are work teams, cross-functional teams, self-managed teams, problem-solving teams, quality circles, virtual teams, and management teams.

2. **Identify the characteristics of an effective team and the different roles played by team members.**

   Two important characteristics are the size of the team and the roles played by its members. Effective teams typically have between five and twelve members, with about seven members being the ideal size. Team members can play task specialist, socio-emotional, dual, or nonparticipator roles. Ideally, teams contain a balance of the first three roles. Research indicates that diverse teams tend to display a broader range of viewpoints and produce more innovative solutions to problems.

3. **Summarize the stages of team development.**

   A team goes through five stages of development: (1) *forming*, an orientation period during which team members get to know one another and find out what behaviours are acceptable to the group; (2) *storming*, during which participants' individual personalities begin to emerge as they clarify their roles and expectations; (3) *norming*, when differences are resolved, members accept one another, and consensus is reached about the roles of the team leader and other participants; (4) *performing*, characterized by problem solving and a focus on task accomplishment; and (5) *adjourning*, where the focus is on wrapping up and summarizing the team's experience and accomplishments.

4. **Relate team cohesiveness and norms to effective team performance.**

   Team cohesiveness is the extent to which team members are attracted to the team and motivated to remain a part of it. Generally, teams with a high degree of cohesiveness tend to be more productive. When cohesiveness is low, morale suffers.

5. **Describe the factors that can cause conflict in teams, and discuss conflict resolution styles.**

   Conflict can stem from many sources: competition for scarce resources, personality clashes, conflicting goals, poor communication, and unclear job responsibilities or team role assignments. Conflict resolution styles cover a continuum from assertive to co-operative. The most effective style varies according to the particular situation. Resolution styles include the competing style, the avoiding style, the compromising style, the accommodating style, and the collaborating style. A team can reduce conflict by focussing on broad goals, clarifying participants' respective tasks and areas of authority, using a mediator, and facilitating effective communication.

6. **Explain the importance of effective communication skills in business.**

   Communication is essential to business. It can be defined as the meaningful exchange of information through messages. Managers spend 80 percent of their time in direct communication with others and the other 20 percent on desk work, much of which is also communication in the form of writing and reading. Communicators need to pay attention to audience feedback, even solicit it, to determine whether their message was perceived in the way they intended.

7. **Compare the different types of communication.**

   Communication takes many forms: oral and written, formal and informal, verbal and nonverbal. While some people feel oral channels allow them to convey their message more accurately, nonverbal cues can distort it. Effective written communication reflects its audience, the channel being used, and the degree of formality that is appropriate. Formal communication channels are those within the chain of command or task responsibility defined by an organization. Informal communication channels are channels, such as grapevines, that exist outside formally authorized channels without regard for the organization's hierarchy of authority. Nonverbal communication plays a larger communication role than most people realize. Generally, when verbal and nonverbal cues conflict, the receivers of the communication tend to believe the nonverbal elements.

8. **Identify and explain several important considerations in international business communication.**

    The ability to communicate cross-culturally is becoming more and more important in business. Communication in low-context cultures tends to rely on explicit written and verbal messages. In high-context cultures, however, it is more likely to depend not only on the message itself, but also on everything

that surrounds it, such as nonverbal cues and the personal relationship between the communicators. Canadian businesspeople must temper their low-context style when in high-context cultures.

9. **Summarize important developments in communications technology and how they affect business communication.**

    Various communications technologies — computers, the Internet, intranets, video conferencing, e-mail, networks — can influence the efficiency of communication by making it easier to create, organize, and distribute messages. They also facilitate international transactions by minimizing time differences and making all areas of the world more accessible.

Key Terms Quiz

problem-solving team
decentralized network
external communication
team
low-context culture
team cohesiveness
work team

listening
cross-functional team
high-context culture
informal communication channels
nonverbal communication
conflict
self-managed team

centralized network
formal communication channels
socio-emotional role
communication
internal communication
grapevine

_____ 1. A small number of people with complementary skills who are committed to a common purpose, approach, and set of performance goals.

_____ 2. A mid-1990s approach in which small numbers of people with complementary skills perform the day-to-day work of the organization.

_____ 3. Temporary combinations of workers who gather to solve a specific problem and then disband.

_____ 4. Employees from different departments who work on specific projects.

_____ 5. Role played by team members who devote their time and energy to providing support for group members' emotional needs and social unity.

_____ 6. The extent to which team members are attracted to the team and motivated to remain a part of it.

_____ 7. A group of employees who work with little or no supervision.

_____ 8. An antagonistic interaction in which one party attempts to thwart the intentions or goals of another.

_____ 9. The meaningful exchange of information through messages.

_____ 10. The skill of receiving a message and interpreting its genuine meaning by accurately grasping the facts and feelings conveyed.

_____ 11. Information channels within the chain of command or task responsibility defined by an organization.

_____ 12. Information channels outside formally authorized channels without regard for the organization's hierarchy of authority.

_____ 13. An internal information channel that transmits information through unofficial, independent sources.

_____ 14. Communication that is transmitted through actions and behaviours.

_____ 15. System of communication through channels within an organization.

_____ 16. The meaningful exchange of information through messages between an organization and its major audiences outside the organization.

_____ 17. Communication of team members through a single person to solve problems or make decisions.

_____ 18. System in which members communicate freely with other team members and arrive at decisions together.

_____ 19. Culture in which communication relies on explicit written and verbal messages.

_____ 20. Culture in which communication depends not only on the message itself, but also on everything that surrounds it.

Other Important Terms

adjourning stage	emoticons	message	quality circle
brainstorming	encoding	noise	receiver
channel	feedback	nonparticipator role	sender
context	forming stage	norming stage	storming stage
decoding	management team	performing stage	virtual team

Review Questions

1. Distinguish among work teams, problem-solving teams, and cross-functional teams.

2. Is there an optimal size for a team? Identify the problems that often occur with large teams.

3. Which team roles are most important in achieving the goals of a team? Which role would you be most likely to assume on a team?

4. Describe each of the five stages of team development. What happens during each stage?

5. List the factors that can lead to team conflict. What resolution styles are identified in the chapter?

6. Draw a diagram of the communication process and label each element. Explain the concept of noise.

7. Compare the different types of communication discussed in the chapter, including oral, written, formal, informal, and nonverbal.

8. Explain why it is important to be an effective communicator in business.

9. Describe how computers and related technologies can affect business communication.

10. Discuss the factors that should be kept in mind when communicating internationally.

Discussion Questions

1. Suppose that you have been asked to create a training program to help employees at a local company improve their teamwork and communication skills. Do a brainstorm. Develop a plan that describes this program.

2. Interview someone from another nation who is visiting or living in Canada. What are this person's most vivid impressions of Canadians? How do work practices and communication styles differ in Canada? Write a summary of the interview.

3. Think back to your most recent experience with being part of a team at work or school. Analyze the team's development. Can you recall specific examples of each stage of development? What were the norms of this group? How would you assess its degree of cohesiveness? How did this affect the team's effectiveness?

4. Keep a record of your communications for one day. Include phone conversations, personal conversations, and mail. Write a two-page report that summarizes your findings and include a description of your personal communication style and patterns.

5. More and more businesses are communicating with foreign customers, colleagues, and vendors via electronic mail. Discuss the advantages and disadvantages of using this channel for international communication.

Answers to Key Terms Quiz

1. team 2. work team 3. problem-solving team 4. cross-functional team 5. socio-emotional team 6. team cohesiveness 7. self-managed team 8. conflict 9. communication 10. listening 11. formal communication channels 12. informal communication channels 13. grapevine 14. nonverbal communication 15. internal communication 16. external communication 17. centralized network 18. decentralized network 19. low-context culture 20. high-context culture

Notes

1. Adapted from "Nortel: The First Century," *Nortel Company History*, **http://www.nortel.com/home/about/mic/ miccohistory.html#know**. All contents copyright © 1996, Nortel. All Rights Reserved. Reprinted by permission.

2. Adapted from "Nortel Teamwork Interview Notes," a personal interview with Northern Telecom conducted by Ben Glover, Algonquin College student.

3. James Treece, "Improving the Soul of an Old Machine," *Business Week*, October 25, 1993, 134–36.

4. John F. Welch, Jr.'s quote is from "Managing for the Nineties," presented at the General Electric Annual Meeting of Share Owners, April 27, 1988, and also quoted in Lynda M. Applegate and James I. Cash, "GE Canada: Designing a New Organization," *Harvard Business School*, Case No. 9-189-138. Copyright © 1989 by the President and Fellows of Harvard College.

5. Colin Campbell, *Where the Jobs Are* (Toronto: Macfarlane Walter & Ross, 1994), 22–24.

6. Ibid.

7. Ibid. See also Gail Rockburne, "Between Friends," *The Globe and Mail*, April 17, 1995, B4.

8. Alan Farnham, "America's Most Admired Company," *Fortune*, February 7, 1994, 50–54.

9. Richard Daft, *Management*, 3rd ed. (Fort Worth, TX: The Dryden Press, 1994), 591–94.

10. Brian Dumaine, "Payoff from the New Management," *Fortune*, December 13, 1993, 103–10.

11. Dawn Baskerville, "Why Business Loves Workteams," *Black Enterprise*, April 1993, 85–90.

12. Ibid.

13. Daft, *Management*, 594–96.

14. David Woodruff, "Saturn: Labor's Love Lost?" *Business Week*, February 8, 1993, 122–24.

15. Ibid.

16. Rod McQueen, "Canada's 50 Best Managed Private Companies: Interweb Printing Corp.," *The Financial Post*, December 14–16, 1996, 36.

17. "Summary of Proceedings," *The Jobs Conference*, Canadian Market and Productivity Centre, April 1994, 50–52.

18. Louis E. Boone, *Quotable Business* (New York: Random House, 1992), 69.

19. Philip Elmer-Dewitt, "Bards of the Internet," *Time*, July 4, 1994, 66–67.

20. Louis E. Boone and David L. Kurtz, *Contemporary Business Communication* (Englewood Cliffs, NJ: Prentice-Hall, 1994), 611.

21. Rod McQueen, "Canada's 50 Best Managed Private Companies: Lauzon Ltd.," *The Financial Post*, December 14–16, 1996, 40.

22. "The World According to Andy Grove," *Business Week/The Information Revolution 1994*, 76–78. See also Giner Trumfio, "The Case for E-Mail," *Sales & Marketing Management*, July 1994, 94–98; and Cheryl J. Goldberg, "Mail Call," *Entrepreneur*, August 1994, 36–39.

23. Carey French, "Yo-Yo Caper Yields a Lesson in E-Mail Utility," *The Globe and Mail*, November 12, 1996, C2.

24. Suzy Parker, "E-Mail Explosion," *USA Today*, July 19, 1994, B1.

25. Andrew Serwer, "Lessons from America's Fastest Growing Companies," *Fortune*, August 8, 1994, 42–60.

26. French, "Yo-Yo Caper," C2.

27. Daft, *Management*, 568–70.

28. Rod McQueen, "Canada's 50 Best Managed Private Companies: Teknion Furniture Systems, Inc.," *The Financial Post*, December 14–16, 1996, 12, 50–52.

29. Thayer Taylor, "Seeing Is Believing," *Sales & Marketing Management*, March 1994, 47–48.

30. Boone and Kurtz, *Contemporary Business Communication*, 8.

31. Jack Russell, "U.S. Fast-Food Giants in Japan Slice Prices," *Advertising Age*, June 13, 1994, 64.

32. Lucent Technologies, Advertising Supplement, "University of Manitoba Views Medical Solutions," *The Globe and Mail*, December 4, 1996, 2.

33. Michael Christie, "Slips of the Tongue Result in Classic Marketing Errors," *Advertising Age International*, June 20, 1994, 15.

34. French, "Yo-Yo Caper," C2.

35. Gail Edmondson, "Wireless Terriers," *Business Week*, May 23, 1994, 117–18.

Chapter 10

Information Technology

After studying this chapter, you should be able to

1. Discuss the role of telecommunications and the information superhighway in business.
2. Explain how the Internet has had an impact on our personal lives and business decisions.
3. Explain the purpose of a management information system and how it aids decision making in business.
4. Distinguish among the three broad categories of computers: mainframes, minicomputers, and microcomputers.
5. Explain the impact of computer networks on information technology.
6. Identify some of the major business applications of computer software.
7. Summarize the major computer/Internet security issues that affect organizations.

IT Is Booming

Learning and training comprise an integral part of the knowledge economy. Canada will provide an environment for lifelong learning in which all Canadians will have access to the widest possible variety of learning opportunities and tools.[1]

This was the vision for Canada as set out by the Information Highway Advisory Council in 1995. Canada is now deeply entrenched in the knowledge-based or information society, and our business community is responding to the Advisory Council's vision. Our information technology (IT) and communications industry is booming. Revenue in the IT sector has expanded from less than $39 billion in 1990 to over $64 billion in 1996. R&D spending was around $2.5 billion annually, and the sector employed about 25 000 workers in 1995. In 1995, Canada exported about $17 billion worth of computers, communications equipment, and electronic components. By world standards, however, we are a small IT player, accounting for only about 1 percent of the world's exports of IT products. But according to Statistics Canada, we have "earned a reputation as a world leader in telecommunications [and have] emerged as a significant producer of software and computer services." So the potential for export growth in this sector remains enormous.[2]

The telephone industry is the largest IT employer, with about 84 000 employees. Next in employment size is the expanding software and computer services segment, with about 77 000 workers. Leading Canadian companies in this group include Corel Corporation, SHL Systemhouse

Matthews' Gospel: Fourteen Rules for Explosive Growth

GROW EXPONENTIALLY OR YOU'LL WITHER AND DIE

In a start-up company aiming for size, growth will not be a measured, ordered thing. If your early growth rates aren't through the roof, you probably won't make it big.

ACT LIKE A PUBLIC COMPANY FROM DAY ONE

If you're planning to go public, learn corporate discipline early. Select a strong board of directors, issue regular quarterly reports, write a rolling five-year plan.

AIM TO CATCH THE "REPLACEMENT WAVE"

This occurs when clients make a wholesale switch from one technology to another and offers the biggest opportunities.

STRIVE TO DOMINATE YOUR NICHE

Aim for market-share leadership. It's the only way you'll earn the hefty profits you'll need to fund future product development.

MOTIVE BY MEANS OF STOCK OPTIONS

Forget the management theory bafflegab about head-patting and "empowerment" if you want your employees to think entrepreneurially.

BEWARE OF "ALIENS"

Don't pick "yes" men you can dominate as board members, but don't pick people alien to your way of operating. "One or two awkward board members can make the life of a CEO completely awful."

PAY YOUR BOARD MEMBERS WITH STOCK OPTIONS, NOT CASH

"That puts their brains in the right gear, so they work for the growth of the company."

NEVER MAKE REVENUE PROJECTIONS

"If you hype a company, there'll be a lot of pressure to justify your performance against what you projected. Analysts are very unforgiving. [If] the numbers are bad, you must be a screw brain."

SEPARATE R&D AND MANUFACTURING

"It's better to have marketing, product management, and R&D people separated from production people, in another building. They're different characters."

AVOID DEBT

A pristine balance sheet reassures customers, who want to know you'll be around to service their equipment and provide them with upgrades.

SAY NO TO MOST ACQUISITIONS

The promised synergies rarely emerge, and management is typically distracted for 6 to 12 months trying to integrate the new firm.

CAREFULLY CALCULATE YOUR RISK/REWARD OUTCOMES

"I'm very bold going after the best-case [scenario], as long as I know if I can live with the worst-case. If I can't, I won't do it."

REMEMBER THE 80/20 RULE

80% of your business will come from the top 20% of your customers. Organize to concentrate on your biggest accounts.

LISTEN TO YOUR CUSTOMERS

The opinions of paying customers are the only opinions that really count.

Source: Michael Salter, "Dream BIG ... then BIGGER," *The Globe and Mail Report on Business Magazine*, June 1996, 59. Reprinted by permission of the author.

Inc., and DMR Inc. of Montreal. Third in terms of employment size is the growing communications equipment industry, with about 58 000 employees as of 1995.[3] This sector includes companies like Northern Telecom (Nortel) Ltd. — highlighted in Chapter 9 — Mitel Corp., and Newbridge Networks Corp.

Newbridge Networks, under the leadership of one of Canada's most respected business gurus, Terry Matthews, is a Canadian success story. In the mid-1980s, Matthews and Michael Cowpland (now CEO of Corel) sold out their ownership in a teetering Mitel — a company they had started in the mid-1970s. Matthews foresaw that the growing volumes of data transmitted over the communications networks would eventually cause congestion and degraded performance. As a result, he formed Newbridge Networks in 1986 and set out to build equipment designed to speed up the electronic transmission of image, video, and multimedia information.

In just ten short years, Matthews had made Newbridge into a global communications player with yearly net earnings of over $200 million (1997). As chairman and CEO of Newbridge, he celebrated a very special Canadian business achievement in December 1996. With the purchase of UB Networks from Tandem Computers Inc., Newbridge went over the $1 billion mark in revenue. As of 1997, Newbridge is well positioned to take a big slice of the world demand for ATM (asynchronous transfer mode) products, a technology for carrying vast amounts of digital information over computer or telecom networks. The global market for ATM products is expected to grow into the billions of dollars by the year 2000. The "Matthews' Gospel" on the opposite page shows some of the reasons for Newbridge's success.

Market analysts agree that it is not an easy feat for a Canadian firm to become a global competitor in the communications sector. According to Bill Fournier of the Evans Research Corporation, a number of factors inhibit a Canadian company from becoming a global player: "lack of capital, skills shortages, high labour costs, R&D underfunding, the brain drain of both new university graduates and experienced talent to the United States, market domination by a handful of established players, an unfavourable tax climate, and small local markets." With the exception of a few scary moments, Matthews has defied these odds.[4]

To learn more about Newbridge, you may wish to visit the company's home page at http://www.newbridge.com.

CHAPTER OVERVIEW

SOMEONE ONCE GAVE the recipe for effective decisions as "90 percent information and 10 percent inspiration." Clearly, obtaining the right information and knowing how to use it are vital to business success — particularly in today's economy.

We have entered a new knowledge-based, digital, and networked economy made up of knowledge consumers and knowledge workers. Canadian companies such as Newbridge Networks have prospered by finding creative ways to deliver information across the world. To an ever-increasing extent, this new economic order relies heavily on the information superhighway, the Internet, computers, and related technologies to store, access, and manage the information. In this chapter, we will look at how global communications technologies, information systems, and computers are transforming our personal lives, the world of business, and the process of decision making.

TELECOMMUNICATIONS AND THE INFORMATION SUPERHIGHWAY

INFORMATION TECHNOLOGIES ARE rapidly changing our personal world and the Canadian business landscape. One of the fastest-growing segments of the information industry is **telecommunications** — *any system in which information or data are sent over a distance through some type of electronic transmission medium.* Telecommunications can involve not only computers, but also such diverse technologies and related industries as telephones, televisions, fax machines, e-mail, satellite

---

→ WAKE-UP CALL

According to Don Tapscott, Canadian author and cyber-guru, considered an international authority on information (or in U.S. vice president Al Gore's words, "one of the world's leading 'cyber-gurus'"), the new economy is a

→ Knowledge economy made up of knowledge workers and knowledge consumers.

→ Digital economy in which physical things can become virtual.

→ Networked economy in which producers and consumers operate directly through digital networks.

Business must undergo a unique transformation in order to compete in the new digital economy.

→ THEY SAID IT

"Already, more Canadians work in the information technology industry – about 300 000 – than in banking, mining, forestry, or automobile assembly. The sector contributes more to the GDP (gross domestic product) – about $40 billion – than pulp and paper and transportation services combined. And it's going to become more pervasive. Globally, information technology is a $10-trillion industry with expectations to double within ten years."

DIANE E. MCGARRY, Chair, President, and CEO, Xerox Canada, Inc.

systems, computer networks, and of course the Internet.

Historically, each of the communications industries built transmission systems for its particular type of communication, developing its own unique route into homes or offices. For example:[5]

- Telephone companies built two-way, point-to-point narrowband or low-bandwidth networks using mainly copper wire.

- Cable companies built broadband or high-bandwidth channels using mainly coaxial cables and fibre optic truck lines, which provided the greater capability needed for video transmission. But, unlike telephone systems, their networks were built for one-way communication only.

- Computer networks were originally designed for transmitting data within and between organizations.

Today there is a global movement to merge these separate and distinct systems into one interoperable network — the so-called **information superhighway** (I-Way) — *merging telecommunications, information, and data systems into a single, enormous network accessible to all consumers and businesses.* The term "information superhighway" is the metaphoric phrase that describes this telecommunications convergence.

Two Forces of Change

Two forces of technological change — fibre optics and digitization — have created a shock wave through the communications and computing industries and shaped the blueprint for the I-Way.

Fibre Optics. In telecommunications, the mode of transmission is evolving from copper wire to **fibre optics** — *a modern transmission technology using lasers to produce a beam of light that can be modulated to carry large amounts of information through fine glass or acrylic fibres.* Fibre optic cable has a high bandwidth, whereas

---

Business Term

√ **Telecommunications**

Any system in which information or data are sent over a distance through some type of electronic transmission medium.

Business Term

√ **Information superhighway**

Single, enormous network merging telecommunications, information, and data systems that can be accessed by all consumers and businesses.

Business Term

√ **Fibre optics**

A modern transmission technology using lasers to produce a beam of light that can be modulated to carry large amounts of information through fine glass or acrylic fibres.

Business Term

√ **Digitization**

The conversion of an analog or continuous signal into a series of ones and zeros, that is, into digital format.

---

copper wires ("twisted pair") have a low bandwidth. Bandwidth is the capacity to move information down a given channel, or the number of signals that can be squeezed into a wire. High bandwidth is required for carrying more complex signals; for example, in the case of full-motion video as opposed to simple voice messages.

The evolution of fibre optic technology, along with a new generation of switches and embedded software, has substantially eliminated bandwidth as a telecommunications constraint. The capacity of optic fibres to transmit data is almost limitless relative to copper. For example, just a single fibre can deliver a million channels of television concurrently — roughly 200 000 times faster than a "twisted pair." Moving large amounts of information required for such uses as videos or X-rays has become increasingly rapid and cost-effective.

Digitization. **Digitization** — *the conversion of an analog or continuous signal into a series of ones and zeros, that is, into digital format* — makes it possible to connect all communication systems into a single, vast network. A unit of information represented by a "0" or "1" is called a binary digit or bit. When information (voice, video, sound, images, etc.) is converted into a digital format it can be transmitted at the speed of light. For example, a human voice can be converted into digital format by sampling it a sufficient number of times. These resulting binary digits can then be stored on a computer or digital storage device (as in the case of voice mail) and reconstructed as an analog wave that can be heard by your ear.

THE INTERNET

How do we access the I-Way? In its simplest form, the superhighway exists in such day-to-day objects as the telephone, television, or personal computer. We also see it in our communications networks. The best-known electronic network is the **Internet (the Net)** — *a series of computer networks with a single point of access that connects the user to an electronic information system that spans the globe.* The Net is quickly emerging as the information superhighway exemplar.

> **Business Term**
>
> √ **Internet (the Net)**
>
> A series of computer networks with a single point of access that connects the user to an electronic information system that spans the globe.

Originally, the most popular use of the Internet was **electronic mail (e-mail):** *a system for sending and receiving written messages from one computer to another via phone lines.* An e-mail system hooked up to the Internet expands the user's address population to literally millions of Net users around the world. E-mail over the Internet has now become such a pervasive part of our lives that e-mail addresses are now listed in telephone books. Canadians can even get their comments to the prime minister in seconds — at the cost of a local call — over the Net.

> **Business Term**
>
> √ **Electronic mail (e-mail)**
>
> A system for sending and receiving written messages from one computer to another via phone lines.

Today the Internet is a ubiquitous part of Canadian culture and business. Even government organizations and departments have a strong presence on the Internet (see the photo). It has the potential to allow each and every Canadian access to information right around

> **DID YOU KNOW?**
>
> **Want to send a message to the prime minister? Try these addresses:**
> → **E-mail address: pm@pm.gc.ca**
> → **Correspondence Web page: http://pm.gc.ca./ prime_minister/contact_pm/index.html-ssi**
>
> In 1997 electronic messages accounted for about one-quarter of Prime Minister Jean Chrétien's mail. Does he read them? "He's given a sampling of what comes across in his e-mail," says spokeswoman Leslie Swartman.
>
> **Want to send a greeting card? Visit the award-winning Prince Edward Island Information Centre at http://www.gov.pe.ca/card/index.html.**

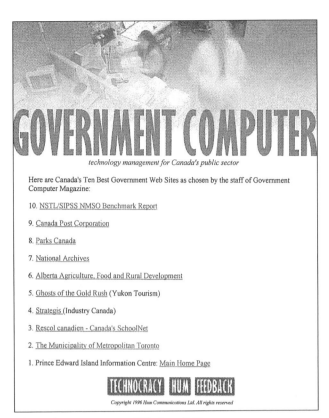

GOVERNMENT COMPUTER

technology management for Canada's public sector

Here are Canada's Ten Best Government Web Sites as chosen by the staff of Government Computer Magazine:

10. NSTL/SIPSS NMSO Benchmark Report

9. Canada Post Corporation

8. Parks Canada

7. National Archives

6. Alberta Agriculture, Food and Rural Development

5. Ghosts of the Gold Rush (Yukon Tourism)

4. Strategis (Industry Canada)

3. Rescol canadien - Canada's SchoolNet

2. The Municipality of Metropolitan Toronto

1. Prince Edward Island Information Centre: Main Home Page

TECHNOCRACY HUM FEEDBACK

The ten best government Web sites, 1996

the world. Once connected to the **World Wide Web (WWW or Web)** — *a system of posting information, much of it connected on the Internet* — the user can listen to songs, view pictures from a museum, read a book, choose a ski vacation, preview the newest cars, or even pay bills. The practical and commercial uses are enormous and increasing every day.

> **Business Term**
>
> √ **World Wide Web**
>
> A system of posting information, much of it connected on the Internet.

Here's what Canadian cyberwhiz Don Tapscott has to say: "Get on the Net! When you do, you'll be joining millions of others in the new digital society. By the end of the decade, more than 1 billion people will be on the Internet. ... If you need help, ask your CIO [chief information officer], IT [information technology] manager, Web manager, or your child — but just do it."[6] Here are some examples of Canadian organizations that are pleased they "just did it":

- Industry Canada is working with the provinces and other SchoolNet stakeholders to ensure that some 23 000 schools, libraries, universities, and colleges are connected over the Net (**http://strategis.ic.gc.ca/engdoc/detail.html**).[7]

- Duthie Books has six stores in Vancouver and a Virtual Bookstore. Users can search and order some 50 000 titles in 150 subject areas and get information on new releases, book awards, and articles (http://www.literascape.com).[8]

- Bolen Books, an independent bookstore in Victoria, now takes more than 150 orders per month through its Web page. Bolen plans to target the tourist market — through its Web page, tourists can order guidebooks before their visit to Victoria or souvenir books after they have returned home (http://www.bolen.bc.ca).[9]

DID YOU KNOW?

Some IT experts claim that much of the Internet activity by employees is a waste of time and corporate resources. For example, they point to a study by Nelson Media Research Inc. that surveyed employee computer logs at IBM, Apple, and AT&T. Together, over a single month in 1996, an estimated 347 workdays were lost because employees spent time visiting the Penthouse Web site.

THEY SAID IT

"Over time, the winners will be those who fully recognize this [Internet] paradigm shift, who figure out how to deliver innovative, high-quality content and transact business more effectively over the Web than by other existing means. But for every winner there will be the also-rans — those who fail to see the Internet as a truly different business medium, as significant as the telephone or the printing press."

BILL GATES, CEO, Microsoft Corporation

- Dei Ex Machina (DEM) of Toronto helps clients provide immediate access to real-estate sites across North America. "One Realtor increased its rate of closure by 60 percent as a result of providing the right information immediately," says Annette Wilde, a founding partner of DEM (http://www.demconsulting.com).[10]

From Internet to Intranet

"Intranets are fundamentally altering the way companies create and disseminate information" says Eric Schmidt, chief technology officer of Sun Microsystems.[11] One of

The World According to Big Shot

BIG SHOT: Slinky, I've made a decision. We have to have a home page. I'll call it "Big Shot's Business File." What do you think?

SLINKY: Great idea, but the name may be a little too long. Why don't you just use your initials?

BIG SHOT: I can live with that. Get somebody to make it happen. Shouldn't take more than a couple of hundred dollars — I think.

→ What do you think of Big Shot's decision?

ROADKILL ON THE I-WAY

Author Don Tapscott, a recognized Canadian expert on electronic commerce, tells us that in this new digital economy, economic benefits will accrue only to those individuals and organizations who can take advantage of new information technologies. In other words, the technological "have-nots" may become roadkill on the Information highway.

Ideally, here is how a typical e-commerce (electronic trade in goods and services) transaction might work. A customer fills in an order form on a computer. At the speed of e-mail, the order is sent through the Internet directly to the retailer's computer system. The system immediately processes the information to create a shipping waybill and packing list, and electronically charges the customer's credit card. In this example, the human element is virtually removed. A low-paid warehouse employee might prepare the shipment and deliver it to the loading dock, but that's about the extent of the labour input. Data processors, bookkeepers, and shipping clerks become redundant.

Within the next five years, as much as 15 percent of retail sales in the world's industrialized countries will be done over the Internet. The issue here is that much of the savings will be in the form of reduced labour costs. Traditional intermediary positions such as travel agents, stockbrokers, and retail sales staff could be significantly reduced.

According to the Organization for Economic Co-operation and Development (OECD), there is a real danger that this shift toward the digital economy could have major employment shocks and threaten to divide the world into two camps — employed and unemployable. The OECD warns that all countries must take an activist approach to promote new job opportunities and career paths, and training to the workforce.

Source: Don Tapscott, *The Digital Economy: Promise and Peril in the Age of Networked Intelligence* (New York: McGraw Hill, 1996); James Baxter, "E-commerce Could Wipe Out Jobs," *Ottawa Citizen*, October 10, 1998, H1, H5.

---

the hottest new business application technologies is the **intranet** — *private computer networks that use the standards and technology of the Internet to distribute internal corporate information.* Privacy is the operative word in the world of intranets, which are off limits to anyone without prior authorization.

Intranets can be used for a variety of business applications from publishing and updating corporate phone books, price lists, and annual reports to delivering video training to employees at their desktops. Technology experts say that the potential savings from intranets are huge, the financial risks are low, and the conclusion is clear: business should move to build an intranet immediately.[12]

According to cyberlord Bill Gates, CEO of Microsoft Corporation, the intranet is fast becoming his firm's main internal communication tool. He says that "sales-analysis data at Microsoft are being accessed five times more often now that they can be reached over our intranet."[13]

Christine Fonden, new media consultant at Bell Sygma Inc., helped build the company's intranet system. She says that in 1995, employees could spend half a month searching for critical background information —

Business Term

√ **Intranet**

Private computer networks that use the standards and technology of the Internet to distribute internal corporate information.

and still could not be sure it was up-to-date. Thanks to the new intranet system, by 1997, some 18 000 staff at Bell could find this same information in under a minute. By the year 2000, an estimated 45 000 Bell employees are expected to have access to the intranet. Graham Silver, a senior consultant, says that the company's intranet is not only faster but cheaper than past information-based technologies, paying for itself within a year. Other Canadian companies that have experimented successfully with intranets are TransCanada Pipelines Ltd., based in Calgary, and International Data Corp. (Canada) Ltd., based in Toronto.[14]

From Intranet to Entranet

The third generation of Internet technology is the "intranet-to-intranet" integration, or the so-called **extranet or entranet** — *a private intranet system that is linked to the outside world of suppliers and customers.* Entranets are carefully controlled openings of private intranets to allow access via the Internet. Access to the

LESSONS FROM THE BEST

NEWCOURT CREDIT TURNS TO JAVA AND THE EXTRANET

Imagine a single personal computer doing business with 1200 users simultaneously. Newcourt Credit Group, a "new economy" Canadian company in Toronto, carries out such transactions using the Extranet, Java script, and a PC server tucked away into a nook of the company's Bay Street offices.

Newcourt's Healthgroup Financial unit lends money to pay for dental work and other medical services not covered by public or private insurance schemes. Newcourt's Web-based Healthline system lets medical office staff complete loan applications on the spot while the patient waits — sometimes a thousand kilometres away. If the loan is approved, a promissory note is generated at the medical office and payment statements are mailed to the borrower.

Since Newcourt uses Java script, users do not even need special PC software to access Newcourt's service.

Standard Web browsers from Netscape or Microsoft will do the job.

Newcourt is a leading company demonstrating that sending and receiving data via the public Internet is not only effective but also efficient compared to the costs of conventional data networks. The cost comparisons become even more economical when Web browsers and servers are used to manage the flow.

Source: Adapted from David Thomas, "Newcourt Credit Turns to Extranet," *The Globe and Mail*, November 12, 1996, C11.

---

entranet is limited and controlled as it is with an intranet. Bell Global Solutions is one of the first companies to put this cutting-edge technology into practice with its "Tactik Electronic Business Solutions." Bell, one of our leading technology companies, believes that entranet technology has widespread commercial and industrial potential. "For example, retailers could use this technology to maintain inventory requirements, submit orders and invoices to partners, and offer on-line catalogue services to customers and partners," says Josée Goulet, vice-president and chief operating officer of Bell Global Solutions.[15]

> **Business Term**
> √ **Extranet or entranet**
> A private intranet system that is linked to the outside world of suppliers and customers.

MANAGEMENT INFORMATION SYSTEMS

"WHAT IS THE sales potential for our brand in South Korea compared with Hong Kong?"

"If we raise the price for the brand by 2 percent, how will it affect sales in both countries?"

> **Business Term**
> √ **Management information system (MIS)**
> An organized method of providing information for use in decision making.

> **Business Term**
> √ **Chief information officer (CIO)**
> Top management executive responsible for directing a firm's MIS and related computer operations.

"How do our wage rates in Halifax compare with similar firms in Vancouver?"

"What are the storage costs for Model XYZ?"

Every day in companies, people are asking questions such as these. An effective information system helps people to answer them. The **management information system (MIS)** *is an organized method of providing information for use in decision making.* Large organizations typically assign *responsibility for directing the firm's MIS and related computer operations* to an executive called the **chief information officer (CIO).** Generally, the CIO reports directly to the chief executive officer (CEO).

Information from a variety of sources — internal and external — is needed to perform almost every company activity. It can make the difference between staying in business or going broke. Keeping on top of changing consumer demands, competitors' actions, and the latest government regulations helps firms fine-tune existing products, develop new winners, and market them effectively.

Databases

The heart of an information system is its **database** — *a centralized, integrated collection of the organization's data resources.* Databases are designed to meet the particular information-processing and retrieval

FUTURE TREND

TELEHEALTH SERVICES

Telehealth means using communications and information technology to deliver health services, products, and education through networks and databases.

According to Industry Canada, the telehealth industry is still embryonic at best. In 1997, Canadian projects were valued at about $500 million and the industry employed about 1700 people. The Canadian sector was comprised of some 300 firms (about twenty percent of companies in the young industry were created in 1997).

Industry Canada estimates that the revenue from this industry could double (from 1997) to reach $1 billion in sales worldwide by the twenty-first century. Employment is expected to almost triple (from 1997) to 5000 people during the same period. Over the next three to five years, the federal and provincial governments alone are expected to spend another $500 million to $750 million on telehealth.

"There's an obvious need for telehealth in Canada because of geography and isolation," says Dr. Brian Haynes of McMaster University in Hamilton, Ontario. Increased demand from an aging population and cost-cutting in health care are driving the need to integrate health networks, especially in Canada and Europe.

Source: Adapted from Dawn Walton, "Telehealth Services," *The Globe and Mail*, October 6, 1998, B13. Reprinted with permission from The Globe and Mail.

---

requirements of decision-makers. They serve as electronic file cabinets capable of storing massive amounts of data and retrieving needed data within seconds. Databases also help firms target their direct marketing efforts by finding out more about prospective customers. For example, in the early 1990s at the Royal Bank, a successful response to a direct mail product offering was about 4 percent. By 1997, a positive direct mail response was as high as 60 percent. This was due to the bank's new Marketing Information File — a $15 million investment in database technology that took four years to build. This file enabled the bank to group its clients into customer profile groups with similar needs. Now, for example, "We look at clients that have a combination of services and if we have a group of clients that have, say, a chequing account, a credit card, and a car loan, and who rent a house and have a certain amount of money on deposit, we then go to [these] clients letting them know we're putting on a new home-buyer seminar," says Charlie Milbury, senior vice-president of marketing for the Royal Bank.[16]

Firms that cannot afford to create and maintain their own databases can subscribe to services that provide databases on specific topics. In addition to such broad-based databases as Prodigy, CompuServe, and Lexis, specialized commercial databases are available to meet

Business Term

✓ **Database**

A centralized, integrated collection of the organization's data resources.

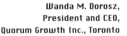

WHERE

The Jobs Are

Wanda M. Dorosz,
President and CEO,
Quorum Growth Inc., Toronto

Break the Logjams

"I still see lots of opportunity in information technology. One example is unlocking logjams and bottlenecks in terms of modem limitations [speed and capacity]. Another is to do anything that increases the bandwidth of the desktop local area networks, right on up to the Net or the worldwide telephone systems.

The second area of opportunity is information technology in the medical area. Look at supplying health-care information over one network. All of the information — clinical, pharmaceutical, family history, methodology changes, new diseases — could be compiled in a database. In a lifetime, a person could have consulted more than twenty doctors. The information must be made available in one spot and be seamless. It can be a matter of life and death."

the specific needs of businesses. For example, Loyalty Management Group Inc. of Toronto maintains a large database collected from the popular Air Miles membership cards. Using the spending patterns collected from Air Miles cardholders helped Shell Canada decide where to phase out full-service gas pumps in Western Canada. Shell kept full-service pumps in areas with a high female customer base and removed them from those areas with more male customers. Air Miles cardholder purchases indicated that women were more likely to use full-service pumps over self-service ones.[17]

BROAD CATEGORIES OF COMPUTERS

THE ENGLISH MATHEMATICIAN William Shanks spent a third of his life computing pi to 707 decimal places — only to make a mistake at the 528th place! Today, computers can duplicate Shanks's work without error in less than five seconds.

A **computer** *is a programmable electronic device that can store, retrieve, and process data.* Once considered exotic, these machines have become an integral part of our personal life and indispensable to business:[18]

- The percentage of employed Canadians using a computer at work increased from 15 percent in the mid-1980s to 50 percent in the mid-1990s.

- Almost 80 percent of all managers used a computer at work in 1994.

- About 10 percent of Canadian households owned a computer in the mid-1980s. By 1995, nearly 30 percent of all Canadian households had a computer.

- Over 55 percent of adult Canadians were able to use a computer in 1994, and an estimated 41 percent had taken a computer course.

Although computers have a way to go to rival the colour TV set (found in 99 percent of Canadian homes), personal computers are outselling TVs, and 70 percent of them are going into the home.[19] Few can argue that technology is, and will continue to be, a dominant force in Canadian life.

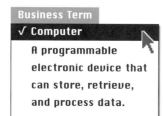

Business Term

√ **Computer**

A programmable electronic device that can store, retrieve, and process data.

Mainframes, Minicomputers, and Microcomputers

Computer hardware consists of the tangible elements of the computer system, including the input devices, the machines that store and process data and perform the required calculations, and the output devices that provide the results to the information user. *Computer software* consists of the sets of instructions that tell the hardware what to do. Computer languages and computer programs — including custom-designed as well as "off-the-shelf" commercial software packages — are both considered software. Popular examples of off-the-shelf software include PowerPoint™, WordPerfect™, CorelDRAW™, and Quicken™. Most PC software is now packaged in a Windows 95™ format. Corel Office Professional™ and Microsoft Office™ are two of the most popular office suites — software packages that unite several software packages in one program.

Based on their size, memory capacity, and processing speeds, computers can be divided into three categories: mainframes, minicomputers, and microcomputers.

- The *mainframe* is the largest and oldest type of computer system. According to many industry observers, mainframes are the technological dinosaurs of the twenty-first century. For example, Nicholas Negroponte, an MIT media technologist, observes that this giant central computer has been almost universally replaced by personal computers. IBM, a name that has been historically synonymous with computer manufacturing and mainframes, has seen its mainframe revenues drop by more than half since 1990. In fact, IBM Canada now collects more than half its revenue by selling services to clients rather than manufacturing large computers.

- The *minicomputer* is an intermediate-sized computer — more compact and less expensive than the mainframe. Intermediate computers are often used in universities, factories, and research labs.

- The *microcomputer* is the smallest type of computer. It is typically called a personal computer (PC) or desktop computer and is equipped with a hard disk drive and monitor.

The distinctions among these three types of computers are blurring due to rapid developments in technology. Today's microcomputers can handle as much work as the huge mainframes of the 1970s. Other machines, called supercomputers, are especially powerful tools that can handle extremely rapid, complex calculations involving

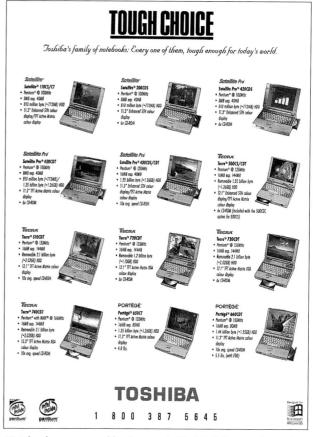

Notebook computers, like the ones in Toshiba's line, are becoming more and more common in the workplace.

thousands of variables. Supercomputers are most commonly used in scientific research.

These advances were made possible by the development of powerful *computer chips* — thin silicon wafers on which integrated circuits (networks of transistors and circuits) are assembled — and the *microprocessor* — a fingernail-sized chip. "Intelligent" features available in today's new cars, toys, and watches also rely on microprocessors. Additional chips containing instructions and data memory are added to convert the microprocessor into a microcomputer.

As technology continues to improve, computers continue to get smaller. Laptop computers are microcomputers that are lightweight enough to be easily portable, and small enough that they can be used on your lap when no desk is available. Today, laptop computers are gradually replacing desktop computers because they are able to provide almost all the information and communication tools you would normally find on a desktop computer, from word processing to faxing, e-mailing, and surfing the Net. An IBM Thinkpad 760ED, the Rolls-Royce of laptops, for example, will let you speak and send data at the same time, allows you to listen to stereo sound, and lets you hook into a video camera or regular TV set. Notebook computers are small enough to slip into a briefcase, and palmtops fit in a shirt pocket and run on ordinary AA batteries. Another hot development in miniaturized computers is the notepad computer, which can "read" handwritten letters, numbers, and drawings.

We have seen computers move out of giant air-conditioned rooms into closets, then onto desktops, and now into our laps and pockets. But is this the end? Not by a long shot, according to Nicholas Negroponte, an

MIT media technologist: "Early in the next millennium your right and left cuff links or earrings may communicate with each other by low-orbiting satellites and have more computer power than your present PC. Your telephone won't ring indiscriminately; it will receive, sort, and perhaps respond to your incoming calls like a well-trained English butler. ... Computing is not about computers any more. It is about living."[20]

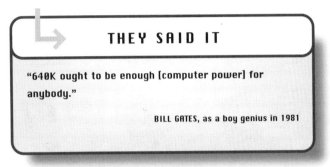

THEY SAID IT

"640K ought to be enough [computer power] for anybody."

BILL GATES, as a boy genius in 1981

COMPUTER NETWORKS

COMPUTING IN THE 1980s was typically one person performing one task on a single system. Today, thanks to computers and the information highway, people obtain and share information from across the world. An important development involves **computer networks**: *systems that interconnect numerous computers so they function individually and communicate with one another*. A network will normally include one or a combination of mainframes, minicomputers, and the Internet. In most cases, such a network has become a required technology tool for business success in today's increasingly competitive environment.

Some companies use computer networks by connecting their different offices and buildings through a **local area network** (**LAN**): *a computer network that connects machines within a limited area* (such as one building or several buildings that are near one another). LANs, the first generation of network computing, are useful in many businesses because they can link minicomputers within an organization and allow them to share printers and information. Internal networks also allow various departments, such as purchasing, finance, and marketing, to make comparisons of actual sales with sales forecasts.

The results of such comparisons often show a need to change production, finance, or marketing plans.

The information highway and Internet technology have led to the second generation of network computing. As we saw in the last section — and thanks to the Internet — companies can now network around the world through intranet and entranet technologies. Some call this new form of networking **collaborative computing**: *a system where employees, business partners, suppliers, and customers can all easily communicate, co-operate, and collaborate via computer*. Boeing's 777 passenger aircraft, rolled out in 1995, is a striking example of the benefits of collaborative networking and the Internet technology. A total of 238 design/build teams worked concurrently, sharing their knowledge instead of applying their skills sequentially. The result? Boeing reduced change, error, and rework costs by more than 50 percent and decreased the plane's time to market. As the Boeing case dramatically attests, the benefits of networking and the Internet can be significant — particularly for megacorporations.[21]

In the fall of 1996, Sun Microsystems Inc. rolled out its JavaStation™, a key element of the firm's vision, the so-called **network computer**: *a personal computer with no hard drive; users reach over their corporate network or the Internet to use application software or files stored on server computers*. With a network computer, applications such as a spreadsheet or word processor are simply downloaded from the server over the network. When required, the work can be regularly saved on the server for employees to access. Potentially, network computers not only improve employee communication, but also result in significant savings — especially in IT administrative costs. For example, consultants estimate that the cost of managing a single desktop computer on a network ranges from $8300 to $11 900 (U.S.) each year. The actual hardware and software expenses account for only about 20 percent of this cost. The remaining 80 percent is spent on the human resources required to install, maintain, and oversee the myriad of other software problems.

Business Term

✓ Collaborative computing

A system where employees, business partners, suppliers, and customers can all easily communicate, co-operate, and collaborate via computer.

Business Term

✓ Computer networks

Systems that interconnect numerous computers so they function individually and communicate with one another.

Business Term

✓ Local area network (LAN)

A computer network that connects machines within a limited area.

Because the network computer contains no software or hard drive, the cost and time of network administration can be significantly reduced. For large organizations with thousands of computers, the savings can be in the millions of dollars. If the network computer gains industry approval and momentum — and there is good reason to believe it will — this new "black box" technology will change the economic model on which the personal computer is based. The "network" could very well become the computer.[22]

For a growing number of companies, a leading-edge technology and a central component of IT strategies and network computing is Sun Microsystems' **Java™**: *a universal computer language that allows all previously incompatible systems to share applications and information.* Many IT experts argue that the new Java™ technology is critical to the success of the network

> **Business Term**
> √ **Network computer**
> A personal computer with no hard drive; users reach over their corporate network or the Internet to use application software or files stored on server computers.

> **Business Term**
> √ **Java™**
> A universal computer language that allows all previously incompatible systems to share applications and information.

computer. In 1996, Forrester Research reported that 42 percent of Fortune 1000 companies questioned in a survey expected Java™ to play a strategic role in their organizations within 1997. The major advantages of Java™ are twofold:[23]

- **Platform-independence.** A technology that can run on any major system: UNIX server, workstation, Macintosh or PC, the new network computers, and the "legacy systems" such as mainframe databases. Java™ also has the ability to "WRITE ONCE, Run Anywhere™"; that is, applications developed on Java™ are designed to run on any system.

- **Network-centricity.** A system where applications and data reside mainly on the network servers and are downloaded to client systems as needed. Applications can be distributed to all users via the corporate intranet.

The development and administration of computer networks will continue to be a critical function of the IT manager. Major functional concerns will be the planning and controlling of the next generation: collaborative, Internet-based networks so that all employees can link up to the system easily and efficiently. Privacy and security will also continue to be major issues. Should all employees in the company be able to access all of the corporate database? Is it safe to give all employees access to the corporation's payroll system? How does a company ensure corporate internal security? How do corporations respect privacy and security when their systems are linked to the Internet? Later in this chapter, we will examine several of these issues.

SOFTWARE APPLICATIONS

MOST OF US are no doubt aware that computers, related software applications, and the information highway have changed how people spend their days, the skills they need, and the leverage they can bring to their work. For example, as we have already discussed, e-mail is a popular Internet tool. Other major software applications that improve the effectiveness and efficiency of our personal lives and the workplace include word

Touted as the "computer of the future," Sun Microsystems' JavaStation™ is expected to change the economic model on which personal computers are based.

James Gosling is flying high these days. For it was a team led by the Calgary-born software developer that brewed up Java, now regarded as the unifying language of cyberspace. No longer does it matter whether users who log onto the Internet have a Macintosh, OS/2, UNIX, or Windows in any of its forms. Any application written in Java will run on any Java-enabled platform.

Gosling's interest in computers showed itself when he was only 13 and he hung around the University of Calgary for an opportunity to use one of the campus machines. That interest led him to graduate studies at Pittsburgh's Carnegie Mellon University. He arrived at Sun Microsystems in 1984, where he wrote NeWS, the Network Extensible Windowing System. It enabled any computer screen to display a program running anywhere else on the network. Well ahead of its time, NeWS was a technical success

although it did not set the world on fire.

By 1991, Gosling was at work on what was to become a programming language for interactive television and the consumer electronics industry. Three years later, the genius of Java shifted the emphasis to the about-to-explode World Wide Web.

The appeal of Java was instant. It offered "applets," much smaller in size than conventional programs. Instead of buying huge applications, many with features never used,

processing, desktop publishing, decision support systems, spreadsheets, fax machines, executive information systems, expert systems, voice processing, multimedia computing, and interactive media and groupware.

Word Processing

One of the most popular business applications involves **word processing**, *the use of computers to type, store, retrieve, edit, and print various types of documents.* If you have ever used a typewriter to write a paper, you know the advantages of using a personal computer to revise what you have written, check spelling, and correct mistakes.

Word-processing software, such as Corel's Word-Perfect™ and Microsoft's Word™, allows companies to handle huge volumes of correspondence, process numerous documents, and personalize form letters. Some firms may use special-purpose computers, called dedicated word processors,

> **Business Term**
> ✓ **Word processing**
> The use of computers to type, store, retrieve, edit, and print various types of documents.

designed exclusively for this purpose. However, word processing more often involves using special word-processing software packages, such as AppleWriter™, Word-Perfect™, MacWrite™, or Microsoft Word™.

Desktop Publishing

A development that takes word processing a step further is **desktop publishing,** *a computer system that allows users to design and produce printed material.* Desktop publishing software combines high-quality type, graphics, and layouts to create output that looks as attractive as documents produced by professional publishers and printers. Advanced equipment can scan photos and drawings and duplicate them on the printed page. Desktop publishing systems often are used to print newsletters, reports,

> **Business Term**
> ✓ **Desktop publishing**
> A computer system that allows users to design and produce printed material.

and form letters. Winning Forms™, produced by Random House, is a book–disk package designed to work in conjunction with many of the major software packages, such as Word for Windows™, WordPerfect™, Lotus 1-2-3™, and Quattro Pro™. It provides templates for many office forms, including mailing labels, invoices, purchase orders, expense reports, business cards, résumés, and press releases. Often firms' advertising and graphic arts departments use this type of software to create brochures and marketing materials. A good desktop publishing system can save a company money by allowing it to produce such documents in-house and to make changes and corrections on-site.

computer users would log onto the corporate intranet or Internet and use only what they need. With Java, they could visit a site, download a "spell checker" or spreadsheet applet, or perhaps one for a car showroom, and then inspect the latest models at home without being bothered by a salesperson.

Quickly, Java was endorsed by many industry leaders including Adobe, Hewlett-Packard, IBM, Oracle, Toshiba, and even Microsoft. Java applets are now found on websites around the world. They range from allowing live news to ticker across monitor screens to providing office productivity tools.

Sun has made Java freely available to individuals and universities. While the company may derive little direct financial benefit initially, Java has enhanced Sun's reputation among Internet users.

And it led Sun to develop its network computer — the JavaStation — which has only minimum memory, a network port, and no hard drive. It provides more economical access to corporate intranets and sells for as little as $1113. Such devices, with their minimal maintenance costs, are changing the face of computing. And it's happening because a quiet Canadian hung around a prairie university as a young boy.

Source: "He's the Father of Java" by Lee Lester appeared in a Sun Microsystems of Canada Inc. advertising supplement for *The Globe and Mail*, produced by The Publishing House (November 20, 1996). Java is a trademark of Sun Microsystems, Inc. Reprinted by kind permission of Sun Microsystems of Canada Inc.

Adobe PageMaker® desktop publishing software offers a professional as well as an accessible way to publish on paper or online.

Decision Support Systems

A **decision support system (DSS)** *is a system that quickly provides relevant facts to help businesspeople make decisions.* It includes software tools that help decision-makers generate the information they need. DSS tools may vary from company to company, but they typically include software that helps people obtain needed information from a database, simulation software that lets employees create computer models to evaluate company performance under different conditions, and presentation software that lets them create graphs and charts.

Business Term

√ **Decision support system (DSS)**

Computer system that quickly provides relevant facts to aid business decision making.

Spreadsheets

An electronic **spreadsheet** *is the computerized equivalent of an accountant's worksheet.* Spreadsheet software *permits businesspeople to manipulate decision variables to determine their impact on such outcomes as profits or sales.* Corel Quattro Pro™ is a popular spreadsheet software package.

A spreadsheet presents a grid of columns and rows that allows information to be organized in a standardized, easily understandable format. As soon as the manager changes a variable, such as price or advertising outlays (see Table 10.1), the computer immediately recalculates all figures to show the impact on expected unit sales or dollar revenues. Since the tedious chore of recalculating and revising figures by hand is done automatically by

Business Term

√ **Spreadsheet**

The computerized equivalent of an accountant's worksheet; computer software that permits businesspeople to manipulate decision variables to determine their effects.

computer, the manager can analyze the impact of dozens of "What if?" alternatives in a matter of seconds.

Fax Machines

Another popular use for computers is the *fax* (short for *facsimile*): an electronic mailing system for sending and receiving written messages over telephone lines. Despite the growth of the Internet, e-mail, and internal computer networks, many Canadian companies are still in love with the fax. A 1996 Gallup poll of 300 large and mid-sized Canadian firms found that most still rely on the fax machine to send documents that are being revised. This study found that many employees — 52 percent in large companies and 62 percent in mid-sized firms — still prefer to have their messages delivered on paper rather than in electronic form. According to one expert, Ken Grant, a vice-president of A.T. Kearney Management Consultants, "We are all creatures of habit. Fax machines are going to be with us for a long time."[24]

Executive Information Systems

Sometimes, specialized information systems are created to address the needs of specific levels of employees. An *executive information system (EIS)* allows top managers to access the firm's primary databases, often by touching

Table 10.1 How a Spreadsheet Works

Fixed Costs Manufacturing	Fixed Costs Marketing	R&D	Fixed Cost	Per-Unit Variable Cost	Sales Price	Breakeven Point in Units
$80 000	$100 000	$170 000	$350 000	$4.00	$8.00	87 500
$80 000	$200 000	$170 000	$450 000	$4.00	$8.00	112 500
$80 000	$100 000	$170 000	$350 000	$3.00	$6.50	100 000

Making pricing decisions concerning a proposed product offers a good illustration of how a spreadsheet works. A relatively simple example demonstrates the ease with which a manager can use a spreadsheet to analyze alternative decisions. Assume a proposed new-product entry will be priced at $8 per unit and can be produced for $4 in variable costs. Total fixed costs of $350 000 include $80 000 for such manufacturing overhead outlays as salaries, general office expenses, rent, utilities, and interest charges; $100 000 for marketing expenditures; and $170 000 for research and development on the product. The spreadsheet calculation reveals that sales of 87 500 units are necessary to cover all costs and break even.

But what if the firm's marketing director persuades other members of the group to increase marketing expenditures to $200 000? A spreadsheet program automatically replaces the $100 000 with $200 000 and calculates the break-even point. Similarly, the break-even point can be determined quickly if there is a reduction in variable costs and a reduction in selling price. Complex spreadsheets may have 50 columns or more, but the spreadsheet makes new calculations as fast as the manager can change the variables.

Figure 10.1 An Expert System

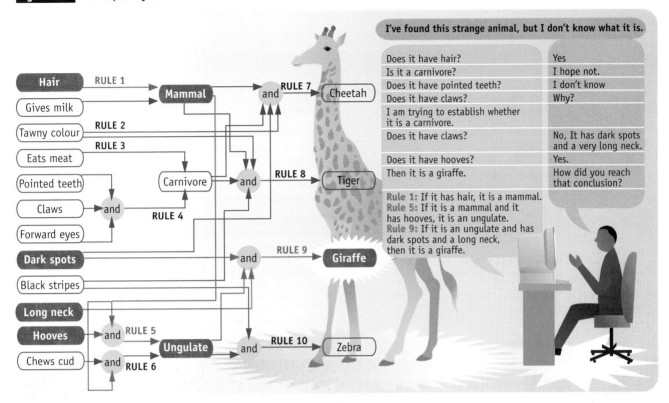

the computer screen or using a mouse. EIS software typically produces easy-to-read graphics with full-colour displays and charts. A typical EIS gives users a choice among many kinds of data, such as the firm's financial statements, sales figures, and stock-market trends for its company and industry. Managers can start by looking at summaries and then request more detailed information if they wish.

Expert Systems

Expert systems *are computer programs that imitate human thinking through a complicated series of "if ... then" rules.* These systems apply human knowledge to specific subject areas in order to solve problems (see Figure 10.1).

Alamo Rent-A-Car Inc. in the United States, for example, uses an expert system to help employees decide how to price its rental cars. The system continually compares Alamo's prices to those of competitors and identifies cases in which Alamo's rates are different.

Business Term

√ **Expert systems**

Computer programs that imitate human thinking through a complicated series of "if ... then" rules.

Business Term

√ **Voice processing**

Voice mail; technologies that use spoken language to send or receive information from a computer.

Voice Processing

Voice processing (or voice mail) involves *technologies that use spoken language to send or receive information from a computer.* Voice processing typically involves using the telephone; for example, an automated telephone ordering system can be used to order catalogue merchandise from some retailers. Voice processing also can improve customer service while helping companies keep their costs down.

Speech recognition systems that allow computers to "understand" and respond to the human voice are still more common in science fiction than in business. At present, no commercially available system exists that instantly can understand a stranger's conversation. Systems first must be "trained" to understand specific individuals' voices and speech patterns. However, there are some voice recognition systems, such as VoiceAssist™, that can, once trained, convert almost anything a certain speaker says to written text. Table 10.2 outlines some common business uses of voice processing.

Table 10.2 Common Business Uses of Voice Processing

Business Uses	Description
Voice-mail equipment	Allows users to record, store, forward, and broadcast voice messages with touch-tone phones.
Voice-mail service	Instead of buying special equipment to handle voice mail, some companies prefer to use outside services.
Voice response gear	Responding to prerecorded cues, callers can instruct a computer to complete a transaction or recite information by pushing the correct key on a touch-tone phone
Audiotex service	Supplies recorded entertainment and information over the phone, sometimes with voice response capabilities.
Automatic call distributor	Parcels out incoming calls to operators.
Speech recognition	Lets computers "understand" and respond to the human voice.

Multimedia Computing

Multimedia computing refers to *the technologies that facilitate the integration of two or more types of media,* such as text, voice, sound, full-motion video, still video, graphics, and/or animation into a single, computer-based application. For example, some experts think that the ordinary telephone is about to undergo a multimedia metamorphosis.

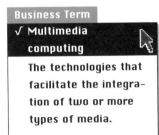

Business Term
√ **Multimedia computing**
The technologies that facilitate the integration of two or more types of media.

Several new devices — using the phone lines for e-mail, Web surfing, and home video conferencing — were introduced at the giant Consumer Electronics Show in Las Vegas in 1997. Corel/Video has introduced an interactive video communications system that allows real-time multimedia communications. This leading-edge

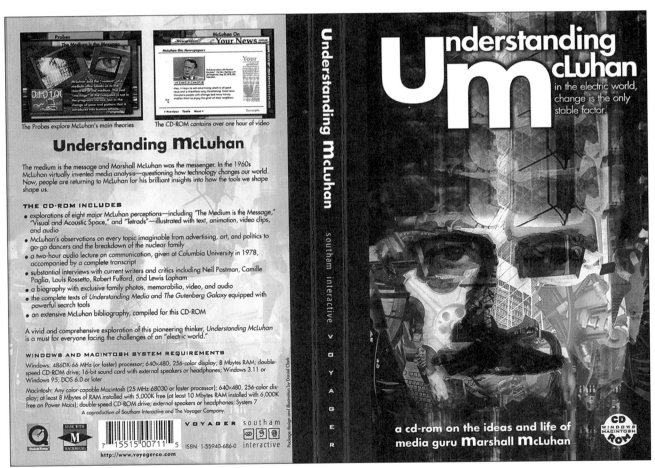

Understanding McLuhan is a CD-ROM about Marshall McLuhan, the Canadian media philosopher and prophet of the information age. Developed by Southam Interactive and manufactured and marketed by Voyager, the CD-ROM is a feast of information, sights, and sounds.

Source: Package design and illustration by Daniel Clark. Reproduced with permission of Southam Inc. and The Voyager Company.

technology was made possible thanks to a joint project with Starvision Multimedia Corp. of Vancouver — a spinoff of Newbridge Networks Corp. Among the more promising business applications for multimedia computing are employee training and business presentations.

Many multimedia applications are programmed on a *CD-ROM* (compact disk–read only memory), because the spiral-type storage is well suited for retrieving continuous blocks of data, such as data converted from music or animation. CD-ROMs are also useful because of their durability and large capacity. Today, CD-ROM technology, the computer, and the Internet allow users to interact over the Net in real time. For example, individuals from around the world can now link up to play any number of computer games.

> **Business Term**
> √ **Groupware**
> Computer software that combines and extends the concept of shared information (a database) with a method for moving data between users (e-mail).

> **Business Term**
> √ **Electronic bulletin boards**
> Public message centres that appear on computer networks.

An especially useful interactive medium is **groupware**, *computer software that combines and extends the concept of shared information (a database) with a method for moving data between users (e-mail).* Groupware allows collaboration among users. IBM's Lotus Notes™ is a popular groupware package. Employees at the accounting firm of Price Waterhouse use it to keep in touch with thousands of co-workers. Lotus Notes™ combines a sophisticated e-mail system with a huge database containing work records and memos. Employees can consult over **electronic bulletin boards:** *public message centres that appear on computer networks.* Here they learn about and obtain information on a variety of services and industries. They also can give their computers standing orders to locate and retrieve the latest news articles on specific topics.

Interactive Media and Groupware

While multimedia involves multiple technologies, interactive media is more focussed on one technology with multiple applications. **Interactive media** involve *program applications that allow users to interact with computers to perform different functions at the same time.* Many experts believe that interactive media will inevitably change the way most people live their lives. Interactive television, for example, allows the viewer to choose between "Seinfeld" and the shopping channel. In addition, purchases can be made using an interactive remote control.

> **Business Term**
> √ **Interactive media**
> Program applications that allow users to interact with computers to perform several different functions at the same time.

The science fiction of yesterday's computerized world is closer to becoming a reality as the television becomes more than an entertainment medium — TV has finally grown to include an increasing number of business and educational applications. In fact, the boundaries between TV and your PC are no longer clear. The PC is becoming more like a TV and the TV is more like a PC. The first sign of this digital convergence was WebTV. Now we can send e-mail, surf the WWW, and play video games right from our TV sets.

WHERE

The Jobs Are

Marc Labrosse, President and CEO, Alex Informatics Inc., Lachine, Quebec, voted Canada's Fastest-Growing Company, 1995, by <u>Profit</u> magazine

Growing with Entertainment and Learning Software

"A growth industry is definitely entertainment and learning software. There is a huge potential for interactive multimedia training and entertainment on-demand over local telecom and cable networks. You'll be able to subscribe or pay-per-use for these services and determine what you watch and when you watch it – with full VCR-like control. Alex is in front of this wave with our software-based Libra™ media server which stores and delivers this high-bandwidth content to thousands of simultaneous users. We're selling our products all over the world. The possibilities are endless."

INFORMATION SYSTEMS AND SECURITY

AS INFORMATION SYSTEMS become more important to business, they also become harder to replace. However, natural disasters, power failures, equipment malfunctions, and human error can wreak havoc with even the most sophisticated system. When computers are connected to a network, a problem at any location can affect the entire network. Organizations need to be prepared with backup plans so they can continue operating if their computer system fails.

While many of these security issues go beyond the scope of this textbook, we will discuss two important security threats: computer crime and viruses. Table 10.3 lists a few general controls that organizations can use to protect their information systems.

Computer Crime

Computers can be effective work tools. Unfortunately, they also can be an effective way to commit crimes. Computer crime falls into three general categories:

Table 10.3 Information Controls

Control	Example
Hardware	Restricting access to machines/terminals; checking for equipment malfunction.
Software	Requiring logs of operating-system activities; restricting unauthorized access to software programs.
Data security	Using passwords; restricting access to terminals to limit access to data files.
Operations	Establishing procedures for running computer jobs correctly; establishing backup and recovery procedures for abnormal or disrupted processing.
Systems development	Requiring management review and audit of each new information system project for conformity with budget, solution requirements, and quality standards; requiring appropriate technical and business documentation for each system.
Management	Establishing formal written policies and procedures; segregating job functions to minimize error and fraud; providing supervision and accountability.

General controls that organizations can use to protect their information systems.

TECHNOLOGY

CORPORATE COMPUTER SYSTEM SECURITY

From an Ernst & Young survey of 1300 chief information officers and other senior information executives.

Key Findings
The increased use of electronic messaging, networked computer systems, and central database resources have made information security systems top priority for management. Among their findings:

➜ Management is paying more attention to information security issues. They noted that

security is "extremely important," and have developed stronger reporting relationships with security professionals.

➜ Organizations are increasingly dissatisfied with decentralized information security administration.

➜ Businesses are making increased use of local area networks and UNIX-based systems, which are most often connected to central computing resources. Still, many organizations are unhappy with the overall security of these client/server services.

➜ As Internet use increases, so do concerns over security. One in five organizations reported attempted or successful break-ins via the Internet.

➜ Viruses caused pain for over two-thirds of survey respondents, though only a small number reported financial loss as a result of infection.

➜ Ninety percent of businesses use some kind of backup and recovery system.

➜ Inadvertent errors were the culprits in security-related financial losses for the 50 percent of companies that

- Data can be changed or invented to produce inaccurate information.

- Computer programs can be changed to create false information or illegal transactions.

- Unauthorized people can access a company's computer system and use it for their benefit.

Every year, North American companies lose over half a billion dollars to computer crime. Often they are reluctant to admit it publicly, fearing the negative image this can give to the public.

Computer Viruses

A related problem involves *computer viruses*, programs that secretly attach themselves to other programs and change them or destroy the data kept on a disk. A virus can reproduce by copying itself to other programs stored on the disk. It spreads as the owner of infected software exchanges software with other users, usually by an electronic bulletin board or by trading floppy disks. Viruses can be programmed to remain dormant for a long time, after which the infection suddenly activates itself.

Sometimes viruses result from pranks that get out of hand. One German student sent a Christmas greeting over a computer network that ended up spreading into IBM's international network and, within hours, attached itself to every mailing list it encountered.

Other viruses involve deliberate crimes. The Michelangelo virus erases data in computers that are used on March 6, the Italian artist's birthday. In one year, 18.2 percent of major North American companies reported being infected by this virus, along with computers in England, the Netherlands, Austria, and South Africa.

To protect against computer viruses, experts recommend the following steps:[25]

- Buy software only if it is in its original shrink-wrapping or sealed container.

- Make backup copies of all new software as soon as you open the package, and store the copies in a location away from the workplace.

- "Quarantine" each new piece of software by reviewing it carefully on a computer that is not connected to a network.

- Restrict access to data and programs wherever possible.

reported suffering them. Eighty percent of these organizations were unable or unwilling to estimate the dollar value of their losses.

→ Less than half of the organizations provide ongoing security awareness or education programs for their employees. Three-quarters, however, have formal security policies.

→ Lack of both human resources and proven security solutions were cited as obstacles to addressing information security concerns.

Source: From an Ernst & Young study, as appearing in Mary Gooderham, "It's Hard to Keep a Secret," *The Globe and Mail*, April 9, 1996, B32. Reprinted by permission of Ernst & Young.

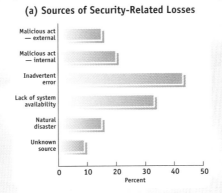

(a) Sources of Security-Related Losses

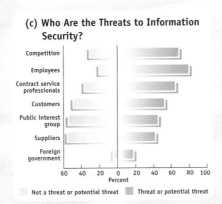

(c) Who Are the Threats to Information Security?

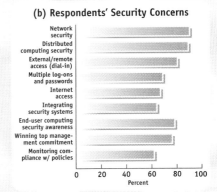

(b) Respondents' Security Concerns

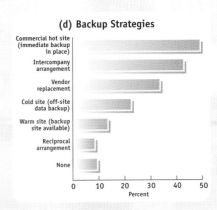

(d) Backup Strategies

CASE EXERCISE

CYBERABUSE

Many companies now empower employees to make decisions and do their work without close supervision or control. Employees are equipped with computers and hooked up to the World Wide Web, giving them global access to information in order to support decision making.

In December 1996, an empowered federal scientist working for the Department of Defence in Ottawa was arrested. He was accused of downloading over 20 000 images of child pornography. This case re-opened public debate about whether the computer activity of employees should be monitored and controlled.

On the one hand, unmonitored Internet access can leave companies open to lawsuits, protests, and the kind of public embarrassment that befell the Department of Defence. It can also lead to workplace inefficiencies and reduced production (see the "Did You Know" box on page 248). Employers estimate that employees who go on-line spend one-third of their time on activities unrelated to their jobs. They use the Internet to send personal e-mail, shop on-line, buy stocks, and conduct other personal financial transactions.

To combat cyberabuse, many employers monitor employee computer files and track e-mail messages. Some firms even monitor these actions without disclosing the eavesdropping. They hire surveillance specialists and install monitoring software to track everything employees do on their computers. For example, a software program called Little Brother™ can track which Web sites an employee visits.

However, some experts say that electronic surveillance by employers has gone too far. Too much security infringes on an individual's right to privacy, a commodity that many workers say is already in short supply. "The potential for abuse is tremendous, but trying to cure that abuse can violate people's privacy," says Frank Work, chief counsel to Alberta's information and privacy commissioner. An International Labor Organization report supports this view: "[M]onitoring and surveillance techniques available as a result of advances in technology make methods of control even more pervasive than ever before, and raise serious questions of human rights."

1. Do you think computer monitoring is an invasion of employees' privacy rights? What are some arguments in favour of and against computer monitoring?

Source: Adapted from Brian Laghi, "Surveillance for Internet Abuse Runs into Employees' Privacy Rights," *The Globe and Mail*, December 14, 1996, A10. Reprinted with permission from The Globe and Mail; Excerpts adapted from *Contemporary Business*, 9th ed. by Louis E. Boone and David L. Kurtz, Copyright © 1998 by The Dryden Press, reprinted by permission of the publisher.

SUMMARY OF LEARNING OUTCOMES

1. **Discuss the role of telecommunications and the information superhighway in business.**

   Telecommunications refers to any system in which information or data are sent over a distance through some type of electronic transmission medium. Telecommunications can involve not only computers, but also such diverse technologies and related industries as telephones, televisions, fax machines, e-mail, satellite systems, computer networks, and of course the Internet. Fibre optics and digitization are two forces of technological change that have shaped the blueprint for the information superhighway — a metaphoric phrase to describe the merging of telecommunications, information, and data networks into a single enormous pathway accessible to all consumers and businesses. This will give businesses and residences access to libraries, databases, teleconferencing, and many other services. The information superhighway will reduce the time necessary to transmit data and speed up the pace of work. It will overcome geographic barriers and restructure business relationships by reducing the need for intermediaries.

2. **Explain how the Internet has had an impact on our personal lives and business decisions.**

   The information superhighway exemplar is the Internet — a series of computer networks with a single point of access that connects the user to an electronic information system that spans the globe. It's a unique business medium, as significant as the telephone or the printing press. For example, thanks to the Internet and related technologies we can now order a book from the local library, buy a pair of jeans, or do our personal banking all from the confines of our homes. The Internet is fundamentally changing the way we communicate, create, and disseminate information. Through Internet systems such as e-mail, the World Wide Web, intranets, and entranets, businesses can now exchange information around the world. Internet technology has the potential to increase sales while reducing costs, and the financial risks are low.

3. **Explain the purpose of a management information system and how it aids decision making in business.**

   Information is a vital element in making business decisions. Effective decisions cannot be made without answers to questions about the internal operations of the firm and the external environment in which it operates. Progressive companies use a planned management information system (MIS) along with the Internet to access past, present, and projected information on internal operations and external intelligence for use in decision making. Such information systems should aid all areas of the organization — production, accounting, marketing, human resources, purchasing, engineering, and finance — in carrying out their decision-making responsibilities.

4. **Distinguish among the three broad categories of computers: mainframes, minicomputers, and microcomputers.**

   The primary bases for distinguishing among the three types of computers are size, memory capacity, and processing speeds. Mainframes are the largest, with the greatest storage capacity and fastest processing speeds. Minicomputers are smaller (about the size of a small filing cabinet), less powerful, and less expensive. Microcomputers, the smallest type of computers, include desktop computers, notepads, and pocket computers that have limited storage systems but are portable. Each type — mainframe, minicomputer, and microcomputer — contains the basic elements of any computer system.

5. **Explain the impact of computer networks on information technology.**

   Computer networks are systems that interconnect numerous computers so they function individually and communicate with one another. A local area network (LAN) is a computer network that connects machines within a limited area. Thanks mainly to the information superhighway and the Internet, companies can now network their internal computer systems with computers from around the world. Some call this new form of networking "collaborative computing."

At the cutting edge of computer networking is a personal computer with no hard drive that is connected to the corporate network or Internet. This "black box," or so-called "network computer," uses application software or files stored on server computers.

6. Identify some of the major business applications of computer software.

Computers are used throughout the private and public sectors; it is difficult to imagine a modern organization operating without them. Examples of important business applications include word processing, desktop publishing, decision support systems, spreadsheets, fax machines, executive information systems, expert systems, voice processing, multimedia computing, and interactive media and groupware.

7. Summarize the major computer/Internet security issues that affect organizations.

Security issues have become a major concern of the management information officer. Two of the traditional security threats are computer crime and computer viruses. Internet security has become a major issue as companies struggle to respect employee privacy while reducing their legal liability and time-wasting abuse.

Key Terms Quiz

chief information officer (CIO)
spreadsheet
Internet (the Net)
electronic mail (e-mail)
local area network (LAN)
management information
  system (MIS)

intranet
computer network
multimedia computing
computer
expert system
telecommunications

groupware
Java™
decision support system (DSS)
fibre optics
interactive media
information superhighway

_____ 1. Organized method of providing information for decision making.
_____ 2. Top management executive responsible for directing a firm's management information system and related computer operations.
_____ 3. Programmable electronic device that can store, retrieve, and process data.
_____ 4. A modern transmission technology using lasers to produce a beam of light that can carry large amounts of information.
_____ 5. A series of computer networks with a single point of access that connects the user to an electronic information system that spans the globe.
_____ 6. Any system in which information or data are sent over a distance through some type of electronic transmission system, typically a telephone line.
_____ 7. System in which interconnected computers can either function individually or communicate with one another.
_____ 8. A single network merging telecommunications, information, and data that can be accessed internally or externally.
_____ 9. A computer network that connects machines within a limited area or organization.
_____ 10. Private computer network that uses the standards and technology of the Internet to distribute internal corporate information.
_____ 11. A universal computer language that allows all sorts of previously incompatible systems to share applications and information.
_____ 12. Computer system that quickly provides relevant facts for use in decision making.
_____ 13. Special computer software permitting manipulation of decision variables to determine their impact.

14. Systems for sending and receiving written messages through computers.
15. Computer programs that imitate human thinking through the use of "if ... then" rules.
16. The technologies that facilitate the integration of two or more types of media.
17. Program applications that allow users to interact with computers to perform different functions at the same time.
18. Computer software that combines and extends the concept of shared information (a networked database) with a method for moving data between users (e-mail).

Other Important Terms

CD-ROM
electronic bulletin boards

extranet
mainframe

microprocessor
voice processing

Review Questions

1. What is telecommunications? Describe its impact on business operations.

2. Explain the term *information superhighway*. Which industries are likely to profit from such a pathway? Which might suffer financially from it?

3. Explain the purpose of a management information system and its functions in an organization.

4. Categorize each of the following as either hardware or software and defend your choices:
   a. CD-ROM
   b. Computer instruction manual
   c. Line printer
   d. A company's customer database
   e. Keyboard
   f. Word-processing program
   g. Groupware

5. Differentiate among the mainframe, the minicomputer, and the microcomputer.

6. Explain the importance and contribution of computer networks and collaborative computing to modern management information systems.

7. List at least two computer applications for each of the following areas of business:
   a. Physical distribution
   b. Production and inventory control
   c. Human resources
   d. Marketing
   e. Finance and accounting
   f. Legal
   g. Customer service

8. Discuss how groupware might change business procedures and working relationships.

Discussion Questions

1. Keep a diary for two or three days, recording each time a computer affects your life. Discuss what you learned from this exercise.

2. A computer programmer was doing contract work for a software publisher when he accidentally acquired a disk infected with a computer virus. Unsuspecting, he ran the infected disk on his office computer. Later,

he reviewed one of the publisher's programs on the same computer and, unknowingly, infected his own company's program. When he returned the program to the publisher, it, in turn, copied the infected program into its nationwide system. Discuss ways to prevent occurrences of this nature.

3. Interview someone who has started using a computer at work. Ask this person to compare his or her job to the way it was before the computer was introduced. How has the job changed? Does this employee feel the computer is an asset, a drawback, or both? Why?

Answers to Key Terms Quiz

1. management information system (MIS) **2.** chief information officer (CIO) **3.** computer **4.** fibre optics **5.** Internet (the Net) **6.** telecommunications **7.** computer network **8.** information superhighway **9.** local area network (LAN) **10.** intranet **11.** Java™ **12.** decision support system (DSS) **13.** spreadsheet **14.** electronic mail (e-mail) **15.** expert system **16.** multimedia computing **17.** interactive media **18.** groupware

Notes

1. Ministry of Supply and Services Canada, *The Challenge of the Information Highway*, Final Report of the Information Highway Advisory Council, Catalogue No. C2-229/7-1995E, xv, September 1995.
2. Statistics Canada, Catalogue No. 15-516-MPE, December 1996, as reported in Bruce Little, "Information Technology Sector Booming," *The Globe and Mail*, December 6, 1996, B11.
3. Based on Statistics Canada 1995 figures, reported in Bruce Little, "Information Technology Sector Booming," B11.
4. Michael Salter, "Dream BIG ... then BIGGER," *The Globe and Mail Report on Business Magazine*, June 1996, 56–60.
5. Ministry of Supply and Services Canada, *The Challenge of the Information Highway*, 2.
6. From an interview, "Cyberwhiz Don Tapscott Is Mapping the Digital Frontier," *Royal Bank Business Report*, November 1996, 22.
7. Ministry of Supply and Services Canada, *The Challenge of the Information Highway*, 5.
8. Ibid., 11.
9. Bolen Books, Advertising Supplement, "Business Grows with On-Line Customers," *The Globe and Mail*, October 23, 1995, C10.
10. "She's Re-Engineering the Ways Companies Do Business," *Royal Bank Business Report*, November 1996, 15.
11. Sun Microsystems of Canada, Advertising Supplement, *The Globe and Mail Report on Business Magazine*, November 1996.
12. Ibid.
13. Bill Gates, "Cyberlord Speaks," *The Globe and Mail Report on Business Magazine*, January 1997, 76.
14. Patrick Brethour, "Savings Lure Companies to Intranets," *The Globe and Mail*, December 11, 1996, B13.
15. Bell Global Solutions, Advertising Supplement, "Net Working," *Canadian Business*, November 1996, 50.
16. Deborah Wilson, "Banks Face Task of Assuring Clients They're Served, not Shadowed," *The Globe and Mail*, December 17, 1996, C1.
17. Terence Belford, "Air Mile Collectors Yield Wealth of Data," *The Globe and Mail*, December 17, 1996, C2.
18. Statistics Canada 1996 study on computer use in the workplace, reported in "The Computer Market," *Royal Bank Business Report*, November 1996, 8.
19. Don Tapscott, *The Digital Economy*, quoted in "Computers at Home," *Royal Bank Business Report*, 8.
20. Nicholas Negroponte, *Being Digital* (New York: Knopf, 1995), quoted in "The Power and the Promise of the Digital Revolution," *Royal Bank Business Report*, November 1996, 5.
21. Boeing, Advertising Supplement, *The Globe and Mail Report on Business Magazine*, November 1996, 45.
22. Geoffrey Rowan, "How Sun's New Computer Changes the Game," *The Globe and Mail*, October 30, 1996, B11.
23. Sun Microsystems of Canada, Advertising Supplement, "Java Changes Everything," *The Globe and Mail*, November 20, 1996, 1.
24. Elizabeth Church, "Business Still Loves the Fax," *The Globe and Mail*, October 11, 1996, B9.
25. Kenneth Laudon and Jane Laudon, *Business Information Systems*, 2nd ed. (Fort Worth, TX: The Dryden Press, 1993), 576.

Production and Marketing

part IV

David K. Foot, Professor of Economics,
University of Toronto

"The best growth market of the future will be

supplying products and services for people

born from 1947 to 1966. ...

Figure out what they'll want. ...

Finally, do not forget the echo children — the teenage

market will also grow in the years ahead."

CHAPTER 11
Marketing Management
and Customer Satisfaction

CHAPTER 12
Creating and Producing World-
Class Goods and Services

CHAPTER 13
Designing and Implementing
Customer-Driven Marketing
Strategies

Marketing Management and Customer Satisfaction

Learning Outcomes

After studying this chapter, you should be able to

1. Discuss how marketing's role in the exchange process creates utility.
2. List the major functions of marketing.
3. Explain the importance of the marketing concept and customer satisfaction in achieving success in the marketplace.
4. Outline methods for obtaining customer feedback and measuring customer satisfaction.
5. Outline how a marketing strategy is developed.
6. Explain the concept of a market.
7. Explain the concept of relationship marketing.
8. Identify the major components of the marketing environment.
9. Discuss why the study of consumer behaviour is important to marketing.
10. Describe the marketing research function.
11. Explain database marketing and the concept of market segmentation.

Build It and They Will Come

Securitex Inc. of Montreal is a small, 55-person, Canadian manufacturer of heavy padded uniforms worn by firefighters. In the summer of 1996, Securitex got a call from The London Fire Brigade, the fire service for London, England, which has about 6400 firefighters. Someone in London had been browsing the Securitex Web page and wanted to know if this Canadian firm would put in a bid for the brigade's $11-million order of new fire suits. This was one of the few inquiries received from Securitex's $12 000 start-up investment in its Web site. Ross Cochran, president of the fire-suit maker, was impressed by the Internet's potential to make a small firm known in foreign markets. He said he had discovered that the benefits of a Web site were not short term: "I don't know how effective it is yet, but my approach is for the long term."[1]

Tilley Endurables and Roots Canada are two other Canadian firms that have taken the leap of faith into the Internet world — both companies are offering online sales of their products. Although, like Securitex, their Web pages have been slow to produce a line-up of cyberspace shoppers, they are cautiously optimistic that eventually their pioneering work will translate into concrete sales and profits.

These leading-edge, entrepreneurial companies understand that the Internet is a different medium — one that will take time and money to bear fruit.[2]

Larger firms like Wal-Mart and Chapters are also jumping on the Web train. In 1996, for example, Wal-Mart announced that it had formed a partnership with Microsoft Corporation to provide products online. Wal-Mart eventually expects to be selling more products in cyberspace than in retail outlets.

Unfortunately, the optimism and longer-term perspective of forward-thinking companies such as Securitex, Roots, and Tilley and retail giants like Wal-Mart are not shared by at least one-third of our business community. Using the Internet remains a question mark for many firms. The "build it and they will come" philosophy isn't working — at least according to many Canadian firms and Internet marketing specialists. A survey by the Toronto-based Tikkanen-Bradley Consulting Group, for example, found that more than one-third of Canadian firms that responded were unhappy with the commercial reaction to their World Wide Web sites. Even though many of the surveyed companies (46 percent) had been on the Web for more than a year, they still found the experience disappointing.[3]

According to A.C. Nielson Canada, about 500 000 Canadians shopped electronically in 1995. This was only about 7.5 percent of the 6.5 million Canadians using the Internet (about 22 percent of the population in 1995).[4] It is these kinds of statistics that have led many techno experts to allude to the enormous commercial potential of the Internet. With the expected double-digit growth in Internet users, few can dispute the long-term revenue potential of cyber commerce.

However, companies that take the plunge and jump on the Net must understand the present-day marketing realities of Web marketing, which include

- **Security.** Many cybercustomers remain leery about providing personal financial information over the Net — they are concerned that a third party will have electronic access to this information. Some experts forecast that continued market penetration of computers and advances in encryption will slowly erode this fear and thus increase the number of electronic shoppers. Nonetheless, the growth of cybershopping will be severely impeded as long as potential customers are afraid.

- **New medium.** Marketing techniques to get the attention of the cybershopper are still at the experimental stages. Unlike television watchers, for example, Net users are active. Strategies must be devised to encourage the Net user to take the initiative to browse a company site.

- **Long-term payoff.** There is little evidence that an Internet presence will produce an immediate payoff. To many experts, Web marketing requires a certain leap of faith.

- **Marketing mix.** The Internet is not a stand-alone marketing tool. It has to be used in conjunction with traditional marketing strategies and print methods.

- **Marketing plan.** Commerce on the Internet should be part of the overall marketing plan of the business. The Internet delivery mechanism must be right for the customer and the business. For example, if most Web surfers are men, this would certainly affect a strategy to sell women's clothing over the Net.

- **Quantification.** As of 1997, most information about Internet users was unaudited and anecdotal. This will change, however — over time, an objective system for measuring the size and characteristics of the Net user will evolve. In the meantime, most companies will have to rely on a "hit and miss" strategy.

CHAPTER OVERVIEW

MARKETING IS ABOUT three words: needs, satisfaction, and benefits.

- **Needs:** There must be a market need for your product or service.

- **Satisfaction:** You must find a way to satisfy this need.

- **Benefits:** You must translate the need-satisfying product or service into a benefit for the customer and the business.

All organizations — profit-oriented or not-for-profit — must serve consumer needs if they are to succeed. Satisfying consumer needs involves more than just placing your company name and logo on a Web page. Marketing is the link between the organization and the consumer — it is the way in which consumer needs are determined and the means by which consumers are informed that the organization can meet those needs.

In addition to selling goods and services, marketing is used to advocate ideas or viewpoints and to educate people. For example, the Canadian Diabetes Association mails out questionnaires that ask, "Are you at risk for diabetes?" and then lists risk factors and common symptoms as well as describing the work of the association.

"Ask five people to define marketing and you will likely get five different definitions. Most of them will be too limited

> **Business Term**
>
> √ **Marketing**
>
> The process of planning and executing the conception, pricing, promotion, and distribution of ideas, goods, and services to create exchanges that satisfy individual and organizational objectives.

CYBERSPACE

Standing in front of a packed theatre at an Internet industry conference, Mark Greene, IBM vice president of electronic payment and certification at the Internet division of Armonk, NY, says 1997 is the year of Internet commerce. He points to the following set of IBM numbers (in U.S. dollars) that forecast explosive growth:

→ 1996: $900 million

→ 1997: $2 billion

→ 2000: $200 billion

→ 2010: $1 trillion

Other experts simply don't agree with Greene's crystal-ball vision of the Internet economic future. They say that it will take years – maybe even decades – before Greene's "pivot year" arrives. Jim Carroll, Canadian cyberspace guru and co-author of The Canadian Internet Handbook, for example, considers himself a "downright sceptic" about online shopping: "I just don't think we're all prepared to drop our lives and rush to the terminal and become dweeb-geek cybershoppers."

and wrong. Because of the visibility of personal selling and advertising, many respondents will say that marketing is selling or that marketing is advertising. But marketing is much more comprehensive than these narrow perspectives."[5] A formal definition of **marketing** *is the process of planning and executing the conception, pricing, promotion, and distribution of ideas, goods, and services to*

create exchanges that satisfy individual and organizational objectives.[6] In this chapter, we examine the role of marketing in organizations and describe how organizations develop a marketing strategy. We also will look at customer satisfaction as a key to organizational profitability and will discuss techniques for obtaining customer feedback and measuring customer satisfaction.

> ### THEY SAID IT
>
> **"Business has only two functions — Marketing and Innovation."**
>
> PETER DRUCKER, business philosopher and author

THE EXCHANGE PROCESS

MARKETING ACTIVITY BEGINS when the exchange process becomes important to society. **Exchange** *is the process by which two or more parties trade things of value, so that each party feels it is better off after the trade.* For example, a consumer "trades" a cheque for $396.96 to Circuit City in exchange for a new colour TV. But where does marketing fit in?

Consider a preindustrial society consisting of two families that each produce their own clothing and food. One of the families is expert at producing clothing; the other consists of skilled farmers. The exchange process allows the two families to concentrate on what they do best and to trade clothing for food and vice versa. This specialization and division of labour leads to increased total production and a higher standard of living for both families. The exchange process could not occur, however, unless each family marketed its products. Marketing is clearly a prime determinant of the overall standard of living. In fact, in advanced societies, marketing costs range between 40 and 60 percent of selling prices.

> **Business Term**
> √ **Exchange**
> The process by which two or more parties trade things of value, so that each party feels it is better off after the trade.

FUNCTIONS OF MARKETING

AS WE HAVE noted, marketing is more than just selling — it is, as Figure 11.1 shows, a complex activity that affects many aspects of an organization and its dealings with consumers. We can think of the functions of marketing in terms of *utility*, which is the want-satisfying power of a good or service. The production function is responsible for creating *form utility* by converting raw materials and other inputs into finished goods and services. The marketing function creates three other types of utility: time, place, and ownership. *Time utility* is created by having a good or service available when the consumer

wants to purchase it. A bank with hours on Saturday illustrates this concept. *Place utility* is created by having a good or service available in the right place when the consumer wants to purchase it. The location of convenience stores and video-rental outlets suggest the importance of place utility. Arranging for an orderly transfer of ownership at the time of purchase creates *ownership utility*. Retailers create ownership utility by accepting currency or credit-card payments, making it easier for customers to purchase merchandise. Marketing adds to the utility of goods and services by performing some basic functions: buying, selling, transporting, storing, standardization and grading, financing, risk taking, and providing market information.

Buying and selling are the exchange functions of marketing. Marketers must study why consumers buy certain goods and services. Indeed, this study of consumer behaviour is critical to the firm's overall success.

Figure 11.1 Eight Basic Functions of Marketing

- Buying
- Selling
- Transporting
- Storing
- Standardization and grading
- Financing
- Risk taking
- Providing marketing information

Transporting involves the physical movement of the product from the seller to the buyer, and storing involves the warehousing of goods until they are needed for sale. Standardization and grading deals with standardizing the description of goods; many industries, such as agricultural products or automotive tires, have specific grading standards for their goods. The financing function involves extending credit to consumers, wholesalers, and retailers.

Risk taking takes into account uncertainties about future consumer behaviour; marketers must be entrepreneurial risk takers in many instances. For example, several major manufacturers currently are spending a lot of time and money developing more energy-efficient furnaces, refrigerators, and cars. Marketers in these companies are betting that consumers will choose a more environmentally friendly product. Finally, marketers collect and analyze market information to determine what will sell and who will buy it.

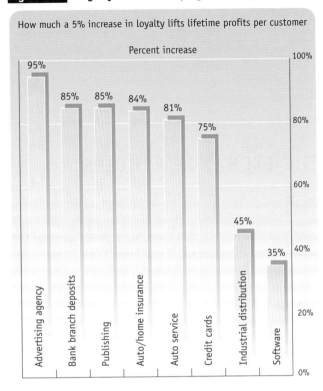

Figure 11.2 Big Payoffs from Keeping Customers

How much a 5% increase in loyalty lifts lifetime profits per customer

THE MARKETING CONCEPT AND CUSTOMER SATISFACTION

IN CHAPTER 6, we discussed the importance of quality in all functions of an organization. In the marketing function, the marketing concept is an important expression of quality. The **marketing concept** can be defined as *adopting a consumer orientation in order to achieve long-term success.* All of the organization's efforts, whether profit-oriented or not-for-profit, are geared to satisfying consumer needs.

Customer satisfaction directly affects a company's profitability. In fact, it is crucial to an organization's continued existence, since a company that fails to provide the same level of customer satisfaction as its competitors will not stay in business for long. As Figure 11.2 illustrates, boosting customer loyalty by just 5 percent translates into a significant increase in lifetime profits per customer. The profit increases range from 35 percent in the software industry to a whopping 95 percent for advertising agencies.

Today's savvy customers want the satisfaction of acquiring goods and services that go beyond the ordinary. They are

Business Term

√ **Marketing concept**

Adopting a consumer orientation in order to achieve long-term success.

Business Term

√ **Added value**

Increased worth of a good or service attained by delivering more than expected – something of personal significance to the customer.

demanding more than just a fair price; they are seeking an added value. *A good or service with* **added value** *attains increased worth by delivering more than expected — something of personal significance to the customer.* If marketers want to compete in today's marketplace, they need to conform to the customer's mind set and standards. In other words, companies have to work harder to make a sale and to satisfy the customer.

Consider Delta Hotels and Resorts, a Canadian company that is renowned for its customer service. In the fall of 1996, Delta went that "extra mile" in its customer service program. It reinvented the concierge by introducing a unique "Delta Privilege Concierge Program." A toll-free 24-hour service gives members of Delta's frequent-guest program exclusive access to a central concierge who will handle their requests personally or forward them to a designated concierge at the appropriate hotel. "This service surpasses the traditional concierge concept usually available only in top-dollar luxury hotels," says Scott Allison, vice-president, marketing for Delta Hotels. "It can be accessed at any time and from anywhere — even if the member is not staying at a Delta hotel when making the request."

The "extra mile" component of the program is this extension of services beyond the four walls of the hotels. A Delta Privilege member, for example, can call the concierge service to have clothes dry-cleaned while on a business trip or, while away at a cottage, have entertainment arranged for visiting clients back home. Delta has reinvented the concierge by taking advantage of modern communication systems, connecting the central concierge in Fredericton to a network of cell phones with its hotels, suppliers, and designated Delta staff to ensure the service is delivered.[7]

Obtaining Customer Feedback

It is imperative for a company to obtain customer feedback. "It is important to get the voice of customers, to capture their words, in order to really understand what they want," remarks consultant Jennifer Brotman.[8] This is often a challenging task, as it can be difficult to determine the best way to obtain and measure clients' feedback.

Most firms use reactive methods, such as toll-free customer service telephone lines, to monitor customer feedback. Far fewer companies use proactive approaches — visiting clients, calling them, or sending out written surveys — to find out how satisfied their customers really are. An example of a proactive approach is that used by Canada Trust, where customer service is "more than a smile." Canada Trust has a program whereby staff randomly telephones customers to evaluate service. At RRSP time, for example, Canada Trust customers are contacted and offered a special consultation and retirement planning advice. A few companies, like Esso Canada, even go to the length of hiring a *mystery shopper*, a professional investigator who poses as a shopper and visits or calls

The World According to Big Shot

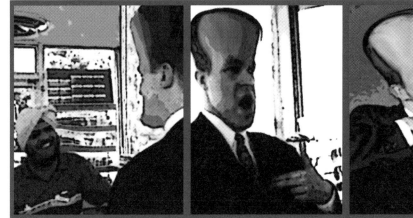

BIG SHOT: What happened to Eric?
JOE: Won't be with us for a couple of days. Lucky he didn't get fired. The mystery shopper got him ... and is he ever steamed!
BIG SHOT: What?
JOE: A company mystery shopper comes in every month now, and if we don't ask the right questions they

suspend us — without pay. We can even get fired! It's part of the company's new customer service strategy. Eric, poor guy, didn't ask the mystery shopper if she wanted a car wash.
BIG SHOT: A mystery shopper? What a great idea. I'm going to get my staff on that tomorrow.

NEXT DAY AT THE OFFICE

BIG SHOT: Slinky, we have to get serious about our customer service. I want you to be our mystery shopper for a couple of days. If somebody's not doing something right, lay them off. If they don't like it, fire them.

SLINKY: Don't you remember, we went virtual two weeks ago — we don't have any employees.
BIG SHOT: Maybe we should start thinking about hiring again.

➜ What do you think of Big Shot's approach to customer service?

Figure 11.3 How Companies Measure Customer Feedback

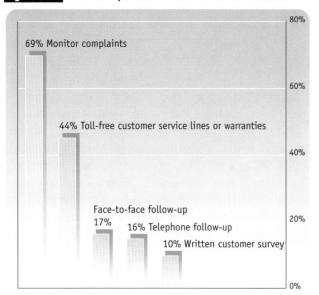

- 69% Monitor complaints
- 44% Toll-free customer service lines or warranties
- Face-to-face follow-up 17%
- 16% Telephone follow-up
- 10% Written customer survey

outlets of the business in order to evaluate the services rendered.[9]

Any method that makes it easier for customers to complain is to a firm's advantage. Customer complaints offer organizations the opportunity to overcome problems and prove commitment to service. Customers often have a stronger commitment to a company after a conflict has been resolved than they would have had they never complained at all. Businesses benefit from treating complaints as wel-

come resources and opportunities to gain innovative ideas for improvement. After all, studies show that while 95 percent of customers don't complain to the company, they end up telling eleven friends and/ or business acquaintances about any negative experiences.

Measuring Customer Satisfaction

Once it has obtained feedback, a firm may initiate a **customer satisfaction measurement (CSM) program**, *a procedure for measuring customer feedback against customer satisfaction goals and developing an action plan for improvement.* These programs can be quite sophisticated and may require the aid of an outside specialist (see Figure 11.3).

CSM programs vary widely, but most include the following steps:

1. Determine what areas are critical to the business and what measurement systems are currently being used.

2. Probe a representative group of customers to learn what factors, or attributes, are important to their use of a good or service.

3. Conduct research to determine the company's performance on the selected attributes.

4. Analyze results to develop action plans.

> **Business Term**
>
> √ **Customer satisfaction measurement (CSM) program**
>
> **A procedure for measuring customer feedback against customer satisfaction goals and developing an action plan for improvement.**

COMPETITIVE STRATEGY

IS TOTAL CUSTOMER SATISFACTION IN RETAILING A MYTH?

The only place I can find service in Canada is in the dictionary — but the dictionary definition is wrong.

I go to The Bay in search of service, defined in the *Penguin Canadian Dictionary* as the function or occupation of being helpful or useful. I stand under the huge sign

that says SERVICE. Nothing happens, nobody appears. I expand my search. I go to Eaton's. I stand under the sign that says SERVICE. Nothing happens. No one appears. The only thing that standing under the sign serves to do is to try my patience.

The usual quest for service goes something like this. I enter the store. There is nobody in sight. I can hear my voice echo through the store. *HHeelloo, ddooees aannyy bbooddyy wwoork hheerree?* You usually have to

search for someone to help you. Finding a salesperson represents phase one of your quest. The next step is finding the product you want. You secure the help of a salesperson. You ask for comparative product information. Which product is better and why? Often the salesperson knows little more than you do.

Getting service over the phone is a whole other source of frustration. It goes something like this: "Hello, I have a problem with. ... "

Marketing in Not-for-Profit Organizations

A substantial portion of our economy is composed of *not-for-profit organizations (NPOs)*. Recall from Chapter 1 that these are firms whose primary objective is something other than returning a profit to their owners. An estimated one out of every ten service workers and one out of six professionals are employed in the not-for-profit sector. This industry is expected to grow as governments across the nation continue to cut budgets and as the "boomers" head into their retirement years. Like profit-seeking firms, not-for-profit organizations may market a tangible good or an intangible service, or both. Canada Post, for example, offers stamps (a tangible good) and mail delivery (an intangible service).

Five types of not-for-profit marketing are person marketing, place marketing, cause marketing, event marketing, and organization marketing. **Person marketing** *refers to a program designed to enhance the favourable opinion of an individual by selected others.* The marketing of a political candidate is an example. Campaign managers conduct marketing research to identify voters and financial supporters and then design promotions, such as advertis-

Business Term

√ **Person marketing**

A program designed to enhance the favourable opinion of an individual by selected others.

Business Term

√ **Place marketing**

Attempts to attract people to a particular area, such as a city, province, or nation.

Business Term

√ **Cause marketing**

The marketing of a social cause or issue.

Business Term

√ **Event marketing**

The marketing of sporting, cultural, and charitable activities to selected target markets.

ing, fund-raising events, and political rallies, to reach voters and donors.

Place marketing *refers to attempts to attract people to a particular area, such as a city, province, or nation.* In addition to marketing themselves as a general vacation destination, some areas advertise to specific market segments. For instance, Jamaica, Bermuda, and Puerto Rico place ads in bridal magazines to catch the attention of brides-to-be who are planning their honeymoons.

Cause marketing *refers to the marketing of a social cause or issue.* This type of marketing covers a wide range of issues, including gun control, birth defects, child abuse, physical fitness, overeating, and alcoholism.

Event marketing *is the marketing of sporting, cultural, and charitable activities to selected target markets.* It includes the sponsorship of such events by firms seeking to increase public awareness and bolster their images by linking themselves and their products to a specific event. Canada, for example, received worldwide recognition by official sponsors and marketing partners when it hosted the Special Olympics in 1997.

Organization marketing *attempts to influence others to accept the goals of, receive*

You explain the problem. "I'm sorry," the person responds, "I'll transfer you to someone who can help you. ... " Click, the line disconnects. Now you've really got a problem: rage.

What irks people even more than the shortage of service is the abundance of *attitude*. We understand that stores are short of staff, but when we do encounter a sales clerk it's not uncommon to get the "Whadya want, don't bug me" attitude. Whatever happened to service with a smile?

Forget the smile for a minute, try just getting a salesperson to acknowledge you. Many salespeople are adept at ignoring customers. They don't come up to you and offer their assistance. In some stores, stocking shelves seems to be a higher priority. A friend of mine related an all-too-familiar story. She went to pay for clothing at one of the big department stores downtown. The cashier was on the phone and in the midst of conversation. My friend waited, simultaneously becoming apprised of the cashier's evening plans. Then the cashier said to the person on the phone, "Just a second," and she turned to my friend. "Do you want that?" My friend nodded. The cashier pro-

ceeded to ring in the sale and arrange her upcoming weekend.

With our increasingly global economy, free trade, and lowered tariff barriers, Canada must improve its service to stay competitive. Perhaps we need to redefine service in Canada. ... I hasten to point out that as Canadians we're all underserviced.

Source: Excerpt from Joanne Milner, "Forget the Smile — Whatever Happened to Service?!" *The Globe and Mail*, November 9, 1994, A24. Reprinted by permission of the author.

the services of, or contribute in some way to an organization. Included in this category are mutual benefit organizations such as churches, labour unions, and political parties; service organizations such as universities and colleges, hospitals, and museums; and government organizations/agencies, such as Canada Post, police and fire departments, and local governments.[10]

Developing a Marketing Strategy

All organizations, whether profit-oriented or not-for-profit, need to develop a marketing strategy to reach customers effectively. This involves analyzing the market, selecting a target market, and developing a marketing mix.

Often a company will develop a marketing plan, which is a written document that expresses the firm's

> **Business Term**
> √ **Organization marketing**
> Attempts to influence others to accept the goals of, receive the services of, or contribute in some way to an organization.

> **Business Term**
> √ **Market**
> People with purchasing power and the ability and authority to buy.

marketing strategy. Again, it is helpful to remember that marketing is about identifying needs, satisfying needs, and providing need-satisfying benefits. Target market, sales and revenue goals, marketing budget, and timing of the marketing-mix elements are included in the marketing plan.

A **market** consists of *people with purchasing power and the ability and authority to buy.* Markets can be classified by the types of products they handle, whether consumer or business products. **Consumer products** *are those goods and services purchased by the ultimate consumer for his or her own use.* Examples include such familiar items as toothpaste, shoes, and CDs. **Business products** — *sometimes called organizational or industrial products — are goods and services purchased to be used, either directly or indirectly, in the production of other goods for resale.* Examples include manufacturing equipment and tools, engineering consulting services, and industrial components. Sometimes an item can be either a consumer or a business product, depending on who buys it and why. The computer you bought for your own use at home is a consumer product, but that same computer, if purchased by a company for use by its office staff, becomes a business product.

Marketers must be familiar with a market's buying patterns and the purchasing behaviour of those involved. This knowledge is critical when marketers deal with consumer and business goods and services.

Having analyzed the market, the next step is to select a **target market** — *the group of consumers toward whom a firm directs its marketing efforts.* Consumer needs and wants vary considerably, and no single organization has the resources to satisfy everyone. Sometimes an organization chooses several target markets for a given good or service. For instance, a college or university might select several target markets for its

> **Business Term**
> √ **Consumer products**
> Goods and services purchased by the ultimate consumer for his or her own use.

> **Business Term**
> √ **Business products**
> Organizational or industrial products; goods and services purchased to be used, either directly or indirectly, in the production of other goods for resale.

HOW TO KEEP A GOOD THING GOING.

Think Ethernet Economy   Think Capacity   Think Multimedia

Think Memory   Think Scan/Copy/Fax   Think Token Ring Performance

Think Productivity   Think Larger Image   Think Portability

Think Capability   Think Communication   Think Fun

Call your IBM Reseller to buy OPTIONS by IBM today!

IBM

Solutions for a small planet

Computers like IBM's ThinkPad are often marketed as both a consumer and a business product.

fund-raising campaign: alumni, wealthy benefactors, foundations, local businesses, and other members of the community.

The final step is creating a marketing mix to satisfy the needs of the target market. The **marketing mix** *is a combination of the firm's product, pricing, distribution, and promotion strategies;* it is the mechanism that allows organizations to match consumer needs with product offerings. We will discuss the marketing mix in more detail in Chapter 13.

Business Term

√ **Target market**

The group of consumers toward whom a firm directs its marketing efforts.

Business Term

√ **Marketing mix**

A combination of the firm's product, pricing, distribution, and promotion strategies.

RELATIONSHIP MARKETING

AN IMPORTANT TREND in marketing centres on the concept of relationship marketing, which is also dealt with in Chapter 13. **Relationship marketing** *is the development and maintenance of long-term, cost-effective relationships with individual customers, suppliers, employees, and other partners for mutual benefit.*[11]

Good relationships with customers can be a vital strategic weapon for a firm. By identifying current purchasers and maintaining a positive relationship with them, organizations can target their best customers more efficiently. As Mitch Kurz, president of ad agency Wunderman Cato Johnson, says, "That's where the money is. ... Without exception, every client's profits are drawn from a relatively small number of its current users." Furthermore, studying current customers' buying habits and preferences can help marketers identify

---

CASE EXERCISE

RELATIONSHIP BUILDING

Positioning is the key to relationship marketing. Marketers must devise strategies to constantly position their product or service in the minds of the customer. Customers must be convinced that a business, product, or service can solve their needs. The key to building long-term customer relationships is to offer something of value that will continuously remind customers how important they are to the business.

Here is how two *Profit* 100 companies position themselves to maintain an enhanced relationship with their customers.

Magnotta Winery Corp. of Vaughan, Ontario has built a wine empire despite its limited advertising budget. While its products have won hundreds of industry awards, Magnotta's wine can only be bought at its five Ontario stores. The company succeeds by getting the most out of every customer who visits. For example, customers are offered tours of the winery. Customers of its Festa Juice Co. are given demonstrations on how to make their own wine. Magnotta also sends out 200 000 newsletters several times a year. The goal here is to convey an image of "real people" business owners who are sincerely interested in their customers and are eager to share their experiences in building the company.

Just Kid'n Children's Wear Ltd. of Langley, British Columbia, has built up a database of over 100 000 customers. Its goal is to establish a one-on-one relationship with each customer, who will feel good about his or her purchase and want to come back again. The information base allows store managers to identify the top twenty customers at each store, to whom they send out handwritten thank you cards with a 10% discount coupon. They also send out birthday cards to their customers' kids, offering a chance to win a free birthday party.

1. Customer retention and building loyal customer relationships is critical. In most cases, simply having the best product is not enough to bring people back. Suppose you were a marketing manager for ABC Inc. First, review the above examples to find a few customer relationship or positioning strategies. Then do some primary research: visit some local businesses, or do a brainstorm. What suggestions would you offer to help the company maintain and build strong customer relationships?

Source: Adapted from Al Ries and Jack Trout, *Positioning: The Battle for Your Mind* (New York: Warner Books, 1987); Rick Spence, *Secrets of Success From Canada's Fastest Growing Companies* (Toronto: John Wiley & Sons, 1997), 78-79, 88-89; http://www.magnotta.com.

potential new customers and keep in touch with them on an ongoing basis.

Information technologies, such as computers, databases, and spreadsheets, help make effective relationship marketing possible. Marketers can maintain databases on current customers' tastes, price ranges, and lifestyles, and can obtain names and other information about good prospects quickly. Spreadsheets allow marketers to answer "what if" questions related to prices and marketing performance.

Service industries, including retailers and airlines, have been in the forefront of relationship marketing since their staffs often meet customers personally. Sears, for instance, builds loyalty and repeat business through its Best Customer plan. "Best customers" are those who come to Sears at least six times a year, spend a large amount there annually, and shop in a variety of departments. According to Al Malony, senior marketing manager for customer marketing, there are 7.2 million best customers, each of whom is worth five to six times more to Sears than a new customer. The plan retains their patronage by offering benefits and privileges, such as guaranteed response to a service call within 24 hours. It has boosted Sears' retention rate by 11 percent and increased sales to the best-customer group by 9 percent.

Air France attempts to build an ongoing relationship with passengers who ride the Concorde several times a year by offering periodic gifts. While this target market may consist of only a few hundred people, they are responsible for $25 million to $30 million of the airline's annual revenues. It is important, of course, to tailor such gifts to the tastes of the market; as Mitch Kurz notes, "These are not the kind of people who are going to be looking for a coupon for $50 off their next $6000 trip." Instead, Air France offers more upscale freebies, such as videocassettes of French director Jean Cocteau's film *Beauty and the Beast.*

Business Term

√ **Relationship marketing**

The development and maintenance of long-term, cost-effective relationships with individual customers, suppliers, employees, and other partners for mutual benefit.

THE MARKETING ENVIRONMENT

RECALL FROM CHAPTER 2 that in selecting a target market and developing a marketing mix, marketers must consider the environmental forces described as

THEY SAID IT

"If I had my life to live over again, I would elect to be a trader of goods rather than a student of science. I think barter is a noble thing."

ALBERT EINSTEIN, physicist

competitive, political and legal, economic, technological, and social/cultural. As Figure 11.4 illustrates, these five external forces provide the framework for planning product, pricing, distribution, and promotion strategies aimed at the target market.

To some extent, all organizations are affected by the external forces in the marketing environment over which they have little or no control. For example, a change in an environmental law could affect some firms' products. Marketers must monitor these factors and assess the impact they will have on goods, services, and marketing practices, adjusting marketing strategies accordingly.

Figure 11.4 The Marketing Environment

Competitive Environment

Marketers must monitor the marketing activities of their competitors continually in order to devise a strategy that will give them a competitive edge. An old marketing tool that is becoming increasingly important again is the *satisfaction and price guarantee,* which many firms use to distinguish themselves from the competition. For example, one of Canada's most respected electronics retailers, Future Shop, has a "You Must Be Satisfied" policy with an "Absolute Lowest Price Guarantee." They promise to "beat" any price advertised by another authorized dealer before and after the purchase.

Satisfaction and price guarantees are not the only ways to attract customers, however — especially in the highly competitive retail market. For years, The Bay has been well known for its "scratch and save days." Holt Renfrew and Co. Ltd. has been known to run special

events on Saturdays, inviting designers to "hold court" with shoppers. Some Rogers Videos stores are now open 24 hours a day and have a "watch bar" that allows customers to preview videos and surf the Internet.

Political and Legal Environment

Federal, provincial, and local governments pass laws that regulate many marketing activities, ranging from package labelling to product safety. These laws are designed to maintain a competitive environment and protect consumers. Marketers must be aware of them in order to comply with them, and noncompliance can result in fines, bad publicity, and even lawsuits. Sometimes external government regulations can have an unexpected positive impact on a business. For example, U.S. lobster marketers lost much of their export market to Japan when the United States increased the minimum size of a legally caught lobster to $3^{1}/_{4}$ inches from $3^{3}/_{16}$ inches (not including the claws). Canada kept the lower limit, one that matches a 1 lb. lobster. Japanese consumers prefer smaller lobsters, so Canadian exports were well received.

Economic Environment

Economic factors, such as inflation, unemployment, and business cycles, influence how much consumers are willing and able to spend as well as what they buy. Marketers' understanding of how economic factors influence consumer buying behaviour allows them to adjust their marketing-mix strategies. For example, during a recession, consumers are more apt to buy basic products with low

TECHNOLOGY

THE SIX MYTHS OF WEB MARKETING

Myth 1: The Web Makes It Easy for Customers to Find You
Truth 1: The Web makes it easy for people to find you *if* they're already looking for you.

→ It's a great way for your existing customers, suppliers, and investors to find you. If you publish your Web address in your print and media ads, people will remember it better than they remember 1-800 numbers.

→ It's also a great way for people to find you if they're looking for something very specific *and* your Web site has been designed to be found. But don't expect people "just looking" to find you —they won't. If you sell women's clothes or pizza or floral arrangements, the odds are very low that a customer is going to bother going to a search to find companies like

yours. Web addresses are like 1-800 numbers — fantastic for people who are already looking for you, but not a first point of contact with most customers.

Bottom Line: There is no foot traffic on the Web: people need to see your Web address somewhere else, and then decide to get in touch.

Myth 2: There's a Market of 40 Million People on the Web
Truth 2: Nobody knows how many people are really on the Web.

→ A senior designer may have eight Internet accounts — most surveys count that eight times, adding up to eight people.

→ More than 100 million people have phones in the U.S. So what? If you list yourself in the phone book, do you think 100 million people are going to pick up the phone and call your business? It doesn't work that way. A Web address is like a 1-800 number. Who your customers are and how they find

you has to do with how you market your business.

Bottom Line: Your market is the same market you had yesterday — the only difference with being on the Web is that now people can reach you through the Web.

Myth 3: The Web Is Fast
Truth 3: The Web is slow.

→ Very slow — about the speed of a fax machine. What's fast about the Web is how quickly you can change the information you make available.

→ The Web is also great for selective reading by your customer. Thus you can put a 300-page catalogue online, and if you have a well-organized site with good search capabilities, your customers can quickly select what they want without having to wade through all 300 pages.

Bottom Line: The Web is good for helping customers find specific items: not for browsing through a

---

prices. Marketers might respond by lowering prices and increasing promotional spending to stimulate demand. Different strategies apply during prosperous times, when consumers are willing to purchase higher-priced goods and services. Marketers then might consider raising prices, expanding distribution, and increasing product lines of these goods and services.

Technological Environment

Changes in technology have a significant impact on how marketers design, produce, price, distribute, and promote their goods and services. New technology can make a

product obsolete, and in today's economy, this can happen very quickly. For example, how many of you remember the slide rule? The gradual introduction of calculators has made this product virtually obsolete — with the exception of some engineering programs. How about DOS (disk operating system)? This operating system was standard for IBM and related desktop computers up to the mid-1990s. Then came Microsoft Windows™ 95 and 97. How many of you use the DOS system now? Almost overnight, DOS began looking for a home in the public archives. In the last chapter, we talked about the new "black box" network computer. Could this new technology and the information highway make the standard desktop with its hard drive obsolete? Bill Gates of Microsoft doesn't think so, but in

whole catalogue when they're not sure what they want.

Myth 4: The Web Is Visual
Truth 4: Most of the Web is text — served up on 3 x 5 cards — with small windows that aren't that easy to read.

→ Get ready to learn a whole new set of design techniques for a medium that gives you all the space you need — carved up into little tiny pieces.

→ Designing artwork for the Web is like designing for television — you have no idea what kind of receiver your viewers have. Graphics designers can talk all they want to about the Web as a visual medium, but it's visual in the way that television is visual, not books and magazines.

Bottom Line: Your most effective visual marketing on the Web is going to done the same way as television ads: with techniques that look good for most people, and allow for individual display variations.

Myth 5: Netscape Is 80 percent of the Web
Truth 5: There are a lot of ways of counting, and none of them are very accurate. The real question is what does *your audience* use?

→ How many people do you want to turn away just because they have last year's computer? Technologists like to ooh and ah over the "wonderful new features" that Netscape or Microsoft or the next big Brand Name Browser brings to the Web. You need to remind them that your target audience may not be the kind of people who buy a new computer system every six months.

Bottom Line: The Web is a broadcast medium, like television or radio. You don't control what kind of display your viewers have. If you design a site that requires the latest and greatest technology to view it, you're going to lose some customers. How many? That depends on your target market.

Myth 6: Designing a Great Web Site Is a Technology Issue
Truth 6: Designing a great Web site is a communications issue: what do you want to say, and who do you want to say it to?

→ Design your message on the Web so that it's simple, it's easy to update, and it creates good communications between you and your customer. Then you're going to find that the Web, with its instant update, easy-to-remember addresses, and reader-controlled selection is even better than a fax.

Bottom Line: The medium may be new, but the message is still the same. You already know your market. The Web is just one more way for your customers to reach you. Treat the Web like a faxback or voice-mail system and let the technologists get the system up and keep it running, but don't give up control of the design.

1981 he thought a computer with 640 K of memory was all he would ever need.

GOOD, BAD, OR UGLY?

The world's largest retailer just announced a massive expansion of its online store. By this time next year, Wal-Mart will be selling more products in cyberspace than it stocks in its physical stores. Along the way, it may kill mom-and-pop stores the way it killed so many mom-and-pop retailers in the real world.

Social and Cultural Environment

In the mid-1990s, Frank and Mary Bouchard formed a company called Personal Weddings. The business was located in a small French community in northern Manitoba. Their home-based business offered five different religious and two secular ceremonies. A few years earlier, a company offering this kind of service would not have been given much of a chance for success. However, given the changes in the socio-cultural fabric of Canada, Personal Weddings may now be quite viable. Consumer and societal values change, and marketers must keep abreast of these kinds of changes to ensure that their marketing strategies are effective.[12]

Concord Pacific Development Corporation, a Vancouver condominium builder, takes a new approach in its advertising by targeting the city's fast-growing Chinese community.

We also want to note that many marketers recognize societal differences between countries, but assume that a homogeneous social environment exists domestically. Nothing could be further from the truth — especially in Canada! We are a mixed society composed of varied sub-markets. Obvious examples are the Quebec and Western Canada market segments. These segments have enough distinctive characteristics that separate marketing programs are often developed for them.

Marketing Products Abroad: Standardization versus Adaptation

Marketing a good or service overseas means choosing between *standardization* — selling the same product to every market — and *adaptation* — modifying products to fit each market.

The advantages of standardization include better marketing performance and lower costs. This approach seems to work best with business goods, such as steel, chemicals, and farm equipment, which tend to be less dependent on each nation's culture. Adaptation, on the other hand, lets companies adapt more effectively to local competition, consumer behaviour patterns, and government regulations. Consumer goods generally require product adaptation because they tend to be more culture-dependent than business products.

> ### THEY SAID IT
>
> "Fifty percent of Japanese companies do not have a marketing department, and 90 percent have no special section for marketing research. The reason is that everyone is considered to be a marketing specialist."
>
> HIROYUKI TAKEUCHI, educator and business writer

Increasingly, companies are even trying to build adaptability into standardized goods and services. In France, you can have a beer with your Burger King Whopper. In Holland, Heineken beer sells at about the same price as mineral water and soft drinks; however, in North America, Heineken has determined that its overseas target market will pay a premium price for the product.[13]

CONSUMER BEHAVIOUR

CONSUMER BEHAVIOUR *consists of actions that are involved directly in obtaining, consuming, and disposing of products, including the decision processes that precede and follow these actions.*[14] This definition includes both consumers and business purchasers. By studying consumer behaviour, marketers can identify consumers' attitudes toward products and how they use the items. This, in turn, helps marketers develop more effective marketing strategies for reaching these people.

Frito-Lay conducts extensive market research to see what people want in a potato chip. The company also studies how, when, and why people eat chips. Sixty-five percent of all chips, the company has found, are eaten in private. "When one is alone on a Friday night, potato chips confer some of the merriment and excitement of snacks eaten previously at a party or other fun event," suggests one psychologist.[15] The company also found that a typical adult eats about 72 potato chips (113 g) in one sitting. Frito-Lay discovered this by renting theatres and offering thousands of moviegoers free tickets and unmarked bags of chips. The company collected the bags when people left and counted the uneaten chips. The result? People apparently felt a bit guilty about eating such an openly unhealthy snack. The tests showed that consumers eat about one-third more chips at a sitting than they admit to in interviews.[16]

Both personal and interpersonal factors influence consumer behaviour. The personal influences on consumer behaviour include people's needs and motives, perceptions, attitudes, learned experiences, and self-concepts. Marketers frequently use psychological techniques to understand what motivates people to buy

> **Business Term**
> √ **Consumer behaviour**
> Actions that are involved directly in obtaining, consuming, and disposing of products, including the decision processes that precede and follow these actions.

WHERE

The Jobs Are

Lise Watier, President,
Lise Watier Cosmetics Inc.,
Montreal, Quebec

What Women Want

"This industry is my destiny and my passion. Women will be buying more cosmetics — make-up, skin care, scents, and body moisturizers — because looking healthy and staying young is more important than ever in our society. It relates to your self-esteem and self-respect, and in a competitive career environment it also plays a role.

The technology today is extraordinary. I have a machine in my office that I use to measure my skin's moisture level every day. I can monitor a cream's performance myself. There are new discoveries every day. We're mixing herbs and natural remedies with biotech, in what is known as biocosmetology."

products and to study consumers' emotional reactions to goods and services. Frito-Lay researchers, for example, show consumers photographs of people in various situations, and ask whether these people are likely to eat potato chips. Some answers: construction workers and people with umbrellas are unlikely to eat chips, while someone playing softball is slightly more likely to eat them. Most likely of all is a person watching television. From such responses, Frito-Lay assembles videotapes depicting "typical" consumers of various Frito-Lay products. A muncher of Lay's potato chips is "affectionate, irresistible, casual, and a fun member of the family." The videos are then shown to copywriters who prepare ads for the company's different product lines.[17]

The interpersonal determinants of consumer behaviour include cultural influences, social influences, and family influences. Such factors often will vary in different countries — even countries that speak the same language, such as Canada and Great Britain.

In its North American ads, Pet Inc. brags that its Old El Paso taco shells are less likely to break apart than those of the competition. In Britain, such claims are meaning-

Featuring beautiful models and using a bit of humour, Baked Lay's, a Frito-Lay product, is promoted as a low-fat snack to people who may be diet-conscious.

less, for a very simple reason: most Britons don't know what a taco is. Indeed, all "finger foods" are much less common in Europe. During Pet's market-research interviews, many Brits asked for a knife and fork prior to eating a taco. Pet's British ads now explain what tacos are and how to make — and eat — them. Today, Old El Paso is a market leader in the British taco market.

Purchasers of business products face a variety of organizational influences as well as their own personal preferences, since many people can play a role in a business purchase. A design engineer may be instrumental in setting the specifications that potential vendors must satisfy. A purchasing manager invites selected companies to bid on the purchase. A production supervisor is responsible for evaluating the operational aspects of the proposals that are received, and the vice president of manufacturing may make the final decision.

> **Business Term**
> ✓ **Marketing research**
> The information function that ties the marketer to the marketplace.

MARKETING RESEARCH

MARKETING RESEARCH *is the information function that ties the marketer to the marketplace.* It provides the information about potential target markets that is necessary to design effective marketing mixes.

Marketers conduct research for five basic reasons:

1. To identify marketing problems and opportunities

2. To analyze competitors' strategies

3. To evaluate and predict consumer behaviour

4. To gauge the performance of existing products and package designs and assess the potential of new ones

5. To develop price, promotion, and distribution plans

Marketing research involves more than just collecting information. Researchers also must decide how to collect the information, interpret the results, and communicate the interpretation to managers for their use in decision making.

Marketing research started in a humorous way. In the early 1900s, Charles C. Parlin was trying to sell advertising space in the *Saturday Evening Post* to the Campbell Soup Company. But the soup company resisted, saying that its product was sold to upscale consumers who paid a pricey 10 cents per can. The *Saturday Evening Post*, by contrast, was viewed as being sold to a working-class audience.

Parlin eventually overcame Campbell Soup's sales resistance by counting empty soup cans in the garbage from different neighbourhoods. He soon found that more soup cans came from working-class neighbourhoods than from wealthier areas. Parlin reasoned that well-to-do people had servants who made soup from scratch. Campbell Soup soon became an advertiser in the *Saturday Evening Post*, and Parlin became the head of the first marketing research department established in the United States.

DID YOU KNOW?

Here's a surprise! According to a 1995 report done by Pollara (formerly called Insight Canada), for the Canadian Imperial Bank of Commerce, 81 percent of small businesses are satisfied with their current bank. Among the dissenters, poor customer service and line-ups, of course, topped the list of complaints at 6 percent.

Obtaining Marketing Research Data

Marketing researchers are concerned with both internal and external data. *Internal data* are generated within the organization. A tremendous amount of useful information is available from financial records, such as changes in accounts receivable, inventory levels, customers, product lines, profitability of particular divisions, or comparisons of sales by territories, salespeople, customers, or product lines.

External data are generated outside the firm and can be obtained from previously published data. Trade associations, for example, publish reports on activities in particular industries. Advertising agencies collect information on the audiences reached by various media. National marketing research firms such as Loyalty Management Group Inc. of Toronto and Compusearch maintain large databases and offer information to organizations on a subscription or contract basis.

Federal, provincial, and local government publications are one of the marketing researcher's most important data sources. The federal government, in particular, maintains a wealth of external marketing data. Much of the federal information is available from its Internet site: http://strategis.ic.gc.ca.[18]

• **Canadian Company Capabilities.** This database includes over 25 000 Canadian company profiles, allowing businesses to search for a firm by product, geographical location, or activity. Businesses can also register their own company and promote their own products or services worldwide, and thus begin to market their company in cyberspace.

• **Trade Data Online.** This source provides reports and graphs on 6000 imports and exports to over 200 countries as well as five-year trends.

• **International Business Information Network.** Here you can obtain contacts, country information, and trade fair venues from around the world.

• **dISTcovery.** Provided are over 35 000 worldwide technologies that can be licensed and are ready for use.

• **Statistical Industry Overviews.** This information source allows a business to compare its company to the average company in its industry sector in areas such as revenues, costs, and so on.

• **CONTACT! — The Canadian Management Network.** This is a source of Canadian contacts for business management advice, skills development, software tools, services, and useful management publications. CONTACT! also hosts online forums where businesspeople and experts can get together electronically to discuss topics of mutual interest.

Statistics Canada is also a valuable federal government source of economic, social, and demographic information. The most frequently used Statistics Canada data source is the Census, which provides statistics on population characteristics such as age, sex, education levels, household size and composition, occupation, employment status, and income. Such information helps marketers to assess the buying behaviour of certain segments of the population, anticipate changes in their markets, and identify markets with growth potential. Data and analyses are provided in a number of different formats: print publications, computer tapes, printouts, diskettes, CD-ROMs, microfilm and microfiche, as well as through an Internet site: http://www.statcan.ca.

In addition to using published data, marketing researchers gather information by conducting observational studies and surveys. In *observational studies*, researchers actually observe the actions of the respondents, either directly or through mechanical devices. For example, traffic counts can be used to determine the best location for a new fast-food restaurant. *People meters* — electronic remote-control devices that record the viewing habits of each household member — are used to check television audience viewership, thereby setting advertising rates.

Some information cannot be obtained through simple observation. When information is needed about attitudes, opinions, and motives, researchers must ask questions by conducting a *survey*. Survey methods include telephone interviews, mail surveys, personal interviews, and focus groups. In a *focus group interview*, eight to twelve people are brought together in one location to discuss the subject being researched. Ideas generated during focus group interviews are especially helpful to marketers in developing new products, improving existing products, and creating effective advertising campaigns.

> **Business Term**
>
> √ **Customer segmentation**
>
> The process of grouping customer data into segments that reflect the goals of the organization.

Database Marketing

The information collected by researchers is valuable only when it can be used to make decisions within the framework of the organization's strategic plan. The more accurate the information collected by researchers, the more effective are the marketing strategies that result. For example, Nissan Canada Inc. maintains an extensive database of information on about 600 000 Nissan owners. From an analysis of this database, the company contacted a select number of Maxima owners and invited them to a special evening to meet and test-drive new models. The result: an astounding 33 percent of the invited guests purchased new cars.[19] As we learned in the last chapter, the Royal Bank experienced up to a 60 percent response rate from its targeted audience in a direct mail program. Highly effective response rates such as these can be attributed to new advances in **database marketing:** *the process of organizing potential customers into groups with similar buying habits and focussing on their needs relative to the organization's business objectives.*

> **Business Term**
>
> √ **Database marketing**
>
> The process of organizing potential customers into groups with similar buying habits and focussing on their needs relative to the organization's business objectives.

One of the main goals of database marketing is relationship marketing, which we discussed earlier in this chapter and will discuss further in Chapter 13. For example, from its database, Nissan knew who its target customers were and their corresponding automotive needs. Nissan created a special relationship when these specific owners were then invited to a unique salon-type evening

staged specifically to satisfy the needs of this target market niche. Relationship marketing is also a key issue for marketing on the Internet. A critical business challenge in Internet marketing is the determination of customer needs through electronic conversation and relationship building, and then being able to satisfy these needs by adding value to the product or service.

According to Dan Legault of the Toronto-based Terren Corp., two effective approaches to database marketing are customer segmentation and activity-based marketing.[20] **Customer segmentation** *is the process of grouping customer data into segments that reflect the goals of the organization*. This kind of data segmentation is exemplified by the Nissan and Royal Bank cases above in which customers were grouped into well-defined categories based on their buying behaviours. **Activity-based marketing** *is the process of tracking individual customer purchases and triggering a response based on this purchase information.*

Canada Post's Addressed Admail™ is a service that provides businesses with a database of information that can help them better define their market.

For example, as we noted in the last chapter, Loyalty Management Group Inc. of Toronto maintains a large database collected from the popular Air Miles membership cards. The spending patterns collected from Air Miles cardholders was the trigger that helped Shell Canada decide where to phase out full-service gas pumps in Western Canada.[21]

MARKET SEGMENTATION

MARKET SEGMENTATION *is the process of dividing the total market into several relatively homogeneous groups.* Both profit-oriented and not-for-profit organizations use market segmentation to help define their target markets.

Figure 11.5 shows that markets can be segmented on a variety of bases. Consumer marketers may divide markets according to demographic characteristics, such as sex, age, and family life-cycle stage; geographic factors; psychographic variables, which involve behavioural and lifestyle profiles; and product-related variables, such as the benefits that consumers seek when buying a product

or the degree of brand loyalty they feel toward it. Business marketers segment markets according to three major criteria: geographic characteristics, customer-based specifications for products, and end-use applications, or the precise way in which the business purchaser will use the product.

Segmentation strategies are important worldwide. In Europe, for instance, Volvo used psychographic research as the basis for developing a small, sporty-style coupe for career women. In Holland, an Amsterdam retailer has taken a product-related approach to segmentation. Witte Tanden-Winkel (translated "White Tooth Shop") sells only dental products like toothbrushes and floss.

It is worth noting that in the past several years, mainstream companies have begun marketing directly to gays and lesbians. Recent print ad campaigns by Benetton, American Express, and Metropolitan Life use same-sex couples, and viewers in some television markets saw two men picking out home furnishings together in an IKEA commercial.

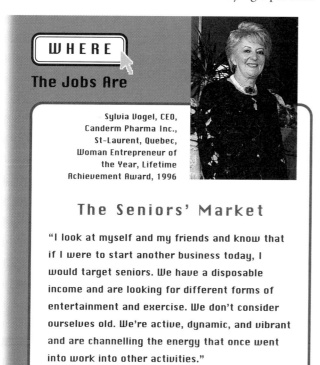

WHERE

The Jobs Are

Sylvia Vogel, CEO, Canderm Pharma Inc., St-Laurent, Quebec, Woman Entrepreneur of the Year, Lifetime Achievement Award, 1996

The Seniors' Market

"I look at myself and my friends and know that if I were to start another business today, I would target seniors. We have a disposable income and are looking for different forms of entertainment and exercise. We don't consider ourselves old. We're active, dynamic, and vibrant and are channelling the energy that once went into work into other activities."

Figure 11.5 Alternative Methods of Segmenting Consumer and Business Markets

Consumer Markets

Demographic   Geographic

Product-Related   Psychographic

Business Markets

Geographic   Customer-Based

End Use

SUMMARY OF LEARNING OUTCOMES

1. **Discuss how marketing's role in the exchange process creates utility.**

    Exchange is the process by which two or more parties give something of value to one another to satisfy felt needs. Marketing is closely linked with the exchange process. It creates utility — the want-satisfying power of a product or service — by having the product or service available when and where the consumer wants to buy it and by arranging for an orderly transfer of ownership. While production creates form utility, marketing creates time, place, and ownership utility.

2. **List the major functions of marketing.**

    The eight basic functions of marketing are buying, selling, transporting, storing, standardization and grading, financing, risk taking, and providing market information.

3. **Explain the importance of the marketing concept and customer satisfaction in achieving success in the marketplace.**

    In the marketing function, the marketing concept — adopting a consumer orientation in order to achieve long-term success — is an important expression of quality. Customer satisfaction — the ability of a good or service to meet or exceed buyer needs and expectations — is the true measure of quality. Customer satisfaction directly affects a company's profitability. It is crucial to an organization's continued existence, since a company that fails to provide the same level of customer satisfaction as its competitors will not stay in business for long.

4. **Outline methods for obtaining customer feedback and measuring customer satisfaction.**

    Companies can obtain customer feedback in many ways, including monitoring complaints, monitoring feedback from warranties and from toll-free phone service lines, visiting clients, calling them, sending out written surveys, or hiring "mystery shoppers." To measure customer satisfaction, a firm may initiate a customer satisfaction measurement (CSM) program. CSM programs involve determining what areas are most critical to the business and what measurement systems are currently being used, probing a representative group of customers, conducting research to determine the company's performance, and analyzing results to develop action plans.

5. **Outline how a marketing strategy is developed.**

    All organizations, whether profit-oriented or not-for-profit, need to develop a marketing strategy to reach customers effectively. This involves analyzing the market, selecting a target market, and developing a marketing mix. Often a company will develop a marketing plan that expresses the firm's marketing strategy.

6. **Explain the concept of a market.**

    A market consists of people with purchasing power and the ability and authority to buy. Markets can be classified by the types of products they handle. Consumer products are those goods and services purchased by the ultimate consumer for his or her own use. Business products (also known as organizational or industrial products) are those purchased to be used, directly or indirectly, in the production of other products for resale.

7. **Explain the concept of relationship marketing.**

    An important trend in marketing centres on the concept of relationship marketing — an organization's attempt to develop long-term, cost-effective links with individual customers for mutual benefit. Good relationships with customers can be a vital strategic weapon for a firm. By identifying current purchasers and maintaining a positive relationship with them, organizations can target their best customers more efficiently. Information technologies, such as computers, databases, and spreadsheets, help make effective relationship marketing possible.

8. **Identify the major components of the marketing environment.**

    The major components of the marketing environment are the competitive, political and legal, economic, technological, and social/cultural environments.

9. **Discuss why the study of consumer behaviour is important to marketing.**

Consumer behaviour consists of actions that are involved directly in obtaining, consuming, and disposing of products, including the decision processes that precede and follow these actions. This definition includes both consumers and business purchasers. By studying consumer behaviour, marketers can identify consumers' attitudes toward products and how they use the items. This in turn helps marketers develop more effective marketing strategies for reaching these people.

10. **Describe the marketing research function.**

Marketing research is the information function that ties the marketer to the marketplace. It provides the information about potential target markets that is necessary to design effective marketing mixes. Marketers conduct research for five basic reasons:
1. To identify marketing problems and opportunities
2. To analyze competitors' strategies
3. To evaluate and predict consumer behaviour
4. To gauge the performance of existing products and package designs and assess the potential of new ones
5. To develop price, promotion, and distribution plans

Research involves more than just collecting information; researchers must also decide how to collect the information, interpret the results, and communicate the results.

11. **Explain database marketing and the concept of market segmentation.**

An important function of the marketing manager's job is database marketing — the process of organizing potential customers into groups with similar buying habits and focussing on their needs relative to the organization's business objectives. There are a number of alternative methods of segmenting or dividing up consumer and business markets. Consumer marketers may divide markets according to demographic characteristics, such as sex, age, and family life-cycle stage; geographic factors; psychographic variables, which involve behavioural and lifestyle profiles; and product-related variables, such as the benefits that consumers seek when buying a product or the degree of brand loyalty they feel toward it. Business marketers segment markets according to three criteria: geographic characteristics, customer-based specifications for products, and end-use applications, or the precise way in which the business purchaser will use the product.

Key Terms Quiz

added value
business products
consumer behaviour
consumer products
cause marketing
marketing concept

relationship marketing
event marketing
exchange
market segmentation
marketing
market

marketing mix
target market
marketing research
organization marketing
place marketing
person marketing

_____ 1. The planning and executing of the conception, pricing, promotion, and distribution of ideas, goods, and services in order to create exchanges that satisfy individual and organizational objectives.

_____ 2. Refers to the process by which two or more parties give something of value to one another to satisfy felt needs.

_____ 3. Consumer orientation designed to achieve long-run success.

_____ 4. The increased worth of a good or service resulting from better-than-expected performance.

_____ 5. Refers to marketing efforts designed to attract the attention, interest, and preference of a target market toward a specific person, such as a political candidate.

_____ 6. Refers to marketing efforts designed to attract people to a particular geographic area.

_____ 7. Refers to marketing efforts designed to promote a cause or social issue.

_____ 8. The marketing of sporting, cultural, and charitable activities to selected target markets.

_____ 9. Refers to the marketing efforts designed to influence others to accept the goals of, receive the services of, or contribute in some way to an organization.

_____ 10. Refers to people with purchasing power and the ability and authority to buy.

_____ 11. Goods and services purchased by the ultimate consumer for his or her own use.

_____ 12. Items purchased to be used directly or indirectly in the production of other goods for resale.

_____ 13. A group of consumers toward which a firm decides to direct its marketing efforts.

_____ 14. Refers to the combination of a firm's product, pricing, distribution, and promotional strategies focussed on selected consumer segments.

_____ 15. Consists of actions that are involved directly in obtaining, consuming, and disposing of products, including the decision processes that precede and follow these actions.

_____ 16. The information function that links the marketer to the marketplace.

_____ 17. Refers to the process of dividing the total market into several relatively homogeneous groups.

_____ 18. An organization's attempt to develop long-term, cost-effective links with individual customers for mutual benefit.

Other Important Terms

activity-based marketing	focus group interview	people meters
customer satisfaction measurement (CSM) program	internal data	place utility
	mystery shopper	survey
database marketing	observational studies	time utility
external data	ownership utility	

Review Questions

1. What type of utility is created by the following?
   a. FedEx shipment of a fast-selling fad item
   b. A corner store
   c. The finishing department of a furniture factory
   d. A company that handles the details of a property transfer

2. List various examples of marketers who are performing each of the eight basic functions of marketing. What, if anything, does this list suggest?

3. Explain the relationship between customer satisfaction and profitability.

4. How successfully do you think the following organizations have adopted the marketing concept?
   a. IBM Canada
   b. The university or college you are attending
   c. Esso
   d. Bell Canada

5. Explain the role of customer feedback in achieving customer satisfaction. What are the primary methods of securing such feedback?

6. Identify the likely target markets of each of the following:
   a. Vancouver Canucks
   b. Midas Muffler
   c. ChemLawn
   d. NordicTrack
   e. Infiniti

7. Find a company that is selling on the Internet. What is it doing right? Wrong?

8. What is meant by a *market*? Distinguish between consumer and business markets.

9. Distinguish between internal and external data.

10. Match the segmentation variables below with the following four bases of consumer market segmentation: (1) geographic segmentation, (2) demographic segmentation, (3) psychographic segmentation, and (4) product-related segmentation.
    a. Lifestyle
    b. Sex
    c. Urban/suburban/rural
    d. Cholesterol-free products

11. List the pros and cons of marketing on the Internet.

Discussion Questions

1. Describe a situation in which you, as a customer, were not satisfied with either a good or a service. How did this experience affect your feelings toward the company? What advice would you give to that company?

2. While Cadillacs are more popular with consumers who are over 50 years of age, younger car buyers feel the vehicle is not sporty enough for them. They are more likely to buy luxury cars, such as the Lexus or BMW. This fact concerns managers at General Motors, who want to reposition their upscale cars to appeal to younger consumers as well. Suppose that you are the marketing manager in charge of developing a plan to achieve this goal. What strategy do you think would be most effective for reaching this market segment? Why?

3. The chapter notes that all organizations, whether profit-oriented or not-for-profit, must serve consumer needs if they are to succeed, and that marketing is an important determinant of a nation's overall standard of living. Do you feel that more university and college students should be encouraged to take marketing classes? Would offering marketing courses at the secondary-school level help? Explain your answer.

4. As we learned in Chapter 2, members of the baby boom generation are a popular target market because there are so many of them. Ten years from now, the consumers in this sizable segment of the Canadian population will be in their fifties and early sixties. Discuss how this demographic trend could affect specific goods and services, such as fast-food restaurants, cosmetics, travel, and soft drinks. What other goods and services would you expect to be affected, and how? Explain your answer.

5. ABC International is an interactive video shopping service that lets consumers call to place telephone orders for roughly 250 000 products. Unlike most home shopping services, ABC customers can comparison shop, via interactive video on their TV screens, for numerous models of the same item and compare prices against those of competitors. Manufacturers ship purchases directly to buyers. "This will go far beyond the Home Shopping Channel, since customers can call up and compare thousands of products," predicts an ABC executive. "The power of television is about to transform retailing forever." Relate ABC's new venture to the chapter's discussion of utility. What type(s) of utility are being created?

Answers to Key Terms Quiz

1. marketing 2. exchange 3. marketing concept 4. added value 5. person marketing 6. place marketing 7. cause marketing 8. event marketing 9. organization marketing 10. market 11. consumer products 12. business products 13. target market 14. marketing mix 15. consumer behaviour 16. marketing research 17. market segmentation 18. relationship marketing

Notes

1. Adapted from Janet McFarland, "Internet Gives Small Firm a Big Reach," *The Globe and Mail*, September 16, 1996, B3.

2. See, for example, Wendy Cukier, "More Anecdotes than Orders from This Web Site," *The Globe and Mail*, April 16, 1996, C9.

3. For further results on the Tikkanen-Bradley Consulting Group's survey, see Geoffrey Rowan, "Internet Not Such a Big Hit for Some Companies: Survey," *The Globe and Mail*, January 22, 1997, B4.

4. Matthew Ingram, "A Cyber Shopper's Guide," *The Globe and Mail*, March 2, 1996, B22.

5. M. Dale Beckman, David L. Kurtz, and Louis E. Boone, *Foundations of Marketing*, 6th Cdn. ed. (Toronto: Dryden, 1997), 4.

6. "AMA Board Approves New Marketing Definition," *Marketing News*, March 1, 1985, 1.

7. Delta Hotels and Resorts, Advertising Supplement, "Re-inventing the Concierge," *The Globe and Mail*, Fall 1996, 1.

8. Faye Rice, "The New Rules of Superlative Service, " *Fortune*, Autumn/Winter 1993, 50–53.

9. "Winning and Dining the Whiners," *Sales & Marketing Management*, February 1993, 73–75.

10. David J. Rachman and Elaine Romano, *Modern Marketing* (Hinsdale, IL: The Dryden Press, 1980), 576; the delineation of person, idea, and organization marketing is proposed by Professors Rachman and Romano, cited in Beckman, Kurtz, and Boone, *Foundations of Marketing*, 429.

11. Adapted from Louis E. Boone and David L. Kurtz, *Contemporary Marketing Wired*, 9th ed. (Fort Worth, TX: The Dryden Press, 1997), 10–15.

12. Adapted from Beckman, Kurtz, and Boone, *Foundations of Marketing*, 26–28.

13. Art Weinstein, "A Primer for Global Marketers," *Marketing News*, June 20, 1994, 4.

14. James F. Engel, Roger D. Blackwell, and Paul W. Miniard, *Consumer Behavior*, 7th ed. (Fort Worth, TX: The Dryden Press, 1993), 4.

15. Robert Johnson, "In the Chips," *The Wall Street Journal*, March 22, 1991, B1–B2.

16. Ibid., B1.

17. Ibid., B2.

18. Industry Canada, *Your Guide to Government of Canada Services and Support for Small Businesses, 1996–1997*, 9–10. This publication and comments survey are available electronically on the World Wide Web at **http://strategis.ic.gc/ca.SSG/mi02983e.html**.

19. Deborah Wilson, "A Guest List with Purchasing Power," *The Globe and Mail*, December 17, 1996, C2.

20. Gordon Arnaut, "The Best Is Still to Come, Data Base Analyst Says," *The Globe and Mail*, December 17, 1996, C3.

21. Terrence Belford, "Air Mile Collectors Yield Wealth of Data," *The Globe and Mail*, December 17, 1996, C2.

Chapter 12

Creating and Producing World-Class Goods and Services

After studying this chapter, you should be able to

1. Explain why product development is important to a firm.
2. List the stages of new-product development.
3. Explain how products are identified.
4. Explain the strategic importance of production and operations management in an organization.
5. Compare mass production with newer production techniques.
6. Discuss how computers and related technologies are revolutionizing product development and production.
7. Outline the major factors involved in choosing plant locations.
8. Describe the major tasks of production and operations managers.
9. Explain the importance of inventory control and just-in-time systems.
10. Discuss the benefits of quality control.

GE's Flex Plan[1]

General Electric is best known for making light bulbs and kitchen appliances. But this industrial giant is likely to take its place in the corporate hall of fame not for its famous products but, instead, for its contribution to management concepts and applications. The company's ability to identify and improve upon good ideas and change or discard failures has enabled GE to prosper when other corporate giants were failing.

Take GE Appliances, for example. This division invested millions to redesign its production operations to achieve the quality levels of Japanese products. GE even instituted a "quality circle" program since workers' suggestions and informal meetings were supposedly driving quality in Japanese companies. As in many North American firms, the programs produced marginal results for General Electric, which found them too restrictive for its workers. In the early 1990s, GE replaced the program with a revised version called Work-Out, in which managers and workers met in a town hall setting. Workers were encouraged to offer radically new ideas regardless of cost. Managers then discussed the suggestions in the group setting.

Unlike quality circles, Work-Out more fully recognized individuals who contributed good ideas. One GE executive estimated that 90 percent of Work-Out ideas have been used. As a result of one suggestion, for example, GE Appliances began building wire racks for its refrigerators rather than buying them from an outside source.

Another Japanese concept that didn't work well for General Electric was the just-in-time system (JIT). Under JIT, inventory levels are minimized by having all suppliers deliver parts on an as-needed basis. This system works well in Japan, where suppliers' facilities are close to their customers. The Japanese invented the system to expose deficiencies in the manufacturing process. If production was kept error-free, inventories could be kept at a minimum.

Many North American companies, like General Electric, missed the point of JIT and concentrated on materials handling to reduce inventories. GE Appliances soon found that low inventory levels of needed parts — 75 suppliers stock 475 parts — prevented the company from filling customer orders on a timely basis. The company has now increased its inventory of some component parts by as much as 24 percent. GE can fill customer orders in 3.6 weeks, compared with a 1990 level of 18 weeks. Still, the company is striving to reduce that number to only three days. Not only is the factory more attuned to customer needs, the benefit of a faster delivery system more than offsets the cost of the higher inventory levels.

What lesson can be learned from General Electric Appliances' experiences? A very important one: what works in one culture may not work in another. However, if a system proved unsuccessful for GE, the company either modified it to specifically fit its needs or discarded it entirely. GE's success is due, in large part, to flexibility: its willingness to experiment, to change, and to adapt.

CHAPTER OVERVIEW

A PRODUCT, which is discussed in more detail in the next chapter, can be defined as *a bundle of physical, service, and symbolic attributes designed to satisfy consumer wants.* The creation of new products is the lifeblood of an organization. Products do not remain economically viable forever, so new ones must be developed to assure the survival of an organization. Each year, thousands of new products are introduced. For many firms, these new products account for a sizable part of sales and profits.

By developing and producing desired goods and services, businesses create utility. *Form utility* is created by converting raw materials and other inputs into finished goods or services. For example, fabric, thread, and zippers are converted into Levi's jeans. The firm's production function is responsible for creating form utility.

In this chapter we will describe the stages of new-product development and examine the strategic role of the production function. We will discuss the importance of product identification through brands and brand names. Finally, we will

look at quality control and new technologies that are revolutionizing the production of goods and services.

STAGES IN NEW-PRODUCT DEVELOPMENT

TODAY, NEW-PRODUCT development is vital. For example, market tests for Sega products show that speed and novelty are key to the company's business. Sega could not survive unless it was on the leading edge of product development. As a result, it creates over 60 new video games and CD-ROMs every year. The company generates ideas for many of its new products by extensive research into the teen and adult markets. Staffers conduct focus groups, visit homes, and even hang out with teens in malls.

Despite its necessity and importance, new-product development is expensive, time-consuming, and risky, since only about one-third of new products become success stories. Products can fail for many reasons: some are not properly developed

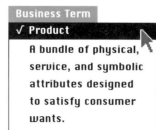

Business Term

✓ **Product**

A bundle of physical, service, and symbolic attributes designed to satisfy consumer wants.

FUTURE TREND

MANUFACTURING FUELS NEW ECONOMY

Annual Growth Rates, 1993–1997

Overall

GNP — 3%

Employment — 2%

Manufacturing

Value of shipment — 9%

Employment — 3%

Electrical/Electronics Industries

Value of shipment — 11%

Employment — 1%

In the 1998 *Profit* 100 survey, manufacturing represented the lion's share of Canada's fastest growing companies. Nearly half of Canada's 100 growth leaders produced goods ranging from bagless vacuum cleaners to Belgian-style beers. "It goes against what most people think about the new economy, but good old manufacturing is alive and well and driving a lot of growth in the Canadian economy," says Michael Fradette of Deloitte Touche Tohmatsu International (DTTI).

According to a DTTI study, Canada's new economy is driven by the manufacturing and telecommunications sectors, which had annual real growths of 6.6 percent and 5.4 percent respectively between 1992 and 1995. Much of this growth is attributed to manufacturers that have geared their operations to meet the needs of the knowledge-based, microchip-driven new economy.

Statistics Canada data also show manufacturing growth during the 1990s.

Between 1993 and 1997, manufacturing shipments grew at about 9 percent per year, and shipments in electrical and electronics products increased at about 11 percent per year. These double-digit growth rates compare with an annual growth for all industries of only 3 percent.

According to these data, high-tech manufacturing may be one of the growth engines to jump-start Canada into the next millennium. However, growth in dollar volume of manufacturing shipments has yet to translate into employment growth. Statistics Canada reports that between 1993 and 1997 employment in the electronics sector grew by only a little over 1 percent a year and in manufacturing by only 3 percent.

Source: Based on a 1996 report by Deloitte Touche Tohmatsu International in Konrad Yakabuski, "Manufacturing Fuels New Economy," *The Globe and Mail*, August 21, 1996, B4. Reprinted with permission from The Globe and Mail; Statistics Canada, http://www.statcan.ca/english/Pgdb/Economy/Manufa.htm.

---

and tested, some are poorly packaged, and others lack adequate promotional support or distribution, or fail because they do not satisfy a consumer need or want.

Most newly developed products today are aimed at satisfying specific customer demands. New-product development is becoming increasingly efficient and cost-effective because marketers use a systematic approach in developing new products.

The new-product development process has six stages (see Figure 12.1):

1. Generating new-product ideas

2. Screening

3. Business analysis

4. Product development

5. Test marketing

6. Commercialization

Each stage in the process requires a "go/no go" decision by management.

Figure 12.1 Stages in New-Product Development

Living up to its motto of "Pioneering New Frontiers™," Pioneer Electronic's new and innovative DVD/Laserdisc player, the DVL-700, is the first of its kind to be sold to consumers.

The starting point in the new-product development process is generating ideas for new offerings. Ideas come from many sources, including customers, suppliers, employees, research scientists, marketing research, inventors outside the firm, and competitive products. The most successful ideas are directly related to satisfying customer needs.

In the second stage, screening, ideas are eliminated if they do not mesh with overall company objectives or cannot be developed given the company's resources. Some firms hold open discussions of new-product ideas among representatives of different functional areas in the organization. In Japan, this cross-functional sharing of ideas within a firm is called *kaizen*.

During the business analysis phase, further screening is done. The analysis involves assessing the new product's potential sales, profits, growth rate, and competitive strengths, and whether it fits with the company's production, distribution, and promotional resources. *Concept testing* — marketing research designed to solicit initial consumer reaction to new product ideas before the products are developed — may be used at this stage. For

example, potential consumers might be asked about proposed brand names and other methods of product identification.

Next, an actual product is developed, subjected to a series of tests, and revised. Tests measure both the product's actual features and how consumers perceive it.

During the test marketing stage, the item actually is sold in a limited area while the company examines both the product and the marketing effort used to support it. Cities or television coverage areas that are typical of the targeted market segments are selected for such tests. Test market results can help managers determine the product's likely performance in a full-scale introduction. Some firms choose to skip test marketing, however, because of concerns that the test could reveal their product strategies to the competition.

COMPANY WATCH

Many successful Canadian firms are forming strategic partnerships and alliances rather than carrying out their own new-product development. Here are just two examples:

→ **N.M. Glegg Water Conditioning Inc. (Guelph, Ontario):** A $100-million firm, and a repeat winner of the <u>Financial Post</u>'s "50 Best Managed Private Companies Award" (1993 and 1996), Glegg uses strategic alliances to expand globally. Its most productive alliance has been with Asaki Glass Company in Japan, in which the two companies undertook a joint R&D program to develop a new EDI (electrodeionization, a new water purification technology) product. Glegg now has a much stronger product development team to compete in the $4-billion global market for pure water treatment equipment.

→ **SMART Technologies Inc. (Calgary, Alberta):** Another winner of the "50 Best Managed Private Companies Award," this $10-million firm partnered with giant semiconducter maker Intel to produce a touch-sensitive interactive electronic whiteboard. "We quickly realized that there were parts of the market that Intel was better at than we would ever be," said David Martin, president of SMART. Now the firm is planning to grow further with Picture Tel Corp., which owns about half the global market for video-conferencing systems.

In the final stage, commercialization, the product is made generally available in the marketplace. Sometimes this is referred to as a product launch. Considerable planning goes into this stage, since the firm's promotional, distribution, and pricing strategies must all be geared to support the new product offering.

PRODUCT IDENTIFICATION

AS NOTED EARLIER, product identification is an important aspect of developing a successful new product. Goods and services are identified by brands, brand names, and trademarks. A **brand** *is a name, term, sign, symbol, design, or some combination thereof used to identify the products of one firm and to differentiate them from competitive offerings.* Brands are important in developing a product's image. If consumers are aware of a particular brand, its appearance becomes advertising for the firm. Pepsi, Mountain Dew, and 7-Up are all soft drinks made by PepsiCo, but each brand possesses a unique combination of name, symbol, and package design that distinguishes it from the others. Successful branding is also a means of escaping some price competition, since well-known brands often sell at a considerable price premium over their competition.

> **Business Term**
> ✓ **Brand**
> A name, term, sign, symbol, design, or some combination thereof used to identify the products of one firm and to differentiate them from competitive offerings.

A **brand name** *is that part of the brand consisting of words or letters included in a name used to identify and distinguish the firm's offerings from those of competitors.* The brand name is the part of the brand that can be vocalized. Many brand names, such as McDonald's, American Express, and IBM, are famous around the world.

A **trademark** *is a brand that has been given legal protection.* The protection is granted solely to the brand's owner. Trademark protection includes not only the brand name but also logos, slogans, packaging elements, and product features such as colour and shape. A well-designed trademark can make a definite difference in how consumers perceive a brand.[2]

> **Business Term**
> ✓ **Brand name**
> That part of the brand consisting of words or letters included in a name used to identify and distinguish the firm's offerings from those of competitors.

> **Business Term**
> ✓ **Trademark**
> A brand that has been given legal protection.

Selecting an Effective Brand Name

Good brand names are easy to pronounce, recognize, and remember: Crest, VISA, and Avis, for example. Global firms face a real problem in selecting brand names, since an excellent brand name in one country may prove disastrous in another. Most languages have a short "a," so Coca-Cola is pronounceable almost anywhere. But an advertising campaign for E-Z washing machines failed in the United Kingdom because the British — and Canadians too, for that matter — pronounce "z" as "zed." Fingos, the brand name for General Mills' meant-to-be-eaten-manually cereal, works well in the United States because it sounds like a play on the English word "fingers." The name would be less successful in Hungarian, however, because it sounds like a common obscenity in that language.[3]

Brand names should give the right image to the buyer. Accutron suggests the quality of an accurate timepiece. Federal Express suggests a fast delivery service with a broad geographic reach. Sometimes, changes in the market's environment require changes to a brand name. Dep Corporation changed the brand name of Ayds diet candy to Diet Ayds because the company was concerned that the old name would remind consumers of AIDS.

Brand names also must be legally protectable. Trademark law specifies that brand names cannot contain words in

One of the most well-recognized names in Ontario and Quebec, Bell Canada's distinctive logo is easy to identify and is especially helpful to pay-phone users, who can spot a Bell phone booth from a distance.

general use, such as "television" or "automobile." Generic words — words that describe a type of product — cannot be used exclusively by any organization. On the other hand, if a brand name becomes so popular that it passes into common language and turns into a generic word, the company can no longer use it as a brand name. Once upon a time, aspirin and linoleum were exclusive brand names, but today they have become generic terms and are no longer legally protectable.

Brand Categories

A brand offered and promoted by a manufacturer is known as a **national brand**, or a manufacturer's brand. Examples are Tide, Jockey, and Gatorade. But not all

> **Business Term**
> ✓ **National brand**
> A brand offered and promoted by a manufacturer.

> **Business Term**
> ✓ **Private brand**
> A brand owned by a wholesaler or retailer.

brand names belong to manufacturers; some are the property of retailers or distributors. A **private brand** (often known as a house, distributor, or retailer label) identifies a product that is not linked to the manufacturer, but instead *is a brand owned by a wholesaler or retailer.* The Sears line of DieHard batteries and Canadian Tire's Mastercraft label are examples.

Many retailers offer a third option, **generic products**, which *are nonbranded items with plain packaging, minimal*

All of Kodak's products, from films to photocopiers, are identified by its family brand name.

labelling, little if any advertising, and that meet only minimum quality standards. Generic products sell at a considerable discount from manufacturers' and private brands. Many consumer goods are available as generic products, such as paper towels, toilet paper, breakfast cereal, and pasta.

Another branding decision marketers must make is whether to use a family branding strategy or an individual branding strategy. A **family brand** *is a single brand name used for several related products.* Kitchen-Aid, Johnson & Johnson, Xerox, and Dole use a family brand name for their entire line of products. When a firm using family branding introduces a new product, both customers and retailers recognize the familiar brand name. The promotion of individual prod-

> **Business Term**
> ✓ **Generic products**
> **Nonbranded items with plain packaging, minimal labelling, and little if any advertising, and that meet only minimum quality standards.**

> **Business Term**
> ✓ **Family brand**
> **A single brand name used for several related products.**

> **Business Term**
> ✓ **Individual branding**
> **Strategy of giving separate products within a line different brand names.**

ucts within a line benefits all the products because the family brand is well known.

Other firms use an **individual branding** strategy by *giving products within a line different brand names.* For example, Procter & Gamble has individual brand names for its different laundry detergents: Tide, Cheer, Dash, and Oxydol. Each brand targets a unique market segment. Consumers who want a cold-water detergent

Labatt's uses individual branding for its line of beers. Ice beer is targeted at the young adults market. Its award-winning package design, a combination of the '70s psychedelic and '90s techno, is meant to appeal to that market segment.

can buy Cheer rather than Tide or Oxydol instead of purchasing a competitor's brand. Individual branding builds competition within a firm and enables the company to increase overall sales.

Figure 12.2 The Production Process

INPUTS	CONVERSION PROCESS	OUTPUTS
• Resources	• Add value	• Goods
• Raw materials		• Services

STRATEGIC IMPORTANCE OF THE PRODUCTION FUNCTION

PRODUCTION *is the use of people and machinery to convert materials into finished goods or services.* Production is a broad term that includes manufacturing, nonmanufacturing, and service industries.

The task of **production and operations management** *is to manage the use of people and machinery in converting materials and resources into finished goods and services.* Services are intangible outputs of the production system and can include outputs as diverse as trash hauling, education, haircuts, and tax accounting. There are almost as many production systems as there are goods and services.

Like marketing, accounting, or human resource management, the production process is a vital business function. Indeed,

Business Term

√ **Production**

The use of people and machinery to convert materials into finished goods or services.

Business Term

√ **Production and operations management**

Managing the use of people and machinery in converting materials and resources into finished goods and services.

without production, none of the other functions would exist. Without a good or service, a company cannot create profits. Without profits, the firm will fail quickly. Yet, the production process is just as crucial in not-for-profit organizations, since it is the good or service that justifies the organization's existence.

In short, the production function adds value to a company's inputs by converting them into marketable outputs (see Table 12.1). This added value turns the outputs into something that customers are willing to pay for. Thus, production and operations management play an important strategic role. Effective management can lower the costs of production, boost the quality of products, and allow the firm to respond dependably to

Table 12.1 Typical Production Systems

Example	Primary Inputs	Transformation	Outputs
Pet-food factory	Grain, water, fish meal, personnel, tools, machines, paper bags, cans, buildings, utilities	Converts raw materials into finished products	Pet-food products
Trucking firm	Trucks, personnel, buildings, fuel, goods to be shipped, packaging supplies, truck parts, utilities	Packages and transports goods from sources to destinations	Delivered goods
Department store	Buildings, displays, shopping carts, machines, stock goods, personnel, supplies, utilities	Attracts customers, stores goods, sells products	Marketed goods
Automobile body shop	Damaged autos, paints, supplies, machines, tools, buildings, personnel, utilities	Transforms damaged auto bodies into facsimiles of the originals	Repaired automobile bodies
County sheriff's department	Supplies, personnel, equipment, automobiles, office furniture, buildings, utilities	Detects crimes, brings criminals to justice, keeps the peace	Acceptable crime rates and peaceful communities

THEY SAID IT

"Production is not the application of tools to materials, but logic to work."

PETER DRUCKER, business philosopher and author

THEY SAID IT

"You can have any colour of car you want as long as it is black."

HENRY FORD, inventor of the assembly line

customers' demands. It also can help companies stay flexible, so they can respond more quickly when customers' demands change.

THE WAY IT WAS — MASS PRODUCTION

THE ERA SPANNING from about 1918 to the 1980s was dominated by manufacturing and mass production.[4] As Table 12.2 illustrates, the world economy was transformed from a commodity into a mass-manufacturing economy. Companies that could feed their domestic consumers with standardized manufactured products would "dine with the upper classes." This era was personified by manufacturing industrialists like Henry Ford and oil baron Henry Rockefeller. A major factor in industrial domination is **mass production,** *the manufacture of products in large quantities through the effective combination of specialized labour, mechanization, and standardization.* Mass production makes large

> **Business Term**
> √ **Mass production**
> The manufacture of products in large quantities through the effective combination of specialized labour, mechanization, and standardization.

> **Business Term**
> √ **Assembly line**
> A manufacturing technique that involves placing the product on a conveyor belt that travels past a number of workstations where workers perform specialized tasks.

quantities of products available at lower prices than would be possible if these products were crafted individually.

Specialization involves dividing work into its simplest components so workers can concentrate on performing one task. Once jobs are separated into smaller tasks, managers can use *mechanization,* the use of machines to perform work, to increase workers' productivity. The third component of mass production, *standardization,* involves producing uniform, interchangeable goods and parts. Standardized parts make it easier to replace defective or worn-out components. If your car's windshield wipers wear out, for instance, you can buy replacement wipers at any auto supply store. Just think how long it would take — and how much more it would cost — if you had to have the replacements specially crafted!

A logical extension of the factors of specialization, mechanization, and standardization is the **assembly line,** *a manufacturing technique that involves placing the product on a conveyor belt that travels past a number of workstations where workers perform specialized tasks,* such as welding, painting, or installing a part.

Table 12.2 The Commodity Economy versus the Mass-Manufacturing Economy		
	THE WAY IT WAS **The Commodity Economy**	**THE WAY IT BECAME** **The Mass-Manufacturing Economy**
Era	Industrial Revolution to circa 1918	1918 to circa 1981
Key Factor	Cheap steel	Cheap energy, especially oil
Four Engines	Textiles, coal, steel, railroads	Autos, machine tools, housing, retailing
Infrastructure	Railroads, shipping, telegraph	Highways, airports, telephones
Leading Economic Indicators	Pig-iron, railroad operating income, inner tube production, coal and coke production, textile mill production, cotton consumption	Industrial production, capacity utilization, machine tool orders, retail sales, housing starts, auto sales

Case 1: Net.Vectoring

How do you get a cybersurfer to stop for your product? Enter net.Vectoring, an innovative technology that marries the telephone with the Internet. The system was developed by S&P Data Corp., a *Profit* 100 company, in alliance with several partners including Bell Canada and Northern Telecom.

Here's how it works. Net shoppers interested in a particular product on a Web site are asked to type in their phone number. Within 30 seconds they automatically get a follow-up call. If the line is busy, a "predictive dialer" will keep calling. Live telemarketers come on the line to help sell the product only when the phone is answered, decreasing labour costs and increasing the productivity of telemarketers by as much as 300 percent. The system increases potential sales and service by allowing companies — small or large — to stay in touch with the customer and sell on the Internet twenty-four hours a day.

Case 2: Co-operating Telcos

There are about 40 small, independent telelphone companies (telcos) in Canada, hundreds in the United States, and thousands around the world. Research and development are critical in the telecommunications industry, but the cost of developing, managing, and upgrading systems can be out of reach for smaller firms. So how can

THE TECHNOLOGY ECONOMY AND PRODUCTION

DURING THE mid-to-late 1980s, the world industrial economy underwent the most significant shift since the cataclysm of the Industrial Revolution. Almost overnight, Canada found itself firmly entrenched in a knowledge-based, technology-driven economy. The new reality of the new *technology* or *"highway" economy* was that our smokestack industries — such as autos, steel, petroleum, and housing — were no longer the growth engines. By the mid-1990s, the average Canadian interacted with more than ten computers a day — in cars,

appliances, entertainment, services like bank machines, and so on. By the next millennium, the average will be more than 1000 interactions per day.[5]

According to Nuala Beck in her insight-packed book *Shifting Gears,* our economy is driven by four engines: computers and semiconductors, the health and medical sector, communications and telecommunications, and instrumentation (see also Table 12.3).[6] Industrial winners in this new economy will be characterized by their technology, innovation, adaptability, customization, and customer focus. Mass-production technology has not been able to respond to this new "highway" reality. Here are three major reasons for this:

- **Change.** Mass-production companies depend on stable market conditions and focus on long production runs. The new economy is characterized by turbulence and change. Long production runs cannot respond to quickly changing consumer demands and market needs.

- **Effectiveness.** Mass-production companies have a tendency to focus on efficiency rather than effectiveness — that is, customer needs. Mass production, while highly efficient for making large numbers of similar products, is less effective in a customer-driven market that requires small batches of different items.

- **Specialization.** In mass production, the key is repetition. The new market requires customization. Specialization through repetitive tasking is not conducive to innovation and change.

Table 12.3 The Way It Is

	Technology Economy
Era	1981 to ???
Key Factor	Cheap chips (microchips)
Four Engines	Computers and semiconductors, health and medical, communications and telecommunications, instrumentation
Infrastructure	The Information highway — telecommunications, fibre optics, LANs and WANs, radio frequencies
Leading Economic Indicators	Computer production, electronic components production, instrumentation sales, high-tech trade balance, knowledge-intensive employment growth, medical starts

they compete with industry giants like Bell, Northern Telecom, and AT&T?

Four telcos in the Maritimes — NBTel, MT&T, Island Tel, and NewTel Communications — found one solution. They've teamed up (formed an alliance) and constructed an information technology "back room." New software and a single server replaced 25 assorted systems ranging from purchasing and inventory management to accounting and payroll. In the process, the four companies also put in place a co-ordinated system to deal with the Year 2000 problem. Jeffrey Read, VP of strategic

alliances and marketing for PeopleSoft Canada Ltd. (the company that installed the administrative system), says that centralizing the functions in communal systems such as this keep consumer prices down and could save each company between 15 to 40 percent a year.

The telcos also found other ways to share technology. For example, they have now adopted a co-operative system to share the same customer care and billing system.

1.   Using the two cases above and other examples provided in the

Technology Economy and Production section below, explain how innovative technology and strategic alliances can improve the competitive position of small and medium-sized firms. Supplement your answer with at least two examples from your local business community.

Source: Case 1: Adapted from Rick Spence, *Secrets of Success From Canada's Fastest Growing Companies* (Toronto: John Wiley & Sons, 1997), 124-25; Case 2: Adapted from Mary Gooderham, "Teaming Up Offers Telcos Rewards," *The Globe and Mail*, October 13, 1998, C2. Reprinted with permission from The Globe and Mail.

WHERE

The Jobs Are

Stephen Van Houten,
President, Alliance of
Manufacturers and
Exporters Canada, Toronto

Mass Customization

"In manufacturing, go after advanced-process technology, which is the products and manufacturing systems used for factory automation. The new robots have infinite variability of motion and action. Japan already has prototypes. They're not bolted to the floor with a limited range of axis and motion. The goal is to increase exponentially the flexibility of the factory, and this is an important step in the drive toward agile manufacturing or mass customization."

According to Beck, successful companies have realized that there are only three ways to grow in the new economy:[7]

1.   Be one of the four driving engines,

2.   Be one of their suppliers, or

3.   Use technology to revitalize an old industry.

The Gagnon brothers of Attraction Corp., for example, used Beck's third option. They used new technology to revitalize an old industry. From Lac-Drolet, Quebec, Attraction Corp. typifies the modern-day production facility. This family-owned business run by four brothers uses a Toyota sewing production system based on the principles of cellular manufacturing. That means specific products for individual clients, short turnaround times, and competitive prices. "We're used to cutting and doing runs as small as two dozen items. Toyota is a computer-driven, just-in-time system that means we cut, embroider, sew, pack, and ship about 10 000 pieces per week," says Gaetan Gagnon, the brother who is the firm's marketing director. Short production runs mean less efficiency than mass production, but Attraction's clients get a customized, made-to-order product.[8]

To be competitive, many Canadian firms are adopting new approaches, such as flexible production, customer-driven production, and the team concept. Mass production and new technologies are not mutually exclusive, however. Many firms have used new technology and production techniques, such as robotics, to improve their mass-production system.

Flexible Production

Many companies now recognize the advantages of flexible, so-called lean, production methods that require fewer workers and less inventory. Table 12.4 compares the traditional, mass-production approach with the newer, more flexible methods. While mass production is most efficient

Table 12.4 Flexible Production versus Mass Production

Flexible Production	Mass Production
Can be profitable making small batches of products.	Profitable only when making large batches.
The product and the process for making it are designed concurrently.	The process is designed after the product has been designed.
Lean inventory turns over fast.	Fat inventory turns over slowly.
Suppliers are helped, informed, and kept close.	Suppliers are kept at arm's length.
Engineers search widely for ideas and technology.	Engineers are insular, don't welcome outside ideas.
Employees learn several skills, work well in teams.	Employees are compartmentalized.
The company stresses continuous small improvements.	The company looks for the big breakthroughs.
The customers' orders pull the products through the factory.	The system pushes products through to the customers.

at making large batches of similar items, flexible production can be cost-effective with smaller batches, too. Flexible production methods also require new approaches to customers, inventory, design, and engineering.

Customer-Driven Production

With customer-driven production, customers' demands determine what retail stores stock and, in turn, what manufacturers make. Japanese firms have implemented this approach in many of their factories, with notable success. As we have seen in the last few chapters, many North American companies have followed suit — Wal-Mart and Proctor and Gamble, for example — and have already linked up their factories and retail distribution. But this new customer-driven era has not stopped here. The information superhighway and Internet technology now allow companies to connect directly to the customer 24 hours a day. Virtual corporations, such as Mbanx, now provide a direct link from the producer to the consumer.

Some experts argue that the advent of the virtual corporation is beginning to erode our traditional store-front retail distribution channels.

Team Concept

Today many production methods challenge the mass-production approach in which specialized workers perform repetitive tasks. This repetition can speed production and allows companies to hire low-skilled workers. Today, however, many companies are emphasizing knowledge and innovation. The team concept combines employees from various departments and functions — such as design, manufacturing, finance, and maintenance

CYBERSPACE

Purolator Courier Ltd. is betting that online commerce will explode into a multibillion-dollar business by the turn of the century. It's aiming for a central role in Canadian online retailing with the introduction in 1997 of pick-up service through its Toronto-based World Wide Web site (http://www.purolator.ca). Retailers, big or small, who want to sell their wares can also link their Web sites to Purolator's. The company says it is able to deliver products directly from manufacturers, eliminating the need for retailers to stock inventory.

COMPANY WATCH

Dream Cycles is a small retail operation selling motorcycle parts and accessories. Owner Frank Stachan keeps in close contact with his customers and found that many of them also wanted a repair service. In response, he took a lesson from the big boys and created a strategic alliance with his long-time friend Rob Ireland, owner of Milwaukee St. Motorcycle Service, a small motorcycle repair business. Some call this a strategic alliance. Frank Stachan and Rob Ireland call it working together — teamwork.

— to work together on designing and building products. The teams also may include people from outside the firm, such as suppliers and customers. This approach is sometimes called *concurrent engineering*, since engineering is done concurrently with design, production, and other functions.

Intelatech Inc. is a Canadian firm based in Mississauga, Ontario, that exemplifies the new breed of producer. Intelatech is a manufacturers' representative for electronic components that sells to such firms as Northern Telecom and Newbridge Networks. According to Michael Ruscigno, president and CEO of Intelatech, his company is successful because "People want faster, cheaper, and smaller. Our customers need to keep looking at their own design to make sure they don't fall behind the competitive curve. We get involved at the design stage and help them get the right product at the right price." To stay ahead, the firm has assembled an information action team consisting of employees from every business area. For example, this team has developed an in-house sales-force automation system that includes opportunity tracking, company profiling, contact management, and time management.[9]

TECHNOLOGY AND THE PRODUCTION PROCESS

LIKE OTHER BUSINESS functions, production has been greatly affected by computers and related technologies. In addition to making the production process more efficient, automation allows companies to redesign their current methods. Production can become more flexible, allowing companies to design and create new products faster, modify them more rapidly, and meet customers' changing needs more effectively. As shown in Table 12.5, important production technologies include robots, computer-aided design (CAD), computer-aided

Table 12.5 Important Production Technologies

Production Technology	Definition	Benefits
Robot	A reprogrammable machine capable of performing a variety of tasks requiring programmed manipulations of materials and tools.	Many production managers have replaced blue-collar workers with these "steel-collar" workers. Robots reduce labour costs and free people from boring, sometimes dangerous assignments.
Computer-Aided Design (CAD)	A process that enables engineers to design parts and buildings on computer screens faster and with fewer mistakes than on paper.	CAD is used to make major and minor design changes and to analyze the design for certain characteristics or problems before the product is made. In this way, potential design deficiencies can be determined and resolved much more quickly, thus improving flexibility and efficiency.
Computer-Aided Manufacturing (CAM)	A process that enables manufacturers to use specially designed computers to analyze the necessary steps that a machine must perform to produce a needed product or part.	CAM improves manufacturing efficiency, reliability, and flexibility. The computer simulates the manufacturing process and detects design errors to be rectified. Ideas can be tested and changed if necessary before the product becomes a reality.
Flexible Manufacturing Systems (FMS)	A facility or process that can be modified quickly to manufacture different products.	FMS improves efficiency. For example, the typical system consists of computer-controlled machining centres to produce metal parts, robots to handle the parts, and remote-controlled carts to deliver materials. All components are linked by electronic controls that dictate what will happen at each stage of the manufacturing sequence — even automatically replacing broken or worn-out drill bits and other implements.
Computer-Integrated Manufacturing (CIM)	The use of computers to design products, control machines, handle materials, and control the production function in an integrated fashion.	CIM is the result of combining robots, CAD/CAM, FMS, computers, and other technologies. CIM improves efficiency, reliability, and flexibility by integrating and controlling various and separate manufacturing processes and functions.

TECHNOLOGY

The "Law of Diminishing Returns" articulated more than a century ago by the great economist Alfred Marshall is still a cornerstone of modern economic theory.

Basically it holds that the profits from any kind of economic endeavour will gradually decline as the scale of activity expands.

The "Law of Diminishing Returns" helped explain how companies (and managers) behave. It provided a theoretical understanding for how market pricing works, and clarified the economic rules for competition between firms. It also explained how competition in a free economy would eventually lead to a stable "equilibrium."

Take a simple example. A farmer finds he can grow coffee and sell it at a tremendous profit. However, as his business grows, he expands to less suitable land and his costs rise. He now has to till the soil and provide irrigation. When other farmers see that he is doing well, they also start to produce coffee. Soon the price for coffee sags. Faced with rising costs and falling prices, the farmer's level of profit diminishes. At some point he finally stops expanding.

When it was first formulated the "Law of Diminishing Returns" was thought to be universally applicable. But today some economists argue that our economy no longer works according to Marshall's famous principle. In fact, argues Prof. Brian Arthur, a "law of increasing returns" applies to an increasing array of high-tech and information-related sectors of economical endeavour.

Arthur is Citibank Professor at the Santa Fe Institute, and the author of *Increasing Returns and Path Dependence in the Economy* (University of Michigan Press, 1994). He has been studying the economic dynamics of the high-tech sector for more than a decade.

According to Arthur, "Increasing returns are the tendency for that which is ahead to get further ahead."

Arthur does not challenge the validity of Marshall's law — just its universality. He readily admits that in an era of bulk production — metal ores, pig iron, lumber, and coffee, for example, the law was an accurate generalization. Coffee plantations were started on the most appropriate land, and did expand to less-fertile ground. And the market actually did end up being shared by many plantations based on the availability of suitable farmland.

---

manufacturing (CAM), flexible manufacturing systems (FMS), and computer-integrated manufacturing (CIM).

CHOOSING THE BEST LOCATION

ONE OF THE major decisions a firm will make is choosing the right place to build a plant. As Table 12.6 illustrates, factors involved in choosing the best location fall into three categories: transportation, human, and physical factors.

Many communities and most major banks require a firm that wants to locate in the vicinity to do an **environmental impact study** that *analyzes how the proposed plant would affect the quality of life in the surrounding area.* Regulatory agencies typically require the study to cover such topics

> **Business Term**
> √ **Environmental impact study**
> Analysis of how a proposed plant would affect the quality of life in the surrounding area.

as impact on transportation facilities; energy requirements; water and sewage treatment needs; effect on natural plant life and wildlife; and water, air, and noise pollution.

Labour costs and the availability of a qualified labour force are important issues. Many electronics firms, for example, are located in Toronto, Cambridge, Calgary, Ottawa, and Montreal, areas that have high concentrations of skilled technicians. Many automakers, on the other hand, are moving their production operations to areas with low labour costs. Germany, for example, ranks as one of the highest among industrialized nations in average hourly labour costs. This is why the country is losing an estimated 100 000 jobs a year. Many of these jobs are migrating to lower-cost labour areas, such as Spain, Portugal, Poland, Hungary, and the Czech Republic.

But important sectors of today's economy work on a different logic — that of increasing returns. In a recent article in the *Harvard Business Review* (July–August 1996), Arthur gives several reasons why this occurs:

1. **Up-front costs.** High-tech products such as pharmaceuticals, computer software, and electronic consumer goods are complicated to design. They typically have R&D costs that are large compared to production costs. Hence [per-unit] costs are very high at small volumes, but fall as quantities increase.

2. **Network effects.** Many products require a network of users to be effective. The firm that is able to dominate the market at the beginning (such as IBM with its DOS system, or VHS in videotape) continues to gain market shares as it becomes the standard.

3. **Customer groove-in.** High-tech products are often difficult to use. They require training. Once a firm has paid for its employees to use WordPerfect, or trained its mechanics to repair an Airbus, it is costly to switch to another system. Those products that gain market advantage stand to gain even more because the costs to the customer of switching are relatively high.

Today's economy shows a paradoxical co-existence of both the old law of diminishing returns and the new law of increasing ones. Mining, transportation, and heavy manufacturing, characterized by big production costs, are still dominated by the law of diminishing returns. But the high-tech sectors operate on the new logic.

Interestingly, the new rules are gradually making their way into the old sectors. Banking is a classic example. At one time, the main costs to a bank were that of operating its many local branches. Just like the coffee plantation, expanding the bank meant moving to less and less profitable locations. But computers are changing this algorithm. The big costs for a bank today are in information technology. And once that investment is made, actual transaction costs are very small.

The new economic rules apply to a wide and growing segment of our economy. Managers who want to be successful need to think carefully about how the new rules of the game are affecting their own industry.

Source: Peter Larson, "Law of Diminishing Returns Doesn't Apply to High-Tech World," *The Ottawa Citizen*, September 7, 1996. Reprinted by permission of Peter Larson, Executive Vice-President, Public Policy Forum.

Table 12.6 Factors in the Location Decision

Location Factor	Examples of Affected Businesses
Transportation Factors	
Proximity to markets	Baking companies or manufacturers of other perishable products, dry cleaners, hotels, or other services for profit
Proximity to raw materials	Mining companies
Availability of transportation alternatives	Brick manufacturers, retail stores
Human Factors	
Labour supply	Auto manufacturers, hotels
Local regulations	Explosives manufacturers, welding shops
Community living conditions	All businesses
Physical Factors	
Water supply	Paper mills
Energy	Aluminum, chemical, and fertilizer manufacturers
Hazardous wastes	All businesses

GOOD, BAD, OR UGLY?

William Coffey, a geography professor at the University of Montreal, researched job and population trends in 152 urban centres across Canada. He found that up to the mid-1990s, the concentration of high-skill jobs in Canada's largest cities increased. Rural areas were not getting their share of the high-tech jobs. "Somewhere along the line, the rural areas have really fallen between the chairs," says Coffey. The futuristic implication of Coffey's research is that the knowledge-based economy may lead to larger "high-tech" urban cores.

Donald Tapscott, author of The Digital Economy, says that he is not surprised by Coffey's findings. But he cautions that this urban trend may not continue due to improvements in communications networks such as interactive video. Tapscott argues that the past may not be a good indicator of the future. His vision of our urban future is smaller cities with the right mix of support services attracting more knowledge-based industries.

Which way is the market taking us? Larger cities or smaller? What do you think, and why?

DID YOU KNOW?

With an output of $12.5 billion of aerospace products in 1996, Canada was the world's sixth-largest supplier in this industry after the United States, France, the United Kingdom, Japan, and Germany. But at current growth rates, Canada should move into fourth place by 2000 with an output of $16.5 billion, according to Peter Smith, president of the Aerospace Industries Association of Canada. There are several reasons for Canada moving up the corporate ladder, including the following:

→ Governments everywhere are cutting defence budgets. Because Canada is a relatively small defence spender, cuts have a smaller effect.

→ Montreal-based Bombardier foresaw a worldwide demand for regional aircraft and moved quickly to position itself as a leader.

→ If the Canadian dollar remains weak against the U.S. dollar, this will continue to spur Canadian exports to the United States. In contrast, the stronger yen and deutschemark are expected to reduce Japanese and German sales to American buyers.

→ Higher social costs in Europe make European companies less efficient.

→ Air travel has grown steadily, more than 10 percent a year in the Asia-Pacific region. Continued growth will fuel worldwide demand for new and replacement aircraft.

TASKS OF PRODUCTION AND OPERATIONS MANAGERS

PRODUCTION AND OPERATIONS management is responsible for overseeing the use of people and machinery to convert inputs (materials and resources) into finished goods and services. These managers have three major tasks. First, they must plan the overall production process. Next, they must determine the best layout for the production facilities and implement the production plan. Finally, they are responsible for controlling the production process to maintain the highest possible quality. Part of the control process involves continually evaluating results. If problems occur, managers should return to the first step and adjust the production process if necessary.

Marketing research studies are used to obtain consumer reactions to proposed products, to test prototypes of new products, and to estimate their potential sales and profitability. The production department is concerned primarily with (1) converting the original product concept into the final product and (2) designing production facilities to produce this new product as efficiently as possible. The new item or service must not only be

THEY SAID IT

Colder weather helps Jarvis Travel increase bookings. "We've got a thermometer hooked up to the telephone. As soon as the temperature goes down, our sales go up."

ROGER JARVIS, president and sole owner, Jarvis Travel Ltd.

accepted by consumers, it also must be produced economically and in a timely fashion in order to assure an acceptable return on company funds invested in the project.

INVENTORY CONTROL

INVENTORY CONTROL *balances the need to have inventory on hand to meet demand with the costs involved in carrying the inventory.* The financial costs of carrying inventory are the funds tied up in it that cannot be used in other activities of the business. Among the expenses involved in storing inventory are warehousing, taxes, insurance, and maintenance. Too much inventory represents wasted money.

But a shortage of raw materials, parts, goods, or sales often means lost production — and delays in production mean unhappy customers if the delays result in late delivery. Firms lose business when they are consistently unable to meet promised delivery dates or when their shelves are empty. These two costs must be balanced to produce acceptable inventory levels; effective inventory control can save a great deal of money.

Just-in-Time System

Ten years ago, the typical factory kept several weeks' worth of parts and supplies on hand. Today, this same plant may have only enough supplies to keep it going for a day. This shortage is not accidental; it is an essential ingredient of the just-in-time system used today by major corporations.

The **just-in-time (JIT) system** *is a broad management philosophy that reaches beyond the narrow activity of inventory control and influences the entire system of production and operations management.* JIT is an approach that seeks to eliminate all sources of waste — anything that does not add value in operations activities — by providing the right part at the right place at the right time. This results in less inventory, lower costs, and better-quality goods and services than the traditional approach.[10]

When applied to inventory control, a JIT system supplies parts to the production line on an as-needed basis. This

> **Business Term**
> √ **Inventory control**
> Balancing the need to have inventory on hand to meet demand with the costs involved in carrying the inventory.

> **Business Term**
> √ **Just-in-time (JIT) system**
> A broad management philosophy that reaches beyond the narrow activity of inventory control and influences the entire system of production and operations management.

approach lowers factory inventory levels and inventory control costs. The JIT system also lets firms respond quickly to changes in the market and employ only the most essential personnel to maintain the inventory. Manufacturers in many industries have adopted JIT, saving billions of dollars. This benefits the economy, since this money can be invested, spent on new-product development, or returned to shareholders as dividends. Says Alan Dawes, who heads operations at GM's auto components group, "There's absolutely no way we're going away from just-in-time."[11]

JIT shifts much of the responsibility for carrying inventory to suppliers operating on forecasts, since they are forced to keep more on hand to be responsive to manufacturers' needs. Suppliers who cannot keep enough high-quality parts on hand often get dropped in favour of suppliers who can.

THE IMPORTANCE OF QUALITY

QUALITY, A CONCEPT discussed in Chapter 6, is just as vital in the product development and production functions as it is in other areas of business. For many of Canada's leading firms, such as Northern Telecom, strict compliance with ISO 9000 standards has provided them with an added competitive/service edge. More companies are realizing that if they build quality into product design from the very beginning, they are more likely to end up with quality products, which are an important aspect of customer satisfaction. Investing more money up front in quality design and development ultimately decreases "costs of quality," or those costs that result from not making the product right the first time. These costs average at least 20 percent of the sales revenues for most companies. Some typical costs of quality include downtime, repair costs, rework, and employee turnover. Systems must be set up to track and reduce such costs. If management concentrates on producing a quality product that satisfies the needs of its customers, a byproduct will be lower costs of quality.

Quality control *involves measuring goods and services against established quality standards.* Such checks are necessary to spot defective products and to see that they are not shipped to customers. Devices for monitoring quality levels of the firm's output include visual inspection, statistical analysis, electronic sensors, robots, and X-rays. A high rejection rate is a danger signal that quality standards are not being met.

But companies cannot rely solely on inspections to achieve quality. A typical factory can spend up to half of its operating budget to identify and fix mistakes. This is both costly and time-consuming. A company instead must identify all processes involved in producing products and work to make them as efficient as possible. This can be done by finding the cause of problems in the processes and eliminating them. If a company concentrates its efforts on improving the processes, a quality product will result.

> **Business Term**
> ✓ **Quality control**
> Measuring goods and services against established quality standards.

THEY SAID IT

"You can hype a questionable product for a little while, but you'll never build an enduring business."

VICTOR KIAM, CEO, Remington Products, Inc.

The World According to Big Shot

SLINKY: Mr. Big, this is serious. We're getting a lot of customer complaints about our widgets not working.

BIG SHOT: Why don't you e-mail them and say we're ISO 9000 approved? Then watch the complaints go down.

SLINKY: But we're not ISO approved.

BIG SHOT: OK. Phone the ISO people and tell them we want to buy one of their little certificates.

→ What do you think of Big Shot's tactic?

SUMMARY OF LEARNING OUTCOMES

1. Explain why product development is important to a firm.

New products are the lifeblood of an organization. Products do not remain economically viable forever, so new ones must be developed to assure the survival of an organization. For many firms, new products account for a sizable part of sales and profits.

2. List the stages of new-product development.

The new-product development process has six stages: (1) generating new-product ideas, (2) screening, (3) business analysis, (4) product development, (5) test marketing, and (6) commercialization. Some firms skip the test marketing stage because of concerns that the test could reveal their product strategies to the competition. Strategic alliances are a common way for many new-generation firms to access new products and production techniques.

3. Explain how products are identified.

Goods and services are identified by brands, brand names, and trademarks. A brand is a name, term, sign, symbol, design, or some combination thereof used to identify the products of one firm and to differentiate them from competitive offerings. A brand name is that part of the brand consisting of words or letters included in a name used to identify and distinguish the firm's offerings from those of competitors. A trademark is a brand that has been given legal protection.

4. Explain the strategic importance of production and operations management in an organization.

The production process is a vital business function. Without a good or service, a company cannot create profits, and it would fail quickly. The production process is also crucial in not-for-profit organizations, since it is the good or service that justifies the organization's existence. Production and operations management plays an important strategic role by lowering the costs of production, boosting the quality of products, and allowing the firm to respond flexibly and dependably to customers' demands.

5. Compare mass production with newer production techniques.

Mass production is the manufacture of products in large quantities through the effective combination of specialization, mechanization, and standardization. Mass production makes large quantities of products available at lower prices than would be possible if these products were crafted individually. However, while highly efficient for making large numbers of similar products, it is less efficient for making small batches of different items. Furthermore, specialization can make workers' jobs boring.

By the mid-1990s, Canada found itself entrenched in a new knowledge-based economy. Mass-production technologies were no longer responsive to this new economic order. Business winners in this new economy will be characterized by their technology, innovation, adaptability, customization, and customer focus. To become more competitive, many firms are adopting new approaches. Flexible production methods require fewer workers and less inventory and are cost-effective with smaller batches too. With customer-driven production, customers' demands determine what retail stores stock and, in turn, what manufacturers make. The team concept combines employees from various departments and functions — such as design, manufacturing, finance, and maintenance — to work together on designing and building products. A common practice today is to include team members from outside the organization — suppliers and customers, for example.

6. Discuss how computers and related technologies are revolutionizing product development and production.

Automation allows companies to design and create new products faster, modify them more rapidly, and meet customers' changing needs more effectively. Important design and/or production technologies include robots, computer-aided design (CAD), computer-aided manufacturing (CAM), flexible manufacturing systems (FMS), and computer-integrated manufacturing (CIM).

7. **Outline the major factors involved in choosing plant locations.**

Factors involved in choosing the best location fall into three categories: transportation, human, and physical factors. Transportation factors include proximity to markets and raw materials, and availability of transportation alternatives. Physical variables involve such issues as water supply, available energy, and options for disposing of hazardous wastes. Human factors include the area's labour supply, local regulations, and living conditions.

8. **Describe the major tasks of production and operations managers.**

Production and operations managers are responsible for overseeing the use of people and machinery to convert inputs (materials and resources) into finished goods and services. This involves three major tasks. First, they must plan the overall production process. Next, they must determine the best layout for the production facilities and implement the production plan. Finally, they are responsible for controlling the production process and evaluating results in order to maintain the highest possible quality.

9. **Explain the importance of inventory control and just-in-time systems.**

Inventory control balances the need to have inventory on hand to meet demand with the costs involved in carrying the inventory. Too much inventory represents wasted money, but a shortage of raw materials, parts, goods, or sales often means lost production and unhappy customers. The just-in-time (JIT) system is a philosophy that seeks to eliminate all sources of waste — anything that does not add value in operations activities — by providing the right part at the right place at the right time. This results in less inventory, lower costs, and better-quality goods and services.

10. **Discuss the benefits of quality control.**

Quality control involves measuring goods and services against established quality standards. Such checks are necessary to spot defective products and to see that they are not shipped to customers. Devices for monitoring quality levels of the firm's output include visual inspection, electronic sensors, robots, and X-rays. Quality is just as vital in product development; investing more money up front in quality design and development ultimately decreases the costs of quality. For many of Canada's leading firms, strict compliance with ISO 9000 standards has provided them with an added competitive/service edge.

Key Terms Quiz

mass production	quality control	production and operations
brand name	trademark	management
generic products	assembly line	production
just-in-time (JIT) system	inventory control	environmental impact study
national brand		

_____ 1. The words or letters that identify a firm's offerings.

_____ 2. A brand that has been given legal protection exclusive to its owner.

_____ 3. A brand that is offered and promoted by a manufacturer.

_____ 4. Nonbranded items with plain packaging and little or no advertising support.

_____ 5. The use of people and machinery to convert materials into finished goods or services.

_____ 6. Managing the people and machinery used in converting materials and resources into finished goods and services.

_____ 7. The manufacture of goods in large quantities as a result of standardization, specialized labour, and mechanization.

_____ 8. The manufacturing technique wherein the product passes through several workstations, each with a specialized task.

_____ 9. The analysis of the impact of a proposed plant location on the quality of life in a specific area.

_____ 10. A system that balances the need to have products on hand with the costs of storing the products.

_____ 11. Continuously stocking items in inventory on an as-needed basis.

_____ 12. The measurement of goods and services against established quality standards.

Other Important Terms

brand	form utility	mechanization	standardization
concurrent engineering	individual branding	specialization	technology economy

Review Questions

1. Why is product development important?

2. Identify and explain the stages in new-product development. Illustrate each stage with a hypothetical example.

3. Differentiate among the terms *brand*, *brand name*, and *trademark*. Cite examples of each.

4. Suggest types of form utility that the following firms might produce:
   a. Delivery service
   b. Sugar refinery
   c. Airline
   d. Family counselling centre

5. Explain why effective production and operations management can provide a strategic advantage for a firm.

6. Describe a mass-production system. What are its advantages and disadvantages?

7. What are the major characteristics of the new economy production processes?

8. Attraction Corp. has a good chance of thriving in the new economy. Why?

9. Why do some experts argue that Canada is well-positioned to compete and prosper in the new "highway" economy?

10. Explain the concept of a flexible manufacturing system.

11. What is the law of diminishing returns, and why might it not be applicable in the high-tech sector?

12. What problems are associated with having too much inventory? With having too little inventory?

13. Relate the tasks of production and operations managers to each of the following. Give specific examples.
    a. Major-league sports facility in the Calgary area
    b. Convenience store
    c. Fish-processing facility
    d. Colour television assembly plant

14. Why is ISO 9000 an important production criterion to Canadian firms?

Discussion Questions

1. Evaluate your city or region as a prospective industrial site and suggest organizations that would be well-positioned to compete and prosper in the new economy.

2. As we learned, Nuala Beck said that there were three ways to compete in the new economy:
   a. Be one of the four driving engines,
   b. Be one of their suppliers, or
   c. Use technology to revitalize an old industry.
   Give an example for each of these competitive strategies. Find a local firm in your community that is ISO 9000 approved. Has ISO 9000 improved its quality and performance?

3. Suggest a brand name for each of the following new products and explain why you chose each name:
   a. A development of exclusive home sites
   b. A low-price term life insurance policy sold by mail

   c. An airline's improved business-class service on Asian routes
   d. A lawn edger that is more durable than its competition

4. Choose a service organization in your community — perhaps a restaurant or department of your school — and evaluate its production process. How efficient is it? Does the resulting good or service meet your standards? Are there any quality-control standards that you might wish to suggest?

5. What is quality control? Suggest ways in which each of the following firms could practise it.
   a. Local bank
   b. City hospital
   c. Amusement park
   d. Clothing manufacturer that exports 50 percent of its goods abroad

Answers to Key Terms Quiz

1. brand name 2. trademark 3. national brand 4. generic products 5. production 6. production and operations management 7. mass production 8. assembly line 9. environmental impact study 10. inventory control 11. just-in-time (JIT) system 12. quality control

Notes

1. Adapted from Amal Kumar Naj, "Some Manufacturers Drop Efforts to Adopt Japanese Technology," *The Wall Street Journal*, May 7, 1993, 1; and Amal Kumar Naj, "GE's Welch Extols Virtues of Being Big — and Small — in a Changing World," *The Wall Street Journal*, February 26, 1993, B5B. Reprinted by permission of *The Wall Street Journal*, © 1993 Dow Jones & Company, Inc. All Rights Reserved Worldwide.

2. Nancy Arnott, "To Know Brands Isn't Necessarily to Love Them," *Sales & Marketing Management*, December 1993, 25.

3. Alison Rogers, "Cheerios Was Taken," *Fortune*, October 18, 1993, 11.

4. Nuala Beck, *Shifting Gears: Thriving in the New Economy* (Toronto: HarperCollins, 1992), 27–31.

5. Lee A. Eckert, J.D. Ryan, and Ronald A. Knowles, *Canadian Small Business: An Entrepreneur's Plan*, 2nd ed. (Toronto: Dryden, 1995), 5.

6. Beck, *Shifting Gears*, 36–38.

7. Nuala Beck & Associates Inc., "Where the Engines Roar — and Sputter," *The Globe and Mail*, October 6, 1992, B2.

8. Rod McQueen, "Canada's 50 Best Managed Private Companies: Attraction Corp.," *The Financial Post*, December 14–16, 1996, 17; and personal interview.

9. Rod McQueen, "Canada's 50 Best Managed Private Companies: Intelatech Inc.," *The Financial Post*, Decmeber 14–16, 1996, 34–36; and personal interview.

10. Norman Gaither, *Production and Operations Management*, 6th ed. (Fort Worth, TX: The Dryden Press, 1994), 39.

11. Howard Gleckman, with Zachary Schiller and James Treece, "A Tonic for the Business Cycle," *Business Week*, April 4, 1994, 57.

Chapter 13

Designing and Implementing Customer-Driven Marketing Strategies

Learning Outcomes

After studying this chapter, you should be able to

1. Contrast relationship marketing with transaction-based marketing.
2. Define the target market and explain the importance of demographics and psychographics in relation to the target market.
3. Explain what a product is; list the components of a product strategy; and identify the classifications of consumer products, business products, and services.
4. Discuss the product mix and the stages of the product life cycle.
5. Describe the importance of pricing strategy.
6. Identify the major components of distribution strategy.
7. Outline the various types of distribution channels, and discuss the factors that influence channel selection.
8. Explain the importance of customer service.
9. Explain how advertising, sales promotion, and public relations are used in promotional strategy, and identify the factors that influence the selection of a promotional mix.
10. Discuss the factors that influence international promotion.

Tough Sell in the New Arena[1]

Change is upon us — and it's fast, furious, and unforgiving. Nowhere is this more evident than in Canada's retail sector, in which marketers try to understand buying behaviour and chart our future shopping patterns. Canadian retailers who do not keep in touch with trends in customer needs will find themselves at a serious disadvantage. The bankruptcy of Consumers Distributing in the fall of 1996 is a painful example of what happens when a company cannot respond fast enough to changing technology and the onslaught of "big box" retailers like Wal-Mart and Future Shop.

During the early 1990s, sales at Consumers remained relatively constant at about $600 million. It even had an operating profit of about $21 million toward the middle of the decade. To the casual observer, Consumers seemed to be holding its own. But most retail experts and senior management at Consumers knew that the company had lost its competitive edge. One only had to observe the result of its "pencil and paper" catalogue strategy on customer service. The company was at a crossroads, and the future of its business and employees was at stake.

While Consumers Distributing closed its doors in the fall of 1996, Future Shop continued to thrive.

According to James McLeod, a merchandising analyst with Richardson Greenshields of Canada, a typical shopping excursion at Consumers for many customers meant flipping through a large catalogue, filling out an order form with a pencil, and standing in a long line-up — only to find out the desired item was out of stock. "Not only did you not get what you wanted, but it cost you time to find that out," said McLeod.

Two major competitive forces sounded a wake-up call in the Consumers marketing department. First there was the onslaught of "big box" retailing, with its high volume/low price strategy. Even Zellers had to rethink its "Where the Lowest Price Is the Law" strategy. Second, the cybermall revolution meant that almost any retailer — large or small — could now offer a catalogue electronically. The overnight popularity of armchair shopping meant that Consumers' archaic pencil and paper retail system had to go. Now customers had the option of shopping at home — on CD-ROM catalogues, for example — and then of simply "clicking in their order." No more walking, no waiting, and no phoning. Cybermalls were beginning to change the face of retailing worldwide.

Senior management at Consumers had to reinvent the company's customer service, distribution, and merchandising strategies. The company had to decide whether to transform Consumers into a big box retailer and/or become a virtual cybermall. But one thing was clear — management had to move quickly. In the retail revolution, the winners are those retailers who can focus on a target market and service a growth niche.

Consumers' retail war plan was this. First, the company built and market-tested a new high-tech superstore in Toronto. This superstore concept was an ambitious attempt to shed Consumers' reputation for spotty service and out-of-stock problems. It featured an expanded product showroom and a touch-screen computer that allowed customers to browse electronically for items and, eventually, pay for purchases with a credit card. Consumers invited retail experts to tour the Toronto prototype. James McLeod had this to say: "It's quite a bit different than anything that I've seen them do in the past. It's almost like a marriage of some traditional retailing and merchandising techniques with the economics of their catalogue-showroom concept." It was reviews like this that led to an aggressive management plan to open 70 such superstores by the end of 1998.

Next, Consumers initiated marketing tests for an electronic version of its catalogue. Using this interactive service, its customers would not have to leave the comfort of their homes. Within the next few years, Consumers planned to create new shelves in cyberspace.

Unfortunately for Consumers, it just didn't move fast enough. In the summer of 1996, the company asked for court protection from its creditors. It was $250 million in debt and needed some additional breathing space to implement its marketing plan. By the fall of 1996, it had failed to convince its financial backers that it could compete in the new retail arena. An impatient group of four banks pulled the plug. Almost overnight, 3700 full- and part-time employees lost their jobs, and some 400 faithful trade suppliers were given little chance of getting any of their money back.

CHAPTER OVERVIEW

THE CONSUMERS DISTRIBUTING debacle reflects the challenge of marketing in the changing Canadian economy. Businesses that do not keep in touch with consumer demands and the vagaries of the marketplace will find themselves going the way of Consumers. In this chapter, we will discuss ways in which organizations can implement responsive marketing strategies that address customers' needs and wants.

Today, marketing revolves around the exchange relationships, and so we begin with a discussion of customer-focussed relationship marketing — one of the most important trends guiding us into the next millennium. Next, we describe the classification of goods and services, the product mix, and the product life cycle. We examine the four elements of the marketing mix — product, pricing, distribution, and promotional strategy — and the role of customer service in developing successful marketing strategies.

FROM TRANSACTION-BASED MARKETING TO RELATIONSHIP MARKETING

AS MARKETING ENTERS the twenty-first century, a significant change is taking place in the way companies interact with customers. The traditional view of marketing as a simple exchange process — a concept that might be termed transaction-based marketing — is being replaced by a different, longer-term approach called relationship marketing.

Traditional marketing strategies focus on individual sales or transactions. The goal is to identify prospects, convert them to customers, and complete sales transactions. **Transaction-based marketing** involves *buyer and seller exchanges characterized by limited communications and little or no ongoing relationship between the parties.*[2] In many ways, Consumers Distributing represented a company whose marketing strategy and culture was mainly transaction-based. The buyer–seller exchanges were characterized by limited communications and little or no ongoing relationship between the customer and the retailer. A customer would come into the store, fill out a form, pass it to a clerk, hope that Consumers had it in stock, and with any luck would walk out with the item. Relationships with the customer were generally sporadic, and often disrupted by conflict.

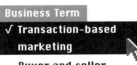

BUSINESS TIP

Marketing today emphasizes networking, creativity, strategic alliances, and partnerships. Three key strategies are

→ Establish a market pull. Integrate customer needs, desires, and marketing strategies into the development of the product or service. The pull of the market – or market demands – is the major factor in determining product and service sales.

→ Own a niche. Focus your knowledge and experience on a specific and targeted customer/business segment, or <u>niche</u>. The idea is to continuously differentiate, create uniqueness in accordance with customer needs, and own this niche.

→ Create relationships. Create customer, supplier, user, and even competitor relationships that will sustain and increase your customer base.

While this transaction-based style of marketing is still widespread, many leading Canadian firms have begun shifting to a new approach — one that looks at customers in a different light. Indeed, they have found that creating long-term relationships with customers pays off in increased sales and decreased marketing costs. Recall from Chapter 11 that *relationship marketing* is the development and maintenance of long-term, cost-effective relationships with individual customers, suppliers, employees, and other partners for mutual benefit.[3] Palmer Jarvis Inc., a Vancouver advertising agency, is another *Financial Post* "Best Managed Private Company." Frank Palmer, the CEO and president, says that it's a buyer's market today, and customers are better educated about what they want and the results they expect. The success of his firm is largely due to relationship marketing: "At the end of the day we're in the business of building relationships. All we have to offer the client is trust."[4]

Relationship marketing is an ongoing, collaborative exchange that creates value

Business Term

✓ **Transaction-based marketing**

Buyer and seller exchanges characterized by limited communications and little or no ongoing relationship between the parties.

and emphasizes co-operation rather than conflict between the parties. Building long-term relationships with consumers and other businesses involves four basic steps:

1. *Identify* who the current and potential customers are.

2. *Analyze* what the needs of the customer are.

3. *Respond* with products and services that the customer wants.

4. *Monitor* by measuring the success of the relationship program.

Developing relationships requires more than "a smile and a promise." To a large extent, relationship marketing depends on developing social ties between buyers and sellers whether the buyers are individuals or other companies. As Figure 13.1 illustrates, all relationships depend on the development of emotional links between the parties, which involves four key dimensions:[5]

- **Bonding.** The mutual interests of the parties must be strong enough to tie them together for the long term.

- **Empathy.** Each party must have the ability to see situations from the perspective of the other party.

- **Reciprocity.** This involves a give-and-take process that creates a web of commitments.

- **Trust.** This is the extent of one party's confidence that it can rely on another's integrity.

Figure 13.1   **Relationship Marketing Orientation**

THE MARKETING MIX

AS WE SAW in Chapter 11, any customer-oriented organization begins its marketing strategy or plan by studying its *target market* — the group of people toward whom the firm markets its goods, services, or ideas with a strategy designed to satisfy their specific needs and preferences.

This target market could be a business or the end user — the customer. JPL International, a Canadian company based in Quebec, targets its hair-care products to professional hair salons, some 30 000 across Canada. "Everything we do, we do for the beauty salons," says

8. When someone does something especially nice or helpful for me, I make it a point to thank them with a personal note or follow-up phone call.

9. I keep in touch with friends, teachers, employers, and co-workers from my past.

10. I am a good listener.

Interpreting Your Answers

If you answered Yes three times or less, your networking skills need work. To build solid networking relationships you have to be willing to give before you expect to receive. Answering Yes four to seven times means that you recognize the importance of developing bonds with others, but you're still uncertain about how to develop them. If you answered Yes eight to ten times, congratulations! You understand some of the key factors involved in creating a network of

contacts who will be willing to help you in the future.

Source: "How Good Are Your Networking Skills?" from *Contemporary Business*, 9th ed. by Louis E. Boone and David L. Kurtz, p. 251, Copyright © 1998 by The Dryden Press, reprinted by permission of the publisher.

Jean Pierre Louis, president and founder of JPL. "In turn, they appreciate the fact that a company takes the time to really listen to their needs and to help them succeed."[6] As we discussed in Chapter 11, the target market for Delta Hotels is the business traveller — the end user.

An understanding of demographics and psychographics helps marketers understand why consumers purchase goods and services.[7] **Demographics** — *the statistical analysis of age, sex, income, education, and the like of a population* — is a major factor that will affect the purchase of consumer goods into the next millennium. The key here is to understand that

- Various age groups will grow faster or slower than the average population.

- These various age cohorts have different purchasing needs.

Canada's changing population profile is shown in Table 13.1. In 1996, the 50+ age group represented about 26 percent of the population. By the year 2011, this group will represent over 33 percent of our total population. We know that 55 percent of disposable income and 80 percent of savings account dollars are controlled by the 50+ group. This kind of demographic pattern shows the impact of the so-called "baby boom" generation —

> **Business Term**
> √ **Demographics**
> The statistical analysis of age, sex, income, education, and the like of a population.

about 10 million Canadians born between 1947 and 1966. Knowing the needs of this demographic age group or cohort can reap huge benefits for the enterprising marketer.

Table 13.1 Canada's Changing Population Profile (millions)

Age	1996	2001	2011
0–4	1 991.5	1 924.3	1 980.1
5–9	2 036.9	2 082.2	2 016.6
10–14	2 035.2	2 124.8	2 104.8
15–19	1 996.3	2 124.5	2 259.2
20–24	2 027.0	2 115.2	2 332.3
25–29	2 217.5	2 177.7	2 392.8
30–34	2 615.4	2 366.4	2 416.1
35–39	2 657.3	2 723.4	2 443.0
40–44	2 377.8	2 716.3	2 544.5
45–49	2 146.6	2 399.6	2 801.9
50–54	1 667.4	2 140.1	2 722.0
55–59	1 327.3	1 651.4	2 362.2
60–64	1 209.4	1 300.9	2 063.6
65–69	1 129.7	1 154.0	1 544.5
70–74	980.4	1 027.1	1 142.5
75–79	704.9	831.9	906.1
80+	842.9	1 017.7	1 398.1
TOTAL	29 963.7	31 877.3	35 420.3

COMPETITIVE STRATEGY

TARGET MARKET — THE NEXUS GENERATION

Businesses, governments, or other organizations trying to reach Generation X soon come up against a major roadblock: no one knows *exactly* who or what Generation X is!

According to some, Generation X is all about the year you were born: 1963, 1969, or (depending on who's talking), 1976. On the one hand, Generation Xers have been described as wanderers, slackers, and couch-potatoes interested only in watching *Simpsons*' reruns; on the other hand, they have been portrayed as the most conservative, hard-working generation since those born during the Great Depression. Similarly, some experts say Xers are serious about marriage, while others see the X-generation as a group reluctant to make commitments.

Robert Barnard disagrees with the term Generation X. As a label, Gen X is widely over-used, ambiguous, and cliché. "It means too many things to too many different people," says Barnard, a 29-year-old Xer

from Toronto. Barnard founded d~Code Inc., a small consulting firm that helps companies and government departments better understand what makes 18- to 34-year-olds tick. In place of the term Generation-X, d~code uses the phrase "Nexus generation" to characterize this target group. Nexus means a bridge or connection; in this case, the connection is between the industrial age and the birth of the information age.

d~Code helps its private- and public-sector clients decipher the aspirations, preferences, and unique features of the age group born at this critical Nexus. It works with them to design marketing, human resource, or public policy strategies that connect with Nexus, consumers, employees, and citizens. In the process, d~Code strives to build bridges across generations.

According to d~Code, there are a few psychographic likes and dislikes of the Nexus generation:

→ For Nexus, financial compensation is not as important as it is to the preceding generations. Nexus ranks quality of life (e.g., longer vacations) and opportu-

nities for on-the-job training ahead of a whopping paycheque.

→ Nexus is more sceptical and has less confidence in traditional institutions such as the Church, the University, the nuclear family, the State, and the Corporation.

→ Nexus is more media-savvy, techno-literate, educated, and worldly than any previous generation.

→ Nexus is composed of "experience seekers" who put off marriage, kids, and house payments longer than those in previous generations.

→ Nexus is more comfortable — and less anxious — about change.

→ Nexus makes up about 32 percent of the voting population.

Sources: Based on personal correspondence with d~Code Inc.; and adapted from Gayle MacDonald, "The Eyes and Ears of a Generation," *The Globe and Mail*, February 4, 1997, B11. Reprinted with permission from The Globe and Mail. Visit d~Code's Web site at **http://www.d-code.com**.

Psychographics — *the first-hand intuitive insight into lifestyles, buying habits, patterns of consumption, attitudes, and so forth of a population* — is also a marketer's key to profiling the target customer. Today, people buy products and services that reflect not only their age, sex, and so on, but also the needs of their lifestyle. For example, two adults with a combined income of $75 000 but with no children (DINKS: **D**ouble-**I**ncome-**N**o-**K**ids) have different spending patterns than two adults earning $75 000 with four children to feed. These two

Business Term
√ **Psychographics**
The first-hand intuitive insight into lifestyles, buying habits, patterns of consumption, attitudes, and so forth of a population.

groups have completely different wants and needs and as a result have different spending patterns. The whys and wants of consumer purchases are what psychographics is all about. Psychographics is about segmenting the population by lifestyles and values, recognizing that people in each segment or slice have different reasons for making a purchase. Table 13.2 outlines some key characteristics of the six Goldfarb Psychographic segments and provides the percentage of the Canadian population that makes up each segment.

Table 13.2 Goldfarb Psychographics

	% of Canadian Population	
	1988	**1996**
A brief outline of some key characteristics for each of the six Goldfarb Psychographic segments follows.		
Day-to-Day Watchers		
Traditional values. Research purchases. Need to be comfortable with products before purchasing. Early followers as opposed to leaders.	22	22
Old-Fashioned Puritans		
Very conservative and traditional. Home and family oriented. Heavily insured. Tend to resist change.	11	13
Disinterested Self-Indulgents		
Hedonistic. Risk takers. Like to be on the leading edge of product innovation. Heavy impulse buyers. Travel.	10	15
Joiner Activists		
Leading-edge thinkers. Willing to spend. Shop most for clothes. Day-to-Day Watchers follow this segment. Heavy pleasure trip takers. Like new technology.	24	27
Responsible Survivors		
Cautious, not risk takers. Enjoy self rewards. Accept direction well. Brand loyal. Heavy TV viewers.	14	11
Aggressive Achievers		
Confident, success oriented. Want to be leaders. Love status-signalling goods. Bargain hunters. Flaunt material possessions.	12	12

After selecting a target market, an organization develops an appropriate marketing mix. Recall from Chapter 11 that the *marketing mix* is a blend of the four strategy elements of marketing decision making — product, price, distribution, and promotion — to satisfy chosen consumer segments. These elements are described in the sections that follow. Each strategy is a variable in the mix; the combination of the variables determines the degree of marketing success.

PRODUCT STRATEGY

AS NOTED IN Chapter 12, marketers broadly define a *product* as a bundle of physical, service, and symbolic attributes designed to satisfy consumer wants. Under this definition, a product is a service and a service

is a product, and in today's market it is sometimes hard to tell the difference. A *product strategy* involves considerably more than just producing a good or service. It also includes decisions about package design, brand name, trademarks, warranties, product image, new-product development, and customer service. Think, for instance, about your favourite soft drink. Do you like it for its taste alone, or do other attributes, such as clever ads, attractive packaging, and overall image also attract you? These other attributes may influence your choice more than you realize.

Classifying Goods and Services

Marketers have found it useful to classify goods and services as either *consumer* or *business*, depending on the purchasers of the particular item. These classifications can be subdivided further, and each type requires a different competitive strategy.

Classifying Consumer Goods. The classifications most typically used for consumer goods are based on consumer buying habits. *Convenience products* are items the consumer seeks to purchase frequently, immediately, and with little effort. Items stocked in 7-Eleven stores, vending machines, and local newsstands are usually convenience products — for example, newspapers, chewing gum, and bread.

Shopping products are those typically purchased only after the consumer has compared competing products in competing stores. Someone intent on buying a new television set may visit many stores, examine perhaps dozens of sets, and spend days making the final decision. *Specialty products* are those that a purchaser is willing to make a special effort to obtain. The purchaser is already familiar with the item and considers it to have no reasonable substitute. The nearest Lexus dealer may be 100 km away, but if you have decided that this is the care you want, you will make the trip.

Note that a shopping product for one person may be a convenience item for someone else. Majority buying patterns determine the item's product classification.

Classifying Business Goods. While consumer products are classified by buying habits, business products are classified based on how they are used and by their basic characteristics. Products that are long-lived and usually are purchased with large sums of money are called *capital items*. Less costly products that are consumed within a year are referred to as *expense items*.

Intel's Pentium® processor, though a computer component part, is targeted at both consumers and businesses. Because of its reputation, many buyers are unwilling to purchase computers that are not marked with the "Intel Inside®" logo.

Installations are major capital items, such as new factories, machinery, and custom-made equipment. Installations are expensive and often involve years of buyer and seller negotiations before a purchase is actually made. *Accessory equipment* includes capital items that are usually less expensive and shorter-lived than installations; examples are hand tools and fax machines.

Component parts and materials are finished business goods that become part of a final product, such as disk drives that are sold to computer manufacturers or tires that are sold to automakers. *Raw materials* are farm and natural products used in producing other, final products; examples include cotton, milk, and iron ore. *Supplies* are expense items used in a firm's daily operation that do not become part of the final product, such as paper clips, light bulbs, and copy paper.

Classifying Services. Services can be classified as either consumer or business services. Child-care centres and shoe-repair shops provide services for consumers, while the Pinkerton security patrol at a factory and Kelly Services' temporary office workers are examples of business services. In some cases, a service can accommodate both consumer and business markets. For example, when Service-Master cleans the upholstery in a home, it is a consumer service, but when it spruces up the painting system and robots in a manufacturing plant, it is a business service.

Marketing Strategy Implications

The consumer product classification is a useful tool in marketing strategy. For example, once a new lawn edger has been classified as a shopping good, marketers have a better idea of its promotion, pricing, and distribution needs. The impact of the consumer products classification on various aspects of marketing strategy is shown in Table 13.3.

Each group of business products, however, requires a different marketing strategy. Because most installations and many component parts are marketed directly from the manufacturer to the buyer, the promotional emphasis is on personal selling rather than on advertising. By contrast, marketers of supplies and accessory equipment rely more on advertising since their products often are sold through an intermediary, such as a wholesaler. Producers of installations and component parts may involve their customers in new-product development, especially when the business product is custom-made. Finally, firms marketing supplies and accessory equipment place greater emphasis on competitive pricing strategies than do other business products marketers, who concentrate on product quality and servicing.

Table 13.3 Relationship between Consumer Products Classification and Marketing Strategy

Marketing Strategy Factor	Convenience Product	Shopping Product	Specialty Product
Store image	Unimportant	Very important	Important
Price	Low	Relatively high	High
Promotion	By manufacturer	By manufacturer and retailers	By manufacturer and retailers
Distribution channel	Many wholesalers and retailers	Relatively few wholesalers and retailers	Very few wholesalers and retailers
Number of retail outlets	Many	Few	Very small number; often one per market area

THE PRODUCT MIX

A PRODUCT MIX *is the assortment of goods and services offered by a firm.* Although Borden Inc. may be best known for its dairy products, the firm's product mix also includes pasta, snack items, niche grocery products (Gallina Blanca dry soups and ReaLemon juice), nonfood consumer goods (Krazy Glue, Elmer's Glue, wallpaper), and specialty business chemicals (plastic film, forest product adhesives, food-wrap items).

The product mix is a combination of product lines and individual offerings that make up the product line. A **product line** *is a series of related products.* Borden's product line of frozen dairy desserts, for example, includes Eagle Brand ice cream, Lady Borden ice cream sand-

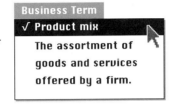

Business Term
✓ **Product mix**
The assortment of goods and services offered by a firm.

Business Term
✓ **Product line**
A series of related products.

wiches, Meadow Gold frozen yogurt and yogurt pops, and Turtles frozen novelties.

Marketers must assess their product mix continually to ensure company growth, to satisfy changing consumer needs and wants, and to adjust to competitors' offerings. To remain competitive, marketers look for gaps in their product lines and fill them with new products or modified versions of existing ones. A helpful tool used by marketers in making product decisions is the product life cycle.

Product Life Cycle

Once a product is on the market, it often goes through a series of four stages known as the **product life cycle** — *introduction, growth, maturity, and decline.* Industry sales and profits vary depending on the life-cycle stage of a product.

Product life cycles are not set in stone: not all products follow this progression precisely, and different products may spend different periods of time in each stage. The concept,

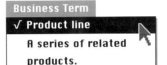

Business Term
✓ **Product life cycle**
Four stages through which a product often passes: introduction, growth, maturity, and decline.

however, as shown in Figure 13.2, helps the marketing planner anticipate developments throughout the various stages of a product's life. Profits assume a predictable pattern through the stages, and promotional emphasis must shift from dispensing product information in the early stages to heavy brand promotion in the later ones.

Stages of the Product Life Cycle. In the *introduction stage,* the firm tries to promote demand for its new offer-

---

BUSINESS TIP

Marketers we know tell us you should be watching out for at least three <u>target customer</u> (TC) groups:

→ **Primary.** This TC is perfect for your business and could be a heavy user. To profile your "heavy" customer, you'll have to use demographics, but you'll also need to consider psychographics.

→ **Secondary.** This one almost slips away before you can focus the camera. Sometimes your secondary TC will lead you to the third customer – who is invisible at first.

→ **Invisible.** This customer appears after you open the doors, after you have the courage to go ahead and start up.

Figure 13.2 Stages in the Product Life Cycle

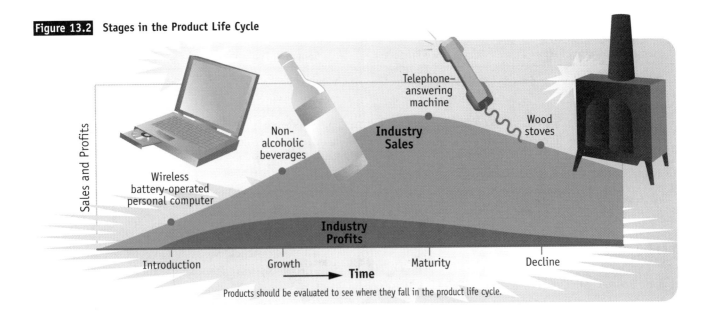

Products should be evaluated to see where they fall in the product life cycle.

ing, inform the market about it, and explain its features, uses, and benefits. New-product development and introductory promotional campaigns, though important, are expensive and commonly lead to losses in the introduction stage. A new product can cost millions of dollars to introduce, but such expenditures are necessary if the firm is to profit later.

During the *growth stage*, sales climb quickly as new customers join the early users who now are repurchasing the item. Word-of-mouth referrals and continued advertising by the firm induce others to make trial purchases. At this point, the company begins to earn profits on the new product. Unfortunately, this encourages competitors to enter the field with similar offerings, and price competition appears.

Industry sales at first increase in the *maturity stage*, but eventually reach a saturation level at which further expansion is difficult. Competition also intensifies, increasing the availability of the product. Firms concentrate on capturing competitors' customers, often dropping prices to further their appeal. Sales volume fades late in the maturity stage, and some of the weaker competitors leave the market. During this stage, firms promote mature products aggressively to protect their market share and to distinguish their products from those of competitors.

Sales continue to fall in the *decline stage*, the fourth phase of the product life cycle. Profits decline and may become losses as further price cutting occurs in the reduced market for the item. The decline stage usually is caused by a product innovation or a shift in consumer preferences.

Marketing Strategy Implications of the Product Life Cycle

The product life cycle is a useful concept for designing a marketing strategy that will be flexible enough to accommodate changing marketplace characteristics. For instance, knowing that the advertising emphasis will change from informative to persuasive as the product faces new competitors during its growth stage helps the marketer anticipate competitive actions and make necessary adjustments. These competitive moves may involve developing new products, lowering prices, increasing distribution, creating new promotional campaigns, or any combination of these strategies.

In general, the marketer's objective is to extend the product life cycle as long as the item is profitable. Indeed, some products can be highly profitable during the later stages of their life cycle, since all of the initial development costs have already been recovered.

One strategy for extending the life cycle is to increase customers' frequency of use; persuading homeowners that they need to have more smoke alarms and flashlights may result in increased purchases by each household. Another strategy might be to add new users; Gerber Products increased the size of its baby-food market by creating specialty foods for foreign consumers, such as strained sushi for Japanese babies and strained lamb brains for Australian infants. Arm & Hammer used a third approach, finding new uses for its product. Arm & Hammer baking soda's original use in baking has been augmented by its newer uses as a toothpaste, refrigerator freshener, and flame extinguisher. A fourth strategy —

Campbell's soups have enjoyed a long life cycle thanks, in part, to creative marketing. Having celebrated their 100th anniversary in 1997, Campbell's soups are still going strong.

changing package sizes, labels, and product designs — works well for Timex Corporation, which supplements traditional wrist-watches with new designs, such as The Lefty and Gizmoz for kids and the large-numbered Easy Reader for people with failing eyesight.

Packaging and Labels

Packaging and labels play an important role in product strategy. Packaging affects the durability, image, and convenience of an item, and is responsible for one of the biggest costs in many consumer products. Cost-effective packaging is one of industry's greatest needs.

Choosing the right package is especially crucial in international marketing, since marketers must be aware of many variables. One variable is cultural preference: African nations, for instance, often prefer bold colours, but flag colours may be preferred (or frowned upon), and red often is associated with death or witchcraft. Package size can vary according to the purchasing patterns and market conditions of a country. In countries

with little refrigeration, people may want to buy their beverages one at a time rather than in six-packs. Package weight is another important issue, since the cost of shipping often is based on weight.[8]

Labelling is an integral part of the packaging process as well. A label in most instances contains

- The brand name or symbol.

- The name and address of the manufacturer or distributor.

- Information about product composition and size.

- Information about recommended uses of the product.

In most Canadian industries, government-set and voluntary packaging and label standards have been developed. The law requires a listing of food ingredients in descending order of the amounts used. Labels of such companies as Del Monte Corporation now show specific food values and include a calorie count and a list of vitamins and minerals. In other industries (such as pharmaceuticals, fur, and clothing), federal legislation requires the provision of various information and prevents

Urban Juice & Soda Co. takes an innovative turn with its soda bottle labels, which vary in images from flavour to flavour, reflecting a philosophy of change and fun — all to appeal to its target market, "Generation 2000." This young company from Vancouver has already won an international labelling award for Wazu, its bottled water.

false branding. The marketing manager must be fully acquainted with these laws, take into consideration language requirements, and ensure that package designs and labels comply with these requirements.[9]

Marketers who ship products to other countries have to comply with the labelling requirements in those nations. For example, in the United States, labelling must meet federal requirements as set forth in the Fair Packaging and Labelling Act (1966) and the Nutrition Labelling and Education Act (1990), which allow consumers to make value comparisons among competitive products. Labelling for other countries should address such questions as: Should the labels be in more than one language? Should ingredients be specified? Do the labels give enough information about the product to meet government standards?

Another important aspect of packaging and labelling is the *universal product code (UPC)*, the bar code read by optical scanners that print the name of the item and the price on a receipt. The advantages of optical scanning include[10]

- Labour saving (because products are no longer individually priced).

- Faster customer check-out.

- Better inventory control, since the scanner can be tied to inventory records.

- Easier marketing research for the industries involved with it.

- Fewer errors in entering purchases at the check-out counter.

PRICING STRATEGY

THE SECOND ELEMENT of the marketing mix is *pricing strategy*. **Price** *is the exchange value of a good or service*. An item is worth only what someone else is willing to pay for it. Pricing strategy deals with the multitude of factors that influence the setting of a price.

Prices help direct the overall economic system. A firm uses various factors of production, such as natural resources, labour, and capital, based on their relative prices. High wage rates may cause a firm to install labour-saving machinery, and high interest rates may lead management to decide against a new capital expenditure. Prices and volume sold determine the revenue received by the firm and influence its profits.

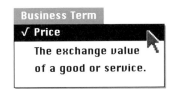

Business Term

✓ **Price**

The exchange value of a good or service.

Consumer Perception of Prices

Marketers must be concerned with the way consumers perceive prices. If a buyer views a price as too high or too low, the marketer must correct the situation. Price–quality relationships and psychological pricing are important in this regard.

Research shows that the consumer's perception of product quality is related closely to the item's price: the higher the price, the better its perceived quality. Most marketers believe this perceived price–quality relationship exists over a relatively wide range of prices, although extreme prices may be viewed as either too expensive or too cheap. Marketing managers need to study and experiment with prices because the price–quality relationship can be of key importance to a firm's pricing strategy.

Many marketers use psychological pricing because they believe certain prices are more appealing than others to buyers. Many retailers believe that consumers are attracted to uneven amounts, so they use prices such as $19.98 or $9.99, rather than $20 or $10. Some stores use prices ending in 1, 2, 3, 4, 6, or 7 to avoid the look of more common prices like $5.95, $10.98, and $19.99.

DISTRIBUTION STRATEGY

THE THIRD ELEMENT of the marketing mix, *distribution strategy*, deals with the marketing activities and institutions involved in getting the right good or service

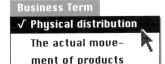

Business Term

✓ **Distribution channels**

The paths that products — and title to them — follow from producer to consumer.

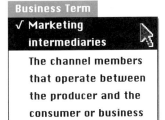

Business Term

✓ **Physical distribution**

The actual movement of products from producer to user.

Business Term

✓ **Marketing intermediaries**

The channel members that operate between the producer and the consumer or business user.

to the firm's customers. Distribution decisions involve modes of transportation, warehousing, inventory control, order processing, and selection of marketing channels. Marketing channels are made up of businesses such as retailers and wholesalers that move a product from producer to final consumer.

The two major components of an organization's distribution strategy are distribution channels and physical distribution. **Distribution channels** *are the paths that products — and title to them — follow from producer to consumer.* They are the means by which all organizations distribute their goods and services. **Physical distribution** *is the actual movement of these products from producer to user.* Physical distribution covers a broad range of activities, including customer service, transportation, inventory control, materials handling, order processing, and warehousing.

Distribution Channels

Distribution channels consist of **marketing intermediaries** (also called *middlemen*), *the channel members that operate between the producer and the consumer or business user.* Marketing intermediaries perform various functions that help the distribution channel to operate smoothly, such as buying, selling, storing, and transporting products; sorting and grading bulky items; and providing information to other channel members. The two main categories of marketing intermediaries are wholesalers and retailers.

Wholesalers

Wholesaling intermediaries *are distribution-channel members that sell primarily to retailers, other wholesalers, or business users.* For instance, Sysco is a wholesaler that buys food products from manufacturers and resells them to restaurants, hotels, and other institutions in the United States and Canada.

Business Term

✓ **Wholesaling intermediaries**

Distribution-channel members that sell primarily to retailers, other wholesalers, or business users.

Wholesaling is a crucial part of the distribution channel for many products, particularly consumer goods. Wholesaling intermediaries can be classified on the basis of ownership; some are owned by manufacturers, some by retailers, and others are independently owned. Most North American wholesalers are independent wholesalers who account for an estimated two-thirds of all wholesale trade.

Retailers

Retailers, by contrast, *are distribution-channel members that sell goods and services to individuals for their own use rather than for resale.* Consumers usually buy their food, clothing, shampoo, furniture, and appliances from some type of retailer. The supermarket where you buy your

IN THE NEWS

WILLY LOMAN IS HISTORY

In 1996, Encyclopedia Britannica — a name synonymous with door-to-door sales — announced it was laying off its home sales force. This action further confirmed the end of a trend — the glory days of the door-to-door direct sales were history.

John Winter, a Toronto retail analyst, says the quintessential door-to-door salesman — captured in Arthur Miller's classic *Death of a Salesman* — have now evolved to a new level. In the 1940s, 1950s, 1960s, and 1970s there were thousands and thousands of these "Avon calling" people. In the nineties, direct sales is still alive and thriving, but few firms make house calls like Willy Loman. Direct selling mainstays like Avon Canada Inc. and Amway of Canada Ltd., or Canadian upstarts like Weekenders, have adjusted to the "ding dong" tactics of the past. House parties, offices,

and technology are now their new stomping grounds — and in many cases their roads are electronic and their doors are on computer screens.

According to Ross Creber, president of the Direct Sellers Association, "Direct-sale companies have simply readjusted their selling approach to be where the consumer is today," and "business has never been stronger." Here are some more facts:

➡ Between 1988 and 1994, sales of the Direct Sellers Association's members — who represent roughly half of all direct sellers in Canada — jumped 116 percent to $1.1 billion.

➡ The number of independent sales reps [in the association] rose 67 percent to 600 000 people. Of these, about 81 percent are women, of whom 78 percent are part-time with the remainder working more than 30 hours per week.

➡ Roughly 53 percent of all sales come from personal care products (cosmetic, skin care, jewellery), 32 percent from home and family-care products, 8 percent from leisure and entertainment products, and the remainder from a cross-section of categories.

➡ About 70 percent of direct sales take place in the home (almost three-quarters by appointment or through group parties), 20 percent in the workplace, and 8 percent at public events such as fairs.

➡ The World Federation of Direct Selling Associations, with members in 43 countries, reports direct selling soared 102 percent between 1988 and 1994 to $67.6 billion (U.S.). The total number of direct-sales people jumped 108 percent to 18 million.

Source: Adapted from Gayle MacDonald, "Who's Still Knocking at the Door?" *The Globe and Mail*, May 6, 1996, B6. Reprinted with permission from The Globe and Mail.

groceries may have bought some of its items from Sysco and then resold them to you.

Retailers are a final link in the distribution channel. Since, traditionally, they are often the only channel members that deal directly with consumers, it is essential they remain alert to customers' needs. It is also important that they keep pace with developments in the fast-changing business environment.

There are two categories of retailers: nonstore and store. *Nonstore retailing* includes direct selling, such as that done by Tupperware and Amway; direct-response retailing, such as the Internet, catalogues, and television shopping; and automatic merchandising, which includes vending machines. The second category of retailers, *store retailing*, accounts for about 90 percent of total retail sales. As Figure 13.3 shows, Canadian retail sales remained relatively constant over the period 1993 to 1996. This was a significant departure from the U.S. experience, which showed continued growth over this same period. There are about 165 000 retail stores in Canada. Table 13.4 lists a few types of store retailers, with examples of each type. Clearly, there are many approaches to retailing and a variety of services, prices, and product lines.

Retailers are subject to constant change as new stores replace older establishments. In a theory called the *wheel of retailing*,

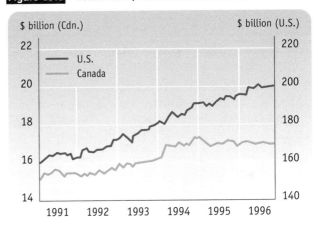

Figure 13.3 **Retail Sales, Canada and the United States**

In 1992 dollars, seasonally adjusted

Business Term

✓ **Retailers**

Distribution-channel members that sell goods and services to individuals for their own use rather than for resale.

new retailers enter the market by offering lower prices made possible through reductions in service. Supermarkets and discount houses, for example, gained their initial market footholds through low-price, limited-service appeals. These new entries gradually add services as they grow, and ultimately become targets for new retailers.

The wheel of retailing shows that business success involves the "survival of the fittest." As we learned in the opening story, Consumers Distributing was a painful

Table 13.4 **Types of Store Retailers**

Type of Retailer	Description	Examples
Variety store	Offers a variety of low-priced merchandise.	Bi-Way, Giant Tiger
Department store	Offers a wide variety of merchandise sold in departmentalized sections (furniture, cosmetics, clothing) and many customer services.	Eatons, The Bay, Sears
Specialty store	Offers a complete selection in a narrow range of merchandise.	Kinney Shoes, Japan Camera, jewellery stores
Convenience store	Offers staple convenience goods, long store hours, rapid check-outs, adequate parking facilities, and convenient locations.	7-Eleven, Mac's Milk, gasoline stations
Discount store	Offers a wide selection of merchandise at low prices and few services.	Giant Tiger, Wal-Mart
Off-Price store	Offers designer or brand-name merchandise of many manufacturers at discount prices.	Winners
Factory outlet	Manufacturer-owned store selling seconds, production overruns, or discounted lines.	Nike outlet store, Black & Decker
Supermarket	Large, self-service store offering a wide selection of food and nonfood merchandise.	IGA, Loblaws
Warehouse club	Large warehouse-style store that sells food and general merchandise at discount prices to people who are part of its associated club membership.	Sam's Club, Price Club/ Costco

LESSONS FROM THE BEST

STRATEGIC ALLIANCES

Partnerships and strategic alliances, particularly in business-to-business transactions, play a major role in relationship marketing programs. Here are two examples.

In 1996, FastLane Technologies Inc., a small software company located in Ottawa's Silicon Valley North, was having trouble recruiting software engineers. Dalhousie University and the Technical University of Nova Scotia saw this as an opportunity to establish a partnership with FastLane and provide jobs for their students. They talked to FastLane about adjusting their courses so that their engineering graduates would be equipped with the kinds of skills FastLane needed. These collaborative discussions were a major factor in convincing FastLane to move almost all its operations and headquarters from Ottawa to Halifax. "In Ottawa we were a small fish in a big pond; here it's completely reversed," said FastLane's CEO and co-founder David Seguin. If the arrangement works out, FastLane will have long-term local access to engineering graduates, and Dalhousie University and the Technical University of Nova Scotia will be able to stimulate local jobs.

In the competitive food service business, many Canadian companies are partnering by sharing space to increase their customer base and reduce leasing expenses. Some Second Cup and Great Canadian Bagel franchises now share space, especially in downtown locations where rent is high. On one side of a room is a Second Cup franchise where you can enjoy coffee and muffins. On the other side is a Great Canadian Bagel where you can munch on a fresh bagel sandwich. A co-operative leasing alliance gives both companies the opportunity to expand their customer base and reduce their leasing costs.

Source: Adapted from James Bagnall, "Firms Move Out to Find Workers," *The Ottawa Citizen*, February 10, 1997, A1, A2; Mario Mota, "Retailers Sharing Space Maximize Customer Base," *The Ottawa Transcript*, January 1997, Vol. 1, No. 1, 1, published by Asset Beam Publishing Ltd., Neapean ON. Reprinted by permission.

example of one Canadian retailer that could not keep up with the times. Canada had another blood-letting example in 1997, this time with the bankruptcy of MMG Management Group of Montreal, a 169-store chain of discount stores. About 1000 jobs were thrown into limbo because of "increased competition and decreased consumer spending," according to Allan MacKenzie, president of Gendis Inc. of Winnipeg, MMG's parent company.[11] In contrast, Canadian Tire made changes to its retailing concept — and prospered. As of 1997, Canadian Tire was a good example of how Canadian firms can successfully compete if they respond to the realities of the new retail landscape.

Teleshopping[12]

Teleshopping or *cybershopping* involves *the selection and electronic purchase of merchandise that has been displayed on computers.* The Internet is quickly growing to become one of the main distribution channels for the teleshopper. In 1996, there were in excess of 12 000 retailers and some 2.5 million people doing business on the Internet. Many argue that we are witnessing just the beginning of a new wave of Internet retail and business-to-business transactions. Canadian cyber guru Don Tapscott, for example, crystal-balls Canada's future in his book *The Digital Economy*. He argues that cybershopping is "coming and there is no stopping it. There will be 1 billion people on the Internet by the end of the end of the decade and all of them shoppers." American "pop" futurist Faith Popcorn, in her book *Clicking*, says that "both computers and TVs are feeding into the armchair ease of electronic shopping." Both authors point to the heavy investment in Internet retailing and home page development by entrepreneurs like Mark Blumes (formerly of Mark's Work Warehouse), large retailers like Wal-Mart and Future Shop, and distributors like Purolator as evidence of this new wave. Other retail analysts and cyber experts are more cautious. They say that teleshopping over the Internet may work for some companies and products — travel companies and book stores, for example, have had some success selling over the Net. But in total, they argue, the expected impact of cyber shopping has been grossly exaggerated. Many say that most consumers will "still want to

Business Term

√ **Teleshopping**

The selection and electronic purchase of merchandise that has been displayed on computers.

go out and see it, touch it, feel it, see how it works." In addition, consumers will not give up the social joys of shopping.

Vertical Marketing Systems

There are some channel members, and even entire channels of distribution, that act quite independently. They have no formal long-term ties to others in the channel, but build relationships with buyers or sellers in an autonomous fashion.

More commonly, other intermediaries have found it desirable to form a **vertical marketing system (VMS):** *a network of channel intermediaries organized and centrally managed to produce the maximum co-operative impact.* In such a system, the co-ordination of the various channel members can produce operation efficiencies, deep market penetration, and greater profits. There are three types of VMS: corporate, administered, and contractual. They are shown in Table 13.5.

Vertical marketing systems produce economies of scale through their size and elimination of duplicated services. For example, a wholesaler such as Oshawa Wholesale often develops a line of private brands to be stocked by members of a voluntary chain. A common store name and similar inventories allow the retailers to achieve cost savings on advertising, since a single newspaper advertisement promotes all retailers in the trading area. IGA, with a membership of about 800 food

Business Term

✓ **Vertical marketing system (VMS)**

A network of channel intermediaries organized and centrally managed to produce the maximum co-operative impact.

Table 13.5 Three Types of Vertical Marketing Systems

Type of System	Description	Examples
Corporate	Channel owned and operated by a single organization	Bata Shoes Firestone Sherwin-Williams Singer McDonald's (partial)
Administered	Channel dominated by one powerful member that acts as channel captain	Kodak General Electric Corning Glass
Contractual	Channel co-ordinated through contractual agreements among channel members	**Wholesaler-Sponsored Voluntary Chain** IGA Canadian Tire Independent Druggists Alliance (IDA) Allied Hardware **Retail Co-operative** Associated Grocers **Franchise Systems** McDonald's (partial) Century 21 Real Estate AAMCO Transmissions Coca-Cola® bottlers Ford dealers

stores, is a good example of this kind of vertical marketing system.[13]

Types of Distribution Channels

Figure 13.4 illustrates the six primary channels of distribution. The first four channels typically are used to distribute consumer goods and services, while the last two commonly are used for business goods and services. Also, a low-priced product usually goes through more intermediaries than a similar product with a higher price tag.

Figure 13.4 The Primary Channels of Distribution

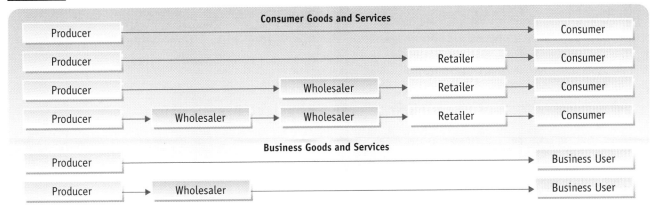

Manufacturing and service industries, however, may use hundreds of channels to distribute their output. Canned foods usually pass through wholesalers and retailers before they reach the grocery store. Books can be sold over the Internet. Weekender's sells most of its clothes at home parties. No one channel is right for every product. The best channel depends on the circumstances of the market and on consumer needs, and it may change over time. In order to stay competitive, marketers must keep their distribution methods up to date.

Selecting a Distribution Channel

The best distribution channel depends on several factors: the market, the product, the producer, and the competition. These factors often are interrelated.

Market factors may be the most important consideration in choosing a distribution channel. Companies must select the degree of market coverage that is most appropriate for their products. Changes in consumer buying behaviour may necessitate a change in distribution-channel strategy. If a product can be sold to more than one market segment, more than one distribution channel may be necessary. In fact, some companies are finding that multiple distribution channels help them sell more, so they sell their products through retailers, mail order, and online computer catalogues.

WAKE-UP CALL

Catalogue shopping is changing and will continue to change on into the next millennium. Dealer-to-dealer network programs, for example, are quickly replacing the infrastructure of store departments and workers who verify, invoice, label, and ship goods. These new programs have the capability of doing everything but picking up and packing your purchase and getting it to the door — and even this is possible at a click of a mouse through such companies as Purolator.

At the leading edge of this branch of the electronic revolution is the network-based program "Smart Catalog" developed by Vicom Multimedia Inc. of Calgary. Says Bob Henderson, purchasing manager at Gulf Canada Resource Ltd. in Calgary, who uses Smart Catalog, "It gives a three-dimensional, pictorial view of a product, eliminates errors in selection, and helps prevent getting the wrong product. We can order online. At the end of the month, we have one invoice for all transactions that are summarized. It's slick." Although these types of multimedia network catalogues may never completely replace touch-and-feel shopping, they certainly add welcome efficiency to business-to-business transactions.

CYBERSPACE

In 1995, Mark Blumes was dumped from the company he founded — Mark's Work Warehouse, a retail chain specializing in work and leisure clothes. Some say the reason for this fall-out was his push to move the company into electronic shopping. Blumes believes that people will eventually opt for the convenience of shopping on the Net: "Imagine your significant other sitting at a computer and in a 3-D virtual experience being able to do all your shopping by pointing and clicking instead of going to the store." Blumes believes that electronic commerce is the wave of the future, and in 1996 he followed his vision by establishing Mark's Club — an Internet, membership-based shopping advantage program. Will he be successful? Only the market and Blumes' business savvy will be able to tell.

Curious? Check it out — see if Mark is still in business. His address in 1997: http://www.marksclub.com.

Performance is a key consideration when choosing a distribution channel. A producer loses customers if its intermediary falls down on the job in promoting or delivering its products. A producer may switch channels if distribution is becoming too difficult or complex.

New technologies are opening up new channels of distribution for all industries. For example, clothing manufacturers, which have long distributed their products through retailers and catalogues, now distribute them using the Internet and TV shopping channels, both of which continue to grow in popularity. Many progressive Canadian businesses are wholesaling and retailing their products using such technologies as multimedia catalogues, intranet, and entranet.

Physical Distribution

Physical distribution, the other component of distribution strategy, involves actually moving goods from producer to user. Physical distribution is important for two reasons. First, such activities account for, on average, about one-fifth the cost of a manufactured product. Reducing the cost of physical distribution can improve productivity and make a company more competitive. Second, customer satisfaction, to a large extent, depends on reliable movement of goods.

COMPANY WATCH

Carlyle Computer Products of Winnipeg is a repeat winner of the Financial Post's "50 Best Managed Private Companies Award." The company supplies computer paper, cut sheet paper, transparencies, inkjet cartridges, ribbons, toner cartridges, power bars, and diskettes to large, small, and home-based businesses. A key component of its distribution strategy is to listen. Carlyle's president, Derek Johannson, does a yearly "if I were president tour." Johannson meets every employee for a twenty-minute one-on-one session to hear their ideas about running the company. In 1996, for example, the distribution department "had specific suggestions regarding how to handle back orders. The ideas had never been brought up through the ranks before," says Johannson. Supply chain acquisitions and capital investment are the other key distribution strategies. In 1995, Carlyle acquired Alberta's largest computer supply company, Western Data Products. It also invested in sophisticated contract management software to track customers' contracts. "In the old days people wanted to see the sales rep across the desk, but clients don't have the time for that anymore. So rather than manage the sales calls, we now manage all contracts," says Johannson.

Physical distribution covers a broad range of activities, including warehousing, materials handling, inventory control, order processing, and transportation. *Warehousing* is the physical distribution activity that involves storing products. *Materials handling* is the physical distribution activity of moving items within plants, warehouses, transportation terminals, and stores. *Inventory control* involves managing inventory costs, such as storage facilities, insurance, taxes, and handling. The physical distribution activity of *order processing* includes preparing orders for shipment and receiving orders when shipments arrive.

The form of transportation used to ship products depends primarily on the kind of product, the distance, and the cost. The physical distribution manager has a number of companies and modes of transportation from which to choose. The five major modes of transportation are railroads, trucks, water carriers, pipelines, and air freight. Some distribution experts have added a sixth mode — electronic. Yes, the I-way is becoming a major competitive weapon in the new economy. The faster methods typically cost more than the slower ones. Speed, reliable delivery, shipment frequency, location availability, handling flexibility, and cost are all important considerations when choosing a mode of transportation.

Order processing and the other physical distribution activities performed by distribution-channel members ensure that customers receive the right products at the right time and the right place. Manufacturers, wholesalers, and retailers have reduced the costs of many physical distribution functions by applying computer-based electronics and automation. Computer linkups that let channel members share information speed up order processing and delivery and help reduce inventory on hand.

Customer Service

Customer service is a vital component of product and distribution strategy. **Customer service standards** *measure the quality of service a firm provides for its customers.* Managers frequently set quantitative guidelines — for example, that all orders be processed within 24 hours after they are received, or that salespeople approach shoppers within two minutes after they enter the store. Sometimes customers set their own service standards and choose suppliers that meet or exceed them. The service standards set by companies for their suppliers are rising as Canadian companies gear up to compete more effectively on a global basis.

The customer service components of product strategy include warranty and repair service programs. A

Business Term

√ Customer service standards

Measurements of the quality of service a firm provides for its customers.

FUTURE TREND

CALL CENTRE BOOM

The call centre industry is booming with more than 500 000 full- and part-time jobs expected to at least double by 2001. Technology combined with a competitive need for improved customer-driven service and sales are the factors driving the boom.

CSB Systems Ltd., a Winnipeg-based Canadian company that specializes in computerizing the manufacturing and distribution sectors, services over 500 North American clients. Its call-centre agents route customer queries, do outbound calls to internal staff, and follow up directly with clients. According to CSB president Dan Stevens, the call centre is really a customer care centre. It gets "customers' questions or ser-vice needs to the right skill set within the right time frame, leveraging our internal resources and skills regardless of [where the customers] reside."

Many Canadians still see working at a call centre as the information-age equivalent to flipping burgers — low-skill, high stress, and low pay. Not so, says Gaylen Duncan, president of the Information Technology Association of Canada. "Call centres are the new economy equivalent of the mail room. They offer a way for young people to learn about products and customer relations, develop communication skills, and deal with stress. The call centre can be a foot in the corporate door that can lead to a full-fledged career."

According to a 1998 study by PricewaterhouseCoopers, new-age call centres act like the central nervous system of a company. Agents must often juggle many different tasks at once, interpret and move customer and electronic information between corporate departments, and respond to customer needs in a professional manner. Many call centres are now becoming the marketing hub of new-age companies.

For more information, check out the International Quality & Productivity Center (IQPC) Web site at **http://iqpc.com/iqpcinfo.htm**.

Source: Adapted from "Call Centre Solution a Partnership for Success," Manitoba Telecom Services Inc., *The Globe and Mail*, September 10, 1998, C1; Tyler Hamilton, "Call Centres Flip their Fast-Food Stereotype," *The Globe and Mail*, October 8, 1998, C9. Reprinted with permission from The Globe and Mail.

warranty is a firm's promise to repair, refund money paid for, or replace a product if it proves unsatisfactory.

Repair services are also important. Consumers want to know that help is available if something goes wrong. Those who shop for home computers, for example, often choose retailers that offer repair services and telephone "help lines." Products with inadequate service backing quickly disappear from the market as a result of word-of-mouth criticism.

PROMOTIONAL STRATEGY

THE FINAL MARKETING mix element, *promotional strategy*, is the function of informing, persuading, and influencing a consumer decision. It is as important to a not-for-profit organization, such as the Heart and Stroke Foundation of Canada, as it is to a profit-oriented company like Future Shop.

> **Business Term**
> **√ Promotional mix**
> The firm's combination of personal selling and nonpersonal selling designed to achieve promotional objectives.

> **Business Term**
> **√ Personal selling**
> A promotional presentation made on a person-to-person basis to a potential buyer.

> **Business Term**
> **√ Nonpersonal selling**
> Advertising, sales promotion, and public relations.

Components of the Promotional Mix

The **promotional mix** *is the firm's combination of personal selling and nonpersonal selling designed to achieve promotional objectives.* **Personal selling** *is a promotional presentation made on a person-to-person basis to a potential buyer. Telemarketing* is personal selling conducted entirely by telephone. Many firms use this method if it is too difficult or too expensive to have salespeople meet all potential customers in person. **Nonpersonal selling** consists of *advertising, sales promotion, and public relations.* Marketers attempt to develop a promotional mix that effectively and efficiently communicates their message to target customers.

For book retailer Chapters, the optimal promotional mix involves a wide range of goods and services designed to encourage customers to stay for a while. Chapters has created a strategic alliance with Starbucks so its customers can browse for hours and relax with a cappuccino or a light snack. Software and multimedia sections attract those interested in nonbook media. Chapters' promotional strategy represents the fastest-growing trend in book retailing.

Advertising

For many firms, advertising is the most effective type of nonpersonal promotion. **Advertising** is *a paid, nonpersonal sales communication usually directed at a large number of potential customers.*

> **Business Term**
> √ **Advertising**
> A paid, nonpersonal sales communication usually directed at a large number of potential customers.

> **Business Term**
> √ **Sales promotion**
> A form of promotion designed to increase sales through one-time selling efforts, such as displays, trade shows, or special events.

> **Business Term**
> √ **Public relations**
> An organization's communications with its customers, vendors, news media, employees, stockholders, government, and general public.

All marketers face the question of how best to allocate their advertising budgets. Cost is an important consideration, but it is equally important to choose the media best suited for the job. All media have their advantages and disadvantages, as Table 13.6 outlines.

Sales Promotion

Sales promotion *is a form of promotion designed to increase sales through one-time selling efforts, such as displays, trade shows, or special events.* Traditionally viewed as a supplement or support to a firm's sales or advertising efforts, sales promotion now has become an integral part of the promotional mix. Sales promotion techniques include point-of-purchase (POP) advertising displays in stores; specialty advertising, such as items imprinted with a company's name and logo; trade shows; samples; coupons; premiums; and contests.

Public Relations

Public relations refers to *an organization's communications with its customers, vendors, news media, employees, stockholders, government, and general public.* Many of

> **THEY SAID IT**
>
> "I learned a long time ago you earn money going where people ain't."
>
> MARK BLUMES, founder of Mark's Work Wearhouse

Table 13.6 Comparing the Advantages and Disadvantages of Advertising Media

Media	Advantages	Disadvantages
Newspapers	Tailored to individual communities; readers can refer back to ads	Short life span
Television	Mass coverage; repetition; flexibility; prestige	High cost; temporary message; public distrust; lack of selectivity
Direct mail	Selectivity; intense coverage; speed, flexibility; complete information; personalization	Expensive; consumer resistance; dependent on effective list
Radio	Immediacy; low cost; flexibility; targeted audience; mobility	Short life span; highly fragmented audience
Magazines	Selectivity; quality reproduction; long life; prestige	Lack of flexibility
Outdoor advertising	Communicates simple ideas quickly; promotes local goods and services; repetition	Too brief; environmental concerns
Internet	Mass coverage; adaptability; interactive; flexible; fast; prestige	Highly fragmented audience; requires constant updates; absence of solid cost–benefit analysis; lots of confusion and media noise

these communication efforts have a marketing purpose. IBM, for example, has received Thailand's prestigious Garuda Award, which recognizes significant contributions to that country's social and economic development. IBM provides personnel and equipment to Thai universities and donates funds to the nation's environmental protection agency.

SELECTING A PROMOTIONAL MIX AND PROMOTIONAL STRATEGY

DEVELOPING THE RIGHT promotional mix is one of the toughest tasks confronting marketers. The following questions provide some general guidelines for allocating promotional efforts and expenditures among personal selling, advertising, sales promotion, and public relations.

- **What is your target market?** For instance, a drill press is sold to the business market, so the manufacturer's strategy must emphasize an effective sales force. By contrast, Scope mouthwash is sold to consumers, so an appealing advertising campaign is more important.

- **What is the value of the product?** Most companies cannot afford to emphasize personal selling in marketing low-priced items like toothpaste, cosmetics, soft drinks, and candy, so they choose advertising instead. Higher-priced items in both business and consumer markets rely more on personal selling. Examples include time-share vacation condominiums and Boeing aircraft.

- **What time frame is involved?** Advertising usually is needed to precondition a person for a sales presentation. An effective and consistent advertising theme may influence people favourably when they are approached by a salesperson in a store. But, except for self-service situations, a salesperson typically is involved in completing the actual transaction. Advertising often is used again after the sale to assure consumers of the correctness of their selection and to precondition them for repeat purchases.

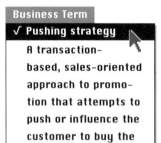

Business Term
√ Pushing strategy

A transaction-based, sales-oriented approach to promotion that attempts to push or influence the customer to buy the product or service.

Business Term
√ Pulling strategy

A relationship-based, positioning approach to promotion that focusses on the long-term needs of the customer.

- **Should you spend your promotional budget on advertising and/or personal selling?** Once this decision is made, you need to determine the level of sales promotion and public relations efforts necessary to market your product.

Push versus Pull Promotional Strategies

The promotional mix choice is related directly to the promotional strategy the firm will employ. The marketer has two alternatives available to meet these goals: a pushing strategy or a pulling strategy. A **pushing strategy** *is a transaction-based, sales-oriented approach to promotion that attempts to push or influence the customer to buy the product or service.* In its purest sense, a company would make a product or offer a service and then expect its salespeople to go out and find a customer to buy it. Sales personnel would be expected to explain to the customer why she or he should carry a particular product or service. You would probably hear sales slogans like "We've got to educate the customer" and "If they only knew what kind of deal they're getting." Under a push promotion strategy, customers are usually offered inducements to buy, such as special discounts, promotional materials, and co-operative advertising allowances. In the last case, the manufacturer shares the cost of local advertising of the product or line with the wholesaler or retailer. All of these strategies are designed to motivate the intermediaries to "push" the good or service to their customers.

A **pulling strategy** *is a relationship-based, positioning approach to promotion that focusses on the long-term needs of the customer.* The ultimate goal of the pulling promotional strategy is to get the customer to come to the supplier or producer with the money and desire to buy. The marketer concentrates on establishing a strong customer relationship based on the needs of the customer, which in turn "pulls" the product or service through the marketing channel. Advertising under a pull environment would focus on informing potential customers of the availability of a product or service since the need has already been determined. A central role of the salesperson is to "add on" to the product or service by establishing a long-term relationship based on the needs of the customer.

INTERNATIONAL PROMOTIONAL STRATEGY

CULTURAL SENSITIVITY AND good homework are crucial when planning international promotional strategies. Strategies that are effective for promoting products and services to Canadian audiences may not work in other countries due to cultural preferences, moral standards, educational levels, and language, all of which influence how ads will be perceived. For example, print ads are less effective in countries with low literacy rates.

Different countries offer different media to advertisers. Television is the most widespread advertising medium in both Europe and Latin America. The most popular advertising spots in Latin America are on prime-time soap operas that are watched by consumers from Brazil to Mexico. In other countries, commercial TV and radio are limited so print advertising is more common, as in Oman, Norway, and Sweden. The major advertising media in China are outdoor posters and billboards, which are usually located near factories.

Another challenge for international marketers is the wide variety of national regulations. Sweden, for example, prohibits television advertising entirely; Germany allows it, but restricts it to fifteen to twenty minutes each day, in blocks of three to five minutes. France and Italy limit the profits that state monopoly systems can make from advertising. Computer manufacturers sometimes have waited up to eighteen months to get air time on French television, which makes advertising this way almost useless for introducing new products.

The World According to Big Shot

PRINCESS: Dad, tell me the truth. Is Santa real?

BIG SHOT: Yes, my Princess. We like to think he is real — in a kind of spiritual way. In business we like to think of him as virtual. That's why he's been so successful over the years. As a matter of fact, I happen to think of him as the world's best marketing manager.

PRINCESS: Oh Daddy, tell me why.
BIG SHOT: Well, OK, here are some of Santa's marketing strategies:

- **Virtual.** His location is somewhere in the North Pole — his e-mail address is santa@gte.net and his mailing address is HOH OHO, North Pole.
- **Vision.** Santa has a driven vision to put a smile on the face of kids across the world.
- **Positioned.** He's well-positioned in a growth niche of a growth market.
- **Relationship marketer.** He has established long-term relationships with kids based on bonding, empathy, reciprocity, and trust. He always keeps his promises — his kids demand it.
- **Promises.** He keeps his promises. He has zero tolerance for mistakes — again, his kids and elves demand it.

- **Partnerships.** Santa has created partnerships with parents around the world. He has also established strategic partnerships — Coke, IBM, and Canadian Tire, to name a few.
- **Advertising.** Santa lets others do his promotion and advertising. He has a "free ink" strategy — no need for him to pay for advertising.
- **Global.** Santa delivers around the world. In 1997, he was even in China with IBM with a special promotion.
- **Corporate identity.** He has a strong corporate identify. His northern attire and image were created by an American artist, Haddon Sundblom, in 1931 — would you believe for a Coke ad?
- **Strong corporate culture.** Santa and his team have FUN — that's their corporate culture.

→ What do you think of Big Shot's analogy?

SUMMARY OF LEARNING OUTCOMES

1. **Contrast relationship marketing with transaction-based marketing.**

Today, marketers have discovered that it pays to retain current customers. Relationship marketing is the development and maintenance of long-term, cost-effective relationships with individual customers, suppliers, employees, and other partners for mutual benefit. In the past, the emphasis on production led companies to focus on individual sales or transactions. Transaction-based marketing involves buyer and seller exchanges characterized by limited communications and little or no ongoing relationship between the parties.

2. **Define the target market and explain the importance of demographics and psychographics in relation to the target market.**

A target market is the group of people toward whom a firm markets its goods, services, or ideas with a strategy designed to satisfy their specific needs and preferences. Demographics and psychographics help marketers understand why consumers purchase goods and services. Demographics is the statistical analysis of age, sex, income, education, and so on of a population. Psychographics is the first-hand intuitive insight into lifestyles, buying habits, patterns of consumption, attitudes, and so forth of a population.

3. **Explain what a product is; list the components of a product strategy; and identify the classifications of consumer products, business products, and services.**

A product is a bundle of physical, service, and symbolic attributes designed to satisfy consumer wants. The product strategy includes deciding on the brand name, product image, warranty, service, packaging, and labelling, in addition to the physical or functional characteristics of the good or service. Goods and services can be classified as consumer or business. Consumer goods are purchased by ultimate consumers for their own use. They can be classified as convenience products, shopping products, or specialty products, based on consumer buying habits.

Business goods are those purchased for use either directly or indirectly in the production of other goods for resale. They can be classified as installations, accessory equipment, component parts and materials, raw materials, and supplies, based on how the items are used and on the product characteristics. Services can be classified as either consumer or business services.

4. **Discuss the product mix and the stages of the product life cycle.**

The product mix is the assortment of goods or services offered by a firm. The four stages products often pass through in their product life cycle are introduction, growth, maturity, and decline. In the introduction stage, the firm tries to promote demand for the product. In the growth stage, sales climb and the company earns profits on the product. In the maturity stage, sales reach a saturation level. In the decline stage, both sales and profits wane. Marketers sometimes can employ strategies that will extend the length of the product life cycle. These strategies include increasing the frequency of use, adding new users, finding new uses for the product, and changing the package size, label, or product design.

5. **Describe the importance of pricing strategy.**

Price is the exchange value of a good or service. An item is worth only what someone else is willing to pay for it. Pricing strategy deals with the multitude of factors that influence the setting of a price. If a buyer views a price as too high or too low, the marketer must correct the situation. Price–quality relationships and psychological pricing are important in this regard.

6. **Identify the major components of distribution strategy.**

The two major components of an organization's distribution strategy are distribution channels and physical distribution. Distribution channels are the paths that products — and title to them — follow from producer to consumer. Physical distribution is the actual movement of these products from producer to user. Physical distribution covers a broad range of activities, including customer service, transportation, inventory control, materials handling, order processing, and warehousing.

7. Outline the various types of distribution channels, and discuss the factors that influence channel selection.

Distribution channels vary in length. Some channels are short, with goods and services moving directly from manufacturer to consumer. Others are longer, involving channel members such as wholesaling intermediaries and retailers. Selecting a channel involves considering various factors, including the product, the market, and the competition.

8. Explain the importance of customer service.

Customer service is a vital component of product and distribution strategy. Customer service standards measure the quality of service a firm provides for its customers. The standards set by companies for their suppliers are rising, as Canadian companies gear up to compete more effectively on a global basis. Customer service components include warranty and repair service programs. Products with inadequate service backing quickly disappear from the market as a result of word-of-mouth criticism.

9. Explain how advertising, sales promotion, and public relations are used in promotional strategy, and identify the factors that influence the selection of a promotional mix.

Advertising is a paid, nonpersonal sales communication usually directed at a large number of potential customers. For many firms, advertising is the most effective type of nonpersonal promotion. Sales promotion consists of the one-time supporting aspects of a firm's promotional strategy. It includes point-of-purchase (POP) advertising, specialty advertising, trade shows, samples, premiums, trading stamps, and promotional contests. Public relations deals with the organization's communications with its various publics. Many of these communications have a marketing purpose. The first decision necessary in the development of a promotional mix is whether to use advertising and/or personal selling. Sales promotion and public relations efforts then are determined. The factors involved in these decisions are the target market, the value of the product, and the timing of advertising.

10. Discuss the factors that influence international promotion.

Cultural sensitivity and good homework are crucial when planning international promotional strategies. Effective strategies for promoting products to Canadian audiences may not work in other countries due to differences in language and culture, media availability, audience characteristics, laws, and product regulations.

Key Terms Quiz

personal selling	transaction-based marketing	physical distribution
pushing strategy	advertising	sales promotion
nonpersonal selling	public relations	product mix
pulling strategy	psychographics	product life cycle
promotional mix	demographics	teleshopping
distribution channels	price	marketing intermediaries

_____   1.   Refers to the movement of goods from producer to user.

_____   2.   The selection and electronic purchase of merchandise that has been displayed on computers.

_____ 3. Advertising, sales promotion, and public relations.

_____ 4. Buyer and seller exchanges characterized by limited communications and little or no ongoing relationship between the parties.

_____ 5. The exchange value of a good or service.

_____ 6. The first-hand insight into lifestyles, buying habits, patterns of consumption, attitudes, and so forth of a population.

_____ 7. The statistical analysis of age, sex, income, education, and the like of a population.

_____ 8. An organization's communications with its customers, vendors, news media, employees, stockholders, government, and general public.

_____ 9. An assortment of products offered by a firm.

_____ 10. Distribution-channel members operating between the producer and the consumer or business producer.

_____ 11. Paths that goods and services and title to them follow from producer to consumer.

_____ 12. Refers to the four stages through which a successful product passes: introduction, growth, maturity, and decline.

_____ 13. A firm's combination of personal and nonpersonal selling designed to achieve promotional objectives.

_____ 14. Refers to the promotional presentation made on a person-to-person basis to a potential buyer.

_____ 15. A relationship-based, positioning approach to promotion that focuses on the long-term needs of the customer.

_____ 16. Refers to a form of promotion designed to increase sales through one-time selling efforts, such as displays, trade shows, special events, and other methods.

_____ 17. A transaction-based, sales-oriented approach to promotion that attempts to push or influence the customer to buy the product or service.

_____ 18. A nonpersonal sales presentation usually directed at a large number of potential customers.

Other Important Terms

capital items
convenience products
cybershopping
decline stage
distribution strategy
growth stage
inventory control
marketing mix

materials handling
maturity stage
niche
nonstore retailing
order processing
promotional strategy
shopping products

specialty products
store retailing
universal product code (UPC)
vertical marketing systems (VMS)
warehousing
warranty
wheel of retailing

Review Questions

1. Explain the differences between relationship marketing and transaction-based marketing. Which approach do you think was used by Consumers Distributing? Why do you think so?

2. What is meant by a product mix? Identify its primary components.

3. Suggest current products that represent each of the stages in the product life cycle. Why did you classify these products as you did?

4. Draw and explain the distribution channels for consumer products and for business products. How does a marketer select a specific channel?

5. Cite a local example (if one exists) of a variety store, department store, specialty store, convenience store, discount store, off-price store, factory outlet, supermarket, and warehouse club.

6. Describe the four key dimensions of relationship marketing.

7. What promotional mix would be appropriate for the following products?
   a. Arc welder
   b. Personal computer
   c. Specialty steel products sold to manufacturers
   d. Landscaping service

8. What type of sales promotion techniques would you use in the following businesses?
   a. Independent insurance agency
   b. Jaguar dealership
   c. Family restaurant
   d. Hardware wholesaler

9. What variables should be considered when selecting a promotional mix? Explain how each variable influences promotional strategy.

Discussion Questions

1. If you were the CEO of Consumers Distributing, what would you have done to save the company?

2. Select a distribution channel for the following:
   a. An infant car seat
   b. An income-tax preparation service
   c. Forklift trucks
   d. Pears

3. Do you think Mark Blumes will be successful with his virtual company, Mark's Club? Why or why not?

4. Describe the best television commercial you have seen in the past year. What made this commercial so effective?

5. Suppose that you are a business owner who wants to start promoting your consumer products in Latin America. Describe the factors that you should consider in planning your promotional strategy.

Answers to Key Terms Quiz

1. physical distribution 2. teleshopping 3. nonpersonal selling 4. transaction-based marketing 5. price 6. psychographics 7. demographics 8. public relations 9. product mix 10. marketing intermediaries 11. distribution channels 12. product life cycle 13. promotional mix 14. personal selling 15. pulling strategy 16. sales promotion 17. pushing strategy 18. advertising

Notes

1. Adapted from John Heinzl, "Consumers Goes Super," *The Globe and Mail*, October 5, 1994, B1. Reprinted with permission from The Globe and Mail.

2. Adapted from Louis E. Boone and David L. Kurtz, *Contemporary Marketing Wired*, 9th ed. (Fort Worth, TX: The Dryden Press, 1997), 10-5.

3. Ibid., 10-4.

4. Rod McQueen, "Canada's 50 Best Managed Private Companies: Palmer Jarvis Inc." *The Financial Post*, December 14–16, 1996, 44.

5. Adapted from Boone and Kurtz, *Contemporary Marketing Wired*, 10-9 to 10-12.

6. Industry Canada, "JPL International," *Participant's Workbook: Strategies for Success* (1992), Catalogue No. C2-198-1992E, 26.

7. Lee A. Eckert, J.D. Ryan, and Ronald A. Knowles, *Canadian Small Business: An Entrepreneur's Plan*, 2nd ed. (Toronto: Dryden, 1995), 40, 41, 84–86.

8. Michael Czinkota and Ilkka Ronkainene, *International Marketing*, 3rd ed. (Fort Worth, TX: The Dryden Press, 1993), 320–24.

9. M. Dale Beckman, Louis E. Boone, and David L. Kurtz, *Foundations of Marketing*, 6th Cdn. ed. (Toronto: Dryden, 1997), 225, 226.

10. Ibid., 226.

11. Michael MacDonald (The Canadian Press), "Retailer's 169-Store Chain Bankrupt," *The Ottawa Citizen*, February 12, 1997, B8.

12. Some information in this section has been adapted from Stuart McCarthy, "Making the Net Work," *The Ottawa Sun*, May 2, 1996, 27–29.

13. Beckman, Boone, and Kurtz, *Foundations of Marketing*, 306–7.

Accounting and Financial Planning

part II

Helen Sinclair, co-founder,
Bankworks Trading Inc., Toronto

"There are a number of things that
Canadian banks do very well.
In terms of our infrastructure, training,
and technological expertise, we're second to none."

Chapter 14

Accounting and Budgeting

Learning Outcomes

After studying this chapter, you should be able to

1. Explain the functions of accounting and its importance to the firm's management and to outside parties, such as owners, investors, creditors, and government agencies.
2. Identify the three basic business activities involving accounting.
3. Explain the need for accounting standards and the three accounting organizations that have input in determining those standards.
4. Differentiate between bookkeeping and accounting.
5. Outline the steps in the accounting process.
6. Explain the functions of the balance sheet and the income statement and the need for a statement of cash flows, and identify their major components.
7. Discuss how the major financial ratios are used in analyzing a firm's financial strengths and weaknesses.
8. Explain the role of budgets in business.
9. Explain the need for international accounting and the importance of uniform financial statements for firms engaged in international business.

Proactive Approach Puts New Polish on the Family Business[1]

Brent Trepel graduated at age 22 from the University of Western Ontario in London, Ontario, with his honours degree in business. Then he jumped in his car and drove west to one of the family jewellery stores.

For the next two years he worked in both the Calgary and Edmonton outlets of Ben Moss Jewellers. And what he found was a near-crisis situation.

"Maybe it was because I was young, but I listened to everybody," Trepel says. "I saw a lot of opportunity at the store level. I realized there was a problem and we had to do something about it. I concluded that if we didn't become proactive, we were going to be in trouble."

The first store had been established in 1910 by Ben Moss, father-in-law of Sidney Trepel, who is chairman and CEO and Brent's father. Sidney ran the company from the 1960s to 1980s, expanding from one store in Winnipeg to 18 in Manitoba, Saskatchewan, and Alberta. But that growth had substantially driven up debt-to-equity ratios and reduced working capital to anorexic levels.

"I understood the importance of financial ratios," says Brent. "I said, 'We don't have options. We can't worry about being nice. If we don't put a plan together, we may not be around.' There was resistance; some people wanted to stick with the old ways, but my father was fantastic. He said: 'Go with it.'"

During the five years from 1986–91, Brent used cash flow to cut the debt–equity ratio in half, slash expenses, and improve working capital by 30 percent.

All the outlets are in malls and sales in each location are consistently 70 percent higher (measured on a dollars per square foot basis) than other stores in the jewellery category in the same mall.

Inventory turnover is 50 percent better than the North American average because each store maintains a light inventory and sets specific turnover objectives. "If a product category is not achieving its turn, we take it out of the assortment," Trepel says.

"I understood the importance of financial ratios. I said, 'We don't have options. We can't worry about being nice.'"

Ben Moss specializes in fine jewellery rather than stocking items that are available in volume in department stores. "You need more showcase space to carry items like giftware, silverware, or costume jewellery. We're focused on using our space efficiently and turning inventory. If something sells, we fill it within a week." Top-selling items have minimum inventory levels so stores never run out.

Ben Moss also offers customers a lifetime trade-up on diamond rings, a 30-day cash refund, and a three-year guarantee on all merchandise. The firm can do custom design work by in-store goldsmiths and it regularly imports new products from Italy and the U.S.

During 1996, the firm's advertising approach has changed. In addition to the traditional newspaper and radio spots, Ben Moss has shifted some ad dollars and added additional funds to produce four-colour, four- and eight-page brochures — one million copies at time — for delivery by Canada Post to targeted neighbourhoods in the spring, fall, and close to Christmas.

In 1996, the number of stores in Ontario was increased from two to six. That's where expansion will continue, with as many as 20 more stores planned over the next five years.

Ben Moss is in the preliminary stage of building a database that will mean, once the information is assembled by next spring, customers will be targeted using their past purchasing history. An engagement ring buyer, for example, could receive a specific offer to purchase an anniversary ring a year later.

Consideration is also being given to expansion into the U.S. "The U.S. is a little bit scary when you look at other Canadian retailers. It's a completely different market. But one store in Fargo or Grand Forks [North Dakota] is a better idea than buying a ten-store chain in Kentucky," Trepel says.

"We might open one store there, try it for three years, make mistakes and learn about the market — but we're still a few years away from that."

CHAPTER OVERVIEW

THE DEGREE TO which Brent Trepel depends on accounting and financial planning to chart a course away from financial ruin is a single example of how today's organizations use this key information tool. The traditional stereotype of an accountant as a pale, bookish male dressed in a white shirt and narrow tie, seated behind a desk in a small office and making notations in a dusty ledger, has been replaced by an image illustrated in the following scene:

> **Business Term**
> ✓ **Accounting**
> The process of measuring, interpreting, and communicating financial information to enable others inside and outside the firm to make informed decisions.

Simone Reynolds carries a leather attaché case to her first meeting with the president and chief officials of Computer Controls Inc., the reportedly fast-growing company she is considering for acquisition as the eighth subsidiary of Reynolds Enterprises. She shakes hands with everyone at the meeting and quickly goes to her seat at the head of the long, polished oak conference table. She immediately opens the attaché case and produces a folder containing a one-page computer printout. "Ladies and gentlemen," she begins, "let's get right to the point. Here is the information I need immediately."

The list is a short one:

1. *Did Computer Controls earn a profit last year?*

2. *What was the taxable income for the year?*

3. *How did Computer Controls raise money last year, and how was it used?*

4. *What were the production costs of the firm's major products?*

5. *What costs were involved in marketing the products?*

6. *How profitable and efficient was each of the firm's three major divisions?*

7. *What is the overall financial position of the company?*

8. *How did last year's operations and current financial position compare with plans made by management at the beginning of the year?*

The president of Computer Controls breathes a sigh of relief. "Thank goodness we've got a good accounting system," he says.

Today's accountants are not mere "bean counters" who work in isolation. They're an integral part of the business team — along with marketers, IT managers, and so on — and good accountants are in high demand. The availability of jobs and the relatively high starting salaries for talented accounting graduates have made accounting one of the most popular business majors on Canadian university and college campuses.

Accounting *is the process of measuring, interpreting, and communicating financial information to enable others inside and outside the firm to make informed decisions.* Like statistics, accounting is a language of business. Both for-profit and not-for-profit organizations are involved in business functions such as financing, investing, and operating activities. Accountants gather, record, report, and interpret financial information that describes the status and operation of a firm and aids in decision making. They must accomplish three major tasks: scorekeeping, calling attention to problems and opportunities, and aiding decision making.

This chapter describes the three basic categories of business activities that all organizations are involved in or influenced by: financing, investing, and operating. The accounting process is explained, followed by a discussion of the development of accounting statements from financial transactions. Methods of interpreting these statements are described, and the role of budgets in planning and controlling is examined.

USERS OF ACCOUNTING INFORMATION

WHILE ACCOUNTANTS ARE the primary providers of financial information, many others are users. So, who are the parties interested in a firm's accounting information? They are, as Figure 14.1 shows, people both inside and outside the firm who rely on this information to help them make business decisions. Inside the business, government agency, or not-for-profit organization, owners and managers are the major users of accounting information, which helps them plan and control daily and long-range operations. Owners of the firm and boards of trustees of not-for-profit groups rely on accounting data to determine how well the firm or agency is being operated. Employees refer to the data in monitoring productivity and profitability, and union officials use the data in contract negotiations.

Figure 14.1 How Accounting Information Is Used

Internal and external users need accounting information to help make effective decisions.

User	Application
• Owners, Stockholders, Potential Investors, Creditors	• To evaluate operations of the firm • To make investment decisions
• Management	• To plan and control
• Employees, Union Officials	• To use in contract negotiations
• Lenders, Suppliers	• To evaluate credit ratings
• Government Agencies, Economic Planners, Consumer Groups	• To evaluate tax liabilities • To approve new issue of stocks and bonds

DID YOU KNOW?

→ Buying on credit is widely viewed by inhabitants of Germany and The Netherlands as living beyond one's means. Schuld, the German term for "debt," also means "guilt."

→ The word "budget" comes from bougette, the French term for a small leather bag in which businesspeople kept their money during the Middle Ages. Budgeting then consisted of counting the money in the bag to see if there was enough to pay expenses.

→ The accounting system used in Russia makes it almost impossible for a manager to determine whether a single item in a product line makes a profit or not. Fixed and variable costs are lumped together and revenues and expenses are not matched.

→ A customer in Rome, Italy, who receives a letter from Canada promising a shipment on 11-6-96 will expect delivery no later than June 11, 1996, six months before the Canadian supplier complies. Unlike the Canadian practice of listing the month first when writing a date, the European dating system lists the day first, followed by the month, and then the year.

Outside the firm, potential investors use accounting information to help them decide whether to invest in the company. Accounting information helps them determine a company's credit rating and gives them insight into a potential client's financial soundness. Revenue Canada and tax officials use it to evaluate a company's tax payments for the year. Government agencies and citizens' groups use such information in assessing the efficiency of a charitable group, local school system, or city museum.

Accounting and the Environments of Business

Accountants play a fundamental role not only in business, but also in other aspects of society. Their work affects each of the environments of business. The importance of accounting information in aiding management in dealing with the competitive and economic environments is clear. Not so obvious is accounting's contributions to understanding, predicting, and reacting to the technological, regulatory, and social/cultural environments.

Accounting information and the interpretation of financial reports affect daily business decisions ranging from adjusting inventory to scheduling work.

COMPANY WATCH

Today, in some business-to-business transactions, even the external customer can make use of a company's financial information and accounting records. RNG Equipment Inc. of Mississauga, one of The Financial Post's "50 Best Managed Private Companies," sells meters, pumps, and hose reels as well as custom designs such as fuel loading systems. RNG allows some of its best customers direct access to the company's mainframe computer for online inventory inquiry as well as order entry. Accounting information also helps RNG form cost-saving alliances with its customers in areas such as equipment supply, service and repair, reporting and information sharing, performance benchmarks, and new products. "Our customers want to reduce the cost of doing business. We've already got the warehousing and computer in place. Instead of going just with the traditional arrangement, we're looking at the total needs — service, inventory, warranty management, and site supervision," says Gord Duncan, president and CEO of RNG.

TECHNOLOGY

TECHNOLOGY MAKES CLEANER ACCOUNTING

Over the past two decades, the bar-code scanning point-of-sale (POS) terminal has become a familiar sight at retail giants ranging from Sears to A&P stores. As technology and competition have pushed down prices, thousands of smaller companies have added these speedy cost-saving devices to their operations. At the beginning of the 1990s, a mainframe POS system carried a $20 000 price tag. Today, a two-computer system can be installed for about a $4000 total investment.

But what does the businessperson get for the $4000 outlay? In addition to replacing the traditional cash register, a simple bar-code scanner will update instantaneously a store's inventory records and accounting data while it performs error-free transactions. However, the real beauty of this technology lies in what it can do in collecting raw data and turning it into decision-oriented information.

In 1997, NCR, a Dayton-based computer maker, unveiled a new-generation POS terminal. It's a self-service check-out system that lets supermarket express lane customers scan, bag, and pay for groceries without a cashier's help. The system uses an automatic teller machine (ATM) and bar-code scanning technology to expedite the check-out process. Not only will this system reduce labour costs, but it also has the capacity to reduce check-out time. "This system makes grocery shopping as easy as banking is today," says Joanne Walter, NCR's vice-president of future retailing systems. "To check out five items

---

Professional accountants often are also called on to provide courts with information in litigation involving embezzlement, misrepresentation, fraud, and misuse of funds. They must be adept in using computerized systems and in teaching managers and workers how to access this information. Twenty-first-century accounting is far different from the bookkeeping stereotype of the past.

BUSINESS ACTIVITIES INVOLVING ACCOUNTING

THE NATURAL PROGRESSION of a business begins with financing, involves investing, and leads to operating the business. All organizations, for-profit and not-for-profit, perform these three basic activities. Accounting plays a key role in each.

- *Financing activities* are necessary to provide the funds to start a business and to expand it in the future. The implications of a firm's financial status go beyond the accounting statements. For example, when the recession hit in 1990–91, Brent Trepel of Ben Moss Jewellers was able to expand the chain west into British Columbia and east into Ontario. The firm's balance sheet was in much better shape than most of its competitors'.[2]

- *Investing activities* are needed to provide valuable assets required to run a business. Ben Moss Jewellers, for example, was able to invest in building a database to target customers using their past history. The company could also afford to give strong consideration to an expansion into the United States.[3]

- *Operating activities* focus on the sale of goods and services, but also consider expenses as an important part of sound financial management. By keeping a sharp eye on inventory, Ben Moss can save carrying costs and leasing costs through reduced retail space.

ACCOUNTING STANDARDS AND THE ACCOUNTING PROFESSION[4]

IN ORDER TO ensure that all users receive accurate information from the accounting system, accountants have developed guidelines or standards for reporting. These standards are referred to as *generally accepted accounting principles (GAAP)* and apply all across Canada. Such standards ensure that accounting is done consistently among businesses. For example, if the owner

and pay for them with a debit card would take 40 seconds."

Such technological advancements make accounting in retailing much cleaner. As Walter mentioned, banking today is made easy thanks to technology. Banks continue to use technology to their advantage. Recent innovations like the automatic banking machines (ABMs) help speed banking transactions. They

→ Reduce costs: transactions typically cost 45 cents at an ABM and more than $1 at the teller's wicket, and

→ Meet customer demand for faster, 24-hour service.

Thus banks around the world are looking at making their ABMs do more. Canadian banks are particularly interested in improving the use of ABMs. And why not? Canadians are the world's No. 1 users of ABMs. ABM transactions account for about 58 percent of routine banking transactions in Canada versus 28 percent in the United States. The Royal Bank has an ABM that can dispense traveller's cheques and U.S. cash. The CIBC has what it calls the Web ABM — an automated banking machine that uses Internet technology to offer a range of new services along with cash withdrawals and bill payment.

It won't be long before ABMs will be able to spit out everything from theatre tickets to stock certificates and savings bonds.

Sources: Adapted from Gale Eisenstodt, "Information Power," *Forbes*, June 21, 1993, 44–45; Larry Stevens, "Point-of-Sales Inventory Systems: Now Ready for Small Business," *Nation's Business*, December 1991, 11; Jim Dillon (Cox News Service), "Check This Out: A Self-Serve Scanner Comes to Grocer's Express Lane," *The Ottawa Citizen*, February 10, 1997, A10; and The Canadian Press, "ABM's Bank on Web," *The Ottawa Sun*, February 21, 1997, 49.

of a shoe store in Halifax was interested in purchasing another shoe store in Vancouver, the owner could compare the financial statements of the two shoe stores and know that the same GAAP were used in the preparation of accounts for both stores.

There are two branches of accounting in Canada, private accounting and public accounting. *Private accountants* are employees of the business. The head of the accounting department is usually called the "controller" or "treasurer" and is considered part of the top management team. The controller or treasurer ensures that all of the bookkeeping and accounting functions of the business are carried out and that the financial statements at the end of the year are prepared in accordance with GAAP.

Public accountants are not employees of businesses; rather, they act independently. They are referred to as "auditors." Their role is to ensure that an organization's financial statements are in fact properly prepared in accordance with GAAP by conducting an audit of the statements. Companies that have bank loans or shares that trade on a stock exchange (for example, the Toronto Stock Exchange) are usually required to have an audit conducted annually. Many users feel that financial statements that have been audited are more reliable than those that have not been audited.

Most private and public accountants in Canada belong to one of three professional accounting bodies. Public accountants belong to the Canadian Institute of

Ideas

Solutions

Results

• Accounting and Auditing
• Actuarial/Benefits/Compensation (Sobeco Ernst & Young)
• Corporate Finance • Corporate Recovery and insolvency
• Forensic and Litigation Accounting
• Management Consulting • Tax

ERNST & YOUNG

Ernst & Young provides a number of accounting and accounting-related services to businesses.

Chartered Accountants (CICA), whose members are referred to as *chartered accountants (CAs)*; or the Certified General Accountants Association of Canada, whose members are referred to as *certified general accountants (CGAs)*. Private accountants belong to the Society of Management Accountants of Canada, whose members are *certified management accountants (CMAs)*.

The Canadian Institute of Chartered Accountants is responsible for researching, setting, and publishing the *CICA Handbook*, from which the generally accepted accounting principles are derived. Members of all three accounting bodies are invited to comment on new standards as they are developed.

All three accounting bodies require their students to undergo rigorous examinations and to have practical experience before granting them their professional accounting designation. All accounting bodies ensure that their students have a thorough understanding of GAAP.

ner is frequently referred to as *management accounting*. Management accounting is tailor-made to the needs of a particular manager and does not have to be governed by GAAP.

> ### THEY SAID IT
>
> "If you owe $50, you're a delinquent account.
> If you owe $50,000, you're a small business person.
> If you owe $50 million, you're a corporation.
> If you owe $50 billion, you're the government."
>
> L.T. WHITE, JR., historian

THE ACCOUNTING PROCESS

ACCOUNTING VERSUS BOOKKEEPING[5]

"**B**OOKKEEPING" AND "ACCOUNTING" are not synonymous.

Bookkeeping deals with *recording transactions in a systematic manner into a series of specially designed records called "journals."* Every time the business makes a sale or pays the rent, the transaction is recorded by the accounting system. A **journal** *is an accounting record that has been designed to record transactions with a minimum of effort.* You keep a journal if you keep a chequebook.

Accounting takes the information that bookkeepers have prepared and organizes this information into coherent financial statements. Therefore, bookkeeping is part, but only part, of accounting. Financial statements are prepared primarily for owners and users who are external to the business, for example, shareholders, creditors, and government. Internal users, such as managers, often require other information that accountants can provide. The process of preparing information to assist managers and owners in operating the company in an efficient and effective man-

Business Term

✓ **Bookkeeping**

Recording transactions in a systematic manner into a series of specially designed records called "journals."

Business Term

✓ **Journal**

An accounting record that has been designed to record transactions with a minimum of effort.

Business Term

✓ **Accounting process**

The procedural cycle used by accountants in converting individual transactions to financial statements.

ACCOUNTING DEALS WITH financial transactions between a firm and its employees, customers, suppliers, owners, bankers, and various government agencies. Weekly payroll cheques result in cash outflows for the compensation of employees. A payment to a supplier results in the receipt of materials needed for the production process. Cash, cheque, and credit purchases by customers generate funds to cover the costs of operations and to earn a profit. Prompt payment of bills preserves the firm's credit rating and its ability to obtain future loans. This *procedural cycle, used by accountants in converting individual transactions to financial statements,* is called the **accounting process.** It involves recording, classifying, and summarizing transactions in order to produce financial statements for the firm's owners, management, and other interested parties. Figure 14.2 summarizes the accounting process.

The Impact of Computers on the Accounting Process

For hundreds of years, the recording, or posting, of transactions was entered manually in a journal, and then the information

Figure 14.2 The Accounting Process

The accounting process involves recording, classifying, and summarizing transaction data in order to create financial statements.

Basic Data

Transactions
Receipts, invoices, and other source documents related to each transaction are assembled to justify making an entry in the firm's accounting records.

Processing

Record
Transactions are recorded in chronological order in books called journals. Brief explanations are given for each entry.

Classify
Journal entries are transferred, or posted, to individual accounts kept in a ledger. All entries involving cash are brought together in the ledger's cash account; all entries involving sales are recorded in the ledger's sales account.

Summarize
All accounts in the ledger are summarized at the end of the accounting period and financial statements are prepared from these account summaries.

Financial Statements

Balance Sheet	Income Statement	Statement of Cash Flows

Intuit's Quicken® products include accounting and bookkeeping software that helps small businesses manage their finances.

26 identifying features that can be accessed for lists and mailing labels. You can also design your own invoices and purchase orders.[6] The integration of accounting and computers in almost every organization and small business requires accountants to be increasingly computer literate.

But computers do more than record and organize data for statements; they also help accountants make sound financial decisions quickly and effectively. In fact, the most important job of the typical private accountant is to communicate this information clearly for use in decision making.

THE FOUNDATION OF THE ACCOUNTING SYSTEM

REMEMBER THAT IN order to provide reliable, consistent, and unbiased information to decision-makers, accountants follow GAAP. These standards are principles that encompass the conventions, rules, and procedures necessary in determining acceptable accounting practices at a particular time. Accountants use GAAP to create uniform financial statements throughout an industry for comparison purposes. Two accounting statements form the foundation of the entire accounting system: the balance sheet and the income statement. The information found in these statements is calculated using the accounting equation and the double-entry system. A third statement, the statement of cash flows, is frequently prepared to focus specifically on the information related to sources and uses of cash for the firm from its operating, investing, and financing activities.

was transferred or posted to individual accounts listed in *ledgers*. However, the computer revolution of the twentieth century has simplified the accounting systems of thousands of firms, both industrial giants and neighbourhood service providers. Fully automated systems, developed by firms such as NCR Corporation, have eliminated most of the recording, classifying, and summarizing tasks once done by hand. As *point-of-sale terminals* replace cash registers, a number of functions can be performed each time a sale is recorded. Not only can such a terminal recall prices from memory and maintain a perpetual inventory count of every item in stock, but it also automatically performs accounting data entries.

Accounting software programs, such as Simply Accounting™ and MYOB Accounting™, are used widely in business today — especially in the small business community. They make possible a "do-it-once" approach, whereby each sale is converted automatically into a journal entry, which then is stored until needed. Up-to-date financial statements and financial ratios then can be requested when needed by the decision-maker. Most of these programs offer much more than just financial or inventory information. For example, MYOB Accounting™ from BestWare provides a database of customer, vendor, and personal contacts. These contacts are characterized by

The Accounting Equation

Four fundamental terms are involved in the accounting equation: assets, equities, liabilities, and owners' equity. An **asset** *is anything of value owned or leased by a business.* Cash, accounts receivable, and notes receivable (amounts owed to the business through credit sales), land, buildings, supplies, and marketable securities are all assets.

An **equity** *is a claim against the assets of a business.* The two major classifications of individuals who have equity in a firm are creditors (liability holders) and owners. A **liability** of a business *is anything owed to creditors* — that is, the claims of the firm's creditors. When the firm makes credit purchases for inventory, land, or machinery, the creditors' claims are shown as accounts payable or notes payable. Wages and salaries owed to employees also represent liabilities (known as wages payable). The **owners' equity** represents the *investment in the business made by owners of the firm, and retained earnings that were not paid out in dividends.*

A strong owners' equity position often is used as evidence of a firm's financial strength and stability. Because equities, by definition, represent the total claims of both owners and creditors against assets, then assets must equal equities:

Assets = Equities
What the business owns = What the business owes

The basic **accounting equation** states that *assets are equal to liabilities plus owners' equity.* It reflects the financial position of any firm at any point in time:

Assets = Liabilities + Owners' Equity

Since financing comes from either creditors or owners, the right side of the accounting equation also represents the financing structure of business.

The relationship expressed by the accounting equation is used to develop two primary accounting statements prepared by every business, large or small: the balance sheet and the income statement. These two statements reflect the current financial position of the firm and the most recent analysis of income, expenses, and

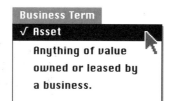

Business Term
√ **Asset**
Anything of value owned or leased by a business.

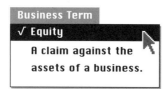

Business Term
√ **Equity**
A claim against the assets of a business.

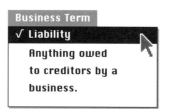

Business Term
√ **Liability**
Anything owed to creditors by a business.

Business Term
√ **Owners' equity**
The investment in the business made by owners of the firm, and retained earnings that were not paid out in dividends.

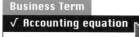

Business Term
√ **Accounting equation**
Basic accounting concept that assets are equal to liabilities plus owners' equity.

profits for interested parties inside and outside the firm. They provide a fundamental basis for planning activities and are used in attracting new investors, securing borrowed funds, and preparing tax returns.

FINANCIAL ANALYSIS

FINANCIAL STATEMENTS provide managers with essential information they need to evaluate the *liquidity* of the organization — its ability to meet current obligations and needs by converting assets into cash; the firm's *profitability*; and its *overall financial health.* The balance sheet and income statement provide an outline on which management can base its decisions. The statement of cash flows tells managers and owners when the business will actually have the funds to pay for its expenses. By interpreting the data provided in these financial statements, the appropriate information can be communicated to internal decision-makers and to interested parties outside the organization, such as investors.

The Balance Sheet

The **balance sheet** shows the *financial position of a company as of a particular date.* It is similar to a photograph comparing a firm's assets with its liabilities and owners' equity at a specific moment in time (see, for example, the sample balance sheet in Figure 14.3). Balance sheets must be prepared at regular intervals, since a firm's managers and other internal parties are likely to request this information on a daily, weekly, or at least once-a-month basis. On the other hand, external users, such as stockholders or industry analysts, typically use this information less frequently, perhaps every quarter or once a year.

Business Term
√ **Balance sheet**
Financial statement that shows the financial position of a company as of a particular date.

Figure 14.3 Sample Balance Sheet

❶ **Current Assets**
Cash and other liquid assets that can or will be converted to cash or used within one year.

❷ **Fixed Assets**
Relatively permanent plant, property, and equipment expected to be used for periods longer than one year.

❸ **Current Liabilities**
Claims of creditors that are to be repaid within one year.

❹ **Long-Term Liabilities**
Debts that come due one year or more after the date of the balance sheet.

❺ **Owners' Equity**
Claims of the proprietor, partners, or stockholders against the assets of a firm; the excess of assets over liabilities.

FIESTA POOLS

Balance Sheet
as of December 31, 199X

ASSETS

❶ **Current Assets**		
Cash	$ 8 000	
Marketable Securities	30 000	
Accounts Receivable	194 000	
Inventory	124 000	
Total Current Assets		$356 000
❷ **Fixed Assets**		
Store Equipment	$ 112 000	
Furniture and Fixtures	40 000	
Total Fixed Assets		$152 000
Total Assets		$508 000

LIABILITIES AND OWNERS' EQUITY

❸ **Current Liabilities**		
Accounts Payable	$ 82 000	
Current Installments of Long-Term Debt	30 000	
Accrued Expenses	14 000	
Income Taxes Payable	12 000	
Total Current Liabilities		$138 000
❹ **Long-Term Liabilities**		
Long-Term Notes Payable	$ 60 000	
Total Long-Term Liabilities		60 000
Total Liabilities		$198 000
❺ **Owners' Equity**		
Common Stock (160 000 shares @ $1)	$ 160 000	
Retained Earnings	150 000	
Total Owners' Equity		$310 000
Total Liabilities and Owners' Equity		$508 000

Fiesta Pools' balance sheet illustrates the accounting equation — assets equal liabilities plus owners' equity.

It is helpful to keep the accounting equation in mind as a diagram that is explained by the balance sheet. Listing the various assets on the balance sheet indicates sources of the firm's strengths — what the business owns. These assets, shown in descending order of liquidity (convertibility to cash), represent the *uses* that management or owners have made of available funds. On the other side of the equation, liabilities and owners' equity indicate what the business owes. Liabilities — what the business owes others — reflect the claims of creditors, such as financial institutions or bondholders that have made loans to the firm; suppliers that have provided goods and services on credit; and others to be paid, such as federal, provincial, and local tax officials. Owners' equity — what the business owes the owners of the business — represents the owners' (stockholders', in the case of corporations) claims against the firm's assets or the

excess of all assets over liabilities. It is important to note that equity is not necessarily cash. It is the dollar value of what the business owes the owners.

Income Statement

While the balance sheet reflects the financial position of the firm at a specific point in time, the income statement is a *flow* statement that reveals the performance of the organization over a specific time period. Resembling a motion picture rather than a snapshot, the **income statement** *is a financial record summarizing a firm's financial performance in terms of revenues, expenses, and profits over a given time period.*

The purpose of the income statement is to show the profitability of a firm during a period of time, usually a

Figure 14.4 Sample Income Statement

❶ **Revenues**
Funds recorded from the sale of goods and services and from interest payments, dividends, royalties, and rents. Grants and contributions can be revenue sources for not-for-profit firms.

❷ **Cost of Goods Sold**
Cost of merchandise or services that generate the firm's revenue; includes *Purchases* section for retailers and *Cost of Goods Manufactured* for producers.

❸ **Selling Expenses**
Advertising, selling, and other expenses incurred in marketing and distributing the firm's output.

❹ **General and Administrative Expenses**
Office salaries and supplies, rent, and other operational expenses not directly related to the acquisition, production, or sale of the firm's output.

❺ **Net Income**
Profit or loss incurred over a specific period; determined by subtracting all expenses from revenues.

FIESTA POOLS

Income Statement
Year Ending December 31, 199X

❶ **Revenues**		
Gross Sales	$600 000	
Less: Sales Returns and Allowances	16 000	
Net Sales		$584 000
❷ **Cost of Goods Sold**		
Beginning Inventory	$130 000	
Purchases during Year	246 000	
Cost of Goods Available for Sale	376 000	
Less: Ending Inventory	112 000	
Cost of Goods Sold		$264 000
Gross Profit		$320 000
Operating Expenses		
❸ Selling Expenses	$150 000	
❹ General and Administrative Expenses	$ 96 000	
Total Operating Expenses		$246 000
Net Income before Taxes		74 000
Less: Income Taxes		14 000
❺ **Net Income**		$ 60 000

Fiesta Pools' income statement shows the firm earned $60 000 on sales of $584 000.

year, a quarter, or a month (see Fiesta Pools' income statement in Figure 14.4). In addition to reporting the profit or loss, it helps decision-makers focus on overall revenues and the costs involved in generating these revenues. Not-for-profit organizations use this statement to see if the organization's revenues and contributions will cover the costs involved in operating. Finally, the income statement provides much of the basic data needed to calculate numerous ratios used by management in planning and controlling the organization (see page 359 for more on these).

The income statement (sometimes called a profit and loss — or P&L — statement) begins with total sales or revenue generated during a year, quarter, or month, and then deducts all of the costs related to producing this *revenue*. Once all costs — administrative and marketing expenses, costs involved in producing the product, inter-

Business Term

✓ **Income statement**
Financial record summarizing a firm's financial performance in terms of revenues, expenses, and profits over a time period.

Business Term

✓ **Bottom line**
The final figure on the income statement – net income after taxes.

est, and taxes, for instance — have been subtracted, the remaining *net income* may be distributed to the firm's owners (stockholders, proprietors, or partners) or reinvested in the company as retained earnings. *The final figure on the income statement — net income after taxes —* is the well-known **bottom line.**

Statement of Cash Flows

In addition to the income statement and the balance sheet, many firms prepare a third accounting statement. Since 1987 all companies listed on organized stock exchanges have been required to prepare a statement of cash flows as part of their annual registration information. In small business, a cash flow is essential. Additionally, major lenders often require it of all firms applying for business loans. As the

Figure 14.5 The Importance of Planning a Cash Flow

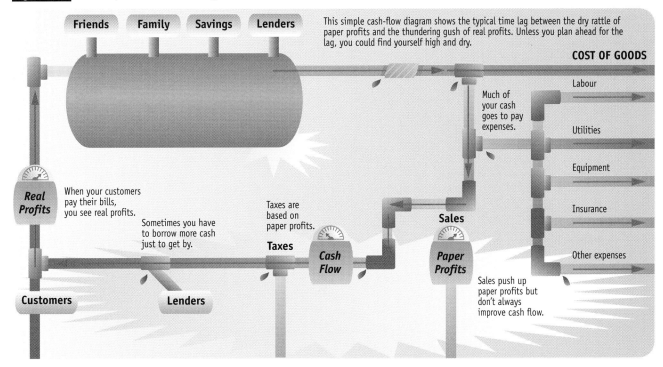

Figure 14.6 Sample Cash Budget

FIESTA POOLS

Sample Cash Budget
January–June 199X

	January	February	March	April	May	June
Beginning Monthly Balance	$ 6 000	$ 6 000	$ 6 000	$ 6 000	$ 6 000	$ 6 000
Add: Cash Receipts	4 000	14 000	12 000	10 000	8 000	18 000
(collections from customers, interest receipts, and other cash inflows)						
Cash Available for Firm's Use	$ 10 000	$ 20 000	$ 18 000	$ 16 000	$ 14 000	$ 24 000
Deduct: Cash Disbursements	10 000	8 000	10 000	12 000	6 000	14 000
(for payroll, materials, income taxes, utilities, interest payments, etc.)						
Preliminary Monthly Balance	$ 0	$ 12 000	$ 8 000	$ 4 000	$ 8 000	$ 10 000
Minimum Required Cash Balance	6 000	6 000	6 000	6 000	6 000	6 000
Excess (or Deficiency)	(6 000)	6 000	2 000	(2 000)	2 000	4 000
Short-Term Investment of Excess			2 000		2 000	4 000
Liquidation of Short-Term Investment				2 000		
Short-Term Loan to Cover Deficiency	6 000					
Repayment of Short-Term Loan		6 000				
Ending Monthly Balance	$ 6 000	$ 6 000	$ 6 000	$ 6 000	$ 6 000	$ 6 000

This sample cash budget covers a six-month period. The firm has set a $6000 minimum cash balance. The cash budget indicates the months in which excess funds will be invested to earn interest rather than remaining idle. It also indicates periods in which temporary loans will be required to finance operations. Finally, it produces a tangible standard for comparing actual cash inflows and outflows.

Table 14.1 Three-Month Cash Flow — DISCovery Bookstore

Step I	OPENING BALANCE	JULY	AUG.	SEPT.
Step II				
1. SALES —		7 800	9 100	11 700
2. —				
3. TOTAL SALES		7 800	9 100	11 700
Step III				
RECEIPTS				
4. CASH IN				
5. — Cash Sales		1 200	1 400	1 800
6. — Receivables Collected				
7. — Loan Proceeds				
8. — Personal Investment				
9. — Sales of Assets				
10. — Equity	80 000			
11. — Loans	35 000			
12. —				
13. Total Cash in (lines 5 through 12)	115 000	9 000	10 500	13 500
Step IV				
DISBURSEMENTS				
14. CASH OUT				
15. — Purchases		5 255	9 880	9 305
16. — Advertising (2%)		200	200	200
17. — Auto and Truck				
18. — Bank Charges and Interest		300	300	300
19. — Insurance		450		
20. — Professional Fees				
21. — Rent		1 200	1 200	1 200
22. — Taxes and Licences				
23. — Telephone		50	50	50
24. — Utilities (Heat, Light, Water)		150	150	150
25. — Wages — Employees				
26. — Principal Draw or Management Salaries		1 600	1 600	1 600
27. — Term Debt (principal portion only)		250	250	250
28. — Purchase Fixed Assets	60 790			
29. — Taxes				
30. — Supplies (1%)		100	100	100
31. — Miscellaneous (3%)		325	325	325
32. — Start-up	44 210			
33. —				
34. Total Cash Out (lines 15 through 33)	105 000	9 880	14 055	13 480
Step V				
SUMMARY				
35. Total Cash In (Line 13)	115 000	9 000	10 500	13 500
36. Plus: Cash Forward (Prev. Mon. — Line 39)		10 000	9 120	5 565
37. Equals: Total Cash Available	115 000	19 000	19 620	19 065
38. Less: Total Cash Out (Line 34)	105 000	9 880	14 055	13 480
39. Equals: Closing Bank Balance	10 000	9 120	5 565	15 585

name indicates, the *statement of cash flows* provides investors and creditors with relevant information about a firm's cash receipts and cash payments during an accounting period. Table 14.1 provides an example of a simple three-month cash flow.

The belt-tightening of the 1990s has left many Canadian blue chip companies with large cash reserves. These firms have been aided in building their cash reserves through a combination of soaring revenues and falling costs: "Our companies are lean and mean and ready to fight, and an awful lot of them are sitting on a lot of cash," said a Vancouver-based fund manager.[7] Table 14.2 lists some examples of cash-rich companies.

Ratio Analysis

Accounting professionals are not simply responsible for preparing financial statements. Of ever greater importance is assisting owners and managers in interpreting these documents by comparing the firm's activities to previous periods and with other companies in the industry. **Ratio analysis** *is one of the most commonly used tools for (1) measuring the liquidity, profitability, extent of debt financing, and effectiveness of the firm's use of its resources and (2) permitting comparison with other firms and with past*

Business Term

✓ **Ratio analysis**

One of the most commonly used tools for (1) measuring the liquidity, profitability, extent of debt financing, and effectiveness of the firm's use of its resources and (2) permitting comparison with other firms and with past performance.

Business Term

✓ **Liquidity ratios**

Ratios that measure a firm's ability to meet its short-term obligations when they must be paid.

performance. Ratios assist the manager by interpreting actual performance and making comparisons with what should have happened. They can be compared with those of similar companies to reflect company performance relative to that of competitors. These industry standards serve as important yardsticks in pinpointing problem areas as well as areas of excellence. Ratios for the current accounting period also may be compared with similar calculations for previous periods to spot any trends that might be developing. Ratios can be classified according to their specific purpose.

Liquidity Ratios. *A firm's ability to meet its short-term obligations when they must be paid is measured by* **liquidity ratios.** Highly liquid firms are less likely to face emergencies in raising needed funds to repay loans. On the other hand, firms with less liquidity may be forced to use high-cost lending sources to meet their maturing obligations or face default.

Two commonly used liquidity ratios are the current ratio and the acid-test ratio. The *current ratio* or *working capital ratio* compares current assets to current liabilities, giving business owners and management information concerning the firm's ability to pay its current debts as they mature. The current ratio of Fiesta Pools can be computed as shown on the next page.

Table 14.2 The Cash Position

Company	Cash on Books $million	Cash per Share $	Share Price 2/21/97 $	Dividends per Share $
George Weston Ltd. (WN/TSE)	250.4	5.53	75.80	0.88
Atco Ltd. (ACO/TSE)	238.2	7.81	25.75	0.52
Brascan Ltd. (BLa/TSE)	1140.0	11.06	31.75	1.04
National Trustco Inc. (NT/TSE)	1630.0	44.12	24.20	0.88
Imperial Oil Ltd. (IMO/TSE)	582.0	3.66	62.20	2.05
DuPont Canada Inc. (DUPa/TSE)	504.9	5.46	33.00	*0.52
Moore Corp. Ltd. (MCL/TSE)	694.3	6.94	30.00	0.94
Molson Cos. Ltd. (MOLa/TSE)	723.5	12.37	24.25	*0.72
E-L Financial Corp. (ELF/TSE)	116.1	30.23	135.00	0.50
PanCanadian Petrol. Ltd. (PCP/TSE)	355.2	125.5	57.25	0.80

* = forecast

$$\text{Current Ratio} = \frac{\text{Current Assets}}{\text{Current Liabilities}} = \frac{\$356\,000}{\$138\,000} = 2.6 \text{ to } 1$$

This means Fiesta Pools has $2.60 of current assets for every $1.00 of current liabilities. In general, a current ratio of 2 to 1 is considered financially satisfactory. This rule of thumb must be considered along with other factors, such as the nature of the business, the season of the year, and the quality of the company's management. Fiesta Pools' management and other interested parties are likely to compare this ratio of 2.6 to 1 to previous operating periods and to industry averages to determine its appropriateness.

The *acid-test* (or *quick*) *ratio* measures the ability of Fiesta Pools to meet its debt on short notice. It calculates quick assets, meaning highly liquid current assets, against current liabilities. It does not include inventory or prepaid expenses — only cash, marketable securities, and in some cases accounts receivable.

Fiesta Pools' current balance sheet lists the following quick assets: cash, $8000; marketable securities, $30 000; and accounts receivable, $194 000. The firm's acid-test ratio is computed as

$$\text{Acid-Test Ratio} = \frac{\text{Quick Assets}}{\text{Current Liabilities}} = \frac{\$232\,000}{\$138\,000} = 1.7 \text{ to } 1$$

Because the traditional rule of thumb for an adequate acid-test ratio is 1 to 1, Fiesta Pools appears to be in a good short-term credit position. However, the same cautions as for the current ratio should be applied here. What would the acid-test ratio look like, for example, if we followed a stricter definition of quick assets — cash plus marketable securities? The quick ratio would now be 0.28 to 1. This new ratio is well below the 1-to-1 requirement. Again, this ratio should be compared with industry averages and with previous operating periods in determining its appropriateness for Fiesta Pools.

Profitability Ratios. Profitability ratios *measure the firm's overall financial performance in terms of its ability to generate revenues in excess of operating and other expenses.* Earnings are compared with total sales or investment. Over a period of time, these ratios also may reveal the effectiveness of management in operating the business. Three commonly used profitability ratios are *earnings per share*, *return on sales*, and *return on equity.*

$$\text{Earnings per Share} = \frac{\text{Net Income after Taxes}}{\text{Common Shares Outstanding}}$$

$$= \frac{\$60\,000}{160\,000} = \$0.375$$

$$\text{Return on Sales} = \frac{\text{Net Income}}{\text{Net Sales}} = \frac{\$60\,000}{\$584\,000} = 10.3\%$$

$$\text{Return on Equity} = \frac{\text{Net Income}}{\text{Total Owners' Equity}}$$

$$= \frac{\$60\,000}{\$310\,000} = 19.4\%$$

The World According to Big Shot

PRINCESS: Dad, a penny for your thoughts?

BIG SHOT: Give me the penny. OK, I was watching the cash flow, and with your penny it just flowed into my hand.

PRINCESS: Dad, which way is the cash flowing in your business?
BIG SHOT: Good question. I think it is flowing the wrong way.

➜ Suggest ways to stop cash from flowing the wrong way.

All of these ratios reflect positively on the current operations of Fiesta Pools. For example, the return-on-sales ratio indicates that the firm realized a profit of 10.3 cents for every $1.00 of sales. Although this ratio varies widely among business firms, Fiesta Pools compares favourably with retailers in general, which average about a 5 percent return on sales. However, this ratio, like the other profitability ratios, should be evaluated in relation to profit forecasts, past performance, or more specific industry averages to better interpret the results. Similarly, while the firm's return of almost 20 percent on equity appears to be satisfactory, the degree of risk present in the industry also must be considered.

> **Business Term**
> √ **Profitability ratios**
> Ratios that measure the overall financial performance of a firm in terms of its ability to generate revenues in excess of operating and other expenses.

Leverage Ratios. The third category of financial ratios, **leverage ratios**, *measure the extent to which a firm is relying on debt financing.* They are of particular interest to potential investors and lenders. If too much debt has been used to finance the firm's operations, problems may arise in meeting future interest payments and repaying outstanding loans. In addition, both investors and lenders may prefer to deal with firms whose owners have invested enough of their own money in the firm to avoid overreliance on borrowing. The *debt-to-owners'-equity ratio* provides answers to these questions.

> **Business Term**
> √ **Leverage ratios**
> Ratios that measure the extent to which a firm is relying on debt financing.

$$\text{Debt to Owners' Equity} = \frac{\text{Total Liabilities}}{\text{Owners' Equity}}$$
$$= \frac{\$198\,000}{\$310\,000} = 64\%$$

Since a debt-to-equity ratio of greater than 1 would indicate the firm is relying more on debt financing than on owners' equity, it is clear that Fiesta Pools' owners have invested considerably more than the total amount of liabilities shown on the firm's balance sheet.

Activity Ratios. The final category of financial ratios, **activity ratios**, *measure the effectiveness of the firm's use of its resources.* The

> **Business Term**
> √ **Activity ratios**
> Ratios that measure the effectiveness of the firm's use of its resources.

most frequently used activity ratio is the *inventory turnover ratio*, which indicates the number of times merchandise moves through the business.

$$\text{Inventory Turnover} = \frac{\text{Cost of Goods Sold}}{\text{Average Inventory}}$$
$$= \frac{\$264\,000}{\$121\,000} = 2.2 \text{ times}$$

Average inventory for Fiesta Pools is determined by adding the January 1 beginning inventory of $130 000 and the December 31 ending inventory of $112 000 (as shown on the income statement) and dividing by 2. The 2.2 turnover rate can be compared with industry standards and used as a measure of efficiency. For retailers, such as furniture and jewellery stores, an annual turnover rate of 1.5 times is about average. For a supermarket, the turnover rate can be as high as once every two weeks.

The four categories of financial ratios relate balance sheet and income statement items to one another and assist owners and management in pinpointing strengths and weaknesses. In large, multi-product organizations operating in diverse markets, today's sophisticated information systems are capable of updating these financial ratios on a daily or even hourly basis. Smaller firms can also obtain this timely financial information using some of the accounting software packages such as MYOB Accounting™, which we discussed previously. Consequently, management and owners must decide on an appropriate review schedule to avoid the costly and time-consuming task of overmonitoring.

BUDGETING

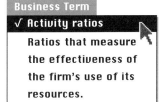LTHOUGH THE FINANCIAL statements discussed in this chapter focus on what has occurred in the past, they are the basis for planning in the future. A **budget** *is a planning and control tool that reflects expected sales revenues, operating expenses, and cash receipts and outlays.* It is the quantification of the firm's plans for a specified future period. Since it requires management to estimate expected sales, cash inflows and outflows, and costs, it serves as a financial blueprint. The budget is the standard against which actual performance is compared.

IN THE NEWS

THE NUMBERS TELL THE STORY

Allan Rothman, an independent pharmacist who runs Clairhurst Pharmacy in Toronto, never takes his eye off the bottom line. "I do my own deliveries, I cut corners like this. To survive, I have to watch every penny," he says. Over the 1990s, independent pharmacists like Allan Rothman struggled to cope with the downward pressure on prices for both prescriptions and other general items in a highly competitive market. "There's been enormous downward pricing pressure on most of the products being sold by pharmacists," says retail analyst Len Kubas. Some of the major reasons for these troubled times included

→ Discount pricing and price wars by general department stores like Loblaws and Wal-Mart.

→ Reduction in prices for dispensing fees.

→ Deregulation of drug prices, giving an enormous benefit to large organizations, which can negotiate bulk deals.

→ Increased pressure from corporate drug plans that are urging employees to fill prescriptions at pharmacies with low dispensing fees.

Financial ratios clearly depict the plight of the independent pharmacist. Dun & Bradstreet did an analysis of 4255 drugstores across Canada with fewer than 50 employees, and excluded corporate-owned stores that were part of large chains. The analysis showed that after-tax return on sales fell to 1.59 percent in 1996 from 2.68 percent in 1992. Return on equity (net worth) fell to 9.5 percent from 17 percent over the same period. The quick ratios were well below 1, and the current ratios were below 2.

Source: Adapted from Janet McFarland, "Pharmacies Face Troubled Times," *The Globe and Mail,* January 27, 1997, B5. Reprinted with permission from The Globe and Mail.

Industry Profile

	1996	1995	1994	1993	1992
1. Quick ratio	0.28:1	0.26:1	0.26:1	0.30:1	0.30:1
2. Current ratio	1.65:1	1.61:1	1.46:1	1.59:1	1.51:1
3. Total liabilities to net worth	71.0%	70.0%	66.5%	82.1%	72.3%
4. Collection period, in days	9.54	9.48	10.66	11.74	11.70
5. Return on sales, after tax	1.59%	1.63%	1.11%	2.00%	2.68%
6. Return on assets, after tax	4.20%	4.36%	4.17%	6.23%	6.92%
7. Return on net worth, after tax	9.53%	9.85%	12.45%	16.57%	17.14%

	At Dec. 31/'96	At Sept. 30/'96	At June 30/'96	At Mar. 31/'96
8. Stability score	5.7	5.7	5.7	5.8
9. Paydex score	61	61	62	63

10. Average number of employees: 12
11. Failure rate for 1995: 1.73%
12. Average annual sales per company: $1 790 837

Footnotes

1. Indicates liquidity: cash and accounts receivable versus current liabilities. A ratio of 1:1 is considered good. Current levels are weak.

2. Also a measure of liquidity: cash, accounts receivable, and inventory versus short-term liabilities. 2:1 is considered good. Current levels are fair.

3. Measures how much debt is leveraged against the worth of the business. Debt levels have remained fairly steady.

4. Measures how quickly a company collects payments from its creditors. The collection period is low in retail.

5. Measures profitability. Current levels are not high.

6. Shows how efficiently a business leverages its assets to make profits. Returns have weakened.

7. Return on equity has fallen significantly.

8. Measures the probability of a company closing in the next six months, measured out of 10, with 10 the safest and 1 the riskiest. In percentage terms, the risk of closure is about 2.58%.

9. Measures how quickly drugstores pay their bills, in number of days. A paydex score of 61 and 70 means companies pay their bills in 45 to 50 days.

Source: Dun & Bradstreet Canada. Reprinted by permission. Visit Dun & Bradstreet's Web site at **http://www.dnb.com**.

Budget preparation is frequently time-consuming and involves many people from various departments of the firm. The complexity of the budgeting process varies with the size and complexity of the organization. Giant corporations, such as Walt Disney, Intel, and Boeing, tend to have more complex and sophisticated budgeting systems. Their budgets serve as a means of integrating the numerous

Business Term

✓ **Budget**

A planning and control tool that reflects expected sales revenues, operating expenses, and cash receipts and outlays.

CYBERSPACE

The Internet can be a good source for picking up financial advice. Here are a few nongovernment sites (1997) worth checking out:

→ Toronto-Dominion Bank: http://www.tdbank.ca

→ Bank of Montreal: http://www.bmo.com

→ Bank of Nova Scotia: http://www.scotiabank.ca

HENRY SPEAKS OUT WITH PASSION

Enhancing shareholder value and executive bonuses is good ... agreed? Not so, according to Henry Mintzberg, one of the world's leading management gurus. He says:

1. Executive bonuses undermine teamwork and focus attention on short-term gain. Since a bonus has no real downside — no basic risk to the executives — it becomes a fundamentally corrupt idea that distorts behaviour. It's just another version of the old boy's network at play.

2. Shareholder value is a one-sided, anti-social concept that has no place in a democratic society. It serves neither social progress nor economic development because societies develop by spreading their benefits, not by concentrating them in the hands of the established wealthy.

What do you think?

divisions of the firm in addition to serving as planning and control tools. Budgeting by firms is similar to household budgeting in that the purpose is to match income and expenses so as to accomplish objectives and correctly time cash inflows and outflows.

CASE EXERCISE

BEAN COUNTERS MUST DO MORE THAN JUST COUNT

Maggie was the owner and president of an expanding manufacturing company, ABC Inc. Her business was profitable, but lately it was running short of cash. It was time for facts. Was she growing the business too fast? Would this pattern continue? Her search for an answer began with an analysis of her financial statements. She called ABC's accounting firm and made an appointment for the next morning.

The morning meeting lasted less than half an hour. Despite the pre-arranged meeting time, the accountant

was in a hurry to get to another appointment. He said he would need at least two weeks to look into the cash shortage problem.

As he backed out, he reminded Maggie that ABC Inc. would have to come up with some extra cash this week to pay for its next business tax installment. This parting statement sent Maggie's blood pressure soaring.

The next evening, Maggie found herself sharing her business frustrations with Steve, her long-time business associate and mentor. "I'm getting a new accounting firm," she began, "but what should I be looking for?" Steve reminded her that both of their businesses had become successful when they learned how to add

value for their customers. Accountants — in fact, any professional who is outsourced — must do the same thing. "The bottom line," Steve said, "is that bean counters must do more than just count. A business can't afford to pay any professional unless that person adds value to the company."

1. Interview at least one business owner and one accountant. Brainstorm a list of ways an accountant or accounting firm could add value to a business.

Source: Adapted from Ron Knowles and Debbie White, *Issues in Canadian Small Business* (Toronto: Harcourt Brace & Company, 1995), 114-15.

Since the accounting department is the organization's financial nerve centre, it provides much of the data used in budget development. The overall master, or operating, budget is actually a composite of numerous sub-budgets for each of the departments or functional areas of the firm. These typically include the production budget, cash budget, capital expenditures budget, advertising budget, and sales budget.

Budgets usually are established on an annual basis, but may be divided monthly or quarterly for control purposes. Since some activities, such as the construction of new manufacturing facilities or long-term purchasing contracts, tend to involve activities extending over several years, longer-term budgets may be used in those cases.

INTERNATIONAL ACCOUNTING

WE LEARNED IN Chapter 10 that Canada's information and communications industries are key growth engines of our economy. The most successful businesses in these sectors, such as Nortel and Newbridge Networks, rely heavily on the export market. Accounting procedures and practices must be adapted to reflect an international environment. Key issues will be the need to translate the financial statement of a global firm's international affiliates, branches, and subsidiaries, and to convert foreign currency transactions to Canadian dollars.

As defined in Chapter 3, an exchange rate is the rate at which a country's currency can be exchanged for other currencies. Like the price of any good or service, currency prices change daily according to supply and demand. These fluctuations affect accounting entries differently than single-currency transactions do. The international firm's consolidated financial statements must reflect any gains or losses that may occur as a result of fluctuations in exchange rates. Financial statements covering two or more countries also need to be consistent to allow for meaningful comparison.

International Accounting Standards

The International Accounting Standards Committee (IASC) was established in 1973 to provide worldwide consistency in financial reporting practices. The IASC is recognized as the sole body with the responsibility and authority to issue pronouncements on international accounting standards. The International Federation of Accountants, formed in 1977, supports the work of the IASC and develops interna-

> ## BUSINESS TIP
>
> See what Canada's four financial Crown corporations can do to help your business grow, including into export markets.
>
> → **Business Development Bank of Canada** (www.bdc.ca). BDC is Canada's small business bank. It plays a leadership role in delivering financial and management services, with a particular focus on the emerging and exporting sectors of the economy. Its products include term loans, working capital for growth, Venture Loans® and venture capital, as well as a counselling program for new exporters called NEXPRO® and ISO registration assistance.
>
> → **Canadian Commercial Corporation** (www.ccc.ca). CCC offers exporters a wide range of services to help Canadian businesses conclude sales, particularly to foreign governments and international agencies. CCC assures contract performance to a foreign customer, enhancing the Canadian exporter's chance of securing a contract on advantageous terms.
>
> → **Export Development Corporation** (www.edc.ca). EDC supports Canada's export trade by helping Canadians compete in world markets. Its risk management services – including insurance, financing, and guarantees – have become an integral part of the export strategies of many small and medium-sized Canadian companies.
>
> → **Farm Credit Corporation** (www.fcc-sca.com). FCC provides a wide range of innovative financing solutions to Canadian agricultural communities. It actively supports farmer-controlled diversification initiatives and value-added agricultural operations within and beyond the farm gate.

tional guidelines for auditing, ethics, education, and management accounting. Every five years, an international congress is held to judge the progress in achieving consistency in standards, with the objective of enhancing comparability between nations and currencies. With the advent of the European Union and the North American trade bloc, the necessity for comparability and uniformity of international accounting standards is becoming widely recognized and soon will be a reality.

SUMMARY OF LEARNING OUTCOMES

1. **Explain the functions of accounting and its importance to the firm's management and to outside parties, such as owners, investors, creditors, and government agencies.**

Accountants measure, interpret, and communicate financial information to owners and other parties inside and outside the firm for effective decision making. They are responsible for gathering, recording, and interpreting financial information for owners and management. In addition, they provide financial information on the status and operation of the firm for use by such outside parties as government agencies and potential investors and lenders.

2. **Identify the three basic business activities involving accounting.**

Accounting plays key roles in (1) financing activities, which are necessary to start a business and to expand it in the future; (2) investing activities, which provide the assets needed to run the business; and (3) operating activities, which focus on the sale of goods and services and on the expenses incurred in operating the business.

3. **Explain the need for accounting standards and the three accounting organizations that have input in determining those standards.**

Accountants have developed "generally accepted accounting principles" (GAAP) to ensure that accounting practices are consistent among firms. There are two branches of accounting: private accountants, who are employees of the business; and public accountants, sometimes referred to as auditors, who are not employees of the business. Private accountants belong to the Society of Management Accountants of Canada. Public accountants belong to the Canadian Institute of Chartered Accountants (CICA) or the Certified General Accountants Association of Canada.

4. **Differentiate between bookkeeping and accounting.**

Bookkeeping is concerned with recording transactions in accounting journals, while accounting organizes this information into financial statements. Account-

ants also deal with management accounting, which is used by owners and internal managers.

5. **Outline the steps in the accounting process.**

The accounting process involves recording, classifying, and summarizing accounting transactions and using this information to produce financial statements for the firm's owners, management, and other interested parties. Transactions are recorded chronologically in journals, posted in ledgers, and then summarized in accounting statements.

6. **Explain the functions of the balance sheet and the income statement and the need for a cash-flow statement, and identify their major components.**

The balance sheet shows the financial position of a company as of a particular date. The three major classifications on the balance sheet represent the components of the accounting equation: assets, liabilities, and owners' equity.

The income statement shows the operations of a firm over a specific period. It focuses on the firm's activities — its revenues and expenditures — and the firm's profit or loss during the period. The major components of the income statement are revenues, cost of goods sold, expenses, and profits or losses.

A statement of cash flows is a third accounting statement required by most firms — especially small and medium-sized businesses — for their operations management. It tells owners, managers, and creditors whether or not the firm can pay its bills.

7. **Discuss how the major financial ratios are used in analyzing a firm's financial strengths and weaknesses.**

Liquidity ratios measure a firm's ability to meet short-term obligations. Examples are the current ratio and acid-test ratio. Profitability ratios assess the overall financial performance of the firm. Earnings per share, return on sales, and return on owners' equity are examples. Leverage ratios measure the extent to which the firm relies on debt to finance its operations, for example, the debt-to-owners'-equity ratio. Activity ratios, such as inventory turnover, measure how effectively a firm uses its resources. Each of these ratios assists management and others by enabling them to compare current company financial information with that of previous years and with industry standards.

8. **Explain the role of budgets in business.**

Budgets are financial guidelines for future periods reflecting expected sales revenues, operating expenses, and cash receipts and outlays. They represent management's expectations of future occurrences based on plans that have been made and serve as important planning and control tools by providing standards against which actual performance can be compared.

9. **Explain the need for international accounting and the importance of uniform financial statements for firms engaged in international business.**

As more Canadian businesses — small and large — search the global marketplace for opportunities, accounting procedures and practices are being adapted to reflect this new international environment. Accountants must take into consideration factors such as fluctuations in exchange rates and inconsistent financial statements between countries. The International Accounting Standards Committee was established to provide worldwide consistency in financial reporting practices and comparability and uniformity of international accounting standards.

Key Terms Quiz

accounting equation	liquidity ratios	owners' equity
bookkeeping	balance sheet	bottom line
accounting	income statement	ratio analysis
accounting process	budget	activity ratios
asset	leverage ratios	liability
equity	profitability ratios	

_____ 1. Measuring, interpreting, and communicating financial information for internal and external decision making.

_____ 2. The systematic recording of business transactions into journals.

_____ 3. Method of converting individual transactions to financial statements.

_____ 4. Anything of value owned or leased by a business.

_____ 5. Claim against the assets of a business.

_____ 6. Claim of a firm's creditors.

_____ 7. Claims of the proprietor, partners, or stockholders against the assets of the firm; the excess of assets over liabilities.

_____ 8. Basic accounting concept that assets are equal to liabilities plus owners' equity.

_____ 9. Statement of a firm's financial position on a particular date.

_____ 10. Financial record of revenues, expenses, and profits of a company over a period of time.

_____ 11. Overall profit or loss earned by a firm.

_____ 12. Use of quantitative measures in evaluating a firm's financial performance.

_____ 13. Ratios measuring a firm's ability to meet its short-term obligations.

_____ 14. Ratios measuring the overall financial performance of a firm.

_____ 15. Ratios measuring the extent to which a firm relies on debt financing in its operations.

_____ 16. Ratios measuring the effectiveness of a firm's use of its resources.

_____ 17. Planning and control tool that reflects expected sales revenues, operating expenses, and cash receipts and outlays.

Other Important Terms

acid-test ratio
certified general accountant (CGA)
chartered accountant (CA)
current ratio
debt-to-owners'-equity ratio
earnings per share

generally accepted accounting
 principles (GAAP)
inventory turnover ratio
journal
liquidity
net income
point-of-sale terminal

private accountant
public accountant
return on equity
return on sales
revenue
statement of cash flows

Review Questions

1. Many accountants show the values for the various items on their firm's income statements in percentages based on net sales rather than showing the actual figures involved. What additional insights would this approach make possible?

2. Identify the three types of assets and the two types of liabilities that appear on a typical balance sheet. Categorize the following account titles:

    a. Mary Ellen Beasley, Capital
    b. Mortgage Payable
    c. Patent
    d. Buildings
    e. Common Stock
    f. Prepaid Expenses
    g. Accounts Payable
    h. Marketable Securities

3. Match each of the accounts listed below with the appropriate accounting categories. Each account may be included in more than one category.

    ____ a. Net Sales
    ____ b. Accounts Receivable
    ____ c. Advertising Expense
    ____ d. Common Stock
    ____ e. Equipment
    ____ f. Marketable Securities
    ____ g. Long-Term Notes Payable
    ____ h. Salaries
    ____ i. Retained Earnings

    1. Current Asset
    2. Fixed Asset
    3. Current Liability
    4. Long-Term Liability
    5. Owners' Equity
    6. Revenue
    7. Expenses

Discussion Questions

1. Who are the major users of accounting information?

2. Describe the role that accounting plays in a firm's financing activities, investing activities, and operating activities.

3. Distinguish between public and private accountants.

4. Explain the steps of the accounting process and the impact of computerization on this process.

5. What is meant by the statement "The balance sheet is a detailed expression of the accounting equation"?

6. Identify the primary purpose of each of the components of the balance sheet and the income statement.

What are the major differences between these statements?

7. Identify the four categories of financial ratios discussed in the chapter, and describe specific ratios included in each category.

8. Explain the similarities and differences between budgeting and the development of accounting statements.

9. What are the primary purposes of budgets?

10. Explain the need for and importance of international accounting.

4. Indicate the ratio that would provide information on
   a. A firm's ability to meet short-term obligations.
   b. A firm's ability to pay current debts.
   c. A firm's ability to pay current debts on short notice.
   d. A firm's overall financial performance.
   e. The amount of profits earned for each share of common stock outstanding.
   f. Net income compared with sales.
   g. Owners' equity.
   h. The firm's use of its resources.
   i. The number of times merchandise moves through the business.
   j. The extent to which a firm relies on financing.
   k. The percentage of owners' investments to debt financing.

5. At the end of the year, Jupiter Enterprises showed the following balances in its accounts:

Land	$ 80 000
Buildings	314 000
Inventory	100 000
Cash	10 000
Accounts Payable	90 000
Marketable Securities	36 000
Retained Earnings	300 000
Common Shares (80 000 shares @ $1)	80 000
Notes Payable	110 000
Equipment	40 000

   a. Prepare a balance sheet for Jupiter Enterprises.
   b. Calculate the current ratio, acid-test ratio, and debt-to-owners'-equity ratio. What conclusions can be drawn from these ratios?

Answers to Key Terms Quiz

1. accounting 2. bookkeeping 3. accounting process 4. asset 5. equity 6. liability 7. owners' equity 8. accounting equation 9. balance sheet 10. income statement 11. bottom line 12. ratio analysis 13. liquidity ratios 14. profitability ratios 15. leverage ratios 16. activity ratios 17. budget

Notes

1. Rod McQueen, "Proactive Approach Puts New Polish on the Family Business," *The Financial Post*, December 14, 1996, 13. Reprinted by permission of The Financial Post.
2. Ibid.
3. Ibid.
4. This section is excerpted from Steven H. Appelbaum and M. Dale Beckman, *Canadian Business: A Contemporary Perspective* (Toronto: Dryden, 1995), ACC 4 to ACC 5. Copyright © 1995 by Harcourt Brace & Company, Canada, Limited. All rights reserved. Reprinted by permission of Harcourt Brace & Company, Canada, Limited.
5. Ibid., ACC 5. Copyright © 1995 by Harcourt Brace & Company, Canada, Ltd. All rights reserved. Reprinted by permission of Harcourt Brace & Company, Canada, Limited.
6. Jane Francis and David Brown, "Accounting," *Profit*, October/November 1996, 33.
7. David Thomas, "Socking Too Much Away for a Rainy Day," *The Financial Post*, February 22, 1997, 5.

Banking and Financial Management

After studying this chapter, you should be able to

1. Identify the functions performed by a firm's financial manager.
2. Describe the characteristics a good form of money should have and list the functions of money.
3. Identify and explain the three principal components of the money supply — M1, M2, and M2+.
4. Explain how a firm uses funds.
5. Compare the two major categories of sources of funds.
6. Identify likely sources of short-term and long-term funds.
7. Identify the major types of Canadian financial institutions and the sources and uses of their funds.
8. Explain the functions of the Bank of Canada and the major tools it uses to increase or decrease the money supply.
9. Explain the purpose and role of the Canada Deposit Insurance Corporation (CDIC) and the Canadian Payments Clearing and Settlement System.
10. Explain some of the major technology changes in the financial sector that have occurred over the 1990s.
11. Discuss how Canadian banks and financial institutions interact with international organizations.

Banking on Your Own[1]

In the spring of 1996, Helen Sinclair joined the 1 million Canadians who have chosen the self-employment option. She left her high-paying and prestigious position as head of the influential Canadian Bankers Association (CBA) and launched a new company — BankWorks Trading Inc.

Sinclair had toyed with the idea of starting her own show for years, but acted only after a job interview with a bank executive when she left the CBA. "We had a lovely conversation and then I told him that the only problem with the job was that I'd have to report to him." Soon after, she called up Danica Lavoie, a former Scotiabank colleague, and asked her to become a minority partner and chief operating officer. Lavoie accepted, and BankWorks was born.

BankWorks is a company that facilitates the trade of know-how among financial institutions both nationally and internationally. It helps build opportunities for North American buyers, to acquire proven technology and products; for suppliers, to recover some of their development costs; and for foreign financial institutions abroad, to acquire world-class know-how quickly and economically. As such, the company focuses primarily on two product lines:

1. **Training programs and courseware.** Canada's financial institutions train more people than any other Canadian industry, and spend more money doing it. Their state-of-the-art courses, ranging from classroom programs to interactive software, are delivered effectively to thousands of employees across six time zones. Building on this demonstrated expertise, BankWorks promotes and markets educational programming to financial institutions both in North America and abroad.

2. **Software, systems, and procedures.** Canada's financial institutions process payments faster and more securely than any other country in the world. This expertise constitutes a competitive advantage that is ideally suited for export, and BankWorks has positioned itself to bring this know-how to the world.

The concept of BankWorks is simple. The company identifies services, technologies, and training products that have already been developed by North American financial institutions. Then it repackages and sells them to an international roster of banks and financial companies that need the expertise. Some industry observers think this idea is a win–win for suppliers, who have the opportunity to recover some of the development costs, and for the buyers, since they can acquire proven products rather than developing them from scratch.

BankWorks made a profit in its first year of operation. It has a good chance at becoming a long-term success. Here are some of the major reasons for Sinclair's success:

- **Influential networks.** BankWorks draws on the research, teaching, and logistics expertise of Canada's financial community and educational institutions. These organizations include the Institute of Canadian Bankers and York University's Schulich School of Business, with its extensive international programming.

- **Respect.** "Helen's well-respected in the banking circles," says her former CBA colleague Al Cooper. "Without question there are people on the inside who might not have always agreed with her, but they respect her talents and abilities."

- **Entrepreneurial spirit.** "She's very entrepreneurial in spirit, ... creative and incredibly hard working," says Joanne De Laurentiis, president of Acxsys Corp., a client company that owns the Interac debit-card system.

- **Focus.** "She never misses a trick," says Robert McIntosh, a former boss at Scotiabank and Sinclair's predecessor at the CBA.

- **Work ethic.** Sinclair has a rigorous fitness regime that gives her the energy to work ten to fifteen hours a day.

- **Partnerships/alliances.** Sinclair knew she needed to have partners, and so teamed up with Danica Lavoie at the very start. BankWorks then formed an alliance with systems consultant United Systems Solutions Inc. — with which it shares office space — to develop expertise in building information management systems for multisite institutions.

- **International banking.** BankWorks is well positioned in the fast-growing international financial market. Its first target was Mexico, which Sinclair and Lavoie believed was ripe for their three areas of expertise: remote banking technology, training programs, and credit risk management.

CHAPTER OVERVIEW

BANKWORKS IS AN exemplary case of how the combination of timing, skills, knowledge, and market need come together to create an opportunity for two Canadian entrepreneurs. Helen Sinclair and Danica Lavoie had the vision to seize a market-driven opportunity and begin the journey to control their own destiny.

To be successful, all businesses require the marketing and managing skills that we discussed earlier in the text. But there is a third skill or function that is equally important — **finance:** *planning, obtaining, and managing a company's use of funds in order to accomplish its objectives most effectively and efficiently.* In the long run, Sinclair and Lavoie knew that adequate start-up funds had to be made available to market and sell their products and services. Like all businesses, they would have to buy materials and equipment, pay bills, purchase additional facilities, and compensate employees. They also knew that they had to start a business in a market that could afford to pay for their services. Lastly, they had to have a financial plan that could prove that their dreams would be translated into profit.

Financial objectives include not only meeting expenses, but also maximizing the firm's overall value, which often is determined by the value of its common stock in the case of an incorporated company like BankWorks. More and more frequently, businesses designate a financial manager to be responsible for both meeting expenses and increasing profits for the firm's stockholders or owners — which is why Sinclair enticed Lavoie with an ownership position to join BankWorks.

In this chapter, we will examine how start-up companies like BankWorks and large companies like IBM

Canada develop and implement financial plans. This chapter focuses on topics such as the role of financial managers, why businesses need funds, and the various types and sources of funds. We also discuss the Canadian banking system, the role of the Bank of Canada, how our money supply is regulated, and the impact of technology on our banking and finance industry. Lastly, we'll examine how our major financial institutions are affecting the fast-growing international finance market.

THE ROLE OF THE FINANCIAL MANAGER

IN THE MODERN business world, effective financial decisions are increasingly important to organizational success. Businesses are placing greater priority on measuring and reducing the costs of conducting business. As a result, **financial managers** — *those responsible for developing and implementing the firm's financial plan and for determining the most appropriate sources and uses of funds* — are among the most vital people on the corporate scene. Their growing importance is reflected in the number of chief executives who were promoted from financial positions. A recent study of major corporations reveals that nearly one in three chief executives has either a finance or a banking background.[2]

Possible job titles for high-ranking financial managers include vice president of finance and chief financial officer (CFO). For start-up companies such as BankWorks, the role of financial manager may be embedded in the responsibilities of the chief operating officer. In most smaller businesses, employees and owners have to wear more than one hat. The way a company's money is managed can reduce the need for financing and, when money is needed, there is a better chance of getting it since investors can see how well the company is handling its finances.[3] In performing their jobs, financial managers continually seek to balance the risks involved with expected financial returns. **Risk** *is the uncertainty of*

Business Term

✓ **Finance**

Planning, obtaining, and managing a company's use of funds in order to accomplish its objectives most effectively and efficiently.

Business Term

✓ **Financial managers**

Managers responsible for developing and implementing the firm's financial plan and for determining the most appropriate sources and uses of funds.

Business Term

✓ **Risk**

The uncertainty of loss.

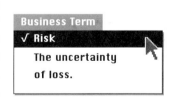

THEY SAID IT

"If you chase money, you'll never catch it. Because it always starts with a dream."

DEBBI FIELDS, founder of Mrs. Fields Cookies, which has about 1000 stores in 10 countries

loss; **return** *is the gain or loss that results from an investment over a specified period.*

A heavy reliance on borrowed funds, however, may raise the return on the owners' or stockholders' investment. The financial manager strives to maximize the wealth of the firm's stockholders by striking a *balance between the risk of an investment and its potential gain.* This balance is called the **risk–return trade-off**. An increase in a firm's cash on hand, for instance, reduces the risk of unexpected cash needs. But cash is not an earning asset, and the failure to invest surplus funds in an earning asset (such as marketable securities) reduces potential return, or profitability.

Business Term

√ **Return**

The gain or loss that results from an investment over a specified period.

Business Term

√ **Risk–return trade-off**

Balance between the risk of an investment and its potential gain.

The Financial Plan

Financial managers develop the organization's **financial plan**, *a document that specifies the funds needed by a firm for a period of time, the timing of inflows and outflows, and the most appropriate sources and uses of funds.* It is based on *forecasts* of labour and production costs, purchasing, and expected sales activities for the period covered. Financial managers and owners use forecasts to determine the specific amounts and

Business Term

√ **Financial plan**

A document that specifies the funds needed by a firm for a period of time, the timing of inflows and outflows, and the most appropriate sources and uses of funds.

timing of expenditures and receipts. The financial plan is built on answers to three vital questions:

1. What funds does the firm require during the next period of operations?

2. How will the necessary funds be obtained?

3. When will more funds be needed?

Some funds will be obtained through selling the firm's goods or services. But funds are needed in different amounts at different times, and the financial plan must reflect both the amount and timing of inflows and outflows of funds. Profitable firms often face a financial squeeze as a result of the need for funds when sales lag, when the volume of credit sales increases, or when customers are slow in making payments. Cash inflows and outflows of a business are similar to those in a household; the members of a household may depend on a weekly or monthly paycheque for funds, but their expenditures vary greatly from one pay period to the next. The financial plan should indicate when the flows of funds entering and leaving the organization will occur and in what amounts.

A good financial plan also involves *financial control*, a process that periodically checks actual revenues, costs, and expenses against forecasts. If significant differences exist between projected figures and reality, it is important to discover them early in order to take corrective action.

CHARACTERISTICS AND FUNCTIONS OF MONEY

PLAYWRIGHT GEORGE BERNARD SHAW once said that the *lack* of money is the root of all evil. Many a businessperson would agree, for money is the lubricant of contemporary business. Firms require adequate funds to finance the company's operations and carry out the plans of management.

Characteristics of Money

Money *is anything generally accepted as a means of paying for goods and services.* Over time, an amazing variety of articles have been used as mediums of exchange at vari-

---

BUSINESS TIP

The financial plan to open and operate a small business is composed of five basic action steps:

Step 1. Create an application and sources of funds table.

Step 2. Create your opening balance sheet.

Step 3. Create your projected cash flow.

Step 4. Determine your projected or pro forma income statement.

Step 5. Calculate end-of-period or year-end balance sheet.

ous times and in various places, including shells, glass beads, fish hooks, teeth, grain, cattle, cocoa beans, paper, and metal — even reproductions of playing cards were legal tender in New France in the eighteenth century when hard currency was scarce.[4] Most early forms of money had a number of serious disadvantages. For example, a cow is a poor form of money for an owner who wants only a loaf of bread and a bottle of wine. Exchange involving the use of money can permit elaborate specialization and provide a general base for purchasing power if the money has certain characteristics. It must be divisible, portable, durable, and difficult to counterfeit, and it should have a stable value.

Divisibility. The dollar can be converted into pennies, nickels, dimes, and quarters. The British pound is worth 100 pence; the German deutsche mark can be traded for 100 pfennigs. These forms of money can be exchanged easily for products ranging from chewing gum to a car because they are so conveniently divisible.

> **Business Term**
> √ **Money**
>   Anything generally accepted as a means of paying for goods and services.

The Currency Museum of the Bank of Canada has a collection of early Canadian money on display.

Portability. The people of Yap on a tiny island in the South Pacific used to publicize the extent of their wealth by placing their stone money at the doorways of their homes. Needless to say, exchanging stones for different items was cumbersome. Today's lightweight, plastic, and electronic currency makes buying and selling a relatively uncomplicated process. For example, many of us now pay for our groceries electronically with a debit card. In seconds your account will be debited and the merchant's account will be credited.

> **DID YOU KNOW?**
>
> The number of debit-card transactions in Canada increased by over 450 percent between 1994 and 1995, amounting to more than $12 billion in 1995.

Durability. A monetary system works more efficiently if it is based on an exchange mechanism that lasts, at least for the foreseeable future. Coins and paper currency satisfy this requirement, in part, because deterioration is slow and replacement is straightforward.

In the 1990s, the Canadian money system, along with that of other developed economies, gradually evolved toward a more "paperless society" characterized by electronic money — the ultimate in durability. Electronic money has a virtually infinite life expectancy and no replacement cost. Canadians are among the world's highest per-capita users of electronic money. For example, in 1995 there were at least a billion automated banking machine transactions. Figure 15.1 illustrates the convenience and efficiency of a paperless transaction.

Difficulty in Counterfeiting. The distribution of counterfeit money could undermine a nation's monetary system by ruining the value of legitimate money. For this reason, all governments make counterfeiting a serious crime and take elaborate steps to prevent it.

The Bank of Canada has sole responsibility for the issue of bank notes (coins and bills) in Canada. To fulfil

> **DID YOU KNOW?**
>
> Do you remember when we used to have $1 and $2 paper bills? Now we have "loonies" and "toonies." That's because metal coins last longer than paper money. A Canadian $2 bill had an average life of approximately 10 months and could be folded some 4000 times without tearing. The annual replacement cost was about $250 million. A metal toonie has a life expectancy of about 20 years and a yearly replacement cost of about $50 million.

Figure 15.1 Journey of an Electronic Data Interchange (EDI) Transaction

Enter data into terminal

Transmits P.O. to supplier

Supplier's PC sends order internally to be shipped

Transmits invoice to ordering company

Out-of-Stock Ordering Company

Software recognizes order and writes a purchase order (P.O.)

Software makes an accounts receivable entry and writes an invoice

its obligations, it is involved in every phase of note design, production, and distribution — a role it assumed in 1935. Not surprisingly, counterfeiting is a primary concern for the Bank. It works closely with currency issuers in other countries, the RCMP, the National Research Council of Canada, and bank-note printing companies to develop designs, processes, and technologies that effectively deter counterfeiting. In the process, Canada has become an internationally acknowledged leader in currency security.

A combination of features protects Canada's bank notes from counterfeiting: the Optical Security Device, the microprint, the multidirectional lines, the subtle shift of pastel colours, the texture of feel of the intaglio print, the planchettes (small green disks) in the paper, and the extremely high quality of the printing.[5]

Stability. A good money system should have a stable value. If the value of money fluctuates, people become unwilling to trade goods and services for it. Inflation is a particular concern for governments around the world. When people fear that money will lose much of its buying power, they begin to abandon it and look for safer means of storing their wealth. As well, the costs of inflation do not fall equally on all members of the population, since some are better able than others to protect themselves against rising prices. Individuals on fixed incomes are among the most vulnerable: at 4.5 percent inflation, a fixed pension will lose half its value in just fifteen years.[6] As we shall see later on in this chapter, price stability — through monetary management — is a major responsibility of the Bank of Canada.

Functions of Money

Money performs three basic functions. First, it serves primarily as a *medium of exchange* — a means of facilitating exchange and eliminating the need for a barter system. Second, it functions as a *unit of account* — a common denominator for measuring the value of all goods and services. Finally, money acts as a temporary *store of value* — a way of keeping accumulated wealth until it is needed to make new purchases. Money offers one big advantage as a store of value: it is highly liquid, meaning it can be obtained and disposed of quickly and easily. The chief advantage of money is that it is immediately available for purchasing products or paying debts.

THE MONEY SUPPLY AND NEAR-MONEY[7]

WHAT IS MONEY? As strange as it may seem, definitions of money differ. **Currency**, or *coins and notes (paper money)*, forms one rather small part — between 4.4 and 5.0 percent, depending on the definition of money used. Chequing accounts are also considered to be money because they are almost instantly available. The Bank of Canada calls these components of the money supply *M1*. More specifically, M1 is the sum of Canadian currency in circulation, metal coins and paper money, and Canadian-dollar **demand deposits** — *accounts from which the depositor can withdraw money "on demand"* —

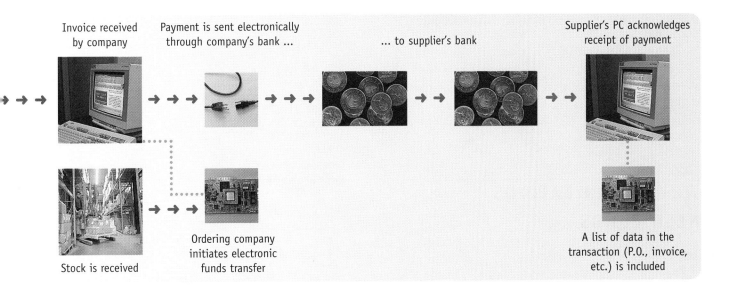

Invoice received by company

Payment is sent electronically through company's bank ...

... to supplier's bank

Supplier's PC acknowledges receipt of payment

Stock is received

Ordering company initiates electronic funds transfer

A list of data in the transaction (P.O., invoice, etc.) is included

in chartered banks, excluding those held by other banks and by the federal government.

This is not the complete picture, however. Another significant group of funds consists of various **notice deposits**, *accounts from which the depositor can withdraw money only after giving notice, usually seven days*. Thus, notice deposits cannot be used in ordinary transactions until they are first converted into chequable deposits or currency. Because these items cannot be used immediately, some economists do not consider them to be money, but instead refer to them as **near-money**: *assets almost as liquid as chequing accounts but that cannot be used directly as a medium of exchange*. Examples of near-money include savings accounts, personal and nonpersonal redeemable fixed-term deposits issued by the chartered banks, share-capital accounts in credit unions (or, in Quebec, *caisses populaires*), and term deposits, guaranteed investment certificates (GICs), and debentures with less than one year to maturity held by trust and mortgage-loan companies. However, these notice deposits can usually be liquidated prior to maturity (usually at some penalty) and therefore

Business Term

√ **Currency**

Coins and notes (paper money).

Business Term

√ **Demand deposis**

Accounts from which the depositor can withdraw money "on demand."

Business Term

√ **Notice deposits**

Accounts from which the depositor can withdraw money only after giving notice, usually seven days.

Business Term

√ **Near-money**

Assets almost as liquid as chequing accounts but that cannot be used directly as a medium of exchange.

can also be considered part of the money supply. These components, plus M1, the Bank of Canada refers to as *M2*.

M2+ is a logical extension of M2. This money measure includes M2 plus all deposits held by the general public at nonbank depository institutions — trust and mortgage-loan companies, credit unions and *caisses populaires*, personal deposits at Alberta Treasury branches and Province of Ontario Savings Offices, life annuities, and money market mutual funds.

There are several other definitions of money, which are discussed in more advanced textbooks. These definitions are related to different emphases on particular functions or properties of money. For example, M3 includes all of M2+ in addition to nonpersonal term deposits and foreign currency deposits of Canadian residents. In summary,

- M1 = Canadian currency in circulation, including metal coins and paper and demand deposits

- M2 = M1 + notice deposits

- M2+ = M2 + all money held at nonbank depository institutions

All of the money in use today is **token money**, that is, *money whose monetary value exceeds the market value of the materials it is made of*. This was not the case when gold coins were in circulation. The present-day monetary system allows a loonie, an official piece of paper such as a $5 bill, or a cheque to work equally well in financial transactions.

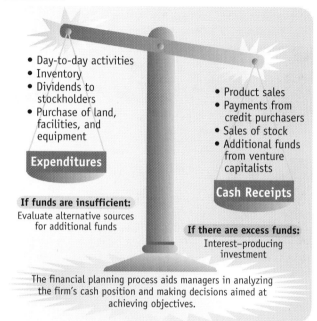

Business Term
✓ **Token money**
Money whose monetary value exceeds the market value of the materials it is made of.

Figure 15.2 Financial Planning Process

- Day-to-day activities
- Inventory
- Dividends to stockholders
- Purchase of land, facilities, and equipment

Expenditures

If funds are insufficient:
Evaluate alternative sources for additional funds

- Product sales
- Payments from credit purchasers
- Sales of stock
- Additional funds from venture capitalists

Cash Receipts

If there are excess funds:
Interest–producing investment

The financial planning process aids managers in analyzing the firm's cash position and making decisions aimed at achieving objectives.

WHY ORGANIZATIONS NEED FUNDS

ORGANIZATIONS REQUIRE FUNDS for many reasons, including running day-to-day business operations, paying for inventory, making interest payments on loans, paying dividends to stockholders, and purchasing land, facilities, and equipment. As Figure 15.2 illustrates, the financial plan identifies the firm's specific cash needs and when they will be needed. Comparing these needs with expenditures and expected cash receipts (from product sales, payments made by credit purchasers, and other sources) will help the financial manager and owner to determine precisely what additional funds must be

obtained at any given time. If inflows exceed cash needs, the financial manager will invest the surplus to earn interest. On the other hand, if inflows do not meet cash needs, the financial manager will seek additional sources of funds.

Generating Funds from Excess Cash

Most financial managers will choose to invest the majority of their firm's excess cash in marketable securities. These often are considered near-money since they are, by definition, marketable and easily converted into cash. Three of the most common types are securities issued by the Bank of Canada, notably Canada Savings Bonds (CSBs), Government of Canada marketable bonds (referred to as Canada bonds), and treasury bills; commercial paper; and certificates of deposit. *Treasury bills* are one of the more popular marketable securities since, as issues of the Canadian government, they are considered virtually risk-free and easy to resell. While *commercial paper* (a short-term note issued by a major corporation with a very high credit standing and backed solely by the reputation of that firm) is riskier than a treasury bill and does not have a well-developed secondary market for resale prior to maturity, it pays the purchaser a higher rate of interest. A *certificate of deposit (CD)* is a short-term note issued by a financial institution, such as a chartered bank, trust company, or credit union. The size and maturity date of a CD vary con-

DID YOU KNOW?

The greatest risk to the payments system arises from large-value payments made between financial institutions on behalf of clients such as manufacturers and their suppliers. Large-value items over $50 000 represent only about one-third of 1 percent of the number of settlements exchanged among banks and other financial institutions, but account for over 94 percent of their value, or approximately $80 billion per day. To reduce the risk associated with the exchange of these huge amounts, Canadian Payments Association (CPA) members have developed an electronic settlement mechanism, which was completed in mid-1997. This settlement system, known as the large-value transfer system (LVTS), offers customers same-day finality of payment, and participants same-day settlement. This means that once a payment has been sent and has passed the system's risk tests, it cannot be returned. This will be supported by netting caps, collateral, and same-day settlement at the Bank of Canada.

siderably and can be tailored to meet the needs of the purchaser. Large CDs in denominations of $100 000 can be purchased for periods as short as 24 hours. At the other extreme, ten-year certificates are available in denominations as low as $100 to $250.

SOURCES OF FUNDS

So far, we have focussed on half of the definition of finance — the reasons organizations need funds and how they use them. But of equal importance to the firm's financial plan is the choice of the best sources of needed funds. Sources fall into two major categories: debt and equity

> **Business Term**
> ✓ **Debt capital**
> Funds obtained through borrowing.

> **Business Term**
> ✓ **Equity capital**
> Funds provided by the firm's owners by reinvesting earnings, making additional contributions, liquidating assets, issuing stock to the general public, or soliciting contributions from venture capitalists.

(see Figure 15.3). **Debt capital** represents *funds obtained through borrowing.* **Equity capital** consists of *funds provided by the firm's owners by reinvesting earnings, making additional contributions, liquidating assets, issuing stock to the general public, or soliciting contributions from venture capitalists.* Equity capital also is obtained from revenues from day-to-day operations and from liquidating some of the firm's assets.

Cash needs vary from one time period to the next, and even established firms may not be able to generate sufficient funds from operations to cover all costs of a major expansion or a significant investment in new equipment. In these instances, the financial manager must evaluate the potential advantages and drawbacks of seeking funds by borrowing. The alternative to borrowing is equity capital, which may be raised in several ways. The financial manager's job includes determining the most cost-effective balance between equity and borrowed funds and the proper blending of short- and long-term funds. See also Table 15.1 for a comparison of factors that need to be considered in deciding the best sources of needed funds.

Short-Term Sources of Funds

At numerous times throughout the year, an organization may discover that its cash requirements exceed available funds. In retailing, for example, the Christmas season

Figure 15.3 Sources of Funds

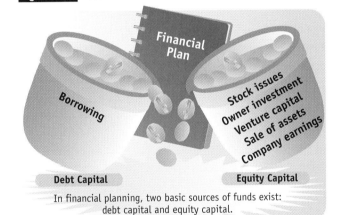

Financial Plan

Borrowing

Stock issues
Owner investment
Venture capital
Sale of assets
Company earnings

Debt Capital   Equity Capital

In financial planning, two basic sources of funds exist: debt capital and equity capital.

Table 15.1 Comparison of Debt and Equity Capital

Four factors are used in making financial decisions concerning whether to use debt capital or equity capital as the major source of funds.

Factor	Debt	Equity
Maturity	Has a specific date when it must be repaid.	Has no maturity date.
Claim on assets	Company lenders have prior claims on assets.	Stockholders have claims only after claims to lenders have been paid.
Claim on income	Lenders have prior claim on a fixed amount of interest, which must be paid before dividends can be paid to stockholders. Interest payments are a contractual obligation of the borrowing firm.	Stockholders have a residual claim after all creditors have been paid. Dividends are not a contractual obligation of the firm.
Right to a voice in management	Lenders are creditors, not owners. They have no voice in company affairs unless interest payments are not received.	Stockholders are the owners of the company, and most are given a voice in the operation of the firm.

may account for at least 60 percent of annual sales. The build of inventory just before the Christmas season may require additional funds to finance it until it is sold. As sales occur during the Christmas season, the incoming funds can be used to repay the suppliers of the borrowed funds. In these instances, the firm's financial manager will evaluate short-term sources of needed funds. By definition, these sources must be repaid within one year.

The major short-term source of funds is *trade credit*, or making open-account purchases from suppliers. A second source is *unsecured bank loans*, for which the business does not pledge any assets as collateral. Another option is *secured short-term loans*, for which the firm must pledge collateral, such as inventory. Large firms with unquestioned financial stability can raise money from a fourth source: by selling commercial paper. Commercial paper typically is sold in denominations of $100 000 with a maturity of 30 to 90 days. Issuing commercial paper to raise funds is usually 1 or 2 percent cheaper than borrowing short-term funds from a bank.

Long-Term Sources of Funds

Short-term sources of cash can be used to meet current needs for cash or inventory, but acquiring another company or making major purchases for such things as land, plant, and equipment will require funds for a much longer period. Unlike short-term sources, long-term sources can be repaid over a period of one year or longer.

A business firm has three long-term financing sources available. One is long-term loans issued by various financial institutions, such as banks, insurance companies, and pension funds. A second source is **bonds:** *certificates of indebtedness sold to raise long-term funds for corporations or government agencies.* A third source is not to borrow but to secure equity capital.

Public Sale of Stocks and Bonds. The sale of stocks and bonds represents a major source of funds for large corporations. Such sales provide cash inflows for the firm and either a share in the ownership (for the stock purchaser) or a specified rate of interest and repayment at a stated time (for bond purchasers). Since stock and bond issues of many corporations are traded on organized securities exchanges, stockholders and bondholders can

easily sell the shares they hold. The use of stock and bond issues to finance corporations is an important decision and is discussed in more detail in the next chapter.

Attracting Venture Capital. Venture capitalists poured record funds into Canadian companies over the 1990s. By the end of 1995, Canada's venture capital industry had $6 billion in funds under management, which was a 21 percent increase from 1994. A survey conducted by Macdonald & Associates Ltd. for the Canadian Venture Capital Association found that start-up companies attracted almost 40 percent of the 1995 pool of venture funds.[8]

Venture or risk capital *is usually provided by outside investors in exchange for an ownership share in the business.* Risk capital funds are usually managed by professionals who normally get the bulk of their money from institutional sources — such as governments, banks, pension funds, life insurance companies, and large corporations. Often a venture capitalist provides management consulting as well as funds, and may be a corporation, a wealthy individual, a pension fund, or a major endowment fund. In exchange for funds, the venture capitalist usually receives shares of the corporation's stock — at relatively low prices — and becomes a part owner of the corporation.

An individual venture capitalist is also known as an "angel" capitalist. One example of an individual or angel venture capitalist is Dennis Bennie, former CEO of Delrina Corp., a software developer. When the company was purchased by Symantec Corp. in mid-1995, Bennie walked away with about $20 million and a few months later began looking for investment opportunities. Using his own money, he formed XDL Capital Corp., a venture capital firm focussing exclusively on Internet technologies. Venture capitalists like Bennie don't usually want to get involved in the day-to-day operations of the companies, but they do want to provide management direction and advice at the board of directors level.[9] According to a study by Professor Riding of Carleton University, these angel capitalists typically invest $50 000 to $500 000. Larger amounts are the domain of the formal money market institutions. As a rule, "Angel investors learn about investments through personal contacts, through a network of business associates, and by word of mouth. They almost always syndicate their investment."[10]

Business Term

✓ **Bonds**

Certificates of indebtedness sold to raise long-term funds for corporations or government agencies.

Business Term

✓ **Venture or risk capital**

Capital usually provided by outside investors in exchange for an ownership share in the business.

Professor Riding estimates that there may be as many as 2000 venture capitalists in Canada today. Each typically receives dozens of proposals every month from businesses seeking funds. Most applications are rejected by these investors, who look for soundly managed firms with unique goods or services in a rapidly growing industry. In recent years, venture capitalists have concentrated in such fields as biotechnology, computers, electronics, and other advanced technologies. The Canadian Venture Capital Association estimated that in 1995, about 64 percent of the total venture capital invested (about $428 million) was directed to these types of fields. The remaining 36 percent ($241 million) was divided among consumer products, manufacturing, and miscellaneous investments.[11]

Leverage. Raising needed cash by borrowing allows the firm to benefit from the principle of **leverage**, *a technique of increasing the rate of return on an investment through the use of borrowed funds.* The concept of leverage can be related to a lever. Like the fulcrum on which a lever rests, the interest payments on borrowed funds are fixed. The key to managing leverage is ensuring that the company's earnings are larger than the interest payments, which increases the leverage on the rate of return on the stockholders' investments. Of course, if the company earns less than its interest payments, stockholders will lose money on their original investments.

As long as earnings exceed interest payments on borrowed funds, financial leverage will allow a firm to increase the rate of return on stockholders' investments.

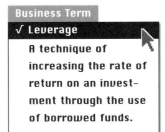

Business Term

√ **Leverage**

A technique of increasing the rate of return on an investment through the use of borrowed funds.

However, leverage also works in reverse. If, for example, Equity Corp.'s (see Table 15.2) earnings drop to $5000, stockholders will earn a 5 percent return on their investment. But, because Leverage Corp. must pay its bondholders $9000 in interest, what appears to be a $5000 gain is actually a $4000 loss for Leverage stockholders. A second problem with overreliance on borrowed funds is that it reduces management flexibility in future decisions.

THE CANADIAN FINANCIAL SYSTEM

T RADITIONALLY, THE CANADIAN financial system has been divided into two categories. *Deposit institutions* accept deposits from customers or members and provide some form of chequing account. This category includes chartered banks and near-banks such as credit unions. The second category is made up of *nondeposit institutions*, such as insurance companies and pension funds, which do not provide chequing/savings account privileges.

THEY SAID IT

"There aren't too many areas in Canada where we can say we have a model for the rest of the world, but I think the banking system is one of them."

SERGE SAUCIER, president and CEO, Raymond, Chabot, Martin, Paré

Table 15.2 How Leverage Works

Leverage Corp.		Equity Corp.	
Common stock	$10 000	Common stock	$100 000
Bonds (at 10% interest)	90 000	Bonds	0
	100 000		100 000
Earnings	30 000	Earnings	30 000
Less bond interest	9 000	Less bond interest	0
	21 000		30 000
Return to stockholders	$\frac{21\,000}{\$10\,000} = 210\%$	Return to stockholders	$\frac{30\,000}{\$100\,000} = 30\%$

The Leverage Corp. obtained 90 percent of its funds from lenders who purchased company bonds. The Equity Corp. raised all its funds through the sale of company stock. Each company earned $30 000. However, Leverage Corp. paid $9000 in interest to bondholders and earned a 210 percent return for its owners' $10 000 investment, while Equity Corp. provided only a 30 percent return on its stockholders' investments of $100 000.

SUCCESS STORY

BANKING STATISTICS: YOU BE THE JUDGE

Some Canadians believe that the profits and assets of our major financial institutions are too large. What do you think?

Source: Adapted from "The Top 1000," *The Globe and Mail Report on Business Magazine,* July 1996, 153 and 155. Reprinted with permission from The Globe and Mail.

Revenue Ranking by Industry

Financial Institution	Revenue ($billions)	Profit ($billions)	Assets ($billions)
Banks (Top 6)			
Royal Bank of Canada (Oct 95)	15.3	1.3	183.7
Canadian Imperial Bank of Commerce (Oct 95)	13.2	1.0	179.2
Bank of Nova Scotia (Oct 95)	12.1	0.9	147.2
Bank of Montreal (Oct 95)	12.1	1.0	151.8
Toronto-Dominion Bank (Oct 95)	8.7	0.8	108.8
National Bank of Canada (Oct 95)	4.3	0.3	48.9
Trust, Savings, and Loan (Top 3)			
CT Financial Services (Dec 95)	4.5	0.3	51.9
Canada Trustco Mortgage (Dec 95)	3.7	0.2	41.7
Montreal Trustco (Oct 95)	1.3	0.4	15.3
Financial Co-operatives (Top 3)			
Desjardins Group (Dec 94)	8.3	0.3	73.9
Caisse Centrale Desjardins (Dec 94)	0.4	0.02	5.4
Vancouver City Savings CU (Dec 95)	0.4	0.2	4.4

The Canadian Banking System

As of October 1996, the Canadian banking system consisted of 52 banks, employed over 207 000 Canadians in more than 8000 branches, housed more than 16 000 automated banking machines, and managed over $900 billion in assets. The federal *Bank Act* recognizes and governs two distinct types of banks: Schedule I, formerly called "Class A" banks; and Schedule II, previously known as "Class B" banks. Schedule I banks are both majority Canadian-owned and widely held, with their shares traded on the major stock exchanges and no one party allowed to own more than 10 percent of the shares. Schedule II banks include all foreign-owned banks and all Canadian-owned banks whose shares are closely held, meaning that one party may hold more than 10 percent of the outstanding shares. As of April 1997, there were 7 Schedule I and 45 Schedule II banks operating in Canada.

Chartered Banks

Chartered banks *are profit-making financial businesses regulated under the Bank Act* that perform two basic functions:

> **Business Term**
> ✓ **Chartered banks**
> **Profit-making financial businesses regulated under the Bank Act.**

1. Buy and sell loans, bills, and bonds (evidences of debt).

2. Provide financial services such as safekeeping of funds; serve as paying and receiving stations for currencies; collect cheques, draft notes, and other obligations for their customers; and perform special advisory services for customers.

Figure 15.4 summarizes the operations of chartered banks.

Services Provided by Banks[12]

Bank services have evolved significantly in recent years to meet customers' needs. As well as the traditional deposit and loan facilities, Canadian banks now administer a myriad of products and services such as credit cards, investment banking, safety deposit boxes, home banking, electronic transfers of money, travellers' cheques, sales of government bonds, and specialized customer services including financial counselling. Banks have now entered the era of niche marketing. For example, they now actively promote specialized functions such as

Figure 15.4   **Operations of Chartered Banks**

investment management, private-banking centres, financial planning and trust services, and investment and mortgage packages.

In recent years, access to banking services has been significantly expanded through the use of automated banking machines (ABMs). Interac, the Canadian ABM system, offers bank cardholders access to cash at over 16 000 (in 1997) machines across the country. In 1994, ABM customers made more than 675 million withdrawals, 110 million deposits, 323 million bill payments, 50 million transfers, and 53 million information requests. Through international alliances, Canadians also have access to cash at over 165 000 ABMs in 67 other countries around the world. In the future, Canadians can expect to see a much wider variety of services. The Canadian Bankers Association (CBA) says that ABMs could very well allow users to access mutual fund deposits and make

loan applications. If regulations permit and there is customer demand, bank ABMs could even sell products such as bus tickets or postage stamps.

Near-Banks

A number of financial institutions other than chartered banks exist both as sources and as users of funds. Trust and mortgage-loan companies, credit unions and *caisses populaires*, for example, provide many of the same services as banks. In particular, these types of financial institutions function as a go-between for savers with funds to lend and people who need to borrow. For this reason they are considered financial intermediaries and are often called *near-banks*. In addition, insurance and pension companies have funds available for business investment. Although they don't compete with the banks for depositors, they do compete in the investment market.

A **trust company** *is a business that acts as a financial trustee and administers funds for individuals and businesses, offering a range of banking services.* Trust companies were originally set up to act as executors of wills, as administrators of estates of living people, as guardians of children, as trustees for bond issues, and so forth. In carrying out their duties to invest the funds in their care, they extended their activities into granting mortgages and other loans. Their acceptance of funds "in trust" has developed into a deposit account system very like that of the chartered banks. Trust companies have gradually expanded the scope of their activities.[13] Throughout the 1980s, assets of major trust companies grew rapidly. However, during the early-to-mid 1990s assets began to signifi-

Some services provided by the Toronto-Dominion Bank.

COMPETITIVE STRATEGY

THE CHANGING FACE OF CANADIAN BANKING

Historically, the Canadian financial sector was divided into four pillars:

1. Banking
2. Trust
3. Insurance
4. Securities

Each set of institutions responsible for each of these functions was required to stay within its own field.

A series of reforms have led to considerable, though not complete, relaxation of these old boundaries. The 1992 revisions to the Bank Act, integrated with changes to federal legislation governing other types of financial institutions, resulted in expanded bank activities both within and outside the financial sector. Banks now have the right to own a broader range of institutions, such as securities dealers, trust firms, and insurance companies. In tune with the new economy, banks today are also allowed to set up networking arrangements with financial institutions in the other pillars of the financial sector and distribute those institutions' products and services in their own branches. For instance, banks may offer their customers the fiduciary services of a trust company (e.g., acting as executor for a will, setting up and managing trust funds). Banks can also own, develop, and manage land through their real-property corporations and may own real-estate firms.

For many years, Canada's chartered banks were required by law to deposit reserve ratios with the Bank of Canada to ensure that they could meet customer withdrawals. Money placed in reserve was termed "idle" money. In 1992, the federal government approved "zero reserve requirements," allowing chartered banks to compete on an equal footing with other financial institutions. Today, Canada's chartered banks police themselves in regard to reserve requirements to meet withdrawals. Banks needing additional funding have lines of credit with the Bank of Canada.

Source: Adapted from Canadian Bankers Association, *Bank Facts, 1996–1997*, October 1996, 16; and Canadian Bankers Association, "Reserve Ratio Deposits Level the Playing Field," *Access Newsletter*, 9609, Issue 22, **http://www.cba.ca/pub/access/9609/ reserve.html**.

cantly decline. The revised federal Trust and Loans Companies Act in 1992 and revisions to the Bank Act gave trust companies almost the same commercial and consumer lending powers as those of the chartered banks. Major Canadian banks and financial institutions responded to this competitive change and other market factors by purchasing most of the major trust companies. Royal Trust, for example, was bought out by the Royal Bank, Montreal Trust by the Bank of Nova Scotia, and Central Guaranty Trust by the Toronto-Dominion Bank. As of 1995, fewer than 35 trust and loan companies were independent of other financial institutions; the big 6 banks owned at least 15 trust and loan companies; and only Canada Trust (held by CT Financial Services, which was 98 percent owned by Montreal's Imasco Ltd.) and National Trust remained as large independent trust companies.[14]

Canada has some 3000 **credit unions** (*caisses populaires*), or *financial co-operatives owned by their members, who are also the shareholders*. They trace their origin to the mutual savings banks in Europe of the eighteenth century and the People's Bank movement of the nineteenth century. The first credit union in North America was founded by Alphonse Desjardins in Lévis, Quebec, in 1900 under its French name, *caisse populaire*. Credit unions spread to the Atlantic region, Ontario, and the West and quickly became a national movement that offered its members a distinctive approach to financial services. Today, more than one in three Canadians are members of credit unions or *caisses populaires*. They have traditionally stressed the virtues of mutuality and thrift, as well as the provision of deposit and credit facilities for the "common people." Credit unions perform many of the regular banking functions and serve as sources

---

Business Term

√ **Trust company**

A business that acts as a financial trustee and administers funds for individuals and businesses, offering a range of banking services.

Business Term

√ **Credit unions (caisses populaires)**

Financial co-operatives owned by their members, who are also the shareholders.

for consumer loans at competitive rates for their members. They tend to be affiliated with companies, unions, professional associations, or religious groups. Their goal is to provide more personalized and accessible banking services to owner members. The close relationship sometimes makes the availability of loans easier because the basis of the loan goes beyond purely objective criteria such as collateral available.[15]

The credit union movement has been most significant in Quebec. This province's largest *caisse populaire* is the Mouvement Desjardins with over 1300 *caisses* within Quebec and another 150 or so in the rest of Canada. (We should note that the 1996 announcement by the Mouvement of its plan to cut 5000 employees from its payroll will probably lead to fewer, more profitable, *caisses* over the latter half of the 1990s.) In 1995, it made almost one-quarter of the commercial loans in Quebec, more than any single bank. Outside of Quebec, the credit union movement is, on the whole, much smaller — although quite healthy in Western Canada. Provinces outside Quebec house about 1000 local credit unions with over 4 million members. Noteworthy is the fact that the credit union movement varies enormously across the country due to differences in provincial regulation and custom. In Saskatchewan, for example, the credit union is the only financial institution in 140 communities. British Columbia houses the Vancouver City Savings Credit Union; with assets exceeding $3 billion (1995), it is one of the larger financial institutions in the country.[16]

Other Nondeposit Financial Institutions

Nondeposit institutions such as pension funds and insurance companies also compete with banks, near-banks, and other investors for investment opportunities. *Pension funds* are established to guarantee members a regular monthly income on retirement or on reaching a certain age. Insurance companies provide protection for insured individual and business policyholders in return for payment of premiums. Both financial institutions are also major sources of long-term loans for corporations, commercial real-estate mortgages on major commercial buildings and shopping centres, and government bonds. Sun Life Assurance of Canada, for example, had revenues of almost $11 billion in 1995. Its invested revenue yielded a profit of over $400 million in 1995.

Business Term

√ **Monetary management**

The control of the money supply in order to promote economic growth and a stable dollar.

The Need for a Central Banking Authority

Up until the 1920s, bank panics often put banks out of business. A bank panic occurred when all of a bank's customers decided to withdraw their money at the same time because of news of bad economic times ahead — or just the rumour of bad times ahead. A bank would be forced to borrow money from another bank, thus spreading the panic through the banking system. In 1933, partly as a result of the stock market crash that precipitated the Great Depression, a royal commission on banking and currency recommended that a central banking authority be established to help ensure the safety and stability of Canada's banking system.

THE BANK OF CANADA[17]

IN 1934, PARLIAMENT passed the Bank of Canada Act, thereby creating a central bank. The Bank of Canada opened its doors in 1935 as a privately owned institution with shares sold to the public. Soon after, a new government introduced an amendment to the Bank of Canada Act to nationalize the institution. The Bank became publicly owned in 1938 and remains that way today. The Bank of Canada Act, which defines the Bank's functions, has been amended many times since 1934, but its preamble has not changed: the Bank still exists primarily "to regulate credit and currency in the best interests of the economic life of the nation."

The Bank of Canada provides a variety of services on behalf of the federal government, such as managing debt, issuing securities on behalf of the government, and managing the government of the nation's foreign exchange reserves. The Bank of Canada is also the federal government's banker and financial adviser. For example, it handles the deposit accounts of the Receiver General (through which flow virtually all the money collected and spent by the federal government). However, **monetary management** — *the control of the money supply in order to promote economic growth and a stable dollar* — still remains the primary objective of the Bank. The Bank's ultimate objective, working through monetary policy, is to enhance the standard of living of Canadians. Formulation and execution of monetary policy for Canada is carried out through several Bank of Canada departments, including the Finan-

DID YOU KNOW?

The Canadian government doesn't have a bank account! Why not? It doesn't have to, because it's not a business.

The Bank of Canada takes care of all the government's banking – and the Bank is not a government department. What this means is that if you lose a government cheque – say, your tax refund – the government cannot put a stop-payment on it. It will eventually issue you another cheque, after requiring you to fill out a lot of paperwork, of course.

Open-Market Operations

A frequently used instrument of the Bank of Canada's monetary management is **open-market operations:** *the buying and selling of government bonds and securities on the open market.* For example, if the government wanted to increase the money supply — to stimulate the economy — it could buy Government of Canada marketable bonds (referred to as Canada bonds or government bonds) on the open market. The exchange of money for bonds would release more funds into the economy, which in turn would increase the money supply and thus the amount available to member banks. Conversely, if the Bank of Canada wanted to slow the economy, it would sell government bonds, which would reduce the overall money supply. The Bank normally uses these open-market operations when small adjustments in the money supply are desired.

cial Markets Department (to handle open-market foreign exchange operations), Research, and Monetary and Financial Analysis. Through its nationwide network of offices and its role as the ultimate clearing agency, the Bank regulates monetary operations in the country.

Although it is a government agency, the Bank of Canada is designed to be fairly free from political interference. The governors of the Bank of Canada have tried to maintain a tradition of independence. Of course the government — as the sole shareholder and the body that is responsible for overall economic policy — has ultimate control over the Bank. There is regular, close consultation between the Minister of Finance and the Governor of the Bank, and in case of serious disagreement, it is the Minister who has the last word.

The Bank has several ways it can influence the money supply. It can, for example, institute credit controls or go out and buy or sell foreign securities. However, the two major instruments of monetary management by the Bank, as shown in Table 15.3, are its open-market operations and adjustments to the bank rate.

Business Term

√ **Open-market operations**

The buying and selling of government bonds and securities on the open market.

Business Term

√ **Bank rate**

The interest rate at which the Bank of Canada will make short-term advances to the chartered banks and money market dealers.

The Bank Rate

As a "banker's bank," the Bank of Canada lends money on a short-term basis to chartered banks and other major financial institutions when they need to make loans. The interest rate charged by the Bank of Canada is the **bank rate:** *the interest rate at which the Bank of Canada will make short-term advances to the chartered banks and money market dealers.*

The banks naturally borrow money from the cheapest sources available, so they will use Bank of Canada funds only if the bank rate is low enough for them to make a profit on the loans they offer to individuals and businesses. When the bank rate is high, the cost of such loans goes up, fewer loans are likely to be made, and money is "tight." Conversely, if the bank rate goes down, more loans are made and the money supply is increased. Changes in the bank rate also produce considerable psychological effects: banks and other lenders tend to change their rates in accordance with movements in the bank rate.

The bank rate therefore affects the money supply and, indirectly, the threat of inflation. It is a blunt instrument that can have a dramatic effect on buying and selling activities, particularly in industries that are highly sensitive to interest rate changes, such as the automobile and housing industries. Changes in the bank rate send messages quickly and effectively to all parts of society

Table 15.3 Bank of Canada Tools and the Economy

Tools	Stimulate the Economy	Slow the Economy
Open-market operations	Buy	Sell
Bank rate	Lower	Raise

about the Bank of Canada's attitude toward and goals regarding the money supply.

Setting the Bank Rate

From 1980 to 1996, the bank rate was set each week at a level equal to the average interest rate established at auctions of three-month Government of Canada treasury bills, plus one-quarter of a percentage point.

As of February 22, 1996, the bank rate is no longer linked to the three-month treasury bill rate. Instead, it is now set at the upper limit of the Bank of Canada's *operating band for the overnight financing rate* — the rate at which major participants in the money market borrow and lend one-day funds. According to the Bank of Canada, a change in the band for overnight rates is a more accurate reflection of the Bank's policy stance:[18]

- **What is the overnight financing rate?** It is the rate at which banks, investment dealers, and other financial market participants borrow and lend funds for one day. It is, for example, the rate paid by investment dealers to finance their holdings of securities from one day to the next.

- **What is the "band" for overnight rates?** In mid-1994, the Bank decided to provide the market with a clearer guide as to its near-term objectives. It also was decided that this guide would be based on the overnight rate, because it is this rate that the bank focuses on in its operations. Specifically, the Bank's operations would be aimed at keeping the overnight rate within a band of half of a percentage point. The band, then, allows some movement of the rate but clearly establishes for the market the upper and lower bounds that the Bank has in mind.

- **How often does the bank rate change?** This depends on when the bank decides to alter its operating policy stance and thus change its band for overnight rates. There were 21 changes in the band between mid-1994 and early 1996.

INSURANCE FOR DEPOSITORS: THE CDIC[19]

WHAT IF YOUR bank fails? Most Canadians had paid little or no attention to the question until the failure of the Canadian Commercial and Northland banks in the 1980s. The last bank failure had been in 1923, although trust companies have also failed. Bank failures can have catastrophic results for depositors. Individuals and businesses deposit money in financial institutions for one major reason: to safeguard their funds, including protection against inflation through interest payments. Few depositors anticipate the collapse of the financial institution itself. However, the remote fear that it might happen and evidence of collapse in other countries have encouraged depositors to lobby for protection against the possible loss of their deposits.

The **Canada Deposit Insurance Corporation (CDIC)** *is a federal government agency that insures deposits up to a maximum of $60 000 for all deposit accounts in one institution and sets requirements for sound banking practices.* As well, joint deposit accounts are insured separately from deposits in one name. Insurable deposits include savings and chequing accounts, guaranteed investment certificates, debentures other than bank debentures, money orders, deposit receipts, and certified drafts or cheques. To be insurable, a deposit must be payable in Canada, in Canadian currency, and must be repayable on demand on or before the expiration of five years. Shareholders, as owners of the bank rather than depositors, are not covered.

Additionally, some provinces insure deposits placed in provincially chartered institutions such as credit unions, *caisses populaires*, and the like. The Deposit Insurance Corporation of Ontario is an example of a provincially chartered institution.

As well as insuring deposits against institutional failures, the CDIC protects the safety of deposits in insured institutions by examining and supervising the financial affairs and management of these institutions; by providing financial and management assistance, it may prevent an institution from failing.

The CDIC was established in 1967. Despite the failures of 1985, deposit insurance is not of such vital importance to the survival of Canadian Schedule I chartered banks. Any bank within the Canadian banking system is part of a huge national operation, and it is unlikely that it would encounter the type of liquidi which is problems that would face a single-unit bank, which are common in

> **Business Term**
>
> √ **Canada Deposit Insurance Corporation (CDIC)**
>
> A federal government agency that insures deposits up to a maximum of $60 000 for all deposit accounts in one institution and sets requirements for sound banking practices.

CASE EXERCISE

PREPARE TO MEET YOUR BANKER

Norbert Bolger of Nor-Built Construction recalls being impressed with his bank initially. But over five years he watched four bank managers breeze through his local branch, and no longer even knew who his account manager was. When Bolger finally went to meet manager number three, he expressed some dissatisfaction with the high interest rate the bank was charging. "It doesn't sound like you want my business," said Bolger, looking for reassurance. "Not really," the banker replied. When Bolger threatened to go elsewhere with his account, the banker said "Go ahead." Bolger recently switched to a new bank.

Although banks are in the business of lending money, they are also responsible to their depositors and stockholders. As such, they are averse to risk taking and choose only the safest deals. Their low target for bad debt losses means they plan to get their money back from 99 out of every 100 loans.

As Bolger learned, it can be difficult for a business to maintain a solid relationship with a bank because bank managers tend to move around a lot. And in the past, they have been very conservative when it comes to accepting new business accounts. This attitude to business is slowly changing, and gradually banks are becoming more receptive to business needs. But, like it or not, business people must learn how to keep the banker happy.

1. Even if you will never need a business loan, chances are that some day you will find yourself on the other side of a bank manager's desk asking for a loan. We want you to prepare to meet your banker. Interview a successful business owner and/or visit a bank. If you were going to start a business or take out a loan, what strategies could you use to build a solid banking relationship now, before you need the money?

Source: Adapted from Rick Spence, *Secrets of Success From Canada's Fastest Growing Companies* (Toronto: John Wiley & Sons, 1997), 166; Lee A. Eckert, J. D. Ryan, Robert J. Ray, and Ronald A. Knowles, *Small Business: An Entrepreneur's Plan*, 3rd Cdn. ed. (Toronto: Harcourt Brace & Company 1999), 208–209.

---

the United States. Deposit insurance is far more important to depositors in the smaller financial intermediaries — the trust companies and credit unions — and places these institutions in a more secure position in competing with banks for the depositor's dollar.

THE CANADIAN PAYMENTS CLEARING AND SETTLEMENT SYSTEM[20]

THE HEAD OFFICES of the banks and major financial institutions support the activities of their networks of branches. They also help to co-ordinate the national payments system, which annually clears a total of 3.8 billion items worth $41 trillion, keeps accurate records for millions of depositors and borrowers, and integrates transactions throughout the entire network.

For example, a cheque drawn on a bank branch in one part of the country and cashed at a branch of another bank elsewhere in the country is usually credited to the depositor's account the same day. This is what clearing is all about: exchanging payment items for sub-sequent settling of accounts among the banks and other financial institutions.

Every working day, the financial institutions clear almost 15 million items that transfer value from one party to another. Most are cheques, but the list also includes direct deposit of paycheques, electronic funds transfer at the point of sale, Canada Savings Bonds (CSBs), money orders, travellers' cheques, mortgage and bill payments, and more.

DID YOU KNOW?

A **cheque** is an authorization to a bank or financial institution to pay from a specific account a certain sum of money to a specific recipient.

Cheques have been written on many curious surfaces. One cheque was written on the shell of a hard-boiled egg and was cashed without trouble at the Canadian Imperial Bank of Commerce. A Western lumberman made out so many cheques on his own brand of shingle that his bank had to construct a special type of filing cabinet for them.

CIBC offers its customers several choices of convenient banking.

Canada's clearing process, a key part of our national payments system, is recognized as one of the fastest and most dependable in the world. The *Canadian Payments Clearing and Settlement System* has been run by the Canadian Payments Association (CPA), in co-operation with the Bank of Canada, since 1980. Banks and other deposit-taking financial institutions that have deposit insurance are members of the CPA.

Together with its members, the CPA is responsible for the development of clearing and settlement rules and standards.

Clearing is handled through regional settlement points of the CPA located in seven major cities across the country. At each point, totals of the day's clearings for each bank's branches in the area are determined and transmitted to other institutions involved in the clearing process. This clearing process also includes the transfer of paper items to the bank against which they are drawn. Each bank then verifies its incoming items and totals. The total balance of each bank's account with the Bank of Canada is then determined; if the bank is short of funds, it borrows from the Bank of Canada.

Bank of Canada settlement accounts are adjusted the next business day by 12:00 noon Eastern time.

CHANGING MARKETS, PRODUCTS, SERVICES, AND TECHNOLOGY

OVER THE 1990s the financial sector was a prime candidate for technological change. Our major banks and financial institutions responded to increased business and consumer demand for information, choice, and convenience with technology and a variety of new products and services. Here are a few examples of technology changes that occurred over the 1990s.[21]

Credit Cards

Credit cards were first introduced by the Diners Club in the spring of 1950. The Diners Club introduced its card to give people the option to "dine now and pay later." The buy-now-pay-later concept worked and today, in Canada alone, about 20 million consumers are armed with Visa or MasterCard. They are able to use these cards in over 950 000 establishments.

During the 1990s, the Canadian credit-card market was characterized by continuous growth, change, and

Figure 15.5   Retail Banking

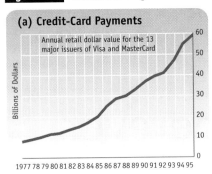

(a) Credit-Card Payments

Annual retail dollar value for the 13 major issuers of Visa and MasterCard

Billions of Dollars

1977 78 79 80 81 82 83 84 85 86 87 88 89 90 91 92 93 94 95

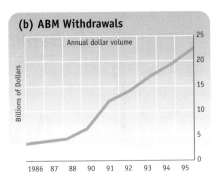

(b) ABM Withdrawals

Annual dollar volume

Billions of Dollars

1986 87   88   90   91   92   93   94   95

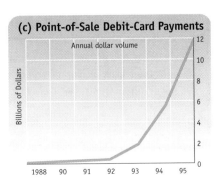

(c) Point-of-Sale Debit-Card Payments

Annual dollar volume

Billions of Dollars

1988   90   91   92   93   94   95

improvement. Every major bank introduced several new credit-card products and services. For example, "premium cards" were introduced to provide, among other things, insurance and travel benefits. Low-rate cards became available for customers who regularly extended payment for their purchases. Partnerships and strategic alliances also played an important role in this change process. For example, agreements between card issuers and other businesses — such as car companies and airlines — called co-branding enabled customers to receive discounts and rewards for using their cards. For most Canadians, the credit card has now become a way of life; and as the graph in Figure 15.5a shows, credit-card payments have simply soared since the late 1970s.

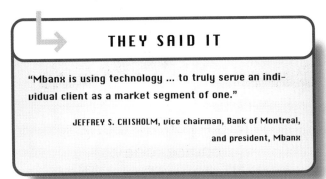

THEY SAID IT

"Mbanx is using technology ... to truly serve an individual client as a market segment of one."

JEFFREY S. CHISHOLM, vice chairman, Bank of Montreal, and president, Mbanx

Home Banking

Home banking and telephone banking now allow customers and businesses to use their personal computers or phones to access many of the bank services in the convenience of their homes. Major financial institutions not only offer the basic range of services — such as account transfers, bill payments, and balance inquiries — but also enhanced services such as stock market

quotes. The financial institutions see home banking as one of the fastest-growing areas of their business.

Debit Cards

The *debit card* offers customers a new way of paying for goods and services. It is similar to a cheque in that it orders a debit from a customer's account and a credit to the merchant. However, the order is made electronically using the same type of card as is used at an *automated banking machine (ABM)* and is accompanied by a personal identification number (PIN) for security. Use of ABMs and debit cards increased annually in the early 1990s (see Figures 15.5b and c).

Smart Cards

Credit and debit cards have a magnetically encoded stripe that holds a customer's account number, expiry date, and other limited information. *Smart cards* incorporate a computer chip that allows the cards to store more information and perform additional functions. An interesting application of the smart card is the so-called "electronic purse." Here, an amount is downloaded from the customer's account and stored in the smart card's computer chip, enabling it to be used to make purchases.

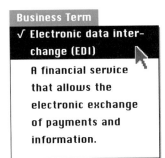

Business Term

√ **Electronic data interchange (EDI)**

A financial service that allows the electronic exchange of payments and information.

Financial Electronic Data Interchange (EDI)

Many corporate clients now *exchange payments and information electronically* through a service called financial **electronic data interchange (EDI)**. This electronic payment system can dramatically reduce the cost to a company of producing a cheque and processing the related paperwork. It also speeds up payment flow.

CDS Debt Clearing Service

The Canadian Depository for Securities (CDS), owned jointly by banks, trust companies, and investment dealers, has automated its system to provide real-time clearing and settlement of securities positions.

INTERNATIONAL BANKING AND FINANCE[22]

CANADIAN BANKS PLAY a strong international role in the increasingly integrated global economy. As Figure 15.6 shows, a few Canadian banks are among the top 100 in the world. Canadian-owned banks have close to 300 foreign branches or private-banking centres and operate in almost 60 countries. They also have working arrangements with thousands of other banks in virtually every country in the world so that trade and other financial transactions can flow smoothly. The role of the correspondent banker is to act as liaison between the Canadian bank and financial institutions in other coun-

tries to ensure that arrangements are made for clients with cross-border transactions.

One-quarter of Canada's gross national product is generated through international trade. Bank activities with foreign clients help to encourage investment, and thus jobs, in Canada, while support for Canadian clients' activities abroad strengthens the key export sector of the economy.

YOU CAN MAKE A DIFFERENCE

Doug Clark is an accountant in a small Ontario town. He was told by his banker that he would only get an increase in his line of credit on the condition that he move his mutual funds (from another financial institution) to the bank. Clark firmly believed this kind of practice was unethical, so in the fall of 1998 he travelled to Ottawa and spoke before the House of Commons finance committee.

Tied selling occurs when a bank makes the granting of a loan to a customer conditional on that individual doing other business with the bank, such as purchasing mutual funds. In 1998, the federal government agreed with Clark and banned the practice of tied selling. This new law, however, applies only to banks and not to other financial institutions.

The World According to Big Shot

PANEL OF BIG SHOTS: If we don't invest in technology and reduce our labour costs, we won't be able to compete with one another.

STUDENT: Where will your sons and daughters find employment?

BIG SHOT: That's a good question. Probably in another country that needs our technology.

➡ How do you see your future in the new digital economy?

Figure 15.6 Size of Major Banks — An International Comparison

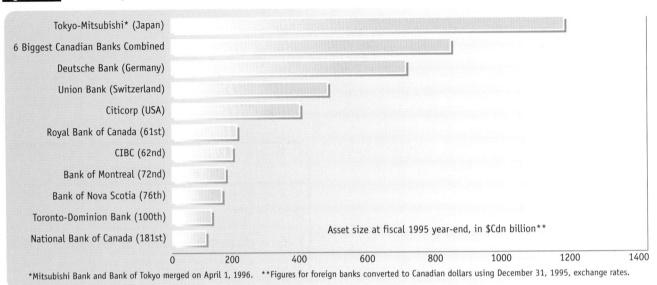

International activities fall under three broad headings: transaction services, risk coverage, and financial services. Although presented here in business terms, many of these activities are familiar to travellers, people studying or living abroad, and prospective immigrants as well.

Transaction services help clients work with businesses beyond their own national borders with, for example, collection services, foreign exchange, travellers' cheques, and international money orders. Risk coverage is designed to reduce the risk associated with international business through guarantees, documentary credits, commercial letters of credit, swaps, and the management of foreign exchange risk. Financial services include a variety of financing arrangements and analysis for clients of financial conditions in the countries that interest them.

To enable Canadian financial institutions to provide more of their foreign-based international services in Canada, international financial centres were established in Montreal and Vancouver in 1988.

SUMMARY OF LEARNING OUTCOMES

1. Identify the functions performed by a firm's financial manager.

The financial manager is responsible for both raising and spending money. As such, a financial manager's major responsibility is to develop and implement a financial plan for the organization. The firm's financial plan is based on a forecast of expenditures and receipts for a specified period and reflects the timing of cash inflows and outflows. The plan includes a systematic approach to determining needed funds during the period and the most appropriate sources for obtaining them.

2. Describe the characteristics a good form of money should have and list the functions of money.

In order to perform its necessary functions, money should possess the following characteristics: divisibility, portability, durability, difficulty in counterfeiting, and stability. These characteristics allow money to perform as a medium of exchange, a unit of account, and a temporary store of value.

3. Identify and explain the three principal components of the money supply — M1, M2, and M2+.

Money, sometimes referred to as M1, is defined broadly as anything generally accepted as a means of paying for goods and services, such as coins, paper money, and demand deposits (chequing accounts). M2 consists of M1 plus near-money, such as savings accounts, term deposits, and GICs. M2+ refers to M2 plus all deposits held by the general public at non-bank depository institutions, such as trust companies and credit unions.

4. Explain how a firm uses funds.

Organizations require funds for many reasons, including running day-to-day business operations, paying for inventory, making interest payments on loans, paying dividends to stockholders, and purchasing land, facilities, and equipment. Most financial managers will choose to invest the majority of a firm's excess cash in marketable securities.

5. Compare the two major categories of sources of funds.

Debt capital represents funds obtained through borrowing. Equity capital consists of funds from several sources, including earnings that have been reinvested in the firm, additional investments by the firm's owners, cash obtained by liquidating some of the company's assets, stock issues, and contributions from venture capitalists.

6. Identify likely sources of short-term and long-term funds.

There are four important sources of short-term funds for business firms. The major short-term source is trade credit, or making open-account purchases from suppliers. A second source is unsecured bank loans. A third is secured short-term loans, for which the firm must pledge collateral. Large firms with unquestioned financial stability can raise money from a fourth source, by selling commercial paper.

Sources of long-term financing include long-term loans that can be repaid over one year or longer, bonds, and equity capital (ownership funds obtained from selling stock in the company, selling company assets, reinvesting company earnings, or from additional contributions by the firm's owners and venture capitalists).

7. Identify the major types of Canadian financial institutions and the sources and uses of their funds.

The Canadian financial system consists of deposit institutions and nondeposit institutions. Deposit institutions such as chartered banks (e.g., the Royal Bank and the Bank of Nova Scotia) and near-banks (e.g., trust and mortgage-loan companies, credit unions and *caisses populaires*) accept deposits from customers or members and offer some form of chequing account. Nondeposit institutions include insurance companies, pension funds, and finance companies; they represent sources of funds for businesses and provide mortgage funds for financing commercial real estate.

8. **Explain the functions of the Bank of Canada and the major tools it uses to increase or decrease the money supply.**

The Bank of Canada provides a variety of services on behalf of the federal government, such as managing debt and foreign exchange reserves. The primary responsibility of the Bank is monetary management: the control of the money supply in order to promote economic growth and a stable dollar. Its primary tools include open-market operations and adjustments to the bank rate. Open-market operations increase the money supply when bonds or treasury bills are purchased, and decrease the supply by their sale. Increases in the bank rate have the effect of reducing the money supply, while decreases have the opposite effect. The Bank of Canada could also influence the money supply through selective credit controls and the purchase and sale of foreign currency.

9. **Explain the purpose and role of the Canada Deposit Insurance Corporation (CDIC) and the Canadian Payments Clearing and Settlement System.**

A major bank failure could have a catastrophic affect on the Canadian economy. Although few depositors anticipate a collapse of any of our major banks or other financial institutions, just in case, the Canada Deposit Insurance Corporation (CDIC) is a federal government agency that provides some insurance for depositors in the case of a bank, credit union, or trust company failure.

Every working day, Canadian financial institutions clear almost 15 million items — such as cheques, mortgages, bill payments, and so on — that transfer value from one party to another. This Canadian Payments Clearing and Settlement System is run by the Canadian Payments Association in co-operation with the Bank of Canada.

10. **Explain some of the major technology changes in the financial sector that have occurred over the 1990s.**

Over the 1990s, our financial sector was a prime candidate for technological change. The credit-card market was characterized by continuous growth, change, and improvment. Home banking, debit cards, and smart cards were introduced. The financial sector also evidenced an improved payments process via financial electronic data interchange (EDI) and an automated system for clearing securities, corporate bonds, and equities through the Canadian Depository for Securities (CDS) Debt Clearing Service.

11. **Discuss how Canadian banks and financial institutions interact with international organizations.**

Canadian banks and financial institutions work closely with international organizations such as the Bank for International Settlements (BIS), the International Chamber of Commerce (ICC), and the International Organization for Standardization (ISO) to ensure safe, quick, and dependable financial transactions in the global marketplace.

Key Terms Quiz

near-money
financial manager
risk–return trade-off
financial plan
finance
money

debt capital
bond
equity capital
leverage
venture or risk capital
chartered banks

electronic data interchange (EDI)
open-market operations
bank rate
credit union (*caisse populaire*)
Canada Deposit Insurance
  Corporation (CDIC)

1. Business function of effectively obtaining and managing funds.
2. Individual in an organization responsible for developing and implementing the firm's financial plan and for determining the most appropriate sources and uses of funds.

_____ 3. Balance between the risk of an investment and its potential gain.

_____ 4. Document that specifies the funds needed by a firm for a period of time, charts inflows and outflows, and outlines the most appropriate uses of funds.

_____ 5. Anything generally accepted as a means of paying for goods and services.

_____ 6. Assets almost as liquid as chequing accounts but that cannot be used directly as a medium of exchange.

_____ 7. Funds obtained through borrowing.

_____ 8. Funds provided by the firm's owners by ploughing earnings back into the firm or making additional contributions, by issuing stock to the general public, or by obtaining contributions from venture capitalists.

_____ 9. Certificate of indebtedness sold to raise long-term funds for corporations or government agencies.

_____ 10. Technique of increasing the rate of return on investment through the use of borrowed funds.

_____ 11. Profit-making financial businesses that are regulated under the Bank Act.

_____ 12. Capital usually provided by outsiders in exchange for an ownership share in the business.

_____ 13. A system that allows the electronic exchange of payments and information.

_____ 14. An instrument of monetary management that includes the buying and selling of government bonds and securities on the open market.

_____ 15. Member-owned financial co-operative that pays interest to depositors, offers share draft accounts, and makes short-term loans and some home-mortgage loans.

_____ 16. The interest rate at which the Bank of Canada will make short-term advances to the chartered banks and money market dealers.

_____ 17. A federal government agency that insures deposits up to a maximum of $60 000.

Other Important Terms

automated banking machine (ABM)	home banking	return
Bank Act	M1	risk
Canadian Payments Clearing and Settlement System	M2	smart cards
	M2+	trade credit
certificate of deposit (CD)	medium of exchange	treasury bills
commercial paper	nondeposit institutions	unit of account
debit card	operating band for the overnight financing rate	unsecured bank loans
financial control		

Review Questions

1. Explain the functions performed by the financial manager. What roles does forecasting play in these functions?

2. Identify the primary uses of cash in an organization.

3. What are the primary uses of short-term financing? Distinguish between unsecured and secured loans.

4. Distinguish between debt capital and equity capital. What are the primary sources of equity capital?

5. Identify the sources for long-term financing. Explain how borrowed funds produce leverage. What impact does borrowing have on an organization's financial performance?

6. Identify the components of the Canadian money supply. What functions are performed by these components?

7. Explain the concept of near-money. Why is it not included as part of the money supply? What is M2+?

8. Explain how the different types of financial institutions can be categorized, and identify the primary sources and uses of funds available in each institution.

9. Explain the major functions of the Bank of Canada. Give an example of how each of the following tools may be used to increase the money supply or to stimulate economic activity:
   a. Open-market operations
   b. Bank rate

10. Summarize recent trends and developments in technology in the financial services sector.

Discussion Questions

1. Joe Valdez timed the opening of his Sandia Mountain Tours to coincide with the annual International Balloon Festival. Valdez knew from the beginning that his enterprise was undercapitalized, but he hoped to cover his need for funds out of cash flow. Sandia Mountain Tours' annual sales volume grew quickly from $80 000 to $326 000, and then to $675 000 and $750 000. This rapid expansion of business involved the addition of many new services, such as overnight and week-long camping trips.

   Cash flow was a constant problem and remains so today. Valdez remarked, "There's a limit to boot-strapping. If you wish to remain a mom-and-pop business, bootstrapping will work, but I wanted more than that. Now I know I should have taken more time and put together more capital before jumping in feet first."

   Analyze and discuss Sandia Mountain Tours' financial management problems. Do you agree with Valdez on "bootstrapping"? Why or why not?

2. Gift shops earn 70 percent of their annual volume just after Thanksgiving and on through Christmas. Given this simple statistic, chart and then explain the cash inflows and outflows for a new gift shop. When would it be most advisable to open a new gift shop? Discuss why.

3. Explain the major reasons why BankWorks Trading Inc. has a reasonable chance of being successful in the long run.

4. Choose a business you would like to start. What short-term and long-term sources of funding would you need? Why? Discuss what business needs are served by each source of funding.

5. Why was the Canada Deposit Insurance Corporation created? Explain its role in the banking system.

Answers to Key Terms Quiz

1. finance **2.** financial manager **3.** risk–return trade-off **4.** financial plan **5.** money **6.** near-money **7.** debt capital **8.** equity capital **9.** bond **10.** leverage **11.** chartered banks **12.** venture or risk capital **13.** electronic data interchange (EDI) **14.** open-market operations **15.** credit union (*caisse populaire*) **16.** bank rate **17.** Canada Deposit Insurance Corporation (CDIC)

Notes

1. Adapted from Gayle MacDonald, "Top Banker Steps Out," *The Globe and Mail*, February 21, 1997, B11. Reprinted with permission from The Globe and Mail.

2. Louis E. Boone, Janelle Emmert Goodnight, and Jeanne Harris, "Leading Corporate America in an Era of Change: A Statistical Profile of Chief Executive Officers," *USA Working Paper*, 1995.

3. Bruche J. Blechman, "Quick Change Artist," *Entrepreneur*, January 1994, 18–21.

4. The Bank of Canada, "Currency Museum," http://www.bank-banque-canada.ca/english/museum.htm.

5. Excerpt from The Bank of Canada, "Bank Note Issue," http://www.bank-banque-canada.ca/english/bnote.htm.

6. The Bank of Canada, "Monetary Policy," http://www.bank-banque-canada.ca/english/monpol.htm.

7. This section is excerpted from Steven H. Appelbaum and M. Dale Beckman, *Canadian Business: A Contemporary Perspective* (Toronto: Dryden, 1995), BAN 7. Copyright © 1995 by Harcourt Brace & Company, Canada, Limited. All rights reserved. Reprinted by permission of Harcourt Brace & Company, Canada, Limited.

8. Gayle MacDonald, "Technology Fuels Venture Capital Boom," *The Globe and Mail*, April 4, 1996, B13.

9. Geoffrey Rowan, "Birth of Venture Capitalist," *The Globe and Mail*, February 26, 1996, B15.

10. Minister of Supply and Services Canada, *Taking Care of Small Business: Report of the Standing Committee on Industry*, October 1994, Catalogue No. XC 39-351/1, 44.

11. MacDonald, "Technology Fuels Venture Capital Boom," B13.

12. This section is adapted from Canadian Bankers Association, "Organization," *Bank Facts*, 1995, http://www.cba.ca/pub/bankfacts/bf2.html#payments. Reprinted by permission of Canadian Bankers Association.

13. Appelbaum and Beckman, *Canadian Business*, BAN 12.

14. Minister of Supply and Services Canada, *Taking Care of Small Business*, 34 and 35.

15. Appelbaum and Beckman, *Canadian Business*, BAN 13.

16. Minister of Supply and Services Canada, *Taking Care of Small Business*, 37.

17. This section is adapted from The Bank of Canada, "Its History," http://www.bank-banque-canada.ca/english/histor.htm; and "Banking Services," http://www.bank-banque-canada.ca/english/bserv.htm.

18. Excerpted with minor changes from The Bank of Canada, "Bank of Canada Changes Basis for Setting Bank Rate," Press Release, February 21, 1996, http://www.bank-banque-canada.ca/english/pr21fe.htm.

19. This section is excerpted from Appelbaum and Beckman, *Canadian Business*, BAN 16–BAN 17. Reprinted by permission of Harcourt Brace & Company, Canada, Limited.

20. This section is excerpted from Canadian Bankers Association, *Bank Facts, 1996–1997*, October 1996, 3 and 4. Reprinted by permission of the Canadian Bankers Association.

21. Some parts of this section are adapted from Canadian Bankers Association, "Looking Ahead," *Bank Facts, 1995*, http://www.cba.ca/pub/bankfacts/bf4.html#changing; and *Bank Facts, 1996–1997*.

22. This section is excerpted from Canadian Bankers Association, *Bank Facts, 1996–1997*, 17–19. Reprinted by permission of the Canadian Bankers Association.

Investors and the Securities Market

Small Business Finds Capital[1]

Certicom Corp. was founded in the early 1990s by three professors from the University of Waterloo. Certicom's products and services are based on elliptic curve technology that protects data, authenticates users, and verifies digital transactions. The company sells its cryptographic solutions to computing and communications firms, helping software developers to create virtually uncrackable security for digital transactions. Today, it seems as though Certicom has a fighting chance of succeeding in the fiercely competitive international market for security technology. It wasn't always that way, however.

Back in 1993, the firm was at a crossroads. It had a well-researched idea, a sound knowledge base, and a technology product in demand by the international market. Certicom's problem was that it needed a major infusion of capital to finance its research and sell its technology internationally. As a result, it made the critical decision to hire Philip C. Deck, a merchant banker, to put its finances in order. "Deck brought Bay Street savvy to encryption and made Certicom's core mathematics marketable," said Bruce MacInnis, the firm's CFO and VP of Finance.

In late 1995, Certicom went public at a price of $3 a share in an $8.1 million offering. The firm obtained an additional $2 million in various federal government technology R&D grants. It also attracted the attention of Microsoft co-founder Paul Allen, who made a $9 million private investment in late 1996. Certicom raised an additional $9 million in another private investment.

As of 1997, this small Canadian firm, led by Phil Deck, was well on its way to being a Canadian success story. The infusion of much-needed start-up capital had allowed Certicom to establish international alliances with such giants as Motorola and Schlumberger Electronic Transaction Group of San Jose, California and licensing agreements with U.S. firms such as Terisa Systems and Tandem Computers. Certicom had 50 employees, an $18 million bank account, and a strong balance sheet.

CHAPTER OVERVIEW

MANY ENTREPRENEURS ENTERING business today are faced with the challenges of financing a new business. For Certicom, an initial stock offering enabled the company to get much-needed investment capital. In fact, this small company would probably not have survived without this inflow of additional funds.

In Chapter 15, we discussed two sources of funding for long-term financial needs: debt capital and equity capital. A major source of long-term debt is bonds, which are usually issued by major corporations and government agencies. Equity capital takes the form of stocks — shares of ownership in the corporation. Stocks and bonds are commonly referred to as **securities** because both represent *obligations on the part of their issuers to provide purchasers with an expected or stated return on the funds invested or loaned.*

Stocks and bonds are bought and sold in two marketplaces. In the **primary market,** *securities are first sold to the public.* The secondary market is the one in which previously issued securities are bought and sold.

Business Term
✓ **Securities**
Stocks and bonds that represent obligations on the part of their issuers to provide purchasers with an expected or stated return on the funds invested or loaned.

Business Term
✓ **Primary market**
Market where securities are first sold to the public.

ment agency may choose to raise funds by issuing bonds. Announcements of these stock and bond offerings appear daily in such business newspapers as *The Financial Post* or *The Globe and Mail* in the form of simple black-and-white announcements called *tombstones.* Governments also use primary markets to generate funds; Canada Savings Bonds, for example, are sold to finance part of the federal deficit, while municipal bonds are issued for various projects such as funding a new city water system.

Although a corporation could market its stock or bond issue directly to the public, most large offerings are handled by financial specialists called investment bankers, or underwriters. An **investment banker** *is a financial intermediary who*

PRIMARY MARKETS

WHEN A CORPORATION needs capital to develop products, expand a plant, acquire a smaller firm, or for other business reasons, it may make a stock or bond offering. A stock offering gives investors the opportunity to purchase ownership shares in the firm and to take part in its future growth in exchange for current capital. In other instances, a corporation or a govern-

---

BUSINESS TIP

When you compound or reinvest the money that you earn, you become wealthier faster. If you reinvest the interest that you earn, here's how much you can save:

THE POWER OF COMPOUNDING

Amount Invested per Month ($)	Number of Years Invested	Annual Rate of Interest (%)	Amount Accumulated after Period ($)
100	10	10	20 484
200	20	10	151 873
300	30	10	687 146
400	30	10	904 195

specializes in selling new issues of stocks and bonds for business firms and government agencies. Investment bankers agree to acquire the total issue from the company or agency and then resell it to other investors. The investment banker underwrites the issue at a discount as compensation for services rendered (for risk incurred and to cover expenses). If the issue is resold at less than the acquired price, the investment banker takes the loss.

> **Business Term**
> √ **Investment banker**
> A financial intermediary who specializes in selling new issues of stocks and bonds for business firms and government agencies.

SECONDARY MARKETS

DAILY NEWS REPORTS of stock and bond trading refer to **secondary markets,** *places where previously issued shares of stocks and bonds are traded.* Such markets are convenient locations for buyers and sellers to make exchanges. The issuing corporations do not receive proceeds from such transactions, and gains and losses affect only the current

> **Business Term**
> √ **Secondary markets**
> Places where previously issued shares of stocks and bonds are traded.

and future owners of the securities. The various secondary markets are discussed later in the chapter.

STOCKS

ALL CORPORATIONS ISSUE stock. Each share of stock represents a share of ownership of a company. Both common and preferred shares represent ownership but bring with them different privileges and offer different rewards. Although every corporation issues common stock, it may also choose to issue preferred stock.

Common Stock

Common stock *is the basic form of corporate ownership whose owners have voting rights and a residual claim on*

FINANCIAL TIP

YOU HAVE TO SAVE MONEY BEFORE YOU CAN INVEST MONEY

Over the last decade, real income for the average Canadian has been declining and personal debt has been increasing. If you want to improve your financial situation, invest, and prepare for your future, you will have to make a decision to increase your savings and reduce your debt. This is the advice of almost every notable financial planner.

How do you save money? To get you started, here are some simple but helpful suggestions — and we're sure you can add to the list.

→ Practise energy conservation — turn off the lights when you don't need them and turn the heat down.

→ Wash only dirty clothes and use cold water.

→ Vacation when the transportation is at a discount.

→ Make your own liquid refreshments — especially after exams and during the festive season.

→ If you use a credit card, pay off the balance each month.

→ Quit smoking.

→ Take your own lunch and bring your own coffee to school and work.

→ Drive and own a car only if you need to.

→ Ride a bike — it's good for your lungs and wallet.

→ Buy secondhand — only you will know.

→ Use coupons and buy in bulk.

→ When shopping, buy only what's on your list.

→ Go out for dinner and a movie at your own home.

→ And the list goes on...

other companies or electing a board of directors. They benefit from company success, and they risk the loss of their investment if the company fails. Since creditors and preferred stockholders are paid before common stockholders, holders of common stock are said to have a residual claim to company assets.

Common stock is sold on either a par or a no-par-value basis. *Par value* is the value printed on the stock certificate of some companies. Because share values change, the par value often soon becomes meaningless, so most firms today issue no-par-value share certificates, with no amount shown. (Par value common shares will likely be abolished, and would apply to preferred shares only.) In either case, the total number of shares outstanding represents the total ownership of the firm, and the value of an individual stockholder's investment is based on the number of shares owned and their market price rather than on an arbitrary par value.

Sometimes confusion results over two other types of value: market value and book value. *Market value* — the price at which a stock is currently selling — is determined easily by referring to the financial pages of the daily newspaper. It usually varies from day to day, depending on company earnings and investor expectations

the firm's assets after all creditors and preferred shareholders have been paid* (see sample in Figure 16.1). Purchasers of shares of common stock — common shareholders — are the true owners of a corporation. In return for their investment, they expect to receive payments in the form of dividends and/or capital gains resulting from increases in the value of their stock holdings.

Common shareholders vote on major company decisions, such as purchasing

Business Term

√ **Common stock**

The basic form of corporate ownership whose owners have voting rights and a residual claim on the firm's assets after all creditors and preferred shareholders have been paid.

Figure 16.1 Sample Common Share Certificate   Front   Back

Share certificates are usually issued as a single engraved sheet with a space on the front for registration in the owner's name and the number of shares owned. After the shares have been purchased, a company's transfer agent (trust company, for example) transfers ownership to the buyer and issues a new share certificate registered in the buyer's name.

about future prospects for the firm. *Book value* is determined by subtracting the company's liabilities from its assets, minus the value of any preferred stock. When this net figure is divided by the number of shares of common stock, the book value of each share is known.

Business Term

√ **Preferred stock**

Stock whose owners receive preference in the payment of dividends and have a claim on the firm's assets before any claim by common stockholders.

Preferred Stock

In addition to common stock, many corporations issue **preferred stock** — *stock whose owners receive preference in the payment of dividends.* Also, if the company is dissolved, holders of preferred stock *have a claim on the firm's assets before any claim by common stockholders.*

In return for this privilege, preferred stockholders usually do not have voting rights and, even when voting rights do exist, they typically are limited to such important proposals as mergers, sales of company property, and dissolution of the company itself. Although preferred stockholders are granted certain privileges over common stockholders, they still are considered owners of the firm and their dividends, therefore, are not guaranteed.

Preferred stock sometimes is issued with a conversion privilege. This *convertible preferred stock* gives stockholders the option of having their preferred stock converted into common stock at a stated price.

Preferred stock usually is issued to attract conservative investors who want the margin of safety in having preference over common stock. Although preferred stock represents equity capital, many companies consider it a compromise between bonds and common stock.

BONDS

CHAPTER 15 DESCRIBED bonds as a means of obtaining long-term debt capital for a corporation and for government agencies. Thus, a *bond* is a certificate that

IN THE NEWS

WHAT'S THE DIFFERENCE AND WHY WORRY?

What is the difference between the federal deficit and the federal debt?

The *deficit* is the amount by which government spending exceeds revenues in any given year. It represents the amount the government must borrow to cover its expenses. The federal deficit for the 1995–96 fiscal year ended March 31, 1996, was $28.6 billion.

The public *debt* is the accumulated total of all past annual deficits and surpluses since Confederation.

As of March 31, 1996, Canada's debt stood at $574.3 billion.

Why should we worry about the deficit and debt?

The federal government has run deficits in 36 of the past 38 years; it has not run a surplus since 1969–70.

According to Finance Canada, here are a few major reasons why we should be worried:

➔ Interest rates are higher because the government must compete with other borrowers to finance the deficit. These higher rates deter investment and consumer spending.

➔ Taxes are also higher to cover growing debt service costs. This in turn discourages investors and entrepreneurs, and thus diminishes growth and job creation.

➔ Canadians get fewer programs and services for their tax dollars — including programs that would create jobs and expand economic growth — as more than one-third of government revenues go toward interest on our debt.

➔ Canada's economic sovereignty is compromised, as economic policy must increasingly take into account the reaction of financial markets.

➔ Our children's future is increasingly mortgaged.

Source: Excerpt from Finance Canada, "Answers to Frequently-Asked Questions," Part 1 (1997), **http://www.fin.gc.ca/faq/afaq1e.html**. Reproduced with the permission of the Minister of Public Works and Government Services Canada, 1997.

Figure 16.2 Sample Bond Certificate   Front   **Back**

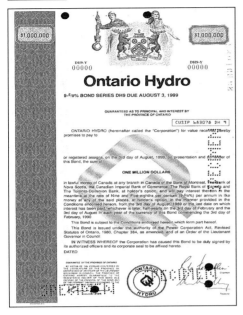
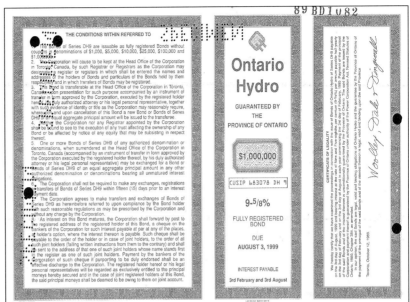

is evidence of a debt, and a contractual obligation of the issuer, so bondholders are creditors, not owners, of a corporation. Figure 16.2 provides a sample bond certificate.

Bonds are issued in denominations ranging from $1000 to $50 000. They indicate a definite rate of interest to be paid to the bondholder and the maturity date. Because bondholders are creditors of the corporation, they have a claim on the firm's assets before any claims of preferred and common stockholders in the event of the firm's dissolution.

Types of Bonds

The potential bondholder has a variety of bonds to choose from. There are, as Figure 16.3 shows, six major types of bonds, each with its own distinguishing characteristics. A **secured bond** *is backed by specific pledges of company assets.* For instance, mortgage bonds are backed by real and personal property owned by the firm, such as machinery or furniture, and collateral trust bonds are backed by stocks and bonds of other companies owned by the borrowing firm.

Since bond purchasers are attempting to balance their financial returns with

> **Business Term**
> ✓ **Secured bond**
> A bond backed by specific pledges of company assets.

> **Business Term**
> ✓ **Debentures**
> Bonds backed only by the reputation of the issuing corporation or government unit.

Figure 16.3 Characteristics of Six Major Types of Bonds

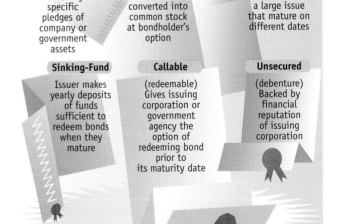

the risks involved, bonds backed by pledges of specific assets are less risky than those without such security. Consequently, a firm will be able to issue secured bonds at lower interest rates than unsecured bonds.

However, a number of companies do issue these unsecured bonds, called **debentures** — *bonds backed only by the reputation of the issuing corporation or government unit.* Only governments and major corporations with extremely sound financial reputations can find buyers for their debentures. Bell Canada, for example, has used debentures to raise several million dollars for its operations.

A Government of Canada bond (or *Canada bond*) represents funds borrowed by the Canadian government. Because they are backed by the full faith and credit of the federal government, government bonds are considered the least risky of all debt obligations. It should be noted, however, that Canada bonds as well as provincial and municipal bonds are technically debentures. That's because governments do not normally pledge any assets or property as security.

In order to entice more speculative purchasers, convertible bonds sometimes are issued by corporations. A *convertible bond* has the option of being converted into a specific number of shares of common stock. The number of shares of stock exchanged for each bond is included in the *bond indenture* — the legal contract containing all provisions of the bond. A $1000 bond might be convertible into 50 shares of common stock. If the common stock is selling at $18 when the bonds are issued, the conversion privilege has no value. But if the stock rises in price to $30, this conversion privilege has a value of $1500. Convertible bonds offer lower interest rates than those lacking conversion provisions and, therefore, reduce the interest expenses of the issuing firm. Some bond purchasers prefer such bonds, even at lower interest rates, due to the potential additional gains if the price of the firm's stock increases.

Rating Bonds

When most people think of investing, they immediately think of the stock market. But it is not the only investment arena available — investors seeking safe instruments in which to put their money often choose the bond market.

Two factors determine the price of a bond: the degree of risk and its interest rate. Since the bondholder is a creditor of the company, he or she has first claim on the firm's assets if it is liquidated. For this reason, bonds are generally less risky than stocks, although not always. To judge the degree of risk in a bond, ask yourself the following:

- Will the company or government agency issuing the bond be able to pay the principal when due?

- Is it able to make the interest payments?

- Is the bond already in default?

In general, the level of risk is reflected in a bond's rating as provided by two Canadian bond rating services: the *Canadian Bond Rating Service* and the *Dominion Bond Rating Service* both provide independent rating services for many debt securities on a subscription fee basis (see Table 16.1). Similar services in the United States, such as Moody's and Standard and Poor's, also have provided ratings on a ranked scale for many years.

The most risk-free bonds are rated A++ (Canadian Bond Rating Service) or AAA (Dominion Bond Rating Service). The scales descend to the so-called *junk bonds*,

Table 16.1 Canadian Bond Rating Service and Dominion Bond Rating Service

Canadian Bond Rating Service	Interpretation	Dominion Bond Rating Service	Interpretation
A++	Highest quality	AAA	Bank investment quality
A+	Very good quality	AA	
A	Good quality	A	
B++	Medium grade	BBB	
B+	Lower medium grade	BB	Mildly speculative
B	Poor quality	B	Medium speculative
C	Speculative	CCC	Highly speculative
D	In default	CC	
S	Rating suspended	C	In default

Canadian Bond Rating Service and Dominion Bond Rating Service help investors balance risks and rewards when purchasing bonds. Ratings of both services may also be modified by a "high" or "low" to indicate the relative standing within a classification and an improving or declining trend within that classification.

and then on to the most speculative issues, which are usually in default.[2] Junk bonds attract investors because of the high yields they offer in exchange for the risk involved. Typically, the safer the bond, the lower the yield. During periods of high interest rates, BB-rated bonds could earn 6 to 7 percent more interest than AAA bonds. Of course, these higher returns also mean higher risk.

The second factor affecting the price of the bond is the interest rate. Other things being equal, the higher the interest rate, the higher the price at which a bond will be bought and sold. But everything else usually is not equal — the bonds may not be equally risky, or one may tie up money for longer periods of time than the other. Consequently, investors must evaluate the trade-offs involved. Another important rule is that when interest rates go up, bond prices go down. This is because bondholders are locked into the coupon rate on the bond.

How Bonds Are Retired

Because bonds have a maturity date, the issuing corporation must have the necessary funds available to repay the principal when the bonds mature. The two most common methods of repayment are serial bonds and sinking-fund bonds.

In the case of *serial bonds*, a corporation simply issues a large number of bonds that mature at different dates. For example, if a corporation decides to issue $4.5 million in serial bonds for a 30-year period, the maturity dates may be established in such a manner that no bonds mature for the first 15 years. Beginning with the 16th year, $300 000 in bonds mature each year until the bonds are repaid at the end of the 30 years.

A variation of the concept of serial bonds is the *sinking-fund bond*. Under this plan, the issuing corporation makes annual deposits of funds for use in redeeming the bonds when they mature. These deposits are made with a *bond trustee,* who has the responsibility of representing bondholders. The deposits must be large enough that, with accrued interest, they will be sufficient to redeem the bonds at maturity.

A *callable bond* has a provision that allows the issuing corporation to redeem it before its maturity date if a premium is paid. For instance, a twenty-year bond may not be callable for the first ten years. Between eleven and fifteen years, it can be called at a premium of perhaps $50, and between sixteen and twenty years it can be called at its face value.

Why issue callable bonds? If a corporation issues 30-year bonds paying 14 percent annual interest and interest rates decline to 10 percent, it is paying more interest than it should. In this instance, it may decide to retire the 14 percent callable bonds and issue new bonds that pay a lower rate of interest. Such actions may be financially sound, even though the firm would incur additional costs in retiring the old bonds and issuing new ones.

SECURITIES PURCHASERS

TWO GENERAL TYPES of investors exist: institutional and individual. An **institutional investor** *is an organization that invests its own funds or those it holds in trust for others.* Included in this definition are insurance companies, pension funds, mutual funds, and chartered banks, as well as other investors, such as not-for-profit organizations and foundations. Institutional investors buy and sell large quantities, often in blocks of at least 10 000 shares per transaction.

> **Business Term**
>
> ✓ **Institutional investor**
> An organization that invests its own funds or those it holds in trust for others.

Individual investors, sometimes called *retail investors*, also play an important role in the securities market. Although they trade in comparatively small quantities, their vast numbers mean they represent nearly half of all the stock market activity. Institutional investors such as mutual funds and insurance companies also have to be aware of the concerns and objectives of the individuals who delegate to them the responsibility of investing their money. At present, about 20 to 25 percent of Canadians invest in the stock market (this percentage could be as high as 35 percent when mutual funds are included), but more are entering it, so the importance of individual investors is likely to continue to grow.

INVESTMENT MOTIVATIONS

WHY DO PEOPLE and institutions invest? For some, the motivation is **speculation** — *the hope of making a large profit on stocks within a short time.* Speculation may take the form of acting on a corporate merger rumour or simply purchasing high-risk stocks, such as low-priced penny stocks (so called because they sell for less than $1 per share). Taeko Rhodes (from the Financial Tip box on page 404) for example, draws the line of comfort at currency trading and the futures market. She said

CASE EXERCISE

GETTING READY TO INVEST

Where does all the money for stocks and bonds come from? From people of course — hard-working Canadians like Taeko Rhodes, an interior designer for Crang & Boake Inc.

Rhodes is typical of the new kind of knowledgeable Canadian investor. She is also a good example of a new breed of female investor (well-educated, professional women generally under the age of 50) who are no longer intimidated by the ups and downs of the equity market. Married or not, they want to manage their own money, and they aren't excited by a portfolio loaded down with safe but boring guaranteed investment certificates and mortgage-backed securities.

Every morning, Rhodes studies the financial section of the newspapers to see how her various stocks and mutual funds are doing. She thinks nothing of calling up her broker in Vancouver every couple of weeks to buy and sell. She's constantly changing her portfolio and often argues against her broker's advice. Much of the time she is right.

Rhodes wasn't always this financially literate: "Thinking about that kind of thing used to give me a headache," she says. When her husband died, she suddenly found herself inundated with all kinds of security statements and complicated transactions that she didn't understand. It was an overwhelming burden — until she took a personal finance course to learn the basics of investing.

Rhodes has learned that investing requires financial self-discipline. For the sake of the future she has put herself on a tight daily budget. Each month, she sets aside $250 for investment and she expects this investment to work for her. Like most good investors, Rhodes employs the services of a financial advisor, who helps her build a balanced financial portfolio that includes some risky investments and some safe investments, depending on her financial goals.

1. Now that you have studied various types of investment options in this chapter, you need to think about applying what you have learned to managing your own money. Do some networking. Interview a financial planner. If you prefer secondary research, pick up a few books on financial planning. Check out the Business Tips box on page 414. You might even do some searching on the Internet. What personal financial strategies would you advise for developing your own financial plan?

Source: Based on personal discussion with Taeko Rhodes, and adapted from Ann Kerr, "A New Breed of Investor," *The Globe and Mail*, October 3, 1995, C1. Reprinted with permission from The Globe and Mail.

---

that after an initial period when "I was doing fad things like buying into a software security company nobody's even heard of" she's now learned to be a lot more conservative.[3]

A second motivation is **investment growth:** *trading in the stock market with a focus on long-term, regular income and/or safety for savings.* In contrast to speculators, these investors do not anticipate making quick profits. Rather, they are interested in steady growth in the value of their stock portfolio that results from the issuing company's sound financial planning. Prudent investors also consider the relative safety of their investment, and returns in the form of dividends and interest consistent with the risk they do take. A major financial goal of Taeko Rhodes, for example, was steady growth. Her investment goal was "at least 10 percent return every year" and, in four years, she achieved her financial objective.[4]

Growth-minded investors are also likely to benefit from stock splits, which typically occur in fast-growing companies such as Wal-Mart. A *stock split*, a recapitalization in which a single share is divided into multiple shares, lowers the price of the stock and makes it easier for new investors to buy.

Still another investment motivation is to use stocks and bonds to supplement income. *The income received from securities investments is called the investor's return, or* **yield**. Yield is calculated by dividing dividends by market price and is normally expressed as a percentage. The yield from any particular security varies with the market price and the dividend payments. Investors motivated primarily by

Business Term

✓ **Speculation**

The hope of making a large profit on stocks within a short time.

Business Term

✓ **Investment growth**

Trading in the stock market with a focus on long-term, regular income and/or safety for savings.

WHERE

The Jobs Are

David Singh, President and
CEO, Fortune Financial
Management Inc.

Financial Services

"Financial services is the fastest-growing industry in North America. It's demographics: we have
more people living longer, so they'll need better
financial planning. You can no longer look to your
company or government to take care of you in
your old age. Today, you have to take responsibility for your financial affairs.

Financial planning will continue to thrive on
the one-to-one, face-to-face approach. Money is
close to people's hearts. I don't see it taking to
the Internet."

WAKE-UP CALL

In the spring of 1977, John Brown, a farmer from the
Eastern Townships of Quebec, nearly lost everything,
including the family house, because he got caught up in
a speculative investment strategy called "buying on
the margin." A <u>margin</u> is the amount paid by a client
when she or he uses credit to buy a security, the balance being borrowed from the broker against acceptable collateral. When you buy stock "on the margin,"
no more than 70 percent of the market value of the
investor's stock portfolio can be bought on credit. The
major risk occurs when the market value of an
investor's stock portfolio drops. That's what happened
to John Brown. When the value of his stock dropped
sharply, he became "under-margined" and was
required to come up with the extra money to maintain
the 50 percent credit ratio. When he could not come up
with the needed cash, his broker was left with the
only remaining option: sell the stock and collect the
balance owing from the sale of the collateral security.
Fortunately, Brown scrambled and was able to put a
second mortgage on his house. His margin account was
put in order and he could only hope that his stock
would not drop any further.

The lesson here is brutal and clear: don't play the
margin game unless you are an experienced stock market player with lots of cash and nerves of steel.

income concentrate on the dividends of prospective
companies or the coupon rate of a bond.

Safety or security is a fourth investment motivation.
Investors whose primary objective is safety for their original investments are likely to purchase high-quality
bonds and preferred stocks. These securities offer substantial protection and are likely to continue paying a
good return on the long-term investment.

Most investors have more than one investment goal.
Investors who emphasize safety of principal may buy
preferred stocks, which
can grow in market value.
Those who buy growth
stocks may choose those
paying at least a 3 percent
yield in order to receive
some short-term return
on the investment.

> **Business Term**
> √ **Yield**
> The income received
> from securities
> investments, or the
> investor's return.

Liquidity and Taxes

In addition to these primary investment goals, investors
have two other factors to consider: liquidity and taxes.
Since the prices of securities can vary widely, investors

cannot count on making a profit whenever they decide
to sell. If liquidity (the speed at which assets can be converted into cash) is important, investors should choose
securities that tend to remain stable in price or that can
be readily sold. Examples of such securities are Canada
Savings Bonds and Government of Canada treasury bills.

Taxes also can influence the investment decision. The
tax that has the greatest impact on investments is the federal and provincial income tax, which is levied on investment income and on capital gains (increases in the value
of assets such as stocks and bonds). Taxes on wealth, such
as taxes paid by property owners on their real-estate
holdings, such as their principal residence, also can affect
specific types of investments. Some investments, like the
purchase of gold or antiques, also may be subject to sales
taxes. Since income tax rates on dividend income are
lower than those on any other kind of income, stocks that
earn dividends have tax benefits.

FINANCIAL TIP

INVESTING YOUR MONEY

Suppose you would like to invest $1500. You are interested in the shares of four companies: Telecommunications Giant, Hardware Supreme, Interprovincial Utilities, and Big Box Department Store. The table below shows recent information on their market prices and dividend rates. If your objective is to achieve immediate income, you will likely buy a stock in Interprovincial Utilities or Telecommunications Giant. We should note, however, that wise investors know that a

company that retains almost none of its earnings, distributing them as dividends instead, may be headed for trouble. Sound companies make it a policy to set aside a portion of their profits for reinvestment.

Source: Steven H. Appelbaum and M. Dale Beckman, *Canadian Business: A Contemporary Perspective* (Toronto: Dryden, 1995), SEC 20. Copyright © 1995 by Harcourt Brace & Company, Canada, Limited. All rights reserved. Reprinted by permission of Harcourt Brace & Company, Canada, Limited.

Market Price and Annual Dividend for Fictitious Companies

Company	Recent Market Price ($)	Recent Annual Dividend ($)	Yield in %
Telecommunications Giant	24.63	1.94	7.90
Hardware Supreme	35.88	0.24	0.67
Interprovincial Utilities	53.00	4.25	8.02
Big Box Department Store	24.88	0.60	2.40

FINANCIAL TIP

HOW CANADIAN TAXPAYERS CAN SAVE MORE MONEY

By investing in dividends as opposed to most other investments you can "take home" more money.

Canadian taxpayers receive preferential tax treatment on divi-

dends received from taxable Canadian corporations. That's because taxpayers who declare dividends are eligible for a federal tax credit. The table below compares after-tax income (1997) for $1000 in dividends as opposed to $1000 in bond interest. This is a general case. The exact amount, for a specific taxpayer, would depend on a

number of factors, such as the specific provincial tax rate, the taxpayer's income, and the prevailing federal tax rate. However, the following example is indicative of the potential savings.

Source: Adapted from the Canadian Securities Institute, *The Canadian Securities Course* (Toronto: 1992), 311–12. Reprinted by permission of the Canadian Securities Institute.

Net (after-tax) Income of $1000 Bond Interest		Net (after-tax) Income of $1000 Dividend Income	
Bond interest income	$1000	Dividend income	$1000
		Gross-up: 25% of $1000	250
Federal tax: 26% of $1000	260	Taxable amount	1250
		Federal tax: 26% of $1250	325
		Federal tax credit: 13.33% of $1250	167
Provincial tax: 53% of $260	138	Federal tax: $325 – $167	158
		Provincial tax: 53% of $158	84
		Total tax: $158 + $84	242
Net after-tax income	$602	Net after-tax income: $1000 – $242	$758

On April 23, 1997, the last shares were traded on the floor of the 145-year-old Toronto Stock Exchange. Hundreds of spectators watched Ted England, a trader with Peters and Co. Ltd., make history by buying 100 shares of Bell Canada before the TSE's trading floor officially closed. Stockbrokers now buy and sell shares over a computer and transmit their orders electronically to the TSE.

SECURITIES EXCHANGES

SECURITIES EXCHANGES ARE the marketplaces for stocks and bonds. At a **stock exchange,** *stocks and bonds are bought and sold.* (Actually, only a small portion of bonds trade on stock exchanges, and this is a new development headed by the Toronto Stock Exchange [TSE]. Bonds normally trade on the dealer network and usually on a "principal" basis.) Although corporations' securities are traded, the corporations are not involved directly, and they receive no proceeds from the sales. The securities traded at organized exchanges already have been issued by corporations.

It is stockbrokers who handle the initial sale to investors and subsequent trading of securities between investors. Only stockbrokers may trade on the stock exchanges. A **stockbroker** *is a securities firm or a registered individual associated with one.* The broker does not usually own the securities that he or she buys and sells, but acts as agent for the buyer or seller and charges a commission for services.

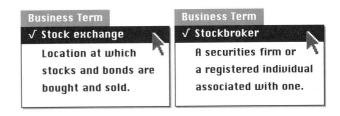

The Toronto Stock Exchange (TSE)[5]

There are five Canadian stock exchanges, but when investors talk about "the stock market," they are usually referring to the Toronto Stock Exchange (TSE), which is the largest in Canada. In order to transact business on the TSE, a brokerage firm must be a member. There are currently about 80 member firms, each having purchased one or more "seats" on the exchange. The current price of a seat is around $200 000. Each representative must meet certain basic qualifications of education and be accepted by the exchange management.

The securities of virtually all the major publicly held companies are listed (traded) on the TSE — approximately 1300 stocks and bonds issued by 850 companies. Several million shares are traded daily. Approximately 75 percent of the dollar value, and 50 percent of the total number, of listed Canadian shares are traded on the TSE.

Other Canadian Stock Exchanges

The remainder of the trading on Canadian exchanges takes place at four regional and local exchanges. The

Table 16.2 Long-Term Investment Objectives of Securities

Type of Security	Investment Objective		
	Safety	Income	Growth
Bonds	Best	Very steady	Usually none
Preferred stocks	Good	Steady	Variable
Common stocks	Least	Variable	Best

Stocks and bonds can be evaluated on the basis of three long-term investment objectives.

largest of these is the Montreal Exchange (ME). The others are in Vancouver, Calgary, and Winnipeg. Often, companies listed on these exchanges are also listed on the TSE. These exchanges trade mainly in the shares of smaller firms operating within a limited geographic area. As well as the shares of larger companies, many smaller, more speculative stocks are often traded here.

Foreign Stock Exchanges

There are about 200 stock exchanges in over 60 nations in the free world. The world's oldest stock exchange is the Amsterdam Stock Exchange, which started trading in 1611. The London Stock Exchange, listing more than 10 000 stocks, goes back to the eighteenth century. The New York Stock Exchange is the world's largest. Many Canadian companies are listed on major foreign exchanges, such as those in Tokyo, Hong Kong, Paris, Zurich, Frankfurt, Johannesburg, Melbourne, and Copenhagen.

DID YOU KNOW?

The Bank of Canada is not a government department. In 1996, it made a cool $1.4 billion in profit, and the money was quietly transferred into general revenue. If only the Bank of Canada had some shares to sell!

The Over-the-Counter (OTC) Market

Individuals who are interested in investing in certain companies may not find their stocks listed on the Toronto Stock Exchange or on any of the other regional exchanges. There are over 2000 securities traded in the **over-the-counter (OTC) market:** *the trading securities not listed on a stock exchange but traded through a network of dealers and brokers.* Actually, the OTC market is not a real place at all. It is simply a method of trading unlisted securities outside the organized securities exchanges. It is a network of securities dealers and brokers throughout Canada who buy and sell unlisted stock and bonds by telephone. Supply and demand, which determine price, are established through regular contact. Securities dealers in the OTC market often purchase shares in their own name.

Business Term
√ **Over-the-counter (OTC) market**
The trading securities not listed on a stock exchange but traded through a network of dealers and brokers.

When a prospective buyer appears, they sell these shares at a profit, if possible. A broker who has none of the wanted shares in inventory will call other brokers to make purchases at the lowest possible price for resale.

The Futures Market

Actual securities are not the only items traded on the stock exchange. A buyer may also invest in futures contracts. **Futures contracts** *guarantee the price at which the number of shares of some stock or amount of some commodity covered by the contract will exchange hands at some specified later date.* Canadian Business describes futures contracts this way:[6]

Unlike options contracts that give the buyer the right (or the option) to purchase or sell a stock, bond, currency, or amount of gold, futures contracts *commit* the holder to take delivery of commodities or financial instruments for a specified price, at some specified date in the future. Few investors actually do take delivery, of course. The game plan for futures players is to keep an alert eye on the price of, say, soybeans, pork bellies, or treasury bills, and, if the price climbs — thus boosting the value of the contract — to unload the contract at a profit. If the price falls, the investor could easily end up in deep financial trouble.

Business Term
√ **Futures contracts**
Contracts that guarantee the price at which the number of shares of some stock or amount of some commodity covered by the contract will exchange hands at some specified later date.

But this is one of the few remaining corners of the investment supermarket where a tough-skinned, financially liquid speculator can hit the jackpot. Cash requirements for futures trading are low — a margin of 5 to 10 percent of the contract price, depending on the commodity or financial instrument and the broker. If you do pay, say, $3000 down on a contract for 5000 bushels of soybeans to be delivered at $6 a bushel next May, however, the margin required to maintain the contract could be raised far and fast if the price of the beans begins to soften. But then, soybeans could soar to $8 a bushel by spring, and your profit on the contract would turn out to be $2 a bushel, or $10 000, minus your $3000 down payment and commission.

ARE SALES COMMISSIONS ETHICAL?

Today's financial consumers want value for their money. They want value-added services provided at reasonable costs. That's why so many investors are taking the do-it-yourself approach of on-line investing or using the services of discount brokerage firms. During the '90s, these new investment options commanded a rising share of securities industry revenues. Full-service brokerages continue to lose ground, in part because some investors simply don't see the need to pay the high commissions being charged by large brokerage firms.

Under fire is the commission payment system that some say puts investors at a disadvantage and strains the integrity of stockbrokers as trusted financial advisors. "Some firms are deliberately trying to hide the fact that many brokers are just salespeople rather than investment advisors," says a former broker who left the business to become an investment consultant. Another broker left because he didn't like the pressure to produce commissions on investments that often didn't benefit his clients. He wanted to build long-term relationships with his customers and develop investment strategies for them. When he started his own firm, this broker decided to charge each client a flat management fee rather than commissions. "I'm getting paid to make money for my clients, not to sell a product," he says.

Many investors aren't aware of the total amount of commissions they pay their brokers each year, because most brokerages don't provide this information to their clients. Nor do they indicate the performance of clients' accounts. Brokerage firms face a dilemma in deciding whether to maintain their commission incentives or abandon them in favour of fee-based systems. Whereas keeping the current system could mean losing more market share, changing the system could result in fewer selling-oriented brokers, and thus smaller company revenues.

1. Do you think brokerage firms should change the way they pay their brokers? What are some arguments for and against?

Source: Excerpt from *Contemporary Business*, 9th ed., by Louis E. Boone and David L. Kurtz, Copyright © 1998 by The Dryden Press, reprinted by permission of the publisher.

The futures market isn't merely a playpen for speculators, though. Those who *sell* the primary contracts are invariably hedgers. A farmer who borrows cash to plant his corn crop could be asked by his bank to sell two futures contracts (5000 bushels each) for September delivery at $2.54 a bushel. In other words, the farmer has locked in his price by selling his corn in advance and the bank's loan is guaranteed, even if the price of corn slumps to $2.00. The price of corn could soar by September, but even so the farmer is assured of his $2.54 a bushel so he can repay his loan.

The largest percentage of commodities futures trading in Canada is done on the Winnipeg Commodity Exchange. Financial futures have been the exclusive preserve of the Toronto and Montreal stock exchanges.

BUYING AND SELLING SECURITIES

INVESTING IN SECURITIES, as distinct from keeping money in a bank account, requires a stockbroker or investment dealer, who buys and sells securities according to the customer's instructions. Suppose you have some money you wish to invest. Usually, you will need $10 000 for a broker, though a discount broker may take you in for $1000. If you do not have a stockbroker, you might ask a friend or colleague to recommend one. Failing that, you can check the stock brokerage firms listed in the *Yellow Pages*. Most cities have offices of major brokerage firms, such as Nesbitt Burns, RBC Dominion Securities of the Royal Bank, and Wood Gundy of CIBC, as well as smaller firms.

Your broker will want to discuss your objectives. Are you looking for short-term profit? long-term gain? both? The broker will then identify a selection of stocks and bonds that seem to meet your needs. When you have decided what, and how much, you want to buy, the broker places the order.

Suppose, for example, that you have dual goals: income and growth. XYZ Company shares may suit you. Your broker can determine the current trading facts on the stock by referring to a computer that has online TSE and other market information.

Stocks are typically traded in multiples known as board lots. A **board lot** *is a trading unit made up of a set* *number of shares; that number depends on the stock price.* For securities priced at $1.00 and over, a board lot equals 100 shares; for those priced between $0.10 and $0.99, a board lot equals 500 shares; and for those priced below $0.10, a board lot equals 1000 shares. You can also buy or sell an **odd lot**, *a number of shares fewer than a board lot.*

In the spring of 1996, the TSE switched to decimal trading. Under the decimal system, stocks now trade in minimum increments of 5 cents. In contrast, the U.S. exchanges (as of 1997) still quote stock trades in fractions of a dollar — with minimum increments of $1/8$ of a dollar or $12 1/2$ cents. There has been some talk in the United States about following the Canadian lead and changing to the decimal system, but as of 1997 this had not happened.[7]

Your broker's information shows the most recent sale price for the stock as well as the current quotation (the bid and ask). The *bid* is the highest price anyone is willing to pay for a stock (for example, $16.25). The *ask* is the lowest price at which anyone is willing to sell the stock (e.g., $16.75). Using this information, you can decide what price you are willing to pay for XYZ shares.

You then authorize your broker to place a market order at the asking price. Or you can place a limit order at some lower price (e.g., $16.50), and your order will automatically be traded if sufficient shares become available at that price or a better one.

The brokerage firm directs your order to the appropriate destination for execution. In the case of the TSE, the days of the hectic floor trading system depicted in the movies have ended. As of 1997, certain orders sent to the TSE are handled by the Computer-Assisted Trading System (CATS), and, at the end of April 23, 1997, the TSE eliminated floor trading. Orders are now entered by traders directly into the market through trading terminals located in the brokerage firm offices. Trades are executed automatically when stock becomes available on the opposite side of the market. Printed trade confirmations are immediately sent to both the buyer's and the seller's brokers.

After your order is filled, your stockbroker will confirm the trade. The brokerage firm will also send you a

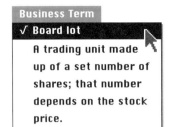

Business Term
√ **Board lot**
A trading unit made up of a set number of shares; that number depends on the stock price.

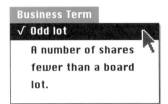

Business Term
√ **Odd lot**
A number of shares fewer than a board lot.

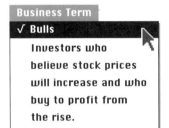

Business Term
√ **Bulls**
Investors who believe stock prices will increase and who buy to profit from the rise.

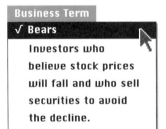

Business Term
√ **Bears**
Investors who believe stock prices will fall and who sell securities to avoid the decline.

written confirmation. Normally you must pay the broker the price of the shares plus the broker's commission within three business days after the day of the trade.

The Costs of Trading

Brokerage firms charge commissions to both buyers and sellers for securities transactions. Charges are usually a percentage of the total value of the trade but can vary among brokers according to volume and services rendered, decreasing as the dollar value of the transaction increases. The fee is a little higher when shares are traded in odd lots to cover the extra paperwork. As with all retailing situations, competition has led to the establishment of discount brokers — especially by our major financial institutions.

Bulls and Bears

Some investors expect the stock market to rise; others, that it will fall. Those investors who believe stock prices will rise are known as **bulls**: *investors who believe stock prices will increase and who buy to profit from the rise.* A market in which stock prices are rising overall is referred to as a *bull market.* In contrast, **bears** *are investors who believe stock prices will fall.* Bears *sell securities to avoid the decline in market prices that they anticipate.* A market in which stock prices are decreasing overall is referred to as a *bear market.*

Regulating Securities Transactions[8]

In Canada there is no federal securities regulatory body (as of 1997). Regulation of securities is principally the responsibility of the provinces — each of which has its own Securities Act and administrators to protect buyers and sellers of securities. In general, the provincial acts use three basic methods to protect investors:

- **Registration of securities dealers and advisers.** In general, every firm underwriting or selling securities must be registered with the provincial authorities.

- **Public company disclosure.** This disclosure usually consists of facts necessary to make reasoned investment decisions, such as financial statements and insider trading reports.

- **Legal enforcement.** Administrators in each province have the legal authority to enforce the securities regulations.

In addition to provincial controls, each of the five stock exchanges possesses self-regulatory powers, and has developed extensive controls over its members through various by-laws and regulations.

A third control mechanism is the *Investment Dealers Association (IDA) of Canada.* The IDA is a national self-regulatory organization that works with the provinces and the various exchanges to ensure the integrity and safety of securities transactions. Association members handle over 95 percent of all investment business in Canada. Through its by-laws and regulations, the IDA controls the type of business carried on and the minimum capital and financial requirements to be maintained by its members.

The basic objective of these controls is to protect investors from securities trading abuses and stock manipulations that have occurred in the past both in Canada and elsewhere by (a) assuring orderly markets and (b) maintaining the financial responsibility of member firms. An important requirement for the protection of investors is the full disclosure of relevant financial information that must be made by companies desiring to sell new stock to the general public. This information is included in a booklet called a prospectus, which must be furnished to purchasers.

Program Trading

Program trading *is a controversial practice in which computer systems are programmed to buy or sell securities if certain conditions arise.* Program trading started as a type of portfolio insurance that allowed market players to hedge their bets with automatic buy or sell orders whenever their stock prices reached a certain level. The practice has become controversial since many peo-

> **THEY SAID IT**
>
> "There are two times in a man's life when he should not speculate: when he can't afford it and when he can."
>
> MARK TWAIN, American author

> **Business Term**
> ✓ **Program trading**
> A controversial practice in which computer systems are programmed to buy or sell securities if certain conditions arise.

> **Business Term**
> ✓ **Insider**
> All directors and senior officers of a corporation and those who may have access to inside or privileged information of a company; also anyone owning 10 percent or more of the voting shares of a corporation.

> **Business Term**
> ✓ **Insider trading**
> Illegal securities trading by persons who profit from accessing nonpublic information about a company.

ple blamed it for the 1987 stock market crash, when the market value of the nation's leading stocks dropped 23 percent in one day. In fact, program trading accounted for only 15 percent of that day's trades. However, it can result in significant price swings in individual stocks when there are numerous buy and sell orders involved, and, for this reason, many people have suggested that it be banned.

Insider Trading

An **insider** refers to *all directors and senior officers of a corporation and those who may have access to inside or privileged information of a company; also anyone owning 10 percent or more of the voting shares of a corporation.* The Canada Business Corporations Act and the various provincial securities laws detail what an insider can and cannot do. **Insider trading** refers to *illegal securities trading by persons who profit from accessing nonpublic information about a company.* In general, an insider who trades must file a report with the provincial administrator and failing to do so would constitute an offence under both federal and provincial acts — usually punishable by fines.

Brokers or Promoters?

The broker who negotiates the purchase of shares of XYZ Company for you is unlikely to push one stock to the exclusion of others. You make your own decisions. Under stock market regulations, the broker should merely provide the service of making the

THE REVOLUTION ON BAY STREET

The late 1980s and early 1990s were some of the most difficult years since the Great Depression for Canada's 120 brokerages — the very symbol of prosperity through much of the previous decade. The horrendous half-decade peaked in 1990, when members of the Toronto Stock Exchange were bludgeoned by the results of the 1987 stock market crash. That year, TSE firms lost $230 million.

Profitability returned in a big way in 1991, largely because of the booming bond market. For the first nine months of 1991, TSE members' profits were $208.7 million, surpassing the previous all-time high of $160 million in 1986. Cyclical activities in the investment industry are not uncommon.

However, Canada's brokerage scene has recently undergone some-thing much more fundamental than an extended bear market. The industry is being reshaped by a number of factors:

→ Deregulation of brokerage fees, ownership, and activities

→ Crisis in public confidence

→ Retreat of the retail investor from the market

→ New technologies

→ Globalization

Deregulation

Commissions were first deregulated in Ontario and Quebec in 1983. Discount investment houses emerged, grabbing an increasing percentage of the market. In 1987, banks were granted the right to buy securities firms, integrating brokerages into a much broader industry. Today, our major banks are major players in the discount brokerage business. Clients of Royal Bank, for example, through its Action Direct discount brokerage subsidiary get a 10 percent discount on all stock and mutual fund transactions.

In 1988, deregulation opened the doors for foreign firms to buy Canadian brokerages and participate in all areas of the Canadian industry. Under revisions to acts governing federally regulated financial institutions, banks, trust and loan, and insurance companies have been granted investment and portfolio management powers. Competition in domestic markets has increased drastically. Large capital-intensive firms, together with new foreign entrants, compete aggressively.

Public Confidence

Internationally, investor confidence has dropped. This has been brought on by some high-profile shady deals. Insider-trading scandals involving the blue-bloods of the industry have rocked the financial markets. In Japan, some of the country's largest dealers were

purchase, offering advice, and perhaps guiding you away from poor investments, but ultimately following your instructions. Stock promoters are interested in gaining investment money for particular firms.

FOLLOWING THE STOCK MARKET

MOST DAILY NEWSPAPERS include several pages of stock market quotations and news from the world of finance. Keeping up-to-date is important for investors because of the dynamic, rapidly changing nature of the market. The volume of sales and closing prices of all stocks and bonds listed on the major exchanges are given. (It takes a little skill to interpret them, however.) More succinct market news is given on many radio and television newscasts.[9] Table 16.3 on page 414 shows a portion of the weekly stock trend summary and an explanation of the symbols.

Stock Indexes[10]

Daily news reports on radio and television often include current stock indexes. A stock index is an average of the market prices of key stocks and thus indicates overall market activity.

The **TSE 300 Composite Index** *is an average of the market prices of the 300 largest stocks listed on the Toronto*

> **Business Term**
>
> √ **TSE 300 Composite Index**
>
> **An average of the market prices of the 300 largest stocks listed on the Toronto Stock Exchange.**

found to have been compensating favoured clients for investment losses.

In Canada, there are growing doubts about the fairness of the stock markets. Institutional players are dominating, pushing retail investors into a diminishing role.

Retail Investor Retreat

Institutional investors such as pension funds can send stocks soaring or plummeting by buying and selling large blocks. For brokerages, growth of institutional trading has meant only one thing — tighter commissions.

New Technologies

The industry is being forced to pour millions of dollars into computers and telecommunications just to remain competitive at home and abroad. Clients are now able to buy and sell shares on their home computers through the Internet and private data networks. Brokers can execute trades directly from their terminals — eliminating the

need for an intermediary within the firm. The combination of more money going into markets and technology is creating opportunities that few are willing to pass up. Most financial institutions say that they expect 30 to 50 percent of their discount brokerage activity to be online by the year 2000. These financial institutions believe those that don't offer online brokerage services will see their best customers go elsewhere: "It's 'table stakes' in this business now" says Bruce Schwenger, president of the Bank of Montreal Investor Services Ltd.

Globalization

Technology has quickened the pace of internationalization. It has linked stock exchanges and brokers from Tokyo to Vancouver and made round-the-clock trading possible. Canadian firms are no longer competing just against one another. They are now up against major brokerage firms around the world. By maintaining foreign offices and

striking global alliances, Canadian brokerages can offer clients portfolios with a more international flavour. The biggest proportion of international trade is made up of debt securities, but experts suggest international equity will soon dominate.

Cyclical trends play a strong role in determining whether a market is a "bear" or a "bull." Consultants from Brendan Wood International Inc. suggest that the investment community must become adaptable to these numerous changes in order to determine "whether to call past successes an indicator of good fortunes ... or the end of a good thing."

Sources: Adapted from Doug Kelly, "The Revolution on Bay Street," *The Financial Post*, January 6, 1992, 4–5; and Geoffrey Rowan, "Banks Take the Plunge into On-Line Trading," *The Globe and Mail*, March 12, 1997, B10. Reprinted with permission from The Financial Post and The Globe and Mail.

Stock Exchange. It is the major Canadian index. The TSE 300 is based on the market prices of 300 stocks listed on the Toronto Stock Exchange that form a cross-section of major companies in the country. Individual stocks sometimes do not rise or fall with the index; however, it does provide a general measure of market activity for a given time period. The arbitrary starting level of the TSE 300 index in 1977 was 1000. The TSE 300 stocks have also been classified by fourteen major industry groups — such as utilities, industrial products, real-estate construction, and so on.

The TSE also introduced a "35" stock index in the late 1980s. The **TSE 35 Composite Index** *consists of 35 of the most widely traded stocks on the Toronto Stock Exchange.* Companies such as the Bank of

Montreal and MacMillan Bloedel Incorporated are included in this list of 35 major firms. Historically the movement of this index has been similar to that of the TSE 300.

The business sections of Canadian newspapers such as *The Globe and Mail* and *The Financial Post* report a range of key market indexes from around the world. As an example, the TSE 300 and the Dow Jones are shown in Figure 16.4.

What happens in one financial market is often reflected in markets around the world minutes later. Thus, investors assess the direction and strength of the market by watching other indexes as well as the TSE 300. One of these is the Dow Jones Industrial Average from the New York Stock Exchange. Others are London's

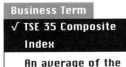

Business Term

√ **TSE 35 Composite Index**

An average of the market prices of the 35 most widely traded stocks listed on the Toronto Stock Exchange.

Table 16.3 How to Read Stock Tables

	① (52-week high/low)		② (Stock)	③ (Sym)	④ (Div)	⑤ (High)	⑥ (Low)	⑦ (Close)	⑧ (Chg)	⑨ (Vol (100s))	⑩ (Yield)	⑪ (P/E ratio)
↑	20.75	8.75	ABC TEC	ABC		20.75	19.85	20.40	+.40	5958		28.7
	15.65	**4.65♣**	**AB CAN**	**AAN**			**13.25**	**12.30**	**12.40**	**-0.90**	**1684**	
	14.85	11.25	AT PLAS	AP	0.18	12.90	12.50	12.50	-.10	70	1.4	12.8

Bold-faced stocks closed yesterday at least 5 percent higher or lower in price than the previous close. Stocks must close at a minimum $1.

<u>Underlined stocks</u> traded yesterday 500 percent or more above their 13-week average daily volume (on Canadian exchanges only).

1. **(Arrow up or down)** — New 52-week high or low in day's trading.
2. **52-week high/low** — Highest and lowest intra-day prices in past 52 weeks.
3. **Stock** — Abbreviated company name.
4. **Sym** — Ticker symbol assigned to issue by exchange; .PR is preferred share, .WT is warrant, .RT is right, .IR is installment receipt, .DB is debenture, .UN is unit, .S means stocks are subject to regulation of the SEC Act, .W means when issued.
5. **Div** — Indicated annual dividend (excluding special dividends).
6. **High** — Highest intra-day trading price.
7. **Low** — Lowest intra-day trading price.
8. **Close** — Closing price.
9. **Chg** — Change between closing price and previous closing board lot price.
10. **Vol** — Number of shares traded in 100s; z preceding figure indicates sales are reported in full.
11. **Yield** — Expressed as percentage, calculated by dividing the dividend by current market price.
12. **P/E ratio** — Price/earnings ratio; current stock price divided by the company's earnings per share from continuing operations for the latest 12 months. The P/E ratio is not shown if greater than 100.

♣ data is supplied by Dow Jones Markets. You can obtain annual reports and, if available, quarterly reports of any companies for which the symbol appears.

Financial Times 100, Tokyo's Nikkei Stock Average, and Hong Kong's Hang Seng Index.

BUSINESS TIP

Before investing your money in stocks or any other securities, make sure you get sound financial advice. If you are a novice investor, you may wish to start by reading

→ <u>Low-Risk Investing in the '90s</u> by Gordon Pape (Scarborough, ON: Prentice-Hall Canada, 1994)

→ <u>The Ultimate Money Guide for Canadians: Investment Strategies That Really Work</u> by Jerry White (Toronto: John Wiley & Sons, 1994)

→ <u>The Banker's Secrets</u> by André Frazer (Toronto: Macmillan Canada, 1997)

Figure 16.4 Key Market Indexes

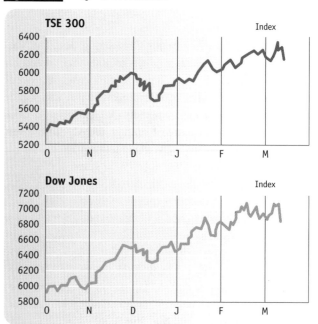

MUTUAL FUNDS

A MUTUAL FUND *is a financial organization that pools investors' money to acquire a diversified portfolio of securities.*

Throughout the 1980s, mutual funds were not a popular investment. Canadians relied mostly on the security and high interest rates from guaranteed investment certificates (GICs) and their daily savings accounts. Over the 1990s, investment strategies changed as interest rates fell and Canadians — especially baby boomers — became more knowledgeable about securities. Mutual funds grew in popularity, becoming one of the major investment choices of the 1990s. By the summer of 1997, about 40 percent of Canadian households owned over $230 billion in about 1100 different mutual funds. Mutual funds have three major attractive features:

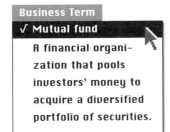

Business Term

√ **Mutual fund**

A financial organization that pools investors' money to acquire a diversified portfolio of securities.

- **Limited risk.** Investors who buy stocks in a mutual fund become part-owners of a large number of companies, thereby lessening the individual risk.

- **Expertise.** Mutual funds are managed by trained, experienced professionals whose careers are based on success in analyzing the securities markets and specific industries and companies.

- **Diversification.** A good mutual fund contains a large number of stocks and bonds or both. So, for example, when you buy 100 units of a mutual fund, you are buying a number of securities the mutual fund manager has already analyzed. This diversification adds to the security and stability of your investment.

There are a wide variety of mutual funds that have many different objectives — each designed to cater to the risk tolerance and objectives of the individual investor. A few examples are[11]

- **Equity funds.** Equity funds buy stocks of several different individual companies from different industries and countries. This diversification lessens your dependence on the performance of a single company or sector. Among equity funds, there are growth and blue chip funds. Blue chip funds buy higher-quality securities with a potential for slower but steadier return. One thing that an investor should know is that equity funds tend to be volatile.

- **Money market funds.** Money market funds invest in the money market, where governments, corporations, and banks borrow. These are low-risk, short-term securities that pay steady interest, although they provide little in the way of capital gains.

A few of the Toronto-Dominion Bank's mutual fund offerings.

- **Mortgage funds.** Mortgage funds invest in residential and commercial mortgages. They offer the chance of a higher rate of return than money market funds and carry less risk than volatile long-term bond funds.

- **Bond funds.** Bond funds buy bonds issued by the federal government, provinces, and large corporations. Bond funds can be volatile depending on the average term to maturity, but they offer the possibility of higher returns.

- **Dividend funds.** Dividend funds invest mainly in dividend-paying preferred shares and are therefore suitable for the investor who needs income. They tend to be less volatile than pure equity funds and, as we have noted, may offer some tax advantages that go with receiving income from dividends rather than from interest.

This market continues to evolve, offering the investor specialized funds that focus on specific sectors such as health, science, and precious metals.

REGISTERED RETIREMENT SAVINGS PLANS (RRSPs)

IN 1957, THE Canadian government created the **registered retirement savings plan (RRSP):** *a retirement savings plan in which the amount invested is tax-deductible and the interest earned on the investment is not taxed until you retire.* The goal was to allow Canadians to shelter their income until they retire. For example, if you were to invest $1000 in an RRSP and your marginal tax rate — the tax rate that applies on the last dollar you earned — was 25 percent, you would save $250 (25 percent of $1000) in income tax. This $1000 would remain in your RRSP account collecting income (which isn't taxed) until you decided to retire and withdraw the money. When you cash out an RRSP you will have to pay taxes on the amount you withdraw as if it were earned income — RRSPs simply defer taxes, they do not eliminate them.

> **Business Term**
>
> ✓ **Registered retirement saving plan (RRSP)**
>
> A retirement savings plan in which the amount invested is tax-deductible and the interest earned on the investment is not taxed until you retire.

The generous tax advantages made RRSPs one of Canada's hottest investment vehicles of the 1990s. In 1995, for example, almost 30 percent of all tax filers contributed some $23 billion to RRSPs. By 1995, there were about 5.5 million RRSP contributors — almost double the 1990 levels. Experts expect this love affair with RRSPs to continue into the next millennium as Canadians gradually begin shifting from government support to personal responsibility.[12]

The maximum taxpayer contribution is 18 percent of the previous year's earned income, less any pension payments, or $13 500, whichever is less. Any Canadian can contribute provided she or he has an earned income and a social insurance number, and files a tax return. To start an RRSP, you have only to visit a major financial institution and fill out the forms. Experts agree that the secrets to RRSP investing are to start early and to exploit the magic of compound interest. For example, at age 12, a single RRSP contribution of $300 compounded each year at 9 percent would grow, tax-free, to almost $29 000 by age 65.

If you should decide to contribute to an RRSP, you should get professional advice. There are numerous kinds of RRSPs you can purchase that give differing levels of income depending on your risk tolerance and long-term goals. For example, Canada Savings Bonds, GICs, mutual funds, and investment property are all eligible for RRSP investments. A growing trend for the more experienced investor throughout the 1990s was the so-called "self-directed" plan, where the individual acts as the manager of the RRSP portfolio. This trend is expected to continue over the next decade as boomers become more concerned about their future retirement.

GUARANTEED INVESTMENT CERTIFICATES (GICs)

ACCORDING TO THE Canadian Bankers Association, **guaranteed investment certificates (GICs)** *are certificates issued by a financial institution giving evidence of a deposit made with it for a fixed maturity, in registered form, and on an interest-bearing basis.*[13] The interest rate is normally higher than the best rate for a premium savings account. Often you find the terms *GIC* and *term deposit* used interchangeably. The main difference is that a GIC is a locked investment that cannot be cashed in before maturity under any circumstances — unless, of course, you sell it to a broker. However, in the case of a term deposit, it is possible to remove your cash early, though with a penalty.[14]

Over the 1990s, GICs remained popular with Canadians despite the growth of mutual funds and the lower interest rates on GICs. They were especially attractive to many investors because of their relative safety and convenience — you can buy GICs at virtually any major financial institution. By the mid-1990s, Canadians had more than $220 billion of their savings invested in GICs.[15] Today, there are many different types of GIC products available, such as escalating GICs, market index GICs, and foreign currency GICs. As noted earlier, GICs can also be purchased for your RRSP portfolio.

> **Business Term**
> √ **Guaranteed investment certificates (GICs)**
> Certificates issued by a financial institution giving evidence of a deposit made with it for a fixed maturity, in registered form, and on an interest-bearing basis.

> **Business Term**
> √ **Canada Savings Bonds (CSBs)**
> Forms of debt issued by the Canadian government that are cashable, with proper identification, at any time at most Canadian financial institutions.

CANADA SAVINGS BONDS (CSBs)

CANADA SAVINGS BONDS **(CSBs)** *are forms of debt issued by the Canadian government that are cashable, with proper identification, at any time at most Canadian financial institutions.* Technically, CSBs are not bonds as such. Bonds are normally secured by assets, and the government does not secure its CSBs. Nevertheless, the general investment community normally refers to CSBs as a bond instrument.

CSBs go on sale each year from the last week of October to the first week of November. Historically, they have been a mainstay of many Canadian investors. The major reasons are

- **Safety.** Returns for CSBs are guaranteed by the government, which make them virtually risk-free.

- **Liquidity.** They are immediately cashable, with interest, at any time after the first three months of purchase.

- **RRSP flexibility.** CSBs became even more attractive to Canadians in 1995 when the Bank of Canada offered them in RRSP form.

The provinces also issue provincial bonds, which pay a little more interest than CSBs but are a little more risky.

The World According to Big Shot

BIG SHOT: I just can't understand what's going on anymore. Business isn't as simple as it used to be.
LITTLE GUY: You mean technology isn't the answer, Dad?
BIG SHOT: I've come to the conclusion that knowledge is the key. So I've paid

my money and I'm going to get my MBA. Told Slinky that yesterday. She can take care of things until I get back.
LITTLE GUY: Be careful Dad, you might have to work.

SLINKY: Goodbye Mr. Big Shot. I WILL take care of things while you're gone. Good luck at school.

→ When do you think your education ends?

SUMMARY OF LEARNING OUTCOMES

1. **Distinguish between primary markets and secondary markets for securities.**

   Primary markets are used by businesses and government units to sell new issues of securities. Secondary markets are where previously issued securities are traded.

2. **Compare common stock, preferred stock, and bonds, and explain why investors might prefer each type of security.**

   As owners, common stockholders have voting rights, but they have only a residual claim on the firm's assets. Preferred stockholders receive preference in the payment of dividends and have first claim on the firm's assets after debts have been paid, but usually do not have voting rights. Bondholders are creditors, not owners, of a corporation.

3. **Identify the four basic motivations of investors and the types of securities most likely to accomplish each objective.**

   The four basic motivations of investors are speculation, growth in the value of the investment, income, and safety. Common stocks are the most risky, but offer investment growth. Preferred stocks have limited growth opportunities, but are reasonably safe and offer a steady income.

4. **Describe the securities exchanges and the way that securities are bought and sold.**

   Securities exchanges are the marketplaces for stocks and bonds. There are five Canadian stock exchanges. Only registered stockbrokers may trade on the stock exchanges. Over 2000 securities are also traded in the over-the-counter (OTC) market, which is a network of dealers and brokers. If you wish to buy or sell stocks, a broker will place the order. Printed trade confirmations are immediately sent to both the buyer's broker and the seller's broker. When your order is filled, the stockbroker will confirm the trade and send you a written confirmation. Normally you must pay within three days after the day of the trade.

5. **Explain methods and institutional responsibilities for regulating securities transactions.**

   Regulating securities transactions is mainly the responsibility of the provincial governments. Provincial acts use three basic methods to protect investors: registration of securities dealers and advisers, public company disclosure, and legal enforcement. As well, each of the five Canadian stock exchanges and the Investment Dealers Association possess self-regulatory powers to protect investors from such illegal activities as trading abuses and stock manipulations.

6. **Explain how investors follow the stock market through commonly reported securities transaction information.**

   Investors can find information on securities in newspapers and on radio and television.

7. **Describe other approaches to investing, notably mutual funds, RRSPs, guaranteed investment certificates (GICs), and Canada Savings Bonds (CSBs).**

   A mutual fund is a financial organization that pools investors' money to acquire a diversified portfolio of securities. Attractive features of this option are limited risk, expert management advice, and diversification. A registered retirement savings plan (RRSP) is a retirement savings plan in which the amount invested is tax-deductible and the interest earned on the investment is not taxed until funds are withdrawn. RRSPs are a popular investment because of the tax savings associated with them and because of growing concern that government and corporate pension plans will not be sufficient for people's retirement years. Guaranteed investment certificates (GICs) are certificates issued by a financial institution giving evidence of a deposit made with it for a fixed maturity, in registered form, and on an interest-bearing basis. GICs are a popular investment vehicle because of their relative safety and convenience. Canada Savings Bonds are forms of debt issued by the Canadian government that are cashable, with proper identification, at any time at most Canadian financial institutions. CSBs are popular because of their safety, liquidity, and RRSP flexibility.

Key Terms Quiz

debenture	TSE 300 Composite Index	bear
speculation	insider trading	registered retirement savings plan
secured bond	yield	(RRSP)
primary market	mutual funds	institutional investor
secondary market	common stock	bull
preferred stock	securities	stock exchange
investment banker		

_____ 1. Stocks and bonds representing obligations of the issuer to provide purchasers with an expected or stated return on investments.

_____ 2. Where new issues of securities are sold publicly for the first time.

_____ 3. Where previously issued shares of stocks and bonds are sold.

_____ 4. Specialist in selling new issues of securities for business and government.

_____ 5. Stock providing owners with voting rights but only a residual claim on company assets.

_____ 6. Stock that provides owners with preferential dividend payment and first claim on company assets after debts are paid, but seldom includes voting rights.

_____ 7. Bond backed by specific pledges of company assets.

_____ 8. Bond backed by the reputation of the issuing corporation or government.

_____ 9. Organization that invests its own funds or funds held in trust.

_____ 10. Purchasing stocks in anticipation of making large profits quickly.

_____ 11. Income received from securities; calculated by dividing dividends by market price.

_____ 12. Location at which stocks and bonds are bought and sold.

_____ 13. Investor who expects stock prices to rise along with market prices.

_____ 14. Investor who expects stock prices to decline along with market prices.

_____ 15. A major Canadian stock index based on the market prices of 300 stocks and 14 different industry sectors.

_____ 16. Financial organizations that use investors' money to acquire a portfolio of securities.

_____ 17. A retirement savings plan in which the amount invested is tax-deductible and the income earned on the investment is not taxed until you retire.

_____ 18. Illegal securities trading by persons who profit from their access to nonpublic information about a company.

Other Important Terms

ask	federal debt	over-the-counter (OTC) market
bid	federal deficit	par value
board lot	futures contract	program trading
bond trustee	guaranteed investment certificate	retail investors
book value	(GIC)	serial bond
Canada bond	Investment Dealers Association	sinking-fund bond
Canada Savings Bond (CSB)	(IDA)	stockbroker
Canadian Bond Rating Service	junk bonds	tombstones
convertible bond	market value	TSE 35 Composite Index

Review Questions

1. In what ways is the secondary market different from the primary market? With which market are investment bankers involved? What role do they play in financial decisions?

2. What is common stock? Explain the alternative methods for evaluating common stock.

3. Explain the major types of bonds issued by corporations and government units. What are the primary methods used in retiring bonds?

4. Identify the four major goals of investors, and suggest an appropriate mix of securities to achieve these goals.

5. Explain the terms "over-the-counter market" and "futures market."

6. Distinguish between the following:
   a. Bulls and bears
   b. Brokers and promoters
   c. Board lot and odd lot

7. Explain how securities transactions are regulated in Canada.

8. What are stock indexes? Would you expect the Dominion Bond Rating Service to be much different from the Canadian Bond Rating Service?

9. How does an investor place an order for common stock? Distinguish between common stock and preferred stock.

10. Explain the major factors that have reshaped Canada's brokerage scene over the 1990s.

11. Explain the advantages and disadvantages of mutual funds, GICs, and Canada Savings Bonds.

Discussion Questions

1. Assume you just inherited $20 000 from your aunt and her will stipulates that you must invest all the money until you complete your education. Prepare an investment plan for the $20 000 inheritance.

2. Assume you are an investment counsellor who has been asked to set up general investment goals for the following individuals, each of whom has adequate current income and about $30 000 to invest. Prepare a short report outlining the proposed investment goals for each person with general suggestions for an appropriate mix of securities.
   a. A 56-year-old retired government employee
   b. A 40-year-old divorced woman with two children
   c. A 19-year-old college student receiving $200 weekly for the next ten years in survivors' insurance benefits
   d. A 26-year-old unmarried person earning $24 000 annually

3. Complete the following table:

Amount Invested per Month ($)	Number of Years Invested	Annual Rate of Interest (%)	Amount Accumulated after Period ($)
100	10	10	_____
200	20	10	_____
300	30	10	_____
400	30	10	_____

Source: Answers contained in André Frazer, *The Banker's Secrets* (Toronto: Macmillan Canada, 1997), 11.

4. Explain why mutual funds were a popular investment tool for many Canadians over the 1990s.

5. A married couple in their late twenties, with two small children and joint annual earnings of $45 000, have decided to invest in stocks that promise growth with a steady return in the form of dividends. They have narrowed the choice of stocks to five and have assembled the data in the table opposite from the past three years.

    Calculate the dividend yield and price/earnings ratio for each stock for each of the three years. Based on your analysis of the data and the risks and rewards involved, recommend one of the five stocks for the couple to purchase.

Year	Company Designation	Average Price per Share	Earnings per Share	Average Dividend per Share
1992	A	$60	$5.12	$2.70
	B	268	13.35	10.00
	C	42	2.17	.05
	D	6	.12	.08
	E	30	3.06	1.70
1993	A	$59	$7.98	$2.80
	B	275	15.94	10.00
	C	45	2.74	.06
	D	8	.22	.10
	E	29	3.20	1.80
1994	A	$72	$9.00	$3.00
	B	320	17.50	10.00
	C	60	3.40	.10
	D	11	.80	.12
	E	42	3.75	2.00

Answers to Key Terms Quiz

1. securities 2. primary market 3. secondary market 4. investment banker 5. common stock 6. preferred stock 7. secured bond 8. debenture 9. institutional investor 10. speculation 11. yield 12. stock exchange 13. bull 14. bear 15. TSE 300 Composite Index 16. mutual funds 17. registered retirement savings plan (RRSP) 18. insider trading

Notes

1. Adapted from Certicom, Advertising Supplement, "How Certicom Found the Solution to Finding Capital," *The Globe and Mail*, March 14, 1997, C11. Reprinted by permission of Certicom. See also Mark Evans, "Certicom Signs Licensing Agreement with Tandem Computer Unit," *Bloomberg Business News*, February 5, 1997; and Mark Evans, "Investors Search for Internet Bargains: Canada Stockwatch," *Bloomberg Business News*, February 5, 1997.

2. The Canadian Securities Institute, *The Canadian Securities Course* (Toronto: 1992), 175–77.

3. Ann Kerr, "A New Breed of Investor," *The Globe and Mail*, October 3, 1995, C3.

4. Ibid., C1.

5. This section through "Bulls and Bears" is excerpted with minor changes from Steven H. Appelbaum and M. Dale Beckman, *Canadian Business: A Contemporary Perspective* (Toronto: Dryden, 1995), SEC 10–14. Copyright © 1995 by Harcourt Brace & Company, Canada, Limited. All rights reserved. Reprinted by permission of Harcourt Brace & Company, Canada, Limited.

6. Donald Coxe, *Canadian Business*, February 1983, 37.

7. Caroline Van Hasselt and Nick Olivari (Bloomberg News),

"TSE Attracts Spotlight for Decimal Trading," *The Ottawa Citizen*, March 18, 1997, C18.

8. This section is adapted from The Canadian Securities Institute, *The Canadian Securities Course* (Toronto: 1992), 254, 413, 414, 421. Reprinted by permission of The Canadian Securities Institute.

9. Appelbaum and Beckman, *Canadian Business*, SEC 15.

10. Parts of this section are excerpted with minor changes from ibid., SEC 17. Copyright © 1995 by Harcourt Brace & Company, Canada, Limited. All rights reserved. Reprinted by permission of Harcourt Brace & Company, Canada, Limited.

11. Excerpt from Doug Kelly, "The Mosaic of Mutual Funds: From Equity to Global," *The Financial Post*, August 21, 1991, 15. Reprinted by permission of The Financial Post.

12. "Facts and Figures about RRSPs," *The Globe and Mail*, February 11, 1997, C6.

13. Canadian Bankers Association, http://www.cba.ca/glossary/G.html.

14. Gordon Pape, *Low-Risk Investing in the '90s* (Scarborough, ON: Prentice-Hall Canada, 1994), 156–65.

15. Ibid.

absolute advantage Situation in which a country holds a monopoly in the marketing of a good or produces it at the lowest cost.

accessory equipment Capital items that are usually less expensive and shorter-lived than installations, such as hand tools and fax machines.

accountability The responsibility of an employee for the results of how he or she performs assignments and the acceptance of the consequences of his or her actions.

accounting The process of measuring, interpreting, and communicating financial information to enable others inside and outside the firm to make informed decisions.

accounting equation Basic accounting concept that assets are equal to liabilities plus owners' equity.

accounting process The procedural cycle used by accountants in converting individual transactions to financial statements.

acid rain Rain containing sulphuric acid produced from the burning of fossil fuels, which kills fish and trees and can pollute groundwater.

acid-test ratio Ratio measuring the ability of a firm to meet its current debt on short notice, calculated by dividing quick (current) assets by current liabilities; also called the quick ratio.

acquisition Situation in which one firm purchases the property and assumes the obligations of another firm.

activity ratios Ratios that measure the effectiveness of the firm's use of its resources.

activity-based marketing The process of tracking individual customer purchases and triggering a response based on this purchase information.

adaptation Modifying products to fit each market.

adaptive planning Planning that allows changes in response to new developments in the business's situation and environment.

added value Increased worth in a good or service that is attained from delivering more than expected—something of personal significance to the customer.

adjourning stage In team development, the phase during which a team focuses on wrapping up and summarizing the team's experience and accomplishments before it disbands.

advertising A paid, nonpersonal sales communication usually directed at a large number of potential customers.

affirmative action Active promotion of programs, policies, and measures designed to ensure an equitable work environment and to rebalance systemic and adverse-effect discrimination.

apprenticeship training Program wherein an employee learns a job by serving as an assistant to a trained worker for a relatively long time period.

arbitration Process of bringing an impartial third party into a union–management dispute to render a legally binding decision.

Asia-Pacific Economic Cooperation Forum (APEC) A group of Pacific Rim economies working to promote open trade.

ask The lowest price at which anyone is willing to sell a stock.

assembly line A manufacturing technique that involves placing the product on a conveyor belt that travels past a number of workstations where workers perform specialized tasks.

asset Anything of value owned or leased by a business.

audience The person or persons who receive a message and interpret its meaning.

authority The power to make decisions and to act on them in carrying out responsibilities.

autocratic leaders Leaders who make decisions on their own without consulting others.

automated banking machine (ABM) Electronic banking machine that permits customers to make banking transactions on a 24-hour basis by using an access code and an ABM card.

balance of payments The overall flow of money into or out of a country.

balance of trade The relationship between a country's exports and imports.

balance sheet Financial statement that shows the financial position of a company as of a particular date.

Bank Act Federal legislation that recognizes and governs Schedule I and Schedule II banks.

bank rate The interest rate at which the Bank of Canada will make short-term advances to the chartered banks and money market dealers.

bears Investors who believe stock prices will fall and who sell securities to avoid the decline.

benchmarking Identifying how business leaders achieve superior performance levels in their industry and continuously comparing and measuring a firm's own performance against these outstanding performers.

bid The highest price anyone is willing to pay for a stock.

board lot A trading unit made up of a set number of shares; that number depends on the stock price.

board of directors The governing authority of a corporation.

bond A certificate of indebtedness sold to raise long-term funds for corporations or government agencies.

bond indenture The legal contract containing all provisions of a bond.

bond trustee Financial institution or individual that has the responsibility of representing bondholders.

book value The value of common stock determined by subtracting the issuing company's liabilities from its assets, minus the value of any preferred stock.

bookkeeping Deals with recording transactions in a systematic manner into a series of specially designed records called "journals."

bottom line The final figure on the income statement—net income after taxes.

brainstorming The establishment of an environment in which innovative thinking can occur.

brand A name, term, sign, symbol, design, or some combination thereof used to identify the products of one firm and to differentiate them from competitive offerings.

brand name That part of the brand consisting of words or letters included in a name used to identify and distinguish the firm's offerings from those of competitors.

budget A planning and control tool that reflects expected sales revenues, operating expenses, and cash receipts and outlays.

bulls Investors who believe stock prices will increase and who buy to profit from the rise.

burnout A mental and physical state characterized by low morale and fatigue.

business All profit-seeking activities and enterprises that provide goods and services necessary to an economic system.

Business Development Bank of Canada Federal Crown corporation that provides financial and management services to small business.

business ethics Standards of business conduct and moral values.

business plan An orderly statement of a business's goals and the means of achieving them.

business products Organizational or industrial products; goods and services purchased to be used, either directly or indirectly, in the production of other goods for resale.

buyer surveys Forecasting technique that collects information from potential buyers based on surveying them.

cafeteria-style benefits System of benefits that offers employees a core package of benefits and then lets them choose extra benefits according to their needs; also called a flexible benefit plan.

callable bond Bond that has a provision that allows the issuing corporation to redeem it before its maturity date if a premium is paid.

Canada bond Also called a Government of Canada bond, represents funds borrowed by the Canadian government.

Canada Deposit Insurance Corporation (CDIC) A federal government agency that insures deposits up to a maximum of $60 000 for all deposit accounts in one institution and sets requirements for sound banking practices.

Canada Savings Bonds (CSBs) Forms of debt issued by the Canadian government that are cashable, with proper identification, at any time at most Canadian financial institutions.

Canadian Bond Rating Service An independent bond rating service for many debt securities that operates on a subscription fee basis.

Canadian Human Rights Act Federal act that guarantees equal opportunity for all Canadians, regardless of race, national or ethnic origin, colour, religion, age, sex, marital status, pardoned offence, or physical handicap.

Canadian Labour Congress (CLC) Canada's largest federation.

Canadian Payments Clearing and Settlement System A clearing process run by the Canadian Payments Association, in co-operation with the Bank of Canada, that clears and processes all the cheques, direct deposits of paycheques, electronic funds transfers, and other financial transactions that occur every day in Canada.

capital A key factor of production consisting of technology, tools, information, and physical facilities; also, the funds that finance the operation of a business.

capital items Business products that are long-lived and are usually purchased with large sums of money.

capitalism The private enterprise system; a system in which private individuals owns the means of production and economic decisions are dictated by the needs of the market.

cause marketing The marketing of a social cause or issue.

CD-ROM Compact disk–read only memory; a popular computer disk for multimedia applications because it stores data in long spirals that are well-suited for retrieving continuous blocks of data.

centralized network Communication of team members through a single person to solve problems or make decisions.

certificate of deposit (CD) A short-term note issued by a financial institution, such as a commercial bank, trust company, or credit union.

certified general accountant (CGA) A public accountant who is a member of the Certified General Accountants Association of Canada.

certified management accountant (CMA) A private accountant who is a member of the Society of Management Accountants of Canada.

chain of command The set of relationships in an organization that indicates who gives direction to whom and who reports to whom.

channel Communication carrier, or medium, through which a sender sends a message to an audience.

chartered accountant (CA) A public accountant who is a member of the Canadian Institute of Chartered Accountants.

chartered banks Profit-making financial businesses regulated under the Bank Act.

chief information officer (CIO) Top management executive responsible for directing a firm's MIS and related computer operations.

classification of organizational objectives A hierarchy of organizational objectives; the prioritization of a firm's objectives that extends from the overall objectives to specific objectives established for each employee.

classroom training Off-the-job training that uses classroom techniques—lectures, audiovisual aids, and so on—to teach employees difficult, high-skill jobs.

code of conduct A company's set of rules for employee behaviour.

code of ethics A statement of a company's values and principles that defines the purpose of the company.

code of practice A statement of a company's values and principles addressed to employees as individual decision-makers.

collaborative computing A system where employees, business partners, suppliers, and customers can all easily communicate, co-operate, and collaborate via computer.

collective bargaining Process of negotiation between management and union representatives for the purpose of arriving at mutually acceptable wages and working conditions for employees.

commercial paper A short-term note issued by a major corporation with a very high credit standing that is backed solely by the reputation of that firm.

committee organization The organizational structure in which authority and responsibility are held jointly by a group of individuals rather than by a single manager.

common market An economic union, a form of economic integration that tries to bring all members' government trade rules into agreement.

common stock The basic form of corporate ownership whose owners have voting rights and a residual claim on the firm's assets after all creditors and preferred shareholders have been paid.

communication The meaningful exchange of information through messages.

communication skills The skills of getting across one's messages to others clearly and interpreting their messages accurately; an important component of effective human relations.

communism Economic system in which property is shared by the people of a community under the planned direction of a strong central government.

comparative advantage Situation in which a country can supply a particular item more efficiently and at a lower cost than it can supply other products, compared with other nations.

competition The battle among businesses for consumer acceptance.

competitive benchmarking Making comparisons with direct product competitors.

competitive differentiation Any aspect of a company or its performance that makes it more successful than its competitors.

component parts and materials Finished business products that become part of a final product.

compressed work week Scheduling work so employees work the same number of hours in fewer days than the typical five.

computer A programmable electronic device that can store, retrieve, and process data.

computer-aided design (CAD) Process that enables engineers to design parts and buildings on computer screens faster and with fewer mistakes than on paper.

computer-aided manufacturing (CAM) Process that enables manufacturers to use specially designed computers to analyze the necessary steps that a machine must perform to produce a needed product or part.

computer chips Thin silicon wafers on which integrated circuits (networks of transistors and circuits) are assembled.

computer-integrated manufacturing (CIM) The use of computers to design products, control machines, handle materials, and control the production function in an integrated fashion.

computer networks Systems that interconnect numerous computers so they function individually and communicate with one another.

computer viruses Programs that secretly attach themselves to other programs and change them or destroy the data kept on a disk.

concept testing Marketing research designed to solicit initial consumer reaction to new-product ideas before the products are developed.

conceptual skills The ability to see the organization as a unified whole and understand how each part of the overall organization interacts with other parts.

concurrent engineering Engineering done concurrently with design, production, and other functions.

conflict Antagonistic interaction in which one party attempts to thwart the intentions or goals of another.

conservation Preserving our declining energy resources.

consumer behaviour Actions that are involved directly in obtaining, consuming, and disposing of products, including the decision processes that precede and follow these actions.

consumer products Goods and services purchased by the ultimate consumer for his or her own use.

consumerism The public demand for business to consider consumer wants and needs in making its decisions.

context The situational and cultural environment surrounding and affecting communication.

contingency planning Planning for emergencies.

contingency theory Theory that argues that management should adjust its leadership style according to the situation at hand.

continuous process improvement The process of constantly studying and making changes in work activities to improve their quality, timeliness, efficiency, and effectiveness.

contract manager A manager hired on a temporary basis.

controlling Evaluating the organization's performance to determine whether it is accomplishing its objectives.

convenience products Products that consumers seek to purchase frequently, immediately, and with little effort.

convertible bond A bond that has the option of being converted into a specific number of shares of common stock.

convertible preferred stock Preferred stock that gives stockholders the option of having their preferred stock converted into common stock at a stated price.

co-operative An organization that is operated collectively by its owners.

corporate culture The value system of an organization.

corporation A legal entity with the authority to act and have liability separate and apart from its owners.

costs of quality Costs associated with poor-quality products and production processes, such as scrap, rework, and loss of customers.

countertrade Negotiated bartering agreements that facilitate exports and imports between countries.

creativity The process of searching for or using novel relationships among objects, people, and ideas; and the process of generating new ideas to deal with change.

credit unions (*caisses populaires*) Financial co-operatives owned by their members, who are also the shareholders.

critical success factors Activities and functions considered most important in gaining a competitive advantage and achieving long-term success.

critical thinking The process of determining the authenticity, accuracy, and worth of information, knowledge claims, or arguments.

cross-functional team Group of employees from different departments who work on specific projects.

Crown corporation A corporation owned by the federal or a provincial government.

currency Coins and notes (paper money).

current ratio Ratio that measures a firm's ability to pay its current debts as they mature, calculated by dividing current assets by current liabilities; also called the working capital ratio.

customer satisfaction The concept that a good or service pleases buyers because it meets their emotional needs and quality expectations.

customer satisfaction measurement (CSM) program A procedure for measuring customer feedback against customer satisfaction goals and developing an action plan for improvement.

customer segmentation The process of grouping customer data into segments that reflect the goals of the organization.

customer service The aspect of competitive strategy that refers to how a firm treats its customers.

customer service standards Measurements of the quality of service a firm provides for its customers.

customs union Form of economic integration that sets up a free trade area, plus a uniform tariff for trade with nonmember nations.

cybershopping The selection and electronic purchase of merchandise that has been displayed on computers; also called teleshopping.

cycle time The time it takes to complete a work process or activity.

database A centralized, integrated collection of the organization's data resources.

database marketing The process of organizing potential customers into groups with similar buying habits and focussing on their needs relative to the organization's business objectives.

debentures Bonds backed only by the reputation of the issuing corporation or government unit.

debit card A card that allows a customer to pay for purchases by electronically ordering a debit from the customer's bank account and a credit to the merchant.

debt capital Funds obtained through borrowing.

debt-to-owners'-equity ratio Ratio that measures the extent to which company operations are financed by borrowed funds, calculated by dividing total liabilities by owners' equity.

decentralized network System in which team members communicate freely with other team members and arrive at decisions together.

decision making Recognizing that a problem or opportunity exists, developing alternative courses of action, evaluating alternatives, selecting and implementing an alternative, and following up.

decision support system (DSS) Computer system that quickly provides relevant facts to aid business decision making.

decline stage The final stage of the product life cycle, when sales and profits decline and may become losses.

decoding The receiver's interpretion of a message.

delayering Reducing the number of corporate layers in the corporate structure.

delegation The act of assigning activities to others in the organization.

Delphi technique Forecasting technique that uses an anonymous panel of individuals from both outside and inside the company to fill out a series of questionnaires until consensus is reached on certain issues.

demand Buyers' willingness and ability to purchase goods and services.

demand deposits Accounts from which the depositor can withdraw money "on demand."

democratic leaders Leaders who involve their subordinates in making decisions.

demographics The statistical analysis of age, sex, income, education, and so on of a population.

departmentalization The subdivision of work activities into units within the organization.

deposit institutions Financial institutions, such as banks and trust companies, that accept deposits from customers or members and provide some form of a chequing account.

deregulation The process of eliminating legal restraints on competition in various industries.

desktop publishing A computer system that allows users to design and produce printed material.

devaluation The fall of a currency's value relative to other currencies or to a fixed standard.

digitization The conversion of an analog or continuous signal into a series of ones and zeros, that is, into digital format.

direct exporting Exporting that is deliberately done and sought out by a business.

distribution channels The paths that products—and title to them—follow from producer to consumer.

distribution strategy The element of the marketing mix that deals with the marketing activities and institutions involved in getting the right good or service to the firm's customers.

Dominion Bond Rating Service An independent bond rating service for many debt securities that operates on a subscription fee basis.

downsizing Laying off employees across the board without changing the basic corporate structure.

downward communication Occurs when someone who holds a senior position in the organization communicates with subordinates.

dual role Role played by team members who contribute to the team's task and support members' socio-emotional needs at the same time.

dumping Selling goods abroad at a price lower than that charged in the domestic market.

earnings per share A profitability ratio that measures the profits earned by a corporation for each share of common stock outstanding, calculated by dividing net income after taxes by the number of common shares outstanding.

ecology The study of the relationships between living things and their environment.

economics The social science of allocating scarce resources and a study of people and their behaviour.

electronic bulletin boards Public message centres that appear on computer networks.

electronic data interchange (EDI) A financial service that allows the electronic exchange of payments and information.

electronic mail (e-mail) A system for sending and receiving written messages from one computer to another via phone lines.

embargo A ban on certain imported or exported products, usually for political rather than economic purposes.

emoticons Little faces called "smileys," used in e-mail messages, that are constructed with punctuation marks and convey some of a message's emotional content.

employee benefits Employee rewards such as pension plans, insurance, sick leave, child care, and tuition reimbursement given entirely or partly at the expense of the company.

employee involvement Practices that motivate employees to perform their jobs better through empowerment, training, and teamwork.

employment equity Ensuring that a business's work force reflects the wider community in terms of the mix of women, visible minorities, Aboriginal people, and people with disabilities.

empowerment The practice of giving employees the authority to make decisions about their work without supervisory approval.

encoding The translation of a message into understandable terms and in a form capable of being transmitted through the communication medium selected by the sender.

encroachment Direct or indirect competition between a franchise chain and an existing franchised outlet.

entranet A private intranet system that is linked to the outside world of suppliers and suppliers and customers; also called an extranet.

entrepreneur The agent of change in the private enterprise system; a person who seeks a profitable opportunity and takes the necessary risks to create a new business.

entrepreneurship The taking of risks involved in creating and operating a business.

environmental impact study Analysis of how a proposed plant would affect the quality of life in the surrounding area.

equilibrium price The price at which supply and demand for a product are equal.

equity A claim against the assets of a business.

equity capital Funds provided by the firm's owners by reinvesting earnings, making additional contributions, liquidating assets, issuing stock to the general public, or soliciting contributions from venture capitalists.

esteem needs In Maslow's hierarchy of needs, the fourth level, which includes the need to feel a sense of accomplishment, achievement, and respect from others.

ethical dilemma A situation in which right or wrong cannot be clearly identified.

European Union (EU) An economic union consisting of twelve European countries working to erase barriers to free trade among its members.

event marketing The marketing of sporting, cultural, and charitable activities to selected target markets.

everyday low pricing (EDLP) A retail business strategy that involves offering low prices for products all the time, made possible by insisting on the lowest possible prices from suppliers.

exchange The process by which two or more parties trade things of value, so that each party feels it is better off after the trade.

exchange control A means of regulating foreign trade by requiring firms to buy or sell only through a country's central bank or other government agency so the government can then allocate, expand, or restrict access to foreign exchange.

exchange rate The rate at which a country's currency can be exchanged for the currencies of other nations.

executive information system (EIS) User-friendly, decision-oriented computer system used by senior management to access the firm's primary databases.

expense items Less costly business products that are consumed within a year.

expert systems Computer programs that imitate human thinking through a complicated series of "if … then" rules.

exponential smoothing A form of trend analysis that considers recent historical data more important than older data in indicating future sales.

export management company A domestic firm that specializes in performing international marketing services as a commissioned representative or distributor for other companies.

export trading company A general trading firm that plays a varied role in world commerce by importing, exporting, countertrading, investing, and manufacturing.

exporting Selling domestic goods abroad.

external communication Meaningful exchange of information through messages between an organization and its major audiences.

external customers People or organizations that buy or use another firm's good or service.

external data Data that is generated outside an organization and can be obtained from previously published data.

extranet A private intranet system that is linked to the outside world of suppliers and customers; also called an entranet.

factors of production The four basic inputs of natural resources, capital, human resources, and entrepreneurship in an economic system.

fair competition Market-controlled competition among businesses; one of the characteristics of the private enterprise system.

family brand A single brand name used for several related products.

family leave Giving employees a leave of absence from work in order to deal with family matters.

fax (facsimile) An electronic mailing system for sending and receiving written messages over telephone lines.

federal debt The accumulated total of all past annual federal government deficits and surpluses since Confederation.

federal deficit The amount by which federal government spending exceeds revenues in any given year.

federation A union of unions that represents the broad interests of the labour movement.

feedback Messages returned by the audience to a sender that may cause the sender to alter or cancel an original message; a response to the sender's communication.

fibre optics A modern transmission technology using lasers to produce a beam of light that can be modulated to carry large amounts of information through fine glass or acrylic fibres.

finance Planning, obtaining, and managing a company's use of funds in order to accomplish its objectives most effectively and efficiently.

financial control A process that periodically checks actual revenues, costs, and expenses against forecasts.

financial managers Managers responsible for developing and implementing the firm's financial plan and for determining the most appropriate sources and uses of funds.

financial plan A document that specifies the funds needed by a firm for a period of time, the timing of inflows and outflows, and the most appropriate sources and uses of funds.

financing activities The business activities dealing with providing the funds to start a business and to expand it in the future.

flexibility Developing scenarios of future activities to be ready to take advantage of opportunities when they occur.

flexible benefit plan System of benefits that offers employees a core package of benefits and then lets them choose extra benefits according to their needs; also called cafeteria-style benefits.

flexible manufacturing system (FMS) A facility or process that can be modified quickly to manufacture different products.

flextime A work-scheduling system that allows employees to set work hours within constraints specified by the firm.

floating exchange rates Exchange rates that vary according to market conditions.

focus Figuring out and then building on what the company does best.

focus group interview A method of gathering marketing research data by bringing eight to twelve people together to discuss the subject being researched.

forecasting The estimation or prediction of a company's future sales or income.

foreign licensing Contract in which a firm allows a foreign company to produce and distribute its products or use its trademark, patent, or processes in a specific geographic area.

form utility Utility created by converting raw materials and other inputs into finished goods and services.

formal communication channels Information channels within the chain of command or task responsibility defined by an organization.

forming stage In team development, an orientation period during which team members get to know one another and find out which behaviours are acceptable to the group.

Forum for International Trade Training (FITT) A Canadian not-for-profit organization whose purpose is to train businesses in international trade skills and help them expand into global markets.

franchise A business agreement that sets the methods a dealer can use to produce and market a supplier's good or service.

franchisee The owner of a small business who is allowed to sell the goods or services of a supplier in exchange for some payment.

franchisor The supplier of a franchise that provides various goods and services in exchange for some payment from franchisees.

free-rein leaders Leaders who believe in minimal supervision and leave most decisions to their subordinates and team members.

Free Trade Agreement (FTA) Agreement designed to gradually reduce and eventually eliminate tariff barriers for many products traded between Canada and the United States.

free trade area Form of economic integration in which participating nations trade freely among themselves without tariffs or trade restrictions.

freedom of choice The right to choose one's employment, purchases, investments, and so on; one of the basic rights of the private enterprise system.

functional benchmarking Making comparisons between the functions of firms in different industries.

futures contracts Contracts that guarantee the price at which the number of shares of some stock or amount of some commodity covered by the contract will exchange hands at some specified later date.

gaps Differences between actual and perceived quality of goods and services.

General Agreement on Tariffs and Trade (GATT) An international trade accord that sponsored a series of negotiations reducing worldwide tariff levels.

general partnership Partnership in which each partner has a hand in managing the business and assumes unlimited personal liability for any debts.

generally accepted accounting principles (GAAP) Standards developed by accountants for reporting businesses' financial information and to ensure that accounting is done consistently among businesses.

generic products Nonbranded items with plain packaging, minimal labelling, and little if any advertising, and that meet only minimum quality standards.

glass ceiling Invisible barrier that keeps women and minorities from advancing to top management.

grapevine Internal information channel that transmits information through unofficial, independent sources.

greenhouse effect Situation where carbon dioxide traps heat in the earth's atmosphere, believed to affect the earth's climate and its ability to support life.

grievance A complaint by a single unionized worker or by the entire union that management is violating some provision of the union contract.

gross domestic product (GDP) The sum of all goods and services produced within a nation's boundaries.

groupware Computer software that combines and extends the concept of shared information (a database) with a method for moving data between users (e-mail).

growth stage The second stage of the product life cycle, when sales climb quickly as new customers join early users.

guaranteed investment certificates (GICs) Certificates issued by a financial institution giving evidence of a deposit made with it for a fixed maturity, in registered form, and on an interest-bearing basis.

hardware The tangible elements of the computer system, including the input and output devices.

Herzberg's two-factor theory Psychologist Frederick Herzberg's theory of motivation that states that maintenance (or hygiene) factors and motivational factors are sources of job satisfaction or dissatisfaction.

hierarchy of organizational objectives Classification and prioritization of a firm's objectives that extends from the overall objectives to specific objectives established for each employee.

high-context cultures Cultures in which communication is likely to depend not only on the message itself, but also on everything that surrounds it.

high-performance human resource management A human resource management strategy characterized by a flexible work organization, a commitment to training, incentives to increase employee involvement, and policies to promote employee–employer collaboration, with the aim of achieving positive outcomes for employment, efficiency, and financial performance of the firm.

highway economy A knowledge-based, technology-driven economy; also called a technology economy.

hiring from within Organizational policy of considering a company's own employees first for job openings.

home banking Banking system that allows customers to use their personal computer or phone to access many bank services.

home-based work Program allowing employees to work at the same job, but at home instead of in the office.

human relations skills "People" skills involving the manager's ability to work effectively with and through people.

human resource management Process of acquiring, training, developing, motivating, and appraising a sufficient quantity of qualified employees to perform activities necessary to accomplish organizational objectives; and developing specific activities and an overall organizational climate to generate maximum worker satisfaction and employee efficiency.

human resources One of the key factors of production, consisting of all the people employed in producing a good or service.

import quota A limit on the quantity of certain products that can be imported.

importing Buying foreign goods and raw materials.

incentive compensation An addition to a salary or wage that is given for exceptional performance.

income statement Financial record summarizing a firm's financial performance in terms of revenues, expenses, and profits over a given time period.

indirect exporting Selling products that are part of another good that is exported.

individual branding Strategy of giving separate products within a line different brand names.

informal communication channels Information channels outside formally authorized channels without regard for the organization's hierarchy of authority.

information superhighway Single, enormous network merging telecommunications, information, and data systems that can be accessed by all consumers and businesses.

insider All directors and senior officers of a corporation and those who may have access to inside or privileged information of a company; also anyone owning 10 percent or more of the voting shares of a corporation.

insider trading Illegal securities trading by persons who profit from accessing nonpublic information about a company.

installations Major capital items, such as a new factory or heavy machinery.

institutional investor An organization that invests its own funds or those it holds in trust for others.

interactive media Program applications that allow users to interact with computers to perform several different functions at the same time.

internal benchmarking Making comparisons between similar functions performed in different departments or divisions within a firm.

internal communication Communication through channels within an organization.

internal customers Individual employees or entire departments within an organization that depend on the work of other people or departments to perform their jobs.

internal data Data generated within an organization.

international business plan A plan formulated by a firm that is entering the international marketplace or considering entering that marketplace.

International Monetary Fund (IMF) International organization that lends money to countries requiring short-term assistance in conducting international trade.

international union A national union with membership outside the country.

Internet (the Net) A series of computer networks with a single point of access that connects the user to an electronic information system that spans the globe.

intranet Private computer networks that use the standards and technology of the Internet to distribute internal corporate information.

intrapreneurship Entrepreneurial-type activity within the corporate structure.

introduction stage The first stage of the product life cycle, when the firm tries to promote demand for its new product.

inventory control Balancing the need to have inventory on hand to meet demand with the costs involved in carrying the inventory.

inventory turnover ratio An activity ratio that measures the number of times merchandise moves through a business, calculated by dividing cost of goods sold by average inventory.

investing activities The business activities that deal with providing the valuable assets required to run a business.

investment banker A financial intermediary who specializes in selling new issues of stocks and bonds for business firms and government agencies.

Investment Dealers Association (IDA) of Canada A national self-regulatory organization that works with the provinces and the various stock exchanges to ensure the integrity and safety of securities transactions.

investment growth Trading in the stock market with a focus on long-term, regular income and/or safety for savings.

ISO 9000 The International Standards Organization's minimum requirements for a quality assurance system to create and promote worldwide quality standards.

Java™ A universal computer language that allows all previously incompatible systems to share applications and information.

job enlargement Expanding a worker's assignments to include additional, but smaller, tasks.

job enrichment Redesigning work to give employees more authority in planning their tasks and deciding how their work is to be done, and allowing them to learn related skills or to trade jobs with others.

job rotation Increasing the number of jobs or tasks an employee performs without increasing the complexity of any one job; the employee rotates through the different jobs in the course of a workday.

job sharing The division of one job assignement between two or more employees.

joint venture Sharing the operation's costs, risks, management, and profits with a local partner; a partnership formed for a specific undertaking that results in the formation of a new legal entity.

journal An accounting record that has been designed in order to record transactions with a minimum of effort.

junk bonds The riskiest, lowest-rated, and most speculative bonds on the market.

jury of executive opinion Forecasting technique that averages the forecasts of top executives from all divisions.

just-in-time (JIT) system A broad management philosophy that reaches beyond the narrow activity of inventory control and influences the entire system of production and operations management.

labour union An organization of employees that has been granted the exclusive legal authority to bargain on behalf of the employees with their employer with respect to the terms and conditions of employment.

leadership The act of motivating or causing others to perform activities designed to achieve specific objectives.

leadership style The way in which a leader uses available power to lead others.

leading Guiding and motivating employees to accomplish organizational objectives.

ledger Book containing individual account information obtained from the journal.

leverage A technique of increasing the rate of return on an investment through the use of borrowed funds.

leverage ratios Ratios that measure the extent to which a firm is relying on debt financing.

liability Anything owed to creditors by a business.

limited partnership Partnership composed of at least one or more limited partners and at least one general partner; the general partner assumes both management duties and the downside risk.

line manager A manager who forms part of the main line of authority that flows throughout an organization, often involved in the critical functions of production, finance, or marketing.

line organization Organizational structure based on a direct flow of authority from the chief executive to subordinates.

line-and-staff organization Organizational structure that combines the direct flow of authority present in the line organization with staff departments that service, advise, and support the line departments.

liquidity The speed at which assets can be converted into cash, and the ability to meet current obligations and needs by converting assets into cash.

liquidity ratios Ratios that measure a firm's ability to meet its short-term obligations when they must be paid.

listening Skill of receiving a message and interpreting its genuine meaning by accurately grasping the facts and feelings conveyed.

local area network (LAN) A computer network that connects machines within a limited area.

local union A labour union that represents union members in a specific area, such as a single community.

lockout A deliberate withholding of labour by an employer to pressure union members into settling a labour dispute or signing a contract.

low-context cultures Cultures in which communication tends to rely on explicit written and verbal messages.

M1 The sum of Canadian currency in circulation, including metal coins and paper and demand deposits.

M2 The sum of M1 plus notice deposits.

M2+ The sum of M2 plus all money held at nonbank depository institutions.

M3 The sum of M2+ plus nonpersonal term deposits and foreign currency deposits of Canadian residents.

macroeconomics The branch of economics that deals with broad issues, such as the overall operation of a country's economy, how to maintain adequate supplies of resources, and so on.

mainframe Largest and oldest type of computer system, offering huge storage capacity and high processing speeds.

maintenance (hygiene) factors In Herzberg's two-factor theory, the lower-level needs—such as working conditions, pay, and job security—that remove job dissatisfaction but are not strong employee motivators.

management The process of achieving organizational objectives in an effective and efficient manner through planning, organizing, leading, and controlling.

management accounting The process of preparing information to assist managers and owners in operating the company in an efficient and effective manner.

management by objectives (MBO) Program that involves employees in setting their own goals, lets them know in advance how they will be evaluated, and bases their performance appraisals on periodic analyses of their progress toward agreed-upon goals.

management-development program Training designed to improve the skills and broaden the knowledge of current and potential managers.

management information system (MIS) An organized method of providing information for use in decision making.

management team Group of managers from various functional departments.

market People with purchasing power and the ability and authority to buy.

market segmentation The process of dividing the total market into several relatively homogeneous groups.

market value Price at which a stock is selling currently.

marketing The process of planning and executing the conception, pricing, promotion, and distribution of ideas, goods, and services to create exchanges that satisfy individual and organizational objectives.

marketing concept Consumer orientation designed to achieve long-term success.

marketing intermediaries The distribution-channel members that operate between the producer and the consumer or business user; also called middlemen.

marketing mix A combination of the firm's product, pricing, distribution, and promotion strategies.

marketing research The information function that ties the marketer to the marketplace.

Maslow's needs hierarchy List of human needs developed by psychologist Abraham H. Maslow arranged in a hierarchy of importance, starting with physiological needs and progressing through safety needs, social needs, esteem needs, and self-actualization needs.

mass customization The ability of companies to customize products and services efficiently and cost-effectively in large quantities.

mass production The manufacture of products in large quantities through the effective combination of specialized labour, mechanization, and standardization.

materials handling The physical distribution activity of moving items within plants, warehouses, transportation terminals, and stores.

matrix organization Organizational structure in which specialists from different parts of the organization are brought together to work on specific projects; also called a project management organization.

maturity stage The third stage of the product life cycle, when sales of the product at first grow, and then reach a saturation level.

mechanization The use of machines to perform work previously done by people, to increase workers' productivity.

mediation Process of settling union–management disputes through recommendations of an impartial third party.

medium of exchange One of the functions of money— a means of facilitating exchange and eliminating the need for a barter system.

merger Situation in which two or more firms combine to form one company.

message A written, oral, or nonverbal communication transmitted by a sender to an audience.

microbusinesses Self-employed individuals and businesses with less than five employees.

microcomputer Smallest type of computer, typically called a personal computer (PC) or desktop computer and equipped with a hard disk drive and monitor.

microeconomics The branch of economics that deals with the study of small economic units, such as individuals, families, and companies.

microprocessor A fingernail-sized computer chip.

middle management Those people responsible for developing detailed plans and procedures to implement the general plans of top management.

middlemen The distribution-channel members that operate between the producer and the consumer or business user; also called marketing intermediaries.

minicomputer Intermediate-sized computer.

mission statement A written explanation of a company's purpose and aims.

mixed economy Economic system that combines government ownership and private ownership.

monetary management The control of the money supply in order to promote economic growth and a stable dollar.

money Anything generally accepted as a means of paying for goods and services.

monopolistic competition Market situation in which firms are able to differentiate their products from those of competitors.

monopoly Market situation in which there are no direct competitors.

morale The mental attitude of employees toward their employer and job.

motivational factors In Herzberg's two-factor theory, higher-level needs—such as the needs for recognition, responsibility, advancement, and growth potential—that influence job satisfaction and motivate employees to excel at their work.

motive Inner state that directs individuals toward the goal of satisfying a felt need.

multicultural diversity The racial and cultural blend within a society.

multimedia computing The technologies that facilitate the integration of two or more types of media.

multinational corporation A firm with major operations outside its home country.

mutual fund A financial organization that pools investors' money to acquire a diversified portfolio of securities.

mystery shopper A professional investigator who poses as a shopper and visits or calls outlets of a business in order to evaluate the services rendered.

national brand A brand offered and promoted by a manufacturer.

national union Labour organization consisting of numerous local chapters.

natural resources One of the key factors of production—anything useful as a productive input in its natural state, such as agricultural land, forests, and mineral deposits.

near-banks Financial intermediaries, including trust companies, mortgage-loan companies, and credit unions/*caisses populaires*.

near-money Assets almost as liquid as chequing accounts but that cannot be used directly as a medium of exchange, such as savings accounts and term deposits.

need Lack of something useful; discrepancy between a desired state and the actual state.

net income Profit or loss incurred over a specific period, determined by subtracting all costs from revenues.

network computer A personal computer with no hard drive; users reach over their corporate network or the Internet to use application software or files stored on server computers.

network organization Organizational structure in which the major functions are broken up into strategic business units (SBUs) or companies that are brokered by a small headquarters or core organization; also called a virtual organization.

niche A specific and targeted customer or business segment.

noise Interference with messages being transmitted, such as poor radio reception, a misunderstanding, or a misinterpretation.

nondeposit institutions Financial institutions, such as insurance companies and pension funds, that do not provide chequing/savings account privileges.

nonparticipator role Role played by team members who contribute little to the team's task or to members' socio-emotional needs.

nonpersonal selling Advertising, sales promotion, and public relations.

nonprogrammed decision Decision involving complex, important, and nonroutine problems or opportunities.

nonstore retailing Direct selling (e.g., Tupperware home parties), direct-response retailing (e.g., the Internet, catalogues, and television shopping), and automatic merchandising (e.g., vending machines).

nonverbal communication Communication that is transmitted through actions and behaviours.

norming stage In team development, the point at which differences among team members are resolved, members accept one another, and consensus is reached about the roles of the team leader and other participants.

North American Free Trade Agreement (NAFTA) A free trade agreement among Canada, the United States, and Mexico that came into effect in 1994.

not-for-profit organizations Firms whose primary objective is something other than returning profits to their owners.

notice deposits Accounts from which the depositor can withdraw money only after giving notice, usually seven days.

objectives Guideposts that managers use to define standards of what the organization should accomplish in such areas as profitability, customer service, and employee satisfaction.

observational studies A method of obtaining marketing research data that involves researchers observing the actions of respondents.

odd lots A number of shares fewer than a board lot.

oligopoly Market in which there are few sellers.

on-the-job training Training employees for job tasks by allowing them to perform them under the guidance of an experienced employee.

open-market operations The buying and selling of government bonds and securities on the open market.

operating activities The business activities that focus on the sale of goods and services but also consider expenses as an important part of sound financial management.

operating band for the overnight financing rate The rate range at which major participants in the money market borrow and lend one-day funds, set by the Bank of Canada.

operational planning Creating the work standards and tasks needed to implement tactical plans.

order processing The physical distribution activity of preparing orders for shipment and receiving orders when shipments arrive.

organization A structured grouping of people working together to achieve organizational objectives.

organization chart Chart showing the authority and responsibility relationships of most organizations.

organization marketing Attempts to influence others to accept the goals of, receive the services of, or contribute in some way to an organization.

organizing Process of blending human, technical, and material resources through a formal structure of tasks and authority.

outsourcing Farming out one or more company operations to outside specialists; relying on outside specialists to perform functions previously performed by company employees.

over-the-counter (OTC) market The trading securities not listed on a stock exchange but traded through a network of dealers and brokers.

owners' equity The investment in a business made by owners of the firm, and retained earnings that were not paid out in dividends.

ownership utility Utility created by arranging for an orderly transfer of ownership at the time of purchase.

par value The value printed on the stock certificate of some companies.

parent company A corporation that owns all or a majority of the stock of another corporation, its subsidiary.

partnership An association of two or more persons who operate a business as co-owners by voluntary legal agreement.

PDCA cycle A step-by-step process of **p**lanning, **d**oing, **c**hecking, and **a**cting.

pension fund Fund established to guarantee members a regular monthly income on retirement or on reaching a certain age.

people meters Electronic remote-control devices that record the television viewing habits of each household member in order to check TV audience viewership and thereby set advertising rates.

performance appraisal Evaluation of an individual's job performance by comparing actual performance with desired performance.

performing stage In team development, the phase characterized by problem solving and a focus on task accomplishment.

person marketing A program designed to enhance the favourable opinion of an individual by selected others.

personal selling A promotional presentation made on a person-to-person basis to a potential buyer.

physical distribution The actual movement of products from producer to user.

physiological needs In Maslow's hierarchy of needs, the basic human needs for food, shelter, and clothing that must be satisfied before higher-order needs can be considered.

place marketing Attempts to attract people to a particular area, such as a city, province, or nation.

place utility Utility created by having a good or service available in the right place when the consumer wants to purchase it.

planning The process of anticipating the future and determining the best courses of action to achieve company objectives.

point-of-sale terminal A computer that has replaced many cash registers that can recall prices from memory, maintain a perpetual inventory count, and automatically perform accounting data entries.

pollution Tainting or destroying a natural environment.

power The ability of one person to influence the behaviour of another.

preferred stock Stock whose owners receive preference in the payment of dividends and have a claim on the firm's assets before any claim by common stockholders.

price The exchange value of a good or service.

price–earnings ratio Current market price divided by annual earnings per share.

pricing strategy The element of the marketing mix that deals with all the factors that influence the setting of a price.

primary market Market where securities are first sold to the public.

private accountant Accountant who is employed by a business other than a public accounting firm.

private brand A brand owned by a wholesaler or retailer.

private enterprise system An economic system founded on the principle that competition among firms determines their success or failure in the marketplace and that this competition, in turn, best serves the needs of society.

private property Property owned by individuals or organizations, the right to which is granted under the private enterprise system.

privatization Converting government-owned companies into privately held firms.

PROBE **Pro**moting **B**usiness **E**xcellence, a benchmarking program developed by IBM and endorsed by Industry Canada.

problem-solving team Temporary combination of workers who gather to solve a specific problem and then disband.

product A bundle of physical, service, and symbolic attributes designed to satisfy consumer wants.

product life cycle Four stages through which a product often passes: introduction, growth, maturity, and decline.

product line A series of related products.

product mix The assortment of goods and services offered by a firm.

product strategy Decisions about package design, brand name, trademarks, warranties, product image, new-product development, and customer service—everything that goes into a good or service.

production The use of people and machinery to convert materials into finished goods or services.

production and operations management Managing the use of people and machinery in converting materials and resources into finished goods and services.

productivity The relationship between the number of units of goods and services produced and the number of inputs of human and other resources necessary to produce them.

profitability The overall financial performance of a firm.

profitability ratios Ratios that measure a firm's overall financial performance in terms of its ability to generate revenues in excess of operating and other expenses; the three commonly used profitability ratios are earnings per share, return on sales, and return on equity.

profits Rewards for the businessperson who takes the risks involved in blending people, technology, and information in creating and marketing want-satisfying goods and services that provide customer satisfaction.

program trading A controversial practice in which computer systems are programmed to buy or sell securities if certain conditions arise.

programmed decisions Decisions involving simple, common, frequently occurring problems for which solutions have already been determined.

project management organization Organizational structure in which specialists from different parts of the organization are brought together to work on specific projects; also called a matrix organization.

promotional mix The firm's combination of personal and nonpersonal selling designed to achieve promotional objectives.

promotional strategy The element of the marketing mix that deals with informing, persuading, and influencing a consumer decision.

protective tariff A tariff designed to raise the retail price of imported items and improve the competitiveness of domestically made goods.

psychographics The first-hand intuitive insight into lifestyles, buying habits, patterns of consumption, attitudes, and so forth of a population.

public accountant Accountant who provides accounting services, including auditing, to other businesses and individuals.

public ownership Enterprise owned and operated by a government unit or its agency.

public relations An organization's communications with its customers, vendors, news media, employees, stockholders, government, and general public.

pulling strategy A relationship-based, positioning approach to promotion that focuses on the long-term needs of the customer.

pure competition Market situation in which there are many firms in an industry close enough in size that no single company can influence market prices.

pushing strategy A transaction-based, sales-oriented approach to promotion that attempts to push or influence the customer to buy the product or service.

qualitative forecasting Forecasting based on subjective judgement and experience.

quality The degree of excellence or superiority of an organization's goods and services.

quality assurance Repeating good performance on every contract through a system of documented procedures that are known, understood, and operated by all personnel, including management, employees, and suppliers.

quality circle A small group of employees from one work area or department who meet regularly to identify and solve problems.

quality control Measuring goods and services against established quality standards.

quantitative forecasting Forecasting based on historical data and mathematical methods.

quick ratio Ratio measuring the ability of a firm to meet its current debt on short notice, calculated by dividing quick (current) assets by current liabilities; also called the acid-test ratio.

ratio analysis One of the most commonly used tools for (1) measuring the liquidity, profitability, extent of debt financing, and effectiveness of a firm's use of its resources, and (2) permitting comparison with other firms and with past performance.

raw materials Farm and natural products used in producing other, final products.

recycling Reprocessing used materials so they can be reused.

re-engineering The process of mapping out delivery chain processes in detail to identify areas in which to reduce cycle time or errors by applying technology in those key steps.

registered retirement savings plan (RRSP) A retirement savings plan in which the amount invested is tax-deductible and the interest earned on the investment is not taxed until you retire.

regulated industry Industry in which competition is either limited or eliminated, and government monitoring substitutes for market controls.

relationship marketing The development and maintenance of long-term, cost-effective relationships with individual customers, suppliers, employees, and other partners for mutual benefit.

research and development (R&D) The scientific process of developing new commercial products.

responsibility Obligation of an employee to perform assigned duties.

retail investors Individual investors in the securities market.

retailers Distribution-channel members that sell goods and services to individuals for their own use rather than for resale.

return The gain or loss that results from an investment over a specified period.

return on equity A profitability ratio that measures the return owners are receiving for their overall investment, calculated by dividing net income by total owner's equity.

return on quality Financial and customer satisfaction benefits derived from investing in quality-improvement programs.

return on sales A profitability ratio that measures the net income earned by a firm on its net sales, calculated by dividing net income by net sales.

revenue Funds received by a business from sales of products and services and from interest payments, dividends, royalties, and rents.

revenue tariff A tariff designed to raise funds for the government.

risk The uncertainty of loss.

risk–return trade-off Balance between the risk of an investment and its potential gain.

robot Reprogrammable machine capable of performing a variety of tasks requiring programmed manipulations of materials and tools.

safety needs In Maslow's hierarchy of needs, the second level of human needs, which includes protection from physical harm, job security, and avoidance of the unexpected.

salary Employee compensation calculated on a weekly, monthly, or annual basis.

sales-force composite A forecast of short-term sales based on salespeople's estimates.

sales promotion A form of promotion designed to increase sales through one-time selling efforts, such as displays, trade shows, or special events.

satisfaction and price guarantee A marketing tool that many retail firms use to distinguish themselves from the competition.

secondary markets Places where previously issued shares of stocks and bonds are traded.

secured bond A bond backed by specific pledges of company assets.

secured short-term loan Short-term source of funds for which the borrower must pledge collateral.

securities Stocks and bonds that represent obligations on the part of their issuers to provide purchasers with an expected or stated return on the funds invested or loaned.

self-actualization needs In Maslow's hierarchy of needs, the highest level of human needs, which includes needs for fulfilment, for realizing one's potential, and for using one's talents and capabilities totally.

self-managed team A group of employees who work with little or no supervision.

sender Participant in communication who composes the message and sends it through a communication channel.

serial bonds Bonds that are issued at the same time but have different maturity dates.

sexism Discrimination against either sex, but primarily occurring against women.

sexual harassment Conduct, comment, gesture, or contact of a sexual nature that is likely to cause offence or humiliation to any employee.

shopping products Products purchased only after the consumer has compared competing products in competing stores.

sinking-fund bonds Bonds whose issuer makes annual deposits of funds for use in redeeming the bonds when they mature.

small business A firm that is independently owned and operated and is not dominant in its field.

Small Business Loans Act (SBLA) Federal program designed to help new and existing businesses obtain term loans directly from their financial institutions for purchasing and improving fixed assets.

smart card Card that incorporates a computer chip that allows it to store more information and more functions than a credit or debit card.

social (belongingness) needs In Maslow's hierarchy of needs, the third level of human needs, which includes the desire to be accepted by members of the family and other individuals and groups.

social responsibility Management philosophy that highlights the social and economic effects of managerial decisions.

socialism Economic system in which government owns and operates the key industries that are considered vital to the public welfare, such as transportation, utilities, and health care.

socio-emotional role Role played by team members who devote time and energy to providing support for group members' emotional needs and social unity.

software Sets of instructions that tell computer hardware what to do.

sole proprietorship A business that is owned by one person.

specialization Dividing work into its simplest components so workers can concentrate on performing one task.

specialty products Products a purchaser is willing to make a special effort to obtain.

speculation The hope of making a large profit on stocks within a short time.

spinoff A completely new company that is formed when a strategic business unit breaks away from its parent firm.

spreadsheet The computerized equivalent of an accountant's worksheet; computer software that permits businesspeople to manipulate decision variables to determine their effects.

staff manager A manager who provides information, advice, or technical assistance to aid line managers; for example, the human resource manager or the director of research.

standardization In marketing, selling the same product to every market; in production, producing uniform, interchangeable goods and parts.

statement of cash flows Information about a firm's cash receipts and cash payments during an accounting period that presents the sources and uses of cash.

statistical quality control A system using statistical procedures to gather and analyze data to pinpoint and correct problem areas.

stock exchange Location at which stocks and bonds are bought and sold.

stock split A recapitalization in which a single share is divided into multiple shares, lowering the price of the stock and making it easier for new investors to buy.

stockbroker A securities firm or a registered individual associated with one.

stockholders People who acquire shares of stock in a corporation, thereby becoming part-owners of the business.

store retailing The major category of retailing, which accounts for about 90 percent of total retail sales.

store of value One of the functions of money—a way of keeping accumulated wealth until it is needed to make new purchaes.

storming stage In team development, the point at which participants' individual personalities begin to emerge as they clarify their roles and expectations.

strategic alliances Partnerships formed between companies to create a competitive advantage.

strategic business units (SBUs) Divisions within a company, each with its own personnel, objectives, products, and planning.

strategic planning The process of determining the primary, longer-term objectives of an organization, adopting courses of action, and allocating the resources necessary to achieve those objectives.

Strategis Industry Canada's comprehensive business information Web site at http://strategis.ic.gc.ca.

strike A refusal on the part of unionized employees to work until a labour dispute is settled or a contract is signed.

subsidiary Corporation with all or a majority of its stock owned by another corporation, its parent company.

supervisory management First-line management; those people directly responsible for the details of assigning workers to specific jobs and evaluating performance.

supplies Expense items needed in a firm's daily operation that do not become part of the final product.

supply Sellers' willingness and ability to provide goods and services for sale in a market.

survey A method of gathering marketing research data by telephone, personal, or focus group interview, or mail survey.

SWOT analysis An organized method of assessing a company's internal strengths and weaknesses and external opportunities and threats.

tactical planning Implementing the activities specified by strategic plans.

target customer The typical consumer toward whom an organization directs its marketing efforts.

target market The group of consumers toward whom an organization directs its marketing efforts.

tariff A tax levied on products imported from abroad.

task specialist role Role played by team members who devote time and energy to helping the team accomplish its goals.

team A small number of people with complementary skills who are committed to a common purpose, approach, and set of performance goals.

team cohesiveness Extent to which team members are attracted to the team and motivated to remain a part of it.

team norm Standard of conduct that is shared by team members and guides their behaviour.

teamwork Employees working together on a project.

technical skills The manager's ability to understand and use the techniques, knowledge, and tools of a specific discipline or department.

technology One of the key factors of production, consisting of the application to business of knowledge based on discoveries in science, inventions, and innovations, including machinery, equipment, and information.

technology economy A knowledge-based, technology-driven economy; also called a highway economy.

telecommunications Any system in which information or data are sent over a distance through some type of electronic transmission medium.

telecommuters Home-based workers who "commute" to work electronically via home computer to their company's computer system.

teleshopping The selection and electronic purchase of merchandise that has been displayed on computers; also called cybershopping.

test marketing Forecasting technique that involves distributing new products in limited test areas to assess the best prices, promotional strategies, and packaging, and then extrapolating the results to a larger region.

Theory X Managerial assumption that employees dislike work and must be coerced, controlled, or threatened to motivate them to work.

Theory Y Managerial assumption that employees like work and, under proper conditions, accept and seek out responsibilities to fulfil their social, esteem, and self-actualization needs.

Theory Z Management approach that views involved employees as the key to increased productivity and an improved quality of work life for the employees.

time management The effective allocation of one's time among different tasks.

time utility Utility created by making a good or service available when the consumer wants to purchase it.

token money Money whose monetary value exceeds the market value of the materials it is made of; all of the money in use today is token money.

tombstones Black-and-white newspaper announcements of stock and bond offerings.

top management The highest level of the management hierarchy, staffed by executives who develop long-range plans and interact with the public and outside entities, like the government.

total quality management (TQM) An approach that involves a commitment to quality in achieving world-class performance and customer satisfaction as a crucial strategic objective.

trade credit Short-term source of funds resulting from purchases made on credit or open account with suppliers.

trademark A brand that has been given legal protection.

transaction-based marketing Buyer and seller exchanges characterized by limited communications and little or no ongoing relationship between the parties.

treasury bills Short-term Government of Canada borrowings issued each week and sold to the highest bidder; virtually risk-free and easy to resell.

trend analysis Mathematical approach to forecasting that assumes that the trends of the past will continue in the future.

trust company A business that acts as a financial trustee and administers funds for individuals and businesses, offering a range of banking services.

TSE 35 Composite Index An average of the market prices of the 35 most widely traded stocks listed on the Toronto Stock Exchange.

TSE 300 Composite Index An average of the market prices of the 300 largest stocks listed on the Toronto Stock Exchange.

unit of account One of the functions of money—a common denominator for measuring the value of all goods and services.

universal product code (UPC) The bar code on products that is read by optical scanners that print the name of the item and the price on a receipt.

unsecured bank loan Short-term source of borrowed funds for which the borrower does not pledge any assets as collateral.

utility The want-satisfying power of a good or service.

value-adding chain A five-step process of adding value for customers and employees that connects the corporate vision to customers' requirements.

venture or risk capital Capital usually provided by outside investors in exchange for an ownership share in the business.

venture capitalist Individual or business organization that invests in promising new businesses.

vertical marketing system (VMS) A network of channel intermediaries organized and centrally managed to produce the maximum co-operative impact.

virtual organization Organizational structure in which the major functions are broken up into strategic business units (SBUs) or companies that are brokered by a small headquarters or core organization; also called a network organization.

virtual team Group of employees who communicate with one another using the computer and in many cases the Internet.

vision The ability to perceive marketplace needs and what an organization must do to satisfy them.

voice processing Voice mail; technologies that use spoken language to send or receive information from a computer.

wages Employee compensation based on the number of hours worked or the amount of output produced.

warehousing The physical distribution activity that involves storing products.

warranty A firm's promise to repair, refund money paid for, or replace a product if it proves unsatisfactory.

wheel of retailing A theory stating that new retailers enter the market by offering lower prices made possible through reductions in service, then gradually add services as they grow, ultimately becoming targets for new retailers.

whistle blowing The disclosure of immoral or illegal acts within an organization.

wholesaling intermediaries Distribution-channel members that sell primarily to retailers, other wholesalers, or business users.

word processing The use of computers to type, store, retrieve, edit, and print various types of documents.

work team Relatively permanent group of employees that consists of a small number of people with complementary skills who perform the day-to-day work of the organization.

worker buyout plans Financial incentives to encourage voluntary retirement or separation of older workers.

working capital ratio Ratio that measures a firm's ability to pay its current debts as they mature, calculated by dividing current assets by current liabilities; also called the current ratio.

World Bank International organization that provides long-term loans to countries for economic development projects.

World Trade Organization (WTO) The multilateral institution charged with the responsibility of developing and administering agreed-upon rules for world trade.

World Wide Web A system of posting information, much of it connected on the Internet.

yield The income received from securities investments, or the investor's return.

zero defects An error-free performance goal that some companies strive for.

Statistics Canada information is used with the permission of the Minister of Industry, as Minister responsible for Statistics Canada. Information on the availability of the wide range of data from Statistics Canada can be obtained from Statistics Canada's Regional Offices, its World Wide Web site at http://www.statcan.ca, and its toll-free access number 1-800-263-1136.

PHOTOS

p. 1: Nuala Beck photo courtesy of Doug Forster. Nuala Beck is quoted in Kara Kuryllowicz, "The Best Businesses to Get into Now," *Profit,* December/January 1997, 57. Reprinted by permission of Nuala Beck and Kara Kuryllowicz.

p. 7: Reprinted by kind permission of the Royal Ontario Museum.

p. 15: Jim Pattison photo courtesy of The Jim Pattison Group.

p. 16: Reproduced by kind permission of Air Canada.

p. 23: Sam Sniderman photo courtesy of Sam The Record Man.

p. 29: Photos by Stirling Ward. Reproduced by kind permission of The Virgin Group of Companies.

p. 31: Reproduced by kind permission of JVC Canada Inc.

p. 32: Don Schafer photo courtesy of Comac Food Group Inc.

p. 33: Reproduced by kind permission of Dimatec Inc.

p. 46 (left): Marlene Conway photo courtesy of Envirolutions Inc.

p. 46 (right): Reproduced by kind permission of Metro Toronto Works Department.

p. 57 (top): George A. Cohon photo courtesy of McDonald's Restaurants of Canada Limited.

p. 57 (bottom): Jane Somerville photo courtesy of Somerville House Books Ltd.

p. 60 (left): Canapress/Peter Dejong.

p. 60 (right): Canapress/Lutz Schmidt.

p. 62: Canapress/Tom Hanson.

p. 79: Michael Cowpland photo by Couvrette/Ottawa, courtesy of Corel Corporation. Michael Cowpland is quoted in Kara Kuryllowicz, "The Best Businesses to Get into Now," *Profit,* December/January 1997, 58. Reprinted by permission of Corel Corporation and Kara Kuryllowicz.

p. 81: CorelVIDEO™: Powerful Enterprise Communications. Reproduced by kind permission of Corel Corporation.

p. 84: Reprinted by kind permission of Norwest Soil Research Ltd.

p. 87: Courtesy of Starbucks Coffee Company.

p. 89: Courtesy of Amex Canada Inc.

p. 90: Anne Sutherland photo courtesy of Royal Bank Financial Group.

p. 99: Pierre Péladeau photo courtesy of Quebecor Inc.

p. 106: Reproduced by kind permission of Louis Garneau Sports Inc.

p. 112: Courtesy of MGMU Communications for Saskatchewan Wheat Pool.

p. 113: Lois Stevenson photo courtesy of Atlantic Canada Opportunities Agency.

p. 117 (left): John Warrillow photo courtesy of Jake Boone for Harcourt Brace & Company, Canada.

p. 117 (right): Reprinted by kind permission of Justin Poy.

p. 122: Michael Bregman photo courtesy of The Second Cup Ltd.

p. 130: Courtesy of Young & Rubicam for Ford Motor Company.

p. 131: From Northern Telecom, *The Anatomy of a Transformation,* 1985–1995, 22. Reproduced by permission.

p. 137: Reprinted by kind permission of Pacific Western Brewing Company.

p. 153: Photo courtesy of d~Code. Quote reprinted by permission of d~Code.

p. 163: James W. Moir photo courtesy of Maritime Medical Care.

p. 171: Reproduced by kind permission of Baranti Group Inc.

p. 172: Reproduced by kind permission of Sun Microsystems of Canada Inc.

p. 176: Reproduced by kind permission of Newbridge Networks Corporation.

p. 180 (left): Reproduced by kind permission of Nokia Mobile Phones.

p. 180 (right): Dunnery Best photo courtesy of Midland Walwyn Capital Inc.

p. 192: Reproduced by kind permission of Communicare Inc. and Psychological Associates Inc.

p. 195: Reproduced by kind permission of Atlantic Canada Careers. Visit Atlantic Canada Careers' Web site at http://www.atl-can-careers.com.

p. 199: Reproduced by kind permission of The Great-West Life Assurance Company.

p. 202: Advertiser: Apple Canada, Agency: BBDO Canada.

p. 205: Alex Urosevic/The Toronto Sun.

p. 218: Reproduced by kind permission of Nortel.

p. 232: Reproduced by kind permission of SAS Institute (Canada) Inc.

p. 234: Reprinted with permission of Ventana Corporation.

p. 247: Lee Hunter, "Ten Best Government Web Sites," *Government Computer Magazine*, 1996, lee.hunter@hum.com. Copyright 1996 Hum Communications Ltd. All rights reserved. Reprinted by permission.

p. 251: Wanda M. Dorosz photo courtesy of Quorum Growth Inc.

p. 253: Courtesy of Toshiba of Canada Limited.

p. 255: Reproduced by kind permission of Sun Microsystems of Canada Inc.

p. 257: Adobe and Adobe PageMaker are trademarks of Adobe Systems, Incorporated.

p. 261: Marc R. Labrosse photo courtesy of Alex Informatics Inc.

p. 269: Reproduced by kind permission of David K. Foot. David Foot is quoted in Kara Kuryllowicz, "The Best Businesses to Get into Now," *Profit,* December/January 1997, 57. Reprinted by permission of David Foot and Kara Kuryllowicz.

p. 278: Advertiser: IBM Canada, Agency: Ogilvy & Mather.

p. 284: Courtesy of Ken Koo Creative Group Inc. for Concord Pacific Development.

p. 285: Lise Watier photo courtesy of Lise Watier Cosmetics Inc.

p. 286: Advertiser: Hostess Frito-Lay, Agency: BBDO Advertising.

p. 288: Reprinted by kind permission of Canada Post Corporation.

p. 289: Sylvia Vogel photo courtesy of Canderm Pharma Inc.

p. 298: Courtesy of Lackey Advertising for Pioneer Electronics.

p. 300: Reproduced by kind permission of Bell Canada.

p. 301 (top): Reprinted courtesy Kodak Canada Inc.

p. 301 (bottom): Courtesy of Tarzan Communications Inc. for Labatt Brewing Company Ltd.

p. 305: Stephen Van Houten photo courtesy of Alliance of Manufacturers & Exporters Canada.

p. 318: Photos courtesy of John Moran for Harcourt Brace & Company, Canada.

p. 324: Reproduced by kind permission of Intel Corporation.

p. 327: Reproduced by kind permission of Campbell Soup Company Ltd.

p. 328: Reproduced by kind permission of Urban Juice & Soda Co.

p. 345: Helen Sinclair photo courtesy of Brian Pieters Photography for Canadian Bankers Association. Photo and quote reprinted by permission of Helen Sinclair, Bankworks Trading Inc.

p. 347: Brent Trepel photo courtesy of Ben Moss Jewellers.

p. 351: Reproduced by kind permission of Ernst & Young.

p. 353: QuickBooks/QuickBooks Pro box shots reproduced by kind permission of Intuit Canada Limited.

p. 373: Courtesy of Zagon Photography and Empire Studio, and The National Currency Collection, Currency Museum of the Bank of Canada.

pp. 374–75: Figure 15.1 photos courtesy of Jake Boone for Harcourt Brace & Company, Canada.

p. 381: Printed with the permission of The Toronto-Dominion Bank.

p. 387: Reproduced by permission of CIBC. Content current between March and October 1997.

p. 405: David Singh photo courtesy of Fortune Financial Group.

p. 407 (left): Mike Peake/The Toronto Sun.

p. 407 (right): Courtesy of Jake Boone for Harcourt Brace & Company, Canada.

p. 415: Printed with the permission of TD Asset Management Inc.

BOXES

p. 5 (left): James Okamura is quoted in Brian Hutchinson, "Merchants of Boom," *Canadian Business*, May 1997, 39.

p. 5 (right): Jeffrey Gandz is quoted in Janet McFarland, "Canada Shines in Global Ratings," *The Globe and Mail*, May 26, 1997, B1.

p. 15: Jim Pattison is quoted in Kara Kuryllowicz, "The Best Businesses to Get into Now," *Profit,* December/January 1997, 56. Reprinted by permission of Jim Pattison and Kara Kuryllowicz.

p. 17: Andrew Spence is quoted in Janet McFarland, "Canada Shines in Global Ratings," *The Globe and Mail*, May 26, 1997, B3.

p. 18: Fred Claridge is quoted in Rod McQueen, "Canada's 50 Best Managed Private Companies: Komex International Ltd.," *The Financial Post*, December 14–16, 1996, 38.

p. 21: Fast Company, as cited in "Neat Job Title," *The Globe and Mail*, April 8, 1997, B13.

p. 22: Ken Blanchard is quoted in Elizabeth Church, "One-Minute Author Keeps on Ticking," *The Globe and Mail*, October 29, 1996, B14.

p. 23: Sam Sniderman is quoted in Kara Kuryllowicz, "The Best Businesses to Get into Now," *Profit,* December/January 1997, 56. Reprinted by permission of Sam Sniderman and Kara Kuryllowicz.

p. 31: Based on personal correspondence with Formal Systems; and Business Development Bank of Canada (BDC), "Canadian Exports Surge: Are You Part of the Success?" *Profit$,* Vol. 17, No. 2, Spring 1997, 1.

p. 32: Don Schafer is quoted in Kara Kuryllowicz, "The Best Businesses to Get into Now," *Profit,* December/January 1997, 58. Reprinted by permission of Don Schafer and Kara Kuryllowicz.

p. 33: Ivor Perry is quoted in Rod McQueen, "Canada's 50 Best Managed Private Companies: Dimatec Inc.," *The Financial Post*, December 14–16, 1996, 27.

p. 37: Neil Nevitte is quoted in Michael Valpy, "The New, Value-Added Canadians," *The Globe and Mail*, October 26, 1996, D5.

p. 39 (bottom): Adapted from David Olive, "Should Business Pick Up the Tab?" *The Globe and Mail*, May 7, 1996, B12.

p. 42: The Society of Management Accountants of Canada, *Codes of Ethics, Practice and Conduct* (Hamilton, ON: The Society of Management Accountants of Canada, 1997), 1. Reprinted by permission of CMA.

p. 43: Excerpt from Vic Parsons, *Bad Blood: The Tragedy of the Canadian Tainted Blood Scandal* (Toronto: Lester Publishing Limited, 1995), back cover. Reprinted by permission of Key Porter Books Limited.

p. 46: Marlene Conway is quoted in Kara Kuryllowicz, "The Best Businesses to Get into Now," *Profit*, December/January 1997, 58. Reprinted by permission of Marlene Conway and Kara Kuryllowicz.

p. 57: Jane Somerville is quoted in Kara Kuryllowicz, "The Best Businesses to Get into Now," *Profit*, December/January 1997, 60. Reprinted by permission of Jane Somerville and Kara Kuryllowicz.

p. 65: François Beaudoin for Business Development Bank of Canada (BDC), "Export Is No Small Business," *Profit$*, Vol. 17, No. 2, Spring 1997, 2.

p. 69: Tom Pugsley and Susan Nation are quoted in Elizabeth Church, "How to Conduct Business in Chile," *The Globe and Mail*, November 15, 1996, B11.

p. 82: Howard Millman is quoted in Corel Corporation, *Annual Report*, 1996, 6.

p. 83: Adapted from Rod McQueen, "Canada's 50 Best Managed Private Companies: Cybermation Inc.," *The Financial Post*, December 14–16, 1996, 24.

p. 87: Roger Jarvis is quoted in Rod McQueen, "Canada's 50 Best Managed Private Companies: Jarvis Travel Ltd.," *The Financial Post*, December 14–16, 1996, 24.

p. 90 (left): Excerpt from Henry Mintzberg, *The Rise and Fall of Strategic Planning* (New York: The Free Press, 1994), 12, 15–19.

p. 90 (right): Anne Sutherland is quoted in Kara Kuryllowicz, "The Best Businesses to Get into Now," *Profit*, December/January 1997, 63. Reprinted by permission of Anne Sutherland and Kara Kuryllowicz.

p. 98: Michael Ruscigno is quoted in Rod McQueen, "Canada's 50 Best Managed Private Companies: Intelatech Inc.," *The Financial Post*, December 14–16, 1996, 12.

p. 99: Pierre Péladeau is quoted in Kara Kuryllowicz, "The Best Businesses to Get into Now," *Profit*, December/January 1997, 58. Reprinted by permission of Pierre Péladeau and Kara Kuryllowicz.

p. 107 (left): Louis Garneau is quoted in Rod McQueen, "Canada's 50 Best Managed Private Companies: The Cycling World's Tour de Force," *The Financial Post*, December 14–16, 1996, 29.

p. 107 (right): Excerpt from "Clear Visions: The Top 40 under 40," *The Financial Post*, April 3, 1997, 22. Reprinted by permission of The Financial Post.

p. 108: Jamie Coatsworth is quoted in Gayle MacDonald, "Top Banker Steps Out," *The Globe and Mail*, February 24, 1997, B11.

p. 110: David Leighton and Donald Thain's book *Making Boards Work* (Whitby, ON: McGraw-Hill Ryerson, 1997) is reviewed in Janet McFarland, "Advice for Directors: 'Don't Back Down,'" *The Globe and Mail*, April 10, 1997, B17.

p. 111: Rick Camilleri is quoted in "Clear Visions: The Top 40 under 40," *The Financial Post*, April 3, 1997, 18.

p. 113: Lois Stevenson is quoted in Kara Kuryllowicz, "The Best Businesses to Get into Now," *Profit*, December/January 1997, 62. Reprinted by permission of Lois Stevenson and Kara Kuryllowicz.

p. 116: Excerpted from Industry Canada, *Your Guide to Government of Canada Services and Support for Small Businesses*. Reproduced with the permission of the Minister of Public Works and Government Services Canada, 1997.

p. 118: Adapted from James Ferrabee for Business Development Bank of Canada, "Does Small Business Have What It Takes?" *Profit$*, Vol. 17, No. 1, Winter 1997, 5.

p. 122 (bottom left): Mac Voisin is quoted in John Southerst, "If You're 'Entrepreneurial,' Forget Franchises," *The Globe and Mail*, May 8, 1995, B5.

p. 122 (top right): Michael Bregman is quoted in Kara Kuryllowicz, "The Best Businesses to Get into Now," *Profit*, December/January 1997, 63. Reprinted by permission of Michael Bregman and Kara Kuryllowicz.

p. 123: Adapted from "When Partners Become Rivals," *The Globe and Mail*, April 18, 1995, B10.

p. 132 (bottom): Ram Charan is quoted in Louis Kraar, "Korea Goes for Quality," *Fortune*, April 18, 1994, 153. See also Stratford Sherman, "Are You as Good as the Best in the World?" *Fortune*, December 13, 1993, 95–96.

p. 135: Leonard Lee is quoted in Paul Adams, "Glenfiddich Profiles in Excellence: Tooling Around," *The Globe and Mail Report on Business Magazine*, January 1996.

p. 140: *Profit Magazine*'s web site featuring Canada's fastest-growing companies, <u>http://www.profit100.com</u>.

p. 142: Excerpt from Quality Management Institute Inc. (QMI), Advertising Supplement, "QMI Guides Canada's Drive to ISO 9000," *The Globe and Mail*, December 16, 1996, 2. Written, designed, and produced by The Publishing House Inc. Reprinted by permission of QMI.

p. 156: Joe Clark is quoted in "What APEC Means to Canada: Towards a New World Order," *The Globe and Mail Report on Business Magazine*, November 1996, 46.

p. 163: James W. Moir is quoted in Kara Kuryllowicz, "The Best Businesses to Get into Now," *Profit*, December/January 1997, 62. Reprinted by permission of James W. Moir and Kara Kuryllowicz.

p. 166: Ron Shay, April 30, 1997. Reprinted by permission.

p. 168: Richard Lipsey is quoted in Bruce Little, "Economist Predicts Booming Future," *The Globe and Mail*, November 6, 1996, B4; Ted Schmidt's view is from his article, "Have You Lived through a 'Worker Imbalance Correction'?" *Catholic New Times*, November 3, 1996, 16.

p. 172: Jayson Myers and the Consortium for Advanced Manufacturing International are quoted in Greg Ip, "Outsourcing Becoming a Way of Life for Firms," *The Globe and Mail*, October 2, 1996, B8.

p. 175: David K. Foot and Daniel Stoffman discuss their book *Boom, Bust & Echo* in their article, "The Great Canadian Job Funk," *The Globe and Mail*, May 25, 1996, D1.

p. 180: Dunnery Best is quoted in Kara Kuryllowicz, "The Best Businesses to Get into Now," *Profit*, December/January 1997, 60. Reprinted by permission of Dunnery Best and Kara Kuryllowicz.

p. 188: John Wright is quoted in Canadian Press, "Canuck Workers Happy with Their Jobs," *The Ottawa Sun*, October 8, 1996, 36. The 1996 Angus Reid poll was sponsored by the Royal Bank of Canada. This phone survey questioned 850 working Canadians between July 29 and August 7, 1996. The results are considered accurate within 3.4 percentage points 19 times out of 20.

p. 205: John Kervin is quoted in Janet McFarland, "Hard Labour Takes Its Toll on Negotiators," *The Globe and Mail*, October 4, 1996, B10.

p. 206: From "An Address by The Honourable Lloyd Axworthy, PC, MP, Minister of Human Resources Development," *Jobs Conference* (Ottawa: Canadian Labour Market and Productivity Centre, April 1994), 58.

p. 207 (left): Judith Maxwell is quoted in "An Address by The Honourable Lloyd Axworthy, PC, MP, Minister of Human Resources Development," *Jobs Conference* (Ottawa: Canadian Labour Market and Productivity Centre, April 1994), 58.

p. 207 (right): Sheelagh Whittaker is quoted in John Heinzl, "Women Take Charge at Canadian Units," *The Globe and Mail*, November 29, 1996, B10.

p. 220: Adapted from http://www.sound.net/~drray/#teamres.

p. 221: Wallace Company Inc.

p. 224: Jacalyn Sherriton and James Stern's *Corporate Culture/Team Culture: Removing the Hidden Barriers to Team Success* (New York: Amacom, 1996) is highlighted in Patti Bond (Cox News Service), "Companies Fail at Teamwork, New Book Claims," *The Ottawa Citizen*, October 26, 1996, J8.

p. 228: Greg Kiessling is quoted in Rod McQueen, "Canada's 50 Best Managed Private Companies: KL Group Inc.," *The Financial Post*, December 14–16, 1996, 31. In 1996, KL Group Inc. had 55 employees. In its seven years of existence, only ten people have left the company.

p. 234: "Employability Skills Profile: The Critical Skills Required of the Canadian Workforce," *Employability Skills Profile*, October 1993, The Corporate Council on Education, a program of the National Business and Education Centre, The Conference Board of Canada.

p. 245 (left): From an interview, "Cyberwhiz Don Tapscott Is Mapping the Digital Frontier," *Royal Bank Business Report*, November 1996, 21.

p. 245 (right): Diane E. McGarry is quoted in "She Said It," *Royal Bank Report on Business*, November 1996, 7.

p. 247 (left): Information on the prime minister is from Jim Bronskill, "PM's Mixed Bag of Requests, Advice, Beefs," *The Globe and Mail*, December 23, 1996, A3.

p. 248 (left): Bill Gates, "The Cyberlord Speaks," *The Globe and Mail Report on Business Magazine*, January 1997, 75.

p. 248 (right): Patrick Brethour and Geoffrey Rowan, "Hitting on Penthouse," *The Globe and Mail*, December 4, 1996, B12.

p. 251: Wanda Dorosz is quoted in Kara Kuryllowicz, "The Best Businesses to Get into Now," *Profit*, December/January 1997, 56. Reprinted by permission of Wanda Dorosz and Kara Kuryllowicz.

p. 253 (left): The IDC survey is reported in Patrick Brethour, "Mainframes Make Moves to Regain Turf: Survey," *The Globe and Mail*, May 28, 1997, B10.

p. 253 (right): Adapted from Geoffrey Rowan, "Time Is Running Out to Fix Year 2000 Computer Problem," *The Globe and Mail*, May 28, 1997, B10.

p. 254: Bill Gates is quoted in "The Power and the Promise of the Digital Revolution," *Royal Bank Business Report*, November 1996, 5.

p. 261: Marc Labrosse is quoted in Kara Kuryllowicz, "The Best Businesses to Get into Now," *Profit*, December/January 1997, 57. Reprinted by permission of Marc Labrosse and Kara Kuryllowicz.

p. 272: Adapted from Patrick Brethour, "Is This the Year for Internet Commerce?" *The Globe and Mail*, January 15, 1997, B12.

p. 281: John Torella's views are reported in Marina Strauss, "What Retailers Will Do to Lure Customers," *The Globe and Mail*, December 5, 1996, B14.

p. 283: http://www.52dnet.com/anchordesk.

p. 285: Lise Watier is quoted in Kara Kuryllowicz, "The Best Businesses to Get into Now," *Profit*, December/January 1997, 63. Reprinted by permission of Lise Watier and Kara Kuryllowicz.

p. 287: Based on a report done by Insight Canada Research for CIBC, appearing in "Tips You Can Use: Dissatisfaction with Banks," *The Globe and Mail*, August 28, 1995, B7.

p. 289: Sylvia Vogel is quoted in Kara Kuryllowicz, "The Best Businesses to Get into Now," *Profit*, December/January 1997, 58. Reprinted by permission of Sylvia Vogel and Kara Kuryllowicz.

p. 298: Based on personal interviews with N.M. Glegg Water Conditioning Inc. and SMART Technologies Inc.; Rod McQueen, "Doing Whatever It Takes to Win Clients," *The Financial Post*, December 14, 1996, 19; and Rod McQueen, "Magic Moment in Vegas," *The Financial Post*, December 14, 1996, 46. Reprinted by permission of The Financial Post.

p. 299: Adapted from Rob Carrick, "Mbanx: Beyond the Hype," *The Globe and Mail*, February 1, 1997, B22.

p. 305: Stephen Van Houten is quoted in Kara Kuryllowicz, "The Best Businesses to Get into Now," *Profit*, December/January 1997, 63. Reprinted by permission of Stephen Van Houten and Kara Kuryllowicz.

p. 306 (left): Adapted from "Courier Starts Virtual Service," *The Globe and Mail*, January 29, 1997, B15.

p. 306 (right): Adapted from "Teamwork, Prices Make Riders Smile," *The Ottawa Sun*, February 4, 1997, 19.

p. 310 (top left): William Coffey's study, "Employment Growth and Change in the Canadian Urban System," 1971–94, was sponsored by the Canadian Policy Research Networks Inc., a nonprofit institute in Ottawa.

p. 310 (top right): Adapted from Allan Swift (The Canadian Press), "Canadian Aerospace Sector Soars to New Heights,"

The Ottawa Citizen, February 3, 1997, A10. Reprinted by permission of The Canadian Press.

p. 310 (bottom right): Roger Jarvis is quoted in Rod McQueen, "Canada's 50 Best Managed Private Companies: Jarvis Travel Ltd.," *The Financial Post*, December 14–16, 1996, 36.

p. 319: Adapted from Lee A. Eckert, J.D. Ryan, and Ronald A. Knowles, *Canadian Small Business: An Entrepreneur's Plan*, 2nd ed. (Toronto: Dryden, 1995), 61. Copyright © 1995 by Harcourt Brace & Company, Canada, Limited. All rights reserved. Reprinted by permission of Harcourt Brace & Company, Canada, Limited.

p. 330: Ross Creber is quoted in Gayle MacDonald, "Who's Still Knocking at the Door?" *The Globe and Mail*, May 6, 1996, B6.

p. 334 (left): Adapted from John Heinzl, "Internet Becomes World's Biggest Car Lot," *The Globe and Mail*, September 23, 1998, B25.

p. 334 (right): Adapted from Andrew Allentuck, "Network Selling: Catalogues are Going Multimedia," *The Globe and Mail*, November 12, 1996, C5.

p. 335 (left): Adapted from Rod McQueen, "Canada's 50 Best Managed Private Companies: Carlyle Computer Products," *The Financial Post*, December 14–16, 1996, 21 and 24. Reprinted by permission of The Financial Post.

p. 337: Mark Blumes is quoted in The Canadian Press, "Online Buying Faces Critics," *The Ottawa Sun*, November 12, 1996, 24.

p. 349 (right): Adapted from Rod McQueen, "Canada's 50 Best Managed Private Companies: RNG Equipment Inc.," *The Financial Post*, December 14–16, 1996, 47. Reprinted by permission of The Financial Post.

p. 363 (left): Based on personal correspondence with the banks; and Advertising Feature, "Where to Pick Up Financial Advice on the Internet," *The Globe and Mail*, January 26, 1996, C2.

p. 363 (right): Adapted from Henry Mintzberg, "Greedy Workers Mimic Managers," *The Globe and Mail*, October 14, 1998, B29.

p. 364: Business Development Bank of Canada (BDC), "Four Financial Crown Corporations on the Web," *Profit$*, Vol. 17, No. 1, Winter 1997, 8. Reprinted by permission of BDC.

p. 371: Debbi Fields is quoted in Rick Spence, "California Dreamin'," *Profit*, February/March 1997, 47.

p. 372: Adapted from Lee A. Eckert, J.D. Ryan, and Ronald A. Knowles, *Canadian Small Business: An Entrepreneur's Plan*, 2nd ed. (Toronto: Dryden, 1995), 235–42. Copyright © 1995 by Harcourt Brace & Company, Canada, Limited. All rights reserved. Reprinted by permission of Harcourt Brace & Company, Canada, Limited.

p. 373 (top): Canadian Bankers Association, "Looking Ahead," *Bank Facts, 1995*, http://www.cba.ca/pub/bankfacts/bf4.html#changing.

p. 376: Excerpted with minor changes from Canadian Bankers Association, *Bank Facts, 1996–1997*, October 1996, 4. Reprinted by permission of the Canadian Bankers Association.

p. 379: Serge Saucier is quoted in BankWorks Trading Inc., "Marketing the Expertise of Financial Institutions," (media kit), 4.

p. 388: Jeffrey S. Chisholm is quoted in the Toronto conference, "The Future of Work," February 25, 1997.

p. 389: Adapted from Susanne Craig, "Ottawa Bans Tied Selling by Banks," *The Globe and Mail*, September 30, 1998, B1. Reprinted with permission from The Globe and Mail.

p. 397: From *The Banker's Secrets* by André Frazer, 11, © 1997. Reprinted by permission of Macmillan Canada.

p. 399: From *The Banker's Secrets* by André Frazer, 29, © 1997. Reprinted by permission of Macmillan Canada.

p. 405: David Singh is quoted in Kara Kuryllowicz, "The Best Businesses To Get into Now," *Profit*, December/January 1997, 56. Reprinted by permission of David Singh and Kara Kuryllowicz.

FIGURES

Figure 1.2: Based on a World Trade Organization (WTO) review released November 19, 1996. See also Madelaine Drohan, "Dependency on U.S. Leaves Canada 'Vulnerable': WTO," *The Globe and Mail*, November 20, 1996, B6.

Figure 1.3a: Bank of Canada statistics. See also April Lindgren, "Fragile Exports," *The Ottawa Citizen*, October 26, 1996, D1.

Figure 1.3b: Adapted from Statistics Canada, *Canadian International Merchandise Trade, 1987–1995*, Catalogue No. 65-001. Statistics Canada information is used with the permission of the Minister of Industry, as Minister responsible for Statistics Canada.

Figure 1.4: Adapted from Statistics Canada, "System of National Accounts: Aggregate Productivity Measures," *The Daily*, June 5, 1997, Catalogue No. 11-001, on http://www.statcan.ca:80/Daily/english/970605/d970605.htm#ART2. Statistics Canada information is used with the permission of the Minister of Industry, as Minister responsible for Statistics Canada.

Figure 1.5: Based on Organization for Economic Co-operation and Development (OECD) semi-annual report, released June 12, 1997. See also Alan Toulin, "Canada Tipped to Lead OECD in Economic Growth," *The Financial Post*, June 13, 1997, 7.

Figure 1.6: Adapted from Statistics Canada, *Household Facilities by Income and Characteristics*, various years, Catalogue No. 13-218. Statistics Canada information is used with the permission of the Minister of Industry, as Minister responsible for Statistics Canada.

Figure 1.7: Canadian Federation of Independent Business, results of Members' Opinions Survey #40, April 1997, as appearing in Gayle MacDonald, "Small Business Gets Connected," *The Globe and Mail*, May 15, 1997, B10. Reprinted by permission of the Canadian Federation of Independent Business.

Figure 2.3: Neil Nevitte, 1990–1991 *World Values* survey. Reprinted by permission. See also Michael Valpy, "The New, Value-Added Canadians," *The Globe and Mail*, October 26, 1996, D5; and Neil Nevitte, *The Decline of Deference* (Peterborough, ON: Broadview Press, 1997).

Figure 2.4: Michael E. Rock, *Ethics to Live By, To Work By* (Toronto: Concept Press, 1992), 40. Copyright © 1992 Holt, Rinehart and Winston of Canada, Limited. All rights reserved. Reprinted by permission of Harcourt Brace and Company, Canada, Limited.

Figure 2.5: *SaskTel 1996 Annual Report*, 2. Reprinted by permission of SaskTel.

Figure 3.1: Minister of Supply and Services Canada, *Canada's International Business Strategy, 1997–1998—Overview,* Catalogue No. C2-226/1-1998E, 5. Reproduced with the permission of the Minister of Public Works and Government Services Canada, 1997.

Figure 3.2: Adapted from the Department of Foreign Affairs and International Trade, *Pocket Facts: Canada,* March 15, 1997. Reproduced with the permission of the Minister of Public Works and Government Services Canada, 1997.

Figures 3.3a & b: Based on an A.T. Kearney survey and appearing in Gayle MacDonald, "Exporters Warned of High U.S. Exposure," *The Globe and Mail,* May 1, 1996, B11. Reprinted by permission of A.T. Kearney Ltd.

Figure 3.4: Adapted from Statistics Canada, *Canada's International Investment Position, 1995,* Catalogue No. 67-202. Statistics Canada information is used with the permission of the Minister of Industry, as Minister responsbile for Statistics Canada. See also Department of Foreign Affairs and International Trade, *APEC: Opening Doors for Canadian Business,* 1996.

Figure 4.1: Reprinted with kind permission of Scotiabank.

Figure 4.5: Adapted from *Management* by Ramon J. Aldag and Timothy M. Stearns, 199–201. Copyright © 1991. By permission of South-Western College Publishing, a division of International Thomson Publishing Inc., Cincinnati, Ohio 45227.

Figure 5.2: Adapted from Sunder Magun (Applied International Economics) for Industry Canada, *The Development of Strategic Alliances in Industries: A Micro Analysis,* Working Paper No. 13, October 1996, Catalogue No. 21-24/14-1996, 4. The views expressed in this working paper do not necessarily reflect those of Industry Canada or the federal government. Reproduced with the permission of the Minister of Public Works and Government Services Canada, 1997.

Figures 5.3a & b: Adapted with the permission of the Minister of Public Works and Government Services Canada, 1997, and by authority of the Minister of Industry, 1997, Statistics Canada, Catalogue 71-529, 1995. This figure appears in Industry Canada, *Your Guide to Government of Canada Services and Support for Small Businesses: Trends and Statistics,* 1996–1997, Catalogue No. C1-10/1997E.

Figure 5.4: Adapted by authority of the Minister of Industry, 1997, Statistics Canada, Catalogue No. 88-202, 1995. This figure appears in Industry Canada, *Your Guide to Government of Canada Services and Support for Small Businesses: Trends and Statistics,* 1996–1997, Catalogue No. C1-10/1997E.

Figure 5.5: Adapted by authority of the Minister of Industry, 1997, Statistics Canada, Catalogue No. 88-202, 1995. This figure appears in Industry Canada, *Your Guide to Government of Canada Services and Support for Small Businesses: Trends and Statistics,* 1996–1997, Catalogue No. C1-10/1997E.

Figure 5.6: Adapted from "Hands On: A Manager's Notebook," *Inc.,* September 1990, 130. Reprinted with permission, *Inc.* magazine, September 1990. Copyright 1990 by Goldhirsh Group, Inc., 38 Commercial Wharf, Boston MA 02110.

Figure 5.7: Adapted from advertisement by Merrill Lynch. Data from U.S. Small Business Administration, Office of Advocacy, *The State of Small Business: A Report of the President,* 1992.

Figure 6.2: Adapted with permission from Jac Fitz-Enz, *Benchmarking Staff Performance: How Staff Departments Can Enhance Their Value to the Customer* (San Francisco: Jossey-Bass, 1993), Figure 1.3, 16. Copyright © 1993 Jossey-Bass Inc., Publishers. All rights reserved.

Figure 6.3: Gallup Canada Inc., 1996, as appearing in Brian Milner, "Survey Finds Pride in Canadian Products," *The Globe and Mail,* December 4, 1996, B8. Reprinted by permission of Gallup Canada Inc.

Figure 6.4: Based on an Angus Reid survey conducted for Royal Bank Human Resources, "Workplace 2000 under Construction: A Snapshot of the New Reality," 1996. Reprinted by permission of the Royal Bank.

Figure 6.6: Adapted from Quality Management Institute Inc. (QMI), Advertising Supplement, "Quality Becomes Job One for Canadian Companies," *The Globe and Mail,* December 16, 1996, 1. Written, designed, and produced by The Publishing House Inc. Reprinted by permission of QMI.

Figure 7.5: Figure from MANAGEMENT, Third Edition (p. 296) by Richard L. Daft, copyright © 1994 by The Dryden Press, reproduced by permission of the publisher.

Figure 7.7a: Figure from MANAGEMENT, Fourth Edition (p. 340) by Richard L. Daft, copyright © 1997 by The Dryden Press, reproduced by permission of the publisher.

Figure 7.7b: The Shamrock Model has been illustrated based on the concept from Charles Handy, *Age of Unreason,* 2nd ed. (London: Century Business Books Ltd., 1991).

Figure 7.8: "Management Aptitude Questionnaire," Copyright Dorothy Marcic 1997; Vanderbilt University, www.marcic.com.

Figure 7.10: Adapted from Michael Salter, "Dream BIG ... then BIGGER," *The Globe and Mail Report on Business Magazine,* June 1996, 60. Reprinted by permission of the author.

Figure 9.2: Adapted from Dawn Baskerville, "Why Business Loves Workteams," **Black Enterprise,** April 1993, 90. Copyright April 1993. Reprinted with permission **BLACK ENTERPRISE Magazine.** The Earl G. Graves Publishing Co., Inc., New York. All rights reserved.

Figure 9.5: Figure from THE NEW COMPUTER USER by David Sullivan, 277, copyright © 1994 by Harcourt Brace & Company, reproduced by permission of the publisher.

Figure 9.6: From Peter March, ed., *Eye to Eye: How People Interact* (Topsfield, MA: Salem House, 1988), 42. Reprinted by permission of Andromeda Oxford Limited, Abingdon, Oxon, England.

Figure 9.7: CONTEMPORARY BUSINESS COMMUNICATION, 607, by Gene Boone and David Kurtz, © 1994. Reprinted by permission of Prentice-Hall, Inc., Upper Saddle River, NJ.

Figure 9.8: TeleGeography, Inc., 1995. Reprinted by permission. http://www.telegeography. com.

Figure 10.1: Adapted from Patrick H. Winston, ARTIFICIAL INTELLIGENCE, 2nd ed. (Figure 6-9, p. 181). © 1992 by Patrick Henry Winston. Reprinted by permission of Addison-Wesley Longman Inc.

Figure 11.2: Adapted from "Big Payoffs from Keeping Customers," *Fortune*, Autumn/Winter 1993, 57. © 1993 Time Inc. All rights reserved.

Figure 11.3: Adapted with permission, *Inc.* magazine (January 1993), 31. Copyright 1993 by Goldhirsh Group, Inc., 38 Commercial Wharf, Boston, MA 02110.

Figure 13.3: Datastream International (Canada) Ltd., with Globe and Mail calculations, as appearing in Marina Strauss, "Retailers Courting Customers," *The Globe and Mail*, December 14, 1996, B5. Reprinted by permission of Datastream International (Canada) Ltd.

Figure 14.5: Adapted from Lee A. Eckert, J.D. Ryan, and Ronald A. Knowles, *Canadian Small Business: An Entrepreneur's Plan*, 2nd ed. (Toronto: Dryden, 1995), 224. Copyright © 1995 by Harcourt Brace & Company, Canada, Limited. All rights reserved. Reprinted by permission of Harcourt Brace & Company, Canada, Limited.

Figure 15.1: Adapted from Canadian Bankers Association, *Bank Facts, 1996–1997*, October 1996, 18–19. Reprinted by permission of the Canadian Bankers Association.

Figure 15.4: Steven H. Appelbaum and M. Dale Beckman, *Canadian Business: A Contemporary Perspective* (Toronto: Dryden, 1995), BAN 11. Copyright © 1995 by Harcourt Brace & Company, Canada, Limited. All rights reserved. Reprinted by permission of Harcourt Brace & Company, Canada, Limited.

Figure 15.5: Canadian Bankers Association, *Bank Facts, 1996–1997*, October 1996, 9. Reprinted by permission of the Canadian Bankers Association.

Figure 15.6: *The Banker* magazine, July 1996, and Canadian bank annual reports, as appearing in The Canadian Bankers Association, *Bank Facts, 1996–1997*, October 1996, 14. Reprinted by permission of the Canadian Bankers Association.

Figure 16.1: Reprinted by permission of Stelco Inc.

Figure 16.2: Reprinted by permission of Ontario Hydro.

Figure 16.3: *The Globe and Mail*, March 14, 1997, B11. Reprinted with permission from The Globe and Mail.

TABLES

Table 1.1: From HUMAN DEVELOPMENT REPORT 1997 by United Nations Development Programme. Copyright © 1997 by the United Nations Development Programme. Used by permission of Oxford University Press, Inc.

Table 1.2: Statistics for all countries, excluding Russia, are from OECD, *Economic Outlook*, June 1997. Reprinted by permission of OECD. Statistics for Russia are from International Monetary Fund, *World Economic Outlook,* June 1997. Reprinted by permission. This table also appeared in Barrie McKenna, "G7 Summit Seen as 'Pageant,'" *The Globe and Mail*, June 16, 1997, B4.

Table 1.3: Adapted from Statistics Canada, *The Daily*, June 5, 1997, Catalogue No. 11-011, on http://www.statcan.ca:80/Daily/english/970605/d970605.htm#ART2. Statistics Canada information is used with the permission of the Minister of Industry, as Minister responsible for Statistics Canada.

Table 1.5: Sunder Magun (Applied International Economics) for Industry Canada, *The Development of Strategic Alliances in Canadian Industries: A Micro Analysis*, Working Paper No. 13, October 1996, Catalogue No. 21-24/14-1996, 27. The views expressed in this working paper do not necessarily reflect those of Industry Canada or the federal government. Reproduced with the permission of the Minister of Public Works and Government Services Canada, 1997.

Table 2.1: The Society of Management Accountants of Canada, *Codes of Ethics, Practice and Conduct* (Hamilton, ON: The Society of Management Accountants of Canada, 1997), 5. Reprinted by permission of CMA.

Table 2.2: Michael E. Rock, *Ethics to Live By, To Work By* (Toronto: Concept Press, 1992), 56. Copyright © 1992 Holt, Rinehart and Winston of Canada, Limited. All rights reserved. Reprinted by permission of Harcourt Brace and Company, Canada, Limited.

Table 3.1: Adapted from "The Top 50 Exporters," *The Globe and Mail Report on Business Magazine*, July 1996, 96. Reprinted with permission from The Globe and Mail.

Table 5.2: Adapted from "The Top 1000," *The Globe and Mail Report on Business Magazine*, July 1996, 141, 153. Reprinted with permission from The Globe and Mail.

Table 5.3: Adapted from Industry Canada, *Your Guide to Government of Canada Services and Support for Small Businesses: Trends and Statistics*, 1996–1997, Catalogue No. C1-10/1997E; and John Manley and Paul Martin for Industry Canada, *Growing Small Businesses*, February 1994, 4. Reproduced with the permission of the Minister of Public Works and Government Services Canada, 1997.

Table 5.4: Based on a study conducted by Thompson Lightstone and Co. for the Canadian Bankers Association, and cited in Industry Canada, *Your Guide to Government of Canada Services and Support for Small Businesses: Trends and Statistics*, 1996–1997, Catalogue No. C1-10/1997E. Reprinted by permission of the Canadian Bankers Association and Thompson Lightstone and Co.

Table 6.1: Based on Malcolm Baldrige Award, as appearing in James Martin, *The Great Transition* (New York: American Management Association, 1995), 245.

Table 6.2: Deming's Fourteen Points for Quality from John Hillkirk, "On Mission to Revamp Workplace," *USA Today*, October 15, 1990, 4B. Copyright 1990, USA TODAY. Reprinted with permission.

Table 6.3: Quality Management Institute Inc. (QMI), Advertising Supplement, "QMI Guides Canada's Drive to ISO 9000," *The Globe and Mail*, December 16, 1996, 2. Written, designed, and produced by The Publishing House Inc. Reprinted by permission of QMI.

Table 6.4: Adapted from Robert C. Camp, *Benchmarking: The Search for Industry Best Practices That Lead to Superior Performance* (Milwaukee, WI: ASQC Quality Press, 1989), 17. Reprinted by permission of the publisher.

Table 7.2: Compiled from *The Financial Post 500*, June 1995 and 1996.

Name Index

Subject Index

READER REPLY CARD

We are interested in your reaction to *Business*, Updated First Canadian Edition, by Louis E. Boone, David L. Kurtz, and Ronald A. Knowles. You can help us to improve this book in future editions by completing this questionnaire.

1. What was your reason for using this book?

    ○ university course   ○ continuing education course   ○ personal interest

    ○ college course   ○ professional development   ○ other

2. If you are a student, please identify your school and the course in which you used this book.

3. Which chapters or parts of this book did you use? Which did you omit?

4. What did you like best about this book?

5. What did you like least about this book?

6. Please identify any topics you think should be added to future editions.

7. Please add any comments or suggestions.

8. May we contact you for further information?

    Name: _____

    Address: _____

    _____

    Phone: _____

    E-Mail _____

(fold here and tape shut)

MAIL ➤ POSTE
Canada Post Corporation / Société canadienne des postes

Postage paid
If mailed in Canada

Port payé
si posté au Canada

Business Reply

Réponse d'affaires

0116870399   01

0116870399-M8Z4X6-BR01

Larry Gillevet
Director of Product Development
HARCOURT BRACE & COMPANY, CANADA
55 HORNER AVENUE
TORONTO, ONTARIO
M8Z 9Z9